THE LIBRARY
ST. MARY'S COLLEGE OF MARYLAND
ST. MARY'S CITY, MARYLAND 20686

D1213810

THE LIBRARY
ST. MARY'S COLLEGE OF MARYLAND
ST. MARY'S CITY, MARYLAND

*Handbook of Evolutionary Psychology*
*Ideas, Issues, and Applications*

# Handbook of Evolutionary Psychology

## Ideas, Issues, and Applications

Edited by

**Charles Crawford**
*Simon Fraser University*

**Dennis L. Krebs**
*Simon Fraser University*

**LEA** LAWRENCE ERLBAUM ASSOCIATES, PUBLISHERS
1998   Mahwah, New Jersey                              London

Copyright © 1998 by Lawrence Erlbaum Associates, Inc.
All rights reserved. No part of this book may be
reproduced in any form, by photostat, microform,
retrieval system, or any other means, without the prior
written permission of the publisher.

Lawrence Erlbaum Associates, Inc., Publishers
10 Industrial Avenue
Mahwah, New Jersey 07430


**Library of Congress Cataloging-in-Publication-Data**

Crawford, Charles.
Handbook of evolutionary psychology / [edited by] Charles Crawford and Dennis Krebs.
      p. cm.
    Rev. ed. of: Sociobiology and psychology. 1987.
    Includes bibliographic references and index.
    ISBN 0-8058-1666-6 (cloth : alk. paper)
    1. Psychology. 2. Sociobiology. 3. Genetic psychol-
ogy. I. Crawford, Charles (Charles B.) II. Krebs, Dennis. III. Title: Sociobiology and psychology.
BF57.H36 1997
155.7—dc21                                          97-16301
                                                        CIP

Books published by Lawrence Erlbaum Associates are
printed on acid-free paper, and their bindings are chosen
for strength and durability.

Printed in the United States of America
10  9  8  7  6  5  4  3  2  1

# Contents

# *Preface*

A decade has passed since the publication of Sociobiology and Psychology: Ideas, Issues, and Applications, the predecessor of this volume. The evolutionary analysis of human behavior has made considerable progress during those years. When the original volume was published, much of the controversy growing out of the study of sociobiology revolved around the putative political implications of applying the theory of Evolution by Natural Selection to the study of human behavior. The intensity of this debate has moderated in recent years because many critics now realize the political ramifications of sociobiology are no more, or no less, than those of other approaches to the study of human behavior, such as behaviorism., psychoanalysis, or cognitive science. Controversy remains, but it is scientific, concerning how to best use the theory of evolution in the study of human behavior and whether any of the current evolutionary approaches to the study of human behavior can be fruitful.

Some researchers, known as *Darwinian anthropologists* or *Darwinian social scientists*, focus on the study of reproductive success in industrialized and current hunter–gatherer societies. They use the methods of animal behavioral ecology to help understand human adaptations and adaptedness. Other researchers, known as *evolutionary psychologists* or *Darwinian psychologists*, focus on the naturally selected design of psychological mechanisms. For them, the application of evolutionary theory to human behavior is concerned with the problems humans encountered in their ancestor environments, the psychological mechanisms natural selection designed to deal with those problems, and the way the evolved psychological mechanisms function in our current environment. Although they use standard methods of psychology in their work, they also call on methods used by anthropologists, behavioral ecologists, and ethologists. Although both approaches are valuable, this book is most representative of those taking a psychological approach to the study of evolution and human behavior.

Psychology spans that part of the behavioral sciences extending from sociology, through social psychology, personality theory, learning, perception, motivation, and developmental psychology, to the biological disciplines of ethology, genetics, and neurophysiology. Because many subdisciplines of psychology have at least some roots in biology, psychology is ideally situated to assist in the integration of evolutionary thinking into the human behavioral sciences. Moreover, psychology has had long and explicit associations with the biological sciences. For 100 years, psychologists have been conducting animal and psychological research and have been attempting to use knowledge gained from animal research to understand humans. The quantitative methods used by evolutionary theorists, ecologists, and population geneticists are shared by psychology. The statistical models of mantel test theory, for example, are similar to those used by quantitative geneticists. Although the study of human reproductive patterns is important, we can now see that sophisticated explanations of human behavior require an understanding of both its ancestral adaptive significance and the proximate psychological mechanisms producing it. An understanding of how animals learn, perceive, and are motivated is required to put these explanations together. Psychology is the discipline that has been most concerned with providing these explanations. Therefore, it is not surprising that psychology has played an increasingly important role in developing integrative explanations of behavior.

The aim of this volume's editors was to compile a volume that would facilitate the development of the evolutionary approach to human behavior by communicating some of the major ideas, issues, and applications of the Theory of Evolution. This volume is intended to be intelligible to senior undergraduates in psychology, anthropology, sociology, and biology, but it is sufficiently sophisticated to be useful to graduate students and professionals desiring an introduction to, or an update on, an exciting new way of thinking about the relation between humans and their environment. The treatment is meant to be thorough. However, the editors endeavored to keep the discussions from becoming too technical.

## ACKNOWLEDGMENTS

Many people helped us put this volume together. In particular, we would like to thank the members of the Evolutionary Psychology Laboratory at Simon Fraser University, who gave valuable advice and criticism. The project received some support from the Social Sciences and Humanities Research Council of Canada grant 410-96-1235 to Charles Crawford and grant 401-94-0345 to Dennis Krebs. Chapters 1 and 9 were written while Charles Crawford was on sabbatical leave at the Center for the Philosophy of the Natural and Social Sciences at the London School of Economics. He thanks Simon Fraser University for the sabbatical leave and the London School of Economics for a congenial and intellectually stimulating atmosphere for thinking and writing.

—*Charles Crawford*
*Dennis L. Krebs*
*Simon Fraser University*

# About the Contributors

**Christopher Badcock**, Sociology Department, London School of Economics.

**J. Michael Bailey**, Department of Psychology, Northwestern University, Evanston, IL.

**Laura Betzig**, Museum of Zoology, University of Michigan, Ann Arbor.

**Derek Bickerton**, Department of Linguistics, University of Hawaii at Manoa, Honolulu.

**David Buss**, Department of Psychology, University of Texas, Austin.

**Charles Crawford**, Department of Psychology, Simon Fraser University, Burnaby, British Columbia.

**Martin Daly**, Department of Psychology, Mcmaster University, Hamilton, Ontario.

**Yuwa Hedrick-Wong**, Horizon Pacific International, Vancouver, British Columbia.

**Mario Heilmann**, Communications Studies, University of California at Los Angeles.

**Harmon Holcomb, III**, Department of Philosophy, University of Kentucky, Lexington.

**Maria Janicki**, Department of Psychology, Simon Fraser University, Burnaby, British Columbia.

**Richard C. Keefe**, Department of Psychology, Scottsdale College, Scottsdale, Arizona.

**Douglas Kenrick**, Department of Psychology, Arizona State University, Tempe.

**Dennis Krebs**, Department of Psychology, Simon Fraser University, Burnaby, British Columbia.

**Bobbi S. Low**, School of Natural Resources and Environment, University of Michigan, Ann Arbor.

**Neil Malamuth**, Communication Studies and Psychology Department, University of California at Los Angeles.

**Geoffrey F. Miller**, Centre for Economic Learning and Social Evolution, University College, London.

**Krista Philips**, Department of Psychology, York University, Downsview, Ontario.

**Irwin Silverman**, Department of Psychology, York University, North York, Ontario.

**Edward K. Sadalla**, Department of Psychology, Arizona State University, Tempe.

**Michele Surbey**, Department of Psychology, Mount Allison University, Sackville, New Brunswick.

**Randy Thornhill**, Department of Biology, University of New Mexico, Albuquerque.

**Andrew Wells**, Department of Social Psychology, The London School of Economics and Political Science, London.

**Margo Wilson**, Department of Psychology, Mcmaster University, Hamilton, Ontario.

# I

# *IDEAS*

Modern evolutionary theory is a vast and complex field of study. Part I of this book introduces readers to those aspects of evolutionary theorizing that have been particularly important during the last decade, and that we believe will continue to be important for some time. Part I in the first edition contained four chapters: "Sociobiology of What Value to Psychology," "Evolution: A Primer for Psychologists," "Sociobiology and Knowledge: Is Evolutionary Epistemology a Viable Option?", and "The Challenge of Altruism in Psychology and Biology." Only the first of these chapters remains. It has been reorganized and expanded in chapter 1 to provide an introduction to evolutionary theory and an orientation to how it is currently being used in the study of human behavior.

The new chapters in Part I, and their level of sophistication, reflect the maturing of the evolutionary analysis of human behavior that has occurred since the publication of the first edition 10 years ago. A primer of evolutionary theory is less necessary now because there are dozens of chapters and books giving introductions to the Theory of Evolution by Natural Selection. Because of the expansion of knowledge on the evolutionary significance of human behavior during the last few years, the philosophical question,

"Does evolutionary theory provide a viable approach to the study of human behavior?" has changed to, "How should evolutionary hypotheses be tested?"

Kinship theory has been at the heart of evolutionary thinking since Hamilton's paper on the subject in 1964. However, its application is not easy. Chapter 2, entitled "Acting for the Good of Others: Kinship and Reciprocity With Some New Twists," explains the basic logic of kinship and reciprocity theory and how they are related. This chapter clarifies many important issues, and results in improved thinking and research in these key areas of modern evolutionary thought.

Darwin's Theory of Sexual Selection, which he developed to help understand sex differences in anatomy and gender differences in behavior, has been a very active area of evolutionary research during the past decade. Many chapters in this book rely on sexual selection for their theoretical orientation. Chapter 3 reviews contemporary thinking on sexual selection and how it is being used by researchers. However, it goes beyond contemporary usage and speculates on how its explanatory power may deeply penetrate into new areas of the study of human behavior.

The life history, the developmental timetable of an organism, the way energy and resources are deployed at different times in the life of an organism is shaped by natural selection. Part I includes the chapter on life-history theory (chap. 4), an area of contemporary evolutionary thinking that holds great promise for guiding future empirical, theoretical, and integrative research on the evolutionary significance of human behavior.

This part concludes with a chapter on human culture because the evolutionary analysis of human culture confronts many of the most difficult issues in the application of evolutionary thinking to human behavior. Hence, this chapter leads to both Parts II and III of this volume.

# The Theory of Evolution in the Study of Human Behavior: An Introduction and Overview

Charles Crawford
*Simon Fraser University*

> *Man with all his noble qualities, with sympathy that feels for the most debased, with benevolence which extends not only to other men but to the humblest of living creatures, with his god-like intellect which has penetrated into the movements and constitution of the solar system—with all these exalted powers—still bears in his bodily frame the indelible stamp of his lowly origin.*
>
> —Charles Darwin (1871/1898)

## RESISTANCE TO EVOLUTIONARY EXPLANATIONS

Early in this century, thinkers such as William James, John Dewey, and Sigmund Freud embraced Darwinism with enthusiasm, but for the past 75 years, a major activity of those involved in the study of human behavior has been "debiologizing" it. Neobehaviorism, social learning theory, cognitive theory, modern psychoanalysis, and, more recently, a variety of postmodernist explanations, as well as politically liberal approaches to the amelioration of social problems, currently dominate the thinking of many academics. Most individuals taking these approaches see little value in ancestral history, human nature, or innate mental mechanisms developing explanations for human behavior.

During the late 19th and early 20th Centuries, there was a strong emphasis on improving society and the lot of those living in it. Because they accepted Jean-Baptiste Lamarck's theory of the inheritance of acquired characteristics, many academic-minded reformers turned to evolutionary theory as a means to reform. They believed that acquired habits, such as prudence, diligence, and restraint, which contributed to successful reproduction in one generation, would be favored by natural selection, and within a few generations, we could all be living in a better society.

Yet, two events occurred just after the turn of the century that shattered these hopes (Degler, 1991). First, August Weisman put forth convincing arguments, supported by some empirical data, that traits acquired during the lifetime of an individual cannot be inherited by his or her offspring. If Weisman was correct, evolution by natural selection did not offer the quick fixes for solving societal problems that early Social Darwinists, such as Herbert Spencer, had expected. Second, the rediscovery of Mendel's laws seemed to provide a sound scientific basis for explaining the biological inheritance of a wide variety of physical and behavioral traits, and suggested that selective breeding of humans could lead to an improvement in society. Weisman and Mendel's discoveries, combined with the desire to produce a better world, sent reformers in two directions (Degler, 1991). Some were attracted to genetic explanations of differences between individuals and groups, and eventually to eugenics, whereas others were attracted to the *tabula rasa* view of human nature. The controversy surrounding Herrnstein and Murray's (1994) *The Bell Curve: Intelligence and Class Structure in American Life* and Wright's (1994) *The Moral Animal: Evolutionary Psychology and Everyday Life* suggests that the intellectual and scientific struggle between these approaches continues, and that the *tabula rasa* view dominates the thinking of the majority of scientists involved in the study of human behavior.

There are political reasons for the widespread resistance to incorporating ideas from evolutionary theory into thinking about human behavior; until recently, a major scientific reason for the wariness was that the theory did not provide a repertoire of useful constructs for formulating detailed explanations of human and animal behavior. Therefore, when the theory of evolution was employed, it was often used as a convenient framework for discussing adaptiveness or as a way to integrate diverse ideas, rather than as a paradigm for developing testable explanations of behavior. During the last three decades, however, the modern synthesis has been enriched by concepts such as inclusive fitness, kin selection, reciprocity theory, and the evolution of life histories, which have made it more applicable to behavior. New techniques for analyzing the formation and nature of adaptations have been developed, such as the theory of evolutionarily stable strategies and optimality theory. Moreover, during the past 5 years, a new discipline focused on the naturally selected design of the mental mechanisms that make up the mind has begun to emerge (Cosmides & Tooby, 1987). It is known as Darwinian or evolutionary psychology.

This introductory chapter begins by reviewing the logic of the Theory of Evolution by Natural Selection and discusses several issues concerned with its use. Then kinship, reciprocity, sexual selection, and the significance of ancestral history are briefly described. The role of genetics in developing evolutionary explanations is controversial so several pages are devoted to some of the related issues. Finally, a bit of time is spent discussing the validation of evolutionary explanations.

## NATURAL SELECTION AND ITS LOGIC

An *adaptation* is an anatomical structure, a physiological process, or a behavior pattern that contributed to ancestral individuals' ability to survive and reproduce in competition with other members of their species (Williams, 1966; Wilson, 1975). *Natural selection*, the process that shapes adaptations, is the differential production or survival of offspring by genetically different members of the population. Darwin's (1859) logic may be explained in terms of the following assumptions and inferences:

*Assumption 1:* All species are capable of overproducing offspring.

*Assumption 2:* The size of populations of individuals tends to remain relatively stable over time.

*Assumption 3:* Resources for supporting individuals are limited.

*Inference 1:* A struggle for existence among individuals ensues.

*Assumption 4:* Individuals differ on traits (i.e., adaptations) that enable them to survive and reproduce.

*Assumption 5:* At least some of the variation in these traits is heritable.

*Inference 2:* There is differential production or survival of offspring by genetically different members of the population, which is, by definition, natural selection.

*Inference 3:* Through many generations, evolution of traits that are more adaptive than others will occur through natural selection.

In summary, some feature of the environment, perhaps the arrival of a new predator or a change in climate, poses a problem for organisms. Genetically based variants, such as longer legs or thicker fur, contribute to reproduction and survival. These assumptions and inferences explain how natural selection provides the solution. Preexisting adaptations, sometimes called *preadaptations*, provide both stepping stones and limits to the solutions natural selection can provide (Gould, 1982). Hence, there are constraints on the "perfection" of the solution natural selection can provide.

This view might be called the phenotypic view of evolution because the focus is on the anatomical structures, physiological processes, or behavior patterns that helped solve the problems faced by the organism. Although at least some of the phenotypic variation must be heritable for natural selection to occur, genetic concepts are not referred to explicitly. However, it is also possible to describe evolution by natural selection in terms of changes in allele frequencies caused by selection, mutation, migration, genetic drift, and other processes. Some scientists favor this more quantitative approach because it enables them to construct precise models of evolutionary processes that may be tested through experimental research, field studies, or computer model simulations. Others believe that the focus of evolutionary work must be on the formation of adaptations. They tend to favor the phenotypic view. However, the two descriptions are complementary, and together they make up the modern synthetic theory of evolution.

## SOME COMMON MISCONCEPTIONS

### Circularity

There are some who still believe that the logic of evolution by natural selection is circular—the fittest survive because they are the fittest. However, this view is incorrect (Sober, 1984). Note that in the prior description of Darwin's logic, the definitions of both *adaptation* and *natural selection* are independent of the assumptions. If one accepts the definitions and can document the validity of the assumptions, then evolution by natural selection follows logically. Darwin extensively documented the validity of the assumptions and, since his time, massive additional evidence for their validity has accumulated (e.g., see Ridley, 1993).

### Nature of Competition

The first three assumptions and their inference do not require that nature be "red in tooth and claw." Differential production or survival of offspring by genetically different members of a population is the basis of evolution by natural selection. Animals use a variety of subtle, and not so subtle, strategies for competing with members of their species. For example, juvenile Florida scrub jays apparently increase their fitness by deferring reproduction for up to 7 years to assist their parents in raising additional broods of siblings (Woolfenden & Fitzpatrick, 1984). In "The Geometry of the Selfish Herd," Hamilton (1971) argued that individual animals in aggregations position themselves in such a way that their risk of predation, relative to others in the aggregation, is minimized.

### Genetic Preprogramming of Evolved Traits

Although Assumptions 4 and 5 require that some trait variation be genetically conditioned for natural selection to occur, they do not imply that the development of evolved traits is genetically preprogrammed. If the ontogeny of a trait is influenced by environmental factors, biologists refer to it as a *facultative trait* and label the genes involved in its development *facultative genes*. For example, the white crowned sparrow must hear an adult male sparrow sing while it is a nestling and it must sing itself as a juvenile if it is to sing a complete song as an adult (Konishi, 1965; Marler, 1984). Moreover, the young sparrow does not, and indeed cannot, learn the song of another species. Apparently, this developmental process ensures that the species' song is learned, but that it can be adjusted to local dialects.

### Acting for the Good of the Group

> Though occasionally, in the territorial or rival fights, by some mishap a horn may penetrate an eye or a tooth an artery, we have never found that the aim of aggression was the *extermination of fellow members of the species* concerned. (Lorenz, 1966, p. 47; emphasis added)

This quotation illustrates Lorenz's assumption, shared by many others, that individuals evolve to act for the good of the group. Similarly, Wynne-Edwards (1962) argued that selection acts on groups rather than on individuals. Models of group selection, although attractive to those attempting to understand the paradox of the existence of "helping" behavior in many species and the inability of "individual fitness"-based evolutionary theory to explain its evolution, have usually foundered on the problem of "cheating" (Williams, 1966).

Consider a number of groups, each made up of individuals who sacrifice some of their reproductive fitness for the good of other group members, competing with each other. Here, a *sacrifice* is defined as any action, such as the provision of food, care, or protection to other group members, that reduces the reproductive success of the performer and increases the reproductive success of the recipient(s). Groups made up of such altruistic individuals may prosper. However, an individual group member possessing a mutation that programmed, or enabled the learning of, the acceptance of helping behavior without reciprocation would leave more offspring than altruistic members of the group. As a result, groups or species made up of individuals acting for the common good would be undermined by mutation from within and by immigration from without. Hence, for group selection to be a viable evolutionary process, groups must appear and disappear at an unrealistically high rate (Maynard Smith, 1976). Although attempts to develop more sophisticated models of group selection are underway (Wilson & Sober, 1994), they do not yet provide a viable alternative to individual and kin selection. Reeve discusses models of group selection in chapter 2 (this volume).

## INCOMPATIBILITY OF EVOLUTIONARY AND NONEVOLUTIONARY EXPLANATIONS

Must evolutionary and nonevolutionary explanations make different predictions? To answer this question consider two sets of explanations. The first set contains explanations that were explicitly constructed with evolutionary theory in mind. The second set contains explanations that were developed without any explicit knowledge of evolutionary theory. However, some of these latter explanations, such as commonsense explanations like, "Blood is thicker than water," and, "It is a wise father that knows his own child," are compatible with evolutionary theory, although they were devised without knowledge of it. Other members of this second set, such as those designed to explain *true altruism*, where fitness costs outweigh benefits, are incompatible with the logic of evolution by natural selection. Thus, the greater set of all explanations that are compatible with evolutionary theory includes all of Set 1 and some overlap from Set 2.

Explanations that are not compatible with evolutionary theory can be thought of as "warp drive" explanations because warp drive is what the crew of the Starship Enterprise use when they wish to violate Einstein's theory of relativity to travel faster than the speed of light. Developing explanations of physical phenomena that violate Einstein's theory of relativity is risky, as is developing explanations about behavior that violate Darwin's theory of evolution by natural selection. Hence, it is likely that any good explanation of behavior will be compatible with an evolutionary explanation, even if it were not explicitly developed from an evolutionary perspective. Although a good explanation of behavior need not have been explicitly constructed from an evolutionary perspective, the contributors to this volume are committed to the proposition that an explicit consideration of evolutionary theory will improve the quality of explanations of human behavior.

Why do they believe this? First, explicit evolutionary thinking can sometimes eliminate certain kinds of errors in thinking about behavior (Symons, 1987). For example, it has been seen that explanations that implicitly assume organisms have evolved to act for the good of their group or species should be treated with considerable skepticism. In addition, use of the theory can sometimes help prevent one from making and accepting *moralistic fallacies*—where one assumes that what *ought* to be actually *is*. Consider some examples. Stepparents ought to treat their natural and stepchildren equally. However, when Daly and Wilson (1980) applied evolutionary thinking to the problem of child abuse, they found that stepparents were a major source of abuse. There ought not to be conflict within families, but Trivers (1974) has used evolutionary theory to help us understand the within-family conflict that has perplexed us for generations. Recently, Haig (1993) argued for the occurrence of mother–offspring conflict during gestation. Men and women ought to have the same intellectual abilities, but Silverman and Eals (1992) have been able to use evolutionary thinking to predict and explain gender differences in some perceptual abilities. A rigorous application of evolutionary theory may help us identify and deal with other *oughts* that contradict reality.

Second, because the theory of evolution explains the evolution of all life forms, concepts developed when using it are likely to be very general. Kinship theory (Hamilton, 1964), parental investment theory (Trivers, 1972), sexual-selection theory (Darwin, 1871/1898), and reciprocity theory (Trivers, 1971), for example, have been used to explain behavior in a great many species of animals. For many, it is intellectually satisfying to use the same theoretical framework, such as kin selection, to help explain sterile castes in worker bees, wasps, and ants (Hamilton, 1964); alarm calling in ground squirrels (Sherman, 1977); helping at the nest in jays (Woolfenden & Fitzpatrick, 1984); suicide in humans (de Catanzaro, 1991); the naming of natural and adoptive children (Johnson, McAndrew, & Harris, 1991); mortality and risk during a crisis year (McCullough & Barton, 1991); genetic relatedness, the biological importance of a decision, and decision rules (Burnstein, Crandall, & Kitayama, 1994); village fissioning among hunter–gatherers (Chagnon & Irons, 1979); and whom new babies are said to resemble (Daly & Wilson, 1982).

Third, and most important, the theory of evolution can be used to help scholars and scientists develop substantive testable predictions about human behavior. Cosmides (1989) used it to make predictions about content effects in logical reasoning. Silverman and Eals (1992) used it to make predictions about gender differences in spatial abilities. Singh (1993) used it to make predictions about preferences for body images. Buss (1994) used it to make predictions about gender differences in mate choice criteria and tactics for acquiring mates. Orians and Heerwagen (1992) used it to make predictions about evoked responses to landscapes. Several chapters in Part III of this book discuss recent research in which various aspects of evolutionary theory were used to derive testable predictions about human behavior.

## SOME ADDITIONAL PRINCIPLES

Although Darwin's logic of natural selection provides the basis of all evolutionary explanations, a number of concepts that were not fully developed in his thinking have been more completely refined during the last few years (e.g., sexual selection, kinship theory, and reciprocity). These concepts are discussed more fully in other chapters in Part I of this book, and they also surface in many chapters in Parts II and III.

### Sexual Selection

Human males and females differ in anatomy, physiology, and behavior. There are at least two sources of selection pressure that interact and complement each other in producing this evolved sexual dimorphism. The production and rearing of offspring may have caused some specialization of roles for ancestral males and females that resulted in selection for sexual dimorphism in physical body size, behavior, and brain development (Kimura, 1987; Tooby & DeVore, 1987). The other evolutionary explanation for sexual dimorphism is Darwin's theory of sexual selection.

*Sexual selection* refers to differences in the ability of individuals with different genotypes to acquire matings. For example, if tall and short males have similar survival, but tall males obtain more matings than short males, then sexual selection is said to be acting on the males. Darwin (1871/1898) argued that sexual selection involves two processes that are usually referred to as *intrasexual selection* and *intersexual selection*.

In intrasexual selection, competition between the members of one sex (usually males) for access to the other sex (usually females) produces selection pressure for increased physical size, organs of threat, and aggressiveness in members of the competing sex, as well as differences between males and females on these traits. Male elephant seals, for example, compete vigorously among themselves for access to females. They are about 60% larger than females and about four times as heavy. Although most males never get near a female during their entire lives, a few male elephant seals may have as many as a hundred females in their harems (LeBoeuf, 1974). The males make no investment in individual offspring, whereas the females provide large quantities of rich milk that contribute to rapid growth of the young. Intersexual selection, which is sometimes called *epigamic selection*, is the result of the members of one sex (usually females) generating competition between members of the other sex by "expressing" choice for a mating partner. The competition results in the elaboration of the traits members of the choosy sex "desire." The tail of the male peacock provides the classic example.

Why do males compete for females, and do females ever compete for males? Trivers (1972) attempted to develop a more general scheme for considering sexually selected traits than the one Darwin employed. He developed the notion of relative parental investment, where parental investment is defined as behavior of a parent toward an offspring that contributes to the offspring's reproduction at the cost of the parent's investment in other offspring. Because the females of most species put relatively greater minimal investment into individual offspring than do males, they are limited in the additional offspring that additional matings can provide to them. Because males put less investment into individual offspring than do females, the former are less limited in the benefits of additional matings. Thus, females are a limiting resource for males, and males can benefit by competing among themselves for access to that resource. Males are usually, but not always, the sexually selected sex.

Exceptions that prove the rule are provided by organisms with gender role reversal such as seahorses, certain frogs, and several species of marsh and shorebirds (including jacanas and phalaropes). In these species, although males make a small investment in sperm, their relative minimal parental investment is large because they take sole responsibility for parental care (Alcock, 1993). As a result, females have evolved to be larger and/or more colorful than the males, and compete among themselves for access to males.

But relative parental investment does not seem to explain why females are often so choosy. Several explanations have been offered. Darwin suggested that the females of some species had a sense of beauty. In his "sexy sons" explanation of female choice, Fisher (1930) argued that females can evolve to favor an arbitrary trait if their sons exhibit the trait and their daughters favor males who exhibit it. Zahavi (1975) argued that certain traits are attractive to females because they provide a handicap that indicates something about the quality of male genes. Thus, the large, brightly colored tail of the peacock may be saying to the female, "Look at my large and beautiful tail. It takes a lot of my resources to grow it. It is cumbersome to maneuver and it may attract predators. But the fact that I have it, despite these costs, shows that I am a vigorous and healthy male and you should choose to mate with me rather than with a male who has a dull, droopy tail." At first, the "sexy sons" and "handicap" arguments were greeted with skepticism. During the last few years, however, the role of ancestral parasites in the evolution of sexuality, the differences between males' and females' reproductive tactics, and how the members of each sex evaluate prospective mating partners have helped us understand how apparent handicaps may provide clues about the fitness of their possessors. In chapter 3, Miller reviews the latest thinking on the origins of sexual dimorphism and its importance in explaining gender differences in behavior.

Are humans a sexually selected species? Men are about 7% larger than women. They are more physically aggressive than women; they die off faster than women at all ages, and they do not live as long as women. They take risks that women consider foolhardy. Men vary more than women in the number of children they produce. Women often invest more in their children than do men. Throughout history, most men have mated monogamously. However, a sample of 849 societies found that 83% are either usually or occasionally polygynous, 16% are monogamous, and 0.5% are polyandrous (Daly & Wilson, 1983). Even in monogamous societies, such as the Hutterites, variance of male reproductive success exceeds that of females (Crawford, 1984). This evidence indicates that humans are a moderately sexually selected species. Several chapters in Part III of this book rely on the theory of sexual selection for their explanations. Buss (chap. 13) uses it in his work on gender differences in mate selection criteria. Daly and Wilson (chap. 14) use it to help explain family violence. It also has implications for Malmuth and Heilmann's (chap. 17) work on coercive sexuality.

### Kinship and Its Ramifications

*Altruistic behavior*, which can be defined as "self destructive behavior performed for the benefit of others" (Wilson, 1975, p. 578), has long been a paradox for evolutionary theorists. According to the logic of natural selection, it should not evolve, but it is widespread in nature. Darwin believed that the "neuter insects," the sterile castes in the bees, wasps, and ants, might be fatal to his theory. However, in 1964, Hamilton elaborated Darwin's solution to the problem and expressed it in the language of modern population biology:

> The social behavior of a species evolves in such a way that in each distinct behavior evoking situation the individual will *seem* to value his neighbors' fitness against his own according to the coefficients of relationship appropriate to that situation. (p. 19; emphasis added)

Hamilton saw that biological altruism can evolve, although it reduces the reproductive fitness of the donor of the help, if it aids the donor's genetic kin, some of whom must inherit the helping allele from a common ancestor of the donor. This statement can be expressed as an equation:

$$Br_1 > Cr_2$$

where $B$ = the benefit to the donor, $r_1$ = the genetic correlation between the donor and the recipient's offspring, $C$ = the cost to the donor, and $r_2$ = the correlation between the donor and its own offspring. In this equation, $r_1$ and $r_2$ represent the probabilities that the individuals in question have an allele that is a copy of one in a common ancestor. Such an allele is described as *identical by common descent*. These probabilities are called *genetic correlations* or coefficients of relatedness between individuals.

Consider the case of an individual who possesses a helping allele $A$ for giving up one offspring to help a full sibling produce three additional offspring. This allele was inherited from the parent of the two sibs. When a gamete is produced, a segregation occurs and only one of each pair of chromosomes is passed on to the fertilized egg. Therefore, the probability that any particular allele in a parent is passed on to an offspring is 0.5. There are two genetic segregations between the donor and any of his or her three additional nieces or nephews that were produced because of the help. Therefore, there is a 0.25 (0.5 × 0.5) chance that any one of them inherits the helping allele possessed by the donor, who is their uncle or aunt. However, there is only one segregation between the donor and his or her one, forgone offspring, resulting in a genetic correlation of 0.5. Putting these numbers into Hamilton's equation produces the following:

$$3(0.25) > 1(0.50)$$
$$0.75 > 0.50$$

Therefore, natural selection can favor the evolution of mechanisms for producing this *altruistic* behavior. Note that both sides of the equation refer to changes in the donor's fitness because of the *altruistic* act. The right side indicates the direct cost to the donor through offspring not produced, whereas the left side indicates the indirect benefits to the donor through offspring that a genetic relative was able to rear because of the help. Thus, Hamilton's altruism is really a special kind of *selfishness*. Those looking to evolutionary theory to provide an explanation for *true altruism*, a behavior that reduces the inclusive fitness of the performer while benefitting that of the recipient, will not find it in Hamilton's equation. As seen later, in a current environment, the action of mechanisms for implementing Hamilton's selfishness can result in something like true altruism.

### Within-Family Conflict

It is instructive to show how Trivers (1974, 1985) applied Hamilton's logic to within-family conflict. Figure 1.1 can be used to compute the probabilities that parents, grandparents, and children possess an allele (say $A$,

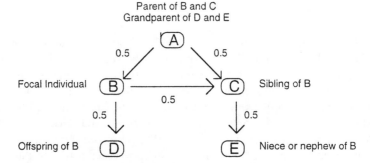

Parent of B and C
Grandparent of D and E

FIG. 1.1. Multiplying along the arrows connecting two individuals gives the probability that they will share an allele by common descent. (A grandparent, A, is equally related to all his or her children, B and C, and to all his or her grandchildren, D and E. However, the focal individual, B, shares an allele with any of his or her children, D, with probability 0.5, and with any of his or her nieces and nephews, E, with probability 0.25. Thus, B is selected to desire an unequal share of A's resources.) From "The Theory of Evolution: Of What Value to Psychology?" by C. B. Crawford, 1989, *Journal of Comparative Psychology, 103,* p. 8. Copyright © 1989 by the American Psychological Association. Reprinted with permission.

or $a$) that is a copy of an allele possessed by a common ancestor. These probabilities are computed by raising 0.5 (the probability that $A$ or $a$ is passed on when a gamete is formed) to the power of the number of genetic segregations (represented as arrows in Fig. 1.1) connecting two individuals. We can see that the genetic correlation between the focal individual and its own offspring is 0.5 because an individual in a sexually breeding species passes one half of its chromosomes onto each of its offspring. We can also see that the genetic correlation between the focal individual and its sibling's offspring (i.e., its niece or nephew) is 0.25 ($0.5^2$) because they are connected by two arrows.

Trivers (1974) used Hamilton's argument—that the behavior of an individual, whether it be a parent, child, or grandparent, is shaped by natural selection to maximize the probability that copies of alleles it carries are replicated through its behavior—to analyze within-family conflict. Because the probability of the focal individual replicating its allele(s) through its own offspring is 0.5 and through its sibling's offspring (its niece or nephew) is only 0.25, natural selection will favor focal individuals that seek an unequal share of their parents' (labeled "grandparent" in Fig. 1.1) resources. Because the parent (grandparent) is equally related to all its children and grandchildren, it will be selected to resist the focal individual's demands.

When the offspring is young, the parent can maximize its fitness by investing in the current offspring at the expense of additional offspring, who would be future siblings of the current offspring. When the offspring is old, it can maximize its fitness if it defers parental investment to this individual in favor of investing in younger offspring. Conflict is most intense at intermediate ages of the focal offspring. During this period, the parent's fitness is increased more by investing in additional offspring, whereas the focal offspring's fitness is increased more by continued parental investment. Thus, the intensity of within-family conflict varies both as a function of genetic relationships and the relative ages of individuals in the family.

Recently, Haig (1993) extended Trivers' thinking by considering three sets of genes that may have different interests: (a) genes in the mother, (b) maternally derived genes in the current child, and (c) paternally derived genes in the current child. Because maternal genes have an equal stake in each child, they will be selected to transfer resources to children as a function of the children's likelihood of reproducing. Genes in the current child have a greater interest in the current child than in future children and will be selected to maximize transfer of resources to the current child. Some genes are imprinted with information about their parental origin. This fact makes the situation more complicated if the mother has children from different fathers because paternally imprinted genes in the current offspring have no stake in offspring fathered by different males. Haig provided arguments and evidence of how these conflicts have influenced the evolution of the female reproductive system and how they can lead to serious health problems for mothers.

The basic logic of kinship theory and its application are explained in chapter 2. In addition, kinship plays a particularly important role in explaining the empirical data in chapter 14 on family violence by Daly and Wilson. The real significance of kinship, however, is that it shifts the emphasis in evolutionary thinking from the individual level to the allele level, and, as has been seen, sheds light on many difficult problems.

**Reciprocity**

Because much behavior, both in animals and humans, includes interactions between individuals who are not genetic kin, additional concepts are necessary for explaining the evolution of social behavior. Darwin recognized the importance of cooperation. However, it was Trivers (1971) who developed the modern theory of reciprocal altruism. Consider the example he used in developing his theory. Suppose you are standing on a dock and you see a man fall into the water and begin to drown. You know that he is not a genetic relative, but you find a life preserver and, by throwing it to him, save his life. Will natural selection favor such action across evolutionary time? If there is even a $\frac{1}{1000}$ chance that you will fall in and drown in your effort to save the drowning man, it would seem that natural selection should select for a preference for ignoring the individual in trouble. Suppose that there is a $\frac{1}{20}$ chance that the roles will be reversed, and that sometime you will need to be saved from a watery death. If there is a greater than $\frac{1}{50}$ chance that the individual you saved will save you, then natural selection can select for the tendency to help the original individual, even though he is not a genetic relative.

In the evolution of tendencies to act reciprocally, because the original helping acts must occur by chance, they would have to be acts of low cost for the donors and provide large benefits for the recipients, or natural selection would eliminate the tendency to perform them, and the system could not get started. Moreover, the roles of donor and recipient must frequently reverse. Finally, the original recipient must be able to recognize the helper so he or she can reciprocate when the roles are reversed. These conditions suggest that reciprocal altruism is most likely to evolve in highly intelligent, closely integrated species. Humans and the higher primates come to mind (Trivers, 1971, 1985).

*Cheating*, accepting help when it is given, but not reciprocating when the roles are reversed, can undermine reciprocity. Trivers (1985) distinguished between two types of cheating. In *gross cheating*, the recipient does not reciprocate or reciprocates so little to the original donor that the benefits are significantly less than the cost of the original donor's act. For example, I am drowning, you find a life preserver, throw it to me, and pull me in. Later, you are drowning and I merely toss you the nearest twig. In *subtle cheating*, both parties reciprocate, but one party reciprocates somewhat less than the other. Both parties benefit, but one consistently benefits more than the other. For example, you and I have lunch once a week. When it is your turn to pay for lunch, we dine at a nice restaurant, but when it is my turn to pay, we dine at the sandwich shop. However, you may not want to terminate the arrangement because you may need a letter of reference from me in the future.

The great benefits received by individuals involved in a reciprocal system will provide strong selection for mechanisms for engaging in reciprocity, but the benefits obtained by gross and, especially, subtle cheating will select for mechanisms for giving back less than one receives. Trivers (1985) argued that, because human reciprocity may span many years and involve thousands of interactions varying on many dimensions, computing the cost–benefit ratios that keep the reciprocal system running requires a complex and subtle psyche. Guilt, fairness, moralistic aggression, gratitude, and sympathy are just some of the feelings and emotions required to make human reciprocal altruism run. Many authors have expanded on Trivers' original notions (Alexander, 1987; Krebs, 1987).

## PROXIMATE MECHANISMS

The mathematical analysis of kinship and reciprocity theory is impressive; it indicates that natural selection may have produced adaptations mediating both cooperation and conflict between genetically related and unrelated individuals. But would not a complicated set of behavioral or mental mechanisms be required to make it all happen? In the late 1980s, Cosmides and Tooby (1987) and Symons (1987) began forcefully arguing that an evolutionary approach cannot be agnostic about the nature of the proximate mechanisms that produce behavior. The result was the beginning of a new area within evolutionary studies. It is known as Darwinian or evolutionary psychology and is concerned with: (a) the stresses that existed in ancestral environments, (b) the proximate mechanisms that evolved to deal with those stresses, and (c) the way those evolved mechanisms function in contemporary environments (Crawford & Anderson, 1989).

### Kin Recognition Mechanisms

If social organisms have evolved the capacity to put their helping behavior where their alleles are, as Hamilton and Trivers assumed, they must possess some proximate mechanisms for kin recognition, and these should be of interest to Darwinian psychologists. Possible mechanisms for kin recognition include spatial distribution (treating individuals in a prescribed geographic area as kin), frequency of association (treating frequent associates as kin), phenotype matching (treating individuals similar to oneself or similar to those with whom one was raised as kin), and recognition alleles (innately treating individuals with a particular genetic marker as kin). They have received attention from both biologists (Holmes, 1986; Waldman, 1986) and psychologists (Porter, 1987).

If small kinship groups were an important feature of human social structure during our evolution, then one or more of the previously described kin discrimination mechanisms may have evolved and may still be influencing our behavior. Understanding the mechanism(s) involved may be critical if we wish to change human behavior through social learning. For example, if spatial distribution or association evolved as mechanisms of human kin discrimination, then encouraging individuals from different ethnic groups to live together in the same geographic area may contribute to ethnic harmony. However, other kin discrimination mechanisms may prescribe different means for achieving ethnic harmony. If treating individuals similar to those with whom one was raised is a human kin discrimination mechanism, then ethnically integrating schools starting with preschools rather than high schools is more likely to lead to ethnic harmony. If treating individuals similar to oneself as kin was an aspect of kin discrimination among our ancestors, then it may be necessary to encourage different ethnic groups to adopt similar accents, manners, customs, and clothing to increase ethnic harmony. Finally, if genetically produced signs evolved among our ancestors to discriminate between kin and nonkin, then producing ethnic harmony may, indeed, be difficult because social learning is not involved.

Research on the evolutionary significance of proximate mechanisms involved in kin discrimination, social exchange, and mate selection is developing rapidly (see Barkow, Cosmides, & Tooby, 1992, for a review of some of this work). However, this focus on proximate mental mechanisms is not without its critics. There is a school of Darwinian-oriented anthropology that focuses on reproduction rather than the inputs and outputs of proximate psychological mechanisms. It has come to be known as Darwinian anthropology or Darwinian social science (e.g., see *Ethology & Sociobiology*, 1990, Volume 11, Number 4/5, which is devoted to this topic). Betzig explains and defends this point of view in chapter 8 (this volume).

## ADAPTATIONS AND THE BEHAVIOR OF INDIVIDUALS

We have seen that an adaptation is an anatomical structure, a physiological process, or a behavior pattern that contributed to ancestral individuals' ability to survive and reproduce in competition with other members of their species (Williams, 1966; Wilson, 1975). The beaks of Darwin's finches, which can be used to characterize the different species of finches living on the Galapagos, provide the classic example of an adaptation. Biologists, who are frequently interested in species' differences and how they were shaped through natural selection, often do not focus on how the concept of adaptation can be used to explain differences in behavior within a particular species. However, when the focus is on the behavior of a single species, as it is in the study of human behavior, the focus must be on how the concept of adaptation can be used to explain differences in behavior manifest by members of the same species.

Consider several examples. In their seminal article, "The Dawn of Darwinian Medicine," Williams and Nesse (1991) gave several examples of how adaptations can help an organism respond differently to differing circumstances. Fever appears to be the result of a specific regulatory mechanism that adjusts body temperature in response to the toxins of some bacteria. When fever is blocked by drugs such as aspirin, resistance to infection may be decreased. Similarly, the sequestering of iron in the

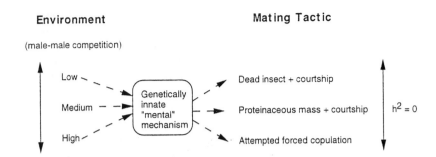

FIG. 1.2. Mating tactics in scorpionflies (*Panorpa sp.*). (The level of male–male competition determines the reproductive tactic used. Heritability of the tactics is zero because all males have alleles for all tactics.) From "The Theory of Evolution: Of What Value to Psychology?" by C. B. Crawford, 1989, *Journal of Comparative Psychology, 103*, p. 15. Copyright © 1989 by the American Psychological Association. Adapted with permission.

liver, which reduces the iron content of the plasma by up to 20%, deprives some bacteria of a vital mineral and inhibits their spread through the body. In both cases, the adaptations adjust bodily functions in response to varying environmental conditions.

Consider a behavioral example in some detail. Figure 1.2 illustrates the mating strategy of the male scorpionfly. The strategy contains three mating tactics: (a) males may obtain a dead insect, present it to a female, and copulate with her as she eats it; (b) they may generate a salivary mass, present it to the female, and copulate with her as she eats it; or (c) if they cannot obtain a dead insect or generate the proteinaceous salivary mass, they may attempt a forced copulation (Thornhill, 1980). In a variety of experimental studies, Thornhill (1980) has shown that all three tactics are available to all adult males, and that it is success in male–male competition that determines the behavior employed to obtain a mating. In these examples, the putative adaptations respond to both external and internal environmental contingencies, producing differences in behavior that contributed to ancestral fitness.

## Adaptations as Decision Makers

Adaptations can be understood in terms of processes for carrying out the cost–benefit analysis an ancestral organism required to survive its daily encounters with problems in its internal and external environment. For example, the fever adaptation can be considered as a set of decision processes for dealing with certain kinds of invading bacteria, such as the rule, "If bacteria A, B, or C is invading the body, raise body temperature

X degrees." Harmful bacteria may be destroyed if the body temperature is raised X degrees, which is beneficial to the individual. Yet, the adaptation has costs as well as benefits. Energy is required to raise the body temperature. Moreover, the rise in body temperature can damage other systems of the body if it is excessive and prolonged. Similarily, the three mating tactics of the male scorpionfly have costs as well as benefits. Even the strong dominant males, who obtain matings by presenting dead insects to females as nuptial gifts, risk broken legs and torn wings in the competition with other males for the dead insects (Thornhill, 1980). Thus, my working definition of an *adaptation* is a set of genetically coded decision processes that enabled ancestral organisms to carry out cost–benefit analyses in response to a specific set of environmental contingencies, and that organized the effector processes for dealing with those contingencies in such a way that gene(s) producing the decision processes would be reproduced better than alternate sets of genes.

When operating in the behavioral domain, we can think of the sets of decision rules as mental mechanisms designed by natural selection for producing the different behaviors required for ancestral survival, growth, and reproduction. Cosmides (1989) coined the term *Darwinian algorithm* for mental mechanisms shaped by natural selection. These "innate school marms," to borrow a phrase from Lorenz (1966), are specialized, innate learning mechanisms that organize experience into adaptively meaningful schemata. When activated by appropriate problem content, they focus attention, organize perception and memory, and call up specialized procedural knowledge that leads to domain-appropriate inferences, judgments, and choices. The mental mechanism producing the mating behaviors of the scorpionfly can thus be considered as an example of a simple Darwinian algorithm. Chomsky's language-acquisition device provides a much more complex example.

## Concurrent and Developmentally Contingent Tactics

The mating behavior of male scorpionflies is an example of a single mating strategy with *concurrently contingent tactics* because the tactics employed depend on current environmental conditions. A strategy may also contain *developmentally contingent tactics*, behaviors that depend on external environmental conditions during development for their functioning (Crawford & Anderson, 1989). Song learning in some species of birds, which requires the song of an adult of the species to be heard during development, and language learning in humans, which also requires that information be obtained during development, provide examples of developmentally contingent tactics.

### Innate and Operational Adaptations

If the organism is living in its natural environment, the operation of its adaptations should contribute to its reproductive success. However, if the organism is living, or has developed, in an environment different from the one in which it evolved, one or more of its adaptations may produce behaviors different from those seen in the ancestral environment. If the current environment differs greatly from the ancestral environment, some adaptations may fail and detract from the lifetime reproductive success of their possessor. In developing this point, it is helpful to distinguish between the innate adaptation and the operational adaptation. *Innate adaptation* refers to species-typical information encoded in genes that directs the development of a phenotype in such a way that the genetically encoded information is passed from generation to generation more efficiently and effectively than information from an alternative set of genes. Yet, all traits require an environment for development. *Operational adaptation* can be defined as the phenotype that develops on the basis of genetic information in conjunction with the internal and external developmental environments of the organism.

Figure 1.3 illustrates how the same innate adaptation may produce quite different behaviors in ancestral and current environments. In the upper part of the figure (labeled "Then"), specific selection pressures on a species produce the innate adaptation, conceptualized as genetically specified innate information-processing mechanisms instantiated in neural hardware. The ancestral developmental environment in conjunction with the innate adaptation produces the operational adaptation—the mental mechanisms that actually produce behavior. The actual ancestral behavior is produced by the operational adaptation as it responds to current ancestral conditions. Now, consider the lower part of the figure (labeled "Now"). The innate adaptation is unchanged, but one or both of the developmental and current environments may differ from those of the ancestral world. As a result, current operational adaptations and behaviors may differ from those of our ancestors.

If the current developmental environment differs from the ancestral developmental environment, then the operational environment may differ from that seen in the ancestral environment. For example, it is likely that practices for educating children have changed greatly since Pleistocene times (Bernhard, 1988). To the extent that our developmental environment helps shape our intellectual abilities, our current abilities may differ con-

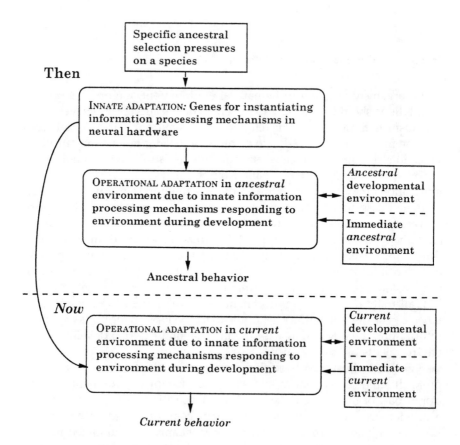

FIG. 1.3. Evolutionary psychology: The relation between ancestral adaptations and current behavior. The evolutionary psychologist's perspective on how the evolved innate adaptation in conjunction with the current developmental and immediate environments produces current behavior. Because there is a clear distinction between ancestral and current environments, and between ancestral and current operational adaptations (although not between ancestral and current innate adaptations), ancestral and current behavior may differ considerably. Although ancestral behavior contributed to ancestral fitness, and hence, the evolution of the innate adaptation, current behavior need not contribute to current fitness. From "The Future of Sociobiology: Counting Babies or Studying Proximate Mechanisms" by C. B. Crawford, 1993, *Trends in Evolution and Ecology, 8,* p. 185. Copyright © 1993 by Elsevier Science Publishers Ltd. Adapted with permission.

siderably from those of our ancestors. Moreover, the intellectual abilities of our descendants may differ from our abilities.

Even if the current and ancestral operational adaptations were identical, it is still possible that the distribution of current information in the ancestral and current environments could differ, and hence different behaviors might been seen in the two environments. Suppose, for the sake of argument, that an operational adaptation for adjusting one's personal level of aggression to the current level of aggression observed in the environment occurred in both ancestral and current children. If the distribution of aggression seen on TV by children differs from the level of aggression that ancestral children would have seen, then the identical operational adaptations may produce quite different levels of aggressive behavior. Thus, from an evolutionary perspective, we should not expect individuals from different cultures to behave similarly, or even individuals in the same culture to always act uniformly.

## Current and Ancestral Fitness

Because ancestral and current operational adaptations and behavior may differ, behaviors that contributed to ancestral fitness may no longer contribute to current fitness. Similarly, behaviors that may contribute to fitness now may not have contributed to it in the past. Although a separation of gender roles, where men hunted and women gathered, may have contributed to ancestral fitness (Tooby & DeVore, 1987), such a separation may no longer contribute to fitness. Moreover, behaviors that contribute to the current fitness of at least some individuals, such as philosophical speculation or conducting academic research, may not have contributed to ancestral fitness. This argument leads many to the conclusion that the study of reproductive fitness in current environments tells us little about evolved adaptations (Crawford, 1993; Symons, 1989; Tooby & Cosmides, 1990b).

The following distinctions may be helpful in clarifying the role of fitness in ancestral and current environments. A *beneficial effect* is an aspect of an adaptation that increases the probability that its carrier will have copies of its alleles represented in succeeding generations; a *detrimental effect* is an aspect of an adaptation that reduces the probability that its carrier will have alleles represented in subsequent generations. If an adaptation's expected beneficial effects are not equal to its expected detrimental effects in a population, then natural selection may be occurring in that population and the adaptation may be evolving. A function is a beneficial effect that existed in an ancestral population, and hence, it can be said to be one of the causes of the evolution of the adaptation. The "thumb–finger" grip, which enables me to manipulate the mouse on my computer (a beneficial effect), and which also enables me to inject dangerous drugs (a detrimental effect), impacts on my current reproductive fitness. Chipping stone tools may have been one of its beneficial effects in an ancestral environment, and hence one of its functions.

Note that if the environment has changed since an adaptation was shaped, the beneficial and detrimental effects in the current environment may not be identical to those in the ancestral environment. The beneficial and detrimental effects and the functions of an adaptation in an ancestral environment tell us something about how that trait evolved and what problem(s) it evolved to solve.

The formation of an adaptation must be distinguished from how it is characterized in a current environment. An *adaptive trait*, such as using the mouse on my computer, is one that has at least one beneficial effect in a current environment. *Adaptiveness* is the degree to which an organism is able to live and reproduce in a given set of environments. *Adaptability* is the degree to which an organism is able to live and reproduce in varying environments. The panda bear has high adaptiveness in bamboo forests only, but the Norway rat has a high level of adaptability, as it thrives in many different environments. These terms help us understand how a trait is related to survival, reproduction, and general functioning in a current environment. Betzig provides an extended discussion of what fitness differences can and cannot tell us about ancestral and current behavior in chapter 8 (this volume).

### Novel Environments and Problematic Behavior

Figure 1.3 also provides some insight into how environmental changes can lead to problematic behavior. Chapter 9 distinguishes between true pathologies, pseudopathologies, and quasinormal conditions. A *true pathology*, such as Huntington's chorea or memory loss due to brain damage, is deleterious in both ancestral and current environments because it compromises the functioning of the operational adaptation in both environments. A *pseudopathology*, such as excessive male jealousy or anorexic behavior in women, has its basis in an adaptation that contributed to ancestral fitness, but, because of changes in the environment in recent evolutionary time, has become maladaptive, unethical, or otherwise harmful.

Finally, *quasinormal behaviors*, such as short birth intervals, large families, or the adoption of genetically unrelated children, are those that would have detracted from ancestral fitness, but may now contribute to well-being and have become culturally acceptable and even encouraged in some cultures. Quasinormal behaviors can arise if the costs and benefits involved in the adaptation have changed in the current environment, resulting in the adaptation processes producing a novel output behavior. Examples of this type of occurrence include increased recreational sexual activity resulting when the cost of undesired pregnancies is reduced through the use of effective birth control methods and shorter birth intervals resulting from changes in lactation patterns, which have reduced the cost of nursing closely spaced children. Quasinormal behaviors may also occur when a novel problem arises in the current environment and is addressed by an adaptation that evolved to solve a similar, but different, problem. These behaviors do not have a basis in evolved innate adaptations, but must depend for their functioning on operational adaptations that evolved to serve other functions. For example, the rearing of genetically unrelated adopted children may employ adaptations that evolved to address the rearing of genetic children. Because the adaptation is being co-opted for a slightly different task than that to which it arose in response, it may not be performing optimally. Although bonding to adopted children occurs through our attachment adaptation, it may be that slight differences in inputs registered by the adaptation process result in attachment mechanisms that are less than optimal.

Because they are not the function of the evolved adaptation, such quasinormal behaviors tend to be unstable and fluctuate across historical time. In addition, there are several factors that might make them problematic. First, the operational adaptations producing them may not be adequate to produce the full suite of behaviors necessary for their optimal functioning, as discussed in the adoption example earlier. Second, the new cost–benefit analysis may function well in the focal adaptation, but less well in other related adaptations, or even produce conflicting outputs among them. Although effective birth control methods may remove some costs associated with recreational sexual behavior, other adaptations, such as those relating to the need to invest in and care for children, or the desire for long-term intimacy, may evaluate such behavior in a negative way and produce feelings of conflict and guilt. Third, because different individuals and groups may have different perspectives of costs and benefits, there are likely to be some people who do not accept such behaviors even when they have attained societal approval. For example, under conditions of scarce resources, group elders may favor a polyandrous mating system, which maximizes overall fitness given the limited resources of the situation. However, it is likely that, within this system, men who are required to share a wife and women who are unable to secure a husband view the situation, with its resulting cost to such individuals, less favorably. In addition, cultural variation across historical time, such as changes in religious values and economic and social trends, may effect the standards for judging the acceptability of such behaviors.

### True Altruism: A Quasinormal Behavior?

There are many examples of behaviors, such as "the good Samaritan" and soldiers throwing themselves on grenades to save their troops, that do not seem to contribute to either the perpetrator's well-being or reproductive fitness. The distinction between innate and operational adaptations and between current and ancestral environments may help with the problem created by these examples of supposed true altruism. One possible explanation is that such behaviors are the result of mental mechanisms selected because they contributed to expected reproductive success in ancestral environments. Although helping a stranger or giving one's life for one's comrades may not contribute to fitness now, analogous actions may have done so in the Pleistocene environment, in which individuals lived in small, interdependent groups. Thus, true altruism may be another example of a quasinormal behavior.


## GENETIC VARIATION AND NATURAL SELECTION

Suppose that identical twins separated at conception were reared in different environments, and that, because of the different environments, their adult personalities and abilities differ greatly. One twin is extroverted, whereas the other is introverted. One is aggressive and the other submissive. One is better at verbal reasoning, whereas the other is better at quantitative reasoning. A common interpretation is that, because the twins are genetically identical, genes are not involved in the production of these differences.

Let us return to Fig. 1.2, which describes scorpionfly mating, to help with the logic of this situation. Suppose that identical triplet scorpionflies are reared in environments differing in levels of male–male competition. Triplet A is reared in an environment high in male–male competition, Triplet B is reared in an environment where male–male competition is absent, and Triplet C is reared in a milieu with moderate male–male competition. How will their behaviors differ? Attempted forced copulation will be absent in the environment of Triplet B, which is free from competition, but it will be the usual tactic in the high-competition environment of Triplet A. The proteinaceous salivary mass will be a frequent mating tactic in the moderate-competition environment of Triplet C, but it will be rare in the low-competition environment of Triplet B.

Because the three male scorpionflies are genetically identical, gene differences between them cannot be contributing to the differences in courtship behavior. But the genes that all three males have, and indeed the genes that every male scorpionfly has, contribute to the development of the behaviors that are seen. Although it is true that the environmental differences are producing the behavioral differences, and that genetic differences are not involved, the environmental differences are acting through the genetically innate information-processing algorithms (Darwinian algorithms) that all male scorpionflies possess (Crawford & Anderson, 1989). Hence, the genes that every male scorpionfly possesses are deeply involved in producing these different behaviors.

Although genetic variation is necessary for a trait to evolve by natural selection, from an evolutionary perspective, it is not the main focus in the study of adaptation (Crawford & Anderson, 1989; Tooby & Cosmides, 1990a). What is of interest is the correlation of the behavioral differences with fitness in the environment in which the trait evolved. Although the different tactics of male scorpionflies do not depend on genetic differences, variation in the tactics is correlated with environmental differences, and with fitness differences in those environments (Thornhill, 1980).

Figure 1.4 illustrates the role of genetic variation in the study of adaptation. At the left of the figure, we see that natural selection acts on ancestral genetic variation in the production of an adaptation. There are two possible results. First, as shown in the lower pathway, genetic variation may remain, and it may be related to fitness-enhancing differences between individuals. There is evidence for genetic differences affecting a wide variety of animal and human behaviors (Plomin, DeFries, & McLearn, 1980). However, although these differences may be real and important, they do not necessarily arise from variation that serves the adaptation's function. For example, although genetic variation may affect social dominance, this variation may not be causally related to differences in social dominance, but may be a fortuitous affect of some other source of genetic variation (Tooby & Cosmides, 1990).

Second, as shown in the upper pathway, genetic variation with respect to the adaptation may be eliminated. Here there are two possible interpretations. The first is that, because genetic variation has been eliminated, current behavior has been freed from genetic influences. This view of the human psyche—that it is a blank slate on which experience writes—is held by many social scientists, and is known as the *tabula rasa* view of the psyche. The second interpretation is that, although natural selection has eliminated genetic variation with respect to the design of the adaptation, thus, making the genetic basis of the adaptation identical for all individuals, the genes that all members of the species now possess still contribute to the behaviors produced by the adaptation. This is the view held by many using the theory of evolution in the study of human behavior (Crawford & Anderson, 1989; Tooby & Cosmides, 1990a). Those who take this view do not argue that genetic differences do not affect behavior, but rather that much of the genetic variation commonly observed occurs at the protein level, rather than at the level of the design

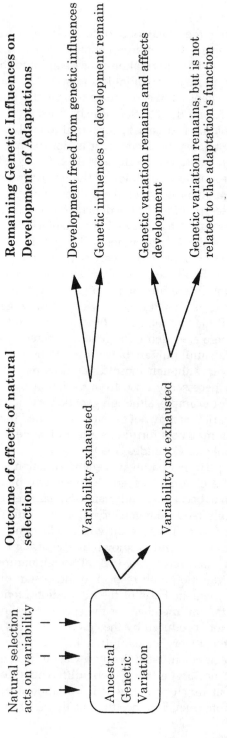

FIG. 1.4. The possible effects of natural selection on ancestral genetic variation. Even if natural selection eliminates genetic variation with respect to an adaptation's function, genes may still affect the functioning of adaptations. In cases where genetic variation affects the expression of an adaptation, these genetically based differences may be unrelated to the adaptation's function. Only in the third case from the top, "Genetic variation remains and affects development," does genetic variation contribute to the functioning of the adaptation.

of the adaptation, and has evolved to protect organs from parasitic infection. Although this variation in protein structure is beneficial, in that it protects the individual from parasites, it may be detrimental to the functioning of the adaptation. Genetic differences between individuals may be the result of genetically caused variations at the protein level, which produce minute lesions that detract from the functioning of the adaptation, but protect organs from attacks by parasites. Thus, in Fig. 1.4, the alternative labeled, "Genetic influences on development remain," which is associated with exhausted genetic variation, would be unlikely in nature. However, the alternative labeled, "Genetic variation remains, but is not related to the adaptation's function" could be relatively frequent in nature. In fact, it is the alternative that is favored by many evolutionary psychologists.

## DEVELOPING EVOLUTIONARY EXPLANATIONS

### Levels of Explanations

Those with an evolutionary orientation are usually interested in ultimate, or why, explanations, rather than proximate, or how, explanations. *Proximate explanations* refer to the immediate factors, such as internal physiology and environmental stimuli, that produce a particular response. *Ultimate explanations* refer to the conditions of the biological, social, and physical environment that, on an evolutionary time scale, render certain traits adaptive and others nonadaptive (Mayr, 1961). For example, consider this question: "Why do ground squirrels hibernate?" The proximate explanation is that hibernation comes about in the current environment because current climatic conditions trigger physiological mechanisms initiating hibernation. Yet, the ultimate explanation is that it is climate, predator pressure, food supply, and so on, acting on an evolutionary time scale, that tell us why squirrels have evolved to hibernate. Considering both levels of explanation may deepen our understanding of the development and significance of a behavior. Let us consider in some detail the value of ultimate explanations.

### Sensation Seeking: The Ultimate Causes

Males die off faster than females at all ages in most species because of disease, trauma, stress, accidents, and murder. Trivers (1985) provided convincing arguments against the notion that the unguarded male Y chromosome is the cause. Zuckerman's theory of sensation seeking (Zuckerman, Buchsbaum, & Murphy, 1980) could provide a proximate explanation. He found that measures of sensation seeking correlate with risk taking in a number of situations and are also related to a variety of behavioral variables, such as sexual experience, interest in new situations, experience with drugs, social dominance, sociability, playfulness, manic–depressive tendencies, and psychopathy. Males score higher than females on measures of sensation seeking. Scores decline after age 16. Sensation-seeking scores are also correlated with strength of initial orienting reflex, augmentation versus reduction of the average evoked brain potential, gonadal hormones, and the enzyme monoamine oxidase. Moreover, many of the correlates of sensation seeking have moderate to high heritabilities.

Zuckerman and his colleagues argued that the bioamines, particularly the catecholamines, that may regulate the sensitivity of reward and activity centers in the limbic system play a central role in sensation seeking. Thus, depending on the level of analysis, gonadal hormones, catecholamines, or sensation seeking can be considered a proximate cause of the sex differences in mortality. Yet, what are the ultimate causes of the excess in male over female mortality?

We have seen that Darwin's theory of sexual selection can help explain sex differences in anatomy and physiology and gender differences in behavior. Can it help explain sensation seeking? In most species, females are a limiting resource for male reproduction, and hence, males evolve tactics for competing for access to them.

In many species, natural selection favors traits that result in a reduction in survival prior to reproduction if those traits increase the reproductive success of those who do survive to mate. For example, diverting resources from growth of the immune system to risky behaviors of threat or aggression could increase the overall fitness of males if it reduced prereproductive male survival by one half, but more than doubled the reproductive success of those who survived. The risky behaviors that led Zuckerman et al. (1980) to postulate a trait of sensation seeking may have contributed to male reproductive success in ancestral populations.

What are the ultimate causes of the gender differences in sensation seeking? Males and females in sexually selected species invest in their offspring in different ways (Thornhill & Alcock, 1983). Females invest more than males in the construction of gametes and in postconception parental investment. These investments limit female reproductive success and are involved in shaping female reproductive adaptations involved in courtship, mating, and the rearing of offspring. Females in sexually selected species are often very selective in their choice of mates.

Males exchange effort and resources for mating (e.g., bride prices in humans and the nuptial gifts provided by some male insects). These exchanges limit their ability to obtain matings. They also invest in risky anatomy (organs of threat), physiology (testosterone impairs some aspects of the immune system), and behavioral displays that help them acquire matings, but that also limit their ability to obtain matings. From an evolutionary perspective, it is the risky male anatomy, physiology, and behavior that are the ultimate causes of the excess in male over female mortality and the gender differences in sensation seeking.

It should be possible to construct a model for predicting species' differences in sensation seeking, risk taking, and differential mortality. Males of species characterized by relatively low postzygotic male parental investment and relatively high costs of obtaining mates would be predicted to exhibit risky anatomy, physiology, and behavior and to suffer higher mortality than females. Psychologists might call them *sensation seekers*. As long as the animals were studied in their natural environment, such a model would require neither knowledge of the biochemistry or physiology of the species, nor constructs such as emotions, motivations, and drives. Instead, it would require information on differences between the sexes in investment in gametes, additional postzygotic parental investment, resources exchanged for a mating, and the elaboration of displays required for obtaining a mating.

Of what value are ultimate explanations to those interested in a single species, such as humans? A consideration of ultimate causation may help us: (a) gain an understanding of the environmental factors that may alter a behavior, which can be used to choose independent variables for the development of within-species models of behavior; (b) unravel the causal sequence between environmental events and manifest behavior; and (c) develop explanations with greater generality. If we assume members of the species have evolved a repertoire of concurrently and developmentally contingent behaviors for dealing with environmental contingencies, we may be able to use some part of evolutionary theory, such as sexual-selection theory in the case of sensation seeking, to help identify crucial environmental variables for models explaining why different individuals behave differently.

Let us continue the example of differential mortality and sensation seeking. Ancestral subordinate males who had difficulty attracting mates because they lacked social status and resources may have increased their fitness by increasing the riskiness of their behavior to obtain these attributes. Younger males who had not yet acquired resources, physical size, social status, and reciprocal relationships with other members of their group might have improved their fitness by engaging in risky behavior. If measures of sensation seeking had been given to such males, we might expect them to have attained relatively high scores on these measures. Thus, an evolutionary perspective can be used to provide hypotheses about the independent variables that could be useful in explaining individual differences in sensation seeking.

A consideration of the ultimate causes of a behavior may help unravel the causal sequence of events between environmental contingencies and behavior. For example, sensation seeking may be a common element in behaviors that males perform in attempts to achieve the social status and resources necessary for obtaining mates in ancestral environments. If this line of reasoning is followed, then gonadal hormones, rather than strength of initial orienting reflex, augmentation versus reduction of the average evoked brain potential, or monoamine oxidase, are likely to be an important proximate biological cause of sensation seeking. Moreover, the ultimate cause analysis further suggests that training in social and technical skills is more likely to be effective than drug therapy in changing behaviors related to risk taking and sensation seeking.

Many of those studying human behavior prefer explanations using proximate, empirically derived variables (Scarr, 1985). For example, sensation seeking is apparently a concept derived from the inspection and analysis of observed data. Although empirically derived concepts have an intuitive and commonsense appeal, and may function reasonably well as predictors within a particular context, they lack generality. If we are to develop theories of behavior that are not situation- and population-specific, we must seek constructs with greater generality. The natural sciences can call on theories such as classical mechanics, the theory of relativity, or the theory of evolution to guide the search for generality in explanations. The prior example illustrates how a consideration of both the proximate and ultimate causes of a behavior can lead to more general explanations and a deeper understanding of the behavior.

## VALIDATING EVOLUTIONARY EXPLANATIONS

The logic of the theory of evolution by natural selection is simple, but using it in the study of human behavior is a challenge. Therefore, it is not surprising that there is controversy over how it can be best employed. See Betzig (1997) for an overall perspective on validating evolutionary explanations of human behavior. Much of the discussion in this chapter has been an exposition of what has become known as *evolutionary psychology*. The majority of this book's authors fall within this perspective. However, it is not the only perspective of how Darwin's ideas should be employed in the study of human nature. The final section of this introductory chapter contrasts the perspective of those who use the approach of behavioral ecology, and who have come to be known as *Darwinian anthropologists* or *Darwinian social scientists,* with their critics, who refer to themselves as *evolutionary* or *Darwinian psychologists.*

Although the proponents of both approaches accept Williams' (1966) conception of adaptation, they differ in their emphasis on: (a) the importance of proximate mechanisms, (b) the relevance of current fitness in the study of adaptation, (c) the role of behavior in explanations, and (d) the nature of proximate mechanisms. These differences lead them to place differential importance on the ancestral environment and to use different research methods in the development of evolutionary explanations (Sherman & Reeve, 1997).

## Darwinian Anthropology

Darwinian anthropologists assume it is unnecessary to invoke specific proximate mechanisms when using evolutionary theory to study behavior. Their focus is on the goals that organisms must achieve if they are to maximize their reproductive success, and the behaviors utilized to achieve those goals. The goals are not to be specified in terms of hunger, fear, love, or anger, but in terms of reproductive fitness. Because they see organisms as inclusive fitness maximizers, much of their research focuses on reproductive differentials, such as those between high- and low-status males in medieval Portugal (Boone, 1986), the number of surviving offspring of good and poor hunters among the Ache, a tribe of Paraguayan hunter–gatherers (Hill & Kaplan, 1988), or the conditions under which polyandry can be advantageous for some Tibetans (Crook & Crook, 1988). They argue that, although the study of proximate mechanisms may occasionally help us understand adaptation, as in kin recognition, it is behavior, not beliefs, values, and sentiments, that maximizes inclusive fitness, and hence, behavior should be the focus of study.

Because of their emphasis on behavior and inclusive fitness maximization, Darwinian anthropologists see less need to focus on the ancestral environment, where adaptations evolved, and its relation to the current environment, where behavior is studied. Let us return to Fig. 1.3 to help understand their perspective. Recall the distinction between innate and operational adaptations, and between the ancestral and current environments depicted in the figure. Darwinian anthropologists view innate adaptations as the genes for a relatively small number of domain-general mechanisms that enable individuals to develop strategies, such as flexible learning and scenario building. In conjunction with tendencies to maximize inclusive fitness, these produce the operational adaptations that address problems in the current environment. Ancestral and current behaviors differ to the extent that different behaviors are required for tracking ancestral and current fitness goals. For Darwinian anthropologists, the line between "then" and "now," as represented in the figure, is less important.

## Evolutionary Psychology

Evolutionary psychologists criticize this approach on several grounds (Cosmides & Tooby, 1987; Symons, 1987). First, they argue that, although adaptations have evolved because they provided ancestral organisms with greater inclusive fitness than alternative adaptations, it is incorrect to say that organisms evolved propensities to maximize their inclusive fitness. Second, although they admit behavior is a manifestation of an adaptation, they argue that behavior is not an adaptation. Therefore, the study of behavior is directed at elucidating the naturally selected design of the proximate mechanisms producing it. Third, they argue that, because the environment of evolutionary adaptedness and the current environment may differ considerably, reproductive differences that contribute to fitness now cannot be used to investigate adaptations that evolved because they maximized ancestral inclusive fitness.

The final point raised by evolutionary psychologists is that, because natural selection can only shape specific mechanisms for dealing with specific ancestral conditions, the human psyche must be comprised of specific mechanisms rather than general mechanisms that can address a wide range of possible problems. Our mechanisms have evolved in response to those problems encountered during the course of their evolution, but have not been designed to anticipate and respond to the wide range of all potential problems that we may encounter in the future. *Evolutionary psychology* is conceptualized as the study of: (a) the conditions in ancestral populations that rendered certain behaviors adaptive and others nonadaptive, (b) the mechanisms natural selection shaped to produce the adaptive behaviors, and (c) the ways these evolved mechanisms function now (Crawford & Anderson, 1989). For evolutionary psychologists, the distinctions between ancestral and current environments, between ancestral and current operational adaptations, between ancestral and current fitness, and between ancestral and current behavior, as shown in Fig. 1.3, are crucial.

The key difference between these two perspectives is the nature of the innate adaptation. Recall the Darwinian anthropologist view discussed in the previous section. This view of the human psyche, as a modified *tabula rasa*, is congenial to most mainstream social scientists. In contrast, evolutionary psychologists argue that the evolution of mental apparatus does not differ from the evolution of other complex adaptations, such as the digestive system. Hence, there is no more reason to believe that the brain is a *tabula rasa*, designed to acquire any abilities necessary for maximizing fitness, than to believe that the stomach is a general digester, designed to extract nutrients from any ingested matter.

## Differences in Research Strategies

In its pure form, Darwinian anthropology focuses on differences in lifetime reproductive success between individuals encountering different environments; it uses the methods of behavioral ecology to study these differences. Evolutionary psychology, in its purest form, uses the methods of evolutionary biology and experimental psychology to study the naturally selected design of psychological mechanisms (Crawford, 1993). Consider how these two types of researchers might approach testing the Trivers–Willard hypothesis (Trivers & Willard, 1973) about the allocation of parental investment to male and female progeny. See Sherman and Reeve (1997) for another perspective on the difference between the two approaches to hypothesis testing.

Trivers and Willard (1973) argued that if variance in lifetime reproductive success of males exceeded that of females, if the relative health and dominance of mothers is passed on to their progeny, and if healthy or dominant males obtain more matings than males lacking these attributes, then females will be selected to allocate investment in progeny as a function of the progeny's health or dominance. For a review of the extensive literature on the validity of the Trivers–Willard hypothesis for both animals and humans, see Sieff (1990). Let us consider one of the animal studies.

In a comprehensive study of red deer, Clutton-Brock, Albon, and Guinness (1986) found considerable support for this hypothesis. Sons born to mothers above median rank were more reproductively successful than their sisters, whereas daughters born to subordinate mothers were more reproductively successful than their brothers. Moreover, the ratio of sons to daughters produced by dominant mothers was higher than that for subordinate mothers. Because the sex ratio and reproductive success were key dependent variables in this study, it is similar to some studies of sex allocation done by Darwinian anthropologists and described in Sieff (1990).

Let us see how an evolutionary psychologist might go about testing the Trivers–Willard hypothesis. First, a selection model with the independent variables of sex differences in variability of reproductive success in males and females and health or status of mother, and the dependent variable of fitness benefits of differential investment in sons and daughters would be developed (Anderson & Crawford, 1992). The independent variables of the model would be varied to provide a description of how sex allocation might have been favored in particular ancestral environments. The model would be used in conjunction with information about the natural history of the species to determine whether a "window of opportunity" could have existed for the evolution of the putative adaptation.

If the results of the modeling suggested that the evolution of the adaptation was plausible, a theory of the nature of the adaptation, specified in terms of decision rules assumed to be instantiated in neural hardware, would be formulated. Here, the dependent variables would be outputs from the decision process affecting such variables as nursing time and the amount of protection from predators given to sons and daughters, rather than fitness measures or behaviors assumed to enhance fitness. In studies on humans, attitudes, values, intentions, and motives would be measured. A decision rule might be something like, "If subordinate and physically weak, be more responsive to the needs of daughters than of sons; if strong and dominant be more attentive to the needs of sons than of daughters." Such a theory requires a model of how the crucial independent variables, which are measures of adaptation-relevant external and internal environmental variables, are represented to the ancestral adaptation. For example, dominance might have been represented in terms of postures, frequency of unreciprocated threat displays, or resources held by different ancestral individuals. Once the decision rules that describe the adaptation and the way the environmental inputs to them are represented to the psyche were specified, the evolutionary psychologist could use the methods of experimental psychology to test predictions from the overall model.

The logic of such an experiment is laid out in Fig. 1.5. In the case of red deer, an experimenter might manipulate status or health of mothers and measure variables related to differential investment in sons and daughters. To strengthen the inferences about the adaptation, predictions from other evolutionary explanations are recommended. For example, Clutton-Brock, Albon, and Guinness (1986) noted that their results could also be explained on the basis of the vulnerable male hypothesis, as a cost of sexual selection. That is, male red deer may have been selected to divert energy from growth of their immune system to growth of their antlers, making them more vulnerable to stress. Thus, what appears to be sex allocation might be nothing more than a fortuitous effect of sexual selection. A series of controlled experiments should enable the researcher to eliminate alternative hypotheses.

If the results of the controlled experiments did not support the proposed explanation, the evolutionary psychologist must attempt to determine where the problem lies. It could reside in the formulation of the selection model, the description of the decision rules that describe the adaptation, the way the crucial environmental variables are represented to the decision

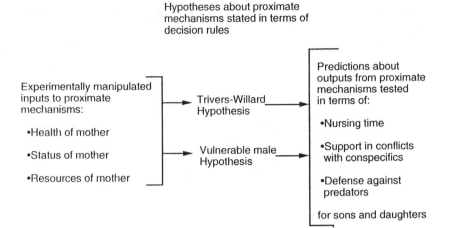

FIG. 1.5. Controlled experimental studies comparing predictions from different hypotheses. Design for experimental studies of putative proximate mechanisms for allocating resources to sons and daughters. Note that the design is strengthened by including predictions from alternative evolutionary hypotheses—in this case, the Trivers–Willard hypothesis and the vulnerable-male hypothesis. Because the design includes random assignment of subjects to treatments, it can be used to make causal statements about the putative adaptation. From "The Future of Sociobiology: Counting Babies or Studying Proximate Mechanisms" by C. B. Crawford, 1993, *Trends in Evolution and Ecology, 8*, p. 186. Copyright © 1993 by Elsevier Science Publishers Ltd. Adapted with permission.

rules, the experimental procedures for data collection, or the inadequacy of the hypothesis being tested. Finally, if both the selection model and experimental studies support the existence of the putative adaptation, evolutionary psychologists would carry out naturalistic observational studies to explore how the adaptation is expressed in a variety of current environments. For humans, cross-cultural studies would be necessary.

Note that the results of the observational studies are contingent on assumptions about the ancestral adaptation and its relation to the current environment. For example, an evolutionary psychologist would claim that the interpretations from Clutton-Brock, Albon, and Guinness' (1986) study are contingent on the assumption that the red deer of Rhum are living in an environment similar to that in which they evolved. If they are not, perhaps because they are being artificially provisioned, their decision processes might not respond according to the Trivers–Willard hypothesis because there are insufficient effective cues in the current environment to activate the adaptation. Completion of modeling, controlled experiments, and observational studies should give the researcher a reasonably comprehensive understanding of the putative adaptation.

Evolutionary psychologists have raised a number of important points that are having considerable impact on the way evolutionary behavior research is being done. However, the methodological approach of the evolutionary psychologists is much more complex than that of the Darwinian anthropologists. Must evolutionary hypotheses always be about mental mechanisms? If so, how specific must these mechanisms be? How important is the difference between the ancestral and current environments? What is the role of behavior in the development of evolutionary explanations? Can studies of current fitness tell us anything about adaptations? These questions have yet to be fully resolved. Their resolution will shape the future of evolutionary studies of human behavior.

## CONCLUSION

The chapters that follow are divided into three sections. Part I expands and elaborates the discussion of kinship, sexual-selection, and life-history theory, introduced in this chapter, because these three topics are currently of both great theoretical and empirical importance in the application of the Theory of Evolution by Natural Selection to the study of human behavior. Part II opens with a chapter on culture because the evolutionary significance of human culture raises many challenging issues that must be confronted when applying evolutionary thinking to the study of human behavior. This chapter is followed by chapters on the place of behavior genetics in evolutionary thinking, evolutionary theory and theories of cognitive architecture, the value of studies of reproductive fitness in current environments, and the functioning of adaptations in ancestral and current environments. Part II concludes with a chapter on hypothesis testing. Part III includes chapters on moral behavior, human development, mate selection, family violence, relation between evolutionary and psychoanalytic thinking, design of cognitive mechanisms, sexual aggression, aesthetics, international conflicts, and gender differences in perceptual abilities. Part III concludes with a chapter on human language.

## REFERENCES

Alcock, J. (1993). *Animal behavior: An evolutionary approach* (5th ed.). Sunderland, MA: Sinauer Associates.
Alexander, R. D. (1987). *The biology of moral systems.* New York: Aldine de Gruyter.
Anderson, J. L., & Crawford, C. B. (1992). Modeling costs and benefits of adolescent weight control as a mechanism for reproduction suppression. *Human Nature, 3,* 299–334.
Barkow, J., Cosmides, L., & Tooby, J. (1992). *The adapted mind: Evolutionary psychology and the generation of culture.* New York: Oxford University Press.

Bernhard, J. G. (1988). *Primates in the classroom: An evolutionary perspective on children's education.* Amherst: University of Massachusetts Press.

Betzig, L. (Ed.). (1997). *Human nature: A critical reader.* New York: Oxford University Press.

Boone, J. L. (1986). Parental investment and elite family structure in preindustrial states: A case study in late medieval–early modern Portuguese genealogies. *American Anthropologist, 88,* 859–878.

Burnstein, E., Crandall, C., & Kitayama, S. (1994). Some neo-Darwinian decision rules for altruism: Weighting cues for inclusive fitness as a function of the biological importance of the decision. *Journal of Personality and Social Psychology, 67,* 773–789.

Buss, D. (1994). *The evolution of desire: strategies of human mating.* New York: Basic Books.

Chagnon, N., & Irons, W. (Eds.). (1979). *Evolutionary biology and human social behavior: An anthropological perspective.* North Scituate, MA: Duxbury.

Clutton-Brock, T. H., Albon, H. D., & Guinness, F. E. (1986). Great expectations: Dominance, breeding success and offspring sex ratios in red deer. *Animal Behavior, 34,* 460–471.

Cosmides, L. (1989). The logic of social exchange: Has natural selection shaped how humans reason? Studies with the Wason selection task. *Cognition, 31,* 187–276.

Cosmides, L., & Tooby, J. (1987). From evolution to behavior: Evolutionary psychology as the missing link. In J. Dupre (Ed.), *The latest on the best: Essays on evolution and optimality* (pp. 277–306). Cambridge, MA: MIT Press.

Crawford, C. (1984). Sex biased parental investment: Findings and frustrations. In *Human reproductive strategies: Empirical tests of evolutionary hypothesis.* Symposium conducted at the meeting of the Animal Behavior Society, Cheney, WA.

Crawford, C. (1993). The future of sociobiology: Counting babies or studying proximate mechanisms. *Trends in Evolution and Ecology, 8,* 183–186.

Crawford, C. B., & Anderson, J. L. (1989). Sociobiology: An environmentalist discipline? *American Psychologist, 44,* 1449–1459.

Crook, J. H., & Crook, S. J. (1988). Tibetan polyandry: Problems of adaptation and fitness. In L. Betzig, M. Borgerhoff Mulder, & P. Turke (Eds.), *Human reproductive behavior: A Darwinian perspective* (pp. 97–114). New York: Cambridge University Press.

Daly, M., & Wilson, M. (1980). Discriminative parental solicitude: A biological perspective. *Journal of Marriage and the Family, 42,* 277–288.

Daly, M., & Wilson, M. (1982). Whom are newborn babies said to resemble? *Ethology and Sociobiology, 3,* 69–78.

Daly, M., & Wilson, M. (1983). *Sex, evolution and behavior* (2nd ed.). Boston: Prindle, Weber & Schmidt.

Darwin, C. (1859). *On the origin of the species by means of natural selection or the preservation of favored races in the struggle for life.* London: John Murray.

Darwin, C. (1898). *The descent of man, and selection in relation to sex* (3rd ed.). New York: Appleton-Century-Crofts. (Original work published 1871)

de Catanzaro, D. (1991). Evolutionary limits to self-preservation. *Ethology and Sociobiology, 12,* 13–28.

Degler, C. (1991). *In search of human nature: The decline and revival of Darwinism in American social thought.* New York: Oxford University Press.

Fisher, R. A. (1930). *The genetical theory of natural selection* (rev. ed.). New York: Dover.

Gould, S. J. (1982). *The panda's thumb: More reflections in natural history.* New York: Norton.

Haig, D. (1993). Genetic conflicts in human pregnancy. *Quarterly Review of Biology, 68,* 495–532.

Hamilton, W. D. (1964). The genetical evolution of social behavior, I and II. *Journal of Theoretical Biology, 7,* 1–52.

Hamilton, W. D. (1971). Geometry of the selfish herd. *Journal of Theoretical Biology, 31,* 295–311.

Herrnstein, R. J., & Murray, C. (1994). *The bell curve: Intelligence and class structure in American life.* New York: The Free Press.

Hill, K., & Kaplan, H. (1988). Tradeoffs in male and female reproductive strategies among the Ache, parts 1 and 2. In L. Betzig, M. Borgerhoff Mulder, & P. Turke (Eds.), *Human reproductive behavior: A Darwinian perspective* (pp. 277–306). New York: Cambridge University Press.

Holmes, W. (1986). Kin recognition by phenotype matching in Belding's ground squirrels. *Animal Behavior, 34,* 38–47.

Johnson, J. L., McAndrew, F. T., & Harris, P. B. (1991). Sociobiology and the naming of adopted and natural children. *Ethology and Sociobiology, 12,* 365–375.

Kimura, D. (1987). Are men's and women's brains really different? *Canadian Psychology, 28,* 133–147.

Konishi, M. (1965). The role of auditory feedback in the control of vocalization in the white-crowned sparrow. *Zeitschrift für Tierpsychologie, 22,* 770–783.

Krebs, D. (1987). The challenge of altruism in biology and psychology. In C. Crawford, M. Smith, & D. Krebs (Eds.), *Sociobiology and psychology: Ideas, issues, and applications* (pp. 81–112). Hillsdale, NJ: Lawrence Erlbaum Associates.

LeBoeuf, B. J. (1974). Male–male competition and reproductive success in elephant seals. *American Zoologist, 14,* 163–176.

Lorenz, K. Z. (1966). *On aggression.* New York: Harcourt Brace.

Marler, P. (1984). Song learning: Innate species differences in the learning process. In P. Marler & H. Terrace (Eds.), *The biology of learning* (pp. 289–309). Berlin: Dahlem Konferenzen.

Maynard Smith, J. (1976). Group selection. *Quarterly Review of Biology, 51,* 277–283.

Mayr, E. (1961). Cause and effect in biology. *Science, 134,* 1501–1506.

McCullough, J. M., & Barton, E. Y. (1991). Relatedness and mortality risk during a crisis year: Plymouth colony, 1620–1621. *Ethology and Sociobiology, 12,* 195–209.

Orians, G. H., & Heerwagen, J. H. (1992). Evolved responses to landscapes. In J. Barkow, L. Cosmides, & J. Tooby (Eds.), *The adapted mind: Evolutionary psychology and the generation of culture* (pp. 555–579). New York: Oxford University Press.

Plomin, R., DeFries, J. C., & McLearn, G. E. (1980). *Behavioral genetics: A primer.* San Francisco: Freeman.

Porter, R. H. (1987). Kin recognition: Functions and mediating mechanisms. In C. B. Crawford, M. F. Smith, & D. Krebs (Eds.), *Sociobiology and psychology: Ideas, issues and applications* (pp. 175–204). Hillsdale, NJ: Lawrence Erlbaum Associates.

Reeve, K., & Sherman, P. (1993). Adaptation and the goals of evolutionary research. *Quarterly Review of Biology, 68,* 1–32.

Ridley, M. (1993). *Evolution.* Oxford, England: Blackwell.

Scarr, S. (1985). Constructing psychology: Making facts and fables for our times. *American Psychologist, 40,* 499–512.

Sherman, P. W. (1977). Nepotism and the evolution of alarm calls. *Science, 197,* 1246–1253.

Sherman, P., & Reeve, K. (1997). Forward and backward: Alternative approaches to studying human social evolution. In L. Betzig (Ed.), *Human nature: A critical reader* (pp. 147–158). New York: Oxford University Press.

Sieff, D. F. (1990). Explaining biased sex ratios in human populations. *Current Anthropology, 31,* 25–48.

Silverman, I., & Eals, M. (1992). Sex differences in spatial abilities: Evolutionary theory and data. In J. Barkow, L. Cosmides, & J. Tooby (Eds.), *The adapted mind: Evolutionary psychology and the generation of culture* (pp. 533–549). New York: Oxford University Press.

Singh, D. (1993). Adaptive significance of female physical attractiveness: Role of waist to hip ratio. *Journal of Personality and Social Psychology, 65,* 293–307.

Sober, E. (1984). *The nature of selection.* Cambridge, MA: MIT Press.

Symons, D. (1987). If we're all Darwinians, what's the fuss about? In C. B. Crawford, M. F. Smith, & D. Krebs (Eds.), *Sociobiology and psychology: Ideas, issues, and applications* (pp. 121–146). Hillsdale, NJ: Lawrence Erlbaum Associates.

Symons, D. (1989). A critique of Darwinian anthropology. *Ethology and Sociobiology, 10,* 131–144.

Thornhill, R. (1980). Rape in *Panorpa* scorpionflies and a general rape hypothesis. *Animal Behavior, 28,* 52–59.

Thornhill, R., & Alcock, J. (1983). *The evolution of insect mating systems.* Cambridge, MA: Harvard University Press.

Tooby, J., & Cosmides, L. (1990a). On the universality of human nature and the uniqueness of the individual: The role of genetics and adaptation. *Journal of Personality, 58,* 17–67.

Tooby, J., & Cosmides, L. (1990b). The past explains the present: Emotional adaptations and the structure of ancestral environments. *Ethology and Sociobiology, 11,* 375–421.

Tooby, J., & DeVore, I. (1987). The reconstruction of hominid behavioral evolution using strategic modelling. In W. G. Kinzey (Ed.), *Primate models for the origin of human behavior* (pp. 183–237). New York: SUNY Press.

Trivers, R. L. (1971). The evolution of reciprocal altruism. *Quarterly Review of Biology, 46,* 35–57.

Trivers, R. L. (1974). Parent–offspring conflict. *American Zoologist, 14,* 249–264.

Trivers, R. L. (1985). *Social evolution.* Menlo Park, CA: Benjamin/Cummings.

Trivers, R. L., & Willard, D. E. (1973). Natural selection of parental ability to vary the sex ratio of offspring. *Science, 179,* 90–92.

Waldman, B. (1986). Preference for unfamiliar siblings over familiar non-siblings in American toad (*Bufo americanus*) tadpoles. *Animal Behavior, 34,* 48–53.

Williams, G. C. (1966). *Adaptation and natural selection: A critique of some current evolutionary thought.* Princeton, NJ: Princeton University Press.

Williams, G. C., & Nesse, R. (1991). The dawn of Darwinian medicine. *The Quarterly Review of Biology, 66,* 1–22.

Wilson, D. S., & Sober, E. (1994). Reintroducing group selection to the human behavioral sciences. *Behavioral and Brain Sciences, 17,* 585–608.

Wilson, E. O. (1975). *Sociobiology: The new synthesis.* Cambridge, MA: Harvard University Press.

Woolfenden, G. E., & Fitzpatrick, J. W. (1984). *The Florida scrub jay: Demography of a cooperative-breeding bird.* Princeton, NJ: Princeton University Press.

Wright, R. (1994). *The moral animal: Evolutionary psychology and everyday life.* New York: Pantheon.

Wynne-Edwards, V. C. (1962). *Animal dispersion in relation to social behavior.* Edinburgh, Scotland: Oliver & Boyd.

Zahavi, A. (1975). Mate selection—a selection for a handicap. *Journal of Theoretical Biology, 53,* 205–214.

Zuckerman, M., Buchsbaum, M. S., & Murphy, D. L. (1980). Sensation seeking and its biological correlates. *Psychological Bulletin, 88,* 187–214.

# 2

## Acting for the Good of Others: Kinship and Reciprocity With Some New Twists

Hudson Kern Reeve
*Cornell University*

Why have humans evolved to help other humans? The answer to this question may seem somewhat trivial because each of us cooperates daily with other humans and repeatedly reaps the emotional and material rewards of such cooperation. Because cooperation is unmysterious to us personally, it appears to lack the explanatory urgency that enshrouds more puzzling forms of human behavior, such as unusual courtship rituals or religious practices. However, at an evolutionary-theoretic level, the answer to why we cooperate is not obvious and even elusive. Evolutionary biologists are keenly aware that cooperation (outside of mating) is infrequent in the animal kingdom—an observation that is broadly consistent with the principle that natural selection should tend to favor selfish, uncooperative phenotypes. Such an argument implies that special mechanisms of natural selection are required to explain the observed cases of cooperation in nature. Darwin understood this, but he was, at best, only partially successful in delineating how such selective mechanisms might work.

This chapter describes the basic modern theory of the special mechanisms promoting the evolution of cooperation, especially cooperation involving "altruistic" helping behavior. After a review of the basic theory, the chapter traces the deep interconnections among the mechanisms (and their various versions) and uses this knowledge to resolve some of the confusions that still haunt discussions and applications of specific theories of cooperation. It also focuses on possible novel ways that the selective mechanisms favoring cooperation have operated (and may still operate) in the context of human social life. Finally, it briefly describes some recent refinements of the evolutionary theory of cooperation that may illuminate ill-understood facets of human social behavior.

We begin by returning to the question of why cooperation or helping behavior should be so puzzling. The evolutionary perspective is as follows: An organism that helps another will likely incur some reproductive cost, such as a loss of resources to allocate to its own offspring (at least temporarily), increased mortality risk, or reductions in other components of Darwinian fitness (i.e., reproductive success). This means that any gene that increases the probability of helping behavior will reduce its frequency in future generations and, ultimately, will be lost unless there is some compensating reproductive benefit (i.e., some additional route by which helping behavior causes a net increase in the underlying gene's frequency). This simple analysis explains why helping behavior is infrequent (i.e., the requisite compensating reproductive benefits occur only in special circumstances) and provides the basis for distinguishing among the special selective mechanisms favoring helping (i.e., the mechanisms are distinguished by the nature of the compensating reproductive benefit).

There currently exist three main classes of selective mechanisms for the evolution of costly helping behavior (henceforth, *helping* is used interchangeably with *altruistic behavior, altruism, cooperative behavior,* and *cooperation*). These classes are: (a) mechanisms based on kinship, (b) mechanisms representing by-product mutualism (or pseudoreciprocity), and (c) mechanisms based on behavioral *reciprocity*. Many theorists have proposed and pressed *neogroup selection* explanations for the evolution of altruism (e.g., Wilson & Sober, 1994), but these do not refer to a logically distinct fourth category of mechanisms. It is later seen that mechanisms (a) through (c) can be framed either in terms of broad-sense individual selection models or in terms of the new group selection models; in other words, the latter two kinds of models are merely alternative pictures of the same mechanisms (Dugatkin & Reeve, 1994).

## MECHANISMS BASED ON KINSHIP: KIN SELECTION

Hamilton (1964) provided a crucial insight into the evolution of altruistic helping by pointing out that altruistic acts directed toward relatives produce a special kind of reproductive compensation. By enhancing the reproduction of relatives, a help-inducing gene is indirectly propagating copies of itself in those relatives. When the relatives are the helper's own offspring, most authors refer to the helping as *parental care,* and the enhancement of propagation of the helping genes is often referred to as a *positive direct effect* of those genes. The power of Hamilton's new theory was that it showed that help-inducing genes benefit in an essentially identical way when the help is directed toward nondescendant relatives, such as siblings. When the latter "indirect" effect is sufficiently strong, the helping gene can spread (increase in frequency) despite decreases in its propagation through the offspring of the individual in which it resides (i.e., the positive indirect effects can outweigh negative direct effects). It is important to note that there is no sense in which indirect effects are less robust than direct effects; the distinction essentially reflects the historical fact that direct effects were recognized earlier than indirect effects (Dawkins, 1979).

The previous verbal presentation of Hamilton's essential idea is intuitively clear to most people; indeed, it is the most common kind of description of Hamilton's theory in elementary textbooks on animal behavior. The problem is that this intuitive clarity has guaranteed neither correct mathematical formulation of Hamilton's theory nor successful quantitative application of the theory to real field data. Consequently, it is necessary that we lay bare the mathematical foundations of Hamilton's kin-selection theory as prophylaxis against the kinds of common confusions that result from imprecise verbal treatments of the theory. This exercise does not require a knowledge of complicated mathematics (algebra will suffice), but instead depends on a consistent, logical approach to the accounting of fitness effects of help-producing genes.

There are two distinct, equally legitimate fitness-accounting methods in kin-selection theory. The same is true for models of reciprocity; moreover, the dual accounting methods for kin selection are logically parallel to those for reciprocity. (It is later argued that much is to be gained by exploiting this correspondence.) In the context of kin selection, the two fitness-accounting methods are distinguished by whether neighbor-modulated fitness or inclusive fitness is used. *Neighbor-modulated fitness* focuses on the reproductive costs or benefits received by an altruist from others (the term *neighbor-modulated* is intended to connote fitness influences from the social environment), whereas *inclusive fitness* focuses on the reproductive benefits and costs dispensed by an altruist to others (the adjective *inclusive* is used to emphasize that effects of altruism on all kin, not just on oneself, are to be combined).

Each of these two fitness measures can be used to predict whether altruistic acts of a given kind will spread and be maintained by natural selection. In fact, we shall see that both methods of accounting fitness lead to exactly the same condition for the spread of altruism (i.e., the now-famous "Hamilton's rule"). Hamilton's rule is the "bottom-line" condition that is ultimately used to predict the evolution of altruism, and this rule is derived using both the neighbor-modulated and the inclusive fitness approaches—in doing so, one sees exactly how these approaches work. (Although the two approaches are fundamentally equivalent, they can differ in their ease of application, depending on the problem. For example, the inclusive fitness approach tends to be the simplest when altruists are specialized individuals that dispense, but do not receive, altruism, and the neighbor-modulated fitness approach tends to be more useful when effects received from altruists combine in complicated ways to affect overall reproductive output.)

### Neighbor-Modulated Fitness

Consider the system of altruists pictured in Fig. 2.1a: Individuals bearing altruism-producing genes dispense benefits of Magnitude $b$ to relatives (arrows between individuals) while incurring reproductive costs of Magnitude $c$ (arrows from altruists to themselves). How does one model the evolution of altruism when such (potentially complicated) networks occur? As Hamilton (1964), Grafen (1982), and Maynard Smith (1982a) pointed out, a sufficient condition for the spread of an altruistic behavior by kin selection is simply that individuals bearing altruism-promoting genes produce more offspring than individuals lacking these genes. For

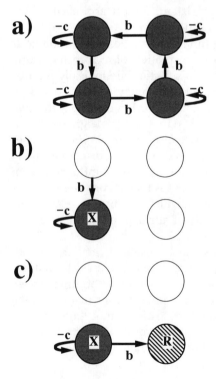

FIG. 2.1. (a) Pictorial model of kin selection; individuals reduce their own reproductive output by $-c$ and increase their kin's output by $b$ (symmetric interactions). (b) Neighbor-modulated fitness focuses on all reproductive effects received by an individual (X). (c) Inclusive fitness focuses on the effects dispensed by the individual (X) both to him or herself and to his or her kin (R), the latter effect devalued by the genetic relatedness.

example, if altruism gene bearers produce an average of 1.5 offspring after dispensing and receiving reproductive benefits, and nonbearers produce an average of only 1.0 offspring after receiving reproductive benefits (if any), the altruist gene obviously will spread in the population. This approach focuses on all reproductive effects received by an individual, as is pictured in Fig. 2.1b for an altruist. The individual's reproductive output in this accounting scheme is called *neighbor-modulated fitness*, because this output is influenced by the effects of interactions with the individual's relatives ("neighbors"). (The term *neighbor-modulated fitness* should not be interpreted to mean that interactants are literal neighbors; "neighbors" are any members of the subpopulation with whom the focal individual may interact.) Neighbor-modulated fitnesses are simply behavior-specific, mean offspring numbers, and thus are essentially the same as the classical fitnesses of population genetics theory.

Let us derive the condition under which altruism initially spreads using neighbor-modulated fitness. An altruist, relative to a nonaltruist, automatically experiences a loss, $c$, in reproductive output. This loss must be more than compensated if the altruism is to begin spreading. In kin selection, reproductive compensation results from the fact that individuals bearing altruism-producing genes are especially likely to receive altruism because the relatives with whom they interact also tend to possess copies of these genes.

What is the expected magnitude of this compensation? Well, if altruism is received, the recipient experiences an increase, $b$, in its reproduction. One must next determine the probability that an individual with the altruistic genes will receive this benefit. When an altruistic gene is just beginning to spread (i.e., when it is rare in the population), two interacting individuals will share the gene only through descent from a common ancestor—the probability that the gene is shared through common descent is known as the *genetic relatedness* between those individuals, and is given the symbol $r$ (see also Exhibit 2.1). Thus, the average reproductive compensation received by an individual with the rare altruism-producing gene from an interactant of relatedness $r$ will be the product $rb$. (For example, if the individual interacts with full sibs, there is a 0.50 probability that it will receive benefits in any interaction. This means that the average benefit received in an interaction will be $0.50[0] + 0.50[b] = 0.50b = rb$.)

Now let us tally up all of these reproductive consequences of altruism to compute the neighbor-modulated fitnesses. Let the "baseline" reproduction of altruists and nonaltruists be equal to $x$. Then, the mean neighbor-modulated fitness of the altruist is $x - c + rb$, and that of the nonaltruist is $x$ (when altruism is rare, almost all nonaltruists will receive no altruistic benefits). The altruism-producing gene will spread if the altruist's neighbor-modulated fitness is higher (i.e., when $x - c + rb > x$ or, simply, $rb >$

Exhibit 2.1.  What is genetic relatedness?

If an individual's relatives are viewed as a mixture of individuals who are genetically like itself and individuals who are a random sample from the population, the fraction of the former is approximately equal to the genetic relatedness $r$, provided selection is not too strong. This statement can be made rigorous in the following way. Let $A$ be the average frequency of the altruism gene in altruists, $p$ be the population average frequency of the altruism gene, and $R$ be the average frequency of the altruism allele in the kin group within which an altruist interacts. Then it can be shown that $Ar'$ $+ (1 - r')p = R$ (Grafen, 1985, 1991), where $r'$ is the "regression measure of relatedness" (so called because it is equal to the slope of the regression of the gene frequency of an individual's group on the gene frequency within the individual). Rearranging the latter equation, $r' = (R - p)/(A - p)$. The regression measure of relatedness is essentially identical to the genealogical measure of relatedness $r$ when selection is not too strong (Grafen, 1985, 1991). This is reasonable because, if $R = p$, the relatedness is zero; if $R = A$, the relatedness is one, as we would expect.

This formulation for genetic relatedness nicely illustrates an important property of genetic relatedness: Relatedness is not a measure of the absolute genetic similarity between two individuals, but of the degree to which this similarity exceeds the background similarity between randomly chosen individuals from the population. (In terms of the equation, relatedness increases with the difference $R - p$.) This feature immediately resolves a still oft-repeated misunderstanding about relatedness, which takes the form: "But if the members of a species share 99% of their genes the relatedness will be so high that indiscriminate altruism by all will be favored." Well, let $p = 0.99$, as conjectured. If the altruism is indiscriminate, $R$ also will equal 0.99 (here the "kin group" is really a random sample of the population). Thus, the relatedness will be zero and indiscriminate altruism cannot evolve—the benefits dispensed to recipients of altruism cannot cause an increase in the frequency of the altruism gene (Dawkins, 1979).

Many recent articles on the methods of estimating genetic relatedness use the regression measure or equivalent measures (for allozyme or microsatellite data, see Queller & Goodknight, 1989; for DNA fingerprint data, see Reeve et al., 1992).

$c$). The latter inequality is the famous Hamilton's rule for the evolution of altruism, which directly expresses the fact that the altruism-producing gene will spread if the average reproductive compensation for an individual bearing the gene exceeds the cost of altruism.

The neighbor-modulated fitnesses calculated earlier are based on only a single interaction; if there are $n$ interactions with interactants of relatedness $r$ (assuming that benefits and costs of multiple interactions simply "add up" to yield overall neighbor-modulated fitness), note that Hamilton's rule is unchanged because the comparison of neighbor-modulated fitnesses $x - nc + nrb > x$ still reduces to Hamilton's rule, $rb > c$. (For simplicity, it is henceforth assumed that $n$ is already included in the variables $c$ and $b$.)

Note that, in the neighbor-modulated fitness method, $r$ is seen as a measure of the probability of received reproductive compensation. Thus, $r$ measures what is called *reception efficiency*. It is later seen that reciprocity has a similar parameter arising from its corresponding accounting scheme.

**Inclusive Fitness**

The inclusive fitness accounting approach is pictured in Fig. 2.1c, in which the focus is not on reproductive effects received, but instead on reproductive effects dispensed, by the individual bearing the altruism-producing gene. The idea is to combine all the dispensed reproductive effects of an individual into an "inclusive fitness" for that individual in a way that correctly predicts the evolution of the altruism (Hamilton, 1964). The proper way to calculate inclusive fitness is the following: Take the baseline personal reproductive output of the individual, add to the latter the effect of the individual's behavior on itself (this sum is called the *personal component* of inclusive fitness), and also add the sum of the effects of the individual's behavior on the reproduction of others, weighted by the individual's genetic relatedness to those other individuals (this weighted sum is called the *kin component* of inclusive fitness). The behavior associated with the higher average inclusive fitness will spread.

Let us apply the definition of inclusive fitness to the initial spread of altruism, when altruists are rare. As earlier, let the average reproductive output of nonaltruists be equal to $x$ offspring. This is also the "baseline" reproductive output for altruists, and thus, the total personal reproductive component for altruists is $x - c$. It then follows from the definition that the average inclusive fitness for altruists is equal to:

$$x - c + rb \tag{1}$$

Altruism should begin to spread (invade) if the inclusive fitness for altruists exceeds the inclusive fitness for nonaltruists (i.e., when $x - c + rb > x$, which simplifies to $rb > c$). The latter condition is just Hamilton's rule again, which verifies the equivalence of the neighbor-modulated fitness and inclusive fitness methods. Note that in the inclusive fitness approach, $r$ represents not the probability of received compensation, as in the neighbor-modulated fitness approach, but rather the probability

Exhibit 2.2.  Neighbor-modulated fitness and inclusive fitness: a numerical example.

Consider the case in which altruists deliver a benefit of 2.1 additional offspring to recipients of their altruistic acts. An altruistic act costs an altruist one offspring. Interactants are noninbred, diploid full siblings ($r = 0.5$). Individuals that are nonaltruistic produce three offspring if they receive no altruism. Thus, $x = 3$, $r = 0.5$, $c = 1$, and $b = 2.1$ (see text). We examine the case in which altruism is nearly fixed in the population (i.e., $u$, the probability that a randomly chosen individual will behave altruistically toward its relatives, is virtually equal to 1.0). The neighbor-modulated fitnesses and inclusive fitnesses are calculated as follows:

Neighbor-modulated fitness of nonaltruist = baseline output + overall probability of receiving altruism from an interactant times the benefit of altruism = $x + (1 - r)ub = 3 + (0.5)(1.0)(2.1) = 4.05$

Neighbor-modulated fitness of altruist = baseline output − cost of altruism + overall probability of receiving altruism × benefit of altruism = $x - c + rb + (1-r)ub = 3 - 1 + (0.5)(2.1) + (0.5)(1.0)(2.1) = 4.1$

Inclusive fitness of nonaltruist = baseline output = $x = 3$

Inclusive fitness of altruist = baseline output − cost of altruism + relatedness times benefit of altruism = $x - c + rb = 3 - 1 + (0.5)(2.1) = 3.05$

Note that, in both fitness schemes, altruism is favored. This result could have been obtained most simply and directly from Hamilton's rule (i.e., $rb > c$), which is here satisfied because $(0.5)(2.1) = 1.05 > 1$ (see also Exhibit 2.3).

that a benefit will be directed toward an individual having the altruism-producing gene. Here, $r$ measures what is called *targeting efficiency*; it is later seen that reciprocity again has a similar parameter in its corresponding accounting scheme.

So far, we have established only the condition for the initial spread of altruism, using both the neighbor-modulated fitness and the inclusive fitness approaches. That is, we have established only the condition for *selective invasion* of a rare mutant gene promoting altruism. Under these special conditions, Hamilton's rule is easily obtained from both the neighbor-modulated and inclusive fitness approaches, and, in fact, the neighbor-modulated and inclusive fitnesses are identical. However, in general, the neighbor-modulated fitness will not equal inclusive fitness when altruism is present in an appreciable frequency in the population. Next, we show how this difference arises, and (more important) that, despite this difference, Hamilton's rule is approximately correct and obtainable from both fitness accounting methods regardless of the frequency of altruism in the population. A numerical example is given in Exhibit 2.2.

## Selective Invasion Versus Selective Maintenance of Altruism

Will Hamilton's rule also describe the conditions under which the altruism-producing gene continues spreading regardless of its frequency (say, when this gene is present in 57% of all individuals in the population)? Fortunately, the answer is yes, at least to a first approximation.

Comparing inclusive fitnesses yields Hamilton's rule, regardless of the frequency of altruism in the population, because there is nothing in the definition of inclusive fitness that makes reference to the frequency of altruism (see the earlier definition). The inclusive fitness of the altruist is always $x - c + rb$, and that of the nonaltruist is always $x$, regardless of how far the altruism genes have spread (i.e., inclusive fitnesses are frequency independent). Thus, the question of immediate concern is whether Hamilton's rule still results from a comparison of neighbor-modulated fitnesses when altruism is not rare. (Answering this question in the affirmative is what allowed Hamilton to validate the concept of inclusive fitness in the first place—i.e., the inclusive fitness approach works because it predicts the same conditions for the spread of altruism that are obtained by using the neighbor-modulated fitness approach, the latter being directly connected to the well-established, classical theory of population genetics.) Recall that when the altruism gene is rare, nonaltruist individuals produce $x$ offspring and altruists produce $x - c + rb$ offspring. However, as altruism spreads, nonaltruists increasingly receive the benefits of altruism (as do bearers of the altruism-bearing gene). Thus, neighbor-modulated fitnesses (but not inclusive fitnesses) are said to be frequency dependent, meaning that their values will depend on the frequency of the altruism-producing gene in the population.

To obtain a general expression for these frequency-dependent neighbor-modulated fitnesses, we first let $u$ be the probability that a randomly chosen individual will deliver a benefit $b$ to an interactant, which has a mean relatedness $r$ to it. Now $u$ obviously will increase with the frequency of the altruism gene in the population, and thus this variable represents the frequency-dependent component of neighbor-modulated fitness. For example, if at a given moment 57% of the members of the population are altruistic toward interactants (which have mean relatedness $r$), then $u = 0.57$.

The next step is to figure out how $u$ should be incorporated into the expression for neighbor-modulated fitness. The key is to use genetic relatedness to infer the probabilities that altruists and nonaltruists will receive the benefits of altruism from the individuals with whom they interact. From the point of view of a given individual, the group of interactants is composed of individuals who are genetically like itself and of individuals who are like a random sample from the population—the fraction of the former is approximately equal to the genetic relatedness $r$, provided selection is not too strong (see Exhibit 2.1). (For example, half of an individual's full sibs will share a copy of one of the individual's genes by common descent from one parent [$r = 1/2$] and the other half will share the gene only to the same extent that it is shared in the general population.) To put this another way, when the mean relatedness among interactants is $r$, a fraction $r$ of a given individual's interactants exhibits the same strategy as that individual (altruism or no altruism), and a fraction $1 - r$ exhibits the same distribution of strategies as would a random sample of the population.

Thus, if an altruist interacts with an individual genetically like itself (probability $= r$), it receives a benefit $b$ with probability $= 1.0$ (these relatives *must* possess altruism genes). If the altruist interacts with an individual that is like a random sample from the population (probability $= 1 - r$), it receives a benefit $b$ with probability $u$ (see the previous definition of $u$). Combining these fitness effects, the average neighbor-modulated fitness for an altruist will be $x - c + rb + (1 - r)ub$. A nonaltruist will receive no benefits from an interactant that is genetically like itself (probability $r$), but can receive a benefit from interactants that are like random samples from the population (overall probability $= [1 - r]u$); thus, the total nonaltruist's neighbor-modulated fitness is $x + (1 - r)ub$. Altruism continues to spread if the altruist's neighbor-modulated fitness is higher (i.e., if $x - c + rb + [1 - r]ub > x + [1 - r]ub$, which simplifies to: $rb > c$, Hamilton's rule again). This establishes that Hamilton's rule is approximately valid at any gene frequency, and consequently, that inclusive fitnesses (which are useful because they are not frequency dependent) yield the approximately correct conditions for the initial invasion, subsequent spread, and maintenance of altruism, at least for the simple model of altruism like that pictured in Fig. 2.1.

How did Hamilton's simple rule emerge again, despite that neighbor-modulated fitnesses are affected by the frequency of the altruism gene? The reason is that the term $(1 - r)ub$, which incorporates the frequency dependence, appears in both the altruist's and nonaltruist's neighbor-modulated fitnesses, and thus cancels out when they are compared. The term appears in both fitnesses because altruists and nonaltruists are equally likely to benefit from altruism dispensed by individuals who are like random samples from the general population; it is only the "extra bit" of altruism received from the "genetically identical" fraction of interactants that gives altruists a special reproductive boost. (See Exhibit 2.2 for a numerical example of the computation of neighbor-modulated fitness, inclusive fitness, and Hamilton's rule.)

## Kin Selection and Behavioral Plasticity:
## Conditional Altruism

The prior model of helping or altruism may seem extremely simplistic, especially if it is to be applied to humans. Surely, it is uncontroversial that humans display extraordinary behavioral plasticity, and that any models assuming simple, "hard-wired" connections between genes and behavior are bound to be inadequate. In particular, if humans display helping behavior toward relatives, surely, it will be highly context-specific (i.e., conditional on both the traits of the individual and the environmental–social circumstances).

A pleasing aspect of kin-selection theory is that its basic structure is unaltered even if altruism is strongly conditional (Parker, 1989). Indeed, the two subsequent sections show that as the conditionality of the altruistic behavior increases, Hamilton's rule becomes a more exact description of the condition for the evolution of altruism and easier to test with actual field data. First, however, let us examine the representation of conditional altruism in kin-selection theory.

Consider the evolution of an altruistic act that occurs only when the organism is in a context E (the context may be defined by body condition, dominance rank, time of the year, cues or signals produced by potential recipients, and so on). We make the plausible assumption that the occurrence of a context is independent of the genes controlling the response to that context (Parker, 1989). It is not difficult to imagine a neural mechanism by which a gene could influence the probability that the helping behavior will be expressed in a specific context E. For example, a mutant altruism-producing gene might strengthen the synaptic connection between a neuron influencing the motor patterns underlying the helping behavior and a sensory neuron or interneuron that carries information about the occurrence of E.

Suppose Context E occurs a fraction $f$ of the time, and that the conditional altruism gene causes individuals in E to increase the reproduction of relatives by an amount $b$. As a first case, assume that dispensers and recipients of altruism are both in E when E occurs (e.g., E might represent a weather condition or a current level of predation). The conditional-altruism gene has no effect when the context is not-E, in which case the average reproductive output of individuals is $a$. This situation is pictured in Fig. 2.2a. If the relatedness between interactants is $r$, the average total neighbor-modulated fitness for a conditional altruist is equal to:

$$f[x + rb - c + (1 - r)ub] + (1 - f)a \qquad (2)$$

This expression is simply the fraction of time in Context E times the neighbor-modulated fitness when in Context E (the latter being exactly the same as the neighbor-modulated fitness calculated in the previous section), plus the fraction of time in Context not-E times the neighbor-modulated fitness while in not-E. The average total neighbor-modulated fitness for a nonaltruist is:

$$f[x + (1 - r)ub] + (1 - f)a \qquad (3)$$

a)

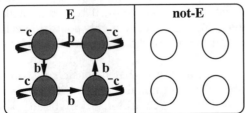

b)

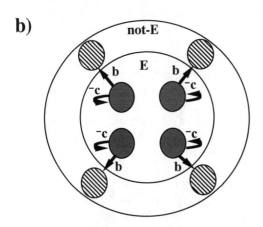

FIG. 2.2. Conditional altruism. (a) context-symmetric altruism toward kin; (b) context-asymmetric altruism toward kin.

The conditional altruist is favored by kin selection when Expression (2) is greater than Expression (3), which, after simplification, becomes the condition $rb > c$ (i.e., Hamilton's rule yet again). We would have arrived at the same result using the inclusive fitness method. The key to this analysis is that what happens in Context not-E is completely irrelevant to the evolution of the behavior. When we exclude consideration of not-E, we essentially return to the model of Fig. 2.1, and inherit all of the theoretical conclusions issuing from that model.

There is a more subtle kind of conditional altruism to be considered. Suppose conditional altruists are in Context E, but that the recipients of their altruism are not (i.e., the symmetry between help givers and help receivers as pictured in Figs. 2.1 and 2.2a is now broken). This situation (pictured in Fig. 2.2b) commonly arises, for example, when a subordinate individual decides to deliver help to a dominant individual—here, dominance ranking defines the context. When will conditional altruism evolve under this context asymmetry?

Let us try the neighbor-modulated fitness approach again, using all of the variables of the original context-symmetric approach. A conditional altruist will be in E a fraction $f$ of the time. Note that the last statement may mean that *every* individual will be in E a fraction $f$ of the time *or* (and this will be important later on) that a fraction $f$ of all individuals will permanently be in E and $(1 - f)$ will permanently be in not-E (or it may mean something in-between these two extremes). The latter distinctions do not matter for our purposes here because in all cases we obtain neighbor-modulated fitnesses by averaging over the genetic outputs of all individuals exhibiting the given behavior. If an asymmetric, conditional altruist is in E (probability $f$), it dispenses, but cannot receive, help, and its reproductive output will be reduced by $c$ units. If the conditional altruist is in not-E (probability $1 - f$), it will receive, but not dispense, help. How much help will it receive when in not-E? It will receive an average of $rb + (1 - r)ub$ units of aid from a single interactant in E (exactly following the logic of the previous section). How many interactants in E will there be for each individual in not-E? The answer is that there will be $f/(1 - f)$ interactants (potential altruism dispensers) in E for every conditional altruist in not-E. (To see the latter, suppose Context E has a frequency $f = ⅓$. This means that, on average, there will be $(⅓)/(1 - ⅓) = 0.50$, or one potentially altruism-dispensing interactant per two altruism-receiving recipients.)

Thus, the overall average neighbor-modulated fitness of the conditional altruist will be equal to the baseline output plus the frequency of Context E times the cost of altruism plus the frequency of Context not-E times the number of interactants in E (each potentially dispensing altruism) for each conditional altruist in not-E times the average aid dispensed by an interactant in E:

$$x + f(-c) + (1 - f)[f/(1 - f)][rb + (1 - r)ub] = \\ x + f(rb - c) + f(1 - r)ub \tag{4}$$

The total average neighbor-modulated fitness for a nonaltruist will be just:

$$x + (1 - f)[f/(1 - f)](1 - r)ub = x + f(1 - r)ub \tag{5}$$

The gene for conditional altruism spreads when Expression (4) is greater than Expression (5)—that is, when $rb > c$. Hamilton's rule works even in this case, and the same result would have been obtained from the inclusive fitness method. In short, conditionality of helping, whether context symmetric or context asymmetric, poses no special problem for the application of Hamilton's rule.

One point should be made about the meaning of $r$ when helpers are permanent (i.e., there is context asymmetry with each individual being permanently either in E or in not-E). In this case, the notions of $r$ as reception efficiency or as target efficiency are no longer interchangeable for the same individual. For the individual in E (a permanent helper), $r$

is to be interpreted strictly as a measure of target efficiency (i.e., as a measure of the likelihood of directing benefits toward possessors of the altruism genes), whereas for the individual in not-E, $r$ is best viewed as a measure of reception efficiency (i.e., as a measure of the likelihood of receiving benefits from altruistic relatives).

## Complications in Kin-Selection Theory: Assumptions Behind Hamilton's Rule

So far, Hamilton's rule, $rb > c$, has been presented as the keystone of kin-selection theory. The rule is easily generalized to encompass interactions with multiple kinds of kin:

$$\sum_{i=1}^{N} r_i b_i > 0 \tag{6}$$

where $N$ is the number of kin plus self, relatedness to self equals one, and the $b_i$s associated with the $i$th kin classes can be either positive or negative (i.e., either benefits or costs to the recipients). Of course, this rule can be applied to the evolution of any phenotype, not just behavioral altruism. However, even the generalized rule has important limitations, as has been pointed out by numerous theoretical population geneticists (see review in Grafen, 1985). In particular, up to now, it has been assumed that (a) costs and appropriately weighted benefits can be added together to determine the overall fitness effect of altruism; (b) selection is weak enough that $r$ is an accurate measure of reception or target efficiency (strong selection can alter the probability that interacting altruists share genes by common descent); and (c) altruism is random according to whether recipients of a given relatedness $r$ actually possess the gene promoting altruism (Grafen, 1984, 1991).

Are these assumptions usually justified? There are some good reasons to believe that they will often apply to humans in particular. The first important point is that if altruism is so strongly context dependent that recipients of altruism do not express the same altruism (e.g., Fig. 2.2b), Assumption (a) of Hamilton's rule will hold (Parker, 1989). Second, departures from the assumption of additivity of costs and benefits will not cause difficulties if a single altruism-promoting gene typically produces only small behavioral effects (which is reasonable because large effects are likely to reduce overall fitness). For example, suppose the cost $c$ and the benefit $b$ combine multiplicatively in the neighbor-modulated fitness, as in the product $(1 - c)(1 + rb) = 1 - c + rb - rcb$. If the effects $c$ and $b$ are small compared to one, then this product is essentially equal to $1 - c + rb$, which is an additive combination of cost and benefit.

Thus, the first assumption is not problematic if selection is sufficiently weak, which brings us immediately to the second assumption that selection must not be so strong that $r$ no longer accurately describes the targeting or reception efficiency. Note that as altruism becomes more strongly context dependent, kin selection operates on a particular altruism-promoting gene only in progressively narrower (less frequent) contexts (i.e., the overall selective effect of the altruism decreases). This point and the first point of the previous paragraph mean that, in organisms capable of sophisticated assessment of internal and external contexts (like humans), conditional altruism will be especially likely to satisfy to Hamilton's rule.

Violations of Assumption (c) would result from altruism being directed specifically either toward or away from relatives possessing copies of the altruism-promoting gene. The first kind of violation is not expected to be frequent because it is difficult to imagine by what mechanism a gene could cause altruism to be channeled specifically to those relatives possessing copies of the same gene (see Dawkins', 1976, fanciful, but instructive, example of "green beard" genes). Moreover, any such gene would achieve effects counter to the evolutionary interests of the majority of genes in the genome (making the former an "outlaw" gene), and thus would be subject to suppression by the latter. For example, a modifier gene that suppressed the dispensing of altruism by an "outlaw" gene, but allowed continued reception of it, could be favored by natural selection (Alexander & Borgia, 1978; Ridley & Grafen, 1981). Finally, altruism-promoting genes that caused altruism to be channeled away from relatives possessing copies of themselves obviously could not spread, and thus need not be considered.

Despite the comforting arguments just presented, theoretical situations inevitably will arise in which one or more of Assumptions (a) through (c) simply will not apply, especially when behaviors of altruists combine to produce nonlinear fitness effects (e.g., as might occur when context-symmetric altruism affects survival of a kin group). What is to be done then? One solution is to use Queller's (1992) general model of kin selection, which is a modification of the neighbor-modulated fitness approach. Queller's method involves calculation of both the partial regression of an individual's reproductive output on the gene frequency of its neighbors (controlling for its own gene frequency; this is equivalent to obtaining $b$ in Hamilton's rule) and the partial regression of an individual's reproductive output on its own gene frequency (controlling for the frequency in neighbors; this is equivalent to obtaining $-c$ in Hamilton's rule). In many cases, we only wish to know under what conditions a mutant gene with certain effects on relatives will be able to invade a population (this simultaneously gives us the invasion conditions for the given behavior and the maintenance conditions for the alternative behavior). A simple, yet general, "rare gene" method is presented in the appendix.

## Testing Kin-Selection Theory With Field Data

Problems often arise when researchers attempt to test kin selection theory with field data (Grafen, 1982, 1984). Especially in the first two decades after Hamilton introduced his theory, field researchers tested kin selection by trying to calculate inclusive fitnesses of animals exhibiting alternative strategies; these calculations occasionally suffered from several flaws (Grafen, 1982). One problem was that researchers would calculate the benefit $b$ of altruism to recipients (see Expression (1)) not as the increase in reproduction resulting from the altruism, but simply as the recipients' total reproductive output. Obviously, the latter error results in a large overestimation of the selective advantage of altruism.

A more subtle error, one that has persisted to the present, occurs when researchers estimate the personal reproductive output (i.e., the baseline output minus the cost, $x - c$; see Expression (1)) simply as the observed number of offspring produced by the altruistic individual. This procedure is incorrect because the observed number of offspring of an altruistic individual may include the effects of the altruist's relatives on its own reproduction, and thus the benefits resulting from altruistic acts will be erroneously "double-counted" (Grafen, 1982). In effect, the neighbor-modulated fitness and inclusive fitness methods are applied simultaneously.

So how does one modify the observed number of offspring to account for benefits received from other altruists? Hamilton (1964), in a key passage, intimated how this might be done by saying that, in his inclusive fitness formulation, the altruist's reproductive output should be stripped of "all components which can be considered as due to the individual's social environment" (p. 8). What, exactly, is the quantity to be stripped? This continues to be the subject of some misunderstanding.

Consider the simple model of context-symmetric altruism in Fig. 2.1 (or Fig. 2.2a). For this model, the altruist's average neighbor-modulated reproductive output, which is just its average offspring production, was found to be equal to $x - c + rb + (1 - r)ub$; the average observed reproductive output of the nonaltruist was equal to $x + (1 - r)ub$. We readily see that the quantity to be stripped to obtain the correct personal reproductive component of inclusive fitness is $rb + (1 - r)ub$ for the altruist and $(1 - r)ub$ for the nonaltruist.

Creel (1990) argued that it is the average benefit received (or dispensed) by a randomly chosen member of the population that should be subtracted from observed personal fitness in the calculation of inclusive fitness. Because this population-average benefit is less than the average benefit received by altruists, this procedure overestimates the altruist's (and underestimates the nonaltruist's) true personal component of inclusive fitness. Creel's subtraction procedure is correct for obtaining the average inclusive fitness for an individual randomly sampled from the population, but not the average inclusive fitnesses for altruists and nonaltruists separately.

The quantity that should be subtracted from observed offspring production to obtain the true personal component of inclusive fitness can depend on whether the altruism is context symmetric (Fig. 2.1) or context asymmetric (Fig. 2.2). For example, even subtracting the term $rb + (1 - r)ub$ from the observed personal reproduction of altruists (which is correct for context-symmetric altruism) is incorrect when there is permanently context-asymmetric, conditional altruism. For example, imagine, in an extreme case, that the altruist in Fig. 2.2b is a permanently nonbreeding, subordinate individual (Context E) helping a dominant breeding relative (Context not-E). To predict whether altruism is favored, we need to compare the inclusive fitnesses of altruists and nonaltruists only when they are in Context E (i.e., when both are subordinates) because their inclusive fitnesses do not differ in Context not-E (i.e., when both are dominants—each with their own subordinates). In other words, no altruism is ever exhibited by any dominant individual (Context not-E), and thus, a dominant individual carrying genes for subordinate altruism has the same inclusive fitness as a dominant individual lacking these genes (to verify this, carefully reread Hamilton's previous definition of inclusive fitness).

Thus, let us examine the inclusive fitnesses of altruistic versus nonaltruistic subordinates (Context E). Because a subordinate altruist does not receive help from another altruist, its observed personal reproductive output (zero in the extreme example) is identical to the personal reproductive component of its inclusive fitness. In other words, nothing needs to be subtracted from the observed reproductive output to obtain a predictive measure of inclusive fitness that accords with Hamilton's original definition. Thus, to the extent that humans (or any animals) exhibit permanently context-asymmetric, conditional altruism, the calculation of the personal component of inclusive fitness is relatively straightforward: Context asymmetry automatically "unveils" the true personal component of inclusive fitness for conditional altruists because their observed reproduction is not confounded by reproductive contributions from other altruists.

So exactly what do we do with field data when altruism is context symmetric? In such cases, there must be an empirical method for determining to what extent an altruist's or nonaltruist's reproduction is affected by other altruists: Either natural observations must be made of reproduction in the absence of influences from other altruists, or reproduction must be measured when help from other altruists is experimentally prevented (these methods are the same as those for determining the effects of altruism on the reproduction of recipients).

The latter methods raise an important question that has been underemphasized in discussions of the field estimation of inclusive fitness. If an altruist receives multiple kinds of help from other altruists, are the effects of all the kinds of help to be subtracted when one calculates the personal reproduction component of inclusive fitness? This issue is particularly relevant to human sociobiology because individual humans typically receive multiple and varied streams of helping behavior from other humans. The answer to the prior question is no: Only the effects of received altruism due to the gene whose evolution is being examined are to be stripped from observed reproduction to obtain the personal component of inclusive fitness. Thus, when Hamilton required that we strip "all components which can be considered as due to the individual's social environment," he meant "all" only in the sense of all effects due to the specific trait in question. This is implicit in the fact that the mathematical definition of inclusive fitness includes only the effects of the behavior being modeled (i.e., the changes in reproductive output relative to a particular, fixed background of reproduction—the baseline reproduction $x$), regardless of what other social influences have contributed to that background. This also means that inclusive fitness is an inherently relative concept, unlike neighbor-modulated fitness. Neighbor-modulated fitness can be measured as absolute offspring number without reference to another behavioral (phenotypic) variant, whereas there is no such "absolute" inclusive fitness. What is stripped from the observed offspring number of a potential altruist to obtain the personal component depends on what alternative traits are being considered, so it is not really meaningful to calculate an individual's absolute inclusive fitness, as is unfortunately attempted in some textbook treatments.

Because Hamiltonian inclusive fitness already implicitly involves a comparison of two phenotypes, a researcher actually does best to forego its calculation and instead just apply Hamilton's rule, which makes the comparison explicit and is easier to apply because it dispenses with the need to worry about the exact magnitude of the personal component of inclusive fitness (Creel, 1990; Grafen, 1982, 1984, 1991). This procedure is illustrated in Exhibit 2.3. Finally, Hamilton's rule applies only when Assumptions (a) through (c) approximately hold. When they do not, researchers must measure the special parameters arising from more general theoretical approaches, such as Queller's (1992) or the rare-gene method (appendix).

Exhibit 2.3. How do we use Hamilton's rule with real data?

Confusion often arises in the application of kin-selection theory to real data (see Grafen, 1982, for discussion of common confusions). Here the correct application of Hamilton's rule to some hypothetical data is illustrated.

The first questions to always ask are: What are the alternative behaviors (strategies) specified by competing alleles at a genetic locus, and What are the numbers of offspring produced by all individuals when each of the alternative behaviors are performed? Consider a focal individual who interacts with a full sibling and a half sibling (all individuals assumed non-inbred and diploid). The focal individual has extra resources that it may altruistically share with its siblings. Because we are interested in whether altruistic behavior by the focal individual (in the given context) will evolve, we tabulate the offspring production of all parties if the focal individual does versus does not engage in the altruistic sharing. To obtain data for the following table, we require observations of reproduction when the altruism occurs and fails to occur, or when it is experimentally prevented (Hamilton's rule always involves a comparison of alternative behaviors):

|  | Offspring Production | |
|---|---|---|
|  | *Focal Individual Altruistic* | *Focal Individual Not Altruistic* |
| Focal individual | 3 | 4 |
| Full sibling | 4 | 2 |
| Half sibling | 2.5 | 2 |

Next, we decide whether the interactions are context symmetric (i.e., the focal individuals and their relatives are in the same context, thus there can be bidirectional flows of altruism) or context asymmetric (i.e., only the focal individual is in an altruism-dispensing context, and thus, altruism flows only from him or her). Because it is only the focal individual who has extra resources to share, the reasonable assumption is that the altruism is context asymmetric, the context being defined by the possession of extra resources. This would be true even if the other siblings aided the focal individual in some way. These additional helping behaviors are likely controlled by different context-sensitive genes, and thus, their consequences are not relevant for understanding the evolution of genes promoting the focal individual's context-specific altruism (i.e., the aid provided by the other relatives are part of the background against which the effects of the focal individual's altruism are being measured).

As a result of the altruistic act, the focal individual's reproductive output changes by $-1$, that of the full sibling changes by $+2$, and that of the half sibling changes by $+0.5$. We now use the expanded form of Hamilton's rule (inequality 6): The relatedness of the focal to him or herself is 1, to the full sibling is 0.50, and to the half sibling is 0.25, so we calculate $(1)(-1) + (0.50)(2) + (0.25)(0.5) = 0.125 > 0$, so the altruism is favored by kin selection. (Note: It would have also been legitimate to use the focal individual's relatednesses to his or her own offspring [0.5], to full sibs' offspring [0.25], and to half sibs' offspring [0.125]. This would not affect the direction of the inequality because it is equivalent to dividing both sides of the inequality by two.)

These two procedures are not equivalent, however, if cross-generational altruism occurs. For example, suppose we are to assess whether a focal female should help her mother raise full siblings: The individual's $r$ to herself is 1.0 and to her mother is 0.50, whereas her $r$ to her own offspring is 0.50 and to her mother's offspring is also 0.50; these two pairs of relatednesses are not proportional to each other. Using offspring relatednesses is correct here because the potential altruist's choice is between rearing two kinds of offspring—sons and daughters versus sisters and brothers. Because of the complication of cross-generational altruism, the best general procedure is to compute relatednesses to interactants' offspring in Hamilton's rule, despite that, in its usual form ($rb > c$), the focal individual's immediate relatedness to herself and other relatives is usually used (West Eberhard, 1975).

## Kin-Recognition Mechanisms

Once kin-selected altruism spreads in a population, subsequent selection should favor behavioral mechanisms that increase $r$ (Hamilton, 1964; i.e., the targeting, or reception, efficiency). These mechanisms are called *kin-rec-ognition mechanisms* (Waldman, 1987). Every kin-recognition mechanism has three components: (a) *the production component*, which refers to the nature and development of kin-recognition cues (Sherman & Holmes, 1985); (b) *the perception component*, which refers to the sensory detection of recognition cues, the comparison of these cues to an internal template used to identify kin, and the nature and development of the internal template (Sherman & Holmes, 1985); and (c) *the action component*, which refers to the nature and determinants of an action taken for a given level of similarity between the recognition cues and the internal template (Reeve, 1989).

Empirical evidence across the animal kingdom suggests that there are two basic kinds of kin-recognition mechanisms, both involving learning of the kin-recognition template (Sherman & Holmes, 1985; Sherman, Reeve, & Pfennig, 1997; Waldman, 1987). In *location* (indirect) *mechanisms*, individuals discriminate among conspecifics based on their locations; the template is learned from cues of locations where kin are reliably found. In *phenotype* (direct) *mechanisms*, individuals discriminate among conspecifics based on their individual phenotypes; the template is based on cues from the individual's kin, its nest, or itself (i.e., from some referent). When the template in phenotype mechanisms is so specific that an individual treats only familiar individuals as kin (i.e., only conspecifics encountered in an early learning period), the mechanism is sometimes called an associational mechanism. When the template is sufficiently generalized that unfamiliar kin can later be recognized, the phenotype mechanism is referred to as *phenotype matching*. Location and phenotype kin-recognition mechanisms are not mutually exclusive; indeed, components of both are expected in dynamically optimal kin-recognition mechanisms (Reeve, 1989).

A current misconception about kin-recognition mechanisms is that true kin discrimination must somehow involve genetically based cues (e.g., Grafen, 1990). The arbitrariness of this requirement can be exposed by viewing kin-recognition mechanisms as strategies by which altruism-producing genes target copies of themselves in recipients. Location or phenotype mechanisms involving environmentally acquired cues can be effective targeting strategies when the altruism-stimulating cues are positively correlated with the relatedness of recipients (Holmes & Sherman, 1982; Sherman et al., 1997). In these cases, the altruism-producing gene does not directly see copies of itself in recipients, but nevertheless promotes its own spread through a chain of positive statistical associations linking the recognition cues at one end with possession of the altruism gene at the other. The situation is no different for a genetically specified cue. Again, the altruism gene spreads via an indirect statistical association between the gene producing the cue and the copy of the altruism gene in the recipient. (Recall from earlier that a gene that manages to directly target copies of itself works against the interest of other genes in the genome, and hence, is subject to intragenomic suppression.)

In humans and other highly social animals, kin-selected altruism can be mediated not merely by indirect cues of recipient kin, but also by intermediary individuals. For example, an altruist may dispense benefits to an individual (whether kin or nonkin) that, in turn (with enhanced probability), dispenses benefits of the same or different kind to the original altruist's kin ("indirect nepotism"; Alexander, 1987). This higher-order kin recognition or nepotism can be of any sequence length; all that is required for spread of the altruistic tendency is that the ultimate recipient of the benefits triggered by the original altruism have the minimal average relatedness for Hamilton's rule or equivalent condition (see appendix) to apply. A simple example of socially mediated nepotism occurs in the eusocial insects. A sterile guard worker that discriminates between sterile nestmate foragers and non-nestmate food robbers is exhibiting bona fide kin-selected kin recognition, albeit kin recognition of second order: A gene that preferentially allows nestmate foragers to enter the colony is ultimately promoting copies of itself in the related brood that receive the collected food. In humans, second-order nepotism may operate when an individual compensates unrelated individuals for helping to rear its offspring under difficult conditions. Undoubtedly, there are more complicated examples in humans that await elucidation (Alexander, 1987).

## MECHANISMS BASED ON BY-PRODUCT
## MUTUALISM AND RECIPROCITY

Considerable theoretical attention has been given to the problem of cooperation among unrelated individuals (see review in Mesterton-Gibbons &
Dugatkin, 1992). The general framework for these investigations is shown
in the left panel of Fig. 2.3a. The "payoff matrix" shows the fitness payoffs
(changes in reproductive output) to Player 1 for either cooperating with or
behaving selfishly toward ("defecting" against) another individual in the
same context and facing the same decisions (Player 2). For example, the
payoff to Player 1 for cooperating with Player 2, given that Player 2
cooperates, is equal to $R$. It is assumed that interaction is context symmetric;
the payoffs for Player 2 would be the same (obtained by simply interchang-
ing its position with Player 1 and reading off the payoffs as earlier).

### By-Product Mutualism

Let us use this simple two-person evolutionary game (Maynard Smith,
1982b) to analyze how cooperation might evolve among unrelated individuals and to understand how such cooperation relates to kin-selected
altruism. The first and most intuitive situation favoring cooperation
would occur if the reward for cooperation $R$ is positive and greater than
the temptation to defect $T$. In such a case, cooperation would be maintained against invasion by defectors because rare defectors would obtain
a lesser payoff ($T$) on interacting with the predominant cooperators than
cooperators would obtain after interacting with each other ($R$).

Thus, if $R > T$, cooperation is said to be evolutionarily stable against
the initial spread (invasion) of defectors, and is called the *evolutionarily
stable strategy* (*ESS*; Maynard Smith, 1982b). By the same logic, cooperation
invades a population of defectors if $S > P$ (the latter invasion condition
is not necessarily the same as the maintenance condition, unlike the case
of kin selection described by Hamilton's rule). Cooperation that spreads
and is maintained in these ways is called *by-product mutualism* (Brown,
1983; Mesterton-Gibbons & Dugatkin, 1992; West Eberhard, 1975). The
essential idea here is that an individual is favored to cooperate regardless
of what his or her partner does (i.e., the enhanced fitness resulting from
the partner's cooperation is merely a fortunate by-product of a cooperative
behavior that would have been favored in any case).

Where, in this model, are the presumed necessary costs of cooperation
or helping? Such costs are already absorbed in the payoffs for cooperation,
$R$ and $S$. In other words, the individual may incur a temporary cost for
cooperation that is automatically compensated after cooperation is completed (regardless of what his or her partner does); the resulting net

## a) single interactions

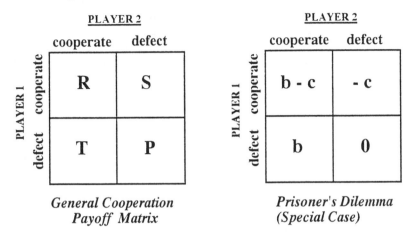

**General Cooperation Payoff Matrix**

**Prisoner's Dilemma (Special Case)**

## b) multiple (iterated) interactions

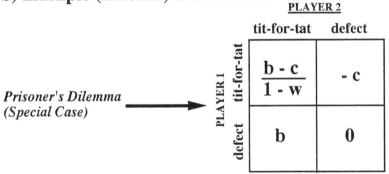

*Prisoner's Dilemma (Special Case)* ➔

FIG. 2.3. Models of the evolution of reciprocity. (a) Payoff matrices for cooperation versus defection: general case (left) and special case of the Prisoner's dilemma (right). R = Reward for cooperating; T = Temptation to cheat; S = Sucker's payoff; P = Punishment for mutual defection. (b) Payoff matrix for tit-for-tat versus defection when there are multiple interactions. $w$ is the probability of future interaction.

payoffs for cooperation are R and S. In by-product mutualism, then, the reproductive compensation is an automatic result of the cooperator's own actions. By-product mutualism is similar to the concept of pseudoreciprocity (Connor, 1986). In *pseudoreciprocity*, an individual helps another at a cost to itself, but the helped individual produces a compensating return benefit as an incidental by-product of its selfish actions after receiving the help. A possible example from animals, including humans, would be the presentation of a nuptial gift to obtain a mate: The cost of the gift may be compensated by a successful bond with a mate; the latter benefit is produced by the gift-accepting mate's selfish pursuit of its best reproductive option (obtaining nutrients or a relatively high-quality mate). Pseudoreciprocity essentially expands the concept of by-product mutualism to include cases where participants have different sets of payoffs (i.e., they are in asymmetric contexts).

## Reciprocity

The case of by-product mutualism is easy to understand. More theoretically fascinating is how cooperation can evolve when there is a constant temptation to cheat (i.e., when an individual would do best by defecting while his or her partner cooperates because such a defector would reap the fruits of cooperation without paying any of its costs, $T > R$). The latter situation corresponds to the classic *Prisoner's dilemma paradigm* for the evolution of cooperation. This paradigm is so named because it logically parallels the problem of whether two isolated prisoners that are accused of a joint crime should each refuse to confess to the crime (cooperate) or to confess and implicate the other (defect). The largest payoff accrues to the prisoner who confesses and implicates the other (as a "prosecution witness" given immunity) while the other refuses to confess, and the smallest payoff accrues to the prisoner who does not confess while the other confesses. Even if both prisoners would do better if both refused to confess (cooperate) than if both confessed (defect), the paradox is that the best strategy is to confess.

Let us analyze this case more formally. In terms of the payoff matrix on the left side of Fig. 2.3a, the Prisoner's dilemma paradigm corresponds to the following ordering of payoffs: $T > R > P > S$ (sometimes the additional assumption $R > [S + T]/2$ is made so that alternation of defection and cooperation does not provide a higher mean payoff than repeated cooperation). Before obtaining the stable outcomes of this evolutionary game, this payoff matrix is converted to one whose parameters correspond to those encountered in kin-selection theory. Following Dugatkin, Wilson, Farrand, and Wilkens (1994), $R = b - c$, $T = b$, $S = -c$, and $P = 0$, as shown in the right-hand payoff matrix of Fig. 2.3a. Here, the benefit of receiving cooperation is $b$, the cost of dispensing cooperation is $c$ ($> 0$), and the highest payoff is obtained if an individual defects while the other cooperates. If the two interactants have only a single interaction, there is only one ESS—to defect. This is seen by noting that the cooperative strategy would be unable to invade a population of defectors (because $-c < 0$) and that cooperators would be invaded by defectors (because $b > b - c$).

Is there any way out of the Prisoner's dilemma—any selective mechanism by which cooperation might be favored under the given conditions? This question has entranced evolutionary theorists, as reflected in the recent explosion of theoretical literature on the subject. The most heralded "solution" to this dilemma brings us to the third selective mechanism favoring cooperation: reciprocity. Trivers (1971) first proposed that cooperation between unrelated individuals might occur when help delivered by one individual to another is later reciprocated, such that both individuals experience a net increase in reproductive success. The solution to the Prisoner's paradox is essentially a specific formulation of Trivers' general notion of reciprocity (or reciprocal altruism).

For reciprocity to evolve under the payoff conditions of the Prisoner's dilemma, it is necessary to assume that there are repeated (iterated) interactions between potential interactants, and that the number of interactions is not fixed, but a random variable (otherwise, the ESS would be to defect on the last interaction, which then makes defection the best strategy on the interaction before the last, and so on, ultimately favoring defection in every interaction). In particular, the probability of future interaction $w$ between two interacting individuals must be positive and above some threshold value. Under the latter conditions, it turns out that a strategy called "tit-for-tat" (TFT; that is, cooperate on the first interaction, then copy the partner's previous behavior on subsequent interactions), can be evolutionarily stable against invasion by the defection strategy (Axelrod, 1984; Axelrod & Hamilton, 1981). TFT is an example of reciprocity. (A recent deluge of theoretical work has shown that various refinements of the basic TFT strategy can yield even more evolutionarily robust forms of reciprocity; e.g., Nowak & Sigmund, 1992, 1993; Sigmund, 1993.)

It is easy to derive the conditions for the evolutionary stability of TFT from the right-hand, single-interaction payoff matrix in Fig. 2.3a. In effect, the single-interaction payoff matrix is converted to a new payoff matrix that gives the average change in reproductive output of TFT strategists versus defectors over multiple interactions (Fig. 2.3b). If the probability of future interaction (given that an initial interaction occurred) is $w$, the average total number of interactions between two individuals will be $1/(1 - w)$.[1] If two TFT strategists meet, they always each obtain $b - c$ fitness

---

[1]Here is an easy way to derive the latter result: Let $I$ be the total expected number of interactions between the two participants. This is equal to one (because at least one interaction is assumed to have occurred) plus the probability of future interaction $w$ times the expected number of future interactions, given that a future interaction occurs. The typical (simplest) assumption is that the probability of future interaction is constant, so that the total expected number of future interactions given that a future interaction occurs is just $I$ again. Putting this all together mathematically, we obtain $I = 1 + wI$. Now we can solve for $I$ to obtain $I = 1/(1 - w)$.

units in every interaction, so the average total fitness change of each will be $(b - c)/(1 - w)$. If two defectors meet, each experiences a fitness change equal to zero. If a TFT strategist meets a defector, the former loses $c$ on the first interaction, becomes a defector, and does not experience any further changes in reproductive success; thus, its payoff is $-c$. If a defector meets a TFT strategist, it obtains a payoff $b$ on the first interaction and 0 thereafter, for an average total payoff of $b$. TFT will be the ESS if defectors cannot invade a population of TFT strategists, which, from the new payoff matrix (Fig. 2.3b), is seen to occur when $(b - c)/(1 - w) > b$ (i.e., when $wb > c$). Thus, TFT is an ESS if the probability of future interaction is sufficiently high (i.e., defectors are unable to invade because their defection deprives them of the substantial cumulative benefits of future cooperation).

Notice the similarity in structure between the latter maintenance condition for TFT and Hamilton's rule for kin-selected altruism; $w$ corresponds to the $r$ in Hamilton's rule. The nature of the reproductive compensation in reciprocity (i.e., help returned from partners) differs from that in kin selection only in the mechanism that guarantees the return help. In reciprocity, return help is assured because only by providing help can partners obtain the benefits of received help in the future; in kin selection, return help is assured (although not necessarily from a helped partner) because partners share the genetic tendency to help (note that $r$ and $w$ are used as reception efficiencies here). It is often said that reciprocity requires a mechanism for detection and punishment of defectors. In TFT-like reciprocity, the punishment need not involve physical retaliation because the loss of benefits from future cooperation by itself is sufficient to discourage defection.

How will kin selection and reciprocity interact? Suppose interactions are always between a pair of relatives with relatedness $r$ (see also Dugatkin et al., 1994). By Hamilton's rule, it can be shown that TFT is uninvadable by defectors if $(w + r)b/(1 + rw) > c$. (Note that this reduces to the condition $wb > c$ for the case of $r = 0$, as derived earlier.)[2] As is intuitive, this inequality is more likely to be satisfied, and thus, cooperation (TFT) is more likely to be an ESS, as the relatedness $r$ between partners increases.

However, now assume that the prior condition is met and that, as a result, the population that consists mostly of TFTs and a small fraction of defectors (D) is maintained only by recurrent mutation. Will TFT be evolutionarily stable against invasion by unconditional altruists (U) (i.e., individuals that are altruistic regardless of interaction history)? Well, TFTs

---

[2]For TFT to be uninvadable by defectors, Hamilton's rule must be satisfied for the behavioral alternatives "TFT in a population of TFT" versus "D in a population of TFT." By Hamilton's rule, "TFT in a population of TFT" is favored when $(b - c)/(1 - w) - b + r[(b - c)/(1 - w) - (-c)] > 0$, which, on rearrangement, yields $(w + r)b/(1 + rw) > c$.

and Us will obtain exactly the same average inclusive fitness payoffs when they interact with each other and with their own kind (because such pairs always cooperate on every interaction). However, TFTs and Us will differ in payoffs when each pairs up with a (rare) defector D. Again, using Hamilton's rule, it can be shown that Us do better than TFTs against Ds if $w(rb - c)/(1 - w) > 0$ (i.e., if $rb > c$). Thus, if $rb > c$, unconditional altruists will invade a population of TFTs (and become established as an ESS, even if the small proportion of Ds persists in the population). Following this reasoning, we infer that TFT (cooperation conditional on prior interaction history) is an ESS if both $(w + r)b/(1 + rw) > c$ and $rb < c$, and unconditional altruism (cooperation regardless of interaction history) is the ESS if $rb > c$.

### Selective Invasion Versus Selective Maintenance of Reciprocity Among Unrelated Individuals

So far only the maintenance condition for TFT has been obtained. What about the invasion condition? From the payoff matrix in Fig. 2.3b, it is seen that the defection strategy is still evolutionarily stable against invasion by TFT strategists (because $-c < 0$). Thus, both TFT and defection are ESSs for the same payoff conditions when there are multiple interactions.

This leaves us with the important problem of how TFT-like reciprocity will become established in the first place. The key to the initial spread of TFT in a population of defectors is that TFT strategists must meet each other with some minimum threshold frequency, so that they can reap enough benefits of cooperation to outreproduce defectors. How might this occur? The standard answer is that if new mutant TFT strategists interact primarily with kin, the TFT strategy will encounter itself often enough that it can invade a population of defectors via kin selection. This solution is not really satisfying for the following reason: Suppose TFT spreads because it is typically directed toward kin of relatedness $r$ ($> 0$) because of some kin-recognition mechanism, and Hamilton's rule is satisfied for TFT versus defection. After kin-selected TFT becomes fixed, will TFT directed toward random (unrelated) individuals now be any easier to evolve? Not necessarily because a new mutant, indiscriminate (nonnepotistic) TFT strategist will obtain an average personal payoff that is some weighted average of $(b - c)/(1 - w)$ and $-c$—the latter occurring when interactions are directed to individuals who do not recognize the mutant strategist as kin. The latter payoff would necessarily be less than the payoff to the predominant nepotistic TFT strategists $((b - c)/(1 - w))$, and the indiscriminate strategy could not spread. There is a possible way out of this problem. The prior model assumes that indiscriminate and nepotistic TFT stategists participate in interactions with the same number of partners. If indiscriminate TFT increases the number of such partners, and if kin-recognition errors are frequent enough that benefits often can be received from nonkin, indiscriminate TFT might be able to spread. It has been noted that TFT strategies have not been documented widely in the animal kingdom (Mesterton-Gibbons & Dugatkin, 1992). Perhaps the restrictiveness of the conditions under which the prior invasion model works is one reason for this.

## Origins of Cooperation Among Unrelated Humans: Some New Suggestions

Although reciprocity may be rare in nonhuman animals, it is obvious that reciprocal cooperation is not uncommon among unrelated humans. In the following text, three novel mechanisms are suggested—mechanisms by which such cooperation is especially likely to become established in highly cohesive social groups like those displayed by humans.

*Spread of TFT Via Errors in Assessment of Cooperative Contexts.* What is desired is some mechanism producing a sufficient frequency of TFTs that TFT directed toward unrelated individuals can further spread. One can easily derive this critical threshold frequency as follows. Suppose that a fraction $f$ of population members are (nonnepotistic) TFTs; the rest are defectors. The average change in the reproductive output of a TFT strategist after interacting randomly with members of the population is thus $f[(b - c)/(1 - w)] + (1 - f)(-c)$. The corresponding payoff for the average defector is $fb + (1 - f)(0) = fb$. The TFT strategy spreads if the former payoff exceeds the latter payoff, which will occur when

$$f > c(1 - w)/w(b - c) \tag{7}$$

or, equivalently, when

$$fwb/[1 - w(1 - f)] > c \tag{8}$$

(Note that Condition (8) has the form of Hamilton's rule, $rb > c$, where $r$ is here equal to $s = fw/[1 - w(1 - f)]$.) The condition for spread includes the maintenance condition as a special case because, when TFT is predominant, $f$ is nearly 1, and Condition (7) reduces to $wb > c$. For TFT to become predominant in a population of defectors, there must be some mechanism by which the proportion of TFTs comes to exceed the critical fraction given by Condition (7).

The first such mechanism can be generated if members of a social group sometimes experience circumstances when cooperation is favored and other circumstances when it is not. TFT can provide a way of assessing from social interactions whether cooperation or defection is currently the best strategy. In particular, assume that by-product mutualism (unconditional cooperation) is the ESS for harsh conditions (i.e., when $R > T$ and $S > P$ in Fig. 2.3a), and defection is the ESS for the Prisoner's dilemma game that applies under mild conditions (i.e., when $T > R$ and $P > S$). (For example, suppose that, when conditions are harsh, two individuals must cooperate in food gathering to survive, whereas, when conditions are mild, an individual gains by defecting against a cooperator.) Further assume that individuals make occasional mistakes in assessing when conditions are harsh versus mild, and thus, whether cooperation or defection is the fitness maximizing strategy. As a result, some individuals in harsh contexts mistakenly defect, and some individuals in mild contexts mistakenly cooperate.

In this situation, TFT can be favored over the error-prone rule, "Cooperate when conditions appear harsh, defect when they appear mild," as a more reliable way of assessing the best action to take under the current conditions. In effect, TFT uses a partner's response (cooperate or defect) to determine the response appropriate to the conditions: If the partner cooperates, the context is likely to be harsh (for which cooperation is always favored); if the partner defects, the context is likely to be mild (for which defection is favored). Moreover, an individual using the error-prone assessment rule risks getting locked into long costly sequences of cooperation with defecting partners (especially arising when mild conditions are mistakenly assessed as harsh); TFT is not vulnerable to such costly sequences. In this way, initially rare TFT can start spreading until the threshold (7) is reached even for mild conditions, with the result that TFT spreads until it becomes the ESS (even if conditions become permanently mild). (The algebraically adventurous can show that when a fraction $e$ of individuals incorrectly assess the prevailing conditions, when the payoff matrix for harsh conditions is $R = b$, $T = 0$, $S = b$, $P = 0$, and when mild and harsh conditions occur equally frequently, then initially rare TFT does better than the error-prone assessment rule if $e > c/(c + b)$, which is less than 1.)

*Spread of TFT Facilitated by Social Learning–Cultural Transmission.* Social learning can promote the initial spread of TFT-like reciprocity. Pollock and Dugatkin (1992) considered a strategy called *observer-tit-for-tat*, in which an individual bases his or her cooperative tendency, in part, on observations of the prior cooperative history of potential partners. This strategy is more easily maintained and more likely to spread than ordinary TFT. Note that, although observer TFT involves learning, the genetic tendency to learn potential partners' propensities for cooperation spreads through selection. (Ordinary TFT involves social observation to a more limited degree because individuals need only observe and remember their partners' behavior on the last interaction.)

A related social mechanism facilitating the spread of TFT arises when members of a group have (as proposed for humans by Alexander, 1979; Flinn & Alexander, 1982) a generalized ability to both assess reproductive benefits of social interactions and differentially copy those behaviors yielding the greatest reproductive payoffs. Let us make the specific assumption that individuals regularly update their assessments of costs and benefits of social interactions. Fortunately, the prior evolution of these abilities seems plausible for individuals in cohesive, complex social groups.

The process is illustrated in Fig. 2.4. Let us assume that an interaction of any sort incurs a small automatic cost $h$ (e.g., due to energy depletion or disease transmission risk), so that the strategy of avoiding interactions altogether invades a population of defectors (defectors receive no benefits from their interactions with each other; Fig. 2.3b). Now, suppose that, because of a shared genetic mutation for (nonnepotistic) TFT, two neighboring individuals engage in reciprocal cooperation. Nearby observers

**a)**

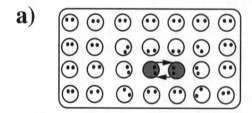

**b)**

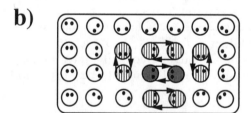

**c)**

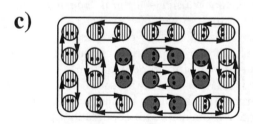

FIG. 2.4. Facilitation of the evolution of cooperation by cultural transmission. (a) Two neighboring individuals (shaded faces) sharing a genetic mutation for TFT engage in reciprocal cooperation. Nearby observers assess that the interaction is beneficial to each member of the cooperating dyad; (b) these observers (vertically hatched faces) begin to cooperate with each other, ultimately resulting (c) in a sufficient fraction of cooperators in the population that the TFT-enhancing genes begin spreading.

will assess that the interaction is beneficial to each member of the cooperating dyad (if $b - c - h > 0$), and these observers will begin to cooperate with each other. If an observer by chance tries to cooperate with a nonobserver, he or she of course, obtain only the small cost $h$, but this does not cause any behavioral changes in the observers of that interaction. Observers of the new cooperative dyads in turn will tend to cooperate with each other, and so on, resulting in a spreading "crystallization" of cooperation throughout the population.

This process may generate a sufficient fraction of cooperators in the population that the TFT-enhancing genes begin spreading (in particular, when $f > h/(b - c)$). Note that, without the spread and fixation of the TFT genes (i.e., the genetic "wave" that follows the cultural "wave"), the population is vulnerable to cultural invasion of the defector strategy because defectors are then seen as reaping the higher payoffs. (For further discussion of cooperation and cultural evolution, see Barkow, 1989; Boyd & Richerson, 1985, 1990; Lumsden & Wilson, 1981.)

*Modification of the Payoff Matrix by a Third Party (Enforced Cooperation).* In cohesive social groups, a third party external to a pair of interactants might experience greater reproductive success if the interactants cooperate than if they do not. For example, a third party may benefit if two other group members cooperate in resource acquisition. The third party may be favored to enforce cooperation by altering the payoff matrix for the two interactants (e.g., reducing, via some form of punishment, the payoff $0$ for mutual defection to some value $-a$ less than $-c$, thereby making it favorable for both interactants to cooperate; Fig. 2.5; see Clutton-Brock & Parker, 1994). The latter model, like the previous one,

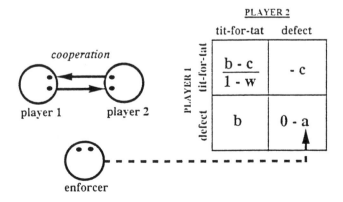

FIG. 2.5. Cooperation enforced by a third party causing a penalty $-a$ for mutual defection.

only works if the interactants are capable of assessing the payoffs for cooperation and defection, and acting so as to maximize their payoffs.

## Reciprocator Recognition Mechanisms

It was noted previously that the condition for the spread and maintenance of reciprocity is formally similar to Hamilton's rule and contains a parameter $s$ (see Condition (8)) that is analogous to the genetic relatedness $r$. Because $r$ can be viewed as either a measure of reception efficiency or targeting efficiency, it should come as no surprise that the reciprocity parameter $s$ can be viewed the same two ways (although reception efficiency—i.e., the efficiency of receiving return benefits—is usually emphasized). In particular, just as selection should favor nepotism genes with increased ability to target closely related relatives, selection should also favor reciprocity genes with increased ability to target true reciprocal altruists (i.e., carriers of reciprocity genes).

In other words, selection will favor reciprocator-recognition mechanisms. A theory of reciprocator recognition is readily obtained by borrowing the theoretical apparatus for kin-recognition mechanisms. Reciprocator mechanisms have the same three components as kin-recognition mechanisms: a *production component*, a *perception component*, and an *action component*. Reciprocator recognition (a) involves learning of an internal template of the individual characteristics of reciprocators or of the locations where they are found, (b) can be based on locational cues, or on genetic or acquired cues of individual phenotypes (Fig. 2.6), and (c) can be mediated by intervening recipients ("indirect" reciprocity; Alexander, 1987).

In kin recognition, cues are used that correlate indirectly with the presence of altruism genes via genetic relatedness of the potential recipient. In reciprocator recognition, cues are used that correlate with the presence of altruism genes via the prior cooperative history of a potential recipient (Fig. 2.6). At first glance, it might seem that accurate memory of an individual's cooperative history would allow fairly direct detection of cooperation genes, leading to the kind of intragenomic conflict presumably suppressing direct detection of altruism genes in relatives (if the latter were even possible). However, there is no such conflict in the case of reciprocity because no gene in the altruist could benefit by eliminating the dispensing of altruism to individuals known to possess a copy of the reciprocal altruism gene. In doing so, the altruism-suppressing gene would be depriving itself of the future reproductive benefits that otherwise would be bestowed by the recipient.

The connection between recipocator-recognition cues and the prior cooperative history of recipients need not be mediated by the altruist's memory of that interaction history. The altruist might also rely on the reputation of the recipient (i.e., verbal reports by others containing infor-

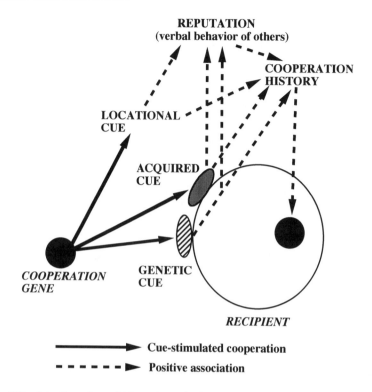

FIG. 2.6. Cues by which reciprocal altruism genes target copies of themselves.

mation about the recipient's interaction history; Alexander, 1987; Dugatkin, 1992; Pollock & Dugatkin, 1992).

Reciprocator-recognition ability will be particularly adaptive when selection maintains a low level of roving defectors (Dugatkin, 1992; Dugatkin & Wilson, 1991). Mobile defectors can obtain the maximal payoff $b$ from multiple "suckered" altruists, without suffering any retaliation, by fleeing after the first interaction. Reciprocator recognition may underlie the formation of diverse kinds of human subgroups, such as professional associations, clubs, communes, and religious organizations. In such cases, recognition may function not only in the detection of "con artists," but also in the identification of individuals most likely to dispense benefits (relatively high $f$ or $w$), individuals likely to dispense the largest benefits ($b$), or individuals with whom the cost of cooperation ($c$) will be least.

To facilitate mutual recognition, it is not surprising that the members of such minisocieties develop special dress or behavioral signals such as passwords, terminologies, and other verbal rituals. On a larger scale, reciprocator recognition might underlie many forms of xenophobia (which is sometimes attributed to kin recognition). The key observation distinguishing kin recognition from reciprocator recognition is whether the recognition is based on kinship or prior interaction history. If both kinship or prior interaction history influence the probability of altruism, disentangling kin from reciprocator recognition will be difficult (e.g., it is conceivable that kin will have cooperated frequently in the past) and probably accomplished only by estimating the costs and benefits associated with both kinds of discrimination.

## THE "NEW" GROUP-SELECTION MODELS
## OF THE EVOLUTION OF COOPERATION

Evolutionary explanations of cooperation based on "good-of-the-species" arguments are usually rejected because natural selection operates most effectively within breeding populations, not between them (Williams, 1966). However, it has been recently urged that evolutionary biologists in general and human sociobiologists in particular should incorporate a "new" brand of group-selection models into their evolutionary thinking (Wilson & Sober, 1994). How do these new models relate to the prior models of kin selection, by-product mutualism, and reciprocity, all of which emphasize selection acting on individuals (i.e., individuals are seen as the vehicles made by genes to propagate themselves; Dawkins, 1982)? It turns out that the "new" group-selection models—in which subgroups of the population, rather than individuals, can be seen as vehicles of selection—are not fundamentally different from the individual-selection models at all. Rather, the neogroup-selection models are generated from an alternative fitness-accounting scheme that merely produces an alternative picture of the same selective processes described by the individual-selection models (Dugatkin & Reeve, 1994). (In the same way, the inclusive fitness and neighbor-modulated fitness accounting schemes of kin selection are not alternative theories, but alternative pictures of the same process.)

The new group-selection models can be translated readily into individual selection models and vice versa. The translation from an individual-selection model to a neogroup-selection model involves (a) identifying a set of interacting individuals as a group, (b) calculating the fitness of a group member relative to those of other group members (rather than relative to all members of the same breeding population, as do individual selectionists), and (c) calculating the fitnesses (overall group outputs) of different kinds of groups relative to each other (Dugatkin & Reeve, 1994). For example, Hamilton's rule could be seen as describing the conditions under which the enhanced output of kin groups due to altruism within these groups compensates for an altruist's reduced fitness relative to nonaltruists within its same group. (The condition summarizing the rare gene method in the appendix can be directly interpreted as referring to within- and between-group fitnesses.) In reciprocity, the *group* is the dyad of potential cooperators; cooperation is maintained when cooperation increases group fitness, and some mechanism of retaliation prevents an altruist's relative fitness within its group from dropping too low. The equivalence of the neogroup- and individual-selection models means that neogroup-selection models cannot be dismissed as old style "good-of-the-species" arguments, but also that they do not represent truly alternative theories of selection (Dugatkin & Reeve, 1994). This chapter ends by briefly summarizing three recent theoretical developments that illuminate previously unexplored aspects of human cooperation.

## RECENT DEVELOPMENTS IN THE THEORY OF COOPERATION

### Intragenomic Conflict

It is well established that conflicts can arise between interacting individuals over the allocation of resources to a third individual who has a different genetic relatedness to each interactant. The classic example is parent–offspring conflict (Trivers, 1974). For example, a mother's offspring usually has a higher relatedness to its own offspring than to the offspring of its siblings. In contrast, the mother has the same relatedness to each of her offspring's offspring. This asymmetry in relatednesses can bring the mother and her offspring into conflict about how resources are to be partitioned during rearing of the offspring. In mother–offspring conflict, the offspring demands a greater proportion of resources for itself than the mother is selected to give. This conflict may be expressed even prenatally as maternal–fetal physiological conflict over the amount of nutrients reaching the fetus through the placenta (Haig, 1993).

Recently, a new wrinkle has been added to the notion of genetic conflicts. Under some conditions, even genes within the same individual theoretically can "disagree" about the optimal social action (i.e., there can be intragenomic conflict; one example was seen in the context of kin recognition). For example, some genes are genetically imprinted (i.e., their expression depends on whether they were inherited from the father or mother; Solter, 1988). Theoretically, these maternally and paternally imprinted genes can be selected to induce different courses of action by the individual in which they reside. Support for this notion comes from an analysis of mother–fetus conflict. When the mother has some probability of mating with more than one male, paternally imprinted genes within the fetus should tend to demand more of the mother's nutrients than would maternally imprinted genes because the paternal genes would have a lower likelihood than maternal genes of having copies in the fetus' other siblings. Remarkably, paternally imprinted genes appear to induce greater development of the placenta (the fetus' nutrient acquisition organ) than do maternally imprinted genes (Haig, 1993).

It is unclear what role genetic imprinting will play generally in the evolution of cooperative human behaviors. However, predictions can be made. For a highly speculative example, heightened aggression or self-ishness of children with unrelated stepfathers might be expected to result from conditional expression of paternally imprinted genes (the reverse for children with stepmothers). The general significance of genetic im-printing is that we may not always be justified in obtaining relatedness values by "averaging" over the relatednesses of paternal and maternal genes; each of the latter may act in accordance with its specific relatedness to interactants.

## Optimal Discrimination Theory

Optimal kin or reciprocator recognition theoretically should be sensitive to the context of recognition, different contexts being distinguished by different rates of encounter with kin or reciprocators or different fitness consequences of cooperating with kin or reciprocators. The problem is shown in Fig. 2.7. Cues for recognizing kin and reciprocators (or their locations) will vary by chance in their dissimilarity to the learned recog-nition template. Consequently, for a given acceptance or cooperation threshold (i.e., level of template-recognition cue dissimilarity below which acceptance occurs and above which rejection occurs), there will be some probability that kin or reciprocators will be erroneously rejected (rejection errors) and some probability that nonkin or nonreciprocators will be erroneously accepted (acceptance errors). The theory that describes the setting of the optimal acceptance threshold (i.e., the threshold that opti-mally balances the two reciprocally related recognition errors) is known as *Optimal Discrimination theory* (Reeve, 1989).

A sampling of predictions from this theory is that, as the relative frequency of encounter with nonkin or nonreciprocators increases, the optimal acceptance threshold should move left (i.e., become more restric-tive). The same prediction holds if the negative fitness consequences of acceptance errors increase in magnitude. As the relative frequency of encounter with kin or reciprocators increases (or as the benefits of coop-eration with kin or reciprocators increase), the optimal acceptance thresh-old should move right (i.e., become more permissive, provided that the

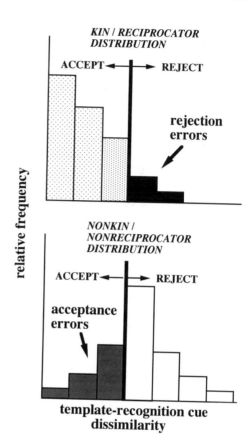

FIG. 2.7. Rejection and acceptance errors for a given setting of the acceptance threshold (level of template-recognition cue dissimilarity below which cooperation is favored and above which rejection is favored).

acceptance of an individual does not markedly reduce the discriminator's ability to accept another partner); it should move left (become more restrictive) otherwise (Reeve, 1989). These predictions could be tested by looking for changing patterns of error probabilities in different recognition contexts. For example, an individual should be less likely to cooperate with another member of a social subgroup of reciprocators when they meet outside the group than when they meet inside the group, even if the payoffs for cooperation are unaltered.

## Social Contract Models

A recent theoretical and empirical focus in nonhuman sociobiology has been the analysis of factors that determine the partitioning of reproduction among breeders in social groups (Emlen, 1982a, 1982b, 1995; Keller & Reeve, 1994; Reeve & Keller, 1995; Reeve & Ratnieks, 1993; Vehrencamp, 1983a). In high-skew societies, actual direct reproduction is concentrated in one or a few dominant individuals in the colony; in low-skew societies, reproduction is distributed more evenly among individuals (Vehrencamp, 1983).

Under some conditions, the dominant breeder may yield reproduction to the subordinate as an inducement to stay in the group and cooperate peacefully (i.e., there can be a "social contract" over reproduction; Reeve & Nonacs, 1992). Previous models of the evolution of this social contract have analyzed how ecological constraints on solitary breeding, relatedness of potential breeders, and productivity advantages of peaceful association should influence the evolutionarily stable reproductive skew in animal groups (Emlen, 1982a, 1982b; Vehrencamp, 1983). Reeve and Ratnieks (1993) recently extended these models by examining how relative fighting ability among breeders will interact with the prior factors to influence the reproductive skew. The general conclusions of the models are that the skew should increase (i.e., reproduction should become less equitable) as the relatedness between dominants and subordinates increases (because subordinates should require a smaller fraction of total reproduction to stay and help a more closely related dominant), the probability of successful solitary breeding by the subordinate decreases (i.e., for stronger ecological constraints), the subordinate's contribution to group productivity increases, and the subordinate's relative fighting ability decreases.

The degree of skew is predicted to influence other key attributes of societies, such as the frequency and intensity of dominance interactions and the division of labor within groups (Reeve, 1991; Reeve & Ratnieks, 1993). For example, when a subordinate of a given fighting ability receives a smaller fraction of the overall reproduction (i.e., the skew is higher), the subordinate should be more likely to aggressively "test" the dominant's strength because the subordinate stands to inherit the large skew if a reversal in dominance occurs. Thus, an understanding of the ultimate factors controlling reproductive skew may enhance our ability to explain and predict the occurrences of different kinds of societies in different ecological and genetic settings.

There are some counterintuitive consequences of the social contract models. Because increased relatedness leads to increased skew, and increased skew can lead to more intense dominance (aggressive) interactions, we are left with the conclusion that increased relatedness within the group can lead to increased intragroup aggression. This result is actually consistent with data on aggression within many societies of social insects and cooperatively breeding vertebrates (Emlen, 1995; Keller & Reeve, 1994; Reeve & Ratnieks, 1993), demonstrating that we can no longer always rely on the simple notion that "increased relatedness leads to increasingly peaceful cooperation."

How might the skew or social contract models be applied to humans? Whenever multiple humans engage in a cooperative enterprise, the social contract models can be used to understand and predict how the benefits of the cooperation will be distributed among the cooperators in an evolutionarily stable way. For example, two predictions are that there will be a more uneven distribution of rewards in favor of the dominant individual as the relative fighting ability of the dominant increases or as the relatedness between the dominant and subordinate individuals increases. The application of social contract models to humans promises to uncover a rich vein of evolutionary insights.

## ACKNOWLEDGMENTS

For valuable discussions and/or comments on this chapter, I thank Charles Crawford, Lee Dugatkin, Steve Emlen, Dennis Krebs, John Peters, David Pfennig, Tom Seeley, Paul Sherman, Janet Shellman-Reeve, and Phil Starks.

## REFERENCES

Alexander, R. D. (1979). *Darwinism and human affairs*. Seattle, WA: University of Washington Press.
Alexander, R. D. (1987). *The biology of moral systems*. Hawthorne, NY: de Gruyter.
Alexander, R. D., & Borgia, G. (1978). Group selection, altruism, and the levels of organization of life. *Annual Review of Ecology and Systematics, 9*, 449–474.
Axelrod, R. (1984). *The evolution of cooperation*. New York: Basic Books.
Axelrod, R., & Hamilton, W. D. (1981). The evolution of cooperation. *Science, 211*, 1390–1396.
Barkow, J. H. (1989). *Darwin, sex and status*. Toronto, Canada: University of Toronto Press.
Boyd, R., & Richerson, P. J. (1985). *Culture and the evolutionary process*. Chicago: University of Chicago Press.
Boyd, R., & Richerson, P. J. (1990). Culture and cooperation. In J. J. Mansbridge (Ed.), *Beyond self-interest* (pp. 111–132). Chicago: University of Chicago Press.
Brown, J. L. (1983). Cooperation—a biologist's dilemma. In J. S. Rosenblatt (Ed.), *Advances in behavior* (pp. 1–37). New York: Academic Press.
Clutton-Brock, T. H., & Parker, G. A. 1994. Punishment in animal societies. *Nature, 373*, 209–216.
Connor, R. C. (1986). Pseudo-reciprocity: Investment in mutualism. *Animal Behaviour, 34*, 1562–1584.
Creel, S. (1990). How to measure inclusive fitness. *Proceedings of the Royal Society of London, Series B, 241*, 229–231.
Dawkins, R. (1976). *The selfish gene*. Oxford, England: Oxford University Press.
Dawkins, R. (1979). Twelve misunderstandings of kin selection. *Z. Tierpsychol, 51*, 184–200.
Dawkins, R. (1982). *The extended phenotype*. Oxford, England: Oxford University Press.
Dugatkin, L. A. (1992). The evolution of the "con artist." *Ethology and Sociobiology, 13*, 3–18.
Dugatkin, L. A., & Reeve, H. K. (1994). Behavioral ecology and the levels-of-selection debate: Dissolving the group selection controversy. *Advances in the Study of Behavior, 23*, 101–133.
Dugatkin, L. A., & Wilson, D. S. (1991). ROVER: A strategy for exploiting cooperators in a patchy environment. *American Naturalist, 138*, 687–701.

Dugatkin, L. A., Wilson, D. S., Farrand, L., III, & Wilkens, R. T. (1994). Altruism, tit for tat and "outlaw" genes. *Evolutionary Ecology, 8*, 431–437.

Emlen, S. T. (1982a). The evolution of helping: I. An ecological constraints model. *American Naturalist, 119*, 29–39.

Emlen, S. T. (1982b). The evolution of helping: II. The role of behavioral conflict. *American Naturalist, 119*, 40–53.

Emlen, S. (1995). An evolutionary theory of the family. *Proceedings of the National Academy of Science, USA, 92*, 8092–8099.

Flinn, M. F., & Alexander, R. D. (1982). Culture theory: The developing synthesis from biology. *Human Ecology, 10*, 383–400.

Grafen, A. (1982). How not to measure inclusive fitness. *Nature, 298*, 425.

Grafen, A. (1984). Natural selection, kin selection, and group selection. In J. R. Krebs & N. B. Davies (Eds.), *Behavioural ecology: An evolutionary approach* (2nd ed., pp. 62–89). Sunderland, MA: Sinauer Associates.

Grafen, A. (1985). A geometric view of relatedness. In R. Dawkins & M. Ridley (Eds.), *Oxford surveys in evolutionary biology* (Vol. 2, pp. 28–89). Oxford, England: Oxford University Press.

Grafen, A. (1990). Do animals really recognize kin? *Animal Behaviour, 39*, 42–54.

Grafen, A. (1991). Modelling in behavioural ecology. In J. R. Krebs & N. B. Davies (Eds.), *Behavioural ecology: An evolutionary approach* (3rd ed., pp. 5–31). Oxford, England: Blackwell.

Haig, D. (1993). Genetic conflicts in human pregnancy. *Quarterly Review of Biology, 68*, 495–532.

Hamilton, W. D. (1964). The genetical evolution of social behaviour: I & II. *Journal of Theoretical Biology, 7*, 1–52.

Holmes, W. G., & Sherman, P. W. (1982). Kin recognition in ground squirrels. *American Zoologist, 22*, 491–517.

Keller, L., & Reeve, H. K. (1994). Partitioning of reproduction in animal societies. *Trends in Ecology and Evolution, 9*, 98–102.

Lumsden, C. J., & Wilson, E. O. (1981). *Genes, mind, and culture*. Cambridge, MA: Harvard University Press.

Maynard Smith, J. (1982a). The evolution of social behaviour—a classification of models. In King's College Sociobiology Group (Eds.), *Current problems in sociobiology* (pp. 29–44). Cambridge, England: Cambridge University Press.

Maynard Smith, J. (1982b). *Evolution and the theory of games*. Cambridge, England: Cambridge University Press.

Mesterton-Gibbons, M., & Dugatkin, L. A. (1992). Cooperation among unrelated individuals: Evolutionary factors. *Quarterly Review of Biology, 67*, 267–281.

Nowak, M., & Sigmund, K. (1992). Tit for tat in heterogeneous populations. *Nature, 355*, 250–253.

Nowak, M., & Sigmund, K. (1993). A strategy of win-stay, lose-shift that outperforms tit-for-tat in the Prisoner's dilemma game. *Nature, 364*, 56–58.

Parker, G. A. (1989). Hamilton's rule and conditionality. *Ethology, Ecology, and Evolution, 1*, 195–211.

Pollock, G., & Dugatkin, L. A. (1992). Reciprocity and the emergence of reputation. *Journal of Theoretical Biology, 159*, 25–37.

Queller, D. C. (1992). A general model for kin selection. *Evolution, 46*, 376–380.

Queller, D. C., & Goodknight, K. F. (1989). Estimating relatedness using genetic markers. *Evolution, 43*, 258–275.

Reeve, H. K. (1989). The evolution of conspecific acceptance thresholds. *American Naturalist, 133*, 407–435.

Reeve, H. K. (1991). *Polistes*. In K. Ross & R. Matthews (Eds.), *The social biology of wasps* (pp. 99–148). Ithaca, NY: Cornell University Press.

Reeve, H. K., & Keller, L. (1995). Partitioning of reproduction in animal societies: Mother–daughter versus sibling associations. *The American Naturalist, 145*, 119–132.

Reeve, H. K., & Nonacs, P. (1992). Social contracts in wasp societies. *Nature, 359*, 823–825.

Reeve, H. K., & Ratnieks, F. A. (1993). Queen-queen conflict in polygynous societies: Mutual tolerance and reproductive skew. In L. Keller (Ed.), *Queen number and sociality in insects* (pp. 45–85). Oxford, England: Oxford University Press.

Reeve, H. K., Westneat, D. W., & Queller, D. C. (1992). Estimating average within-group relatedness from DNA fingerprints. *Molecular Ecology, 1*, 223–232.

Ridley, M., & Grafen, A. (1981). Are green beard genes outlaws? *Animal Behavior, 29*, 954–955.

Sherman, P. W., & Holmes, W. G. (1985). Kin recognition: Issues and evidence. In B. Holldobler & M. Lindauer (Eds.), *Experimental behavioral ecology and sociobiolgy* (pp. 437–460). Sunderland, MA: Sinauer.

Sherman, P. W., Reeve, H. K., & Pfennig, D. W. (1997). Recognition systems. In J. Krebs & N. Davies (Eds.), *Behavioral ecology: An evolutionary approach* (4th ed., pp. 69–96). Oxford, England: Blackwell.

Sigmund, K. (1993). *Games of life*. Oxford, England: Oxford University Press.

Solter, D. (1988). Differential imprinting and expression of maternal and paternal genomes. *Annual Review of Genetics, 22*, 127–146.

Trivers, R. L. (1971). The evolution of reciprocal altruism. *Quarterly Review of Biology, 46*, 35–57.

Trivers, R. L. (1974). Parent–offspring conflict. *American Zoologist, 14*, 249–264.

Vehrencamp, S. L. (1983). Optimal degree of skew in cooperative societies. *American Zoologist, 23*, 327–335.

Waldman, B. (1987). Mechanisms of kin recognition. *Journal of Theoretical Biology, 128*, 159–185.

West Eberhard, M. J. (1975). The evolution of social behavior by kin selection. *Quarterly Review of Biology, 50*, 1–33.

Williams, G. C. (1966). *Adaptation and natural selection*. Princeton, NJ: Princeton University Press.

Wilson, D. S., & Sober, E. (1994). Reintroducing group selection to the human behavioral sciences. *Behavioral and Brain Sciences, 17*, 585–608.

## APPENDIX: THE RARE GENE METHOD
## FOR MODELING THE INVASION
## OF A GENE AFFECTING RELATIVES

When the altruism-producing allele (variant gene) is rare, the regression measure of relatedness $r'$ (see Exhibit 2.1) is approximately equal to $(R - 0)/(A - 0) = R/A$. Because the allele is rare, virtually all carriers will be heterozygotes (i.e., carry just one copy of the allele), so that $R/A = [0.5$ times (fraction of kin that carries the allele)$]/0.5 =$ fraction of kin that carries the allele. Thus,

$$r = \text{fraction of kin group that carries the allele} \qquad (9)$$

Let $a'$ be the total number of mutant alleles in pooled, mutant-containing kin groups after selection, and let $M' =$ the total number of all alleles in pooled, mutant-containing kin groups after selection, given that the mutant allele produces the effect; let $a$ and $M$ be the same quantities under the assumption that the mutant allele produces no effect. Let $N$ be the total number of alleles from all nonmutant kin groups after selection. The frequency of the mutant allele after selection will increase if and only if:

$$a'/(M' + N) > a/(M + N) \qquad (10)$$

which is equivalent to

$$M'(a'/M')/[M' + N] > M(a/M)/[M + N] \qquad (11)$$

Because $N \gg M, M'$, Condition (11) becomes, approximately,

$$(M'/M)(a'/M') > a/M \qquad (12)$$

From Condition (9), it is known that $a/M = r/2$ and $a'/M' = f'/2$, where $f'$ is the fraction of individuals possessing the mutant allele in mutant-containing kin groups after selection. Substitution of these expressions into Condition (12) yields the invasion condition:

$$(M'/M)f' > r \qquad (13)$$

If there are $k$ kinds of mutant-containing kin groups, each with their own specific values of $M'/M$ and $f'$, the latter condition becomes

$$\sum_{i=1}^{K} q_i e'_i f'_i > r \qquad (14)$$

where $q_i$ is the relative frequency of the $i$th kind of mutant kin group, and $e'_i$ is the reproductive output of the $i$th mutant kin group divided by the corresponding output in the absence of the effect of the mutant allele. (Note that $M'/M$ can be viewed, from the perspective of the neogroup-selection theories, as a measure of relative between-group fitness, and $f'/r$ as a measure of relative within-group fitness, of the altruistic strategy—altruism spreads when the product of these fitnesses exceeds the standard fitness of 1.)

Let us try to derive Hamilton's rule as a special case, using Condition (13) together with the assumption of weak selection and additivity of costs and benefits. $M'/M$ will equal $[r(x - c + rb) + (1 - r)(x + rb)]/x$ because mutants in the kin group [proportion $r$] will produce an average of $x - c + rb$ offspring per individual if altruism occurs and an average of $x$ offspring if it doesn't occur), and $f'$ will approximately equal $r(x - c + rb)/[r(x - c + rb) + (1 - r)(x + rb)]$. Substitution into Condition (13) thus yields $r(x - c + rb)/x > r$, or $rb > c$, Hamilton's rule.

# 3

## How Mate Choice Shaped Human Nature: A Review of Sexual Selection and Human Evolution

Geoffrey F. Miller
*Centre for Economic Learning and Social Evolution*
*University College London*

The application of sexual-selection theory to human behavior has been the greatest success story in evolutionary psychology, and one of the most fruitful and fascinating developments in the human sciences over the last two decades. Ironically, this development would have seemed absurd only 20 years ago. At that time, many biologists considered sexual selection through mate choice to be Darwin's least successful idea: If not outright wrong, it was at most a minor, uninteresting, even pathological evolutionary process. At that time, any "Darwinization" of the human sciences would have had to rely on natural selection theory, which bears much less directly on human social, sexual, and cultural behavior.

Instead, something remarkable happened: Sexual-selection theory was revived over the last two decades through the combined efforts of researchers in theoretical population genetics, experimental behavioral biology, primatology, evolutionary anthropology, and evolutionary psychology. Today, although natural selection theory serves as the conceptual and rhetorical foundation for evolutionary psychology (see Tooby & Cosmides, 1990, 1992), sexual-selection theory seems to guide more actual day-to-day research (see Buss, 1994; Ridley, 1993; Wright, 1994).

This chapter reviews the current state of sexual-selection theory, and outlines some applications to understanding human behavior. Sexual-selection theory has been revived so recently that, although extraordinary opportunities exist for further research, many old misconceptions persist. These include the mistaken ideas that sexual selection: (a) always produces sex differences, (b) does not operate in monogamous species, (c) is weaker than natural selection, and (d) had nothing to do with the evolution of human intelligence, language, or creativity. One goal of this chapter is to dispel some of these myths, and to bring evolutionary psychology up to date with respect to the biological literature on sexual selection. It reviews the history and basic theory of sexual selection; contextualizes human mate choice by covering sexual selection in primates and hominids; surveys some possible roles of mate choice in shaping the human body, the human mind, and human culture; and concludes with some academic and existential implications of applying sexual-selection theory to understand human nature.

## HISTORY OF SEXUAL-SELECTION THEORY

Darwin (1859, 1871) realized that his theory of natural selection through differential survival could not explain extravagant male traits, such as the peacock's tail, because such traits actually decrease survival ability. Rather, he reasoned that in a sexually reproducing species, any heritable traits that help in competing for sexual mates will tend to spread through the species, even if they somewhat compromise survival. This process of sexual selection may favor, for example, better sensory and motor abilities for finding mates, gifts and ornaments to attract them, weapons and bluffs for repelling same-sex competitors, endurance for lasting through the breeding season, and genitals and gametes that maximize fertilization rates. Within the sexual-selection process, Darwin distinguished between male competition for female mates (which typically gives rise to weapons) and female choice of male mates (which typically gives rise to gifts and ornaments). Yet, he recognized that female choice and male competition are often two sides of the same coin because mate choice by one sex usually implies competition by the other sex, either through direct "interference competition" (e.g., physical fights over the opposite sex) or indirect "exploitation competition" (e.g., scrambles to find and seduce the opposite sex before someone else does). Darwin had no real explanation of why males usually compete harder for mates than females do—why males court and females choose—although he offered a staggering amount of evidence that this pattern holds from insects through humans (Darwin, 1871).

Sexual selection was a radical idea for several reasons. First, it was a truly novel concept. Whereas the theory of natural selection had been anticipated by many 18th- and 19th-century thinkers, such as Jean-Baptiste de Lamarck, Etienne Geoffroy Saint-Hilaire, Frederic Cuvier, Thomas Malthus, and Robert Chambers (see Richards, 1987), and was codiscovered by Alfred Russell Wallace (1870, 1889), the notion that mate choice could shape organic form was without scientific precedent. Second, sexual selection embodied Darwin's conviction that evolution was a matter of differential reproduction, rather than differential survival. Animals expend their very lives in the pursuit of mates, against all the expectations of natural theology. Third, Darwin recognized that the agents of sexual selection are literally the brains and bodies of sexual rivals and potential mates, rather than the insensate features of a physical habitat or biological econiche. Psychology haunts biology with the spectre of half-sentient mate choice shaping the otherwise blind course of evolution (see Miller, 1994; Miller & Todd, 1995). For Darwin (1871), the choice of mates by female animals was no different in kind from artificial selection by human breeders:

> All animals present individual differences, and as man can modify his do-mesticated birds by selecting the individuals which appear to him the most beautiful, so the habitual or even occasional preference by the female of the more attractive males would almost certainly lead to their modification; and such modification might in the course of time be augmented to almost any extent, compatible with the existence of the species. (pp. 750–751)

Because female animals exercised most mate choice, and sexual selection through mate choice came very close to creative, conscious artificial selection by humans, Darwin's ideas put females in a very powerful evolutionary role—a role that made most (male) Victorian biologists deeply uncomfortable. Thus, male competition was widely accepted by Darwin's peers as an important, necessary, and general evolutionary process, but the possibility of female choice driving evolution was almost universally mocked and dismissed (Cronin, 1991).

For example, even Wallace (1870), the codiscoverer of natural selection, was deeply skeptical about sexual selection through female choice. He doubted that the perceptual systems of female animals could shape male courtship ornaments, and viewed such ornaments as arising from a simple male "surplus of strength, vitality, and growth-power which is able to expend itself in this way without injury" (Wallace, 1889, p. 293). Wallace's skepticism is strange because his insightful analyses of camouflage, mim-icry, and warning coloration all presupposed a form of "perceptual selec-tion" by female (and male) predators hunting prey (see Wallace, 1870, 1889). If female predators could shape the evolution of bright warning colors in their prey, why couldn't they shape the evolution of bright courtship colors in their males? Even now, we hear echoes of Wallace's fallacious surplus-of-energy argument in most psychological and anthro-pological theories about the "self-expressive" functions of human art, music, language, and culture.

After Darwin (1871), sexual selection received such a frosty reception from Wallace and others that it was virtually forgotten (Cronin, 1991;

Mayr, 1972). The Modern Synthesis of Mendelian genetics and Darwinism in the 1930s viewed male competition as a subclass of natural selection while continuing to reject female choice. Sexual ornaments were assumed to intimidate other males, or were "species-recognition markers" to help animals avoid cross-species mating (e.g., Cott, 1940; Huxley, 1938). Sexual selection remained hidden in biology's blind spot for many decades. The reasons are clear in retrospect. Sexual selection is hard to analyze mathematically. Behaviorist psychology ignored evolution, denied instincts, and disregarded the ecological validity of psychology experiments, so was not prone to doing realistic experiments on mate choice. A fallacious form of group selectionism viewed costly courtship ornaments as "bad for the species," and therefore, implausible. Freud's vain attempt to leapfrog past Darwin without really understanding sexual selection (see Sulloway, 1979) led to psychoanalysis supplanting evolutionary biology as the early 20th century's leading account of human sexuality. Not least, persistent sexism in biology denied the power of female choice until the 1970s (see Miller, 1993). However, during sexual selection's long exile from biology, it was sometimes adopted by early evolutionary psychologists such as Edward Westermark (1903) and Havelock Ellis (1905, 1934), who used it to explain many aspects of the human body and mind.

R. A. Fisher (1915, 1930) was one of the few biologists to take sexual selection seriously. He viewed mate preferences as legitimate biological traits subject to heritable variation, and this insight led him to postulate a process he called *runaway sexual selection*. In runaway, an evolutionary positive feedback loop gets established between female preferences for certain male traits, and the male traits themselves. Given a nudge in the right direction (e.g., an initial bias in female preferences), Fisher's model could account for the wildly exaggerated male traits seen in many species, such as the peacock's plumage. However, Fisher did not explain the evolutionary origins of female preferences, nor did he develop formal genetic models of runaway sexual selection. Huxley's (1938) hostile, deeply confused critique of Fisher's theory, and of sexual selection in general, consigned the field to continued neglect until the 1970s.

Sexual selection's revival has been swift, dramatic, and unique. Darwin's idea is, to my knowledge, the only major scientific theory ever to have been accepted after a century of condemnation. A centenary volume on sexual selection (Campbell, 1972) drew some attention to Darwin's neglected ideas. Trivers (1972) finally explained why males court and females choose, when he pointed out that the higher levels of necessary "parental investment" by females of most species make females a limiting resource over which males must compete: Sex differences in parental investment drive sex differences in the intensity of sexual selection. Zahavi (1975) set off intense debate with his "handicap principle," suggesting that the extravagance and costliness of many sexual ornaments function to guarantee their reliability as displays of genetic quality (e.g., only healthy peacocks can afford to grow such huge, handicapping tails). The debate over sociobiology (Wilson, 1975) attracted interest in the evolution of social and sexual behavior. The new population genetics models of O'Donald (1980), Lande (1981), and Kirkpatrick (1982) showed the mathematical feasibility of Fisher's runaway sexual-selection process. New behavioral experiments on animals showed that females of many species do exhibit strong preferences for certain male traits (e.g., Andersson, 1982; Catchpole, 1980; Moller, 1988; Ryan, 1985). Important edited volumes appeared on sexual-selection theory (Bateson, 1983; Bradbury & Andersson, 1987), and on sexual selection in insects (Blum & Blum, 1979) and humans (Betzig, Borgerhoff Mulder, & Turke, 1988). Eberhard (1985) argued that the only feasible explanation for the wildly complex and diverse male genitalia of many species is female choice for certain kinds of genital stimulation. Finally, primatologists began to appreciate the role of sexual selection in primate social systems (e.g., Byrne & Whiten, 1988; De Waal, 1982; Dunbar, 1988; Smuts, 1985), and Symons (1979) applied sexual-selection theory to humans more thoroughly than ever before. Once biologists started taking the possibility of female choice seriously, evidence for its existence and significance came quickly and ubiquitously (see Andersson, 1994; Cronin, 1991).

Currently, sexual selection is one of the fastest growing and most exciting areas of evolutionary biology and animal behavior. Recent biological work permeates the journals *American Naturalist, Animal Behavior, Behavioral Ecology and Sociobiology, Evolution, Heredity, Journal of Theoretical Biology, Nature*, and *Science*. Research on sexual selection in humans appears most often in the journals *Behavioral and Brain Sciences, Ethology and Sociobiology, Human Nature*, and *Psychological Review*. The best recent theoretical and empirical review of sexual selection is Andersson (1994); the best historical review is Cronin (1991). Darwin's (1871) foundational work, *The Descent of Man, and Selection in Relation to Sex*, still rewards careful and repeated reading. Accessible introductions to sexual selection in humans include Batten (1992), Buss (1994), H. Fisher (1992), Daly and Wilson (1988), Ridley (1993), and Wright (1994).

It is important to understand the peculiar history of sexual-selection theory because virtually all of 20th-century psychology, anthropology, paleontology, primatology, and cognitive science, as well as the social sciences and humanities, developed without recognizing that sexual selection could have played any important role in the evolution of the human body, human mind, human behavior, or human culture. Since biologists have embraced sexual selection, we must face the possibility that most current theories of human behavior and culture are inadequate because they may have vastly underestimated the role of sexual competition, courtship, and mate choice in human affairs.

## MATE CHOICE CRITERIA AND SEXUAL SELECTION MECHANISMS

The simplest way to review the current state of sexual-selection theory is to explore the different kinds of criteria that animals can use to choose mates. This is because we can often view sexual competition within each sex as an outcome of mate choice by the other sex—if *choice* is understood broadly to include processes both conscious and unconscious, and both psychological and physiological. Recently, there have been two major schools of thought about mate choice criteria. Champions of Zahavi's (1975) handicap principle have emphasized selection for *genetic indicators*—also called *good genes, good sense,* or *healthy offspring* selection. Champions of R. A. Fisher's (1930) runaway process have emphasized selection for *aesthetic displays*—also called *good taste* or *sexy son* selection. In evolutionary biology, these different mate choice criteria are often considered competing models of how sexual selection works, but there is now sufficient evidence for each (see Andersson, 1994) that they can be considered well-established, often complementary selective forces. Of course, mate choice can favor many other important qualities, including parental ability and resources (see Clutton-Brock, 1991; Hoelzer, 1989; Price, Schluter, & Heckman, 1993), fertility (e.g., sperm quality in males or fecundity in females; see Baker & Bellis, 1995; Singh, 1993), optimal genetic distance (to avoid inbreeding with close relatives or outbreeding with the wrong species; see N. Thornhill, 1991, 1993), and similarity in appearance, behavior, and personality (see Buss, 1985; Rushton, 1989; Thiessen & Gregg, 1980). Yet, before discussing these various classes of mate choice mechanisms, one must understand their origins.

### The Origins of Mate Preferences

Mate choice is the behavioral outcome of mate preferences. These preferences are usually "mental adaptations" implemented as complex neural circuits, and constructed through the interaction of many genes and environmental conditions, which bias mating in favor of individuals with certain perceivable traits. In most species, such systems may function without conscious awareness, deliberation, or complex aesthetic feelings. Yet, we might expect mate choice to be among the least unconscious of an animal's decisions because it requires the integration of such diverse information, and has such important fitness consequences. Mate choice operates by rejecting some potential mates and accepting or soliciting to others. In almost all species, females can effectively resist copulation attempts by unwanted males; in many species, females actively solicit copulations from desired males. Likewise, males actively pursue desired females and ignore solicitation attempts by unwanted females. Although sexual harassment of females is common in nature, "successful" rape seems fairly rare, being reported in only a small collection of species such as ducks, squid, dolphins, orangutans, and humans (Brownmiller, 1975; Rodman & Mitani, 1987; R. Thornhill & N. Thornhill, 1992). Generally, mutual choice and mutual cooperation are necessary for breeding.

Why do these mechanisms for mate choice evolve? Being choosy requires time, energy, and intelligence, and these costs of mate choice can impair survival and can decrease the likelihood of sexual selection operating at all (Pomiankowski, 1987; Reynolds & Gross, 1990). The basic rationale is that random mating is stupid mating. It pays to be choosy because in a sexually reproducing species, the genetic quality of your mate will determine half the genetic quality of your offspring. Ugly, unhealthy mates yield ugly, unhealthy offspring. By forming a joint genetic venture with an attractive, high-quality mate, one's genes are much more likely to be passed on. Even modern women who deny the "role of genes in human behavior" tend to choose their sperm donors quite carefully (see Scheib, 1994). Mate choice is simply the best eugenics and genetic screening that female animals are capable of carrying out under field conditions, with no equipment but their senses and their brains.

Mate choice mechanisms can evolve through direct selection for mate choice efficiency (i.e., better preferences lead to more or better offspring), and through three other less predictable, less adaptive processes: (a) mutation, (b) genetic drift, and (c) genetic linkage with another trait that is undergoing genetic drift, natural selection, or sexual selection. These last three processes typically produce harmful changes in mate choice mechanisms, so usually are selected out. But some changes will persist, through chance, utility, or Fisher's runaway effect. The unpredictability of these three processes is important in explaining the diversity of sexually selected ornaments across similar, closely related species (Eberhard, 1985; Miller & Todd, 1995).

The following sections review some of the major kinds of mate choice and sexual selection. But in addition to the mate choice criteria discussed later, most animals also have mechanisms to ensure that they mate with partners of the appropriate species, sex, age, and genetic distance, at an appropriate place and time (see Andersson, 1994; Bateson, 1983).

## Selection for Indicators

Probably the most fundamental form of sexual selection is mate choice for various "indicators" of viability (likelihood of survival) and fertility (likelihood of reproduction). These can take many forms. Almost any perceivable bodily or behavioral trait can function as an indicator, revealing age, health, nutritional status, size, strength, aggressive dominance, social status, disease resistance, or overall vigor. Such indicators may reveal both heritable genetic traits that would be passed on to offspring (selection for "good genes") and chances that the mate will survive to give provisioning, protection, and support to offspring (selection for "good parents").

No one is surprised when animals avoid mating with the dead, injured, or sick. All such mating decisions must rely on observable cues of viability. The idea of indicators is that the cues used in such assessments will tend to be exaggerated over eons of mate choice. Weak, ambiguous, unreliable, incidental cues of being non-dead and non-sick will become strong, clear, reliable, specially adapted indicators of being vigorous and healthy. For example, dead peacocks have rather drab tails. Peacocks with inferior tails get eaten more often by predators (Petrie, 1992). So tail quality probably reflects some underlying physiological quality that correlates with predator escape ability, and that could be inherited by offspring. This gives an incentive for peahens to choose males for tail quality, and for peacocks to display large, healthy tails as vigorously as possible (Petrie, Halliday, & Sanders, 1991). Other classic examples of indicators include color and condition of bird plumage in other species (Hamilton & Zuk, 1982; Moller, 1988), loudness and complexity of bird song (Catchpole, 1980, 1987), antler size and symmetry (e.g., Goss, 1983), and raw body size (Ryan, 1985). Yet, almost any body part or behavior that is expensive to produce, and that varies in magnitude, can serve as an indicator.

The importance of indicators in sexual selection has been emphasized by R. A. Fisher (1915), Williams (1966), and Zahavi (1975). Indicators, like animal signals in general, are subject to the *handicap principle*—the game-theoretic constraint that they must be costly in order to be reliable because, if not, they can be faked too easily (Zahavi, 1975, 1991). Indicators evolve most easily when they are condition dependent, such that healthier animals grow bigger or better indicators (e.g., larger, more colorful tails), or are revealing, such that healthier animals take better care or make better use of the indicators they have (e.g., the tails are better groomed and better displayed).

Despite initial skepticism about the handicap principle, computer simulations and mathematical models have helped convince most biologists that condition-dependent and revealing indicators are common outcomes of sexual selection. For example, simulations by Andersson (1986) showed that condition-dependent indicators could evolve even in perfectly monogamous species, given viability differences of only a few percent. An important mathematical analysis by Iwasa, Pomiankowski, and Nee (1991) confirmed that indicators can evolve under sexual selection even if mate preferences are costly, as long as mutations are usually harmful. Other, more recent models suggest that good parenting indicators can evolve to display even nonheritable resources, such as good territories (Grafen, 1990; Heywood, 1989; Hoelzer, 1989; Price et al., 1993). Thus, not all indicators are necessarily advertising genetic quality; they could simply be advertising resources and health relevant to raising offspring. Indicators often evolve better when runaway sexual selection is also operating on the relevant traits and preferences (Andersson, 1986; Heywood, 1989; Pomiankowski, 1988; Tomlinson, 1988). However, indicators alone, even without the runaway process, can suffice for the evolution of extravagant male ornaments and extreme female preferences (Grafen, 1990). See Andersson (1994) for a comprehensive review of indicator models and data.

The idea of genetic indicators has been criticized because of the lek paradox (e.g., Kirkpatrick, 1987; Maynard Smith, 1976; Pomiankowski, 1987, 1995; Reynolds & Gross, 1990; Williams, 1975). *Leks* are aggregations of animals such as sage grouse, where females pick their mates very carefully from among dozens of males displaying in large groups, and females receive nothing but sperm from the males they choose. The most attractive male sage grouse may achieve over 30 matings in a single morning, whereas average males usually win none (Boyce, 1990). Under such intense selection for attractive traits, we might expect the preferred traits to go to fixation (100% frequency) in the gene pool very quickly (R. A. Fisher, 1930). Once fixated, there would be no further incentive for females to be choosy because all of the males should have the same genes, and hence, be equally attractive. Indicators would become irrelevant once the population became genetically homogenous, without any heritable variation in fitness or attractiveness.

However, three processes can maintain heritable fitness variation: temporal variation in selection, spatial variation in selection, and mutation pressure (see Andersson, 1994). Temporally varying selection can result from co-evolution between ecological competitors, between predators and prey, or, perhaps most important, between hosts and parasites (Hamilton, Axelrod, & Tanese, 1990; Hamilton & Zuk, 1982; Low, 1990). Spatially varying selection in different geographic areas, combined with migration, can maintain heritable variation in a population. Mutation pressure can also maintain heritable fitness variation because most mutations are harmful and give rise to an excess of low-fitness individuals (Charlesworth, 1987; Kondrashov, 1988; Lande, 1981; Rice, 1988). Indeed, genetic models show that indicators evolve more easily under biased mutation (Iwasa et al., 1991). Some recent studies even suggest that sexually selected traits have much higher heritabilities and genetic variances than naturally selected traits, despite strong directional selection (Moller & Pomiankowski, 1993; Pomiankowski, 1995; Wilcockson, Crean, & Day, 1995). The importance of heritable fitness variation is also confirmed by experiments in which females who are allowed to choose their mates have offspring with higher phenotypic (and, by inference, genetic) quality than females not allowed to choose (e.g., Partridge, 1980; Reynolds & Gross, 1992). Through female choice, males have been forced to evolve clear windows onto the quality of their genes, so that females can weed out the bad ones. In this sense, females shape males to function as a kind of genetic sieve for the species (Atmar, 1991; Michod & Levin, 1988): out with the bad genes, in with the good.

## Selection for Aesthetic Displays

Some traits have been shaped as aesthetic displays, sometimes in addition to functioning as indicators. Aesthetic displays play on the perceptual biases of receivers to attract attention, provoke excitement, and increase willingness to mate. That is, seducers manipulate perceptions. The perceptual biases open to manipulation can arise in two, often complementary, ways. They may already exist as *latent preferences*—side effects of previous evolutionary processes, reflecting basic psychophysical effects, general principles of perception, or perceptual adaptations to particular environments—and they may co-evolve with the courtship traits they prefer, through Fisher's runaway process.

Several species have been shown to have latent preferences for particular ornaments, although the ornaments have not yet evolved in the species. Burley (1988) showed that female zebra finches prefer males whose legs have been experimentally decorated with red or black plastic bands, but males with blue and green bands were rejected. Basolo (1990) showed that female platyfish prefer males with colorful plastic "swords" glued on the ends of their tails, suggesting that this preference also predated the evolution of such ornaments in their close relatives the swordtails. Ryan (1985, 1990) found that female frogs of some species prefer the courtship calls (deep "chuck" sounds) of male frogs if they are played back at artificially lowered frequencies, as if produced by extralarge frogs. Ridley (1981) suggested that tails with multiple eye spots, such as those of the peacock and the Argus pheasant, play on a widespread responsiveness to eyelike stimuli in animal perception.

In response to such findings, several theorists have emphasized the role of perceptual biases in sexual selection, using terms such as *sensory drive* (Endler, 1992, 1993), *sensory trap* (West-Eberhard, 1984), *sensory exploitation* (Eberhard, 1985; Ryan, 1990), *signal selection* (Zahavi, 1991), and *the influence of receiver psychology on the evolution of animal signals* (Guilford

& Dawkins, 1991; see also Enquist & Arak, 1993). As any perceptual psychologist might predict, animals typically prefer displays that are louder, larger, more colorful, more frequent, more varied, and more novel than average (Miller, 1993; Ryan & Keddy-Hector, 1992). But such perceptual biases may also vary substantially across species, in accord with ecological specializations of the perceptual systems. For example, birds that eat blue berries may evolve blue-sensitive eyes, which would tend to favor blue ornaments, whereas birds that eat red berries may evolve red-sensitive eyes that favor red ornaments. These perceptual specializations may help explain the rapid divergence of sexually selected traits across closely related species (Endler, 1992, 1993). The effectiveness of aesthetic displays in courtship supports Dawkins and Krebs' (1978) theory that animal signals often evolve to manipulate receivers in the signaler's interest, not to communicate truthful information (as indicators do) for the benefit of both.

But latent preferences are not necessary, according to R. A. Fisher's (1930) runaway theory. Even chance fluctuations in mate preferences, combined with a strange kind of evolutionary positive feedback loop, could produce extreme mate preferences and exaggerated courtship traits (see Miller & Todd, 1993; Todd & Miller, 1993). Suppose that mate preferences vary somewhat randomly within a bird population, so that, in one particular generation, some females happen to prefer long tails on males whereas others do not care. Suppose male tail length also varies randomly. Could the preference (for long tails) and the trait (of having a long tail) evolve together in a positive feedback loop? This possibility was first considered and dismissed by Morgan (1903) to ridicule Darwin's sexual-selection theory:

> Shall we assume that . . . those females whose taste has soared a little higher than that of the average (a variation of this sort having appeared) select males to correspond, and thus the two continue heaping up the ornaments on one side and the appreciation of the ornaments on the other side? No doubt an interesting fiction could be built up along these lines, but would anyone believe it, and if he did, could he prove it? (cited in Andersson, 1994, p. 24)

R. A. Fisher (1930) believed it, but could not prove it:

> The two characteristics affected by such a process, namely plumage development in the male and sexual preference in the female, must thus advance together, and so long as the process is unchecked by severe counterselection, will advance with ever-increasing speed. (p. 152)

Recent population genetics models (e.g., Kirkpatrick, 1982; Lande, 1981; Pomiankowski, Iwasa, & Nee, 1991) have finally proved it:

Females that prefer to mate with long-tailed males will mate with such males more often than females that prefer short-tailed males. Following mating and genetic recombination, the genes for long-tail preference and the genes for the long tail itself will become correlated: an individual carrying a gene for long tails will tend to carry a gene for the corresponding preference. (Kirkpatrick, 1987, pp. 74–75)

The argument looks a bit circular, but then all positive feedback processes look a bit circular. The only thing keeping runaway going is the "momentum" conferred by genetic linkage and the risk to individuals of failing to display exaggerated traits or choosy preferences given that momentum. The peacock's tail grows longer and longer because of a despotic treadmill of fashion: "Each peahen is on a treadmill and dare not jump off lest she condemn her sons to celibacy" (Ridley, 1993, p. 135). However, the treadmill does not go on forever: Eventually, runaway would be counteracted by the survival costs of elaborate ornaments (R. A. Fisher, 1930). At evolutionary equilibrium, the survival costs of an ornament should balance the reproductive advantages (Kirkpatrick, 1982).

Runaway can happen in any sensory modality. Animals' eyes respond to color and form on tails and faces; ears respond to loud, complex songs by birds and whales; noses respond to intense pheromones such as musk deer scent; skin responds to grooming, foreplay, and genital stimulation. Electric fish may even respond to galvanic courtship (Kramer, 1990). Yet, there is much more to animal cognition than low-level sensation, so courtship behaviors may have evolved to play on higher level mental processes of categorization, symbolism, memory, expectation, communication, and curiosity (Miller, 1993).

Runaway is a fairly robust and pervasive force that emerges even in genetic models of indicators (Kirkpatrick, 1992; Pomiankowski et al., 1991), but it is also a highly stochastic process, quite sensitive to initial conditions, and therefore, capable of explaining the capricious divergence of sexual ornamentation observed across species (Eberhard, 1985; Miller & Todd, 1993, 1995). The three basic assumptions of Fisher's model have been moderately well supported by recent empirical work (see Andersson, 1994): (a) individuals with large sexual ornaments have higher mating success, but lower survival than those with smaller ornaments (all else being equal); (b) the relevant traits and preferences show heritable genetic variation; and (c) there is genetic linkage between the relevant traits and preferences (e.g., Bakker, 1993; Houde & Endler, 1990). The runaway process is also supported by findings that some animals copy each others' mate choices, as if following an arbitrary fashion rather than a reliable indicator (Balmford, 1991; Dugatkin, 1992; Pruett-Jones, 1992).

## Selection for Sperm Competition

Sexual selection does not stop when copulation begins. Indeed, gonads and genitals are the clearest expressions of sexual selection because they are most directly responsible for fertilization, and they typically serve no survival functions. The traditional view that "primary sexual characters" such as penises are "necessary for breeding and hence are favored by natural selection" (Andersson, 1994, p. 14) is misleading. If sexual competition and mate choice can affect genitals, then genitals can be shaped by sexual selection.

In many species, females mate with more than one male, so sperm competition becomes important: Males evolve larger testicles, larger ejaculates, faster swimming sperm, various devices to remove previous competitors' sperm from the female reproductive tract, and various plugs to keep future competitors' sperm excluded entirely (Parker, 1984). The results can be dramatic: The male North Atlantic right whale reputedly has 2,000-pound testicles to pump out gallons of semen and billions of sperm per ejaculate.

In primates, testicle size increases with intensity of sperm competition across species (Harcourt & Harvey, 1984); female chimpanzees are highly promiscuous, so male chimpanzees have evolved large 4-ounce testicles. Male humans have medium-sized testicles by primate standards, and produce a respectable 400 million sperm per ejaculation, suggesting that ancestral females had multiple lovers within a month fairly often (Baker & Bellis, 1995).

Female choice does not always stop when copulation starts. Eberhard (1985) argued that male genitals often function as "internal courtship devices" to stimulate females into accepting sperm from the copulating male. The length, variety, and vigor of human copulation suggests that this type of internal courtship has been highly elaborated in our species. Human female orgasm may function partially to suck sperm into the uterus, thereby promoting fertilization by sexually exciting males (Baker & Bellis, 1995).

## Selection for Provisioning, Territories, and Protection

Females can gain nongenetic benefits from mate choice by favoring males that offer material gifts (Searcy, 1982). The main examples of such provisioning come from male insects giving nuptial gifts such as spermatophores or caught prey (see R. Thornhill & Alcock, 1983), male birds provisioning offspring and building nests in socially monogamous bird species (see Clutton-Brock, 1991), and sex-for-meat exchanges (e.g., prostitution and marriage) in humans (H. Fisher, 1982, 1992). Male provisioning is useful to females because it eases the nutritional and energetic burden of producing eggs, and gestating and feeding young. However, male provisioning of females during courtship is not common across species, and male provisioning of offspring after birth is quite rare, except in monogamous birds (Clutton-Brock, 1991). Often, male provisioning may represent mating effort more than paternal effort, if females prefer males that have provisioned previous offspring (Seyfarth, 1978; Smuts, 1985). Biologists may often mistake the grudgingly generous stepfather for the committed dad.

Selection for direct provisioning must not be confused with the more common pattern of selection for good territories that happen to be defended by particular males. Socioecologists have long recognized that female animals tend to distribute themselves around their habitat to exploit the available food resources and protect themselves against the local predators, and the males distribute themselves to exploit the available females as reproductive resources (Davies, 1991; Dunbar, 1988). In such cases, males often fight to exclude competitors from prime territories, and females prefer to mate with males that hold prime territories. Such systems are called *resource defense polygyny*, because males that are successful at excluding other males from areas desired by females will reap a disproportionately high number of offspring with multiple females. Male territoriality can be viewed in two ways: as female choice in favor of sexy, healthy, high-status, land-holding aristocrats, or as female acquiescence to a Machiavellian protection racket, where violent, harassing males extort sex for access to food, and then leave females with all the burdens of parenting.

Males can sometimes serve as convenient, if unreliable, protectors from predators or other males. Thus, mate choice in favor of protectors is especially favored in species where females and/or infants are subject to strong predation risk or strong risk of infanticide by rival males (see Hausfater & Hrdy, 1984). Again, the *protection racket* metaphor may be apt: Males extort sex in exchange for a commitment not to kill a female's offspring and a willingness to keep other males from killing them. Moreover, much of what appears to be protection behavior by males may function as mate guarding to minimize sexual competition from rival males, and may not reflect female choice. Biologists have recently begun taking a darker view of male provisioning, territoriality, and protection behavior—a view surprisingly concordant with recent feminist analyses of human patriarchy, prostitution, marriage, sexual exploitation, and the economic oppression of women (see Brownmiller, 1975; Buss & Malamuth, 1996; Haraway, 1989; Lancaster, 1991; Smuts, 1991).

## Summary of Sexual Selection Modes

The scope of sexual selection through mate choice is rather broad. It can operate in almost any animal species capable of making discriminations among potential mates and in responding more positively toward some than toward others. Mechanisms that cause selective mating can arise from several sources, both as adaptations in their own right and as side effects of other adaptations (e.g., as sensory biases). Once in place, these mechanisms can influence the evolution of sexual ornamentation and courtship behaviors. If the selected trait correlates with general viability as a conditional or revealing handicap, and if genetic variance in viability is maintained somehow (e.g., by biased mutation or co-evolution), then Zahavi's handicap principle will work to elaborate both trait and preference (Iwasa et al., 1991). Even if the selected trait is purely ornamental, does not correlate with general viability, and as long as genetic variance in the trait is maintained, then Fisher's runaway process can elaborate both trait and preference (Pomiankowski et al., 1991). Often, Zahavi's and Fisher's processes will be mutually reinforcing, such that a trait is elaborated both as a viability indicator that increases offspring survival rates and an aesthetic ornament that increases offspring attractiveness. For example, "a peacock's tail is, simultaneously, a testament to naturally selected female preferences for eye-like objects, a runaway product of despotic fashion among peahens, and a handicap that reveals its possessor's condition" (Ridley, 1993, pp. 161–162). These processes can operate even in the face of substantial natural selection to evolve costly male traits and costly female preferences. Sexual selection will work in pseudomonogamous and polygynous species through differential mating success, and will work in truly monogamous species if animals mate assortatively with respect to viability indicators, or if animals that mate earlier have more offspring (Darwin, 1871; Kirkpatrick, Price, & Arnold, 1990).

## SEX DIFFERENCES AND SEXUAL SELECTION

Sexual selection through mate choice would be expected to operate in any sexually reproducing lineage, regardless of whether there were distinct sexes such as males and females. If hermaphrodites exercise mate choice, they can evolve sexual ornaments. Thus, sexual selection does not necessarily require or produce sex differences.

However, in almost all sexually reproducing lineages on earth, distinct sexes have evolved, consisting of males that produce small gametes called sperm and females that produce large gametes called eggs. Bateman (1948) and Trivers (1972) pointed out that, because females invest more matter and energy into producing each egg than males invest in producing each sperm, eggs form more of a limiting resource for males than sperm do for females. Thus, males should compete more intensively to fertilize eggs than females do to acquire sperm, whereas females should be choosier than males. Males compete for quantity of females, and females compete for quality of males. In short, males court and females choose (see Daly & Wilson, 1983; Reynolds & Harvey, 1994; Trivers, 1985).

In female mammals, the costs of internal fertilization, gestation, and long-term lactation are especially high, leading to even more striking differences between male competitiveness and female choosiness. For example, the minimum parental investment by female humans under ancestral conditions would have been a harrowing 9-month pregnancy followed by at least 2 years of breastfeeding and baby carrying (Shostak, 1981); whereas the minimum paternal investment would have been a few moments of copulation and a teaspoonful of semen (Symons, 1979). The result is an enormous difference in maximum lifetime reproductive success. King Moulay Ismail the Bloodthirsty, a medieval king of Morocco, sired over 800 children by the women in his harem; the first emperor of China, around 3,000 years ago, was reputed to have sired even more through his much larger harem (Betzig, 1986). By contrast, the world record for a woman is 69 children, many of whom were triplets (Daly & Wilson, 1983). Even under relatively egalitarian tribal conditions, some men can father several dozen children by several different women, whereas no woman bears more than 10 or so children (Chagnon, 1983).

Thus, a man's reproductive success generally increases with his number of sexual partners (in the absence of contraception), whereas a woman reaches her reproductive limit rather quickly as her number of sexual partners increases. This is because males can opt out of parental investment in a way that women cannot—nature cannot enforce child support laws any better than modern governments. Of course, women under ancestral conditions probably used abortion and infanticide to avoid maternal investment during difficult times (see Hausfater & Hrdy, 1984), but they could not induce another woman to bear a child for them. Maternal investment was obligatory in hominids, whereas paternal investment was not.

There are usually trade-offs between courtship effort and parental effort. Males usually invest more in the former and females more in the latter. In females, the marginal costs of sexually selected traits will be higher (because the demands of maternal investment push females closer to their physiological limits) and their benefits will be lower (because males are less choosy), so females often invest less time and energy in growing and displaying such traits than males do. The result is *sexual*

*dimorphism*—a sex difference in the expression of the courtship or reproductive trait. The most ancient and reproductively central sexual dimorphisms are usually qualitative: Males have testicles, whereas females have
ova. More recently evolved courtship traits usually retain only quantitative dimorphism: Many male birds have longer, brighter feathers than
females, but females often retain some discreet ornamentation. Female
mammals have breasts, but males retain nipples. All the qualitative sexual
dimorphisms started out as quantitative ones.

Sexual dimorphism is a common, but not necessary, outcome of sexual
selection. Two major factors limit sexual dimorphism: the mutuality of
mate choice, and genetic linkage between the sexes. The effects of mutual
choice are easy to understand: If both males and females are somewhat
choosy and somewhat competitive, as in many monogamous species, then
sexual selection will apply to males and females roughly equally, and
sexually selected ornaments and indicators will evolve to similar magnitudes in each. Whenever males must invest time, effort, and energy in
courtship, they have incentives to be at least slightly choosy about which
females they choose to court, but male choice has been studied only rarely,
and may have often been overlooked. For example, Trail (1990) observed
that, in about a quarter of lek-breeding birds (which provide the best
opportunities for female choice), ornaments are equally elaborate in males
and females, suggesting that male choice was operating as well. Also,
whenever high-quality males are in short supply, females have an incentive to compete with each other to attract and retain such males. Competition to retain the paternal investment and protection of male partners
will also lead to substantial variance in the number of offspring raised to
maturity by females; measuring variance in number of offspring born
would completely miss a major stage of female reproductive competition,
which occurs after birth (Dunbar, 1988; Miller, 1993). Males also vary less
in their lifetime reproductive success than in their day-by-day success
because male success follows a typical life-history trajectory (adolescent
frustration, young adult violence, older adult coalition-building, and gradual senescence). Therefore, short-term measures will overestimate variance in male reproductive success and underestimate female variance
(Dunbar, 1988). Thus, sexual selection often applies to both sexes, and
can drive the evolution of indicators and aesthetic displays in both.

Especially under monogamy, mutual mate choice can yield strong
sexual selection without much sexual dimorphism. Sexual selection can
work in monogamous species if the sex ratio is skewed, if extrapair
copulations undermine the putative monogamy, or, most important, if
mates differ in genetic quality (Darwin, 1871; R. A. Fisher, 1930). For
example, if animals mate assortatively with respect to quality (e.g., the
healthy marry each other, leaving the unhealthy no option but to marry

other unhealthies), then indicators of genetic quality can still evolve under sexual selection (see Darwin, 1871). Thus, traits that improve the ability to compete for mates will be favored even under strict monogamy (Jones & Hunter, 1993; Kirkpatrick et al., 1990). Moreover, female competition over mates will be stronger under monogamy, so females may evolve ornaments as extravagant as those of males. Mate choice must also be somewhat mutual in species that use interactive courtship displays (which ethologists used to call *pair-bonding rituals*), such as coordinated dances, song duets, mutual sexual foreplay, and conversations (Miller, 1993). Only the pure Fisherian runaway process is undermined by monogamy because it depends on some individuals obtaining a disproportionate number of mates.

Genetic linkage between the sexes also constrains the evolution of sexual dimorphism. Because males and females within a species grow from similar genes and developmental mechanisms, most traits are homologous (developmentally and anatomically similar) across sexes, and the male trait cannot initially evolve separately from the female trait. This constraint holds for any traits that still have quantitative, rather than qualitative, sexual dimorphism. Sons will tend to inherit their mothers' mate preferences and daughters will tend to inherit their fathers' sexually selected traits. Darwin (1871) called this the "Law of Equal Inheritance": All else being equal, even if only one sex is exercising selective mate choice, both the selected traits and the selective preferences will tend to be expressed in both sexes. For example, if female choice favored large penises over many generations in some species, the clitoris (female homolog of the penis) would tend to enlarge along with the penis, assuming no other selection operated on the clitoris.

Lande (1980, 1987) showed that this sort of genetic linkage between the sexes makes the evolution of sexual dimorphism a very slow process. Typically, sexual dimorphism evolves a few orders of magnitude slower than do sexually selected traits. For example, Rogers and Mukherjee (1992) applied Lande's model to data on the cross-sex heritability of human height and other body dimensions. They found that, if female choice alone were favoring tall males and males were not selecting females for height, sexual dimorphism in height would evolve around 65 times slower than height. That is, female height would increase over 98% as fast as male height increases, purely as a correlated response to selection on males. This argument also applies to sexually selected behavioral and mental traits: Any female choice for some courtship capacity in the male would be expected to produce a correlated response in the female. In an extraordinary passage, Darwin (1871) revealed his belief in the importance of mate choice in human mental evolution, and in the importance of genetic linkage between the sexes:

It is fortunate that the law of equal transmission of characters to both sexes prevails with mammals; otherwise it is probable that man would have become as superior in mental endowment to woman, as the peacock is in ornamental plumage to the peahen. (p. 874)

Now that we have reviewed sexual-selection theory, we can explore how that theory applies to primates, hominids, and modern humans.

## SEXUAL SELECTION IN PRIMATES

To a first approximation, ecological circumstances determine mating patterns in primates. Generally, the distribution of food determines the distribution of females, and the distribution of females determines the distribution of males. When females must forage on their own, males disperse to pair with the lone females, giving rise to monogamy. This pattern is fairly rare in primates, being restricted to gibbons, some lemurs, and some African and South American monkeys. When females can afford to forage in small groups to protect each other against female competitors, predators (Dunbar, 1988), and infanticide by strange males (Hrdy, 1979), a single male can exclude other males from each female group. This gives rise to the common "harem system" of unimale polygyny, as in hamadryas baboons, colobus monkeys, some langurs, and gorillas. Unimale polygyny usually imposes strong sexual selection for aggressiveness, including male size, strength, and weaponry (e.g., large canine teeth), resulting in high degrees of sexual dimorphism in body size and behavior. When females can forage in larger groups (of more than 10 or so), males must usually form coalitions to exclude other males from the female group, resulting in a complex system of multimale polygyny, as in some baboons, macaques, ring-tailed lemurs, howler monkeys, and chimpanzees. In multimale polygyny, males compete at several levels: female promiscuity leads to sperm competition; female preferences for dominant males lead to status competition, individual aggressiveness, and coalition formation; and female preferences for nice males lead males to groom females, protect their offspring, and guard them from other males (see De Waal, 1989). Hominids and humans probably evolved in fairly large groups under multimale polygyny, thus, the focus here is on sexual selection in large-group primates.

Male primates fight more often and more intensely when estrus females are in their group. These fights usually result in a linear dominance hierarchy among the males, with high-ranking males usually obtaining more matings because they can chase lower ranking males away from estrus females (Silk, 1987). However, lower ranking males can use a number of alternative mating strategies because females often prefer novel males, long-term friends, and ex-dominant older males to the current dominant male (Smuts, 1985, 1987). Sometimes, these alternative strategies are as successful as achieving high dominance rank, although they may often be making the best of a bad situation. Males can also form coalitions to take over groups, repel outside males, achieve higher dominance rank within groups, and acquire estrus females (Smuts, 1987). Male primates often use different strategies at different ages, as their physical and social powers wax and wane (Dunbar, 1988).

Given multimale, multifemale primate groups, how does mate choice work? Female primates can exercise choice by joining groups that contain favored males, initiating sex with them during estrus, supporting them during conflicts, and developing long-term social relationships with them. Females can reject disfavored males by refusing to cooperate during copulation attempts, driving males away from the group, or leaving the group. But female mate choice criteria remain obscure for most primate species. In contrast to modern humans, female primates rarely favor males that can provide resources or paternal care of offspring. The sporadic male care that is observed, such as watching, carrying, and protecting infants, may represent mating effort rather than paternal investment (Seyfarth, 1978; Smuts, 1985) because it is often performed by a male unlikely to be the father of the infant, who is interesting in mating with the infant's mother.

Rather, the only consistent female preferences observed have been for high-ranking males capable of protecting females and offspring from other males; specific males with whom a special short-term consortship or long-term friendship has been formed through mutual grooming and affiliation, and male food-giving and infant protection; and new males from outside the group, to avoid inbreeding and protect against the infanticide they might commit if they knew that none of the local offspring was theirs. Clearly, these criteria conflict somewhat: High-ranking males have insufficient time to maintain special friendships with all local fe-males, and new males, by definition, cannot yet be long-term friends, nor can they attain high rank immediately. In addition, females may choose to mate promiscuously, to maximize sperm competition, and to confuse paternity, thereby inducing several males to protect the offspring and guard against infanticide (Hrdy, 1979; Small, 1993). Despite Darwin's (1871) discussion of sexual selection for the various beards, tufts, and colorful hair styles that adorn male primates, female choice for aesthetic displays and indicators has rarely been investigated in primates, perhaps because the relevant sexual selection theory has been developed only recently. However, female primates often exhibit preferences that cannot be accounted for on the basis of male rank, age, novelty, grooming effort, or protection effort. Sometimes primates just seem to like each other based on appearance, behavior, and personality.

Although primates follow the general animal pattern of male sexual competition and female choosiness, female competition and male mate choice are also important (Smuts, 1987). In monogamous callitrichids, such as marmosets and tamarins, females compete to form pairs with quality males and drive off competing females. In unimale polygynous systems, the dominant male's sperm becomes a limiting resource, and high-ranking females prevent low-ranking females from mating through aggression and harassment (Small, 1988). In multimale groups, females compete to form consortships and friendships with favored males. Such patterns of female competition suggest some degree of male mate choice. When the costs of sexual competition and courtship are high, as they are for most primates, males have incentives to be choosy about how they allocate their competitive effort, courtship effort, and sperm among the available females. Males compete much more intensely for females who show signs of fertility, such as sexual maturity, estrus behavior, absence of lactation, and presence of offspring (Smuts, 1987). Male primates almost always avoid adolescent, low-ranking, nulliparous (no-offspring) females, and prefer older, high-ranking, multiparous (several offspring) females who have already demonstrated their fertility, viability, social savvy, and mothering skills. Marriage (i.e., legally imposed, lifelong monogamy) has overturned this male mate choice pattern in modern human societies by pushing males to compete for unmarried, nulliparous young women of unproven fertility and uncertain status—a recent pattern that Symons (1979), Buss (1989, 1994), and others have projected into the ancestral past. Like females, male primates also show strong individual preferences for particular mates with whom they have developed special relationships (Smuts, 1985). The myth that romantic love is a recent invention of Western patriarchy denies not only the warm sexual relationships of humans in other cultures and historical epochs, but also those of other primate species.

In summary, sexual selection in multimale, multifemale primate groups is intense because the social context of mating is so complex and dynamic. Both sexes compete, are choosy, have dominance relations, and form alliances. Sexual relationships develop over weeks and years, rather than minutes. Under these relentlessly social conditions, reproductive success came to depend on mental capacities for "chimpanzee politics" (De Waal, 1982, 1989), "Machiavellian intelligence" (Byrne & Whiten, 1988), "special friendships" (Smuts, 1985), and creative courtship (Miller, 1993), rather than simple physical ornaments and short-term courtship behaviors, as in most other animals.

## SEXUAL SELECTION IN HOMINIDS

It is hard to reconstruct sexual selection patterns in extinct animals because mate preferences and courtship behaviors do not fossilize. However, it seems reasonable to suppose that the primate tradition of intense sexual selection within highly social groups persisted in our hominid ancestors, with ever-larger group sizes, and ever more complex relationships and sexual strategies. We are the products of this primate heritage refracted through a unique hominid sequence of habitats and econiches (Foley, 1987), combined with the unpredictable effects of runaway social competition for Machiavellian intelligence (Byrne & Whiten, 1988; Dunbar, 1992) and runaway sexual selection for various courtship behaviors (Miller, 1993).

Fossils and genetic markers suggest that hominids diverged from other anthropoid apes around 6 million years ago (mya), leading to increasing bipedalism, group size, and omnivory in the sequence *Australopithecus ramidus*, *A. afarensis*, and *A. africanus*. By two mya, hominids had divided into two main branches (see Foley, 1987): *Paranthropus* (also known as *Australopithecus*), including *P. robustus* and *P. boisei*, and *Homo*, including successively *Homo habilis* (2.0–1.8 mya), *Homo erectus* (1.8–0.5 mya), and *Homo heidelbergensis* (400,000–120,000 years ago). This latter type split into two species (see Stringer & Gamble, 1993): the Neanderthals (*Homo neanderthalensis*; 200,000–40,000 years ago), and modern *Homo sapiens* (120,000 years ago to the present). Because the Pleistocene period covers the era from two mya until recently, and *Homo sapiens* probably evolved and migrated out of Africa quite recently (see Gamble, 1993), hominids and humans are largely a product of Pleistocene Africa.

Mating among our ancestors probably occurred in the context of small, mobile hunter–gatherer tribes. As with most primates, social life was probably centered on matrilines (female kin groups and their offspring), with the males largely fending for themselves, hovering around the periphery, and trying to insinuate themselves into the powerful female bands (see Dunbar, 1988). Under these conditions, the central mating problem for males was inseminating mature, attractive, viable, fertile females (Buss & Schmitt, 1993). The central mating problem for females was obtaining good sperm and genes from high-quality males, and perhaps some provisioning and protection from a few males whose presence was not more trouble than it was worth. Equally unlikely are the tough-minded view of the Pleistocene as a brutal, male-dominated era of continuous warfare, frequent rape, and anarchy (e.g., Ardrey, 1976), and the tender-minded picture of lifelong pair-bonded monogamy and heavy male investment (Lovejoy, 1981). Male scientists have been reluctant to recognize that, for the most part, adult male hominids must have been rather peripheral characters in human evolution, except as bearers of traits sexually selected by females for their amusement value or utility.

Hominids probably did not live in discrete tribes with mutually exclusive and stable memberships, well-defined territories, or coherent group movements. Social organization was more complex and multilayered, as it is in other primates (Dunbar, 1988). Thus, mates may have been chosen not from within the small bands that characterize day-to-day foraging, but from the much larger congregations that occurred at special times (e.g., food-rich seasons) and places (e.g., water sources). Social and sexual relations were probably at least as fluid, complex, and ad hoc as they are today, with plenty of polygamy, serial monogamy, and infidelity (see H. Fisher, 1992; Ford & Beach, 1951; Lockard & Adams, 1991; Shostak, 1981). Without marriage, mortgages, or money, why stick with just one lover during a lifetime? Given this social complexity and fluidity, each sex probably evolved a multitude of flexible strategies for pursuing their mating goals (Buss & Schmitt, 1993; Simpson & Gangestad, 1992). An individual's current strategy might depend on his or her personal attributes (e.g., age, health, attractiveness, parenting skills, social skills, and seduction skills), the state of his or her kin network and social network (e.g., number of dependable child-care helpers), and various ecological conditions (e.g., reliability and patchiness of resources, foraging costs, and dangers) and demographic conditions (e.g., operational sex ratio).

Primates, and especially hominids, are extremely "K-selected" taxa: We have much slower development, larger bodies, fewer offspring, higher survival rates, and longer life spans than more "r-selected" taxa, such as insects, fish, or rodents (Harvey, Martin, & Clutton-Brock, 1986). The more K-selected the species, the more important sexual selection usually becomes compared with natural selection (Miller & Todd, 1995). We might expect that, as hominids evolved to be more and more K-selected, the relative importance of sexual selection increased. K-selection usually reduces the relative energetic demands of reproduction on the female, and almost eliminates the need for male help, because slow gestation spreads maternal investment over a longer period, and small litters of large, well-developed offspring are easier to care for. However, human brains grow so large that infants must be born relatively immature to fit through the female pelvic canal: "Human gestation is really 21 months long, with 9 months in the uterus followed by 12 months in the mother's care" (Martin, 1992, p. 87). The helplessness and expense of human infants increases both the nongenetic and genetic benefits from mating: Choosing males for their provisioning and protection abilities eases the energetic burden of motherhood, but choosing males for their indicators of genetic quality and aesthetic displays reduces the risk of producing sickly, unattractive offspring that may never reproduce. Thus, whereas infant dependency favors male provisioners, infant expense favors males with good genes and good displays. Foley (1992) provided life-history and nutritional evidence that the latter was more important: Human infants do not grow using more energy per month than other ape infants, as paternal provisioning would have made possible; they simply grow for a longer time. Such data undermine the common assumption that male hunting was somehow important in feeding infants and mothers, and in supporting the energetic costs of encephalization (cf. Buss, 1992, 1994; Knight, Power, & Watts, 1995; Lovejoy, 1981).

Many people assume that the opportunities for mate choice would have been severely limited under ancestral conditions, due to the supposed prevalence of arranged marriages; the exchange of women as chattel between families and tribes; the influence of cultural rules concerning incest, outbreeding, marriage, monogamy, and adultery; and the generally low status of women under patriarchy. Yet, there is good archaeological and ethnographic evidence that many of these factors arose within the last 10,000 years, where they arose at all (see H. Fisher, 1992). The economic and geographic demands of agriculture distorted human mate choice patterns because agriculture requires long-term investment in preparing and maintaining a plot of land, and thereby reduces the physical and social mobility that underlay the free choice of sexual mates in hunter–gatherer tribes. Modern mating behavior may not accurately reflect ancestral patterns of sexual selection. Hence, the next section reviews modern human morphology, which, being less influenced by culture, is more reliable evidence of ancestral mate choice patterns.

## SEXUAL SELECTION AND HUMAN MORPHOLOGY

Humans show sexual dimorphism in several traits. Compared with females, males on average have more height and mass, more upper-body strength, higher metabolic rates, more facial and bodily hair, deeper voices, larger brains, and riskier life histories, with higher juvenile mortality, later sexual maturity, and earlier death (Ankney, 1992; Daly & Wilson, 1983, 1988; Ghesquiere, Martin, & Newcombe, 1985; Rushton, 1995; Short & Balaban, 1994). Our moderate size dimorphism is consistent with our species having evolved under a moderately polygynous mating system, with more intense sexual competition between males than between females (Fleagle, Kay, & Simons, 1980; Martin, Willner, & Dettling, 1994). But human bodies reveal much more than just the degree of ancestral polygyny; they indicate a wide array of mate choice criteria used by our male and female ancestors.

Compared with other anthropoid apes, humans have less hair on their bodies, more on their heads, whiter eyes, longer noses, larger ear lobes, more everted lips, smaller and safer teeth, more expressive faces, more dextrous hands, and better developed pheromone systems (Margulis & Sagan, 1991; Miller, 1993; Morris, 1985; Napier, 1993; Stoddart, 1990). Also, compared with other primates, male humans have rather long, thick, and flexible penises, larger beards, and sometimes baldness later in life; female humans have greatly enlarged breasts and buttocks, a greater orgasmic capacity, and continual "sexual receptivity" throughout the monthly cycle. Many of these traits show hallmarks of having evolved under the capricious power of sexual selection: They are uniquely elaborated in our species, show considerable sexual dimorphism, are grown only after puberty (sexual maturity), become engorged and displayed during sexual arousal, are manifestly valued as sexual signals, and are selectively elaborated through ornament and makeup (Miller, 1993; Morris, 1985). Such traits probably evolved both as indicators (of fertility, viability, age, health, and lack of infestation by pathogens and parasites) and aesthetic displays (that play on preexisting or co-evolved perceptual biases). Sexual-selection research has focused particularly on the human face, breasts and buttocks, the penis, and the clitoris. These are examined in turn.

The human face is a major target of selective mate choice during all stages of courtship, from flirtation through face-to-face copulation. Research on human facial aesthetics has boomed in the last few years (Alley & Cunningham, 1991; Brown & Perrett, 1993; Langlois & Roggman, 1990; Perrett, May, & Yoshikawa, 1994), revealing that average faces are attractive, but that females with more *neotenous* (childlike) faces, including large eyes, small noses, and full lips, are still more attractive, as are males with testosterone-enlarged features, such as high cheekbones, strong jaws, strong chins, and large noses (R. Thornhill & Gangestad, 1993). Bilateral symmetry is another important determinant of facial beauty because symmetry correlates with *developmental competence*—resistance to disease, injury, and harmful mutations that cause fluctuating asymmetry during development (Moller & Pomiankowski, 1993; R. Thornhill & Gangestad, 1993). Also, as Darwin (1872) emphasized, human facial musculature is uniquely well developed for displaying a variety of expressions, many of which are used in courtship.

Darwin (1871) assumed that genitals evolve purely through natural selection for fertilization ability, but Eberhard (1985, 1991) demonstrated a substantial role for female choice in the evolution of male genitalia. The human penis is a prime example: Men have the longest, thickest, and most flexible penises of any living primate. Gorillas, orangutans, and chimpanzees have very thin "filiform" penises that are less than 3 inches long when fully erect, and made rigid by muscular control combined with a *baculum* (penis bone). By contrast, human penises average over 5 inches long and 1.25 inches in diameter, and use an unusual system of vasocongestion (blood inflation) to achieve erection (Sheets-Johnstone, 1990; Short, 1980). The size and flexibility of the human penis is more likely the result of female choice than sperm competition because sperm competition generally favors large testicles, as in the small-penised chimpanzee (Baker & Bellis, 1995; Harcourt & Harvey, 1984; G. Parker, 1984; Smith, 1984).

The female clitoris is anatomically homologous to the male penis; although its structure probably did not evolve directly under male mate choice, clitoral orgasm has two important roles in sexual selection. First, as a female mate choice mechanism, clitoral orgasm favors males capable of providing high levels of sexual stimulation. Over the short term, orgasm promotes vaginal and uterine contractions that suck sperm into the uterus and minimize postcoital "flowback" therefrom (Baker & Bellis, 1995). Over the long term, pleasurable orgasms promote future copulations with the favored male through reinforcement learning and emotional attachment. Some male scientists (e.g., Gould, 1987; Symons, 1979) have questioned whether human female orgasm is an adaptation at all because it can be hard to achieve. However, it makes sense for a "choosy clitoris" to produce orgasm only given substantial foreplay and emotional warmth because this would reinforce only sex with males who have the willingness and skill to provide the right kinds of sexual stimulation. Thus, the sexual dimorphism between penis and clitoris could be viewed as a direct physical manifestation of the two components of Fisher's runaway process: a highly elaborated male trait (the penis) designed to stimulate, and a highly discerning female preference (the clitoral orgasm) designed to respond selectively to skillful stimulation. The second role of clitoral orgasm is to advertise happiness to lovers. Given that orgasms come hard, only when sex is long, varied, and exciting, rather than brief, mechanical, and perfunctory, orgasms can serve as fairly reliable indicators of female sexual satisfaction, commitment, and fidelity. Thus, some aspects of female orgasm may have evolved through male mate choice to promote male certainty of paternity (and hence male protection and investment). If so, we can understand why females advertise their orgasms through clear tactile, visual, and auditory signals, such as strong vaginal contractions and hip movements, the sexual blush over face and chest, and passionate vocalizations (see Morris, 1985).

Female human breasts and buttocks have undergone sexual elaboration through mate choice by males. These organs store substantial amounts of fat, so could function as indicators of female nutritional status, and hence fertility (Low, Alexander, & Noonan, 1987; Szalay & Costello, 1991). Singh (1993) showed that men prefer women who display a low waist-to-hip ratio (WHR), ideally about 0.70, concordant with enlarged buttocks indicating

sufficient fat reserves and a narrow waist indicating nonpregnancy. Permanent enlargement of breasts and buttocks is also fairly effective at conceal-
ing ovulation (Margulis & Sagan, 1991; Szalay & Costello, 1992). Females
who do not reveal their menstrual or lactational cycles may benefit from
male uncertainty by being able to solicit male attention and investment even
when they are not really fertile: "From hairy, flat-chested ape to modern
buxom woman . . . males were kept guessing about when females were
ovulating" (Margulis & Sagan, 1991, p. 96). More generally, the loss of a
specific estrus period, combined with concealed ovulation and continuous
sexual receptivity, may have allowed females to attract more continuous
attention (e.g., protection, provisioning, social support) from males, even
when they were not ovulating (Alexander & Noonan, 1979; H. Fisher, 1982;
Hrdy, 1981, 1988; Hrdy & Whitten, 1987; Tanner, 1981).

Sexually selected morphological features are important to the study of
evolution and human behavior for three main reasons. First, there is no
sharp division between body and brain: Apparently simple bodily
adaptations also have physiological, neurological, and psychological
features. The richly innervated penis, clitoris, nipple, and mouth are as
much psychological organs as physical objects. Second, the mate choice
mechanisms that assess bodily features are easy to study experimentally,
and may lead to insights about mate choice with respect to more complex
mental and behavioral traits. Finally, body features reveal patterns of
ancestral mate choice relevant to understanding human mental evolution.
Mate choice by males has shaped female breasts, buttocks, and orgasms;
mate choice by females has shaped male body size, beards, and penises.
Mutual mate choice has probably influenced human hair, skin, eyes, lips,
ears, face shape, hands, and pheromones. If our male and female ancestors
were both selecting for bodily traits, it seems likely that they were also
both selecting for mental and behavioral traits. By overcoming the
Cartesian split between body and mind, we can better appreciate the role
of mate choice in shaping both.

## SEXUAL SELECTION AND HUMAN MENTAL EVOLUTION

> Most evolutionary anthropologists now believe that big brains contributed
> to reproductive success either by enabling men to outwit and outscheme
> other men (and women to outwit and outscheme other women), or because
> big brains were originally used to court and seduce members of the other
> sex. (Ridley, 1993, p. 20)

Could sexual selection have shaped not only the human body, but the
human mind? Darwin (1871) clearly thought so, but most 20th-century

theorists have viewed natural selection as the exclusive director of human mental evolution. Even those who granted a role to sexual selection focused more on male sexual competition than on mate choice. Chance (1962) suggested that sexual selection would have favored young males who show intelligence and caution in challenging dominant males, and in forming coalitions to take territories and intimidate females. Fox (1972) argued along similar lines that sexual selection would have favored male hunting prowess, leadership, and tool making. Alexander (1971) viewed organized warfare for possession of females and mating-relevant resources as a major force in human evolution. Caspari (1972) considered oratory as an arena of male competition, and suggested a role for sexual selection in the evolution of language. In a fairly sketchy, but provocative, article, S. Parker (1987) proposed that sexual selection could help account for the evolution of bipedalism, canine reduction, tool making, fire using, shelter construction, and language. This emphasis on male competition made sense when Darwin's theory of female choice was still considered unfounded. But given the resurgence of interest in mate choice in other species, perhaps the role of mate choice in human mental evolution deserves another look.

But why bother with sexual selection? What is wrong with the traditional story that natural selection just generally favored intelligence, learning, tool making, and culture? The problem is that the evolution of big brains is so rare, so recent, so capricious, and seemingly so unrelated to the demands of habitat or econiche (Miller, 1993). Brain size in our lineage has tripled over the last 2 million years, reflecting the evolution of unprecedented mental and behavioral capacities. Over 3 million years ago, our ancestors were already successful, social, fairly bipedal, tool-making hunter–gatherers on the African savanna, and they had brains only slightly larger than the chimpanzee's. Then, 2 million years ago, for no apparent reason, brain size started growing exponentially in our lineage, but not in other closely related hominid species who shared the same habitat, such as *Paranthropus boisei* and *robustus*. Encephalization then stopped about 100,000 years ago, again for no apparent reason, long before the Neolithic revolution in technology and art 40,000 years ago. Extreme encephalization also happened in some species of cetaceans (dolphins and whales) and proboscids (elephants) living in quite different environments, but has not occurred in other primates living in quite similar environments (e.g., baboons, chimpanzees, *Paranthropus* hominids).

The speed, uniqueness, and capriciousness of this encephalization process have prompted many theorists to accept that human mental evolution must have been driven by some sort of positive feedback process that is sensitive to initial conditions. There have been two traditional contenders. In the runaway social competition model (Byrne & Whiten, 1988; Humphrey, 1976; Whiten, 1991; also see Miller, in press), hominids got smarter to predict and manipulate each other's behavior, leading to a social intelligence arms race between mind reading and deception. In the runaway gene–culture co-evolution model, hominids got smarter to learn and use material culture (e.g., tools and survival techniques), which was itself evolving (Durham, 1991; Lumsden & Wilson, 1982; Wills, 1993). Yet these theories overlook the clearest and best established case of positive feedback evolution in nature: runaway sexual selection. The runaway process is a good fit to the human evolution data because it begins and ends unpredictably, without much relation to the external environment, but it is extremely powerful and directional once underway (Miller, 1993; Miller & Todd, 1993).

As was seen earlier, hominid social life probably allowed considerable scope for mate choice by both males and females. Our ancestors lived in hunter–gatherer tribes that probably had rather fluid, complex, and polygynous mating patterns—rather different from the modern ideals of lifelong monogamy and nuclear family. The mate choice patterns permitted by tribal life could have favored several classes of courtship behaviors that function as indicators: *viability indicators,* which demonstrate physical health, energy, and freedom from disease, deformity, or deleterious mutation; *age indicators,* which reveal age, reproductive status, and survival prospects; *social-success indicators,* which reveal social skills for dominance, competition, aggression, deception, peace making, communication, and unpredictability; and *cognition indicators,* which reveal mental capacities for perception, attention, memory, planning, and creativity. In addition, perceptual biases in mate choice could have favored aesthetic displays of complex, interesting, innovative behaviors that are less closely correlated with fitness in other domains. Together, these forms of mate choice could have set up runaway sexual selection for more complex and creative behavioral courtship displays, such as stories, myths, jokes, rituals, dance, music, art, and sexual foreplay.

If the brain evolved through runaway sexual selection, what were the relevant traits and preferences? Two uniquely elaborated aspects of the human brain are its creativity (Boden, 1991, 1994; Campbell, 1960; Freyd, 1994) and its neophilia, or love of novelty (Zuckerman, 1984). Perhaps creativity became a trait subject to sexual selection by neophilia as a mate preference. More technically, mental capacities for generating *protean* (adaptively unpredictable) courtship displays may have been subject to neophilic mate preferences in both sexes (on proteanism, see Driver & Humphries, 1988).

Neophilia influences mate choice in many species. Darwin (1871) observed that "mere novelty, or slight changes for the sake of change, have sometimes acted on female birds as a charm, like changes of fashion with us" (p. 813). Males of many species are more sexually excited by novel females (Dewsbury, 1981). Females of several bird species prefer males who display larger song repertoires with greater diversity and novelty (Catchpole, 1980, 1987; Podos, Peters, Rudnicky, Marler, & Nowicki, 1992). Such neophilic mate choice may account for the creativity of male blackbirds, nightingales, sedge warblers, mockingbirds, parrots, and mynahs. Small (1993) emphasized neophilia in primate mate choice: "The only consistent interest seen among the general primate population is an interest in novelty and variety" (p. 153). Neophilia (termed *openness*) is one of the "Big Five" personality traits in humans (see Buss, 1991), and shows moderate heritability (Plomin & Rende, 1991; Zuckerman, 1984).

Of course, in modern society, human neophilia is the foundation of the art, music, television, film, publishing, drug, travel, pornography, fashion, and research industries, which account for a substantial proportion of the global economy. Before such entertainment industries amused us, we had to amuse each other on the African savanna, and our neophilia may have demanded ever more creative displays from our mates. This hypothesis can explain the mysterious cultural capacities that are universally and uniquely developed in humans, such as language, music, dance, art, humor, intellectual creativity, and innovative sexual play. These are all highly valued during mate choice and highly useful during courtship. Such displays all use a uniquely human trick: the creative recombination of learned semantic elements (e.g., words, notes, movements, visual symbols) to produce novel arrangements with new emergent meanings (e.g., stories, melodies, dances, paintings). This trick allows human courtship displays not just to tickle another's senses, but to create new ideas and emotions right inside their minds, where they will most influence mate choice.

The gradual evolution of language was especially important because it allowed hominids to display complex ideas and images to one another using an increasingly complex, structured, open-ended, combinatorial system (Pinker, 1994). Language gave potential mates a unique window into each other's minds, and so allowed much more direct sexual selection on the mind. Also, language permits gossip, which can transform mate choice from an individual decision to a social decision that integrates information from family and friends. With language and gossip, courtship displays need not be observed directly; they need only be witnessed by someone who can talk later to potential mates. The feedback loop between sexual selection, language complexity, and mental complexity was probably the mainspring of human mental evolution.

The lack of sexual dimorphism in human mental capacities is not a fatal problem for this sexual-selection theory. We would expect men and women to have similar minds given the genetic linkage between the sexes, the mutuality of mate choice, the interactiveness of courtship behaviors (e.g., conversation, dance, and musical dueting), and the overlap between perceptual capacities for judging complex behaviors (e.g., understanding language) and motor capacities for generating complex behaviors (e.g., speaking language). The general notion of mental evolution through mate choice has been presented more fully elsewhere (Miller, 1993, 1994, 1995, in press; Miller & Pratto, 1992; Miller & Todd, 1993, 1995; Todd & Miller, 1993).

A methodological problem arises: How could one demonstrate that a mental adaptation really evolved through mate choice? As shown earlier, sexually selected human bodily traits can be identified by being uniquely elaborated in our species, growing only after puberty, becoming engorged and displayed during sexual arousal, being selectively elaborated through ornament and makeup, being manifestly valued as sexual signals, and showing sexual dimorphism. Similar criteria for special design features can also be applied to mental and behavioral traits. If a behavior is uniquely human, is selectively displayed by adult humans during courtship and sexual competition, is displayed in different forms and frequencies by males and females, and is clearly valued as a sexual display, then it is worth investigating as a sexually selected adaptation. By these adaptationist criteria, many aspects of human cognition and culture would thus fall under the rubric of courtship behavior: language, art, music, humor, acting, mimicry, metaphor, sports, games, ritual, myth, ideology, religion, politics, and science. More generally, sexually selected adaptations are expected to show complex organization specially attuned to reliably, efficiently, and flexibly perform certain functions in sexual competition and/or courtship (on adaptations, see Tooby & Cosmides, 1990; Williams, 1966). Such adaptations can also be identified through the comparative method (Harvey & Pagel, 1991) by examining the distribution of traits across related species with known phylogenies, to discern when and where evolutionary innovations occurred. New methods in cognitive neuroscience (see Gazzaniga, 1995) should also allow localization of the mental adaptations underlying these courtship capacities, and comparison to homologous structures in other primates.

One might also check whether such adaptations are currently under sexual selection, by seeing whether the trait shows heritable variation (e.g., a moderate coefficient of additive genetic variation; see Moller & Pomiankowski, 1993) and whether individuals exhibiting one form of the trait have greater mating success (e.g., number of copulations, partners, or offspring) than individuals exhibiting other forms. One might also show that individuals can (consciously or unconsciously) discriminate among variants of the trait and do exhibit a preference for one variant. To further establish that a trait functions as an indicator, one must show that variants of the trait correlate with some indicated quality, such as age, health, fertility, or social status. To establish that a trait is evolving at least partially under the runaway process, one must show genetic linkage between the trait and the corresponding preference. However, all such questions of utility in current societies are a bit tangential to the question of adaptive function under ancestral conditions.

## SEXUAL SELECTION AND HUMAN CULTURE

Theories of human mental evolution are theories of human nature, and theories of human nature are the foundation of psychology, the social sciences, and the humanities (Tooby & Cosmides, 1992). So, if sexual selection played a major, but little appreciated, role in shaping human evolution, and if sexually selected traits are the most central, distinctive, and long-overlooked components of the human mind, then the standard model of human nature used in the social sciences and humanities probably focuses too heavily on the economics of survival and not enough on the mental, material, and cultural demands of courtship. Sexual competition probably underlies many political, economic, sociological, anthropological, criminological, cultural, ideological, religious, moral, and artistic phenomena (e.g., see Barkow, 1989; Betzig, 1986, 1992; Daly & Wilson, 1988; L. Ellis, 1993; Frank, 1985; Ridley, 1993; Wright, 1994), but it has been almost entirely overlooked as an explanatory principle. Instead, culture has become the dominant explanation for all human social and communicative behavior, despite its vagueness as a scientific concept (see Cosmides & Tooby, 1994; Sperber, 1994; Tooby & Cosmides, 1992). Rather than viewing culture as the reason for individual human behavior, we might view culture as an emergent phenomenon arising from sexual competition among vast numbers of individuals pursuing different mating strategies in different display arenas.

For example, only sexual-selection theory can provide a coherent, noncircular account of *cultural dimorphism*: Why have males always dominated political, economic, and cultural life in every known society? Most feminist theories of patriarchy simply beg the question by viewing male power as a self-sustaining tradition, without offering any plausible explanation of its origins. Traditional religious, reactionary, and sexist ideologies also beg the question, by invoking unexplained natural or divinely ordained sex differences. Yet, if most economic behavior is mating effort by males to acquire material resources for attracting and provisioning females, and if most cultural behavior is male mating effort to broadcast courtship displays to multiple female recipients, then cultural dimorphism is easily explained by sexual selection.

The age and sex demographics of cultural production are almost the same as the demographics of homicide (Miller, 1995; see also Daly &

Wilson, 1988): Males produce about an order of magnitude more art, music, literature, and violent death than women, and they produce it mostly in young adulthood. This suggests that, like violent sexual competition, the production of art, music, and literature functions primarily as a courtship display. For males, the mating benefits of public cultural displays are large because every additional short-term mating achieved through impressing some receptive female represents a substantial increase in expected fitness. Because male reproductive success can be virtually unlimited, the amount of energy and time that talented men are motivated to invest in cultural displays should be virtually unlimited. For example, although the gifted guitarist Jimi Hendrix died at age 27 from a drug overdose, he had affairs with hundreds of groupies, and fathered children in the United States, Germany, Britain, and Sweden. Composer J. S. Bach fathered 8 children by his first wife and 11 by his second. The sexual conquests of Picasso, Chaplin, and Balzac are legendary. As every teenager knows and most psychologists forget, cultural displays by males increase their sexual success.

However, for females, the genetic benefits of public cultural displays are smaller because their maximum reproductive success is constrained directly by their maternal investment ability (i.e., the time required for pregnancy and lactation), not by the number of short-term matings they can achieve. Rather than broadcasting her courtship displays to all males indiscriminately and risking sexual harassment from undesirables, it may be more effective for a woman to narrowcast her courtship displays to a few select males who are capable of giving her the long-term care, attention, and resources she wants. This could be called the *Scheherezade strategy*, after the woman who retained a sultan's intellectual attention, sexual commitment, and paternal investment by inventing fantastic stories throughout 1,001 nights. Thus, cultural dimorphism is much more likely to reflect a difference in motivation and sexual strategy than a difference in basic mental capacity.

## CONCLUSION

In sexually reproducing species, all genes must propagate through the gateway of sex, and mate choice is the guardian of that gateway. For this reason, sexual courtship was probably central in human evolution, and remains central in modern human life. However, sexual selection has long been overlooked in the human sciences, partially because evolutionary biologists were skeptical about Darwin's most innovative theory until quite recently, and partially because various ideological biases kept sex marginalized as a topic too messy, too mystical, too embarrassing, and too arousing for scientific analysis. We have to face the possibility that, if human evolution was a film, it would be X-rated.

This chapter reviewed the history of sexual-selection theory, the diversity of mate choice criteria (selection for indicators, aesthetic displays, sperm competition, provisioning, territories, and protection), the logic and limits of sex differences, the patterns of sexual selection in primates and hominids, and the parts of the human body, human mind, and human culture that have probably evolved through sexual selection. This is all only the tip of the *sexberg*: a snapshot of the sometimes eager, sometimes resistant human sciences trying to absorb an unexpectedly large and potent body of biological theory and evidence. However, the rapture will be mutual because a new appreciation of sexual selection allows the tightest possible fit between well-established biological theory and data, universal and important aspects of human nature and human psychology, and universal and important aspects of human culture and social life. This integration, although necessary for future progress, will be difficult for the social sciences and humanities because it undermines and replaces some of their cherished models of human nature (e.g., Freud, Marx, social constructivism), and because it demands research concerning the adaptive functions rather than just the proximate mechanisms of human social, sexual, and cultural behavior. Yet, if we recognize the role of sexual selection in the evolution of human intelligence, creativity, and culture, perhaps some of the old dichotomies—passion–reason, mind–body, nature–culture, sex–science—can finally be reconciled.

Future histories of science will probably look back at our era as a critical point during which human self-understanding was challenged and re-cast more deeply than ever before. Although the conceptual novelties of Copernicus, Adam Smith, Marx, Einstein, and Freud have lost their revolutionary edge, the Darwinian revolution continues to dig deeper and more sharply into the human soul (see Dennett, 1995; Ridley, 1993; Wright, 1994). Just when we thought we were comfortable with the idea of blind natural selection shaping human nature, the eerie, half-sentient process of sexual selection came back from the dead, more powerful and ubiquitous than ever. A full recognition of the role of mate choice and sexual competition in human affairs and human evolution may shake not only our psychology, but our psyches. It remains to be seen whether we have the intellectual creativity, the sexual self-confidence, and the existential courage to pursue these inquiries to their completion.

## ACKNOWLEDGMENTS

The author's research was supported partly by NSF-NATO Post-Doctoral Research Fellowship RCD-9255323. For institutional support, thanks to the University of Sussex, the University of Nottingham, the London School of Economics, the Max Planck Society, and the Economic and Social Research Council. For guidance and illuminating discussions, thanks to Rosalind Arden, David Buss, Charles Crawford, Leda Cosmides, Helena Cronin, Martin Daly, Robin Dunbar, Chris Knight, John Maynard Smith, John Tooby, and Andrew Pomiankowski.

## REFERENCES

Alexander, R. D. (1971). The search for an evolutionary philosophy of man. *Proceedings of the Royal Society of Victoria, 84*(1), 99–120.

Alexander, R. D., & Noonan, K. M. (1979). Concealment of ovulation, parental care, and human social evolution. In N. A. Chagnon & W. Irons (Eds.), *Evolutionary biology and human social behavior: An anthropological perspective* (pp. 402–435). North Scituate, MA: Duxbury Press.

Alley, T. R., & Cunningham, M. R. (1991). Average faces are attractive, but very attractive faces are not average. *Psychological Science, 2*(2), 123–125.

Andersson, M. (1982). Sexual selection, natural selection, and quality advertisements. *Biological Journal of the Linnaean Society, 17,* 375–393.

Andersson, M. (1986). Evolution of condition-dependent sex ornaments and mating preferences: Sexual selection based on viability differences. *Evolution, 40,* 804–820.

Andersson, M. (1994). *Sexual selection.* Princeton, NJ: Princeton University Press.

Ankney, C. D. (1992). Sex differences in relative brain size: The mismeasure of woman, too? *Intelligence, 16,* 329–336.

Ardrey, R. (1976). *The hunting hypothesis.* New York: Atheneum.

Atmar, W. (1991). On the role of males. *Animal Behavior, 41,* 195–205.

Baker, R. R., & Bellis, M. A. (1995). *Human sperm competition.* London: Chapman & Hall.

Bakker, T. C. M. (1993). Positive genetic correlation between female preferences and preferred male ornament in sticklebacks. *Nature, 363,* 255–257.

Balmford, A. (1991). Mate choice on leks. *Trends in Ecology and Evolution, 6,* 87–92.

Barkow, J. (1989). *Darwin, sex, and status.* Toronto, Cananda: University of Toronto Press.

Basolo, A. L. (1990). Female preference predates the evolution of the sword in swordfish. *Science, 250,* 808–810.

Bateman, A. J. (1948). Intra-sexual selection in *Drosophila. Heredity, 2,* 349–368.

Bateson, P. (Ed.). (1983). *Mate choice.* Cambridge, England: Cambridge University Press.

Batten, M. (1992). *Sexual strategies: How females choose their mates.* New York: Putnam.

Betzig, L. (1986). *Despotism and differential reproduction: A Darwinian view of history.* Hawthorne, NY: Aldine.

Betzig, L. (1992). Roman polygyny. *Ethology and Sociobiology, 13,* 309–349.

Betzig, L., Borgerhoff Mulder, M., & Turke, P. (Eds.). (1988). *Human reproductive behaviour: A Darwinian perspective.* Cambridge, England: Cambridge University Press.

Blum, M. S., & Blum, N. A. (Eds.). (1979). *Sexual selection and reproductive competition in insects.* New York: Academic Press.

Boden, M. (1991). *The creative mind.* New York: Basic Books.

Boden, M. (Ed.). (1994). *Explorations in creativity.* Cambridge, MA: MIT Press.

Boyce, M. S. (1990). The Red Queen visits sage grouse leks. *American Zoologist, 30,* 263–270.

Bradbury, J. W., & Andersson, M. B. (Eds.). (1987). *Sexual selection: Testing the alternatives.* New York: Wiley.

Brown, E., & Perrett, D. I. (1993). What gives a face its gender? *Perception, 22,* 829–840.

Brownmiller, S. (1975) *Against our will: Men, women, and rape.* New York: Simon & Schuster.

Burley, N. (1988). Wild zebra finches have band-color preferences. *Animal Behavior, 36,* 1235–1237.

Buss, D. M. (1985). Human mate selection. *American Scientist, 73,* 47–51.

Buss, D. M. (1989). Sex differences in human mate selection: Evolutionary hypotheses tested in 37 cultures. *Behavioral and Brain Sciences, 12*(1), 1–49.

Buss, D. M. (1991). Evolutionary personality psychology. *Annual Review of Psychology, 42,* 459–491.

Buss, D. M. (1992). Mate preference mechanisms: Consequences for partner choice and intrasexual competition. In J. H. Barkow, L. Cosmides, & J. Tooby (Eds.), *The adapted mind: Evolutionary psychology and the generation of culture* (pp. 249–266). Oxford, England: Oxford University Press.

Buss, D. M. (1994). *The evolution of desire: Human mating strategies.* New York: Basic Books.

Buss, D. M., & Malamuth, N. (Eds.). (1996). *Sex, power, conflict: Evolutionary and feminist perspectives.* Oxford, England: Oxford University Press.

Buss, D. M., & Schmitt, P. (1993). Sexual strategies theory: An evolutionary perspective on human mating. *Psychological Review, 100*(2), 204–232.

Byrne, R., & Whiten, A. (Eds.). (1988). *Machiavellian intelligence: Social expertise and the evolution of intellect in monkeys, apes, and humans.* Oxford, England: Oxford University Press.

Campbell, B. (Ed.). (1972). *Sexual selection and the descent of man, 1871–1971.* Chicago: Aldine-Atherton.

Campbell, D. (1960). Blind variation and selective retention in creative thought as in other knowledge processes. *Psychological Review, 67,* 380–400.

Caspari, E. (1972). Sexual selection in human evolution. In B. Campbell (Ed.), *Sexual selection and the descent of man* (pp. 87–104). Chicago: Aldine-Atherton.

Catchpole, C. K. (1980). Sexual selection and the evolution of complex song among European warblers of the genus *Acrocephalus*. *Behavior, 74,* 149–166.

Catchpole, C. K. (1987). Bird song, sexual selection and female choice. *Trends in Evolution and Ecology, 2,* 94–97.

Chagnon, N. (1983). *Yanomamo: The fierce people* (3rd ed.). New York: Holt, Rinehart & Winston.

Chance, M. R. A. (1962). Social behavior and primate evolution. In M. F. A. Montagu (Ed.), *Culture and the evolution of man* (pp. 84–130). Oxford, England: Oxford University Press.

Charlesworth, B. (1987). The heritability of fitness. In J. W. Bradbury & M. B. Andersson (Eds.), *Sexual selection: Testing the alternatives* (pp. 21–40). New York: Wiley.

Clutton-Brock, T. H. (1991). *The evolution of parental care.* Princeton, NJ: Princeton University Press.

Cosmides, L., & Tooby, J. (1994). Origins of domain specificity: The evolution of functional organization. In L. A. Hirschfeld & S. A. Gelman (Eds.), *Mapping the mind: Domain specificity in cognition and culture* (pp. 85–116). Cambridge, England: Cambridge University Press.

Cott, H. B. (1940). *Adaptive coloration in animals.* London: Methuen.

Cronin, H. (1991). *The ant and the peacock: Altruism and sexual selection from Darwin to today.* Cambridge, England: Cambridge University Press.

Daly, M., & Wilson, M. (1983). *Sex, evolution, and behavior* (2nd ed.) Boston: Willard Grant Press.

Daly, M., & Wilson, M. (1988). *Homicide.* New York: Aldine.

Darwin, C. (1859). *On the origin of species by means of natural selection.* London: John Murray.

Darwin, C. (1871). *The descent of man, and selection in relation to sex* (2 vols.). London: John Murray.

Darwin, C. (1872). *The expression of the emotions in man and animals.* London: John Murray.

Dawkins, R., & Krebs, J. R. (1978). Animal signals: Information or manipulation? In J. R. Krebs & N. B. Davies (Eds.), *Behavioral ecology: An evolutionary approach* (pp. 282–309). Oxford: Blackwell Scientific.

Davies, N. B. (1991). Mating systems. In J. R. Krebs & N. B. Davies (Eds.), *Behavioral ecology: An evolutionary approach* (3rd ed., pp. 263–294). London: Blackwell Scientific.

De Waal, F. (1982). *Chimpanzee politics.* New York: Harper & Row.

De Waal, F. (1989). *Peacemaking among primates.* Cambridge, MA: Harvard University Press.

Dennett, D. (1995). *Darwin's dangerous idea.* New York: Simon & Schuster.

Dewsbury, D. A. (1981). Effects of novelty on copulatory behavior: The Coolidge effect and related phenomena. *Psychological Bulletin, 89,* 464–482.

Driver, P. M., & Humphries, N. (1988). *Protean behavior: The biology of unpredictability.* New York: Oxford University Press.

Dugatkin, L. (1992). Sexual selection and imitation: Females copy the mate choice of others. *American Naturalist, 139,* 1384–1389.

Dunbar, M. (1988). *Primate social systems.* London: Croom Helm.

Dunbar, R. (1992). Neocortex size as a constraint on group size in primates. *Journal of Human Evolution, 22*(6), 469–493.

Durham, W. H. (1991). *Coevolution.* Stanford, CA: Stanford University Press.

Eberhard, W. G. (1985). *Sexual selection and animal genitalia.* Cambridge, MA: Harvard University Press.

Eberhard, W. G. (1991). Copulatory courtship and cryptic female choice in insects. *Biological Review, 66,* 1–31.

Ellis, H. (1905). *Sexual selection in man.* Philadelphia: F. A. Davis.

Ellis, H. (1934). *Man and woman: A study of secondary and tertiary sexual characters* (8th ed.). London: Heineman.

Ellis, L. (Ed.). (1993). *Social stratification and socioeconomic inequality: Vol. 1. A comparative biosocial analysis.* London: Praeger.

Endler, J. A. (1992). Signals, signal conditions, and the direction of evolution. *American Naturalist, 139,* S125–S153.

Endler, J. A. (1993). Some general comments on the evolution and design of animal communication systems. *Philosophical Transactions of the Royal Society of London, B, 340,* 215–225.

Enquist, M., & Arak, A. (1993). Selection of exaggerated male traits by female aesthetic senses. *Nature, 361,* 446–448.

Fisher, H. (1982). *The sex contract.* New York: W. Morrow.

Fisher, H. (1992). *Anatomy of love: The natural history of monogamy, adultery, and divorce.* New York: Simon & Schuster.

Fisher, R. A. (1915). The evolution of sexual preference. *Eugenics Review, 7,* 184–192.

Fisher, R. A. (1930). *The genetical theory of natural selection.* Oxford, England: Clarendon.

Fleagle, J. G., Kay, R. F., & Simons, E. L. (1980). Sexual dimorphism in early anthropoids. *Nature, 287,* 328–330.

Foley, R. (1987). *Another unique species: Patterns in human evolutionary ecology.* Harlow, England: Longman Scientific & Technical.

Foley, R. (1992). Ecology and energetics of encephalization in hominid evolution. In A. Whiten & E. M. Widdowson (Eds.), *Foraging strategies and the natural diet of monkeys, apes and humans* (pp. 63–72). Oxford, England: Oxford University Press.

Ford, C. S., & Beach, F. A. (1951). *Patterns of sexual behavior.* New York: Harper & Row.

Fox, R. (1972). Alliance and constraint: Sexual selection in the evolution of human kinship systems. In B. Campbell (Ed.), *Sexual selection and the descent of man, 1871–1971* (pp. 282–311). Chicago: Aldine-Atherton.

Frank, R. (1985). *Choosing the right pond.* Oxford, England: Oxford University Press.

Freyd, J. J. (1994). Circling creativity. *Psychological Science, 5*(3), 122–126.

Gamble, C. (1993). *Timewalkers: The prehistory of global colonization.* Phoenix Mill, England: Alan Sutton.

Gazzaniga, M. (1995). *The cognitive neurosciences.* Cambridge, MA: MIT Press.

Ghesquiere, J., Martin, R. D., & Newcombe, F. (Eds.). (1985). *Human sexual dimorphism.* Washington, DC: Taylor & Francis.

Goss, R. J. (1983). *Deer antlers: Regeneration, function, and evolution.* New York: Academic Press.

Gould, S. J. (1987, February). Freudian slip. *Natural History,* 14–19.

Grafen, A. (1990). Biological signals as handicaps. *Journal of Theoretical Biology, 144,* 517–546.

Guilford, T., & Dawkins, M. S. (1991). Receiver psychology and the evolution of animal signals. *Animal Behavior, 42,* 1–14.

Hamilton, W. D., Axelrod, R., & Tanese, R. (1990). Sexual reproduction as an adaptation to resist parasites (A review). *Proceedings of the National Academy of Sciences, USA, 87,* 3566–3573.

Hamilton, W. D., & Zuk, M. (1982). Heritable true fitness and bright birds: A role for parasites? *Science, 218,* 384–387.

Haraway, D. (1989). *Primate visions; Gender, race, and nature in the world of modern science.* New York: Routledge & Kegan Paul.

Harcourt, A. H., Harvey, P. H., Larson, S. G., & Shout, R. V. (1991). Testis weight, body weight and breeding systems in primates. *Nature, 293,* 55–57.

Harvey, P. H., Martin, R., & Clutton-Brock, T. (1986). Life histories in comparative perspective. In B. B. Smuts, D. L. Cheney, R. M. Seyfarth, R. W. Wrangham, & T. T. Struthsaker (Eds.), *Primate societies* (pp. 181–196). Chicago: University of Chicago Press.

Harvey, P. H., & Pagel, M. D. (1991). *The comparative method in evolutionary biology.* Oxford, England: Oxford University Press.

Hausfater, G., & Hrdy, S. B. (Eds.). (1984). *Infanticide: Comparative and evolutionary perspectives.* New York: Aldine.

Heywood, J. S. (1989). Sexual selection by the handicap mechanism. *Evolution, 43,* 1387–1397.

Hoelzer, G. A. (1989). The good parent process of sexual selection. *Animal Behaviour, 38(6),* 1067–1078.

Houde, A. E., & Endler, J. A. (1990). Correlated evolution of female mating preferences and male color patterns in the guppy *Poecilia reticulata. Science, 248,* 1405–1408.

Hrdy, S. B. (1979). Infanticide among animals: A review, classification, and examination of the implications for the reproductive strategies of females. *Ethology and Sociobiology, 1,* 13–40.

Hrdy, S. B. (1981). *The woman that never evolved.* Cambridge, MA: Harvard University Press.

Hrdy, S. B. (1988). The primate origins of human sexuality. In R. Bellig & G. Stevens (Eds.), *The evolution of sex* (pp. 101–136). San Francisco: Harper & Row.

Hrdy, S. B., & Whitten, P. L. (1987). Patterning of sexual activity. In B. B. Smuts, D. L. Cheney, R. M. Seyfarth, R. W. Wrangham, & T. T. Struthsaker (Eds.), *Primate societies* (pp. 370–384). Chicago: University of Chicago Press.

Humphrey, N. (1976). The social function of intellect. In R. Byrne & A. Whiten (Eds.), *Machiavellian intelligence* (pp. 13–26). Oxford, England: Oxford University Press.

Huxley, J. S. (1938). The present standing of the theory of sexual selection. In G. R. de Beer (Ed.), *Evolution: Essays on aspects of evolutionary biology* (pp. 11–42). Oxford, England: Clarendon.

Iwasa, Y., Pomiankowski, A., & Nee, S. (1991). The evolution of costly mate preferences: II. The "handicap" principle. *Evolution, 45(6),* 1431–1442.

Jones, I. L., & Hunter, F. M. (1993). Mutual sexual selection in a monogamous seabird. *Nature, 36,* 238–239.

Kirkpatrick, M. (1982). Sexual selection and the evolution of female choice. *Evolution, 36,* 1–12.

Kirkpatrick, M. (1987). The evolutionary forces acting on female preferences in polygynous animals. In J. W. Bradbury & M. B. Andersson (Eds.), *Sexual selection: Testing the alternatives* (pp. 67–82). New York: Wiley.

Kirkpatrick, M. (1992). Direct selection on female mating preferences: Comments of Grafen's models. *Journal of Theoretical Biology, 154,* 127–129.

Kirkpatrick, M., Price, T., & Arnold, S. J. (1990). The Darwin–Fisher theory of sexual selection in monogamous birds. *Evolution, 44*(1), 180–193.

Knight, C., Power, C., & Watts, I. (1995). The human symbolic revolution: A Darwinian account. *Cambridge Archaeological Journal, 5*(1), 75–114.

Kondrashov, A. (1988). Deleterious mutations as an evolutionary factor: III. Mating preference and some general remarks. *Journal of Theoretical Biology, 131,* 487–496.

Kramer, B. (1990). Sexual signals in electric fish. *Trends in Ecology and Evolution, 5,* 247–250.

Lancaster, J. B. (1991). A feminist and evolutionary biologist looks at women. *Yearbook of Physical Anthropology, 34,* 1–11.

Lande, R. (1980). Sexual dimorphism, sexual selection, and adaptation in polygenic characters. *Evolution, 34,* 292–305.

Lande, R. (1981). Models of speciation by sexual selection on polygenic characters. *Proceedings of the National Academy of Sciences, USA, 78,* 3721–3725.

Lande, R. (1987). Genetic correlation between the sexes in the evolution of sexual dimorphism and mating preferences. In J. W. Bradbury & M. B. Andersson (Eds.), *Sexual selection: Testing the alternatives* (pp. 83–94). New York: Wiley.

Langlois, J. H., & Roggman, L. A. (1990). Attractive faces are only average. *Psychological Science, 1*(2), 115–121.

Lockard, J. S., & Adams, R. M. (1991). Human serial polygyny: Demographic, reproductive, marital, and divorce data. *Ethology and Sociobiology, 2,* 177–186.

Low, B. (1990). Marriage systems and pathogen stress in human societies. *American Zoologist, 30,* 325–339.

Low, B., Alexander, R. M., & Noonan, K. M. (1987). Human hips, breasts, and buttocks: Is fat deceptive? *Ethology & Sociobiology, 8,* 249–257.

Lovejoy, C. O. (1981). The evolution of man. *Science, 211,* 341–350.

Lumsden, C. J., & Wilson, E O. (1982). Precis of genes, mind, and culture. *Behavioral and Brain Sciences, 5,* 1–37.

Margulis, L., & Sagan, D. (1991). *Mystery dance: On the evolution of human sexuality.* New York: Summit Books.

Martin, R. (1992). Primate reproduction. In S. Jones, R. Martin, & D. Pilbeam (Eds.), *The Cambridge encyclopedia of human evolution* (pp. 86–90). Cambridge, England: Cambridge University Press.

Martin, R. D., Willner, L. A., & Dettling, A. (1994). The evolution of sexual size dimorphism in primates. In R. V. Short & E. Balaban (Eds.), *The differences between the sexes* (pp. 159–200). Cambridge, England: Cambridge University Press.

Maynard Smith, J. (1976). Sexual selection and the handicap principle. *Journal of Theoretical Biology, 57,* 239–242.

Mayr, E. (1972). Sexual selection and natural selection. In B. Campbell (Ed.), *Sexual selection and the descent of man, 1871–1971.* Chicago: Aldine-Atherton.

Michod, R. E., & Levin, B. R. (Eds.). (1988). *The evolution of sex: An examination of current ideas.* Sunderland, MA: Sinauer.

Miller, G. F. (1993). *Evolution of the human brain through runaway sexual selection.* Doctoral dissertation, Stanford University Psychology Department. (Available through UMI Microfilms.)

Miller, G. F. (1994). Exploiting mate choice in evolutionary computation: Sexual selection as a process of search, optimization, and diversification. In T. C. Fogarty (Ed.),

*Evolutionary computing: Proceedings of the 1994 Artificial Intelligence and Simulation of Behavior (AISB) Society Workshop* (pp. 65–79). New York: Springer-Verlag.

Miller, G. F. (1995, June). *Darwinian demographics of cultural production.* Paper presented at the Human Behavior and Evolution Society 7th annual meeting, University of California, Santa Barbara.

Miller, G. F. (in press). Psychological selection in primates: The evolution of adaptive unpredictability in competition and courtship. In A. Whiten & R. W. Byrne (Eds.), *Machiavellian intelligence II.* Oxford, England: Oxford University Press.

Miller, G. F., & Pratto, F. (1992, July). *Political ideology as a form of sexual display.* Paper presented at the Human Behavior and Evolution Society 4th annual conference, Albuquerque, NM.

Miller, G. F., & Todd, P. M. (1993). Evolutionary wanderlust: Sexual selection with directional mate preferences. In J.-A. Meyer, H. L. Roitblat, & S. W. Wilson (Eds.), *From animals to animats: 2. Proceedings of the 2nd International Conference on Simulation of Adaptive Behavior* (pp. 21–30). Cambridge, MA: MIT Press.

Miller, G. F., & Todd, P. M. (1995). The role of mate choice in biocomputation: Sexual selection as a process of search, optimization, and diversification. In W. Banzaf & F. Eeckman (Eds.), *Evolution and biocomputation: Computational models of evolution* (pp. 169–204). New York: Springer-Verlag.

Moller, A. P. (1988). Female choice selects for male sexual tail ornaments in the monogamous swallow. *Nature, 332*(6165), 640–642.

Moller, A. P., & Pomiankowski, A. (1993). Fluctuating asymmetry and sexual selection. *Genetica, 89,* 267–279.

Morgan, T. H. (1903). *Evolution and adaptation.* New York: Macmillan.

Morris, D. (1985). *Bodywatching: A field guide to the human species.* New York: Crown Books.

Napier, J. (1993). *Hands* (rev. ed.). Princeton, NJ: Princeton University Press.

O'Donald, P. (1980). *Genetic models of sexual selection.* Cambridge, MA: Cambridge University Press.

Parker, G. A. (1984). Sperm competition and the evolution of animal mating systems. In R. L. Smith (Ed.), *Sperm competition and the evolution of animal mating systems* (pp. 1–60). New York: Academic Press.

Parker, S. T. (1987). A sexual selection model for hominid evolution. *Human Evolution, 2*(3), 235–253.

Partridge, L. (1980). Mate choice increases a component of offspring fitness in fruitflies. *Nature, 283,* 290–291.

Perrett, D. I., May, K. A., & Yoshikawa, S. (1994). Facial shape and judgments of female attractiveness. *Nature, 368,* 239–242.

Petrie, M. (1992). Peacocks with low mating success are more likely to suffer predation. *Animal Behavior, 44,* 585–586.

Petrie, M., Halliday, T., & Sanders, C. (1991). Peahens prefer peacocks with elaborate trains. *Animal Behavior, 41,* 323–331.

Pinker, S. (1994). *The language instinct.* London: Allen Lane.

Plomin, R., & Rende, R. (1991). Human behavioral genetics. *Annual Review of Psychology, 42,* 161–190.

Podos, J., Peters, S., Rudnicky, T., Marler, P., & Nowicki, S. (1992). The organization of song repertoires in song sparrows: Themes and variations. *Ethology, 90*(2), 89–106.

Pomiankowski, A. (1987). The costs of choice in sexual selection. *Journal of Theoretical Biology, 128,* 195–218.

Pomiankowski, A. (1988). The evolution of female mate preferences for male genetic quality. *Oxford Surveys in Evolutionary Biology, 5,* 136–184.

Pomiankowski, A. (1995). A resolution of the lek paradox. *Proceedings of the Royal Society of London, B, 260*(1357), 21–29.

Pomiankowski, A., Iwasa, Y., & Nee, S. (1991). The evolution of costly mate preferences: I. Fisher and biased mutation. *Evolution, 45*(6), 1422–1430.

Price, T. D., Schluter, D., & Heckman, N. E. (1993). Sexual selection when the female directly benefits. *Biological Journal of the Linnaean Society, 48*, 187–211.

Pruett-Jones, S. (1992). Independent versus non-independent mate choice: Do females copy each other? *American Naturalist, 140*, 1000–1009.

Reynolds, J. D., & Gross, M. R. (1990). Costs and benefits of female choice: Is there a lek paradox? *American Naturalist, 136*, 230–243.

Reynolds, J. D., & Gross, M. R. (1992). Female mate preference enhances offspring growth and reproduction in a fish, *Poecilia reticulata. Proceedings of the Royal Society of London, B, 250*, 57–62.

Reynolds, J. D., & Harvey, P. H. (1994). Sexual selection and the evolution of sex differences. In R. V. Short & E. Balaban (Eds.), *The differences between the sexes* (pp. 53–70). Cambridge, England: Cambridge University Press.

Rice, W. R. (1988). Heritable variation in fitness as a prerequisite for adaptive female choice: The effect of mutation-selection balance. *Evolution, 42*, 817–820.

Richards, R. J. (1987). *Darwin and the emergence of evolutionary theory of mind and behavior.* Chicago: University of Chicago Press.

Ridley, M. (1981). How the peacock got his tail. *New Scientist, 91*, 398–401.

Ridley, M. (1993). *The red queen: Sex and the evolution of human nature.* New York: Viking.

Rodman, P. S., & Mitani, J. C. (1987). Orangutans: Sexual dimorphism in a solitary species. In B. B. Smuts, D. L. Cheney, R. M. Seyfarth, R. W. Wrangham, & T. T. Struthsaker (Eds.), *Primate societies* (pp. 146–154). Chicago: University of Chicago Press.

Rogers, A. R., & Mukherjee, A. (1992). Quantitative genetics of sexual dimorphism in human body size. *Evolution, 46*(1), 226–234.

Rushton, J. P. (1989). Genetic similarity, human altruism, and group selection. *Behavioral and Brain Sciences, 12*, 503–559.

Rushton, J. P. (1995). *Race, evolution, and behavior: A life history perspective.* New Brunswick, NJ: Transaction.

Ryan, M. J. (1985). *The Tungara frog: A study in sexual selection and communication.* Chicago: University of Chicago Press.

Ryan, M. J. (1990). Sexual selection, sensory systems, and sensory exploitation. *Oxford Surveys of Evolutionary Biology, 7*, 156–195.

Ryan, M. J., & Keddy-Hector, A. (1992). Directional patterns of female mate choice and the role of sensory biases. *American Naturalist, 139*, S4–S35.

Scheib, J. (1994). Sperm donor selection and the psychology of female choice. *Ethology and Sociobiology, 15*(3), 113–129.

Searcy, W. A. (1982). The evolutionary effects of mate selection. *Annals Rev. Ecol. Syst., 13*, 57–85.

Seyfarth, R. M. (1978). Social relationships among adult male and female baboons: 1. Behavior during sexual courtship. *Behaviour, 64*, 204–226.

Sheets-Johnstone, M. (1990). Hominid bipedality and sexual selection theory. *Evolutionary Theory, 9*(1), 57–70.

Short, R. V. (1980). The origins of human sexuality. In C. R. Austin & R. B. Short (Eds.), *Reproduction in mammals* (Vol. 8, pp. 1–33). Cambridge, England: Cambridge University Press.

Short, R. V., & Balaban, E. (Eds.). (1994). *The differences between the sexes.* Cambridge, England: Cambridge University Press.

Shostak, M. (1981). *Nisa: The life and words of a !Kung woman.* Cambridge, MA: Harvard University Press.

Silk, D. (1987). Social behavior in evolutionary perspective. In B. B. Smuts, D. L. Cheney, R. M. Seyfarth, R. W. Wrangham, & T. T. Struthsaker (Eds.), *Primate societies* (pp. 318–329). Chicago: University of Chicago Press.

Simpson, J. A., & Gangestad, S. W. (1992). Sociosexuality and romantic partner choice. *Journal of Personality, 60,* 31–52.

Singh, D. (1993). Waist-to-hip ratio (WHR): A defining morphological feature of health and female attractiveness. *Journal of Personality and Social Psychology, 65*(2), 293–307.

Small, M. (1988). Female primate sexual behavior and conception: Are there really sperm to spare? *Current Anthropology, 29*(1), 81–100.

Small, M. (1993). *Female choices: Sexual behavior of female primates.* Ithaca, NY: Cornell University Press.

Smuts, B. B. (1985). *Sex and friendship in baboons.* New York: Aldine.

Smuts, B. B. (1987). Sexual competition and mate choice. In B. B. Smuts, D. L. Cheney, R. M. Seyfarth, R. W. Wrangham, & T. T. Struthsaker (Eds.), *Primate societies* (pp. 385–399). Chicago: University of Chicago Press.

Smuts, B. B. (1991). Male aggression against women: An evolutionary perspective. *Human Nature, 3,* 1–44.

Sperber, D. (1994). The modularity of thought and the epidemiology of representations. In L. A. Hirschfeld & S. A. Gelman (Eds.), *Mapping the mind: Domain specificity in cognition and culture* (pp. 39–67). Cambridge, England: Cambridge University Press.

Stoddart, D. M. (1990). *The scented ape: The biology and culture of human odour.* Cambridge, England: Cambridge University Press.

Stringer, C., & Gamble, C. (1993). *In search of the Neanderthals: Solving the puzzle of human origins.* London: Thames & Hudson.

Sulloway, F. J. (1979). *Freud, biologist of the mind: Beyond the psychoanalytic legend.* New York: Basic Books.

Symons, D. (1979). *The evolution of human sexuality.* Oxford, England: Oxford University Press.

Szalay, F. S., & Costello, R. K. (1991). Evolution of permanent estrus displays in hominids. *Journal of Human Evolution, 20,* 439–464.

Tanner, N. M. (1981). *On becoming human.* Cambridge, England: Cambridge University Press.

Thiessen, D., & Gregg, B. (1980). Human assortative mating and genetic equilibrium: An evolutionary perspective. *Ethology and Sociobiology, 1,* 111–140.

Thornhill, N. W. (1991). An evolutionary analysis of rules regulating human inbreeding and marriage. *Behavioral and Brain Sciences, 14,* 247–293.

Thornhill, N. W. (Ed.). (1993). *The natural history of inbreeding and outbreeding.* Chicago: Chicago University Press.

Thornhill, R., & Alcock, J. (1983). *The evolution of insect mating systems.* Cambridge, MA: Harvard University Press.

Thornhill, R., & Gangestad, S. W. (1993). Human facial beauty: Averageness, symmetry, and parasite resistance. *Human Nature, 4*(3), 237–269.

Thornhill, R., & Thornhill, N. W. (1992). The evolutionary psychology of men's coercive sexuality. *Behavioral & Brain Sciences, 15,* 363–421.

Todd, P. M., & Miller, G. F. (1993). Parental guidance suggested: How parental imprinting evolves through sexual selection as an adaptive learning mechanism. *Adaptive Behavior, 2*(1), 5–47.

Tomlinson, I. P. M. (1988). Diploid models of the handicap principle. *Heredity, 60,* 283–293.

Tooby, J., & Cosmides, L. (1990). The past explains the present: Emotional adaptations and the structure of ancestral environments. *Ethology and Sociobiology, 11*(4/5), 375–424.

Tooby, J., & Cosmides, L. (1992). The psychological foundations of culture. In J. H. Barkow, L. Cosmides, & J. Tooby (Eds.), *The adapted mind: Evolutionary psychology and the generation of culture* (pp. 19–136). Oxford, England: Oxford University Press.

Trail, P. W. (1990). Why should lek-breeders be monomorphic? *Evolution, 44*(7), 1837–1852.

Trivers, R. (1972). Parental investment and sexual selection. In B. Campbell (Ed.), *Sexual selection and the descent of man 1871–1971* (pp. 136–179). Chicago: Aldine.

Trivers, R. (1985). *Social evolution.* Menlo Park, CA: Benjamin/Cummings.

Wallace, A. R. (1870). *Contributions to the theory of natural selection.* London: Macmillan.

Wallace, A. R. (1889). *Darwinism: An exposition of the theory of natural selection, with some of its applications.* London: Macmillan.

West-Eberhard, M. J. (1984). Sexual selection, competitive communication, and species-specific signals in insects. In T. Lewis (Ed.), *Insect communication* (pp. 283–324). New York: Academic Press.

Westermark, E. (1903). *The history of human marriage* (3rd ed.). London: Macmillan.

Whiten, A. (Ed.). (1991). *Natural theories of mind.* Cambridge, MA: Basil Blackwell.

Wilcockson, R. W., Crean, C. S., & Day, T. H. (1995). Heritability of a sexually selected character in both sexes. *Nature, 374*(6518), 158–159.

Williams, G. C. (1966). *Adaptation and natural selection.* Princeton, NJ: Princeton University Press.

Williams, G. C. (1975). *Sex and evolution.* Princeton, NJ: Princeton University Press.

Wills, C. (1993). *The runaway brain: The evolution of human uniqueness.* New York: Basic Books.

Wilson, E. O. (1975). *Sociobiology: The new synthesis.* Cambridge, MA: Harvard University Press.

Wright, R. (1994). *The moral animal: Evolutionary psychology and everyday life.* New York: Pantheon.

Zahavi, A. (1975). Mate selection—a selection of handicap. *Journal of Theoretical Biology, 53,* 205–214.

Zahavi, A. (1991). On the definition of sexual selection, Fisher's model, and the evolution of waste and of signals in general. *Animal Behaviour, 42*(3), 501–503.

Zuckerman, M. (1984). Sensation seeking: A comparative approach to a human trait. *Behavioral and Brain Sciences, 7,* 413–471.

# 4

# *The Evolution of Human Life Histories*

Bobbi S. Low
*University of Michigan*

Organisms live their lives in a staggering diversity of ways. Not only ecologically, but in the very patterns of their lives, there is great diversity. Across nonhuman species, there are asexual species, species with one sex, two sexes, and more than two sexes. There are species in which a single individual is two sexes, either concurrently or sequentially; species that live only minutes and species that live for centuries; species that breed once and die and species that breed repeatedly; species that have single young and species that lay thousands of eggs at a time. It is easy for those of us who specialize in human behavior and evolution to remain unaware of the sheer scope of this diversity. Yet human life histories are unusual, and occasionally unique, in ways that are instructive in the context of all this diversity. This chapter describes the ways in which humans are typical, and unusual primates, and uses natural selection theory to explore why we differ in the particular ways we do.

Life-history theory is a subset of natural selection theory. It argues that the characteristics we see represent trade-offs in allocating effort between survival and current reproduction; between current versus future reproduction; and, within current reproduction, among offspring of different sex, size, and number. As in any zero-sum game, what an organism spends in one endeavor cannot be spent in another. Life histories, the patterns of birth, growth, and death that we see, are thus the outcome of competing costs and benefits of different activities at any point in the life cycle. Two recent syntheses of life-history theory (Roff, 1992; Stearns, 1992) identified

131

the following life-history traits as central to any analysis: size at birth, growth pattern, age and size at maturity, allocation of reproductive effort, age schedules of birth and death, and number and sex ratio of offspring. The trade-offs among these traits (e.g., energy spent on reproduction cannot be spent on growth) lead to a variety of patterns in, for example, mating, parental care, and senescence.

At first, the diversity in other species, rich as it is, may seem unrelated to the relatively tame variation in human lifetimes. It is argued here that it is not. Life-history theory lies at the heart of understanding diversity, dealing as it does with natural selection, adaptation, and constraint. Human life histories are diverse and unusual among primates in several regards. We mature strikingly late; no other primate, even the largest and slowest maturing, takes more than a decade to mature. Our offspring are extremely large compared with the mother's size, and they are, as any mother will tell you, ridiculously altricial, or helpless; by the time a human infant rolls over for the first time, an infant chimpanzee is playing among its friends, moving freely about. The complexity and diversity of human social systems foster even more life-history diversity within our species— so that the costs and benefits of different parental care patterns, for example, differ among societies within humans. If natural selection indeed shapes the specifics of life histories, what are the driving forces that lead to our differences and similarities to other primates?

## ALLOMETRIC BACKGROUND: THE IMPACT OF SIZE

Some phenomena are so strongly size related that this aspect swamps other patterns. For example, animals that are as large as adults take longer to grow to that adult size than small animals. These effects of size ("allometric" relationships) play a major role in shaping life-history patterns. In mammals, most life-history timing variables and many physiological variables scale against body weight with a slope of about 0.25 (Harvey & Read, 1988; see also Harvey & Pagel, 1991). Simply knowing the size of an organism tells you a great deal about many things in its life. If you know the size of an adult female, you can predict with some accuracy, for example, the likely size of her offspring at birth (Harvey, Martin, & Clutton-Brock, 1986). Why this remarkably consistent size effect? Size-specific mortality is important. In the context of life-history analysis, the timing of many events is strongly driven by age-specific mortality patterns (e.g., Charlesworth, 1980; Charnov, 1991; Roff, 1992; Stearns, 1992), and small organisms have higher age-specific mortality; they simply tend to be more at risk than larger organisms. Thus, smaller species within appropriate taxonomic categories are, *ceteris paribus*, likely to mature earlier and have shorter gestation lengths and interbirth intervals than larger species.

Many differences are simply size related, but this size effect can be used to discover which differences are interesting because they are not size related. Harvey, Martin, and Clutton-Brock (1986) compared the "relative value" of a number of life-history traits in primates (including humans), which describes the variable after the effects of size have been removed. One can then ask: Does this trait follow the pattern one would expect from size alone? If not, what other factors are important? This technique allows one to compare human patterns with those of other primates, without the complication of size differences.

### Size at Birth, Altriciality, and Growth Rates

In general, monkeys and apes larger than 1 kg have single offspring, and show a rather tight correlation between mean offspring weight and mean maternal weight (Leutenegger, 1979; Stearns, 1992): Bigger mothers have larger offspring. Within this pattern, however, human offspring are 38% larger, and are carried in utero about 11% longer, than predicted from maternal size (Harvey et al., 1986). Further, human babies continue to grow rapidly for a long time after birth, compared with other primates. While human infants are growing rapidly, they remain markedly altricial, compared with offspring in other primate species. Typically among vertebrates, altricial young are naked, helpless, and often blind (e.g., Case, 1978; Nice, 1962; Ricklefs, 1983). Mammal species with strong predation pressure against which parental care is ineffective—many ungulates like deer, caribou, cattle—are relatively precocial; babies can run within an hour or two of birth. Primates, in contrast, are relatively altricial.

More work on growth versus precociality has been done within birds than within mammals. Nestlings of altricial bird species are fed by their parents, and they grow much faster than the offspring of precocial species (Ricklefs, 1974, 1975, 1979a, 1979b, 1983). This suggests that rapid growth may be a selective advantage of altricial development (Ricklefs, 1983; see also Alexander, 1990): Offspring that simply sit in a safe place and grow can grow faster than infants that must forage for themselves and run from predators. Although this observation seems relevant for humans, because they are both helpless and fast-growing, Dienske (1986) and Alexander (1990) doubted that growth potential alone is the advantage for humans, for a variety of reasons. Alexander (1990) speculated that early physical precociality in humans is traded off for later mental precociality; that is, humans grow fast and remain helpless, but it is actually mental and psychological development useful in later complex social situations, rather than simply size, that is at issue.

The brains of human infants are also large and fast-growing. In primates, neonatal brain size is highly correlated with neonatal body size ($r$

= 0.99; Harvey et al., 1986; Jolly, 1985). However, adult human brains are 83% larger than would be predicted from size (Harvey et al., 1986; see also Martin, 1983). Humphrey (1976) and others have argued that this large brain size has been favored by the importance of intelligence in social evolution—that the uncertainties and risks of social life require more complex intellectual skills than, say, simply avoiding predation and finding food. This is consistent with the general pattern that social species have somewhat larger brains than predicted by size alone; humans are simply extreme. Human brain size has roughly doubled over about 2 million years. This is a surprisingly slow evolutionary rate of increase, and some scholars argue it reflects serious constraints on brain size. The brain is metabolically expensive; in a resting human, brain tissue consumes 20% of the energy budget, compared with 9% for a resting chimpanzee, or 2% for a typical marsupial (Hofman, 1983; see review by Smith, 1990, 1992).

Human babies are born with brains 40% larger than expected, and their brains continue to grow rapidly for another year (Harvey et al., 1986; Martin, 1983), contrasting with the pattern of other primates, in which brain growth slows significantly soon after birth. This pattern may represent some trade-off in optimal human brain size and bipedalism; perhaps bipeds face particular difficulties in giving birth to large-brained offspring, but large brains are highly advantageous for humans. A big brain appears to have been highly advantageous through human evolution.

*Development and Time to Maturity.* Both size at birth and growth rate contribute to time to maturity (e.g., Roff, 1992). Because human infants are relatively large at birth and grow rapidly, we would expect them to mature early, but this is not so. Human females are 45% older at sexual maturation than would be expected from size (Harvey et al., 1986). However, age at sexual maturation is strongly influenced by age-specific mortality (e.g., Roff, 1992; Stearns, 1992). Young women are subfecund for several years; they are less fertile, very nutrition-sensitive, and suffer greater infant loss than women in their late teens and early 20s (e.g., Lancaster, 1986). Even in societies in which a girl is married before puberty, and in which there is no evidence of deliberate fertility limitation, she is unlikely to have her first child before her midteens. Again, some scholars argue that this late maturity reflects the complexity of raising a successful human infant; thus, girls who matured later not only had greater physical reserves to contribute to their children, but also more experience to bring to child training.

Although we are longer-lived, bigger, and begin reproducing later than, for example, chimpanzees, our interbirth intervals are relatively short. For example, chimpanzee females are likely to have their first offspring at 10 to 11 years, and have an average interbirth interval of 60 months. In contrast, women are likely to be much older at the birth of their first child, but the average interbirth interval for surviving offspring is shorter than for chimpanzees; it ranges from 30 to 45 months, whether among hunter–gatherers (Harvey et al., 1986), 19th-century Swedes (Low, 1991), or 19th-century Germans (Knodel, 1988). In modern developed nations, because lifetime number of children is low (1–3 in Western Europe and the United States), the interval is growing longer.

In iteroparous (*repeated birth*) mammals with seasonal breeding, interbirth intervals are obviously multiples of a year. Biologically interesting patterns, nonetheless, occur. For example, red deer mothers, after the birth of a son, are likely to "skip" a year's pregnancy (Clutton-Brock, 1991), reflecting the greater costs of producing a son, compared with producing a daughter. In many mammals, there is typically little variance in fertility across age classes for females, although male variation can be extreme. Humans have nonseasonal breeding, short interbirth intervals, and quite uneven fertility across age. Age-specific fertility, for both men and women, is strongly influenced by cultural factors (e.g., Juliet was only 12 years old when she was to be married—typical for that time period in Europe).

*Maturation Patterns.* Smith (1991, 1992) noted other oddities in the pattern of human developmental life-history events, compared with other primates. Comparing *Pan*, *Australopithecus*, and *Homo* (from *H. habilis* to modern humans), the time from birth to eruption of the first permanent tooth has increased by 3 years, the time to completion of permanent dentition has increased by 10 years, and life span has increased by 30 years (e.g., Smith, 1991). As Harvey et al. (1986) noted, humans are weaned at ages 40% younger than would be expected from size alone. In other primates, weaning is closely associated with first molar eruption; if human mothers waited to wean until children's molars erupted, they would wean their children at 6 to 8 years. We are born big, grow fast, wean early, but mature late.

In primates, as the face and teeth mature more slowly and infants are weaned later and later, the proportional reproductive periods of life tend to shift (Smith, 1992). Primate species that take longer to develop their teeth (extended somatic effort) show proportionately younger age at first reproduction and proportionately shorter gestation lengths and interbirth intervals. But humans are anomalous here, also, maturing later than other species with late dental maturation, and, as noted earlier, having shorter interbirth intervals than predicted.

Most placental mammals are "live fast, die young" species: After they complete dental maturation, the epiphyses of the long bones close and sexual maturation follows. Oddly, however, long-lived species such as most primates (including humans) mature sexually before dental maturation is complete (Smith, 1992). Slow-growing species can be at great risk of dying before sexual maturation (e.g., Charnov, 1991; Harvey & Nee, 1991; Promislow & Harvey, 1990; Roff, 1992; Stearns, 1992). Life-history theory argues that shifting sexual maturation younger may help reduce the period of risk of death before reproduction. Yet this very problem leads back to the conundrum: Why do humans mature so late for their size? Most scholars suggest that patterns of social cooperation and complexity are relevant because they affect age-specific mortality patterns, but this is a largely unanalyzed problem.

## CURRENT VERSUS FUTURE REPRODUCTION

A central life-history trade-off is that between current and future reproduction. On the one hand, in stable or increasing populations, offspring produced now mature earlier than future offspring, and thus have higher reproductive value (Fisher, 1958). On the other hand, high current reproductive effort carries costs: reduced chances of survival and lowered future reproduction (e.g., Lessells, 1991; Roff, 1992; Stearns, 1992). Thus, own survivorship is traded off against value of offspring.

Across primates, both age at first reproduction and degree of iteroparity (repetition of reproduction) are allometric. Small species are less safe even as adults, and their general pattern is early investment in reproduction, despite its associated costs to future reproduction. That is, "mature early and spend a lot in reproducing even if it kills you, for the future is uncertain." Humans delay maturation considerably, but there is across- and within-population variations. As noted earlier, age-specific mortality influences timing of reproduction; in risky environments, current reproduction is heavily favored over delayed reproduction. In humans, social perception of these factors might be important (e.g., Lancaster, 1994). For example, Geronimus (1987, 1991) argued that most teenage mothers in the United States today are members of an urban economic underclass (which suffers higher age-specific mortality than many other groups) who may well be optimizing their fertility schedules in a life-history context. Similarly, Chisholm (1993) suggested that across- and within-population variation in age at first birth might be related to individual perception of environmental uncertainty: Individuals raised in environments they perceive as risky for their long-term success (e.g., adolescents in inner-city environments with high mortality rates) may choose to reproduce early, even if this reduces their chances of high fertility or their ability to invest in the children they produced.

## Concealed Ovulation and Menstruation

Concealed ovulation in humans has puzzled biologists for some time. In other primates, a female's reproductive status is relatively easy to assess: Female ovulation is typically associated with estrus bleeding and often with highly conspicuous perianal swellings. Female advertisement signals female receptivity. Human females are unusual in a number of ways (although other primates may approach these conditions; Alexander & Noonan, 1979). Menstrual bleeding is not associated with the fertile period of ovulation; female receptivity can be continuous, and unrelated to ovulatory state; and ovulation is practically undetectable in most women.

Female humans are potentially sexually receptive throughout their cycle, rather than just at the time of ovulation. As a result, conceptions per copulation are much lower in humans than in other mammals, including other primates. Most women cannot detect ovulation themselves. When a couple wishes to track ovulation to bias the likelihood of having a son versus a daughter (there is some evidence that copulations immediately before, during, and immediately after ovulation produce male-biased sex ratios, whereas copulations during the rest of the cycle are female-biased, or 1:1), they must use somewhat intrusive methods unlikely to have been common in our evolutionary history (e.g., testing the vaginal mucosa for *spinbarkheit*, or viscosity). Burley (1979) suggested that natural selection conceals ovulation to counter "a human or prehuman conscious tendency among females to avoid conception through intercourse near ovulation" (p. 835). Alexander (1979) made a suggestion similar to Burley's about the concealment of ovulation from the female herself. Hrdy (1981) suggested that concealment allows for "paternity confusion"; in primates in which females are receptive for a period longer than the ovum is fertilizable, and in which males may give some (relatively low-cost) paternal care to infants, female receptivity-without-certain-fertility might allow females to garner care for infants from more males than the one who is the father. That is, males' only cue to potential fatherhood is having mated with a female, so males who have mated with females are more willing to give some paternal care. Alexander and Noonan (1979) argued that concealed ovulation may have enabled females to force desirable males into consort relationships long enough to preclude the male's access to other matings, and simultaneously raised his confidence of paternity, making expensive paternal investment more profitable.

Menstruation, separated as it is from ovulation, cannot signal simple receptivity or immediate presence of ovulation. Profet (1993) suggested that menstruation evolved to protect the uterus and oviducts from sperm-borne pathogens by dislodging endometrial tissue and delivering immune cells to the uterine cavity. However, Strassmann (1994) pointed out that the degree of bleeding in primate females is phylogenetically patterned, and shows no apparent correlations with appropriate ecological and social factors (e.g., degree of promiscuity); and there is no pattern to pathogen presence during the menstrual cycle (as would be predicted if the menses rid the uterus of pathogens). Strassmann noted that metabolic rate is approximately 6% to 9% higher during the luteal phase of the menstrual cycle. She calculated the energy costs of maintenance of the endometrium versus shedding and regeneration. As she pointed out, for women in traditional societies, who cycle relatively less (being pregnant or in post-partum amenorrhea most of the time) than modern women, the energetic efficiency of shed-and-replace may be greater than that of constant maintenance.

Finally, although menstruation is separated from the fertile period, it may still signal something about a woman's fertility. Strassmann (1991) suggested that the menstrual taboos (such as menstrual hut visits) of some societies, which make a woman's status public, advertise several things: nonpregnancy, resumption of fertility after postpartum amenorrhea, and (with the cessation of observation of menstrual taboos), infecundability because of pregnancy or menopause. Strassmann suggested that public menstrual taboos may also function as anticuckoldry tactics: By signaling menstruation, women advertise their reproductive status to husbands, affines, and other observers. This has three consequences: Men can assess paternity probability better and direct paternal investment to their advantage, adulterous pregnancies are more easily detected and punished, and men can avoid marrying already pregnant women.

Today, humans may be changing the environment in novel ways that affect reproductive patterns. Whitten (1992), reviewing demographic data and historical trends in human sexual behavior, suggested that the chemical revolution, with its legacy of environmental pollutants known to influence steroidal activity, may have produced fundamental shifts in human reproduction. For example, dizygotic twinning and age at menarche have changed in a coordinated fashion, co-varying with changes in diet and production of specific chemicals.

## SEX DIFFERENCES IN REPRODUCTION: MATING VERSUS PARENTAL EFFORT

In most mammals, including humans, the sexes differ in age at first reproduction, adult size, and life expectancy at birth. These differences arise from the selective pressures accompanying polygyny and any impact of male size in male–male competition that is so important in most polygynous species. In humans, the pattern is further influenced by sociocultural patterns; for example, in many societies, older polygynous men promulgate rules to preclude young men's access to young women of high reproductive value (e.g., Low, 1990a; Murdock, 1949; Whyte, 1978, 1979).

In life-history theory, sex differences result from trade-offs. At any moment, an organism might spend its effort on maintaining its soma, or body (*somatic effort*: thermoregulation, eating, avoiding predators, etc.), or it might spend *reproductive effort*, either in attracting a mate (*mating effort*) or in caring for offspring (*parental effort*). In any particular environment, for an organism of a particular age, some patterns of expenditure are better than others in their effect on survival and reproduction. Further, in most species, it pays individuals to specialize in either mating or parental effort—the behaviors that make one successful in mating are often mutually exclusive of the behaviors that promote parental success (reviewed by Low, 1993a, 1994; see also Daly & Wilson, 1983). In most species, mating specialists are likely to be male and parental specialists are likely to be female. This tendency is particularly pronounced in mammals, including humans, probably because females are specialized to produce milk for early nutritional care.

This specialization has profound and not immediately obvious implications. If one sex specializes in getting mates and the other in investing in offspring, the two are likely to behave quite differently, for mating and parental effort show very different reproductive "return curves" (reproductive success gained per unit of resources or status acquired, or effort spent; see Low, 1993a). Mating effort has a high fixed cost; typically, a male must establish himself as successful (e.g., growing antlers, fighting for dominance or a territory) before he can even get his first mate. Parental effort shows a more linear return curve: Each additional offspring is likely to cost about as much as the first (although in highly polygynous species, the return curves for making sons, versus daughters, reflect the adult mating versus parental return curves; see review by Frank, 1990).

This dichotomy creates a strong bias in polygynous species: Far fewer males than females actually reproduce, but the most successful male may have an order of magnitude more offspring than the most reproductively successful female. For example, among elephant seals, over 80% of males fail to reproduce; the most reproductive female had 11 offspring in her lifetime, whereas the most successful male had over 90 (LeBoeuf & Reiter, 1988). Because males typically experience more variance in reproductive performance than females, their stakes are higher: Delayed maturation of males, to achieve larger size and competitive ability, is common (and typical of humans). Great expenditure and risk may be profitable for males, so risky behavior and conflict are male endeavors in polygynous species like humans.

Physical intrasexual conflicts (more frequently by males, in humans as in other mammals) are more likely to escalate to lethal levels than conflicts arising from other sorts of individual selection. Human male reproductive variance typically exceeds female variance, as in other mammals, resulting in striking sex differences in aggressiveness, promiscuity, and risk taking (e.g., Boone, 1986, 1988; Daly & Wilson, 1983, 1984, 1985, 1987, 1988; Low, 1988, 1990a, 1993a; Low & Clarke, 1992; Smith & Boyd, 1990). This difference, of course, is what prompted Darwin (1871) to treat sexual selection differently from ordinary natural selection. Darwin was perplexed that males often seemed to do expensive and risky things that got them killed. The secret, of course, is that when the mating stakes are high, and success is rare, expensive and risky behavior can be profitable—but this tends to be true for mating (usually male) effort, not for parental effort.

Women are rarely found in high-risk occupations like warfare (Low, 1993b). Through evolutionary history, men have often been able to gain reproductively by warring behavior; women almost never have been able to do so (see review by Low, 1993b). But women warriors are not unknown. During the 17th, 18th, and 19th centuries, women occasionally disguised as men and fought in the ranks of infantry and cavalry regiments (Holmes, 1985). Most often, this appeared to be a device allowing women to follow their men (e.g., Keegan, 1987). Thus, social-environmental factors could influence trends and patterns.

Not surprisingly, there are trends toward sexual dimorphism in behavior, as well as physical traits, because resources are useful in different ways to achieve mating versus parental success. That is, sexual dimorphism in the usefulness of resources and power to aid reproduction is the critical factor. Cross-culturally, men in many societies can make enormous direct reproductive gains through access to power, status, and great amounts of resources, but it is not clear to what extent women can do so (Low, 1990a); this parallels the reproductive ecology of resource control and status in other polygynous species. In the few societies in which women wield substantial public power, as opposed to informal influence, they show no clear reproductive gain from doing so. In fact, there is frequently a conflict between political and direct reproductive gain for women. In matrilineal and double descent systems, women's power appears to accrue to their sons, who may reap reproductive benefit (e.g., Low, 1992). In other systems, women's direct gains are not clear, but when power gives access to substantial resources, women in power can make reproductive gains through their sons or nepotistically.

## Male Resource Control and Fertility

As is true for the males of most mammalian species, men's age-specific fertility is related to resource access and control. Men who control significant resources frequently are able to marry and start families earlier, and to marry younger (higher reproductive value) women and more women; all of these strategies translate into higher lifetime fertility, compared with other men—hence men's tendency to strive for wealth and power in politics and war. A concomitant result is that fewer men than women in any generation may reproduce at all.

Successfully polygynous men, of course, are likely to have more children than monogamously married men. For men in most societies for which there is information, men's resources are clearly related to their age at first reproduction, age-specific fertility, and lifetime fertility (e.g., Hill, 1984). Richer Turkmen had more wives and more children than poorer Turkmen (Irons, 1979). In the pastoral Mukogodo of Kenya, wealth enhances men's reproductive success (Cronk, 1991). Similarly, the Meru use livestock for bridewealth, and richer men can marry more wives (Fadiman, 1982). In societies as diverse as the Hausa (Barkow, 1977), Trinidadians (Flinn, 1986), and Micronesian islanders (Turke & Betzig, 1985), status and wealth correlate with male reproductive success. Among the Kipsigis, a man's lifetime reproductive success was significantly correlated with the size of his agricultural plot and pastoral herd—both correlated with his ability to make substantial bridewealth payments (Borgerhoff Mulder, 1988a, 1988b).

In societies in which resources appear to be economically indefensible, men may arrange to exchange women for women, rather than resources for women (e.g., Flinn & Low, 1986). In societies such as the Ache (Hill & Kaplan, 1988; Kaplan & Hill, 1985) and the Yanomamö (Chagnon, 1979, 1982, 1988), few physical resources are owned, but even here, status represents a resource. Among the Ache, men who are good hunters not only get more matings than other men, but more of their children survive (Hill & Kaplan, 1988). In the Yanomamö, male kin available for coalitions also represent a resource, and men manipulate kinship terms in ways that make more women available for mates; this also renders powerful men available as coalition partners (Chagnon, 1979, 1982) so that reproductive success is uneven. In Yanomamö, the most successful methods of gaining wives include being a member of a powerful kin group and gaining recognition as a revenge killer (Chagnon, 1988). Among the polyandrous Toda, the centrality of a man's status in the kinship network is related to his reproductive success (Hughes, 1988).

Even in monogamous societies, wealthier men are likely to marry younger women (Low, 1990b), and daughters of wealthy families may be considered marriageable years before poorer women (Drake, 1969). A man's wealth trajectory is important; in some societies, men born into poor families who, nonetheless, become wealthy have extraordinarily high fertility (Low, 1994). As Josephson (1993) has shown, however, these gains may not be carried on into subsequent generations of the lineage.

In the 19th century, family sizes fell dramatically in Europe and North America (the "demographic transition"), reducing variance in fertility. This phenomenon raises the question of whether wealth any longer correlates with reproduction. The positive correlation between men's resources and lifetime reproductive success appears to have held through the demographic transition (Low & Clarke, 1992), but results from contemporary societies are mixed (Low et al., 1992; Pérusse, 1993). There are both methodological and conceptual complications. As Low and Clarke (1992) noted, studies using proxy measures rather than actual resource control (e.g., Birdsall, 1980, who used total fertility rate, TFR, and gross national product, GNP, both population measures; and Vining, 1986, who used individual education, IQ, etc.), often find negative results (although Birdsall's within-country data suggest a positive correlation between wealth and resources within societies). Studies that examine lineages (e.g., Mueller, 1991), individual patterns (Rank, 1989), and some census data (Daly & Wilson, 1983) typically find positive results. A careful recent lineage study of men in Albuquerque (Kaplan, Lancaster, Bock, & Johnson, 1993) finds little evidence of any remaining connection between resource control and fertility. Contraception technology further complicates the issue. In modern societies, when sexual access rather than fertility is measured, richer men clearly have more sexual access than poorer men (Pérusse, 1992). Obviously, although men's wealth may ensure sexual access, when effective contraception exists, access may not translate into fertility (Kaplan et al., 1993; Pérusse, 1993).

In past human environments, then, men almost certainly profited reproductively from resource acquisition. Today there is some evidence that reduced fertility, combined with greater per capita investment in offspring, is a highly effective parental strategy in competitive environments (e.g., Kaplan, 1994; Low, 1993a). The "game" may no longer be simply numbers of offspring, but offspring who control more of the available resources. This may explain much of the variation in demographic transitions: Industrialization is only one factor (and not a certain one) that might increase the competitiveness needed for children to become established themselves (e.g., Low, 1993a; Low et al., 1992); social and ethnographic phenomena can be important.

The two sexes may have different costs and benefits with regard to this particular parental strategy: Males with few resources might still do best by trying to maximize matings without much investment, whereas females and better-off parents of both sexes are likely to be more concerned with effective longer term investment. Finally, we live in a novel environment, which may well foster nonadaptive "runaway" consumption, independent of fertility.

## Female Resources and Fertility

In some other social primates (those in which males disperse and females remain in their natal group), female status not only translates into increased access to resources, but is also heritable. Male mammals typically do not provide food for their offspring to any great extent. In humans, the general pattern is that societies tend to be patrilocal (men stay, women move). Women provide much (often most) of the subsistence, which is usually shared by kin (parental effort), whereas male hunting effort often seems to function as mating effort (e.g., Hawkes, 1991; Hill & Kaplan, 1988). Hawkes (1991) provided important insights into male, versus female, cooperation and sharing of food. In examining foraging patterns of the Ache, she found that (male) hunters who were more successful received more attention from group members, and fared better reproductively. Men often hunted in ways that look inefficient from standard optimal foraging perspectives, but Hawkes suggested that such men may have been pursuing a (high risk–high gain) "showoff" strategy that suffered more variance in calories, but produced big, flashy hunting successes, and thus, more sexual access to the women men sought.

Thus, male resource acquisition increases male fertility at the "high end" of reproductive variation: High amounts of resources make the most successful males very successful. For the wives of such polygynous men, fertility may be uneven. In a number of societies, second and subsequent wives, for whatever reasons, have fewer children than first wives (e.g., Daly & Wilson, 1983). Women's independent resource access makes more difference as parental effort to avert failure at the low end of the variation. Women need enough resources to raise healthy children and resource scarcity is critical. However, through most of our evolutionary history, it has not profited women to strive for great amounts because they could not convert such excess resources directly into reproductive gain, as men could (e.g., Low, 1992, 1993a, 1993b).

How do women in traditional societies most effectively transform resources into reproductive success? Bailey et al. (1992) found that, among the Efe, women's ovarian function and resulting birth schedules showed a seasonal pattern that correlated only with food availability—a clear physiological reproductive response to changing ecological conditions. Interbirth interval similarly responds to ecological conditions and the balancing of effort and risk. !Kung women have interbirth intervals of about 4 years (Blurton Jones & Sibley, 1978). Because predators are prevalent, !Kung women, who depend on bush foods, may carry their children at least occasionally for up to 6 years. Blurton Jones (1986, 1987), using a model of "backload" (weight of child plus foraged material), could predict interbirth intervals and mortality patterns. The number of successful descendants was maximized for bush-living women not by maximizing rate of births, but by responding to the conflict between production of a new child versus the cost of such production on the survivorship of other children. !Kung women living in compounds, not dependent on bush foods, showed quite different birth schedules.

Among the Ache (e.g., Hurtado, Hawkes, & Hill, 1985; Hurtado et al., 1992), the Hiwi (Hurtado et al., 1992), and the Ye'kwana (Hames, 1988), nursing women can forage less than others, and this was probably broadly true through human evolution. In some societies, these costs are partially defrayed by peer or sibling child care, and the availability of such peer or sibling caregivers can have an impact on a mother's lifetime fertility. On Ifaluk, for example, a woman's lifetime fertility was correlated with the sex of her first two children: Women whose first two children were girls had greater lifetime fertility than others (Turke, 1988). Because daughters assist in child care on Ifaluk, mothers whose first children are daughters defray some costs.

In some societies, wealth could be used to defray these costs by hiring wet nurses. A dramatic example is given by Hrdy (1992), who found that interbirth interval, fertility, and infant mortality all varied with mother's status. The richest women had very short interbirth intervals, very high fertility, and low infant mortality. The linear relationship between the cost of a wet nurse and infant survivorship meant that the richest women, who could afford the best wet nurses, fared best. Among the bourgeois, complexities created more variation in pattern. Poor women had longer interbirth intervals, lower fertility, and high infant mortality; the wet nurses fared worst of all, with very long interbirth intervals, very low fertility, and very high infant mortality.

In Western industrial nations today, women's work, although in the marketplace rather than the field, still conflicts with child care. Fertility may show a nonlinear relationship to the wealth women earn for themselves. Very poor women (many single mothers on welfare) have lower age-specific fertility at all ages than all other women (Rank, 1989), perhaps reflecting the importance of effective investment. Highly educated women, particularly those who hold professional positions, also have low fertility (Kasarda, Billy, & West, 1986); these women remained in school for longer than most women, they married later, and fewer of them married. Their children, however, tended to be well invested. For women earning their own income, an age-old conflict is magnified; maternal investment in one child may come at the expense of investment in others. What is invested in work cannot be invested in child care. Here we have few data, and more work is needed. Most studies do not distinguish household income by source; yet we need these data to understand the ecology of fertility in modern societies.

## SINGLE-PARENT VERSUS BIPARENTAL CARE

The prior logic leads to the suggestion that female humans, like other female primates, will frequently bear the burden of offspring-specific true parental investment (Trivers, 1972). In other primates, male parental care ranges from absent to occasional. But male mammals, and particularly male humans, can be quite caring of young. The economic defensibility or availability of resources seems to be important (e.g., Kurland & Gaulin, 1984; Low, 1989); if parental resources are predictable and defensible, males are more likely to attempt to control these and use them to attract females and invest in offspring. If resources are not economically defensible, females and juveniles become autonomous units (cf. Hill & Low, 1990; Low, 1989). Uniparental (usually female) care is favored if young are precocial, food is readily harvestable, and predation rates are either low or so high that parents are unable to deter predators. These are all situations in which increased parental investment cannot affect juveniles' probable success (cf. Lancaster, 1989; Lancaster & Lancaster, 1987; Low, 1978).

Male parental care, from food provisioning to protection, may have been important in the evolution of a number of unusual human life-history attributes. Remember that humans are peculiar in the scheduling of fertility, compared with other primates: They are altricial, fast growing, late maturing, and have relatively good juvenile survival, but have short interbirth intervals. Perhaps these unusual attributes interact with significant male economic contributions to mother and child, which allow high age-specific fertility for females despite the great requirements of large, altricial offspring.

Even today, the promise of male parental care appears to influence fertility patterns. In the United States from 1975 to 1981, 65% of pregnancies among unmarried women were terminated by abortion, compared with about 10% among pregnant married women (Henshaw, Forrest, & Blaine, 1984). A child conceived by an unmarried woman may be delivered only if resources are available from sources other than self-support. In a study of teenagers comparing terminators to those who got married or gave birth while remaining single, Leibowitz, Eisen, and Chow (1985) found that 42% of women who expected financial help bore the child, compared with 11% of women who had no help ($p < .01$; data re-analyzed by Hill & Low, 1990). Similarly, 57% of women who had state financial aid bore the child versus 29% of those who did not ($p < .05$). Thus, single women on welfare may be more likely to bear children than single women with no support. Still, Rank (1989) has found that single mothers on welfare, lacking male or familial investment, have lower age-specific fertility at all ages than other women.

Is male care always true parental investment—care that, once given to one child, cannot be given to another (Trivers, 1972)? Some scholars argue that monogamy may result from the relative benefits of particular patterns of male paternal care that preclude other matings; monogamy only occurs when the benefits of true parental investment outweigh the benefits of seeking other matings. Yet, monogamy is rare among humans (Murdock, 1967), and polygyny is the most common marriage system. Male care can occur in polygynous systems, and women (or their families) may be choosing for male resource control or other qualities (e.g., Lancaster & Kaplan, 1992). Smuts and Gubernick (1992) note that male care of and association with young in primates occurs not only in monogamous breeding systems, but in single-male and multimale polygynous systems. They suggested that male care of infants may represent an evolved form of mating effort, entailing a mutually advantageous, reciprocal relationship between a male and a female. This would mean that male care probably preceded the pair bond in evolutionary time, and that, even today, some male investment in children may represent mating, as well as parental, effort. Certainly male investment patterns seem to respond to the relative effect of male mating, versus parental, effort on male reproductive success (Lancaster & Kaplan, 1992).

## FERTILITY AND CHILDREN'S PRODUCTIVITY

Across other primates, females and their young are relatively independent economic foraging units. Male reproductive success is likely to vary with male status, which does not translate into increased offspring nutrition. Female reproduction is constrained by the demands of parental investment. In humans, because both parents may contribute to the food base and because children may forage, there has been some exploration of the possibility of children defraying their own costs (i.e., fertility should be higher when children can forage more than they eat). The patterns seen are consistent with the behavioral ecological hypothesis that resources contribute to reproductive success (Low, 1989, 1990b; Low & Clarke, 1992), but not consistent with the children-as-resource-producers hypothesis (e.g., Hammel, Johansson, & Gunsberg, 1983). Even in hunter–gatherer societies, grandmothers are still producing for their grandchildren; resources always flow down to descendants, in the societies in which measurements have been made (e.g., Hawkes, O'Connell, & Blurton Jones, 1989), rather than eventually reversing and flowing "up," as Caldwell (1982) suggested. Often, data exist to test between these hypotheses. For example, in agricultural societies, if children were perceived by parents as producers, not only land owners but land workers should have higher fertility. Yet land *owners* typically have higher fertility and larger resulting families no matter what the economic times; and landowners' family size shows less variance than that of nonlandowners (Cain, 1985; Hayami, 1980; Hughes, 1986; Low & Clarke, 1991; McInnis, 1977; Pfister, 1989a, 1989b; Voland, 1990). Land ownership apparently provides a more reliable resource control, a buffer against hard times. Here, too, is an area in which further data could help clarify and test conflicting hypotheses.

## ALLOCATION AMONG OFFSPRING

Variation in ecological or resource parameters affects the reproductive costs and benefits of investment in current versus future offspring, and among current offspring. For example, environmental unpredictability is important: If future chances are uncertain, an individual profits more from continued investment in the current offspring than in curtailing that investment for the sake of potential future offspring. Some offspring are worth more to parents than others, and all offspring are expected to attempt to divert parental investment to themselves at the expense of their siblings (parent–offspring conflict; Trivers, 1974).

Birth order and sex are two important offspring characteristics that can influence the parents' costs and benefits for investment. Older (earlier born) offspring have fewer chances to die before becoming reproductive than younger offspring, and thus have higher reproductive value (Fisher, 1958). It is not surprising, then, that parents might favor some offspring over others, especially when resources are limiting. "Choice" among offspring may be seen even at physiological levels. Subtle maternal responses (e.g., adjustment of blood flow to the uterus) during pregnancy fit a life-history model of lifetime reproductive optimization (Peacock, 1990, 1991).

### Sex Biases in Investment

In many polygynous species, including humans, male offspring are more expensive energetically to raise than female offspring (Daly & Wilson, 1983; Trivers & Willard, 1973); they are carried longer *in utero,* they are larger at birth, they nurse more and more frequently, and they are weaned later. Trivers and Willard (1973) argued that, in polygynous species under such conditions, females in good nutritional condition are more likely to bear sons than daughters. A more broadly applicable statement might be: When variance in reproductive success of one sex exceeds that of the other (as in elephant seals or any polygynous species), or when parental investment can influence the reproductive success of one sex but not the other (as in baboons), there should be a correlation between parental condition and investment in that sex (cf. Clutton-Brock, 1991).

Trivers and Willard (1973) assumed that mother's physiological condition (resources available to rear a successful offspring) would decline with age. In nonhuman species, and in many preindustrial societies and developing countries, this is appropriate. Whenever the nutritional condition of mothers does not decline with age, a male bias in sex ratio might be found in older mothers (Low, 1991; Williams, 1966). In polygynous species with repeated reproduction, as with primates, if a female's condition is good, a male bias is predicted to be profitable as the female nears the end of her reproduction—to invest more heavily, with a greater potential reproductive profit if successful (e.g., male-biased sex ratios for older female gorillas; Mace, 1990). In 19th-century Sweden, mothers over age 35 showed a sex-ratio bias toward sons, and mothers under 25 toward daughters (Low, 1991). Such patterns underlie other influences (e.g., parental sex preference; Kishor, 1993; Knodel, 1988).

Perhaps no other species exhibits the degree of resource transfer that can take place through inheritance within human families. In societies with heritable goods, the size of a family and the sex of siblings may influence men's and women's ability to marry at appropriate times somewhat differently. Resource control is an effective and widespread strategy for men in acquiring mates.

Resource inheritance biases are important because they can influence survivorship and likelihood of reproduction, especially for sons. Inheritance is frequently biased by legitimacy, birth order, and sex: Resources are funneled into older sons and to sons at the expense of daughters. Within polygynous marital systems, inheritance is strikingly male-biased (Hartung, 1982), precisely the pattern predicted if male reproductive success varies more than female reproductive success, and male success is influenced by resource control. In many societies, earlier born sons tend to inherit the greatest proportion of the resources, even where more equal distribution is stipulated by law (e.g., 19th-century Sweden). Among 15th- and 16th-century Portuguese nobles, the proportion of ever-married men and women decreased with birth order, as did fertility for married individuals (Boone, 1986, 1988). In Sweden, women's lifetime reproduction decreased as their number of siblings increased (Low, 1991; Low & Clarke, 1992). For men, only the number of brothers mattered, suggesting that brothers represent resource competitors for men, and that as total sibship size increases for women, they are more likely to be drawn into caring for their siblings (regardless of sex), at some cost to their own reproduction.

Voland (1984) examined the effect of father's status on children's survival in a 19th-century German parish. The overall sex ratio of children born was almost exactly even. Deaths during the first year of life due to parental neglect were status-related: For farmers, daughters were likely to be considered less desirable than sons, and therefore suffered higher mortality; for other classes, the reverse appeared to be true. Thus, Voland has evidence of uneven parental investment tied to the perceived value of each sex for parents in different classes. In India, too, sex biases in survivorship exist, influenced by cultural and economic considerations, and the resulting perception of the value of children of each sex (Kishor, 1993). Kinship systems and female labor force participation are of primary importance. Such patterns can vary; in Sweden during the same period, Low (1991; see also review by Low et al., 1992) found the typical mammalian pattern: Daughters survived better than sons.

There may be important sex-investment biases in contemporary society. In contemporary Tennessee, sons in higher status families fare better than others (Abernethey & Yip, 1990). Among polygynous Mormons, sex ratio and parental status are correlated, as predicted by Trivers and Willard (Mealey & Mackey, 1990). Gaulin and Robbins (1991) found a series of other Trivers–Willard effects in contemporary U.S. society. They examined interbirth interval, birth weight, and proportion of children nursed as they related to income and the presence of an adult male in the household. They found that as income increased, so did interbirth interval and percent breastfed—for sons, but not daughters. For all seven of their measures, patterns differed for sons versus daughters: Daughters received relatively more from low-investment mothers, and sons got more from high-investment mothers.

### Abortion, Infanticide, Abandonment, and Neglect

Parental withdrawal of investment seems at first obviously counterselective. In other species, it is typically not parents, but reproductive competitors (e.g., males taking over a harem), who commit infanticide (e.g., langurs: Hrdy, 1974, 1978, 1979; lions: Packer & Pusey, 1983, 1984). In some female-bonded primate species, powerful matrilines may harass subordinate females and wound or kill their offspring (Wasser & Barash, 1983). Across primate species, the overwhelming majority of infanticides is committed by immigrant males, or males who do not belong to the victim's social group (Struhsaker & Leland, 1986). In humans also, stepparents are more likely to abuse or neglect children than genetic parents (Daly & Wilson, 1984, 1985, 1987).

Yet, parents can commit infanticide, abortion, and abandonment. Because each infant requires great investment, investment biases, even to the extent of infanticide, can sometimes be reproductively profitable (Daly & Wilson, 1988). Selective reasons for terminating investment in an offspring include: mother's ability to invest, mother's access to additional resources (family, mate), child's ability to succeed, and the economic and reproductive value of other existing or possible future children. Cross-culturally, deformed or seriously ill newborns are at great risk for infanticide (Daly & Wilson, 1988). Similarly, when circumstances reduce a mother's chance of successful investment (e.g., too-close births, twins, lack of an investing male), infanticide or neglect (e.g., Bugos & McCarthy, 1984; Daly & Wilson, 1988) is more likely. Abortion, too, appears more common in circumstances in which the birth of an additional child is likely to reduce the mother's lifetime reproductive success (Hill & Low, 1990; Torres & Forrest, 1988). As women age and their reproductive value declines, termination of investment is less likely. Even attitudes toward abortion in our society are related to the proportion of women in any group who are "at risk" of unwanted pregnancy (Betzig & Lombardo, 1991).

In some societies, a sex preference in infanticide exists; this represents a conundrum if it becomes widespread and persistent, as Fisher (1958) noted, because the rare sex comes to be more valuable in any marriage market. Laland, Kumm, and Feldman (1994) have shown that persistent sex-preferential infanticide may feed back and influence the birth sex ratio. Many cases of long-term sex-biased infanticide may simply be maladaptive, but there are examples that suggest evolved parental strategies. In a detailed study of female-biased infanticide among the Inuit, Smith and Smith (1994) concluded that parents may be trying to match their number of sons with local prevailing sex ratios. Dickemann (1979, 1981) found pertinent biases in sex preference in hypergynous societies. In these societies, women may marry up and men down, but the reverse is not allowed. Thus, daughters are valuable to lower-class families, but costly to upper-class families. Dickemann found that there was no single within-society sex bias, but that in high-status families daughters were killed. These patterns, Dickemann argued, probably also represent a Trivers–Willard effect. It is possible, too, that (otherwise rare) male-biased infanticide occurred in high-status families (Parry, 1979).

Patterns of child abandonment, like infanticide and abortion, reflect such selective considerations as a mother's ability to invest in the child (including own health, familial resources, economic conditions), and the child's health, legitimacy, and sex (e.g., Silk, 1980, 1987). When children are given up by their parents for adoption in traditional societies in Oceania and West Africa, it is most often to close consanguineal kin; parental investment may continue. Parents who give up their children often do so only temporarily (Silk, 1987). Child abandonment in historical France (Fuchs, 1984), Spain (Sherwood, 1988), and Russia (Ransel, 1988) appears related to economic factors and mother's abilities. Similarly, Boswell's (1990) historical overview of child abandonment reveals that 46% (29/63) of cases he examined were related to maternal ability to invest, despite great variation in time, country, and other circumstances; when resource allocation and offspring quality were considered, selective reasons were apparent in 77% of cases ($^{49}\!/_{63}$).

## LIFE SPAN AND SENESCENCE

Among primates, humans are relatively long lived (maximum life span of 115 years vs. 29 for macaques and 44 for chimpanzees; Stearns, 1992). We live 83% longer than would be predicted from our size (Harvey et al., 1986). Harvey et al. noted Sacher's (1959) finding—that bigger brained primates live longer—although they pointed out that other measures such as adrenal gland weight (Economos, 1980) correlate even better than brain weight with longevity, and correlational analyses do not suggest any appropriate causality. It is still not clear why we are so long lived. Medical advances are not the answer; most evidence suggests that people in traditional societies also had long lives (e.g., Early & Peters, 1990; Hill & Hurtado, 1991; Howell, 1979; see Hill & Hurtado, 1991, for a review). The current weight of evidence suggests that, although reduction of accidental death, for example, has changed human life expectancy slightly, the existing maximum life span is not a product of medical advance, but of human evolution. One important inference from this is that there is little chance medical science will be able to change human life span.

In humans, as in other primates and most mammals, males senesce and die sooner than females, and the survivorship curves of the two sexes are quite different. Older explanations argued for "male vulnerability" because males are the heterogametic sex (Hutt, 1972)—they have an "unprotected" Y chromosome. But such suggestions do not explain the fact that, for example, males in many bird species (in birds, females are heterogametic) still die sooner than females. In fact, the correlation is with breeding system, and the cause is the different payoffs for males and females of risky mating effort. In polygynous species, especially those with limited or no male parental care, males evolve to be mating specialists, with the attendant high fixed costs and risks of failure. In such systems, risk-taking males are predicted to have higher death rates, and indeed they do.

Old humans do die eventually, but first, like old soldiers, they begin to "fade away." This raises the issue of why organisms senesce and why they do so at such varying rates. Older explanations like "wearing out" and "toxin accumulation" would not predict rate differences. Species should all senesce at similar rates, and that is simply not true. Older group-level "adaptive" explanations (e.g., death clears the way for others; Curtis, 1963) simply do not make sense. Arguments that senescence is selectively irrelevant (e.g., Comfort, 1956) do not explain why senescence actually begins at the age of first reproduction, not late in life.

Williams (1957) and Hamilton (1966) first pointed out that, other things being equal, longer life should be favored by natural selection. Senescence arises, in part, because of pleiotropic effects (a single gene can have multiple effects). Natural selection favors genes with favorable early effects. Because reproductive value (Fisher, 1958) declines from the age of first reproduction, at some age selection cannot distinguish between simple early good effects and early good effects accompanied by later (pleiotropic) deleterious effects; these later costs affect fewer individuals in any population (due to age-specific mortality schedules), and they affect a smaller proportion of the reproductive lives of those remaining individuals. In this way, deleterious genetic effects late in life accumulate; as we age, if it is not one complaint, it is another. Senescence, then, is a cost, not an evolved phenomenon—we senesce because we are stuck with it.

Human senescence is unusual in another way as well. All physiological systems senesce, and reproductive function is no exception (e.g., Dunbar, 1987). Yet, human female reproductive function decays decades earlier than other systems in either sex (including male reproductive function; e.g., Gaulin, 1980). Most human physiological systems decay at a steady rate from about age 30, and function at age 65 is about 60%–70% of maximum (e.g., Mildvan & Strehler, 1960). Among most mammals, female reproductive function decays at about the same rate as other systems (Smith & Polacheck, 1981), and even very old females retain some fertility. Another way to say this is that female life expectancy at age of first reproduction is usually not longer than expected reproductive life (Nishida, Takasaki, & Takahata, 1990).

But human females lose reproductive function dramatically after age 30 (see Hill & Hurtado, 1991, which combines data from Wood, 1990, and Mildvan & Strehler, 1960). Women in natural fertility (noncontracepting) societies show maximum fertility between ages 20 and 30; fertility then declines to zero between ages 45 and 50 (Ravenholt & Chao, 1974; Wood, 1990, reviewed by Hill & Hurtado, 1991). In other mammals, the oldest females might spend 10% of their lives after their last birth; in contrast, human females live perhaps a third of their years after menopause. In developed nations today, average age at menopause (reproductive system senescence in women) is about 50.5 years (Snowden et al., 1989). Whether this represents a shift from patterns in traditional societies is unclear.

Such a difference in rate of senescence among systems is quite rare. A few other species (none primate) show long life either in very low-fecundity condition or after something similar to menopause—total reproductive senescence. Female elephants (Croze, Hillman, & Lang, 1981) and perhaps horses show increasing length of interbirth interval with age. In toothed whales (Marsh & Kasuya, 1986) and some strains of laboratory mice (Festing & Blackmore, 1971; Jones, 1975), female reproductive function appears to cease entirely well before the end of life, as in humans.

An intuitively appealing hypothesis is that, in species such as elephants, horses, and humans, in which offspring may depend for some time on their mother, it may pay older females to shift from production of additional offspring to continued high-level care of existing offspring. As noted earlier, in traditional societies, grandmothers continue to contribute to the well-being of their families (Hawkes et al., 1989; Hurtado & Hill, 1990; Lancaster & King, 1992). In other primate species, grandmothers help their kin (Cheney & Seyfarth, 1990; Fairbanks & McGuire, 1986). Children born to very old men but young mothers might survive better than children born to older women, if the nature of male and female parental investment differs between the sexes. Hill and Hurtado (1991) have performed the most direct tests of the grandmother hypothesis. They were unable to falsify it, but their calculations suggest that, under reasonable assumptions, the reproductive gains would be greater for women's continued reproduction, rather than a switch to care of existing kin. This leaves us with a puzzle requiring more research. It seems unlikely that if continued reproduction were reproductively profitable it would be impossible.

## HUMANS AS PRIMATES

In some ways, humans are a typical large social primate, but important aspects of our physiology, life history, and demography are unusual. Many of these, from menopause to dental maturation, reflect our evolutionary history, but their functional significance is still not well understood. We evolved as group-living, polygynous, intelligent, and highly social primates, with late maturation, short interbirth intervals, and very long lives, although with reproductive senescence in females. Our large brains and high intelligence are almost certainly related to many of these traits. Our social complexity makes analysis complicated. Perhaps analyzing our life history in the context of primate life histories will be useful in beginning to understand why our lives are shaped as they are.

## REFERENCES

Abernethey, V., & Yip, R. (1990). Parent characteristics and sex differential infant mortality: The case in Tennessee. *Human Biology, 62*(2), 279–290.

Alexander, R. D. (1979). *Darwinism and human affairs.* Seattle: University of Washington Press.

Alexander, R. D. (1990). *How did humans evolve? Reflections on the uniquely unique species.* Special Publication No. 1, Museum of Zoology, University of Michigan.

Alexander, R. D., & Noonan, K. (1979). Concealment of ovulation, parental care, and human social evolution. In N. A. Chagnon & W. Irons (Eds.), *Evolutionary biology and human social behavior: An anthropological approach* (pp. 402–435). North Scituate, MA: Duxbury Press.

Bailey, R. C., Jenike, M. R., Ellison, P. T., Bentley, G. R., Harrigan, A. M., & Peacock, N. R. (1992). The ecology of birth seasonality among agriculturalists in central Africa. *Journal of Biosocial Science, 24,* 393–412.

Barkow, J. H. (1977). Conformity to ethos and reproductive success in two Hausa communities: An empirical evaluation. *Ethos, 5,* 409–425.

Betzig, L. B., & Lombardo, L. H. (1991). Who's pro-choice and why. *Ethology and Sociobiology, 13,* 49–71.

Birdsall, N. (1980). Population growth and poverty in the developing world. *Population Bulletin, 35*(5), 3–46.

Blurton Jones, N. (1986). Bushman birth spacing: A test for optimal interbirth intervals. *Ethology and Sociobiology, 7,* 91–105.

Blurton Jones, N. (1987). Bushman birth spacing: Direct tests of some simple predictions. *Ethology and Sociobiology, 8,* 183–203.

Blurton Jones, N., & Sibley, R. M. (1978). Testing adaptiveness of culturally determined behavior: Do Bushman women maximize their reproductive success by spacing births widely and foraging seldom? In N. Blurton Jones & V. Reynolds (Eds.), *Human behavior and adaptation* (Symposium No. 18 of The Society for the Study of Human Biology, pp. 135–157). London: Taylor & Francis.

Boone, J. L., III. (1986). Parental investment and elite family structure in preindustrial states: A case study of late medieval-early modern Portuguese genealogies. *American Anthropology, 88,* 859.

Boone, J. L., III. (1988). Parental investment social subordination and population processes among the 15th and 16th century Portuguese nobility. In L. Betzig, M. Borgerhoff Mulder, & P. Turke (Eds.), *Human reproductive behaviour: A Darwinian perspective* (pp. 201–220). Cambridge, England: Cambridge University Press.

Borgerhoff Mulder, M. (1988a). Reproductive success in three Kipsigis cohorts. In T. H. Clutton-Brock (Ed.), *Reproductive success* (pp. 419–435). Chicago: University of Chicago Press.

Borgerhoff Mulder, M. (1988b). Kipsigis bridewealth payments. In L. L. Betzig, M. Borgerhoff Mulder, & P. Turke (Eds.), *Human reproductive behaviour: A Darwinian perspective* (pp. 65–82). Cambridge, England: Cambridge University Press.

Boswell, J. (1990). *The kindness of strangers: The abandonment of children in Western Europe from late antiquity to the Renaissance.* New York: Vintage Press.

Bugos, P. E., & McCarthy, L. M. (1984). Ayoreo infanticide: A case study. In G. Hausfater & S. B. Hrdy (Eds.), *Infanticide: Comparative and evolutionary perspectives* (pp. 503–520). New York: Aldine.

Burley, N. (1979). The evolution of concealed ovulation. *American Naturalist, 114,* 835–858.

Cain, M. (1985). On the relationship between landholding and fertility. *Population Studies, 39,* 5–15.

Caldwell, J. (1982). *Theory of fertility decline.* New York: Academic Press.

Case, T. J. (1978). Endothermy and parental care in the terrestrial vertebrate. *American Naturalist, 112,* 861–874.

Chagnon, N. A. (1979). Is reproductive success equal in egalitarian societies? In N. A. Chagnon & W. Irons (Eds.), *Evolutionary biology and human social behavior: An anthropological perspective* (pp. 374–401). Boston: Duxbury.

Chagnon, N. A. (1982). Sociodemographic attributes of nepotism in tribal populations: Man the rule-breaker. In Kings' College Sociobiology Group (Eds.), *Current problems in sociobiology* (pp. 291–318). Cambridge, England: Cambridge University Press.

Chagnon, N. A. (1988). Life histories blood revenge and warfare in a tribal population. *Science, 239*, 985–992.

Charlesworth, B. (1980). *Evolution in age-structured populations.* Cambridge, England: Cambridge University Press.

Charnov, E. L. (1991). Evolution of life history variation among female mammals. *Proceedings of the National Academy of Sciences, 88*, 1134–1137.

Cheney, D., & Seyfarth, R. (1990). *How monkeys see the world.* Chicago: University of Chicago Press.

Chisholm, J. S. (1993). Death, hope, and sex: Life-history theory and the development of reproductive strategies. *Current Anthropology, 34*(1), 1–46.

Clutton-Brock, T. H. (1991). *The evolution of parental care.* Princeton, NJ: Princeton University Press.

Comfort, A. (1956). *Ageing: The biology of senescence.* New York: Rinehart & Winston.

Cronk, L. (1991). Wealth status and reproductive success among the Mukogodo of Kenya. *American Anthropology, 93*(2), 345–360.

Croze, H., Hillman, A. K., & Lang, E. M. (1981). Elephants and their habitats: How do they tolerate each other? In C. W. Fowler & T. D. Smith (Eds.), *Dynamics of large mammal populations* (pp. 297–316). New York: Wiley.

Curtis, H. J. (1963). Biological mechanisms underlying the aging process. *Science, 141*, 686–694.

Daly, M., & Wilson, M. (1983). *Sex evolution and behavior* (2nd ed.). Boston: Willard Grant Press.

Daly, M., & Wilson, M. (1984). A sociobiological analysis of human infanticide. In G. Hausfater & S. B. Hrdy (Eds.), *Infanticide: Comparative and evolutionary perspectives* (pp. 487–502). New York: Aldine.

Daly, M., & Wilson, M. (1985). Child abuse and other risks of not living with both parents. *Ethology and Sociobiology, 6*, 197–210.

Daly, M., & Wilson, M. (1987). Children as homicide victims. In R. J. Gelles & J. B. Lancaster (Eds.), *Child abuse and neglect: Biosocial dimensions* (pp. 201–214). New York: Aldine.

Daly, M., & Wilson, M. (1988). *Homicide.* Hawthorne, NY: Aldine.

Darwin, C. (1871). *The descent of man, and selection in relation to sex* (2 vols.). London: John Murray.

Dickemann, M. (1979). The ecology of mating systems in hypergynous dowry societies. *Social Science Information, 18*, 163–195.

Dickemann, M. (1981). Paternal confidence and dowry competition: A biocultural analysis of purdah. In R. D. Alexander & D. W. Tinkle (Eds.), *Natural selection and social behavior* (pp. 417–438). New York: Chiron Press.

Dienske, H. (1986). A comparative approach to the question of why human infants develop so slowly. In J. G. Else & P. C. Lee (Eds.), *Primate ontogeny, cognition, and social behavior* (pp. 147–154). London: Cambridge University Press.

Drake, M. (1969). *Population and society in Norway: 1735–1865.* Cambridge, England: Cambridge University Press.

Dunbar, R. (1987). Demography and reproduction. In B. B. Smuts, D. L. Cheney, R. M. Seyfarth, R. W. Wrangham, & T. Struhsaker (Eds.), *Primate societies* (pp. 240–249). Chicago: University of Chicago Press.

Early, J. D., & Peters, J. F. (1990). *The population dynamics of the Mucajai Yanomamo.* New York: Academic Press.

Economos, A. C. (1980). Brain-life span conjecture: A re-evaluation of the evidence. *Gerontology, 26*, 82–89.

Fadiman, J. A. (1982). *An oral history of tribal warfare: The Meru of Mt. Kenya.* Athens, OH: Ohio University Press.

Fairbanks, L. A., & McGuire, M. T. (1986). Determinants of fecundity and reproductive success in captive vervet monkeys. *American Journal of Primatology, 7,* 27–38.

Festing, M. F. W., & Blackmore, D. K. (1971). Life span of specified pathogen-free (MRC Category 4) mice and rats. *Laboratory Animal Bulletin, 5,* 179–192.

Fisher, R. A. (1958). *The genetical theory of natural selection* (2nd rev. ed.). New York: Dover.

Flinn, M. V. (1986). Correlates of reproductive success in a Caribbean village. *Human Ecology, 14,* 225–243.

Flinn, M. V., & Low, B. (1986). Resource distribution social competition and mating patterns in human societies. In D. Rubenstein & R. Wrangham (Eds.), *Ecological aspects of social evolution* (pp. 217–243). Princeton, NJ: Princeton University Press.

Frank, S. A. (1990). Sex allocation theory for birds and mammals. *Annual Review of Ecology and Systematics, 21,* 13–55.

Fuchs, R. (1984). *Abandoned children: Foundlings and child welfare in nineteenth-century France.* Albany: SUNY Press.

Gaulin, S. J. (1980). Sexual dimorphism in the post-reproductive lifespan: Possible causes. *Human Evolution, 9,* 227–232.

Gaulin, S. J. C., & Robbins, C. J. (1991). Trivers–Willard effect in contemporary North American society. *American Journal of Phys. Anthropol., 85,* 61–68.

Geronimus, A. T. (1987). On teenage childbearing and neonatal mortality in the United States. *Population and Development Review, 13,* 245–279.

Geronimus, A. T. (1991). Teenage childbearing and social and reproductive disadvantage: The evolution of complex questions and the demise of simple answers. *Family Relations, 40,* 463–471.

Hammel, E. A., Johansson, S., & Gunsberg, C. (1983, Winter). The value of children during industrialization: Sex ratios in childhood in nineteenth-century America. *Journal of Family History,* pp. 400–417.

Hamilton, W. D. (1966). The moulding of senescence by natural selection. *Journal of Theoretical Biology, 12,* 12–45.

Hartung, J. (1982). Polygyny and inheritance of wealth. *Current Anthropology, 23,* 1–12.

Harvey, P., Martin, R. D., & Clutton-Brock, T. H. (1986). Life histories in comparative perspective. In B. B. Smuts, D. L. Cheney, R. M. Seyfarth, R. W. Wrangham, & T. Struhsaker (Eds.), *Primate societies* (pp. 181–196). Chicago: University of Chicago Press.

Harvey, P. H., & Pagel, M. D. (1991). *The comparative method in evolutionary biology. Oxford series in ecology and evolution.* Oxford: Oxford University Press.

Harvey, P. H., & Read, A. F. (1988). How and why do mammalian life histories vary? In M. S. Boyce (Ed.), *Evolution of life histories: Pattern and process from mammals* (pp. 213–232). New Haven, CT: Yale University Press.

Hawkes, K. (1991). Showing off: Tests of another hypothesis about men's foraging goals. *Ethology and Sociobiology, 11,* 29–54.

Hawkes, K., O'Connell, J. F., & Blurton Jones, N. G. (1989). Hardworking Hadza grandmothers. In V. Standen & R. A. Foley (Eds.), *Comparative socioecology* (pp. 341–366). London: Blackwell.

Hayami, A. (1980). Class differences in marriage and fertility among Tokugawa villagers in Mino Province. *Keio Economic Studies, 17*(1), 1–16.

Henshaw, S. K., Forrest, J. D., & Blaine, E. B. (1984). Abortion services in the United States. *Family Planning Perspectives, 16,* 119–127.

Hill, E. M., & Low, B. (1990). Contemporary abortion patterns: A life history approach. *Ethology and Sociobiology, 13,* 35–48.

Hill, J. (1984). Prestige and reproductive success in man. *Ethology and Sociobiology, 5,* 77–95.

Hill, K., & Hurtado, M. (1991). The evolution of premature reproductive senescence and menopause in human females: An evaluation of the "Grandmother Hypothesis." *Human Nature, 2*(4), 313–349.

Hill, K., & Kaplan, H. (1988). Tradeoffs in male and female reproductive strategies among the Ache. In L. Betzig, M. Borgerhoff Mulder, & P. W. Turke (Eds.), *Human reproductive behaviour: A Darwinian perspective* (pp. 277–289). Cambridge, England: Cambridge University Press.

Hofman, M. A. (1983). Energy metabolism, brain size, and longevity in mammals. *Quarterly Review Biology, 58*, 495–512.

Holmes, R. (1985). *Acts of war: The behavior of men in battle.* New York: The Free Press.

Howell, N. (1979). *Demography of the Dobe !Kung.* New York: Academic Press.

Hrdy, S. B. (1974). Male-male competition and infanticide among the lemurs (*Presbytis entellus*) of Abu Rajasthan. *Folia Primatology, 22*, 19–58.

Hrdy, S. B. (1978). Allomaternal care and the abuse of infants among Hanuman langurs. In D. J. Chivers & P. Herbert (Eds.), *Recent advances in primatology* (Vol. 1). New York: Academic Press.

Hrdy, S. B. (1979). Infanticide among animals: A review classification and implications for the reproductive strategies of females. *Ethology and Sociobiology, 1*, 13–40.

Hrdy, S. B. (1981). *The woman that never evolved.* Cambridge, MA: Harvard University Press.

Hrdy, S. B. (1992). Fitness tradeoffs in the history and evolution of delegated mothering with special reference to wet-nursing abandonment and infanticide. *Ethology and Sociobiology, 13*, 409–442.

Hughes, A. L. (1986). Reproductive success and occupational class in eighteenth-century Lancashire England. *Social Biology, 33*, 109–115.

Hughes, A. L. (1988). *Evolution and human kinship.* Oxford, England: Oxford University Press.

Humphrey, N. K. (1976). The social function of intellect. In P. P. G. Bateson & R. A. Hinde (Eds.), *Growing points in ethology* (pp. 303–325). Cambridge, England: Cambridge University Press.

Hurtado, A. M., Hawkes, K., & Hill, K. (1985). Female subsistence strategies among Ache hunter-gatherers of eastern Paraguay. *Human Ecology, 13*, 1–28.

Hurtado, A. M., Hill, K., Kaplan, H., & Hurtado, I. (1992). Tradeoffs between food acquisition and child care among Hiwi and Ache women. *Human Nature, 3*, 185–216.

Hurtado, M., & Hill, K. (1990). Seasonality in a foraging society: Variation in diet, work effort, fertility, and the sexual division of labor among the Hiwi of Venezuela. *Journal of Anthropological Research, 46*, 293–346.

Hutt, C. (1972). *Males and females.* London: Penguin.

Irons, W. (1979). Cultural and biological success. In N. Chagnon & W. Irons (Eds.), *Evolutionary biology and human social behavior: An anthropological perspective* (pp. 257–272). North Scituate, MA: Duxbury.

Jolly, A. (1985). *The evolution of primate behavior* (2nd ed.). New York: Macmillan.

Jones, E. C. (1975). The post-reproductive phase in mammals. In P. van Keep & C. Lauritzen (Eds.), *Frontiers of hormone research* (Vol. 3, pp. 1–20). Basel: Karger.

Josephson, S. C. (1993). Status, reproductive success, and marrying polygynously. *Ethology and Sociobiology, 14*, 391–396.

Kaplan, H. (1994). Evolutionary and wealth flow theories of fertility: Empirical tests and new models. *Population and Development Review, 20*(4), 753–791.

Kaplan, H., & Hill, K. (1985). Hunting ability and reproductive success among male Ache foragers: Preliminary results. *Current Anthropology, 26*, 131–133.

Kaplan, H., Lancaster, J., Bock, J. A., & Johnson, S. E. (1995). Fertility and fitness among Albuquerque men: A competitive labor market theory. In R. I. M. Dunbar (Ed.), *Human reproductive decisions: Biological and social perspectives* (pp. 96–136). New York: Macmillan.

Kasarda, J. D., Billy, J. O. G., & West, K. (1986). *Status enhancement and fertility: Reproductive responses to social mobility and educational opportunity.* New York: Academic Press.

Keegan, J. (1987). *The mask of command.* London: Jonathan Cape.

Kishor, S. (1993). May God give sons to all: Gender and child mortality in India. *American Sociological Review, 58,* 247–265.

Knodel, J. (1988). *Demographic behavior in the past: German village populations in the 18th and 19th centuries.* Cambridge, England: Cambridge University Press.

Kurland, J., & Gaulin, S. (1984). The evolution of male parental investment: Effects of genetic relatedness and feeding ecology on the allocation of reproductive effort. In D. M. Taub (Ed.), *Primate paternalism* (pp. 259–306). New York: Van Nostrand Reinhold.

Laland, K. N., Kumm, J., & Feldman, M. W. (1994). Gene-culture coevolutionary theory: A test case. *Current Anthropology, 36*(1), 131–156.

Lancaster, J. B. (1986). Human adolescence and reproduction: An evolutionary perspective. In J. Lancaster & B. Hamburg (Eds.), *School-age pregnancy and parenthood: Biosocial dimensions* (pp. 17–37). New York: Aldine de Gruyter.

Lancaster, J. B. (1989). Evolutionary and cross-cultural perspectives on single-parenthood. In R. W. Bell & N. J. Bell (Eds.), *Sociobiology and the social sciences* (pp. 63–72). Lubbock, TX: Texas Tech University Press.

Lancaster, J. B. (1994). Human sexuality, life histories, and evolutionary ecology. In A. S. Rossi (Ed.), *Sexuality across the life course* (pp. 39–62). Chicago: University of Chicago Press.

Lancaster, J. B., & Kaplan, H. (1992). Human mating and family formation strategies: The effects of variability among males in quality and the allocation of mating effort and parental investment. *Topics in Primatology, 1,* 21–33.

Lancaster, J. B., & King, B. J. (1992). An evolutionary perspective on menopause. In V. Kerns & J. K. Brown (Eds.), *In her prime: New views of middle-aged women* (2nd ed., pp. 7–15). Urbana: University of Illinois Press.

Lancaster, J. B., & Lancaster, C. B. (1987). The watershed: Change in parental-investment and family-formation strategies in the course of human evolution. In J. B. Lancaster, J. Altmann, A. S. Rossi, & L. R. Sherwood (Eds.), *Parenting across the lifespan: Biosocial dimensions* (pp. 187–205). New York: Aldine de Gruyter.

LeBoeuf, B., & Reiter, J. (1988). Lifetime reproductive success in Northern elephant seals. In T. H. Clutton-Brock (Ed.), *Reproductive success: Studies of individual variation in contrasting breeding systems* (pp. 344–383). Chicago: University of Chicago Press.

Leibowitz, A., Eisen, M., & Chow, W. K. (1985). An economic model of teenage pregnancy decision-making. *Demography, 23,* 67–77.

Lessells, C. (1991). The evolution of life histories. In J. Krebs & N. B. Davies (Eds.), *Behavioural ecology: An evolutionary approach* (3rd ed., pp. 32–68). Oxford, England: Blackwell Scientific.

Leutenegger, W. (1979). Evolution of litter size in primates. *American Naturalist, 114,* 881–903.

Low, B. (1978). Environmental uncertainty and the parental strategies of marsupials and placentals. *American Naturalist, 112,* 197–213.

Low, B. (1988). Comments on White's "Rethinking polygyny." *Current Anthropology, 29,* 563.

Low, B. (1989). Occupational status and reproductive behavior in nineteeth-century Sweden: Locknevi Parish. *Social Biology, 36,* 82–101.

Low, B. (1990a). Sex power and resources: Ecological and social correlates of sex differences. *International Journal of Contemporary Sociology, 27,* 49–73.

Low, B. (1990b). Occupational status landownership and reproductive behavior in nineteenth-century Sweden: Tuna parish. *American Anthropologist, 92,* 457–468.

Low, B. (1991). Reproductive life in nineteenth century Sweden: An evolutionary perspective on demographic phenomena. *Ethology and Sociobiology, 12,* 411–448.

Low, B. (1992). Sex, coalitions, and politics in pre-industrial societies. *Politics and the Life Sciences, 11*(1), 63–80.

Low, B. (1993a). Ecological demography: A synthetic focus in evolutionary anthropology. *Evolutionary Anthropology, 1993,* 106–112.

Low, B. (1993b). An evolutionary perspective on war. In H. Jacobson & W. Zimmerman (Eds.), *Behavior, culture, and conflict in world politics* (pp. 13–56). Ann Arbor, MI: University of Michigan Press.

Low, B. (1994). Men in the demographic transition. *Human Nature, 5*(3), 223–253.

Low, B., & Clarke, A. L. (1991). Family patterns in 19th century Sweden: Impact of occupational status and land ownership. *Journal of Family History, 16*(2), 117–138.

Low, B., & Clarke, A. L. (1992). Resources and the life course: Patterns through the demographic transition. *Ethology and Sociobiology, 13*, 463–494.

Low, B., Clarke, A. L., & Lockridge, K. (1992). Toward an ecological demography. *Population Development Review, 18*, 1–31.

Mace, G. M. (1990). Birth sex ratio and infant mortality rates in captive western lowland gorillas. *Folia Primatology, 55*(3–4), 156–165.

Marsh, H., & Kasuya, T. (1986). Evidence for reproductive senescence in female cetaceans. *Report of the International Whaling Commission, Special Issue, 8*, 57–74.

Martin, R. D. (1983). *Human brain evolution in an ecological context.* 52nd James Arthur Lecture on The Evolution of the Human Brain. New York: American Museum of Natural History.

Mealey, L., & Mackey, W. (1990). Variation in offspring sex ratio in women of differing social status. *Ethology and Sociobiology, 11*, 83–95.

McInnis, R. M. (1977). Childbearing and land availability: Some evidence from individual household data. In R. Lee (Ed.), *Population patterns in the past* (pp. 201–227). New York: Academic Press.

Mildvan, A. S., & Strehler, B. L. (1960). A critique of theories of mortality. In B. L. Strehler (Ed.), *The biology of aging* (pp. 45–78). New York: American Institute of Biological Sciences.

Mueller, U. (1991). Social and reproductive success: Theoretical considerations and a case study of the West Point Class of 1950. ZUMA: Zentrum für Umfragen, Methoden und Analysen.

Murdock, G. P. (1949). *Social structure.* New York: The Free Press.

Murdock, G. P. (1967). *Ethnographic atlas.* Pittsburgh, PA: University of Pittsburgh Press.

Nice, M. M. (1962). Development of behavior in precocial birds. *Transactions of the Linnean Society of New York, 8*, 1–211.

Nishida, T., Takasaki, H., & Takahata, Y. (1990). Demography and reproductive profiles. In T. Nishida (Ed.), *The chimpanzees of Mahale Mountains.* Tokyo: University of Toykyo Press.

Packer, C., & Pusey, A. E. (1983). Adaptations of female lions to infanticide by incoming males. *American Naturalist, 121*, 716–728.

Packer, C., & Pusey, A. E. (1984). Infanticide in carnivores. In G. Hausfater & S. B. Hrdy (Eds.), *Infanticide: Comparative and evolutionary perspectives* (pp. 31–42). New York: Aldine.

Parry, J. P. (1979). *Caste and kinship in Kangara.* London: Routledge & Paul.

Peacock, N. (1990). Comparative and cross-cultural approaches to the study of human female reproductive failure. In C. J. Rousseau (Ed.), *Primate life history and evolution* (pp. 195–220). New York: Wiley-Liss.

Peacock, N. (1991). An evolutionary perspective on the patterning of maternal investment in pregnancy. *Human Nature, 2*(4), 351–385.

Pérusse, D. (1993). Cultural and reproductive success in industrial societies: Testing the relationship at the proximate and ultimate levels. *Behavioral and Brain Sciences, 16*, 267–322.

Pfister, U. (1989a). Proto-industrialization and demographic change: The Canton of Zurich revisited. *Journal of Economic History, 18*, 629–662.

Pfister, U. (1989b). Work roles and family structure in proto-industrial Zurich. *Journal of Interdisciplinary History, 20*, 83–105.

Profet, M. (1993). Menstruation as a defense against pathogens transported by sperm. *Quarterly Review of Biology, 68*, 335–386.

Promislow, D., & Harvey, P. (1990). Living fast and dying young. A comparative analysis of life history traits among mammals. *Journal of Zoology, 220*, 417–437.

Rank, M. A. (1989). Fertility among women on welfare: Incidence and determinants. *American Sociological Review, 54*, 296–304.

Ransel, D. (1988). *Mothers in misery: Child abandonment in Russia.* Princeton, NJ: Princeton University Press.

Ravenholt, R. T., & Chao, J. (1974). World fertility trends. Population Reports, Series J, #2, George Washington University Dept. of Medical and Public Affairs, Washington, DC.

Ricklefs, R. E. (1974). Energetics of reproduction in birds. In R. A. Paynter, Jr. (Ed.), *Avian energetics, Publication of the Nuttall Ornithological Club, 15*, 152–297.

Ricklefs, R. E. (1975). The evolution of cooperative breeding in birds. *Ibis, 117*, 531–534.

Ricklefs, R. E. (1979a). Adaptation, constraint, and compromise in avian postnatal development. *Biological Reviews, Cambridge Philosophical Society, 54*, 269–290.

Ricklefs, R. E. (1979b). Patterns of growth in birds: V. A comparative study of development in the starling, common tern, and Japanese quail. *Auk, 96*, 10–30.

Ricklefs, R. E. (1983). Avian postnatal development. In D. S. Farner, J. R. King, & K. C. Parkes (Eds.), *Avian biology* (Vol. 7, pp. 1–83). New York: Academic Press.

Roff, D. A. (1992). *The evolution of life histories: Theory and analysis.* New York: Chapman & Hall.

Sacher, G. A. (1959). Relation of lifespan to brain size. In G. E. W. Wolstenholme & M. O'Connor (Eds.), *The lifespan of animals* (pp. 115–141). Boston: Little, Brown.

Sherwood, J. (1988). *Poverty in eighteenth-century Spain: Women and children of the Inclusa.* Toronto, Canada: University of Toronto Press.

Silk, J. B. (1980). Adoption and kinship in Oceania. *American Anthropologist, 82*, 799–820.

Silk, J. B. (1987). Adoption and fosterage in human societies: Adaptations or enigmas? *Cultural Anthropology, 2*, 39–49.

Smith, B. H. (1990). The cost of a large brain. *Behavior and Brain Sciences, 13*(2), 365–366.

Smith, B. H. (1991). Dental development and the evolution of life history in Hominidae. *American Journal of Physical Anthropology, 86*, 157–174.

Smith, B. H. (1992). Life history and the evolution of human maturation. *Evolutionary Anthropology, 1*(4), 134–142.

Smith, E. A., & Boyd, R. (1990). Risk and reciprocity: Hunter-gatherer socioecology and the problem of collective action. In E. Cashdan (Ed.), *Risk and uncertainty in tribal and peasant economies* (pp. 167–191). Boulder, CO: Westview Press.

Smith, E. A., & Smith, S. A. (1994). Inuit sex-ratio variation: Population control, ethnographic error, or parental manipulation? *Current Anthropology, 35*(5), 595–624.

Smith, T., & Polacheck, T. (1981). Reexamination of the life table for northern fur seals with implications about population regulatory mechanisms. In C. W. Fowler & T. D. Smith (Eds.), *Dynamics of large mammal populations* (pp. 99–120). New York: Wiley.

Smuts, B. B., & Gubernick, D. J. (1992). Male-infant relationships in nonhuman primates: Paternal investment or mating effort? In B. S. Hewlett (Ed.), *Father-child relations: Cultural and biosocial contexts.* Chicago: Aldine de Gruyter.

Snowden, D. A., Kane, R. L., Beeson, W., Burke, G. L., Sprafka, J. M., Potter, J., Jacobs, D. R., & Phillips, R. L. (1989). Is early natural menopause a biologic marker of health and aging? *American Journal of Public Health, 79*, 709–714.

Stearns, S. (1992). *The evolution of life histories.* Oxford: Oxford University Press.

Strassmann, B. I. (1991a). The function of menstrual taboos among the Dogon: Defense against cuckoldry? *Human Nature, 3*(2), 89–131.

Strassmann, B. I. (1991b). Sexual selection, paternal care, and concealed ovulation in humans. *Ethology and Sociobiology, 2*, 31–40.

Strassmann, B. I. (1994, June). *The evolution of menstruation.* Paper presented at the Human Behavior and Evolution Society meetings, Ann Arbor, MI.

Struhsaker, T. T., & Leland, L. (1986). Colobines: Infanticide by adult males. In B. B. Smuts, D. L. Cheney, R. M. Seyfarth, R. W. Wrangham, & T. T. Struhsaker (Eds.), *Primate societies* (pp. 83–98). Chicago: University of Chicago Press.

Torres, A., & Forrest, J. D. (1988). Why do women have abortions? *Family Planning Perspectives, 20*(4), 169–176.

Trivers, R. L. (1972). Parental investment and sexual selection. In B. Campbell (Ed.), *Sexual selection and the descent of man 1871–1971* (pp. 136–179). Chicago: Aldine.

Trivers, R. L. (1974). Parent-offspring conflict. *Quarterly Review Biology, 46*, 35–57.

Trivers, R. L., & Willard, D. E. (1973). Natural selection of parental ability to vary the sex ratio. *Science, 179*, 90–92.

Turke, P. W. (1988). Helpers at the nest: Childcare networks in Ifaluk. In L. Betzig, M. Borgerhoff Mulder, & P. Turke (Eds.), *Human reproductive behaviour: A Darwinian perspective* (pp. 173–188). Cambridge, England: Cambridge University Press.

Turke, P. W., & Betzig, L. L. (1985). Those who can do: Wealth status and reproductive success on Ifaluk. *Ethology and Sociobiology, 6*, 79–87.

Vining, D. R. (1986). Social versus reproductive success: The central theoretical problem of human sociobiology. *Behavioral Brain Sciences, 9*, 167–216.

Voland, E. (1984). Human sex-ratio manipulation: Historical data from a German parish. *Journal of Human Evolution, 13*, 99–107.

Wasser, S. K., & Barash, D. (1983). Reproductive suppression among female mammals: Implications for biomedicine and sexual selection theory. *Quarterly Review Biology, 58*, 513–535.

Whitten, P. L. (1992). Chemical revolution to sexual revolution: Historical changes in human reproductive development. In T. Colburn & C. Clement (Eds.), *Chemically-induced alterations in sexual and functional development: The wildlife-human connection* (pp. 311–334). Princeton, NJ: Princeton Scientific Publishing.

Whyte, M. K. (1978). Cross-cultural codes dealing with the relative status of women. *Ethnology, 17*, 211–237.

Whyte, M. K. (1979). *The status of women in pre-industrial society.* Princeton, NJ: Princeton University Press.

Williams, G. C. (1957). Pleiotropy, natural selection, and the evolution of senescence. *Evolution, 11*, 398–411.

Williams, G. C. (1966). *Adaptation and natural selection.* Princeton, NJ: Princeton University Press.

Wood, J. W. (1990). Fertility in anthropological populations. *Annual Review of Anthropology, 19*, 211–242.

# 5

*Evolutionary Approaches to Culture*

Maria G. Janicki
Dennis L. Krebs
*Simon Fraser University*

The existence of human culture entails a challenge for evolutionary theorists motivated to explain human behavior. Human behavior is unique because it is influenced by both genetic and cultural information. Traditionally, social scientists have assumed that culture and the learning mechanisms through which people acquire culture constitute systems that have somehow superseded evolved dispositions in the human species. This assumption is unacceptable to evolutionary theorists, who consider the capacity for culture, along with evolved psychological mechanisms that mediate the learning and transmission of cultural information to have been naturally selected. This chapter reviews several models of the relations between biology and culture advanced by evolutionary theorists, then compares and contrasts them. To a greater or lesser extent, these models will offer answers to the following questions:

- What is the relation between biological and cultural evolution? Does culture affect biological evolution and vice versa? Do evolved dispositions give rise to or constrain culture? To what extent are cultural traits selected in terms of their contributions to individuals' inclusive fitness? Are cultural traits sometimes biologically maladaptive, and if so, why?

- What are the psychological mechanisms and processes that mediate the selection and transmission of culture?

- What is the relation between genetic and cultural influences on human behavior? Do they exert independent or interacting effects? Can humans, armed with a capacity for culture, release themselves from the constraints imposed by their genetic heritage?

163

All models reviewed here accept the premise that the human capacity for culture arose through natural selection because of the fitness benefits it conferred on our ancestors. This capacity includes cognitive abilities for symbolic representation, language, abstract thinking, social learning, and communication, as well as physical abilities for speech and cultural displays.[1] All models take exception to assumptions inherent in traditional anthropological and sociological approaches to culture, such as individuals are passive recipients of their culture; culture has more control over human nature than vice versa; culture has superorganic properties that can only be explained in terms of itself (e.g., White, 1949), and culture alone is an adequate explanation for variations in human behavior.

These commonalities notwithstanding, the models may differ on the positions they advance on the following issues: what culture is, and how it is best divided into units; the extent to which cultural traits are biologically adaptive; the relationship between genes, the mind, environment, and culture; the extent to which cultural processes constitute a system of inheritance independent of genetic inheritance; sources of cross-cultural similarities and differences; and the nature of the psychological mechanisms involved in the learning of culture.

The first section of this chapter reviews seven models of the relation between biology and culture. The first three models offer different evolutionary perspectives on culture in general: (a) cultural evolution as analogous to, but independent of, biological evolution; (b) culture as the product of inclusive fitness maximizers; and (c) culture as the product of evolved minds. The remaining are four different coevolutionary models that focus on the dual and interdependent processes of biological and cultural evolution. The second section compares and evaluates the models reviewed; the third section offers a brief synopsis.

## EVOLUTIONARY MODELS OF THE RELATION BETWEEN BIOLOGY AND CULTURES

### Independent but Analogous Processes

Although one might expect all evolutionary theorists to assume that culture is guided by genetically based dispositions, well-known evolutionary biologist Richard Dawkins (1976) argued that biological and cultural processes constitute independent systems of inheritance. Although

---

[1]For additional reading on the origins of cultural capacity, see Graubard (1985), Rindos (1986), and Spuhler (1959). Among the models reviewed in this chapter, Barkow (1989), Boyd and Richerson (1985), and Lumsden and Wilson (1981) also feature discussions on this topic.

independent, Dawkins considered the two systems analogous, and he believed that biological evolution supplies a good model for the processes of cultural change.

In *The Selfish Gene*, Dawkins (1976) advanced a compelling case for using genes as the unit of selection in evolutionary analyses. Analogously, Dawkins labeled the unit of cultural selection a *meme*. Memes are the smallest unit of cultural information that can be copied and transmitted from brain to brain among individuals, and can influence the carriers' phenotype. Examples of memes are: ideas, fashions, information, thoughts, theories, songs, a method of irrigation, and pieces of art. Dawkins viewed cultural change as an evolutionary process in which memes are differentially selected. In agreement with Dawkins, Dennett (1990) argued that meme selection is a process that conforms to the laws of natural selection exactly.

## Similarities Between Memes and Genes

Dawkins identified several similarities between memes and genes. First, both are replicators—they make copies of themselves. As replicators, both memes and genes belong to the codical or information domain (Williams, 1992). Second, errors can occur in the copying process of both memes and genes, which in turn can produce mutations or variations in the information each carries. Third, both are differentially replicated and, as a result, undergo a selection process. Fourth, like genes, memes are in competition with their alleles. As a consequence, some memes, such as the works of Shakespeare, survive longer than others in the "meme pool," and can be said to have a high survival value. Ball (1984) classified memes into dominant and recessive alleles. Recessive meme alleles are those that are "remembered but not believed or acted upon" (p. 148). A meme allele can be both dominant and recessive at different times and in different minds, depending on which other memes are present. Finally, as with genes, memes may link up with one another if they are mutually reinforcing. Dawkins (1976) discussed the popularity of the "God meme" in cultures worldwide, and its possible linkage to the "blind faith" meme, which together reinforce each other, producing a co-adapted meme complex.

## Differences Between Memes and Genes

There are, however, several important differences between memes and genes. The first relates to the media of transmission and storage. In biological evolution, there is only one type of interactor (also called *vehicles* or *survival machines*)—the individual organisms that transmit the replicators (genes) to future generations. In contrast, cultural replicators (memes) can be carried in and stored on innumerable types of interactors, such as a pattern of ink on paper or the digital information on a computer disk. Second, instead of competing to be passed onto offspring, memes compete for placement in limited spaces, such as the attention of human brains and coverage in various media. Third, memes can be transmitted from individual to individual by innumerable means, such as through the spoken or written word, mass media, or the Internet, and they can be stored in countless sources. Finally, in contrast to genetic transmission, which proceeds slowly, generation by generation, mimetic or cultural transmission is rapid and Lamarckian (Wilson, 1979). Dramatic cultural change may occur in a single generation.

## Memes and Fitness

In response to the question, "What qualities in genes foster their selection and propagation?", evolutionary theorists point to the ability of genes to contribute to the survival and reproduction of their interactors. Unlike many evolutionary scientists, Dawkins (1976) did not believe that the contributions of memes to biological fitness necessarily enhance their power to replicate. In this sense, Dawkins' model involves an "uncoupling" of biological and cultural evolution. According to Dawkins, once the human brain evolved through natural selection, it created an environment in which a new type of selection could occur independently of natural selection. Dawkins argued that it is a waste of time to search for the reproductive benefits of possessing certain memes. Rather, he suggested that memes, including cultural traits, evolve simply because they are advantageous to themselves. For example, memes with psychological appeal, such as the God meme, will have a higher fecundity than memes that do not. Dennett (1990) suggested that many memes have high survival value because of their value in our society, such as the memes for environmental awareness, honesty, and music. However, Dennett acknowledged that socially unappealing memes, such as those contributing to racism, graffiti, and terrorism, also may persist, even though they are disavowed by the majority. Dennett (1990) advanced the interesting idea that some memes have intrinsic characteristics that reinforce their perpetuation. For example, challenges or denials of conspiracy theories are seen as evidence for their validity.

## Interaction Between Memes and Genes

According to Dawkins (1976), memes and genes may reinforce or oppose one another with respect to their effects on genetic reproduction and control of phenotypic behavior and ideas. For example, a cultural rule opposing incest may reinforce biologically evolved dispositions to avoid inbreeding. In contrast, memes for ideas such as celibacy may oppose genetically based reproductive interests. Inasmuch as genes have been selected in terms of their ability to foster their own replication, they may be considered to be selfish. Genetic selfishness can contribute to selfish dispositions within individuals. Theorists such as Dawkins (1976) and Campbell (1983) believe cultural prescriptions may override such selfish dispositions. Indeed, Dawkins closed the final chapter of the first edition of *The Selfish Gene* with the statement, "We are built as gene machines and cultured as meme machines, but we have the power to turn against our creators. We, alone on earth, can rebel against the tyranny of the selfish replicators" (1989, p. 201). If we can break free from of our genetic heritage, as Dawkins suggested, all cultural products need not be adaptive.

## Memes as Viruses of the Mind

In effect, memes use the human brain, which evolved biologically through natural selection, as a host. In this sense, they may be considered to be parasitic. As Dawkins (1989) stated, parasitic memes act by "turning [one's brain] into a vehicle for the meme's propagation in just the way a virus may parasitize the genetic mechanisms of a host cell" (p. 192). Dawkins (1993) suggested the human mind is an excellent host for viruslike parasitic memes that manipulate it into making and spreading copies of themselves. Dawkins cited as evidence the tendency, especially in children and young adults, to follow what the majority of others (or significant figures) are doing, adducing "crazes" such as hula-hoops and reversed ball-caps as examples. Dennett (1990) suggested that people may not always be masters of their own ideas, able to manipulate, accept, and discard them as they wish. He gave the examples of an annoying song that keeps replaying itself in people's heads, a writer who feels the characters of a novel "had a life of their own," and poems that "write themselves." Dennett further suggested that we *are* our memes—our minds are a composite of the ideas we have ingested over our lifetime.

   This chapter returns to the idea of a separate cultural selection process when it reviews the coevolutionary models. But first it describes a model that contrasts sharply with the one advanced by Dawkins.

## CULTURE AS THE PRODUCT
## OF INCLUSIVE FITNESS MAXIMIZATION:
## DARWINIAN ANTHROPOLOGY

In his book *Darwinism and Human Affairs*, biologist Richard Alexander (1979) asked: "to what extent can culture be understood by thinking in terms of individuals striving to maximize their genetic reproduction?" (p.

67). This question is central in an evolutionary perspective that views humans as predisposed to behave in ways that will maximize their inclusive fitness and, consequently, expects most behavior to be adaptive. For convenience, this perspective is referred to as *Darwinian anthropology*, a label given by Symons (1989). The methods of Darwinian anthropologists include deriving behavioral predictions from theories of evolutionary biology, and gathering behavioral data to test these predictions. Behavioral models incorporating inclusive fitness as a variable are also formulated to generate predictions.[2] Examples of cultural behaviors of interest to Darwinian anthropologists are status-seeking and resource accrual, with respect to their effects on male reproductive success (e.g., Irons, 1979b; Turke & Betzig, 1985).

## Definition of Culture

According to Darwinian anthropologist William Irons (1979a), the human capacity for culture is an adaptation that enables individuals to track their environment and adaptively adjust their behavior as conditions change. Culture is a tool or vehicle of genetic replication (Alexander, 1979). Irons (1979a) viewed individuals as actively weighing, even if unconsciously, the value of behavioral choices in terms of their consequences for biological fitness. Darwinian anthropologists define culture in terms of behavior because behavior has the most direct influence on reproductive success. They consider other aspects of culture, including ideas and beliefs, important only with respect to their influence on behavior. An interesting implication of this theory is that people may develop customs that enhance their biological fitness, but as the drive to maximize fitness is largely unconscious, the customs are explained in terms of other, often religious or moral, reasons.

## Cross-Cultural Differences and Cultural Change

Culture and social structure are seen as outcomes of the strategies individuals invoke to maximize their biological fitness in particular environments (Irons, 1979b). Different behavioral strategies are selected in different environments, producing cross-cultural differences in customs. Irons (1979a) does not believe environments elicit particular preprogrammed adaptive responses. Rather, he argued that humans have a unique ability to create behavioral innovations in response to environmental demands and opportunities, including those that were not present when the human mind evolved. Thus, Irons attributed cross-cultural

---

[2]Because these methods are similar to those used by behavioral ecologists who study animal behavior, this discipline is sometimes referred to as *human behavioral ecology*.

variations in behavior to adaptive flexibility rather than to genetic differences between cultures. If cross-cultural differences in customs are due to environmental differences in fitness-enhancing opportunities, it follows that customs, or culture, should change when fitness-relevant aspects of environments change. Irons (cited in Cronk, 1995) adduced a great deal of evidence that they do.

## Mechanisms Mediating Adoption and Transmission of Culture

Because Darwinian anthropologists focus on behavior, their cultural models do not emphasize evolved mental mechanisms as much as some other models do. However, Darwinian anthropologists' contention that humans behave as if they were maximizing their inclusive fitness implies the existence of domain-general psychological mechanisms able to assess the fitness consequences of actions. With respect to the adoption of cultural traits, Alexander (1979) proposed a "social learning mechanism" that causes individuals to be physiologically or psychologically reinforced by pleasant interactions with particular individuals. Flinn and Alexander (1982) proposed more specific decision rules that guide people to imitate successful others and be more willing to accept advice from those who are interested in their success than from those with whom their interests conflict.

In summary, Darwinian anthropologists see culture as an outcome of the actions of individuals motivated to maximize their inclusive fitness under certain ecological and social conditions. Darwinian anthropologists acknowledge the possibility of some current behaviors being maladaptive. In such cases, the fault may lie in natural selection's inability to compensate for random or nonrandom genetic effects, random environmental fluctuations, or the strength and speed of relevant environmental changes (Betzig, 1989).

It is interesting to note that the role of culture in behavioral analyses is not emphasized by all Darwinian anthropologists. For example, Betzig (chap. 8, this volume) argues that behavioral models that incorporate a fitness measure as a variable, and "have dispensed with culture altogether," have successfully predicted and explained several behavioral patterns.

## EVOLVED MINDS GENERATING AND REACTING TO CULTURE: EVOLUTIONARY PSYCHOLOGY

Throughout writings that outline the evolutionary psychology perspective, Tooby and Cosmides (1990) have argued that the mind is composed of evolved psychological information-processing mechanisms that were shaped by natural selection in ancestral environments. These mental mechanisms evolved in response to particular adaptive problems faced by early humans, such as the need to attract a mate, acquire a language, detect cheaters in social exchange, and avoid predators. The ancestral environment, also referred to as the *environment of evolutionary adaptedness* (EEA),[3] is the enduring social and physical conditions under which a particular adaptation arose (Tooby & Cosmides, 1990). Evolutionary psychologists argue that there has not been sufficient time for natural selection to change the complex mental mechanisms that evolved in hunter–gatherer conditions in the Pleistocene era. This point has two important implications. First, in contrast to Darwinian anthropologists, evolutionary psychologists would not be surprised to find maladaptive behaviors in the current environment. Second, given that current behavior may not be adaptive, studying the structure of mental adaptations should be of more use than studying adaptiveness of behaviors (Symons, 1989).

## Nature of Evolved Mental Mechanisms

Evolutionary psychologists describe the innate mechanisms of the mind in terms of decision rules or algorithms. They reject the possibility of a mind consisting of domain-general, content-independent mechanisms. According to evolutionary psychologists, to carry out everyday tasks, our minds require specialized knowledge about the world in the form of domain-specific psychological mechanisms that regulate our thoughts and actions. The mind can be divided into many distinct (although interacting) modules, containing cognitive mechanisms that process information from specific content areas. For example, evolutionary psychologists propose that there are modules specializing in reasoning in social exchange and mate choice (see Barkow, Cosmides, & Tooby, 1992).

Evolutionary psychologists assume that evolved mental mechanisms have little or no genetic variability, thus constituting part of a universal human nature. These mechanisms are viewed as sensitive to environmental contingencies, both developmental and concurrent, and as capable of guiding development and activating appropriate behavioral strategies and responses. As such, evolutionary psychology has been described as an environmentalist discipline (Crawford & Anderson, 1989). It follows that most evolutionary psychologists view individual differences in behavior as the outcome of varying environmental inputs to the evolved mechanisms.

---

[3]The *EEA* is defined as "not a place or a habitat, or even a time period. Rather it is a statistical composite of the adaptation-relevant properties of the ancestral environments encountered by members of ancestral populations, weighted by their frequency and fitness-consequences" (Tooby & Cosmides, 1990, pp. 386–387). The term was originally conceived of (and coined) by Bowlby (1969).

The model of the mind advanced by evolutionary psychologists has been compared metaphorically to a Swiss-army knife or jukebox, where the mental tool or mental recording used is contingent on the type of task to be solved and the environmental conditions the organism is faced.

## Culture in General

In contrast to what they called the *Standard Social Science model*, Tooby and Cosmides (1989, 1992) asserted that individuals are neither born with blank slate minds nor are they capable or learning all skills, behaviors, and attitudes with equal ease. Most important, individuals are not passive recipients of their culture. According to evolutionary psychologists, cultural information—including behaviors, symbolic representations, and cognitions—is both generated and responded to by the evolved mental programs in our minds.

## Components of Culture

In general, Tooby and Cosmides (1992) defined culture as ". . . any mental, behavioral, or material commonalities shared across individuals . . . regardless of why these commonalities exist" (p. 117). More specifically, they factored culture into three components: metaculture, evoked culture, and epidemiological culture.

*Metaculture.* Although people in different cultures across the world may differ in their customs and beliefs, many human universals exist, such as the tendency to interpret the actions of others in terms of beliefs and desires, the ability to comprehend and speak a language, the tendency to associate preferentially with a mate and close kin, and feeling grief after a loss. These universals are a product of shared evolved psychological mechanisms that were shaped by natural selection in response to regularities in human social life throughout the EEA. Tooby and Cosmides (1992) used the term *metaculture* to refer to: these shared evolved mechanisms, the interactions of these mechanisms with those of others in the population, the interaction of these mechanisms with relevant aspects of the social and physical environment, and the impact of these mechanisms on human life. In other words, *metaculture* refers to the outcome of the interactions of individuals' universal human cognitive structures. This common metacultural structure allows for both the communication among individuals from different cultures and the transmission of particular cultural traits within a culture.

*Evoked Culture.* Universal evolved psychological mechanisms are expected to be responsive to contingencies in the developmental and immediate environment. According to Tooby and Cosmides (1992), *evoked culture* is the aspect of culture produced when shared mental mechanisms operating in different environments evoke different behavioral patterns or attitudes in response to different environmental contingencies, or the same patterns in response to the same environmental contingencies. Responses of evolved mechanisms to similar local environments contribute to within-group similarities and between-group variability. For example, when language-acquisition mechanisms are activated in differing linguistic environments, individuals develop different languages. Differences in attitude toward food sharing may be the result of differences in the socioecological conditions affecting food quality, variability, and availability.

*Epidemiological Culture.* The ability to socially learn from others and the transmission of cultural information are made possible by evolved mental mechanisms. Tooby and Cosmides (1992) referred to the product of these processes as *epidemiological culture* or *adopted culture*. These two labels are chosen over *transmitted culture* to emphasize that individuals actively learn cultural standards more often than they actively transmit them. Other theorists, such as Cavalli-Sforza and Feldman (1981), also have described cultural transmission in epidemiological terms because of the resemblance between cultural transmission and the spread of contagious diseases. Mental mechanisms mediating social learning evolved because, in many circumstances, social learning was more cost-effective than learning from individual experience.

### Cultural Change

Tooby and Cosmides (1992) explained cultural change in terms of the interaction between the evoked and epidemiological aspects of culture. Environmental changes create changes in the appeal of particular customs or ideas that may, in turn, be transmitted through social learning. For example, a change in the nutritional environment caused by a famine might evoke new (and now more appealing) attitudes toward food that are spread by transmission, leading to cultural change (Tooby & Cosmides, 1992). Considering the interaction of evoked and transmitted aspects of culture helps explains why cultural traits change over time (as conditions change), rather than being copied identically from generation to generation. It also explains why there are similarities between certain cultures—because of shared environmental elements.

Tooby and Cosmides (1992) acknowledged that psychological processes alone cannot constitute a complete theory of culture. Although an understanding of the human psyche is paramount, a complete theory of culture must include group-level processes of cultural transmission. Other theorists have been more attentive to this level of analysis. The next section highlights their work.

## LUMSDEN AND WILSON'S EPIGENETIC APPROACH

Lumsden and Wilson (1981) advanced a coevolutionary model based on the idea that frequencies of genes and cultural units (culturgens) in the population exert reciprocal influences on each other, with a neurological model of the mind mediating the relationship. Lumsden (1989) defined culture as "a system of socially learnable knowledge shared among members of a society" (p. 15). Lumsden and Wilson (1981) labeled the unit of culture a *culturgen*, which they defined as "transmissible behaviors, mentifacts, and artifacts" (p. 7). They gave food items, carpenter's tools, and marriage customs as examples.

Lumsden and Wilson's model of the relation between genetic and cultural influences on culturgens differs from other coevolutionary models in its focus on epigenesis: the process through which genetic factors affect the development of children under the influence of environmental inputs. According to Lumsden, infants are exposed to all kinds of environmental input, including the culturgens of other members of society, but they are biologically evolved to attend to, register, process, and remember information about only a relatively small portion of such input, in only a relatively limited number of ways. For example, humans perceive only a small part of the electromagnetic spectrum and parse it up into only a relatively small number of colors.

### Epigenetic Rules

Epigenetic rules are evolved constraints on development that "help to match the developmental needs of the individual to the contents of the social system, assembling knowledge, attitudes, and beliefs into an evolutionarily competitive phenotype" (Lumsden, 1989, pp. 13–14). Epigenetic rules are genetically based mechanisms that induce preferences in the developing infant for certain culturgens over others and that cause infants to be prepared to learn some things and resist learning others. Thus, epigenetic rules are mechanisms of selection that determine the contents of the culture to which future generations are exposed. Lumsden (1989) commented that the operation of epigenetic rules does not make cognition and behavior genetically determined. Rather, cognition and behavior are outcomes of the interaction between evolved rules and experience.

## Gene–Culture Translation and Genetically Based Differences Among Cultures

*Gene–culture translation* refers to the "effect of the genetically determined epigenetic rules of individual cognitive and behavioral development on social patterns" (Lumsden & Wilson, 1981, p. 100). Lumsden and Wilson moved from the individual level (at which epigenetic rules operate) to the societal level of culture simply by adding the cumulate effects in individuals of the adoption and use of particular culturgens. The theorists speak of ethnographic curves based on the proportion of members in particular societies using a given culturgen.

## Coevolutionary Circuit

Tying the components of their model together, Lumsden and Wilson described a coevolutionary circuit based on the following sequence of processes: Genetically determined epigenetic rules influence individual learning and adoption of various culturgens, which in turn influence individual behavior. The distribution of culturgens internalized by the individuals in a society constitutes its culture. This culture (i.e., the proportions of particular culturgens in a society) then becomes part of the selection environment, which produces changes in the frequency of genes and the epigenetic rules they produce.

## Model of the Mind

Lumsden and Wilson (1981) outlined a complex model of the mind, described as having "a strong tendency to generalize episodic memory [specific people, objects and actions] into concepts and higher-level entities, which then constitute the 'nodes' or reference points in long term semantic memory [related concepts and meanings]" (p. 245). Nodes are organized into networks that form schemata, and plans of action that constitute the meaning or knowledge structures of the human mind, which are used to guide behavior. Culturgens are represented in long-term memory as node-link structures. Epigenetic rules, responding to individual experience, govern the probability that particular nodes will become linked.

## Genetic Differences, Cultural Diversity, and Cultural Change

Lumsden and Wilson reasoned that genetic differences among cultures may have evolved under certain conditions. In particular, given differences in the adaptiveness of different culturgens in different environments, natural selection would favor individuals in one environment who possessed a genetically based learning bias toward a particular culturgen, and favor individuals in another environment who possessed a bias toward an alternative culturgen. If the two environments remained constant for 50 generations, or 1,000 years, and the gene pools did not mix, selection would produce a genetically based difference between the two populations in the learning bias. Lumsden and Wilson called this the 1,000-year rule.

Evolved constraints on learning may induce cultural change because they induce individuals to learn certain types of information and not others. As new ideas, or culturgens, are introduced into a culture, epigenetic rules determine which ones are selected, retained, and therefore passed onto future generations. Lumsden (1989) argued that evolved constraints not only facilitate cultural diversity, but that they are necessary for it. These constraints likely underlie the ability of children to learn their culture with relative ease.

### Is Culture Adaptive?

The learnability of culturgens is not necessarily correlated with their adaptiveness: People can learn behaviors and ideas that do not enhance—and may detract from—their inclusive fitness. This may arise, in part, from differences between the adaptiveness of culturgens in ancestral and current environments. Preferences that were selected in ancestral environments because they enhanced fitness may fail to perform this function in current environments.

### Some Examples of Evolved Constraints

Lumsden offered the preferences and forms of learning involved in stranger anxiety, incest avoidance, nepotism, nonverbal communication, music, and language as examples of evolved constraints (influenced by epigenetic rules). Consider the example of language. Linguists have established that, although general learning mechanisms such as modeling and reinforcement may affect the acquisition of language, such mechanisms cannot account for phoneme discrimination, the acquisition of transformational grammar, and other universal features of language acquisition. Children simply could not learn all the complexities of language as fast as they do or in the way they do through reinforcement and modeling without innate mechanisms. The common language errors that young children make have provided evidence that they are prepared to process linguistic information in only certain ways.

## Recent Revisions in Lumsden's Model

In recent years, Lumsden has tried to improve on what he called the *beanbag genetics metaphor* for culture—based on the idea that culture consists of little particles of information. Lumsden believed this metaphor fails to account for human creativity, the ease with which various aspects of culture are interpreted, and the transition to macroevolutionary trajectories in gene–culture systems. Responding to a draft of this chapter, Lumsden wrote, "When I started my work in this area mid-70's, evolutionary psychology was a rather quaint backwater. . . . You'd be surprised how hard I had to work just to convince people that 'mind' in any form recognizable by cognitive science merited a place in the story of genes, culture, and how they interact" (personal communication on January 23, 1997). See Lumsden (1988), Lumsden (1991), and Findlay and Lumsden (1988) for more recent accounts of Lumsden's model of gene–culture coevolution.

The next section turns to another gene–culture coevolutionary model. Lumsden and Wilson used the term *coevolutionary* to mean reciprocal effects of cultural and genetic change, whereas Durham (1976) did not believe the effects are always reciprocal and interactive.

## DURHAM'S COEVOLUTIONARY MODEL

Durham's coevolutionary model has evolved over time. Therefore, in summarizing Durham's perspective, this section distinguishes between his early and recent models. Durham's models can be classified as *dual inheritance*, a term coined by Boyd and Richerson (1976). Like Dawkins, dual-inheritance theorists acknowledge that behavioral phenotypes are influenced by two independent systems of inheritance: biological and cultural. In contrast to Dawkins, Durham viewed cultural selection as complementary to genetic selection.

## Durham's Early Model

Like Irons (1979a), Durham (1976) hypothesized that individuals select cultural variants based on their effects on inclusive fitness. Durham (1979) proposed that the selection of cultural traits is influenced by several biases that favor adaptive choices. Four such biases include:

1. *Learned biases.* When children are socialized to follow cultural norms and practices, they develop biases that assist them in selecting cultural traits and values that are adaptive and "for their own good."
2. *Bias of satisfaction.* We are biased toward favoring those traits that produce pleasant mental or physical feedback. Feelings of satisfaction are likely correlated with adaptive choices.[4]
3. *Bias in the learning structures and functions of the human brain.* Individuals have a cognitive bias favoring the selective retention of more-versus-less adaptive cultural traits. For example, people seem to easily develop phobias to natural dangers.
4. *Circumstantial bias.* When parents are primarily responsible for enculturating their children, any cultural traits or information that enhance survival and reproductive success will tend to be passed onto more children, thus differentially propagated.

There are two corollaries to Durham's early hypotheses (Durham, 1991). First, cultural behaviors with relatively large fitness effects (benefits or costs) are better explained with reference to inclusive fitness than are cultural behaviors with relatively small fitness effects. Second, the prior biases may be overridden or prevented from functioning by force, resulting in the maintenance of maladaptive cultural practices.

### Durham's Recent Model

The two main ways in which Durham (1991) revised his earlier model were by: (a) defining culture in terms of information, and (b) elaborating on the forces of cultural change and the relation between genes and culture. In his new model, Durham defined culture as shared ideas, values, and beliefs in the minds of humans. He viewed cultural units (which, following Dawkins, he labeled *memes*) as socially transmitted information that has the potential to guide behavior. Cultural changes involve the adoption of particular memes over their alternatives, which Durham terms *allomemes.* Durham advocated the use of ideational units in cultural analyses because, he argued, cultural information is only one of the guiding forces influencing behavior. Genetic information and environmental circumstances are others. Using behavioral traits as cultural units muddies the distinction between cultural forces and cultural products.

---

[4]Durham's bias of satisfaction appears functionally similar to Alexander's (1979) social learning mechanism.

## Forces of Transformation

Durham used the term *transformation* to encompass all the forces and processes (genetic and cultural) of cultural change within an established cultural system. As Durham (1991) stated, both genes and memes "share the same basic properties of instructing phenotypes and of being transformed sequentially through replication in a given environment" (p. 185). Durham's transformation forces are illustrated in Fig. 5.1. Durham described two main kinds of transformation force: nonconveyance and conveyance. *Nonconveyance forces* increase the frequency of a given allomeme without transmission among members of a population. Durham subdivided nonconveyance forces into three subtypes: recurrent innovation (analogous to mutation), migration, and cultural drift (increasing the frequency of one allomeme due to the loss of others caused by random memory lapses or random death). *Conveyance forces* increase the frequency of a given meme through social transmission. They include natural selection, choice, and imposition. Natural selection increases the frequency of a given meme if the carrier has a "greater than average" number of children and the meme is successfully (socially) transmitted to them. Choice refers to the individual's selection of memes by the active process of discriminative decision making. Imposition, on the opposite end of a continuum with choice, involves the spread of cultural units due to the imposed choices of others.

## Cultural Selection

Durham defined the cultural fitness of an allomeme in terms of its expected rate of social transmission, relative to other allomemes. Cultural selection operates primarily by decision making, which is guided by primary and

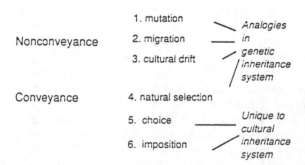

FIG. 5.1. Forces of transformation in Durham's (1991) coevolutionary model. Nonconveyance forces increase meme frequencies without social transmission. Conveyance forces increase meme frequencies through social transmission and are proposed by Durham to be the primary influences on cultural change.

secondary values. Primary values have a genetic basis and are influenced by evolved preferences and psychological mechanisms. They develop within each individual through an interaction between the nervous system and the environment (Durham, 1991). When primary values are the most important influences on decision making in cultural selection (by choice or by imposition), primary value selection is occurring.

Secondary values are culturally based and drawn from collective experience and social history. Durham gave social conventions and rules of thumb as examples. Secondary value selection occurs when cultural selection is most influenced by secondary values. Durham's (1991) first main hypothesis is that secondary value selection is more important than primary value selection in inducing cultural change. Because secondary values are memes that influence the selection of other memes, Durham (1991) argued that a culture system has the capability of self-selection (i.e., the cultural system "can influence the direction and rates of its own evolutionary change"; p. 201). For example, individuals will be biased toward selecting cultural variants that fit the existing cultural values.

## Modes of Relations Among Genes and Culture

Durham's second hypothesis is that there are five distinct modes of relations among genes and culture, which are outlined in Fig. 5.2. These include two interactive modes, wherein genotypes and allomemes influence each other's fitness values directly, and three comparative modes,

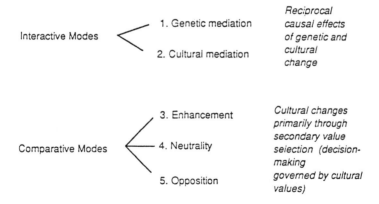

FIG. 5.2. Five modes of interaction between genes and culture in Durham's (1991) coevolutionary model. Durham argued that genes and culture may have, but need not always have, reciprocal effects on each other. The interactive modes describe the reciprocal gene-culture interactions, whereas the comparative modes describe a comparison of a meme's effects on cultural fitness with its effects on inclusive fitness (in nonreciprocal interactions).

wherein cultural changes are produced by decision making based on existing cultural values (secondary value selection). Durham claimed that his model covers coevolution in a broader sense than Lumsden and Wilson's (1981) model, which includes only the two interactive modes.

*Interactive Modes.* The two interactive modes are cultural and genetic mediation. Durham (1991) stated that cultural mediation occurs "whenever a cultural difference in memes within or between populations creates a behavioral difference that, in turn, causes a difference in the reproduction of genotypes" (p. 226). Durham cited the relationship between history of dairying and lactose absorption as an example of cultural influence on genotypes. Genetic mediation occurs when genetically based primary values influence the selection of allomemes. In this mode, genetic changes within groups (or differences between groups) can lead to cultural differences, or, conversely, genetic similarity of populations can cause cultural similarity. Durham argued that the cultural selection of basic color terms is a good example of genetic mediation because the evidence suggests similarity in color encoding is determined by genetic similarities among people.

*Comparative Modes.* Durham argued that the ability of existing memes to influence the cultural fitness of other memes through the process of secondary value selection allows for the possibility of three additional modes of relationship between genes and culture: enhancement, opposition, and neutrality. He labeled them *comparative modes* because the cultural fitness of the allomemes are compared with their inclusive fitness consequences. Enhancement occurs when the cultural values of a population produce high cultural fitness effects in an allomeme that also has high inclusive fitness effects. Opposition occurs in circumstances where allomemes that confer high cultural fitness have suboptimal inclusive fitness effects. In the neutrality mode, allomemes do not differ in their inclusive fitness effects, although they may differ in cultural fitness. In this mode, cultural change neither promotes not detracts from biological fitness.

### Principle of Congruence

Durham's (1991) third hypothesis states, "The main but not exclusive effect of the human decision system is to promote a general pattern of positive covariation between the cultural fitnesses of allomemes and their inclusive fitness values for the 'selectors' " (p. 209). Durham argued that secondary cultural selection should tend to influence culture in a biologically adaptive manner. Because of a long history of cultural selection of reproductively advantageous secondary values, evaluations influenced by primary values should be congruent with those influenced by secondary values. Durham called this generalization the *principle of congruence.* In other words, given conditions of choice, people should tend to select, using primary or secondary values, allomemes that benefit inclusive fitness.

Although Durham emphasized the importance of social values and decision making in cultural selection and transmission, he contended that these processes lead to the selection of biologically adaptive cultural elements. The next section reviews the original dual-inheritance theorists, Boyd and Richerson, who argued that cultural transmission processes can lead to the adoption of maladaptive as well as adaptive cultural elements.

## DUAL-INHERITANCE THEORY

Boyd and Richerson (1985) produced mathematical models akin to those used in population genetics to demonstrate that cultural beliefs are influenced by both cultural and genetic transmission forces. In agreement with other evolutionary theorists, Boyd and Richerson suggested that evolved predispositions play an important role in shaping behavior and culture. However, as their models have demonstrated, nonsociobiological forces can have a significant impact on beliefs, values, and behavior within a culture—sufficient to lead to the adoption of maladaptive cultural variants. Richerson and Boyd (1989) argued that, to supply a complete explanation of human behavior, one must first distinguish between genetic and cultural processes and then determine how they interact with regard to individual decision making, cultural, and genetic evolution.

### Definition of Culture

Like Durham (1991), Boyd and Richerson (1985) defined culture in ideational terms: "Culture is information capable of affecting individuals' phenotypes which they acquire from other conspecifics by teaching or imitation" (p. 33). A person's *cultural repertoire* is the information that he or she culturally inherits, and is analogous to the genotype that contains inherited genetic information. Specific elements of the cultural repertoire are referred to as *cultural variants*. Boyd and Richerson excluded behavior from their culture definition because it is seen as contingent on the interaction of cultural and genetic dispositions and particular environmental conditions.

## Genetic and Cultural Transmission

Transmission of genetic information always travels from parent to child. However, this is only one form of transmission for cultural information. Borrowing terminology from Cavalli-Sforza and Feldman (1981), Boyd and Richerson (1985) classified parent–child transmission of cultural information as *vertical*; cultural influence from members of the previous generation other than the parents (e.g., teachers) as *oblique*; and cultural influence from members of one's own generation (e.g., peers) as *horizontal*. Nonvertical transmission is asymmetric with respect to genetic transmission.

## Transmission of Culture: Individual Versus Social Learning

Boyd and Richerson (1985) distinguished between individual learning and social learning. *Individual learning* is considered a process that produces variations in phenotypes in response to environmental contingencies, a capability all organisms possess. In humans, individual learning involves assessment of situations and learning on one's own, often by trial and error. Individual learning is governed by rules that reject some behaviors and accept others (e.g., the rules of operant conditioning). Information learned in this way perishes with the learner, and is not a key factor in cultural inheritance. Boyd and Richerson (1985) suggested cultural inheritance is based primarily on *social learning*, defined as "the transmission of stable behavioral dispositions by teaching or imitation" (p. 40). Cultural variants spread by social learning are more similar to genes than individually learned variants because cultural variants can be inherited and transmitted over consecutive generations (Richerson & Boyd, 1992).

## Interaction Between Genetic and Cultural Evolution

Boyd and Richerson proposed several ways in which genes and culture may interact. Over long periods of time, evolved predispositions can influence the selection, retention, and transmission of cultural traits; because these evolved predispositions are selected within a cultural context, culture can influence their nature. On a shorter time scale, cultural variants whose evolution is mainly controlled by biologically evolved predispositions coevolve with cultural variants whose evolution is guided mainly by nonsociobiological processes.

## Factors Shaping Culture

*Genetically Inherited Predispositions.* Richerson and Boyd (1989) argued that behaviors produced by evolved predispositions are directed toward the attainment of fitness-enhancing goals, such as seeking sexual gratification, attaining social approval, and reducing hunger. Individuals evaluate (consciously or unconsciously) alternative beliefs, values, and attitudes, and select those they sense will best satisfy their evolved goals (a process known as *direct bias*, to be discussed later). As such, some behavioral variation across cultures can be explained in terms of people making different adaptive behavioral choices in different sociocultural contexts. Like Tooby and Cosmides (1992), Richerson and Boyd (1989) argued that understanding cultural evolution requires knowledge of the evolved pre-dispositions that affect the choice of cultural variants selected. Conversely, genetic changes cannot be understood without attending to the cultural beliefs within a population, which contribute to the social environment under which biological selection operates.

*Nonsociobiological Effects.* Richerson and Boyd (1989) argued that evolved predispositions are not the only factors that affect the selection and retention of cultural traits. Under certain conditions, nonsociobiologi-cal processes—processes that are not associated with promoting genetic fitness—can exert important influences. For example, when many alter-native cultural variants are available, it may be difficult to deter-mine, through individual learning, which will best serve evolved goals. Relying on alternative methods of selecting these variants, such as social learning, may be more adaptive in the long run, even if maladaptive traits are adopted in some instances. Richerson and Boyd gave religious or political affiliation as examples of beliefs or attitudes that may be weakly affected by evolved predispositions (and be acquired through social learning), but still have strong effects on behavior. For whatever reason, when the effect of evolved goals and predispositions on cultural choice is weak, culture may become more like an independent system of inheritance. In these cases, population-level processes such as cultural group selection, which is shortly discussed, may play an important role in cultural evolution.

## Key Forces of Cultural Evolution:
## Decision-Making Forces

According to Boyd and Richerson (1985), the driving forces of cultural evolution include random forces (mutation and drift), natural selection, and decision-making forces. Decision-making forces are considered to be "the most important difference between the evolutionary processes of the genetic and cultural systems" (Richerson & Boyd, 1992, p. 91). Boyd and Richerson divided these decision-making forces into two main categories: guided variation and biased transmission. Biased transmission is further

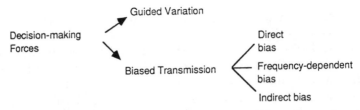

FIG. 5.3. Boyd and Richerson's (1985) decision-making forces. Guided variation and direct bias tend to favor the spread of adaptive cultural variants, whereas frequency-dependent and indirect bias may lead to the adoption of maladaptive variants.

divided into direct bias, frequency-dependent bias, and indirect bias. These forces are illustrated in Fig. 5.3, and are described as the following.

*Guided Variation.* Guided variation of cultural traits occurs when people modify culturally inherited information to better suit the local environment based on individual learning from their own experience. The modified behavior or information may then be imitated and culturally transmitted. Hence, the cultural variants that are socially transmitted have been "guided" by individual learning. Under conditions in which behavior is determined mainly by individual learning, guided variation allows populations to adapt relatively quickly and effectively to changing environments.

*Biased Transmission.* This refers to variations in transmission that occur when information is transmitted through social learning. As social learning theorists have demonstrated, people do not copy others indiscriminately. Boyd and Richerson (1985) identified three types of bias that influence which beliefs and behaviors people copy, and therefore transmit culturally.

1. Direct Biases. In directly biased transmission, individuals choose the cultural variant they believe is most suitable for their needs. For example, people may choose to wear a bicycle helmet because of its safety value. Direct biases are similar to guided variation, except direct biases are dependent on existing variation in cultural traits, whereas in guided variation, individuals generate alternatives for themselves through individual learning. Boyd and Richerson (1985) suggested the guiding criteria influencing direct bias and guided variation could be "inherited genetically or culturally or learned independently" (p. 136). When decision making strongly depends on naturally selected guiding criteria, and the cultural environment is similar to that in which the guiding rules were selected, direct bias (and guided variation) will usually cause adaptive

cultural variants to spread (Richerson & Boyd, 1992). If these conditions are not met, direct bias and guided variation may select for maladaptive traits. In their writing, Boyd and Richerson usually considered the outcome of these two processes to be adaptive.

2. Frequency-Dependent Biases. Frequency-dependent biases induce people to choose cultural traits based on their frequency in the population (e.g., choosing to wear a bicycle helmet after most people wear them). Imitating the most common traits may be an adaptive strategy when the traits are difficult or costly to evaluate, but can also lead to the adoption of maladaptive behaviors.

3. Indirect Biases. Indirect biases direct people to select cultural variants based on the use of the variants by particular types of people. For example, one might choose to imitate the behavior, or be influenced by the beliefs, of someone who is admired, respected, and considered wise, or who has high prestige or status. An example of the potentially maladaptive effects of this bias would be a person choosing not to wear a bicycle helmet because individuals they admired did not wear one.

## Is Culture Adaptive?

Boyd and Richerson attempted to distinguish between forces that promote adaptive cultural choices and those that promote maladaptive choices. In general, the greater the reliance on social learning, the greater the opportunity for maladaptive variants to be adopted. Because evolved predispositions often influence the choices mediated by guided variation and direct biases, these processes tend to lead to the adoption of adaptive beliefs and behaviors. However, when it is too difficult or too costly for people to evaluate cultural variants in terms of their fitness benefits, people will tend to rely on indirect and frequency-dependent bias.[5] According to Boyd and Richerson (1985), these processes, along with asymmetric transmission,[6] can increase the frequency of cultural variants that have lower fitness than other variants. In summary, according to Boyd and Richerson, our reliance on social learning is usually adaptive, but can

---

[5]In a recent paper, Boyd and Richerson (1995) evaluated the argument that social learning evolved because of its cost-effectiveness. Using mathematical models, they concurred with Rogers' (1989) findings that disputed this argument. However, after changing the models to allow for selective learning, Boyd and Richerson (1995) demonstrated that "social learning can be adaptive if it makes individual learning more accurate or less costly" (p. 125).

[6]For example, one may choose to devote considerable time and energy to a career (an idea likely transmitted horizontally), rather than to raising a large family. Hence, asymmetric transmission (horizontal or oblique), which is more frequent when parental influences wane, may lead to the adoption of maladaptive cultural variants.

lead to the adoption of maladaptive behaviors or ideas. Whether this occurs depends on the leash linking culture with the evolved dispositions governing decision making.

## Interaction of Genetic and Cultural Evolution

Richerson and Boyd (1989) distinguished among four possible scenarios of gene–culture interaction: (a) culture is kept on a leash by evolved predispositions and, as a result, culture tracks fitness; (b) evolved predispositions are kept on a leash by the evolution of cultural norms that create systems of reward and punishment, which govern the expression of the dispositions; (c) harmful cultural variants (such as smoking) may arise and be able to attract imitators, similar to Dawkins' parasitic memes. Natural selection may respond by favoring evolved predispositions that protect individuals from adopting some of the harmful traits, leading to a continuing coevolution of parasite and host in a gene–culture evolutionary arms race; and (d) genes and culture may coevolve through a series of mutually beneficial interactions.

All of these scenarios are considered common, but Richerson and Boyd (1989) considered the last one most important because of the success of the human species. Although they have identified several means through which cultural transmission can lead individuals off the adaptive track, the theorists conclude that individual and social learning together allow individuals to track environmental changes more quickly than genes can, at a lower information cost, and with fewer errors than individual learning alone (Richerson & Boyd, 1992). Another important conclusion of Boyd and Richerson's work is that, because behaviors and beliefs are subject to both cultural and genetic forces, observed behaviors or cultural patterns may be genetically optimal, culturally optimal, both, or neither.

## An Example of Frequency-Dependent Transmission: Cultural Group Selection

One of the most important products of frequency-dependent transmission is cultural group selection, which Boyd and Richerson suggested accounts for the evolution of cooperation on a large scale among nonrelatives in the human species. The process of cultural group selection requires that humans inherit some portion of their cultural beliefs, values, and goals from individuals who have a cultural influence on them (this process has also been referred to as *conformist transmission*; Richerson & Boyd, 1989). Groups of hominids that contained relatively high frequencies of cultural inducements to cooperate may have fared better than groups that did not. Also, beliefs that improved group stability and viability tended to persist because the groups did. Frequency-dependent biases tend to increase the amount of cultural variability between groups relative to that within groups, which in turn can cause selection between groups to favor cultural traits that promote group over individual success. Cultural group selection is an example of a mutualistic interaction of genes and culture. From the cultural viewpoint, "selfish" genes are harnessed in the service of a group-selected cultural unit. From a genetic perspective, selfish genes use their leash on cultural evolution to produce an efficient system to police an extensive, generalized system of reciprocal altruism (similar to Alexander's, 1987, notion of indirect reciprocity). Richerson and Boyd (1989) argued that cultural evolutionary models are better predictors of human cooperation than models derived solely from kinship theory (Hamilton, 1964) and direct reciprocity theory (Trivers, 1971).

## BARKOW'S COEVOLUTIONARY MODEL

In the book *Darwin, Sex, and Status*, Barkow (1989) presented his coevolutionary model of relations between biology and culture. Barkow reviewed definitions of *culture* supplied by other scholars and derived three basic components: (a) socially transmitted (b) information (c) that is organized in a system. Culture, which is the largest system of socially transmitted information, may be made up of smaller systems, often called *subcultures*. Barkow distinguished between culture, which he viewed as a population-level phenomenon, and the internalization of culture, which occurs at an intraindividual level. According to Barkow (1989), culture "is not the cause of anything" (p. 142). It is simply a set of information whose meaning is shared.

### The Intra-Individual System

The heart of Barkow's analysis of the relation between genes and culture lies in his model of the intervening psychological processes. Barkow decried "genes for" explanations of behavior, and suggested such explanations be avoided by identifying the mental structures that mediate relations between genes and culture. To explain relations between genes and culture, Barkow created a metaphor called the *intra-individual system* based on a distributed, parallel information-processing model of the brain. The intra-individual system consists of five interacting information-processing components—goals, plans, codes, cognitive maps, and self-representations—and their subsystems. Examples of basic goals are reproduce, obtain nutrition, seek prestige, and create cognitive maps of the physical and social universe. Achieving such goals requires the creation of subgoals such as find food and have sex.

Plans are behaviors in service of goals. Eating is a plan that serves the goal obtain nutrition, and buying food is a subplan serving the eating plan. A subplan might involve finding a job to obtain money to buy food. As illustrated, goals and plans tend to be organized hierarchically. Codes are cognitive structures that organize information and enable communication. Examples of basic codes are those that structure perception, color vision, the deep structure of language, and myths. Like goals and plans, codes have subcodes. For example, particular languages are subcodes of the language code.

Cognitive maps constitute the fourth component of the intra-individual system. Cognitive maps are internal representations of external reality, akin to computer simulation models used to make predictions. They are also called the *mazeway* by Wallace (1970), who stated that "every human brain contains, at a given point in time, a unique mental image of a complex system of dynamically interrelated objects" (p. 15). Such cognitive maps, or mazeways, include values, representations of objects—including the self, other people, and animals—and conceptions of how various physical, social, and religious systems work. The information contained in our basic cognitive maps, including a great deal of social information, was selected in ancestral environments in terms of its fitness-enhancing ability. Individuals' cognitive maps are akin to groups' culture.

The final component of the intra-individual system is representations of self. One of the most important objects people seek to locate in their cognitive maps is themselves. According to Barkow (1989), "an organism with a model of external reality that includes a representation of itself will experience consciousness. When that internal representation of self becomes sufficiently complex, it will subjectively experience self-consciousness" (p. 103).

In Barkow's model, basic goals, plans, and codes are culturally universal. But the further down the hierarchy of subgoals, subplans, and subcodes one goes, the more environmentally and culturally variable they become. It follows that biological factors play the most important role in determining basic goals, plans, and codes, and cultural factors play the most important role in determining subgoals, subplans, and subcodes.

To summarize, Barkow (1989) stated, "I do not argue that the mind actually works in terms of goals, plans, and codes: rather, I believe that the brain's functions are conducted by specialized processors or subsystems (some would use the term 'modules') that use algorithms that generate behavior *usefully conceptualized* in terms of subplans and subgoals associated with adaptive problems" (p. 106).

### Relations Between the Intra-Individual System and Culture

Barkow suggested that, to understand culture, one must distinguish among the ways in which different categories or types of culturally provided information are processed in the intra-individual system. Natural selection favors the ability to replicate subcodes such as language with high fidelity because there is little adaptive advantage in changing or challenging the fundamental ways in which people structure reality and communicate information (subaspects of subcodes such as slang, which serve functions other than communication, may, however, change rapidly through selection). In contrast, natural selection favors the tendency to challenge, revise, and reinvent subgoals and subplans. People are constantly finding better ways of achieving adaptive ends, especially as environments change. One of the most important determinants of which subgoals and subplans individuals adopt is the extent to which the subgoals and subplans enable people to satisfy multiple needs. According to Barkow, cultures differ mainly in the extent to which they provide different recurring subgoals and subplans. Individuals also may differ in the extent to which they are disposed to select and respond to the particular subgoals and subplans available in their cultures, which, in part, gives rise to individual differences in personality.

According to Barkow, the basic cosmology contained in an individual's mazeway, or cognitive map, is almost as resistant to cultural change as subcodes are. The ways in which people represent their worlds are developed at an early age and built on, forming highly organized, deep cognitive structures. However, in situations of social and ecological breakdown, when people's world view is no longer predictive—when their subgoal and subplans do not succeed—people may synthesize a new world view, often preached by a charismatic leader.

### Cultural Selection

Subgoals and subplans that work are retained in the information pool of cultures; those that do not are discarded. It follows that cultures are dynamic: There is constant, ongoing competition among the subgoals and subplans people create and refine. Ecology plays a role in the selection of culture, but the role it plays is less causal than constraining in nature.

### Are We Motivated to Enhance Our Inclusive Fitness?

Basic goals—our primary needs and motives—and basic plans—the basic ways in which we satisfy them—have been built into our minds through natural selection. These goals and plans enabled our ancestors to maximize their inclusive fitness, and they usually enable us to maximize our inclusive fitness today. However, this does not mean that individuals are consciously driven by the personal intention of maximizing their inclusive fitness. For example, Barkow suggested that people may circumvent the goal of reproduction through the use of contraceptives. Barkow identified four processes that may mediate the evolution of culturally maladaptive traits: elites may appropriate ideas; information may be mistransmitted; environments may change, rendering previously adaptive traits maladaptive; and there may be maladaptive side effects of otherwise fitness-enhancing aspects of culture.

## Cultural Universals and Cultural Diversity

Barkow dealt with the cultural universality/cultural diversity polarity in terms of the various levels in his hierarchy of the intra-individual system. Basic goals, plans, and codes are culturally universal and environmentally stable: They are built into the human psyche and organize the behaviors of all people everywhere. Such universal components of human nature dominate the behavior of newborns. However, as babies mature, they develop subgoals, subplans, and subcodes based on the particular input from their particular environments and cultures (e.g., particular languages). As the subgoals and subplans become increasingly derivative (removed from basic goals and basic plans), they become increasingly derived from culture.

## Attention and Learning

Barkow suggested that the things to which we attend determine to a great extent the aspects of culture that influence us. He argued that, in general, we are evolved to attend to the aspects of our environment—such as information about food sources, predators, potential mates, and status—that enhanced our ancestors' fitness. We do not have the kind of willful control over our attention that many scholars assume, yet undoubtedly have experienced when various kinds of biologically basic imagery have intruded on their academic ruminations.

Barkow was critical of the concept of learning, and preferred to think of it in terms of the ways in which information is processed in the intraindividual system. Barkow argued that subgoals and subplans are constrained by learning biases built in by natural selection of the structures that mediate them. Such biases are directed toward the enhancement of inclusive fitness, at least as operationalized in our ancestral environment. In general, things we experience as pleasureful enhanced our ancestors' fitness, and things we experience as painful detracted from it. However,

Barkow argued that the limbic system may override the learning-based neocortical system (e.g., parents often risk their lives to save their children, or men fly into uncontrollable rages when they believe their mates are cheating on them).

## COMPARISONS AND EVALUATIONS

The preceding sections presented several evolutionary approaches to the understanding of culture and cultural evolution. Table 5.1 summarizes the important ideas from each approach. This section briefly outlines the main similarities and differences among the approaches and provides critiques of each.

## THE MEMETIC APPROACH

Dawkins (1976) argued that the process of cultural selection has become uncoupled from the process of biological selection. He suggested that successful memes are those that best promote their own replication, not ones that are linked to biological fitness. Memes can be considered parasitic in the way they manipulate their hosts.

Of the theorists discussed here, Dawkins is unique in arguing that cultural selection has become uncoupled and completely independent of biological selection. Most other theorists argue that the human mind, which was shaped by natural selection, is in some way disposed to, or at least able to, select cultural traits in terms of their adaptive value.

Dawkins' differentiation of two inheritance systems is compatible with dual-inheritance models; indeed, Dawkins' ideas can be considered forerunners of these models. However, dual-inheritance models differ from Dawkins' model in allowing that genetic predispositions may play a greater role in cultural selection than Dawkins allows, and that cultural fitness may be more closely associated with biological fitness.

Several theorists (e.g., Daly, 1982; Tooby & Cosmides, 1989) have challenged the biological evolution analogy of cultural change (used by Dawkins and the dual-inheritance theorists). Boyd and Richerson (1985) and Durham (1991) acknowledged some of the differences between biological and cultural evolution, especially the Lamarckian and multidirectional nature of cultural transmission and the inclusion of choice or bias in the selection process, and have built these differences into their models. Dawkins (1986) acknowledged that the analogy is imperfect, but argued that there is sufficient commonality between the two processes to make

TABLE 5.1
Summary of Evolutionary Culture Theories

| Theory | Definition of Culture | Adaptive Function of Culture | Means of Transmission | Mechanisms, Constraints, Biases | Selection and Retention | Relation Between Biology and Culture | Relation Between Culture and Behavior |
|---|---|---|---|---|---|---|---|
| Dawkins' meme model | No specific definition given. Culture can be broken down into informational units, or memes (Dawkins, 1976). | The capacity for culture evolved through natural selection; however, memes may have no adaptive value. | Memes are replicated through imitation and can be transmitted through various media. | None given. | Memes with attributes that increase their likelihood of being imitated and adopted will be favored. | Cultural and biological selection processes are uncoupled. | Memes are capable of influencing behavior of their carriers. In this sense, they are considered parasitic. |
| Darwinian anthropology | The outcome of the actions of individuals motivated to maximize their inclusive fitness in particular environments (Irons, 1979b). | Culture enables individuals to track fitness in varying environments. | Social learning. | Social learning mechanism (Alexander, 1979). Learning incorporating value-based decision rules (Flinn & Alexander, 1982). | Individuals continually make behavioral choices that maximize their inclusive fitness. | Culture adaptively tracks fitness in varying conditions. Biologically based fitness calculators have direct influence on cultural patterns. | Culture defined in terms of behavior. Culture and behavior not clearly differentiated. |

| | | | | | | |
|---|---|---|---|---|---|---|
| Evolutionary psychology (Tooby & Cosmides, 1992) | Includes mental, behavioral, or material commonalities shared across individuals, and is the product of evolved psychological mechanisms. Can be factored into evoked, epidemiological, and metaculture. | Evoked culture allowed ancestral individuals to adaptively respond to varying environmental conditions. Adopted culture allowed for low-cost information gathering. | Social learning. | Evolved mental mechanisms are involved in the operation of evoked culture, epidemiological culture, and metaculture. | Evolved mechanisms may make some traits more appealing under certain conditions. | All aspects of culture are both generated by and responded to by biologically inherited mental mechanisms. | Mental mechanisms link culture to behavior. |
| Lumsden & Wilson's co-evolutionary theory | "The sum total of mental constructs and behavior . . . transmitted from one generation to the next" (Lumsden & Wilson, 1981, p. 3). Cultural units are culturgens—transmissible behaviors, mentifacts, and artifacts. | Culture usually enhances inclusive fitness, but may be maladaptive. | Social learning. Translation: the expression at the societal level of the cumulative effects of the transmission process at the individual level. | Epigenetic rules are evolved constraints that affect the probability of an individual using one culturgen as opposed to another. | Culturgens are processed through a sequence of epigenetic rules. | Genes and culture have reciprocal influences on each other. | Cultural rules and behavior treated as if they were isomorphic. |

(Continued)

TABLE 5.1
(Continued)

| Theory | Definition of Culture | Adaptive Function of Culture | Means of Transmission | Mechanisms, Constraints, Biases | Selection and Retention | Relation Between Biology and Culture | Relation Between Culture and Behavior |
|---|---|---|---|---|---|---|---|
| Durham's co-evolutionary theory | Shared ideas, values, beliefs, etc. in the minds of humans. A pool of information that is both public (socially shared) and prescriptive (guides behavior) (Durham, 1991). Memes: ideational cultural units. | Cultural system acquires a set of standards based on primary and secondary values that increasingly select genetically advantageous variants (Durham, 1991). | Social learning. Conveyance forces (natural selection, choice, imposition) increase the frequency of a given meme through social transmission. | Various selection biases: learned biases, satisfaction bias, bias favoring more adaptive cultural traits, circumstantial bias (Durham, 1979). | Cultural selection retains cultural variants that enhance inclusive fitness (Durham, 1979). Cultural selection operates by decision making guided by genetically and culturally inherited values. The latter, secondary value selection, is most important (Durham, 1991). | Five modes of relationship: cultural mediation, genetic mediation, enhancement, opposition, and neutrality. Gene–culture relations need not always be reciprocal and interactive. | Distinguishes culture (ideational form) from behavior. Culture and behavior not necessarily isomorphic. |

| | | | | | | |
|---|---|---|---|---|---|---|
| Boyd & Richerson's dual-inheritance theory | "Information capable of affecting individuals' phenotypes which they acquire . . . by teaching or imitation" (Boyd & Richerson, 1985, p. 33). | Evolved mechanisms allow individuals to determine which cultural beliefs and behaviors best satisfy evolved goals. Social learning mechanisms allow for cost-effective learning of adaptive traits under certain conditions. | Social learning. | Biased transmission: direct bias, indirect bias, and frequency-dependent bias. | See previous. | Four types of interaction: Culture is constrained by evolved predispositions; evolved predispositions are constrained by culture; harmful cultural variants co-evolve with host defenses; genes and culture co-evolve in mutually beneficial way. | "The relationship between culture and behavior is similar to the relationship between genotype and phenotype in noncultural organisms" (Boyd & Richerson, 1985, p. 36). Behavior is the outward manifestation of culture. |
| Barkow's co-evolutionary theory | "A system of socially transmitted information" (Barkow, 1989, p. 140). | Most aspects enhance inclusive fitness, but some aspects may be maladaptive. Several explanations for the evolution of culture are discussed, including autopredation and sexual selection. | Multiple means, depending on the type of cultural information in question. | Goals, plans, codes; evolved psychological information-processing mechanisms. | Depends on the type: cultural information in question and the level (basic vs. sub). Natural selection favors higher fidelity replication of codes than goals or plans. | Reciprocal co-evolution of genes and culture. | Culture affects behavior when processed through mental mechanisms. |

knowledge of biological evolution useful for understanding cultural change.

Durham (1979) and Ball (1984) challenged the idea that parasitic memes may render individuals helpless victims of their culture. They argued that, because capacity for culture was naturally selected, it must include the capacity to evaluate and reject harmful memes. Durham (1991) suggested that harmful memes are usually removed through cultural self-selection processes; when they are present, it is usually due to social imposition or imperfections in our decision-making system (see Durham, 1991, for a detailed discussion of these imperfections).

## DARWINIAN ANTHROPOLOGY AND EVOLUTIONARY PSYCHOLOGY

### Darwinian Anthropology

This evolutionary approach focuses on the adaptiveness of behavior and cultural traits. The capacity for culture is seen as having the adaptive function of tracking fitness in varying environments. Most cultural behavioral patterns are expected to be adaptive. Measures or estimates of fitness or reproductive success are sometimes used in modeling and predicting the behavior patterns of various cultural groups.

### Evolutionary Psychology

Evolutionary psychologists study the domain-specific psychological mechanisms that were shaped by natural selection in ancestral environments. These mechanisms produce and regulate evoked culture, epidemiological (transmitted) culture, and metaculture. Evolutionary psychologists argue that examining the design of mental adaptations (evolved mechanisms) is more useful than focusing on the adaptiveness of current behaviors because the current environment has changed greatly from the ancestral one.

### Similarities and Differences Between Darwinian Anthropology and Evolutionary Psychology

Richerson and Boyd (1989) identified several similarities between Darwinian anthropology and evolutionary psychology. Both approaches reject the idea that genetic variation is responsible for cross-cultural variability in behavior patterns. Both agree that our capacity for culture was selected because it served an adaptive function in the past, and both agree that this capacity is regulated by universal evolved mechanisms and predispositions. However, the two perspectives differ in their interpretation of the nature of these mechanisms. Darwinian anthropologists view mechanisms as domain-general inclusive fitness motivators that calculate fitness costs and benefits and adjust behavior adaptively in varying environments, whereas evolutionary psychologists view evolved mechanisms as domain-specific, designed to solve problems that early humans faced.

Differences in interpretations of how evolved mechanisms shape behavior and culture give rise to different predictions of human behavior and culture (Crawford, 1993; Richerson & Boyd, 1989). Darwinian anthropologists expect the predominant cultural beliefs and values to maximize inclusive fitness. In contrast, evolutionary psychologists do not necessarily expect evolved mechanisms that were shaped in ancestral environments to function in adaptive ways in the current environment. For example, in our current society, exposure to high levels of violence on television and in films may activate an ancestral adaptation that sets levels of aggression in accordance with levels experienced during development, maladaptively inducing children to behave unnecessarily aggressively.

## Criticisms of Darwinian Anthropology

Symons (1992), an outspoken critic of Darwinian anthropology, has argued that adaptive effects of current behavior may be fortuitous effects rather than an indication of an underlying adaptation; currently maladaptive behaviors observed today (e.g., eating copious amounts of sugary foods) may be the result of an adaptation that would have enhanced our ancestors' fitness in their environment (e.g., eating ripe fruits at their peak of nutritional value), but do not enhance our fitness in the current environment (where nonnutritious sweets are plentiful).

In response to such criticisms, Darwinian anthropologists have argued that there is value in studying adaptiveness and reproductive success in current environments because the most plausible explanation for current adaptiveness is that these behaviors benefited fitness in the past and were naturally selected. For example, Betzig (1989) suggested that other explanations, such as random evolutionary forces (e.g., drift), random environmental forces (e.g., learning errors), nonrandom evolutionary forces (e.g., pleiotropy), or nonrandom environmental forces (culture), are weak in comparison. In addition, argued Betzig, the effects of these other forces are more likely to produce maladaptive than adaptive behaviors.

Betzig (chap. 8, this volume) argues that it is easier to measure selection pressures and fitness effects in the present than to estimate them in ancestral populations. Betzig asserts that models incorporating selection pressures that shaped a trait (e.g., predation levels) are valuable in studying adaptations. According to Betzig, such models have been successful at predicting traits in a variety of cultures. Some examples are age at maturity and the relations between material inheritance and mating systems.

Irons (1990) attacked the assumption that the current environment has changed so much that we would not expect current behavior to be adaptive. He noted that all adaptations are affected by specific environmental elements and unaffected by others. The fact that there is some environmental novelty in the present does not necessarily mean all adaptations are dysfunctional (see Crawford, chap. 9, this volume).

## Criticisms of Evolutionary Psychology

Evolutionary psychology has been criticized for its reliance on the narrowly defined and somewhat ambiguous concept of the ancestral environment (EEA). The difficulty lies in finding an appropriate exemplar of ancestral human life, which is necessary for making predictions about adaptations. Betzig (chap. 8, this volume) argues that basing a model on the behavior of current hunter–gatherer groups is problematic because of the variability in behavioral patterns across such groups. Irons (1990) argued that the idea that we spent 99% of our existence as hunter–gatherers may be inaccurate, noting that behaviorally and neurologically modern humans did not appear until 50 to 35 thousand years ago, near the end of the Pleistocene. Only then did evidence of cultural practices such as art and local traditions appear. If we consider only the time during which *Homo sapiens* displayed a capacity for culture, the amount of time spent as Pleistocene hunter–gatherers is reduced to 70% to 80% of our history, making our time spent in relatively novel environments 20%–30%.

Tooby and Cosmides' (1992) model of evoked culture has been criticized for being too simple to predict and explain complex cultural dynamics. Their model is weak at explaining diversity within a population of individuals that experience the same environmental conditions.

## Combining Darwinian Anthropology
## and Evolutionary Psychology

Some theorists (Irons, 1990), ourselves included, believe evolutionary studies of human behavior are most productive when both evolutionary psychology and Darwinian anthropology are combined. To enhance our understanding of human nature and culture, the adaptiveness of current behavior and the structure of mental mechanisms should be investigated. Studying adaptiveness can shed light on the adaptations of the mind. Studying the structure of the mind's mental mechanisms is necessary for understanding the current functioning of these adaptations.

## COMPARISONS AMONG COEVOLUTIONARY THEORIES

- *Boyd and Richerson's Dual-Inheritance Theory.* Using mathematical models, Boyd and Richerson (1985) have shown that behavior may be transmitted through both cultural and genetic means. Behavior may be optimal or suboptimal, either culturally or biologically (i.e., in various combinations). Cultural evolution is distinct from biological evolution, although the two processes undergo similar forms of selection and the two may coevolve.

- *Lumsden & Wilson's Coevolutionary Theory.* Lumsden and Wilson (1981) postulated a reciprocal interaction between genes and culture. Epigenetic rules, as evolved constraints, bias the adoption of cultural traits, or culturgens, during development of the individual. The corresponding effects of individual behavior and cognition on societal patterns (translation) contribute to the environment in which natural selection may modify the underlying epigenetic rules, with the entire circular process being referred to as the *coevolutionary circuit.*

- *Durham's Coevolutionary Theory.* Durham's (1991) cultural transmission model considers genetic and cultural influences on the transmission and selection of ideational cultural units. Focusing on the human decision-making system, Durham proposed cultural values have the most important influence on cultural selection. However, he expected cultural units that are favored by such a system to enhance both cultural and biological fitness. Five modes of relationship between genes and culture are outlined.

- *Barkow's Coevolutionary Theory.* Barkow's model distinguishes among genetic, cultural, environmental, and psychological processes, and attempts to explain how they relate to each other in an integrated system. Barkow (1989) suggested people process different kinds of cultural information (goals, plans, codes) in different ways, and that they develop cognitive maps to represent reality. Barkow accepted that most aspects of culture were selected because they enhanced the inclusive fitness of our ancestors, but that many aspects of modern culture may be maladaptive.

### Similarities Among Cultural Transmission Models

These coevolutionary models can be classified as dual inheritance because they recognize biological and cultural determinants of behavior. Durham's (1979) and Lumsden and Wilson's (1981) models feature behavioral trait units, whereas Boyd and Richerson's (1986), Barkow's (1989), and Durham's (1991) feature ideational units.

Lumsden and Wilson (1981) and Durham (1976, 1979) assumed that cultural transmission, selection, and evolution are constrained, to some extent, by genetic transmission, natural selection, and biological evolution (Holcomb, 1993). Richerson and Boyd (1989) argued that genetic predispositions can keep culture on a leash, often leading to highly adaptive behaviors. However, cultural selection processes that are not strongly genetically influenced can lead to maladaptive behaviors. Consequently, Richerson and Boyd (1989) concluded that human evolution is fundamentally different from the evolution of other organisms. Durham (1991) found this conclusion to be anti-Darwinian.

Boyd and Richerson (1985) noted several similarities between their theory and other models. For example, they suggested that several of the biases that Durham (1979) proposed correspond to the mechanisms of direct bias or guided variation they defined. Durham (1991) suggested that Boyd and Richerson's frequency-dependent bias and indirect bias play a role similar to "choice" in his model. Barkow (1989) and Durham (1991) similarly discussed how people may be forced by others to adopt maladaptive variants.

### Differences Among Coevolutionary Models

Although the coevolutionary models posit biases, rules, or predispositions that influence cultural choices, the models differ in how hard-wired they assume these mechanisms are. Lumsden and Wilson (1981) advanced the strongest position, arguing that individuals have a direct genetic propensity to acquire some cultural traits rather than others. Other theorists allow that individuals may choose among cultural traits, guided both by motivations shaped by natural selection and values influenced by culture.

Boyd and Richerson (1985) criticized Lumsden and Wilson's 1,000-year rule, in which cultural groups experiencing different selection pressures could acquire genetic differences in 50 generations. According to Boyd and Richerson, such genetic differentiation could occur only if there were strong and persistent selection pressures favoring different cultural variants, and if the two groups existed in isolation. The rarity of such conditions diminishes the importance of the 1,000-year rule. (For similar critiques of Lumsden and Wilson's model, see Maynard Smith & Warren, 1982.)

### Major Criticisms of the Coevolutionary Models

Critics have identified two significant weaknesses of the coevolutionary/dual-inheritance models. First, such models fail to supply adequate detail about the specific psychological mechanisms individuals use to evaluate, adopt, and transmit cultural elements (Barkow, 1989; Cronk, 1995;

Daly, 1982; Daly & Wilson, 1989; Flinn & Alexander, 1982; Tooby & Cosmides, 1989). Although Richerson and Boyd (1989) acknowledged the importance of evolved predispositions in shaping culture, they defined them in terms of general evolved goals rather than well-defined decision rules or cognitive algorithms. According to Barkow (1989), Boyd and Richerson need to specify when selection will favor specific biases, under what environmental conditions each will be elicited, and which would be favored or more prominent during different stages of the life cycle. Durham (1991) did not elaborate on the biases he proposed in his 1979 paper. Lumsden and Wilson (1981) gave some insight into the nature of secondary epigenetic rules, using cognitive biases and heuristics as examples.

The second major criticism of coevolutionary models is that they imply a passive view of the individual (Barkow, 1989; Cronk, 1995; Daly, 1982; Daly & Wilson, 1989). Although most models focus on individual decision making, the processes involved—whether they be frequency-dependent bias (Boyd & Richerson) or secondary value selection (Durham, 1991)—do not seem to portray people as active, strategizing, goal-seeking individuals (Daly, 1982; Daly & Wilson, 1989). Rarely is there a discussion of how people manipulate culture in their own interests, as has been suggested by Cronk (1995). Cronk criticized cultural transmission models (as well as inclusive fitness-maximizing models) for failing to account for the discrepancies between the ideational aspect of culture—what people say— and the behavioral aspect of culture—what people do. Cronk noted that people often behave in fitness-maximizing ways, yet describe attitudes or beliefs that are discrepant with their behavior—an occurrence that is not explained by the cultural transmission models. In keeping with the view of the individual as an evolved strategist, cultural transmission theorists need to incorporate key evolutionary ideas, such as sexual selection, parental investment, and kinship theory (Daly & Wilson, 1989).

## CONCLUSIONS

Each of the models reviewed herein increases our understanding of culture. We side with Barkow (1989), Boyd and Richerson (1985), Dawkins (1976), and Durham (1991) in defining the units of culture in terms of information, rather than in terms of behavior. Defining culture in this way enables investigators to distinguish between cultural influences on behavior and other types of influences.

Some models reviewed here analyze culture from the viewpoint of the individual, whereas other models emphasize group-level processes. We believe that a complete explanation of cultural phenomena requires descriptions of processes at both levels. At the individual level, it is important to recognize that we are evolved to use culture to advance our interests, as Alexander (1979), Barkow (1989), and Cronk (1995) suggested. Cronk (1995) adduced evidence that one of the primary functions of culture is to manipulate others. In agreement with other evolutionary theorists, we believe it is valuable to view culture as a tool.

Also at the individual level, we need to understand the cognitive mechanisms that mediate the creation, adoption, transmission, and change of culture, as evolutionary psychologists suggest. However, we find ourselves somewhat disappointed in the paucity of mechanisms identified by evolutionary psychologists pertaining specifically to cultural selection and change. Indeed, advocates of other theoretical perspectives, such as Durham (1979) and Flinn and Alexander (1982), appear to have gone further than evolutionary psychologists toward detailing decision rules that influence the adoption of cultural traits. Others, such as Boyd and Richerson (1985), have at least provided an outline of several transmission biases, although the decision rules involved have not been clearly defined.

At the group level, a complete model of culture should include a description of the forces influencing cultural transmission, an analysis of patterns of information flow, and an analysis of the social dynamics within a group that can influence cultural patterns (e.g., imposition by subgroups). An analysis of cultural evolution at the group level has been tackled best by Boyd and Richerson (1985), whose mathematical models focus on transmission processes. Durham (1991) provided insight into how power relations affect cultural dynamics.

## Distance Between Biology and Culture

One of the most important issues an evolutionary account of culture must address pertains to the strength of the relation between biological and cultural selection. Evolutionary theorists have supplied good explanations of such aspects of culture as mate choice (Buss, 1989), risk taking and violence (Wilson & Daly, 1985), and patterns of helping behavior (Essock-Vitale & McGuire, 1980) exclusively in terms of principles of evolution, without any reference to cultural mechanisms. However, purely biological models will not be able to supply a full account of human behavior without reference to cultural processes for four main reasons.

First, as pointed out by several theorists, we are evolved to learn from others, and much of what we learn from them is culture. Although we genetically inherit the mechanisms that regulate and guide social learning, what we learn—the content of culture—may become uncoupled from the evolved constraints, as Richerson and Boyd (1989) proposed.

Second, rapidly progressing cultural change and innovation may produce an environment to which we are poorly adapted. In recent years, several writers (e.g., K. Bailey, 1996; Bernhard, 1988; Nesse & Williams, 1994; Wright, 1995) explored the question of whether there is a mismatch between our hunter–gatherer brains and the modern environment we live in, and, if so, what the effects are. For example, K. Bailey (1995, 1996) and K. G. Bailey (1996) asserted that biological and cultural evolution were closely matched during most of our evolutionary history; however, during the past 40,000 years, massive cultural and environmental changes have caused current humans to become mismatched with their cultural and physical environments. Culture and neoculture (e.g., as reflected in technological advances such as air travel) have become increasingly independent of (decoupled from) our biological heritage. Bailey believes mismatches between biologically and culturally evolved needs and goals to be the central source of psychopathology in modern societies.

In a similar vein, Wright (1995) suggested that the changes in our social and living environments from ancestral times (e.g., the large proportion of single-occupant households, isolation of family units, and deterioration of social networks) has led to increased feelings of social isolation and increased risk of depression and domestic violence. In addition, in the book *Primates in the Classroom*, Bernhard (1988) argued that characteristics of modern school systems—providing a single role model (the teacher) and a single age cohort (classmates), separating students from the rest of society, and teaching material that cannot readily be applied to the real world—are poorly matched to students' evolved needs and learning skills. With reference to everyday work, Bernhard and Glantz (1991) suggested that employees will be most productive when the workplace contains features familiar to most hunter–gatherer bands, such as a sense of belonging, recognition, self-reliance, communal loyalty, reciprocity, meaningful activity, leadership, and authority. Crawford (chap. 9, this volume) examines issues related to mismatch theory more deeply than this chapter, questioning some of the theory's assumptions.

Third, even if biologically inherited dispositions are capable of influencing cultural attitudes and practices in response to environment changes, as evolutionary psychologists and Darwinian psychologists expect, adaptive cultural changes will not occur immediately. Boyd and Richerson (1985) argued that *cultural inertia*—a property of culture systems that is analogous to phylogenetic inertia in biological evolution—will impose a time lag on cultural change in response to any force of change. As a result of the lag time: "we expect to observe not only the persistence of old traits in new environments, but also different responses on the part of historically different groups to new circumstances" (Boyd & Richerson, 1985, p. 59). In other words, the influences of cultural inertia and cultural history can help account for some of the variation in human cultural patterns that is not fully explained by exclusively biological models of human behavior.[7]

The final limitation of exclusively biological accounts of culture is associated with variations in the fitness value of different cultural traits. In situations where adoption of one cultural variant over another has relatively little impact on fitness, models derived from evolutionary biology may be less useful than models that analyze culture in terms of a separate cultural inheritance system (e.g., Boyd & Richerson, 1985; Dawkins, 1976; Durham, 1991). For example, dual-inheritance models might be more effective than evolutionary psychology or Darwinian anthropology models in explaining changes in popular culture, including fashion and music trends. Investigating the history of each trend and modeling the patterns of transmission may be more helpful than using models drawn from evolutionary biology alone. Although cultural transmission theories are the most useful in these cases, evolutionary theory is nevertheless essential for obtaining the most complete explanation of cultural phenomena. Evolutionary theory may not provide much insight into which fashions may be popular next year, but psychological mechanisms that evolved by natural selection continue to mediate fitness-enhancing behavior related to gender, status, occupation, and so on.

In conclusion, we hope we have demonstrated the value of an evolutionary perspective to the explanation of culture. We believe that the evidence unequivocally establishes that no account of culture can be complete without reference to natural selection and inclusive fitness. As Dawkins and others have shown, the mechanisms of biological evolution supply useful tools for understanding the mechanisms of cultural evolution. In addition, as other researchers and theorists have shown, biological factors exert powerful influences on the selection, transmission, retention, and change of at least some aspects of culture.

## REFERENCES

Alexander, R. D. (1979). *Darwinism and human affairs*. London: Pitman Publishing Ltd.
Alexander, R. D. (1987). *The biology of moral systems*. New York: Aldine de Gruyter.

---

[7]Cultural inertia may be an inherent property of cultural systems, as Boyd and Richerson (1985) suggested, but maintaining the status quo can also be an individual strategy. Alexander (1979) argued that it is in individuals' biological interests to direct their efforts toward using and exploiting their cultures, rather than changing them, because existing cultures have been selected to maximize the fitness of the individuals who created and adopted them.

Bailey, K. (1996, February). Mismatch theory 1: Basic principles. *ASCAP Newsletter, 9*(2), 7–9.

Bailey, K. G. (1995, July). Mismatch theory and paleopsychopathology. In C. B. Crawford (Chair), *Environmental "Mismatch," Stress, and Pathology*. Symposium conducted at the annual meeting of the Human Behavior and Evolution Society, Santa Barbara, CA.

Bailey, K. G. (1996). *Human paleopsychopathology*. Manuscript in preparation.

Ball, J. A. (1984). Memes as replicators. *Ethology and Sociobiology, 5*, 145–161.

Barkow, J. (1989). *Darwin, sex, and status: Biological approaches to mind and culture*. Toronto: University of Toronto Press.

Barkow, J. H., Cosmides, L., & Tooby, J. (Eds.). (1992). *The adapted mind: Evolutionary psychology and the generation of culture*. New York: Oxford University Press.

Bernhard, J. G. (1988). *Primates in the classroom: An evolutionary perspective on children's education*. Amherst: University of Massachusetts Press.

Bernhard, J. G., & Glantz, K. (1991). Management theory. In M. Maxwell (Ed.), *The sociobiological imagination* (pp. 53–70). New York: State University of New York Press.

Betzig, L. (1989). Rethinking human ethology: A response to some recent critiques. *Ethology and Sociobiology, 10*, 315–324.

Bowlby, J. (1969). *Attachment and loss*. New York: Basic Books.

Boyd, R., & Richerson, P. J. (1976). A simple dual inheritance model of the conflict between social and biological evolution. *Zygon, 11*, 254–262.

Boyd, R., & Richerson, P. J. (1985). *Culture and the evolutionary process*. Chicago: University of Chicago Press.

Boyd, R., & Richerson, P. J. (1995). Why does culture increase human adaptability? *Ethology and Sociobiology, 16*(2), 125–144.

Buss, D. (1989). Sex differences in human mate preferences: Evolutionary hypotheses tested in 37 cultures. *Behavioral and Brain Sciences, 12*(1), 1–14.

Campbell, D. T. (1983). The two distinct routes beyond kin selection to ultrasociality: Implications for the humanities and social sciences. In D. L. Bridgeman (Ed.), *The nature of prosocial behavior*. Orlando, FL: Academic Press.

Cavalli-Sforza, L. L., & Feldman, M. W. (1981). *Cultural transmission and evolution*. Princeton, NJ: Princeton University Press.

Crawford, C. B. (1993). The future of sociobiology: Counting babies or studying proximate mechanisms. *Trends in Ecology and Evolution, 8*(5), 183–186.

Crawford, C. B., & Anderson, J. L. (1989). Sociobiology: An environmentalist discipline? *American Psychologist, 44*(12), 1449–1459.

Cronk, L. (1995). Is there a role for culture in human behavioral ecology? *Ethology and Sociobiology, 16*(3), 181–205.

Daly, M. (1982). Some caveats about cultural transmission models. *Human Ecology, 10*, 401–408.

Daly, M., & Wilson, M. (1989). Homicide and cultural evolution. *Ethology and Sociobiology, 10*(1–3), 99–110.

Dawkins, R. (1976). *The selfish gene*. New York: Oxford University Press.

Dawkins, R. (1982). *The extended phenotype: The gene as the unit of selection*. San Francisco: Freeman.

Dawkins, R. (1986). *The blind watchmaker*. New York: Penguin.

Dawkins, R. (1989). *The selfish gene* (new ed.). New York: Oxford University Press.

Dawkins, R. (1993). Viruses of the mind. In B. Dahlbom (Ed.), *Dennett and his critics: Demystifying mind* (pp. 13–27). Cambridge, MA: Blackwell.

Dennett, D. C. (1990). Memes and the exploitation of imagination. *The Journal of Aesthetics and Art Criticism, 48*(2), 127–135.

Durham, W. H. (1976). The adaptive significance of cultural behavior. *Human Ecology, 4,* 89–121.

Durham, W. H. (1979). Toward a coevolutionary theory of human biology and culture. In N. A. Chagnon & W. Irons (Eds.), *Evolutionary biology and human social behavior: An anthropological perspective* (pp. 39–59). North Scituate, MA: Duxbury Press.

Durham, W. H. (1991). *Coevolution: Genes, culture, and human diversity.* Stanford, CA: Stanford University Press.

Essock-Vitale, S., & McGuire, M. (1980). Predictions derived from the theories of kin selection and reciprocation assessed by anthropological data. *Ethology and Sociobiology, 1,* 233–243.

Findlay, C. S., & Lumsden, C. J. (1988). The creative mind: Toward an evolutionary theory of discovery and innovation. *Journal of Social and Biological Structures, 11,* 3–55.

Flinn, M. V., & Alexander, R. D. (1982). Culture theory: The developing synthesis from biology. *Human Ecology, 10,* 383–400.

Graubard, M. (1985). The biological foundations of culture. *Journal of Social and Biological Structures, 8,* 109–128.

Hamilton, W. D. (1964). The genetical evolution of social behavior: II. *Journal of Theoretical Biology, 7,* 17–52.

Holcomb, H. R., III. (1993). *Sociobiology, sex, and science.* New York: SUNY Press.

Irons, W. (1979a). Natural selection, adaptation, and human social behavior. In N. A. Chagnon & W. Irons (Eds.), *Evolutionary biology and human social behavior: An anthropological perspective* (pp. 4–39). North Scituate, MA: Duxbury.

Irons, W. (1979b). Cultural and biological success. In N. A. Chagnon & W. Irons (Eds.), *Evolutionary biology and human social behavior: An anthropological perspective* (pp. 257–272). North Scituate, MA: Duxbury.

Irons, W. (1990). Let's make our perspective broader rather than narrower: A comment on Turke's "Which humans behave adaptively, and why does it matter?" and on the so-called DA-DP debate. *Ethology and Sociobiology, 11,* 353–360.

Lumsden, C. J. (1988). Gene-culture coevolution: A test of the steady-state hypothesis for gene-culture translation. *Journal of Theoretical Biology, 130,* 391–406.

Lumsden, C. J. (1989). Does culture need genes? *Ethology and Sociobiology, 10,* 11–28.

Lumsden, C. J. (1991). Culture as a semantic fractual: Sociobiology and thick description. *Journal of Ideas, 2,* 11–18.

Lumsden, C. J., & Wilson, E. O. (1981). *Genes, mind, and culture: The coevolutionary process.* Cambridge, MA: Harvard University Press.

Maynard Smith, J., & Warren, N. (1982). Models of cultural and genetic change. *Evolution, 36*(3), 620–627.

Nesse, R. M., & Williams, G. C. (1994). *Why we get sick: The new science of Darwinian medicine.* New York: Vintage Books (Random House).

Richerson, P. J., & Boyd, R. (1989). The role of evolved predispositions in cultural evolution. *Ethology and Sociobiology, 10,* 195–219.

Richerson, P. J., & Boyd, R. (1992). Cultural inheritance and evolutionary ecology. In E. A. Smith & B. Winterhalder (Eds.), *Evolutionary ecology and human behavior* (pp. 61–92). New York: Aldine de Gruyter.

Rindos, D. (1986). The evolution of the capacity for culture: Sociobiology, structuralism, and cultural selectionism. *Current Anthropology, 27*(4), 315–332.

Rogers, A. R. (1989). Does biology constrain culture? *American Anthropologist, 90,* 819–831.

Spuhler, J. N. (Ed.). (1959). *The evolution of man's capacity for culture.* Detroit, MI: Wayne State University Press.

Symons, D. (1989). A critique of Darwinian anthropology. *Ethology and Sociobiology, 10,* 131–144.

Symons, D. (1992). On the use and misuse of Darwinism in the study of human behavior. In J. Barkow, L. Cosmides, & J. Tooby (Eds.), *The adapted mind: Evolutionary psychology and the generation of culture* (pp. 137–159). New York: Oxford University Press.

Tooby, J., & Cosmides, L. (1989). Evolutionary psychology and the generation of culture: Part I. Theoretical considerations. *Ethology and Sociobiology, 10*, 29–49.

Tooby, J., & Cosmides, L. (1990). The past explains the present: Emotional adaptations and the structure of ancestral environments. *Ethology and Sociobiology, 11*, 375–424.

Tooby, J., & Cosmides, L. (1992). The psychological foundations of culture. In J. Barkow, L. Cosmides, & J. Tooby (Eds.), *The adapted mind: Evolutionary psychology and the generation of culture* (pp. 19–136). New York: Oxford University Press.

Trivers, R. (1971). The evolution of reciprocal altruism. *The Quarterly Review of Biology, 46*, 35–57.

Turke, P. W., & Betzig, L. L. (1985). Those who can do: Wealth, status, and reproductive success on Ifaluk. *Ethology and Sociobiology, 6*, 79–87.

Wallace, A. F. C. (1970). *Culture and personality* (2nd ed.). New York: Random House.

White, L. A. (1949). *The science of culture: A study of man and civilization.* New York: Farrar, Straus & Giroux.

Williams, G. C. (1992). *Natural selection: Domains, levels, and challenges.* New York: Oxford University Press.

Wilson, E. O. (1979). Biology and anthropology: A mutual transformation? In N. A. Chagnon & W. Irons (Eds.), *Evolutionary biology and human social behavior: An anthropological perspective* (pp. 511–518). North Scituate, MA: Duxbury.

Wilson, M., & Daly, M. (1985). Competitiveness, risk taking, and violence: The young male syndrome. *Ethology and Sociobiology, 6*, 59–73.

Wright, R. (1995, August 28). The evolution of despair. *Time Magazine*, pp. 32–38.

# II

## *ISSUES*

Much of the material in the Ideas part (Part I) is not very controversial. Yet, there are conceptual issues involved in the application of the theory of evolution to the study of human behavior that are particularly important, and over which there is much controversy. In the first edition, Donald Symons opened the Issues part with a chapter on the value of evolutionary explanations of human behavior. He argued that Darwinism can do more than merely rule out certain views of the mind: It can guide research, prevent certain kinds of errors, inspire new questions, and call attention to aspects of the mind that are normally too mundane or uniform to be noticed. Specifically, it can lead us to anticipate a brain/mind composed of numerous, specific, complex mechanisms, rather than simple, general mechanisms of association or symbol manipulation, and may be especially useful in guiding research on the mechanisms of feeling. But he also considered the level of resolution that we may obtain when using evolutionary theory, and questioned the limits of the application of evolutionary theory when it is used to elucidate the details of proximate mechanisms. This chapter provided, and in our opinion continues to provide, much of the agenda of evolutionary scientists studying human behavior. The chapters in the current part reflect some of the challenges of this agenda.

The chapters in Part II deal with some of the central issues in the application of the Theory of Evolution to the study of human behavior. The issues discussed in these chapters are not yet resolved. When they are resolved, we believe the solutions will shape the study of the evolution of human behavior for decades.

Geneticists focus on how gene differences produce differences in behavior. Evolutionists focus on how genetically conditioned adaptive mechanisms enable organisms to adapt to varying environmental circumstances. The chapter entitled "Can Behavior Genetics Contribute to Evolutionary Behavioral Science?" (chap. 6) discusses the controversies over the role of genetics in evolutionary studies of human behavior. Chapter 7, "Evolutionary Psychology and Theories of Cognitive Architecture," explores the interrelation of cognitive science and computer models of thought with evolutionary theory in the development of evolutionary explanations of mental functioning. These two chapters focus on how two sciences, genetics and cognitive science, relate to evolutionary studies of behavior.

The last three chapters in this part deal with important methodological issues. Although ancestral adaptations came into being because they contributed more to lifetime reproductive success than alternative adaptations, the value of studying reproductive success in currently existing populations is controversial. The third chapter in Part II, "Not Whether to Count Babies, But Which Babies to Count?" (chap. 8), argues that appropriate studies of current reproductive success can be useful in the study of human behavior. The environment in which humans evolved no longer exists, and the adaptations that evolved in past environments must function in the current world. The penultimate chapter in Part II, "Environments and Adaptations: Then and Now" (chap. 9), discusses the nature of the environment of evolutionary adaptedness (EEA), and questions how much we have to know about it to study the evolutionary significance of human behaviors. This part closes with a chapter on testing evolutionary hypotheses (chap. 10).

# 6

## Can Behavior Genetics Contribute to Evolutionary Behavioral Science?

J. Michael Bailey
*Northwestern University*

Since the quantitative synthesis accomplished by Fisher, Wright, and Haldane, genetics and evolutionary selection theory have been inextricably linked. The link is not merely historical. For example, the journal *Evolution* commonly publishes articles concerning population genetic findings in nonhuman species. In contrast, the relatively recent disciplines of human behavior genetics and evolutionary behavioral science have developed virtually independently. The most representative journals of the two disciplines, *Behavior Genetics* and *Ethology and Sociobiology*, respectively, have little author overlap. Representative books from each discipline (e.g., Barkow, Cosmides, & Tooby, 1992; Neale & Cardon, 1992) ignore the other. Ironically, there is much more overlap among the disciplines' opponents (e.g., Gould, 1981; Gould & Lewontin, 1978; Lewontin, Rose, & Kamin, 1984) than among their practitioners.

Why has there been such little mutual influence between two such seemingly related disciplines? Besides their relative youth—perhaps there has simply been insufficient time—there are at least two important reasons. First, it is impossible to perform many experiments on humans that could provide evolutionarily relevant data. For example, institutional review boards take a dim view of selective breeding experiments using human subjects. Second, to date, human behavioral geneticists and evolutionists have focused on attributes of a population's behavior that are at best independent and at worst in opposition. Behavior geneticists are concerned with a population's variance—specifically, whether that variance is attributable to genetic or environmental variation. However, human behavioral evolutionists have been primarily concerned with providing adaptationist accounts of behavior that is characteristic of all, or most, humans. Behavior geneticists cannot investigate phenotypes that show no variation, and behavioral evolutionists concerned with central tendencies have mostly behaved as if the variation around those tendencies is an annoyance. The one type of variation studied by many evolutionists—sex differences—is not amenable to behavior genetics investigations. Human behavioral evolutionists have begun to pay more attention to trait variation (Buss, 1994; Gangestad & Simpson, 1990; Tooby & Cosmides, 1990). Furthermore, a debate has recently begun among human behavioral evolutionists regarding whether behavior genetics and evolutionary behavioral science (insofar as the latter is concerned with adaptation) can be meaningfully integrated (Tooby & Cosmides, 1990; Wilson, 1994). This important debate remains unresolved.

This chapter has three main purposes: to review the methods and findings of contemporary human behavior genetics; to survey factors that maintain genetic variation, including the controversial idea of "adaptive genetic variation" (Tooby & Cosmides, 1990; Wilson, 1994); and, finally, to address genetic and evolutionary approaches to behavioral differences between ethnic groups.

## CONTEMPORARY BEHAVIOR GENETICS: AN OVERVIEW

### Behavior Genetics Methodologies

The most basic goal of behavior genetics studies is to determine whether a trait of interest runs in families, and, if so, why. The large majority of available studies have used the general strategy of finding at least two groups of relatives that differ in their degree of genetic or environmental relatedness, and then correlating relatedness with phenotypic similarity. For example, biological siblings reared apart are as similar, genetically, as those reared together, but the latter are more similar, environmentally. If the rearing environment makes a difference for a trait of interest, then biological siblings reared together should be more similar for the trait than those reared apart.

The conceptually simplest study is the family study. For a continuous trait such as intelligence, such studies typically proceed by obtaining measurements on at least two relatives per family (e.g., parents and offspring, or siblings) and then correlating those measurements across families. For categorical phenotypes (i.e., an observable trait that is either present or absent) such as schizophrenia, researchers first assemble two groups of index cases (initially ascertained subjects with the traits, often called *probands*), one with and one without the phenotype. They then assess the prevalence of the trait in the probands' relatives. Family studies are useful to quantify the degree of familial aggregation of a trait. They are also potentially useful to detect Mendelian patterns of transmission signifying major gene effects, primarily sex-linked recessive or dominant and autosomal (i.e., on a chromosome other than X) recessive or dominant. In general, family studies of sufficient size nearly always have found evidence for familial aggregation. For behavioral traits, they have not been very helpful in detecting Mendelian genic effects, perhaps because such effects are rare. The mere detection of familial aggregation is, of course, insufficient to reach a genetic conclusion because a characteristic (e.g., Catholicism) can be familial for other reasons. To quantify the roles of genes and environment in explaining why a trait runs in families, it is necessary to employ more sophisticated designs, including twin and adoption studies.

The twin study has been the most frequently used design for disentangling genetic and environmental influences on human behavior. The most compelling kind of twin study examines phenotypic similarity of monozygotic (MZ) twins separated at birth, or shortly afterward, and as such, actually combines twin and adoption methodologies. Unfortunately, the total number of twins reared apart who have been studied has been small. Thus, the more common study includes twins who have been reared in the same family. By examining the relative similarity of MZ cotwins compared with dizygotic (DZ) cotwins, it is possible to estimate the importance of genetic and environmental factors. This kind of twin study requires the assumption that environmental factors that influence the trait of interest are no more similar for MZ than for DZ twins (the *equal environments assumption*).

Adoption studies focus on pairs of individuals who are genetically related but environmentally unrelated (e.g., parents and their adopted away biological offspring) or those who are environmentally related but genetically unrelated (e.g., adoptive siblings). If genes are important for a trait, then genetically related but environmentally unrelated relatives should be similar.

Before considering environmental hypotheses, it is useful to distinguish between two types of environment: shared and nonshared. The shared environment consists of those aspects of the environment typically shared by siblings reared in the same family and works to make siblings more similar to each other. Shared environmental factors could include parental characteristics such as socioeconomic status, religion, childrearing attitudes, and emotional stability. Traditionally, social science explanations of individual differences in behavior have stressed the importance of shared environment. Examples include schizophrenogenic mothers, middle class values, and broken families. In contrast, the nonshared environment consists of those environmental factors that are uncorrelated even for siblings reared together. These would include, for example, influential teachers and peer groups not shared by siblings, birth order, and parental favoritism. The nonshared environment operates to make siblings, even identical twins, different from each other.

Simple behavior genetics analyses typically apportion phenotypic variance to genetic, shared environmental, and nonshared environmental causes. The proportion of phenotypic variance attributable to genetic differences between people is called *heritability* of a trait. Similarly, shared and nonshared environmentality are the proportions of phenotypic variance attributable to differences in people's shared and nonshared environments, respectively. Heritability, shared environmentality, and nonshared environmentality each range from 0 to 1, and in the simplest model behavior geneticists examine, they sum to 1.

Two types of heritability should be distinguished in an evolutionary context. Narrow sense heritability is the proportion of phenotypic variance attributable to additive genetic factors. Additive genetic factors cause a trait to "breed true" from parents to offspring, and thus the presence of additive genetic variance is necessary for evolution to occur. In contrast, nonadditive genetic factors include sources of genetic variance that do not cause parents and offspring to be similar. These include dominance variance (i.e., variance due to the action of dominant and recessive genes, genes whose effects are represented statistically as the interaction between two alleles at one locus or genetic location) and epistasis (i.e., variance due to the interaction of genes at different loci).

Dominance variance, when present, is evidence that a trait has been subject to directional selection (i.e., selection for either high or low values of the trait). To see why, consider a disadvantageous trait (e.g., cystic fibrosis) caused by homozygosity for a recessive allele, c (i.e., one must have two copies of the same gene to have the trait; one must have genotype cc). Natural selection will make the trait rarer so that, eventually, most copies of c will be in heterozygous individuals (i.e., individuals who have only one copy of c). These individuals are normal, and thus, their copies of c are immune from natural selection. Only when two such individuals mate and produce affected offspring can natural selection see the disadvantageous alleles. As c becomes rarer, such matings do as well. Inbreeding depression, or inferiority of offspring of matings by genetic relatives, is due to the fact that relatives tend to share the same disadvantageous recessive alleles. Conversely, a trait's response to inbreeding can provide evidence that the trait has undergone directional selection. For example, offspring of matings between first cousins tend to have lower IQ, suggesting that higher IQ has been evolutionarily selected (Agrawal & Jensen, 1984).

Broad sense heritability is the proportion of phenotypic variance attributable to all genetic factors, both additive and nonadditive. Cystic fibrosis is highly influenced by genes, yet parent–offspring resemblance for the disorder is low. This means that cystic fibrosis has a high broad sense heritability, but a low narrow sense heritability. In contrast, height is both highly genetic and phenotypically familial—tall parents tend to have tall children. Height's heritability is high in both the narrow and broad sense. Fisher's (1958) fundamental theorem states that selection removes additive genetic variance, and thus should diminish narrow sense heritability. In other words, selection causes a population to be increasingly homogeneous for advantageous genes (and hence, uses up genetic variation). But this is true only to the extent that advantageous genes cause parent–offspring resemblance. Dominance variance, a major component of nonadditive variance, is uncorrelated between parents and offspring, and hence, is immune from selective pressures. Indeed, a high ratio of nonadditive to additive heritability is one indication that a trait has been under selection. Broad sense heritability is most intuitively estimated as the correlation between MZ twins reared apart. This is because MZ twins share all their genes, and thus would have identical additive and nonadditive genetic influences, and relatives reared separately, in random environments, share no environmental influences. More commonly, broad sense heritability is estimated as twice the difference between MZ and DZ twin correlations using twins reared together because they are more common. Subtracting the correlations before doubling them controls for environmental similarity of relatives reared together. Doubling the difference allows estimation of the full genetic contribution. (The MZ genetic correlation is 1.0, and the DZ correlation is approximately .50. Thus, $2*[1.0 - .50] = 1.0$.) Narrow sense heritability can be estimated as twice the correlation between biological first-degree relatives (ideally, parents and offspring) who have been reared separately.

The importance of shared environment for a given trait is most directly tested as the correlation between adoptive siblings for the trait. The importance of nonshared environment is most directly indicated by the degree to which the MZ twin correlation is less than 1.0 (although measurement error will also diminish the correlation) because only the non-shared environment can cause MZ twins to differ.

Heritability and environmentality estimates have a number of limitations. (Despite accusations to the contrary [e.g., Lewontin, Rose, & Kamin, 1984], these limitations are widely acknowledged by behavior geneticists.) First, heritability and environmentality are not intrinsic qualities of a trait, but rather they reflect the distribution of trait-relevant genes and environments in a specific population at a given time. Change the distribution of genes and environments, and heritabilities and environmentalities will change. For example, in highly genetically homogeneous populations, people are so similar genetically that most phenotypic variation will be due to environmental differences. Conversely, as environments become more equal within a population (e.g., as economic inequality diminishes), heritability will tend to increase (this argument has been developed fully by Herrnstein, 1973). Second, high heritability does not imply that a trait is difficult to change, although it does suggest that manipulating environmental factors that already vary considerably (e.g., income) will not change the trait substantially. Third, although positive heritability does imply that there are genes for the studied trait, this is true only in a restrictive sense. Many people assume that heritability findings show a direct genotype-to-phenotype pathway. Actually, genes code for proteins not behaviors, although proteins and their products can, and do, affect behavior. Thus, a gene for a behavioral trait is one whose different alleles are causally associated with different levels of the trait, regardless of how complicated the genotype-to-phenotype pathway. For instance, Maynard Smith has pointed out that in the only meaningful sense of genes for anything other than proteins, it is perfectly defensible to speak of a gene for shoe-tying ability (Maynard Smith, 1993; for example, consider an allele that allows one individual's fingers to be relatively nimble). Furthermore, a trait could be highly heritable, yet require sychosocial input in its development. For example, suppose a gene affected attractiveness, which in turn affected one's success interacting with the opposite sex, which affected one's self-esteem. Self-esteem would thus be somewhat heritable even though the genotype-to-phenotype pathway required social input. Behavior geneticists refer to such developmental processes as *gene–environment correlation* (Plomin, DeFries, & Loehlin, 1977).

Regarding environmentality, it is important to emphasize that environment cannot be equated with socialization. There is also a biological environment that includes, for example, some intrauterine factors, disease, head injuries, and diet. The usual behavior genetics analyses cannot distinguish between social and biological environmental factors. Indeed, one of the most important limitations of such analyses is their inability to elucidate the mechanisms through which genetic and environmental factors have their effects.

## Do Methodological Limitations Render Behavior Genetic Estimates Meaningless?

A potentially more damaging criticism, of heritability estimates especially, is that their computation requires assumptions that are false, rendering the estimates meaningless. Reading some critiques of quantitative behavior genetics (Block & Dworkin, 1976; Feldman & Lewontin, 1975; Lewontin, Rose, & Kamin, 1984) could leave one the impression that behavior genetics—especially human behavior genetics—is quite sloppy methodologically. Although human behavior genetics has not reached the methodological rigor of genetics performed on more pliant subjects, such as yeast, c. elegans, and mice, its practitioners have explicated and tested the necessary assumptions of their analyses and recognized their limitations as well as any other behavioral science discipline.

For example, deriving heritability estimates from the study of twins reared together requires the aforementioned equal environments assumption—that the environmental factors that affect a trait are no more similar within MZ pairs than within DZ pairs. Superficially, this assumption seems unlikely to be true. Because MZ twins appear more physically similar than DZ twins, and because they are treated more similarly by their parents (Loehlin & Nichols, 1976), MZ twins' environments would appear to be more similar, thus violating the equal environments assumption. However, it is likely that the respects in which MZ twins' environments are especially similar are unimportant in the development of many, perhaps most, interesting traits. Furthermore, the equal environments assumption can be tested empirically. For instance, studies have shown that among MZ twins, those whose parents treated them quite similarly are no more similar in intelligence, personality, or psychopathology than are other twins (e.g., Loehlin & Nichols, 1976; Kendler et al., 1993; Plomin, DeFries, & McClearn, 1989). MZ twins who are frequently mistaken for each other are no more similar in their behavior than are other MZ twins (Loehlin & Nichols, 1976). DZ twins whose parents mistakenly believe they are MZ twins are only as similar as other DZ twins. Findings using MZ twins reared apart (whose similarity cannot be due to parental shaping) are similar to those using twins reared together. To the extent that it has been tested, the equal environments assumption appears to be valid.

Another complaint about behavior genetics methodology is that the statistical models employed are naive. For example, gene–environment interaction (i.e., different genotypes having different effects in different environments) and gene–environment correlation are typically ignored (Layzer, 1974), and indeed most studies of humans have had insufficient statistical power to detect such effects (Wahlsten, 1990). However, animal studies having adequate power have yielded few appreciable gene–environment interactions (Plomin, 1990). Furthermore, even the presence of such effects does not invalidate heritability analyses (Plomin, 1990), although it may indeed complicate them (Plomin et al., 1977).

## Molecular Behavior Genetics

The molecular revolution that has had such a huge impact on biology in general has begun to affect behavior genetics as well. The two main strategies that have been employed so far are linkage and association analysis. Linkage aims to map genes onto chromosomal regions. If two relatives both have the same phenotype (e.g., schizophrenia), they probably share any genes that contribute importantly to the phenotype. If so, they have a high likelihood of sharing the larger chromosomal segment that contains the gene. Thus, for example, Hamer et al. (1993) showed that gay brothers were more likely than chance (which is 50%) to share the chromosomal region, Xq28, suggesting that a gene influencing male sexual orientation lies within that chromosomal region. If so, future linkage studies will narrow the width of the genetic confidence interval. Association analysis looks for correlations between a trait and the presence or absence of specific alleles. There have been claims, for example, that alcoholism is associated with the A1 allele of the D2 dopamine receptor gene (Noble & Paredes, 1993), although these claims are controversial (Gelernter, Goldman, & Risch, 1993).

Molecular techniques have the potential to identify specific genes affecting behavior. Identification of genes will eventually allow the elucidation of mechanisms by which genes affect behavior. Thus, molecular techniques are potentially very powerful. Unfortunately, at this early stage of their application, their promise has not been realized. Indeed, to date, not a single molecular finding concerning behavior has been widely accepted as valid by the scientific community, and several highly publicized findings have failed to replicate (Risch & Merikangas, 1993). This is in part because the number of studies examining any one trait has been relatively small. But it could also reflect the likely possibility that genes underlying behavior variation are typically of small effect, and thus, are difficult to detect.

## Behavior Genetics Findings

It is impossible here to provide an adequate summary of the huge behavior genetics literature. However, it is possible to make some general statements that appear to characterize that literature. First, behavioral traits that have been well studied (e.g., with large samples and good measures) have been found to be moderately heritable, with typical findings in the range from .25 to .75. Among the traits whose moderate heritabilities have been established beyond reasonable doubt are intelligence (Herrnstein & Murray, 1994), schizophrenia (Gottesman, 1991), manic depression (Tsuang & Faraone, 1990), alcoholism (Cloninger, 1987; Kendler et al., 1992), extraversion, and neuroticism (Eaves et al., 1989; Loehlin, 1992). Although less well established, heritability findings have also been reported for the following noteworthy traits: religiosity (Waller et al., 1990), social attitudes (Tesser, 1993), time spent watching television (Plomin, Corley, DeFries, & Fulker, 1990), and divorce (McGue & Lykken,

1992). The fact that divorce appears to be moderately heritable illustrates that genotype-to-phenotype pathways may be complicated. Presumably, between the protein products of relevant genes and the filing of divorce papers, a variety of personality traits, attitudes, and preferences intervene.

There was a time when findings that behavioral traits are moderately heritable were surprising, given the prevailing environmental bias in the social sciences and the relative dearth of behavior genetics studies. However, due to the relentless barrage of behavior genetics studies yielding similar findings, rejecting the null hypothesis that heritability is equal to zero is no longer very interesting. Indeed, the convincing, replicable demonstration that a well-measured behavioral trait has a heritability of zero would be much more interesting. Appreciable genetic variation underlying behavioral variation is the rule, not the exception. Much of this variation appears additive, although nonadditive genetic variation has been detected in traits such as extraversion (Loehlin, 1992; Tambs et al., 1991).

The second generalization concerns whether genetic variation is attributable to a small number of genes of large effect or a large number of genes of small effect. Although this question is difficult to answer definitively, most evidence is consistent with the many genes possibility. Unfortunately, this evidence is mostly negative in nature. Replicable findings that single genes contribute importantly to behavioral variation have not materialized so far, despite intensive efforts. Neither careful animal studies using methodologies that might detect major genes, such as recombinant inbred strain studies, nor human linkage studies have borne fruit for behavioral phenotypes (Plomin, 1990).

A third, recently recognized pattern in behavior genetics concerns the nature of environmental influence. Although studies invariably find that environment is an important determinant of trait variation, the environment appears to operate primarily to make siblings different from, rather than similar to, each other (Rowe, 1994a). In other words, the most important environmental factors appear to be those that cause differences between MZ twins reared together. Data for this contention come from several sources. Most important are studies of adoptive siblings, who are typically not much more similar, if at all, than strangers. MZ twins reared together are typically only slightly more similar, if at all, than MZ twins reared apart. Evidently, shared familial environmental events do not generally make much of a difference. In other words, traits typically run in families for genetic, rather than environmental, reasons. Exceptions include religious affiliation (denomination rather than degree of religious commitment; Eaves, Martin, & Heath, 1990) and some social attitudes (Rowe, 1994a). The preeminence of the nonshared environment (compared with shared environment) may be evolutionarily sensible. Rowe (1994a) argued that so much valuable knowledge can be acquired from nonrelatives that a gene causing children to learn only, or primarily, from their parents would not be successful.

The nature of the within-family environment is unclear. Although it is clear that parents treat offspring differently from each other, the direction of causation is uncertain (Rowe, 1994a). That is, siblings may behave differently due to genetic reasons, eliciting different responses from their parents. Birth order is a within-family environmental influence that has been shown to be important for some traits such as revolutionary thinking (Sulloway, 1995). Molenaar, Boomsma, and Dolan (1993) argued that much of apparent within-family environmental variation may be attributable to random developmental processes.

## THE PARADOX OF GENETIC VARIATION

Fisher's (1958) fundamental theorem of natural selection states: "The rate of increase in fitness of any organism at any time is equal to its genetic variance in fitness at that time" (p. xxx). One implication of the theorem is that a trait's narrow sense heritability constrains the response to selection for the trait. Indeed, one way of computing heritability is to measure response to selection. Conversely, traits that have undergone consistent and intense selection should have relatively low narrow sense heritabilities. That is, natural selection causes individuals to become genetically similar to each other, at least with respect to those traits that affect reproductive success and survival. Thus, some have argued that traits showing high additive heritabilities are evolutionarily unimportant (Tooby & Cosmides, 1990). I have noted that behavior geneticists typically find moderate heritabilities. Does this mean that behavior geneticists are typically studying evolutionarily neutral traits—genetic junk?

Studies of animals in natural populations suggest that the answer is "no." Mousseau and Roff (1987) reviewed narrow sense heritability estimates for wild, outbred animal populations, comparing heritabilities of life history traits to those of morphological traits. Because life history traits concern the most important aspects of organisms' reproductive lives, such as age of first reproduction, typically number of offspring per pregnancy, and life span, they presumably have a history of strong selection. Morphological traits, such as limb size, have probably been subject to less intense selection, on average. Consistent with the fundamental theorem, heritabilities of life history traits were significantly lower (mean heritability of .262 vs. .461 for morphology). However, in general, heritabilities of the life history traits were also appreciable, indicating that in natural populations substantial genetic variation is maintained in the face of selection. One of the major goals in contemporary population genetics has been to discover why, contrary to Fisher's fundamental theorem, the link between selection strength and additive heritability is modest. Fisher's theorem requires a number of assumptions, which evidently are not all typically met.

### Factors Maintaining Genetic Variation

The following factors help to explain how heritability can be appreciable despite selection.

*Heritability Is a Ratio.* Heritability is the ratio of additive genetic to phenotypic variance. As such, heritability can be high even if there is little additive genetic variance, provided that phenotypic variance is low. For example, there is evidence that male sexual orientation is somewhat heritable (Bailey & Pillard, 1991). Because homosexuality is associated with greatly diminished reproduction (Bell & Weinberg, 1978), the existence of alleles that cause homosexuality is puzzling. However, even if the heritability of male sexual orientation is moderate, the absolute genetic variation is very small because phenotypic variation in sexual orientation is quite small. Perhaps 98% of men have a heterosexual orientation (Billy, Tanfer, Grady, & Klepinger, 1993). It is not difficult to imagine scenarios whereby it is difficult for selection to wring out the last few "gay genes" (e.g., epistatis, in this case unfavorable interactions between otherwise favorable alleles). The low prevalence of homosexuality strongly suggests that selection has favored genes for heterosexuality, even if sexual orientation remains moderately heritable.

*Mutation.* Because even the highest mutation rates are low, it has often been assumed that mutation cannot help much in explaining how genetic variation persists despite selection. However, Lande (1976) has shown that, in polygenic systems (i.e., trait values are determined by many genes, each of small effect), considerable genetic variation can be maintained. Briefly, mutation induces genetic variation that may be temporarily hidden, even under stabilizing selection, by linkage between alleles of negatively correlated effects. Recombination eventually breaks the linkage, releasing hidden genetic variation. Because the traits are polygenic, affected by genes at many different loci, there is ample opportunity for trait-relevant genes to mutate. The degree to which mutation can help to maintain polygenic variation remains controversial (Maynard Smith, 1989).

*Spatial-Temporal Heterogeneity in Optimal Phenotypes.* Patchy environments can cause the optimal phenotype (hence the optimal genotype) to vary. If individuals from different patches interbreed, this introduces genetic variation into at least one of the patches. Contemporary America is an extreme example of this, with people whose genotypes are optimized for quite different environments brought together (arguably) into one population. There is likely more genetic diversity in contemporary America than in any other human population, ever.

Temporal variation in optimal genotype also helps maintain genetic variation. For example, it is plausible that temporal variation in food availability has helped maintain heritable variation related to obesity. In times of famine, those with efficient metabolism and greater fat storage—those with "thrifty genotypes" (Neel, 1962)—would have been more likely to survive. In more plentiful times, they may have been at a disadvantage, as are obese people in modern societies (Diamond, 1992).

Pathogens help ensure genetic diversity across time (Tooby & Cosmides, 1990). The most pathogen-resistant genotype at one time is unlikely to remain the most resistant at a much later time. The most resistant genotype at Time 1 will become increasingly prevalent, and pathogens will evolve to attack it optimally. Hosts will then evolve to elude the pathogens, and so a different genotype will be optimal at Time 2. (A similar argument has been used to explain the frequency of sexual reproduction despite the twofold cost of sex [Hamilton, 1980], the fact that sexual reproduction allows only half the number of offspring per individual, compared with parthenogenetic reproduction. Indeed, there is considerable overlap between explanations of genetic variation and sexual reproduction.)

*Antagonistic Pleiotropy.* Most genes have manifold phenotypic effects. An allele that has an evolutionarily advantageous effect with respect to one trait may have a disadvantageous effect with respect to another. For example, in some species, genotypes that reproduce the earliest may be relatively short-lived (Rose & Charlesworth, 1980). The antagonistic pleiotropy hypothesis of aging—that genes that confer early benefits are responsible for many of aging's detrimental effects (Williams, 1957)—is another example.

*Heterosis.* Cases of heterozygotic advantage maintaining genetic variation in single-locus systems are well established, the classic case being maintenance of the allele that in homozygous form causes sickle cell anemia. The likely frequency of such cases is more controversial (Maynard Smith, 1989), as is the ability of heterosis to maintain genetic variability in polygenic systems (Roff, 1992).

*Balance Between Selection at Different Levels.* Maynard Smith (1989) pointed out that genetic variation can be maintained due to a negative association between genetic effects at different levels of selection. Some cases of meiotic drive, in which a gene biases its likelihood of being transmitted (e.g., a Y-linked gene impedes the formation of sperm carrying the X chromosome) may be examples. More relevant to human behavior, individuals who exploit their kin may outreproduce their close relatives (thus increasing the frequency of the exploitive gene), but decrease the average fitness of their kin (hence decreasing its frequency).

*Frequency-Dependent Selection.* Perhaps the most interesting potential explanation of the persistence of genetic variation, at least from the perspective of evolutionary behavioral science, is that part of the variation represents different genetically based life-history strategies. This possibility raises a number of complex issues, some of which are addressed in the next section. Assuming this possibility is plausible, why doesn't the best strategy win? The classic solution to this problem is that how good a strategy is may depend on its frequency. One strategy may be best until it becomes too frequent, at which point another strategy works better. Consider, as a very speculative human example, law-abiding versus criminal strategies. If few people are criminals, then few people will have guns in their houses to deter thieves, and the risk to criminals will be relatively low. As the frequency of crime increases, more people will buy guns, and criminal strategies will become increasingly risky and less successful.

The maintenance of genetic variation by pathogen pressure is also an example of frequency-dependent selection. Because pathogens evolve to exploit the most common genotypes, rare host genotypes are the most fit. As they become more common, they become less fit.

## Are There Genetically Based Life-History Strategic Differences Among Humans?

A large proportion of individual differences in human behavior is attributable to genetic differences. Does any of this variation reflect different behavioral life-history strategies maintained by processes such as frequency-dependent selection? There are at least two such strategies: male and female. These strategies are ultimately genetically caused, and, as Fisher pointed out, frequency-dependent selection maintains a more-or-less equal sex ratio (with some interesting exceptions).

But what about other salient behavioral variation? Do introverts and extraverts represent different life-history strategies? Are women who engage in casual sex pursuing a genetically based, frequency-dependent selected strategy? Are psychopaths genetically programmed to pursue an exploitive strategy? We do not yet know the answers to these questions, but the general issue of "adaptive genetic variation" among humans has been intensely debated (Tooby & Cosmides, 1990; Wilson, 1994). Following Wilson (1994), *adaptive* (alternatively, *coordinated*) genetic variation is used here to refer to genetic variation that is the product of natural selection. Such variation is not only allowed by evolutionary processes, but is created by them.

Tooby and Cosmides (1990) provided the most formidable argument against the possibility of adaptive genetic variation. The argument concerns the genetics of polygenic systems. Most human behavioral variation is polygenic. Two genetically determined alternative strategies will differ at many genetic loci, across several chromosomes. The problem with the co-evolution of two alternative strategies (or the later evolution of one strategy after the first has been established) is that the fortuitous combinations of genes will be broken apart during recombination (especially when individuals with the two different optimal genotypes mate). For example, assume that *Dads* (dependable mates, high investment) and *Cads* (undependable mates, low investment) represent two possible genetically determined life-history strategies. These strategies are behaviorally complex and surely would differ, on average, at many loci. Whenever someone with a Dad genotype mated with someone with a Cad genotype (or anyone with a genotype different from Dad), the adapted genotypes would both be destroyed. Assortative mating would help preserve the genotypes, but assortative mating behavior is highly complex, polygenic, and subject to the destructive influence of recombination.

Wilson (1994) argued that Tooby and Cosmides were premature to dismiss the possibility of adaptive genetic variation. Simulations (Wilson, 1994) and empirical data (Brodie, 1989) have shown that complex polymorphisms can be maintained in a population if their fitnesses are sufficiently high, even if intermediate forms have relatively low fitness. For example, Brodie (1989) has shown that there is a genetic correlation between color pattern and escape tactic among garter snakes. Mottled snakes tend to remain motionless under threat, in contrast to striped snakes, who flee in a straight line. This correlation appears to arise because intermediate phenotypes (e.g., mottled snakes who flee in a straight line) have lower fitness. (The fitness function is saddle shaped.) Nevertheless, the two most common types have fitnesses high enough to ensure that genetic variation is maintained, and to prevent the population from becoming monomorphic.

At least two other processes can generate and maintain coordinated genetic variation. First, pleiotropic genes whose effects are complimentary will be favored by selection. Thus, an allele that increases both strength and aggressiveness will fare better than one that decreases strength but increases aggressiveness. Second, tightly linked genes that have complementary effects will be favored. The classic example concerns mimicry in butterflies (Maynard Smith, 1989). The ability of palatable butterflies to mimic distasteful species is controlled by several tightly linked genes, sometimes called a *supergene*. Both pleiotropy and linkage explanations of adaptive genetic variation depend on seemingly unlikely coincidences—that mutations induce a fortuitous genetic correlation between two or more traits. It is difficult to estimate how frequently such fortuitous mutations arise.

Although, as noted, the two sexes represent different genetic strategies and human sexual differentiation is surely influenced by many genes, the evolution of the sexes was distinct in one important respect. In mammalian sexual differentiation, a gene on the Y chromosome determines the early hormonal environment, and is in this sense a single gene switch. Sexual differentiation has evolved by the selection of genes that do different things in the two different early hormonal environments (such genes interact epistatically with the sex determination gene). The genetic *variation* that determines if our life-history strategy will be male or female is monogenic, not polygenic. Evolution of this kind of genetic variation is less problematic than coordinated polygenic variation. For such types to evolve, the genetic switch must have an appreciable phenotypic influence that is correlated with evolutionarily relevant variation.

To conclude this discussion of adaptive genetic variation, Tooby and Cosmides (1990) were correct that such variation, when polygenic, poses some explanatory difficulties. Nevertheless, Wilson (1994) was certainly correct that it is premature to reject the possibility of adaptive genetic variation for human behavioral traits.

## Is There But One (Contingent) Human Nature?

Adaptive genetic variation is not the only possible cause of adaptive phenotypic variation. People sometimes assume that behavioral adaptations are fixed and inflexible, but there is no reason why this must be true. A gene can code for phenotypic flexibility, given environmental input. For example, people may possess the ability to assess their own mate value (Landolt, Lalumiere, & Quinsey, 1995), and are likely to pursue different mating strategies on the basis of what they infer. A woman who infers from others' reactions to her that she is beautiful is likely to pursue her life differently than a woman who infers that she is plain. A boy born to parents who cannot invest much in his future may be more likely than other boys to pursue a criminal career. Moreover, these decisions (for they are surely mostly unconscious) may be made using a species-typical adapted mental algorithm. That is, human nature may be contingent, programmed such that fundamentally different circumstances lead to fundamentally different outcomes. Still, by this model, we all possess the basic architecture to pursue different strategies. Crawford and Anderson

(1989) endorsed this general model when he argued that sociobiology is an environmentalist discipline.

The evolution of a contingent human nature simply requires that, across generations, humans are regularly exposed to different environments in which different strategies would work best. Genes that have different, optimal, effects in different environments (i.e., which show gene–environment interaction) are selected. It was already noted that genes that affect sexual differentiation have been selected this way. It is also possible that genes have been selected to yield different phenotypes contingent on information about one's own genetic endowment. In their discussion of this possibility, which they referred to as "reactive heritability," Tooby and Cosmides (1990) offered the example of an evolved program to be more aggressive when one has a stronger body, but to be less aggressive when one has a weaker body. One's strength is likely to be a highly genetic trait. If so, and given the evolved program, trait aggression would also be highly heritable. This would be so even if the evolved program were species-typical, and hence, not at all heritable. (In this example, there remains the issue of why there would be genetic variation in strength to begin with. The explanation might entail factors already discussed, such as antagonistic pleiotropy.)

## Empirical Exploration of Evolutionary Hypotheses of Phenotypic Variation

Can one distinguish empirically between adaptive genetic variation and a universal human nature's contingent responses to different environments? The first step in either case is to specify hypotheses regarding how particular behavioral variation is adaptive. Only recently have evolutionary behavioral scientists begun to do this systematically (e.g., Mealey, 1995).

Behavior genetics analyses could provide evidence relevant to the existence of coordinated genetic variation. First, multivariate genetic analyses could examine the extent to which trait covariation is due to genetic or environmental factors. If trait covariation is due to coordinated genetic variation, then the covariation should primarily be due to genetic, rather than environmental, factors. Evidence for strong assortative mating for a phenotype would also be consistent with a coordinated genetic variation account because assortative mating slows the breakup of fortuitous combinations of genes.

Regarding environmentally contingent relations between genotype and phenotype, the analysis of MZ twins exposed to different life circumstances could be illuminating. MZ twins reared apart are uncorrelated for both shared and nonshared environment, and thus would be ideal to examine the possibility that the same genotype will yield different phenotypes under different environments. For example, Belsky, Steinberg, and Draper (1991) argued that early family disruption is a valid signal that early reproduction is a preferable life-history strategy. Consistent with their theory, women whose parents were divorced had earlier menarche than women from intact families. However, as they acknowledged, it is possible that the correlation between early menarche and parents' marital dissolution is genetic. A study of MZ twins reared separately—one twin by an intact family and one by a divorced family—would be the ideal test that the aforementioned relation is environmentally mediated, as a contingent hypothesis would predict. Because MZ twins reared separately are so rare, biological siblings reared apart are a more realistic population to study, and could also provide a definitive test. Even MZ twins reared together could be useful, provided that the environmental contingencies could plausibly differ between individuals reared together. This could be true, for example, if severe early illness were hypothesized to trigger an alternative life-history pattern.

## THE EVOLUTION OF GROUP DIFFERENCES

The debate between those who believe adaptive phenotypic variation could reflect adaptive genetic variation (e.g., Wilson, 1994) and those who believe that virtually all adaptive phenotypic variation is environmentally contingent (e.g., Tooby & Cosmides, 1990) concerns phenotypic variation within a single population. If two or more populations are reproductively isolated for a sufficiently long time, and if their environments are sufficiently different, it is a virtual certainty that genetic differences will emerge between them. That is, adaptive genetic variation between populations (in contrast to that within populations) is unproblematic and, indeed, to be expected. In principle, behavior genetics methods could be used to determine the degree to which average group differences are genetic in origin.

### Behavior Genetics and Ethnic Differences

The study of ethnic differences in behavioral traits has a controversial history in behavior genetics. Arguably, contemporary behavior genetics was born with Arthur Jensen's notorious 1969 article, "How Much Can We Boost IQ and Scholastic Achievement?", in which he argued that the one standard deviation Black–White IQ difference is substantially genetic in origin. The controversy has largely been due to political concerns (about whose legitimacy I defer comment), but there are also serious methodological and scientific issues, which are briefly mentioned here.

Most research related to possible genetic behavioral differences between ethnic groups has concerned the aforementioned Black–White IQ difference. The greatest impediment to knowing the proportion (if any) of the difference that is genetic is the confounding of relevant genetic and environmental factors. Across people, the hypothetical cultural factors that might be causing the difference are almost perfectly confounded with the hypothetical genetic factors. In America, those whose genetic heritage is most recently from Africa are nearly all labeled *African American*. Thus, it is difficult to determine whether such labeling (and its associated consequences—e.g., racial prejudice) affect IQ, or if African Americans would have lower IQ independent of those factors. To be sure, researchers have made some progress in narrowing the range of acceptable explanations. Neither socioeconomic status (SES), education differences, nor test bias can explain much of the IQ difference (Herrnstein & Murray, 1994).

There is little, if any, direct evidence of a genetic difference, however. Findings that IQ is heritable within the White and African-American populations do not necessarily mean that the group difference reflects genetic differences, because in principle, the causes of within- and between-groups variation can be independent. However, it is not obvious, a priori, that within- and between-groups variation should be independent (Turkheimer, 1991), and the fact that IQ has similar correlates within both groups suggests, but does not prove, that similar processes affect its development in both (Rowe, 1994b). More direct tests have focused on the relation between degree of African ancestry and IQ (e.g., Scarr, Pakstis, Katz, & Barker, 1977). These tests have been inconclusive, however, because they have had insufficient power to detect the small relations predicted, given likely parameter values (Jensen, 1981). As molecular behavior genetics progresses, alleles associated with high IQ will be identified. This will allow a test of whether the allelic frequencies differ between ethnic groups.

## Evolutionary Approaches to Group Differences

Most large genetic group differences, whether morphological or behavioral, are the result of different selection pressures among the different groups. This is especially true of polygenic traits because genetic drift (chance fluctuations in allele frequencies due, for example, to outward migration) is unlikely to cause large polygenic differences between groups. Random drift of genes will mean that half of changes in gene frequency will cause a trait to increase, and half will cause the trait to decrease. It would be statistically unlikely that enough random changes would be in the same direction to cause substantial phenotypic changes.

In contrast, very modest selection pressures can cause large differences, given a long enough time. Loehlin, Lindzey, and Spuhler (1975) gave the following example: Suppose that IQ has moderately high heritability (approximately .60), and that high IQ is relatively advantageous to reproduction and/or survival (alternatively, that low IQ is disadvantageous). Assume that two reproductively separated groups differ slightly in the relation between IQ and fitness, which is a normal threshold function. Specifically, assume that in Population A, the point at which an individual incurs a 2.5% reproductive disadvantage corresponds to an IQ of about 60, and the point at which he incurs a 97.5% disadvantage corresponds to an IQ of about 40. (In contemporary America, individuals with IQs of 60 are considered mentally retarded, and those with IQs of 40 are considered severely retarded.) In Population B, the corresponding IQs are 65 and 45, respectively; thus, selection pressure is slightly greater in Population B. In 100 generations (approximately 2,000 years), the mean IQ of Population B will be four points higher, and in 400 generations (8,000 years), it will be a full standard deviation higher. This model is unrealistic in assuming that the relation between IQ and fitness would be constant over time, and the narrow sense heritability assumed is probably too high, but the general point remains true: Small differences in selection can cause large group differences.

Rushton (1995) offered an evolutionary hypothesis regarding the origins of a wide variety of behavioral differences between Black, White, and Asian populations. The argument uses the ecological distinction $r$ versus $K$ strategies. Organisms that are $r$ strategists devote more resources to "gamete production, mating behavior, and high reproductive rates" (Rushton, 1995, p. 199). In contrast, $K$ strategists emphasize "high levels of parental care, resource acquisition, kin provisioning, and social complexity" (Rushton, 1995, p. 199). Rushton argued that Asians have been most $K$ selected, African Americans most $r$ selected, and Whites have been subject to intermediate degrees of $r$ and $K$ selection. Specifically, he speculated that, as humans emerged from Africa into colder regions, the harsher environment selected for $K$ strategists. Rushton offered as data a wide variety of race differences, based on his interpretation of $r$ and $K$ strategies, that show African Americans to be the most $r$ selected and Asians the most $K$ selected.

Rushton's general approach is potentially useful. Valid deduction and confirmation of hypotheses using evolutionary theory would both increase the likelihood that relevant ethnic differences were genetic and strengthen evolutionary hypotheses. However, there are difficulties with his specific ambitious hypotheses and methods. First, the theory of $r$ and $K$ strategies is not well articulated (Harpending, in press). As a result, it is less clear than Rushton acknowledged which specific predictions follow from the general hypothesis that ethnic groups differ on an $r$–$K$ continuum. For example, Rushton believed that group differences in IQ are consistent with his hypothesis. Why should it follow, however, that individuals selected for mating effort should be less intelligent? It is not obvious that finding mates, impressing them, deceiving them, and so on require less intelligence than do acquiring resources and caring for children.

Regarding Rushton's methods, it is problematic that his tests involve only three groups. Given that three groups differ, the probability is one sixth that they differ in Rushton's predicted order. This is not an impressive level of statistical significance. The best comparative analyses employ many more data points (e.g., Finlay & Darlington, 1995; Harcourt, Harvey, Larson, & Short, 1981). Within both the Mongoloid and Caucasoid races, there has been variation in subpopulations' historical exposure to harsh climate. Thus, in principle, it is possible to investigate Rushton's hypotheses within race, using finer distinctions than the three major races. This would be a more impressive test of his theory.

Rushton emphasized the sheer number of traits consistent with his theory. However, many of the phenotypes he examined may not be independent within the races. For example, IQ and criminality are correlated within both African Americans and Whites (Wilson & Herrnstein, 1985). Traits that are intercorrelated within races due to pleiotropy (genes' having more than one phenotypic effect), for example, cannot count as independent tests of his evolutionary theory. To the extent that such trait nonindependence obtains, the length of the lists showing the predicted ordering is less impressive than Rushton argued. One way to examine this possibility is to see whether traits of interest covary within families. Is a sibling who is less intelligent than another also less law abiding? Does the sibling who has sex the earliest also tend to have the highest number of sex partners? If so, then respective differences between races cannot independently count as evidence for $r$–$K$ theory.

## CONCLUSIONS

Despite the success of evolutionary behavioral scientists in predicting trends, they have been much less successful in addressing the substantial variation that is invariably found. Behavior geneticists have shown that a great deal of this variation is genetic in origin. This would seem to suggest that behavior geneticists could contribute to evolutionary behavioral science. It may be time to see if they can, or if the two disciplines are destined for scientific reasons to remain distant cousins.

## REFERENCES

Agrawal, N., & Jensen, A. R. (1984). Effects of inbreeding on Raven Matrices. *Behavior Genetics, 14,* 579–585.

Bailey, J. M., & Pillard, R. C. (1991). A genetic study of male sexual orientation. *Archives of General Psychiatry, 48,* 1089–1096.

Barkow, J. H., Cosmides, L., & Tooby, J. (1992). *The adapted mind: Evolutionary psychology and the generation of culture.* New York: Oxford University Press.

Bell, A. P., & Weinberg, M. S. (1978). *Homosexualities: A study of diversity among men and women.* New York: Simon & Schuster.

Belsky, J., Steinberg, L., & Draper, P. (1991). Childhood experience, interpersonal development, and reproductive strategy: An evolutioanry theory of socialization. *Child Development, 62,* 647–670.

Billy, J. O. G., Tanfer, K., Grady, W. R., & Klepinger, D. H. (1993). The sexual behavior of men in the United States. *Family Planning Perspectives, 25,* 52–60.

Block, N. J., & Dworkin, G. (1976). *The IQ controversy.* New York: Pantheon.

Brodie, E. D. (1989). Genetic correlations between morphology and antipredator behaviour in natural populations of the garter snake Thamnophis ordinoides. *Nature, 342,* 542–543.

Buss, D. (1994). Individual differences in mating strategies. *Behavioral and Brain Sciences, 17,* 581–582.

Cloninger, C. R. (1987). Neurogenetic adaptive mechanisms in alcoholism. *Science, 236,* 410–415.

Crawford, C. B., & Anderson, J. L. (1989). Sociobiology: An environmentalist discipline? *American Psychologist, 44,* 1449–1459.

Diamond, J. M. (1992). Diabetes running wild. *Nature, 357,* 362–364.

Eaves, L. J., Martin, N. G., & Heath, A. C. (1990). Religious affiliation in twins and their parents: Testing a model of cultural inheritance. *Behavior Genetics, 20,* 1–22.

Feldman, M. W., & Lewontin, R. C. (1975). The heritability hang-up. *Science, 190,* 1163–1168.

Finlay, B. L., & Darlington, R. B. (1995). Linked regularities in the development and evolution of mammalian brains. *Science, 268,* 1578–1584.

Fisher, R. A. (1958). *The genetical theory of natural selection.* New York: Dover.

Gangestad, S. W., & Simpson, J. A. (1990). Toward an evolutionary history of female sociosexual variation. *Journal of Personality, 58,* 69–96.

Gelerntner, J., Goldman, D., & Risch, N. (1993). The A1 allele at the D2 dopamine receptor gene and alcoholism. A reappraisal. *Journal of the American Medical Association, 269,* 1673–1677.

Gottesman, I. I. (1991). *Schizophrenia genesis.* San Francisco: Freeman.

Gould, S. J. (1981). *The mismeasure of man.* New York: Norton.

Gould, S. J., & Lewontin, R. C. (1978). The spandrels of San Marco and the Panglossian Paradigme: A critique of the adaptationist programme. *Proceedings of the Royal Society of London, 205,* 581–598.

Hamer, D. H., Hu, S., Magnuson, V. L., Hu, N., & Pattatucci, A. M. L. (1993). A linkage between DNA markers on the X chromosome and male sexual orientation. *Science, 261,* 321–327.

Hamilton, W. D. (1980). Sex versus non-sex versus parasite. *Oikos, 35,* 282–290.

Harcourt, A. H., Harvey, P. H., Larson, S. G., & Short, R. V. (1981). Testis weight, body weight and breeding system in primates. *Nature, 293,* 55–57.

Harpending (in press). Review of Rushton. *Evolutionary Anthropology.*

Herrnstein, R. J. (1973). *IQ in the meritocracy.* Boston: Little, Brown.

Herrnstein, R. J., & Murray, C. (1994). *The bell curve: Intelligence and class structure in American life.* New York: The Free Press.

Jensen, A. R. (1969). How much can we boost IQ and scholastic achievement? *Harvard Educational Review, 39,* 1–123.

Jensen, A. R. (1981). Obstacles, problems, and pitfalls in differential psychology. In S. Scarr (Ed.), *Race, social class, and individual differences in IQ* (pp. 483–514). Hillsdale, NJ: Lawrence Erlbaum Associates.

Kendler, K. S., Heath, A. C., Neale, M. C., Kessler, R. C., & Eaves, L. J. (1992). A population-based twin study of alcoholism in women. *Journal of the American Medical Association, 268,* 1877–1882.

Kendler, K. S., Neale, M. C., Kessler, R. C., Heath, A. C., & Eaves, L. J. (1993). A test of the equal-environment assumption in twin studies of psychiatric illness. *Behavior Genetics, 23,* 21–28.

Lande, R. (1976). The maintenance of genetic variability by mutation in a polygenic character with linked loci. *Genetic Research, 26,* 221–235.

Landolt, J. A., Lalumiere, M. L., & Quinsey, V. L. (1995). Sex differences in intra-sex variations in human mating tactics: An evolutionary approach. *Ethology and Sociobiology, 15,* 3–24.

Layzer, D. (1974). Heritability analyses of IQ scores: Science or numerology? *Science, 183,* 1259–1266.

Lewontin, R. C., Rose, S., & Kamin, L. J. (1984). *Not in our genes.* New York: Pantheon.

Loehlin, J. C. (1992). *Genes and environment in personality development.* Newbury Park, CA: Sage.

Loehlin, J. C., Lindzey, G., & Spuhler, J. N. (1975). *Race differences in intelligence.* San Francisco: Freeman.

Loehlin, J. C., & Nichols, R. C. (1976). *Heredity, environment, and personality.* Austin, TX: University of Texas Press.

Maynard Smith, J. (1989). *Evolutionary genetics.* New York: Oxford University Press.

Maynard Smith, J. (1993). *The theory of evolution.* New York: Cambridge University Press.

McGue, M., & Lykken, D. T. (1992). Genetic influence on risk of divorce. *Psychological Science, 3,* 368–373.

Mealey, L. (1995). The sociobiology of sociopathy: An integrated evolutionary model. *Behavioral and Brain Sciences, 18,* 523–599.

Molenaar, P. C., Boomsma, D. I., & Dolan, C. V. (1993). A third source of developmental differences. *Behavior Genetics, 23,* 519–524.

Mousseau, T. A., & Roff, D. A. (1987). Natural selection and the heritability of fitness components. *Heredity, 59,* 181–197.

Neale, M. C., & Cardon, L. R. (1992). *Methodology for genetic studies of twins and families.* Dordrecht, Netherlands: Kluwer.

Neel, J. V. (1962). Diabetes mellitus: A "thrifty genotype" rendered detrimental by "progress." *American Journal of Human Genetics, 14,* 353–362.

Noble, E. P., & Paredes, A. (1993). Recent developments in alcoholism: Molecular biology and behavior. *Recent Developments in Alcoholism, 11,* 345–362.

Plomin, R. (1990). The role of inheritance in behavior. *Science, 248,* 183–188.

Plomin, R., Corley, R., DeFries, J. C., & Fulker, D. W. (1990). Individual differences in television viewing in early childhood: Nature as well as nurture. *Psychological Science, 1,* 371–377.

Plomin, R., DeFries, J. C., & Loehlin, J. C. (1977). Genotype-environment interaction and correlation in the analysis of human behavior. *Psychological Bulletin, 84,* 309–322.

Plomin, R., DeFries, J. C., & McClearn, G. E. (1989). *Behavioral genetics: A primer.* New York: Freeman.

Risch, N., & Merikangas, K. R. (1993). Linkage studies of psychiatric disorders. *European Archives of Psychiatry and Clinical Neuroscience, 243,* 143–149.

Roff, D. A. (1992). *The evolution of life histories: Theory and analysis.* New York: Chapman & Hall.

Rose, M., & Charlesworth, B. (1980). A test of evolutionary theories of senescence. *Nature, 287,* 141–142.

Rowe, D. C. (1994a). *The limits of family influence: Genes, experience, and behavior.* New York: Guilford.

Rowe, D. C. (1994b). No more than skin deep: Ethnic and racial similarity in developmental process. *Psychological Review, 101*, 396–413.

Rushton, J. P. (1995). *Race, evolution, and behavior: A life history perspective.* New Brunswick, NJ: Transaction.

Scarr, S., Pakstis, A. J., Katz, S. H., & Barker, W. B. (1977). Absence of a relationship between degree of white ancestry and intellectual skills within a black population. *Human Genetics, 39*, 69–86.

Sulloway, F. (1995, June–July). *Birth order and evolutionary psychology: A meta-analytic overview.* Paper presented at the seventh annual meeting of the Human Behavior and Evolution Society, Santa Barbara, CA.

Tambs, K., Sundet, J. M., Eaves, L., Solaas, M. H., & Berg, K. (1991). Pedigree analysis of Eysenck Personality Questionnaire (EPQ) scores in monozygotic (MZ) twin families. *Behavior Genetics, 21*, 369–382.

Tesser, A. (1993). The importance of heritability in psychological research: The case of attitudes. *Psychological Review, 100*, 129–142.

Tooby, J., & Cosmides, L. (1990). On the universality of human nature and the uniqueness of the individual: The role of genetics and adaptation. *Journal of Personality, 58*, 17–68.

Tsuang, M. T., & Faraone, S. V. (1990). *The genetics of mood disorders.* Baltimore: Johns Hopkins University Press.

Turkheimer, E. (1991). Individual and group differences in adoption studies of IQ. *Psychological Bulletin, 10*, 392–405.

Wahlsten, D. (1990). Insensitivity of the analysis of variance to heredity-environment interaction. *Behavioral and Brain Sciences, 13*, 109–120.

Williams, G. C. (1957). Pleiogropy, natural selection, and the evolution of senescence. *Evolution, 11*, 398–411.

Wilson, D. S. (1994). Adaptive genetic variation and human evolutionary psychology. *Ethology and Sociobiology, 15*, 219–236.

Wilson, J. Q., & Herrnstein, R. J. (1985). *Crime and human nature.* New York: Simon & Schuster.

# 7

# Evolutionary Psychology and Theories of Cognitive Architecture

Andrew Wells
*The London School of Economics and Political Science*

Evolutionary psychology (Barkow, Cosmides, & Tooby, 1992; Buss, 1995) is an approach to understanding the mind that draws on two profoundly important theories. The first is Darwin's theory of evolution by natural selection, which underpins the idea that psychological mechanisms are adaptations (cf. Darwin, 1859, 1871). Darwin's theory explains how complex biological organisms can be constructed by natural selection operating on heritable differences between individuals that affect reproductive fitness. The second theory on which evolutionary psychology draws is the theory of computation, which underpins the treatment of psychological mechanisms as information processors and minds as computers. The originator of the modern theory of computation was the mathematician Alan Turing (cf. Turing, 1936–1937). Turing developed the abstract definition of a universal computer on which contemporary computer science is founded, and was able to prove some fundamental theorems about the capacities and limitations of symbolic information-processing systems. The universal machine concept is as important for our thinking about the nature of machines as natural selection is for thinking about the origins of complex biological systems.

This chapter examines the integration of biological and computational thinking with respect to theories of cognitive architecture. The use of the term *architecture* in this context derives from the design of computers, rather than buildings. In computer science, the term *architecture* refers to the overall design of the software, and especially the hardware of a computer. In cognitive science, the term *architecture* refers to the overall design of the software and hardware of the mind, and a theory of cognitive architecture needs to consider the range of purposes for which the mind was shaped by natural selection, the nature and capacities of its different systems, and the means of communication among them. A focus on cognitive architecture is, essentially, a focus at the level of the individual mind, rather than at the level of the parts of the individual mind or at the level of the group or other social structure of which the individual is, in turn, a part. However, to focus on the individual is not to deny the importance of the other levels of analysis. Indeed, one way to think of the individual level of analysis is as a bridge between the lower level analysis of parts and the higher level analysis of social structures.

This chapter begins by outlining its structure. Following this introduction, it discusses digital computer architectures, which provide a possible model for human cognitive architecture. Then it introduces two primary constraints on theories of cognitive architecture, which are called the evolutionary constraint and the universality constraint. The discussion of these constraints serves to frame the issues of the nature of mental representations and the sources of behavioral flexibility, which are central to the chapter. Following the discussion of constraints there is an outline of the central features of evolutionary psychology, which relate to theories of cognitive architecture. Evolutionary psychologists hypothesize that cognitive architecture consists essentially of an aggregate of adaptations that are special-purpose, evolved psychological mechanisms. Although this proposal clearly meets the evolutionary constraint, it does not appear to meet the universality constraint. Next, the chapter outlines one of the principal ways in which cognitive scientists have deployed computational ideas in forming theories of cognitive architecture. This is the idea that minds are physical symbol systems. The symbol systems approach meets the universality constraint, but appears to be incompatible with the evolutionary constraint.

The conclusion drawn from the discussions of the symbol systems and evolutionary psychology approaches is that an adaptationist theory of cognitive architecture, which is compatible with both constraints, requires new understandings of the nature of mental representation and of the relationship between computation and thinking. It is argued here that just such a new understanding can be securely grounded using Turing's analysis of computation and the Turing machine model. A new approach to the Turing machine model provides a more suitable foundation for an adaptationist theory of cognitive architecture than either symbol systems or the current computational thinking of evolutionary psychologists. In particular, it offers a much more plausible picture of the relation between evolved psychological mechanisms and culture and a convincing account of the nature of human behavioral flexibility.

## PROGRAMMABLE COMPUTER ARCHITECTURE

The architecture of most digital computers is an obvious candidate model for human cognitive architecture. It is sometimes called the *von Neumann architecture* after the mathematician John von Neumann, who was one of the pioneers of computer science in the 1940s. One can think about the principal features of the von Neumann architecture in the context of the personal computer. The most important hardware components of the personal computer are the processor, the memory (including both RAM and disk drives), and the communications devices (e.g., the monitor, keyboard, mouse, CD-ROM drive, audio equipment, fax, modem, joystick, etc.). Then there is software. An operating system, which is the software on which everything else depends, is essential. The choice of other software depends on the user's requirements.

Although the technology has changed radically since the 1940s, in terms of the size and speed of the components, the basic design pattern has remained the same. von Neumann would recognize his design principles in today's personal computers. The key to the success of the von Neumann architecture is not that there are no alternatives, but that there is something fundamental about the design. Personal computers, along with the first machines built to von Neumann's specifications, and modern supercomputers are all, essentially, instances of what are called *universal machines*. It was already mentioned that we owe the universal machine concept to Turing, who developed it before there were any electronic computers; the chapter returns to Turing's analysis later. It is easier, however, to introduce the concept of universality in the context of familiar machines like personal computers. The relevant sense of *universal* can be defined initially as "capable of being applied to a great variety of uses" or "general purpose," and what needs to be understood is the sense in which a machine like a personal computer is general purpose. After all, there are all sorts of things that you cannot do with them. The key point is that von Neumann machines are programmable.

One significant aspect of programmability is that it promotes behavioral flexibility. The tasks that a programmable machine can do are determined primarily by its programs and only secondarily by the characteristics of its physical equipment and the environmental input it experiences. A program is a sequence of instructions that is stored in memory and executed by the processor. It determines how the computer functions from moment to moment. To change the task performed requires changing the program, rather than physically rebuilding the machine. A program specifies the functional relationship between the input a machine receives and the output it produces. Thus, a programmable machine is one in which the functional relationship between input and and output can be modified.

A second significant point about programmability is that programs frequently include symbolic representations of aspects of the external world. In cases where the interaction between a program and the external world is at all complex, such representations may be essential for the program to function correctly. One of the cornerstones of cognitive theory is the idea that human mental representations are of the same kind as the representations used by computers.

Both these points about programmability can be illustrated in the familiar context of word processing. As I type these words, the relationship between keyboard and monitor is under the control of the Word Perfect software, which I use for word processing. The software is responsible for the fact that when I press the sequence of keys marked H, O, R, S, E, in that order, the word *horse* appears on the screen. It is essential to understand that this sensible relationship between key presses and output to the screen is specified by the Word Perfect software, and not by the hardware of the machine. As far as the hardware is concerned, it could just as easily output Z when I press A. The memory and processor of a computer are classic examples of the *tabula rasa*, or blank slate. Without a program, no relationship is specified between input and output. This does not mean, of course, that there are no physical connections between input and output systems. There is a vast amount of complex electronics, but its purpose is to support any relationship between input and output, which is specified in a program.

Consider how keyboards, programs, and VDU displays work together. Alphabetic characters are represented in a computer's memory in a numeric code called the *ASCII code*. For example, A is ASCII code 65. When a key is pressed, the hardware keyboard controller generates a number called a *scancode*, which identifies the key. In a DOS-based machine, the scancode is passed to part of the operating system called the *BIOS*, which interprets the scancode and stores the appropriate ASCII code in an area of memory called the *keyboard buffer*. To translate a key press into a pixel pattern on the screen, the processor has to be told by its controlling program to read the ASCII code from the keyboard buffer, set up a pattern in the video display memory, and make the video display hardware put the pattern on the screen. Thus, there is the following sequence of events: key press, scancode generation, ASCII code generation, VDU pattern generation, and VDU pattern display. Crucially, the link between the ASCII code in the keyboard buffer and the VDU pattern produced for output is controlled by a program. There is no direct physical linkage between keyboard and VDU like that between the keys and hammers on a typewriter. This means that the conventional relationship between key presses and VDU display patterns can easily be changed by the controlling program. It takes just a few lines of programming to output Z for input A, Y for B, and so on.

The relationship between input and output in a programmable system is fully modifiable because input from physical devices is delivered to programs in the form of uninterpreted codes, which can be associated in arbitrary ways with the codes that drive output devices. This point is quite general and extends beyond the simple example of ASCII codes and video monitors to embrace coded input from and output to any kind of peripheral device. The indirectness and malleability of the relationship between input (I) and output (O) in a programmable system shows that it is quite possible to build in completely arbitrary or positively harmful I/O functions. This is an important general point. When one thinks about general-purpose machines like computers, one tends to think of the range of useful purposes to which they can be put. What one also needs to bear in mind to get a complete picture is the even larger range of completely useless functions that a computer can be programmed to execute. Tooby and Cosmides (1992) suggested that this breadth of flexibility makes general-purpose computer architecture an implausible candidate model of human cognitive architecture.

The second significant point about programmable architectures can also be illustrated in the context of word processing: General-purpose memory can be used to construct internal representations of the environment in which a machine is operating to enhance its performance. Consider the word-wrap feature that all modern word processors have. Word wrap ensures that a word is not broken at the end of a line. If it is too long to fit on the current line, the whole word is moved to the next line. The point of the example is not that word wrap is a particularly significant operation, but that it illustrates a general point about the need for models to support complex functions. Only very simple functions can be supported without some kind of model or representation of the operating environment of the program.

Word wrap is complex enough to require a model of the screen environment. What kind of model is needed to implement word wrap? To begin with, a representation of a line is essential. Without one it is impossible to determine when the end has been reached. One good way to represent a line is as a fixed length array of character locations. With such a representation, the ends of the line are specified by the bounds of the array. Representations of a word and of the possible separators between words are also needed. The simplest model takes the space character as the separator and every other character, apart from control characters, as part of a word. Given the representations of line and word, the operations to be carried out must also be represented. What needs to be done is roughly as follows; as characters are typed, they must be stored in the array representation of the line, as well as being sent to the screen. As each character is received, a test is made to determine whether the end of the line has been reached. When the end of a line is reached, the program must determine whether the current character is part of a word or separator. If it is a separator, word wrap is not needed. If it is part of a word, the program needs to backtrack through the representation of the line to the most recent separator, delete the part of the word already sent to the screen, start a new line, print the part word at the beginning, and update the representation.

The enhanced capabilities that can be provided by building internal models of the environment have costs as well as benefits. Part of what makes a model complex is the way in which the representation and the world it models interact. In the case of word wrap, for example, the internal representation of the line must be constantly updated, otherwise it loses synchrony with the onscreen display. This sort of interaction is very much the norm, and is one of the reasons that writing large programs that work properly is such a difficult business. Another difficult problem with internal models is determining whether a model explicitly represents everything about a real system that is needed to make the model work properly. There is a line of theorizing in robotics (cf. Brooks, 1991) that suggests that building complex internal models is the wrong way to approach the synthesis of intelligent behavior, and that robots should be constructed to interact directly with the real world, rather than with representations of it. The adaptationist approach to cognitive architecture, which is outlined later, takes a similar view.

To summarize the discussion of programmability so far, two key points have been made. First, programmable machines are those in which the relationship between input and output is flexible and modifiable because it is controlled by a program; a corollary of this point is that the general-purpose nature of a programmable machine allows for the implemented relationship to be arbitrary with respect to the contingencies of the environment in which the machine operates. The second key point is that complex operations can be performed by constructing internal representations or models of the environment.

These points serve to introduce a slightly more general discussion. It is clear that many different relationships between input and output can be implemented in a programmable machine. A good question to ask is, how many? The answer, which we owe to Turing, is that there is a countable infinity in principle. They are called the *computable functions*. In practice, the number of different programs that could be run on any given machine is limited by the size of its memory; but given the size of current computer memories, the practical limitation is not serious. In principle, any one programmable machine can implement exactly the same set of functions as any other, and it is for this reason that computers are called *universal machines*. However, the fact that a computer is a universal machine does not mean that it can implement absolutely any input–output relationship. One of the other important discoveries that Turing made was that there are some noncomputable functions. For readers who are interested in understanding more of the fascinating technical background, there are numerous introductory texts on the theory of computation. Minsky (1967) and Lewis and Papadimitriou (1981) are particularly useful. For practical details about hardware, Norton (1995) is very informative about real personal computer architectures.

Thus far, this chapter has discussed programmable machines in the familiar context of personal computers, which have very limited equipment like keyboards and mice for communicating. To get a full picture, it is important to think about what programmability implies with respect to other peripheral communications devices, like visual sensors and robot arms and legs. No one has yet managed to write programs to control a completely autonomous mobile computer with a full set of senses, but programmability suggests that such extensive capabilities are possible. In principle, a programmable architecture can function with any kind of physical equipment that provides input in the form of symbolic codes and can be controlled by output of the same kind. Thus, programmable input–output relationships could plausibly underpin human behavioral capacities. The fact that we have different physical equipment from that commonly found in computers is not an objection in principle.

This section on programmable computer architecture concludes with a focus on the architecture of processors and the relationship between processors and programs. A processor is a special-purpose device designed to carry out a specific set of instructions, called its *instruction set*. Many of the instructions perform basic arithmetic operations like addition and subtraction. However, there are also logical operations, including conditional operations that allow the processor to test whether a specific condition holds, and to do one thing if it does and another if it does not. The logic operations are what make computers more than just glorified adding machines. The instruction sets of different processors have different numbers and types of instructions. Early processors typically had tens of instructions in their instruction sets, whereas modern processors may have hundreds. A processor also has a small memory that consists of a set of registers. The registers enable the processor to store intermediate results while carrying out calculations. The storage provided is enough for efficient instruction execution, but is small by contrast with the main memory.

Because the instruction set of a processor is a small, fixed repertoire of basic instructions, more complex operations have to be composed as sequences of the basic instructions. That is what programs are. Thus, programs have a dual function. They both encode representations of the external environment and provide sequences of instructions to drive the processor. The processor's view of programs is very different from the programmer's view. The programmer, in theory, views the task as a whole, whereas the processor views the task on an instruction by instruction basis. Moreover, the instructions for the processor have to be coded as binary patterns in what is known as *machine language*. Processors simply cannot deal with the English-like syntax of high-level programming languages. Programmers, in their turn, find it very hard to write machine language. The solution has been to develop programs that translate from high-level languages like BASIC or Pascal into machine language.

One other important point that is later discussed and developed further, is the way in which programming languages and processors are designed with each other in mind. If they were evolved systems, we would want to think of them as co-adapted. Although high-level programming languages try, as far as possible, to hide details of the processor from the programmer, and thus, to allow the programmer to work at a level of abstraction that suits the domain of application of a program, ultimately a program must be expressed as a sequence of instructions in the machine language of the processor. This is an absolute requirement, but the traffic is not all one way. As processor design has developed, instructions have been built in to support particular kinds of high-level operations. Thus, for example, the instruction set of the Intel 8086 processor—an ancestor of the 80486 and Pentium processors, which power a significant percentage of the current generation of personal computers—included a set of string manipulation instructions that its predecessor the 8080 lacked, specifically to simplify the compilation of high-level language string processing operations and to improve their execution speeds (Morse, 1982).

To summarize, a programmable architecture of the kind found in digital computers is a general-purpose control system that can, in principle, implement an infinite number of different input–output relationships known collectively as the *computable functions*. Programs are implementations of computable functions that are stored as symbolic representations in memory and are executed, when in machine language form, by a central processor. Processors communicate indirectly with the environment via coded input and output. Complex functions require internal models of the operating environment. The peripheral equipment available affects the tasks that can be carried out in practice, but does not limit what can be done in principle.

## CONSTRAINTS ON THEORIES OF COGNITIVE ARCHITECTURE

A particularly useful way to frame the issues that are at stake is in terms of constraints on theories of cognitive architecture. Constraints are conditions that a theory must meet if it is to give an adequate account of what it sets out to explain. Two of the obvious constraints on theories of human cognitive architecture are that the mind is a product of biological evolution, and that it is capable of remarkable behavioral flexibility, including apparently indefinitely complex information processing.

The first of these constraints can simply be called the *evolutionary constraint*. There is no serious debate about the truth of the evolutionary constraint, but it is difficult to understand exactly how it impinges on the study of minds. For example, Newell (1980) suggested that "one real problem with the evolution constraint is that we know it gives rise to an immense diversity of systems (organisms). It is not clear how to get it to generate systems that are shaped at all to mind-like behavior" (p. 140). This is an assessment that many other theorists would share. Given the wide range of systems, some with minds and some without minds, which have been produced by evolution, why should we expect our evolutionary background to provide any specific clues to the nature of the human mind? Humans are also constrained by the need to breathe air, but we do not expect this constraint to be particularly informative about the nature of the mind.

Evolutionary psychologists, however, claim that the evolutionary constraint is a powerful source of information about the nature of psychological mechanisms, and one that allows us to form predictive hypotheses about current behavior. The central point is that evolutionary theory leads to a view of psychological mechanisms as autonomous, special-purpose entities crafted to solve specific adaptive problems. This is a productive view for two reasons. First, it suggests that the task of understanding the mind can be undertaken on a piecemeal basis, adaptation by adaptation. Second, it suggests an experimental methodology. The first step is to provisionally identify an adaptive problem that our ancestors might have faced. This requires imaginative reconstruction of the likely demands of the ancestral environment. The second step is to form a hypothesis about the nature of an adaptation that might solve the putative adaptive problem. The third step is to form a hypothesis about the behavioral effects that might spring from the interaction of the hypothesized adaptation and the contingencies of the current environment. The fourth step is to design experiments to test the behavioral hypothesis. A notable example of this methodology in practice is the study by Cosmides (1989), in which the existence of an adaptation to detect opportunities for cheating in social exchanges was hypothesized. The adaptive problem was the uncertainty of food supplies resulting from chance factors affecting individuals, and the hypothesized adaptation was for reciprocal food sharing within the social group to even out the effects of chance. The cheating-detection mechanism was needed to ensure that debts were repaid. Without such a mechanism, reciprocity would be vulnerable to invasion by defectors and could not become a stable strategy. Successful counterintuitive predictions about the current operation of the cheater-detection mechanism were couched in terms of expected performance on content-specific forms of the Wason selection task.

The question of how to characterize the requirement for substantial behavioral flexibility has a clear answer in terms of the capacities of universal computers and can, for this reason, be called the *universality constraint*. Recall from the earlier discussion of universality that there is a countable infinity of programs, hence the behavioral flexibility of universal machines is almost unlimited. Moreover, universal machines are as flexible in their behavior as it is possible for mechanical systems to be; therefore, we can be confident that if we require theories of mind to specify cognitive architectures that are computationally universal, they will be capable of sufficient flexibility of behavior. More significant, computational universality appears to be a necessary feature of an adequate theory of cognitive architecture. The weakest argument for this point is that humans can quite clearly emulate universal machines. Newell (1990) discussed this and other, more substantial, arguments.

The central issue with which this chapter is concerned can therefore be thought of as the development of a theory of cognitive architecture that meets both the evolutionary constraint and the universality constraint. This is a difficult task because the two constraints seem, at first sight, to be mutually incompatible. The evolutionary constraint leads in the direction of special-purpose mechanisms, and thus, in the direction of task-specific behavior rather than universality; whereas the universality constraint leads in the direction of general-purpose mechanisms, and thus, in the direction of maximal behavioral flexibility but away from the space of designs that seem plausible given the evolutionary constraint.

## EVOLUTIONARY PSYCHOLOGY

Evolutionary psychology emphasizes human cognitive architecture as a product of evolution. Thus, a proposed theory of cognitive architecture "must be able to account for the solution of the broad array of distinct problems inherent in reliable reproduction over thousands of generations under ancestral conditions" (Tooby & Cosmides, 1992, pp. 108–109). Considering the range of problems that our ancestors must have solved, Tooby and Cosmides compiled an impressive list that is worth quoting at length.

> Over the course of their evolution, humans regularly needed to recognize objects, avoid predators, avoid incest, avoid teratogens when pregnant, repair nutritional deficiences by dietary modification, judge distance, identify

plant foods, capture animals, acquire grammar, attend to alarm cries, detect
when their children needed assistance, be motivated to nurse, select conspecifics as mates, select mates of the opposite sex, select mates of high
reproductive value, induce mates to choose them, choose productive activities, balance when walking, avoid being bitten by venomous snakes, understand and make tools, avoid needlessly enraging others, interpret social
situations correctly, help relatives, decide which foraging efforts have repaid
the energy expenditure, perform anticipatory motion computation, inhibit
one's mate from conceiving children by another, deter aggression, maintain
friendships, navigate, recognize faces, recognize emotions, cooperate, and
make effective trade-offs among many of these activities, along with a host
of other tasks. (Tooby & Cosmides, 1992, p. 110)

Evolutionary psychologists convincingly argue that the way evolution
has solved these problems is by selecting specialized mechanisms, essentially one mechanism per problem. According to this view, human genotypes contain genes for all these mechanisms, and human phenotypes
have many of them in place at birth, although some require maturation,
tuning to the specifics of the environment and learning, and others are
expressed later in the course of individual lifetimes.

The proposal that our cognitive architecture consists of a set of adaptations is clearly consonant with the evolutionary constraint. The question we
need to ask is whether it also meets the universality constraint. This is a
serious question because, "specialized mechanisms can be very successful
and powerful problem-solvers, but they achieve this at the price of addressing a narrower range of problems than a more general mechanism" (Tooby
& Cosmides, 1992, p. 112). The solution they offered is based on aggregating
more and more special-purpose machines.

The solution to the paradox of how to create an architecture that is at the
same time both powerful and more general is to bundle larger numbers of
specialized mechanisms together so that in aggregate, rather than individually, they address a larger range of problems. Breadth is achieved not by
abandoning domain-specific techniques but by adding more of them to the
system. (Tooby & Cosmides, 1992, p. 113)

The notion that an aggregate of adaptations is more powerful than the
individual adaptations that constitute it can be understood in at least two
ways. The extra power might simply be additive; an aggregate of $N$
adaptations solves $N$ adaptive problems, whereas each adaptation solves
only one adaptive problem. More interesting, however, is the possibility
of interactions among the members of an aggregate to produce compound
or complex adaptations. Visually guided reaching would be a possible
compound adaptation for a system that had independently evolved both
the capacity to see and reach for objects. Visually guided reaching involves

the parallel activation of individual adaptations, but there might also be interactions that relied on the sequential activation of individual adaptations. A capacity like hunting appears to be a clear case; the hunter must find a spoor, identify, track, and then tackle the prey animal, and so forth.

However, the aggregation of adaptations is not the only means of achieving behavioral flexibility. Tooby and Cosmides (1992) suggested that the more specialized mechanisms there are in place, the more likely it is that general-purpose mechanisms will also be useful. "The more alternative content-specialized mechanisms an architecture contains, the more easily domain-general mechanisms can be applied to the problem spaces they create without being paralyzed by combinatorial explosion" (Tooby & Cosmides, 1992, p. 113). Thus, they concluded that:

> what is special about the human mind is not that it gave up "instinct" in order to become flexible, but that it proliferated "instincts" [i.e., adaptations] . . . which allowed an expanding role for psychological mechanisms that are (relatively) more function general. (Tooby & Cosmides, 1992, p. 113)

Although this solution is no doubt partly correct, it is questionable whether it can lead to the satisfaction of the universality constraint as it stands. The proposed existence of relatively more general mechanisms operating alongside highly specialized adaptations raises as many questions as it solves. What, precisely, a relatively general mechanism is, how such mechanisms might evolve, and how the combination of these with specialized adaptations makes possible the behavioral flexibility of a universal machine are questions that the proposal does not answer. Evolutionary psychology needs a more detailed theory of cognitive architecture to tackle these, and other, problems.

## THE SYMBOL SYSTEMS APPROACH TO COGNITIVE ARCHITECTURE

The symbol systems approach to cognitive architecture has been developed over more than a quarter of a century primarily by Newell and Simon (cf. Newell, 1980, 1990; Newell & Simon, 1972, 1976). Throughout its development, one of the central features of the approach has been an emphasis on computational universality. "A physical symbol system is an instance of a universal machine" (Newell & Simon, 1976, p. 117); "Symbol systems form a class—it is a class that is characterized by the property of *universality*" (Newell, 1980, p. 147); "Symbol systems are a form of universal computational system" (Newell, 1990, p. 76). Thus, symbol systems satisfy the universality constraint by definition. If a machine or organism is not a universal computer, it is not a symbol system.

Because they are universal machines, symbol systems are programmable, and this is taken as the explanation for their behavioral flexibility. "When we seek to explain the behavior of human problem solvers (or computers for that matter), we discover that their flexibility—their programmability—is the key to understanding them" (Newell & Simon, 1972, p. 870). Thus, the symbol systems approach claims that human cognitive architecture is computationally universal and programmable. The focus on the similarity between human cognitive architecture and the architecture of computers is deliberate and quite specific. Like a computer, a symbol system has a memory, a processor, inputs, outputs, and symbol structures. Symbol structures are programs and representations of objects and events in the external environment. The key characteristics of a symbol system, again mirroring the computer case, are the modifiability of the relationship between inputs and outputs to take account of changing circumstances, and the capacity for activities such as planning and problem solving, which require the manipulation of internal representations independently of the state of the external environment.

The symbol systems approach treats mental representations in humans as symbolic representations, such as those that make programmable computer systems powerful. The idea that mental representations are symbolic representations that are processed in the same way as representations in computers provides a potential solution to a long-standing problem about the nature of thought. The notion of a mental representation as a symbol structure in an internal machine language is attractive and intuitively appealing. Representations allow us to work out the consequences of potential actions without actually having to engage in them, which is presumably highly adaptive; they also allow us to solve problems by concentrating on specific aspects of them.

The classical problem with the idea of mental representations has been the danger of an infinite regress of representing systems. A representation is always a representation for someone. Thus, the postulation of mental representations seemed to lead to the requirement for an inner person, or *homunculus*, whose task was to understand the representations. The mind of the homunculus had to have its own representations, which required a further homunculus to understand them and so forth. What the architecture of programmable computers shows is that the circle can be broken. The idea that the mind is organized as a universal machine thus meets the requirements of the universality constraint and solves the problem of mental representation.

Given that the symbol systems approach manifestly satisfies the universality constraint, the question to ask is whether it also satisfies the evolutionary constraint. If it does, it provides a potentially satisfactory account of human cognitive architecture. At first sight, the prospect is promising. Symbol systems theorists explicitly recognize the evolutionary constraint. Moreover, other theorists with evolutionary leanings endorse the approach. Pinker (1994), for example, said that the symbol systems hypothesis "is as fundamental to cognitive science as the cell doctrine is to biology and plate tectonics is to geology" (p. 78).

Although symbol systems theorists acknowledge the evolutionary constraint, it is not clear that the architecture of symbol systems is, in fact, compatible with it. The primary characteristic of a symbol system is its computational universality, and the difficulty this poses is that universal architecture is general purpose. One reason for the staggering success of the computer industry is that computers can be made to do any task for which a program can be written, ranging from displaying digitized images to controlling interplanetary satellites to word processing chapters on evolutionary psychology. The crux of the issue, as far as the evolutionary constraint is concerned, is that such virtuoso, general-purpose functionality is possible only because computer architecture is not geared to the solution of any specific adaptive problem and will always be outperformed by a mechanism specialized for a given problem. This makes it difficult to see how universal architecture could have evolved because evolution selects just those mechanisms that solve adaptive problems better than their competitors. Moreover, universal architecture requires the existence of at least an abstract specification of a specialized mechanism for any function that it computes. Thus, its mode of functioning seems to deny the possibility of a direct evolutionary origin.

A further argument against the symbol systems approach is based on the idea that programmability is incompatible with the evolutionary constraint because it conflicts with other characteristics of evolved systems. This argument is the work of computer scientist Michael Conrad, who has made an extensive study of the principles of biological computation over more than 20 years. Conrad argued that there is a trade-off principle that shows that computational efficiency and evolutionary adaptability are incompatible with programmability:

> A system cannot at the same time be effectively programmable, amenable to evolution by variation and selection, and computationally efficient. The von Neumann computer opts for programmability. The trade-off theorem suggests that an alternative domain of computing is in principle possible, where programmability is exchanged for efficiency and adaptability. Biological systems, as the products of evolution, must operate in this alternative domain. (Conrad, 1985, pp. 464–465)

The essence of Conrad's view of the relation between programmability and evolvability is that programmability imposes constraints on the structure of a computational system that are incompatible with the modifiability required for evolution. Informally, we can get a feel for the issues by considering the well-known brittleness of programs and hardware, which is their inability to tolerate structural changes while remaining functional. As every programmer knows, a single alteration in the code of a program is usually sufficient to prevent it from operating correctly or even from operating at all. Similarly, a single bit error in the hardware of a computer can lead to major malfunctioning. Small structural changes tend to lead to large changes in behavior, the great majority of which are deleterious to the functioning of the system. Why is this a consequence of programmability? One of the problems is the discrete and nonredundant nature of program encodings. The economy and power of the symbolic representations that allow a programmer to communicate a desired program exactly to a universal machine appear to preclude the modifiability that evolution requires.

Conrad's approach makes this and other issues more formal. He considered three attributes of computational systems: programmability, efficiency, and evolutionary adaptability. His arguments lead to the conclusion that high computational efficiency and high evolutionary adaptability are both incompatible with programmability. Conrad argued that evolutionary adaptability (i.e., the capacity to survive in uncertain environments as a result of the operation of variation and selection mechanisms) requires both evolutionary flexibility and what he called gradual transformability.

Evolutionary flexibility is essentially a measure of the capacity of a system to undergo changes to its structure while continuing to solve a particular class of adaptive problems. The greater the number of such structural changes that a system can sustain, the greater its evolutionary flexibility. The types of structural change that are relevant depend on the system under consideration. Conrad mentioned single mutations or crossover events in DNA and single alterations of code in computer systems as examples.

The concept of gradual transformability links structural changes to a system with changes in its behavior. For a system to evolve, it must be capable of undergoing at least one structural change that either improves its behavior immediately or is one of a series of sustainable changes that eventually leads to an improvement in its behavior. Structural changes are likely to be sustainable if they result in small, rather than large, changes in behavior, and Conrad defined a system as being *gradually transformable* if it undergoes only a small change in behavior as a result of a structural change. The question then is what constitutes a small change in behavior. This question has no general answer, but Conrad suggested that, in the context of evolution, it is reasonable to think of the behavior of two systems as differing by a small amount if each solves approximately the same class of adaptive problems or performs adequately in approximately the same set of environments.

Conrad showed that programmable systems are not, in general, gradually transformable, using an argument that is similar to Turing's celebrated proof of the unsolvability of the "halting problem" (for details, see Conrad, 1988, pp. 297–298). The argument shows that the class of programmable systems, considered as a whole, fails to meet a necessary condition for evolutionary adaptability, and this suggests that minds are not programmable systems because minds are the products of an evolutionary process.

Conrad also discussed the question of efficiency. It is a commonplace notion that evolution does not produce optimal designs, and there are many instances where evolution's solution to a problem could be improved. The vertebrate eye, in which the retina is back to front, is a classic example of a design that could be improved. However, the fact that evolution does not produce optimal designs does not mean that the designs produced are not efficient. The visual system again serves as a good example. The photoreceptors that transduce light are extremely sensitive. Rods that are specialized for night vision give a detectable response to single photons (Sterling, 1990), and the system as a whole functions over a remarkably wide range of light intensities.

Conrad discussed efficiency in terms of the number of interactions between particles in a system that are used for computation relative to the maximum number of interactions that are possible in a system with the same number of particles, and showed that the efficiency of systems that are constrained to be programmable is much lower than the efficiency of those that are not so constrained. A less technical appreciation of the lower efficiency of programmable systems can be achieved by considering the differences between programmable and nonprogrammable systems. A nonprogrammable system responds directly to its inputs, whereas a programmable system requires those inputs to be translated into a coded form that its processor can deal with and also needs a program to specify the task it is to carry out. These overheads mean that a programmable system inevitably consumes more resources than a nonprogrammable system specially designed for a given task, and is thus less efficient at carrying out that task. The overheads can be greater or lesser according to the design of the programmable machine, but they are always there. The flexibility of universal simulation capacity is bought at the cost of a decrease in efficiency.

Despite the appeal of the symbol systems approach, and despite its commitment, in principle, to the evolutionary constraint, it is not clear that the architecture of symbol systems meets the evolutionary constraint because the fundamental claim is that the mind is a programmable architecture of essentially the same type as a digital computer. The most plausible conclusion to draw is that the mind is not a symbol system.

## TOWARD AN ADAPTATIONIST THEORY
## OF COGNITIVE ARCHITECTURE

If the mind is not a symbol system, as Conrad's and other arguments strongly suggest, there is a need for an alternative approach to cognitive architecture that meets both the evolutionary constraint and the universality constraint. This section outlines some ideas that may prove fruitful in this regard. A good place to begin is with the problems with both symbol systems theory and evolutionary psychological theory. The central problem with the symbol systems approach is the claim that the memory medium is general purpose and programmable. This claim is implausible on evolutionary grounds. The central problem with the evolutionary psychology approach, by contrast, is that it provides no satisfactory account of how the universality constraint might be met. It is not clear what range of behavioral flexibility is possible on the basis of an aggregate of specialized mechanisms evolved to solve specific problems, even with the addition of relatively more general mechanisms, as Tooby and Cosmides proposed, and this theoretical opacity compares unfavorably with the clarity of the symbol systems approach in this respect. It is also not clear how a bundle of special-purpose adaptations can support the general memory capacity that humans have. Nevertheless, the idea that cognitive architecture is based on an aggregate of adaptations is plausible and seems likely to be essentially correct. The question is how to extend this idea within a computational framework to meet the universality constraint.

The answer proposed here starts from the assumption that it is a mistake to suppose that humans have both a programmable symbolic memory and a processor like a computer, but instantiated in neural tissue rather than in silicon. The correct claim, I believe, is that the brain is essentially just a processor. Recall from the discussion of digital computer architecture what processors are like. They have a fixed set of hard-wired, special-purpose operations—called an instruction set—and a small memory consisting of a set of registers. The registers provide limited temporary storage that facilitates the efficient operation of the processor. Thus, one should think of the set of adaptations that evolutionary psychologists consider to be the basis of cognitive architecture as the instruction set of a processor designed by evolution and of human working memory as the registers of this processor. The evolved processor is, among other things, a symbol processor par excellence, but the symbol structures it processes are external (i.e., things like books and pictures).

The combined system of neural processor and external symbol structures meets both the evolutionary constraint and the universality constraint. The evolved part of the system is an aggregate of adaptations, whereas the system as a whole is undoubtedly a universal computer because it has the capacity to carry out symbolic instructions coded in a symbolic notation that is rich enough to encompass the computable functions. Every time one consults a map to determine where to go, cooks a meal using a recipe book, or consults a reference manual to find out how to get a software system to do something, one is carrying out essentially the same sort of process that a computer carries out when it executes a program. One implication of this approach is that an adequate theory of human cognitive architecture must include not just the brain of the cognizer, but also the external symbolic artefacts with which the cognizer interacts. For a rather similar view based on a study of navigation practices, see Hutchins (1995). The approach can also be related to Dawkins' (1982) notion of the extended phenotype: "an animal artefact, like any other phenotypic product whose variation is influenced by a gene, can be regarded as a phenotypic tool by which that gene could potentially lever itself into the next generation" (p. 199). What are books if not animal artifacts?

The theoretical justification for treating a human brain combined with an external symbolic resource as a computer comes from Turing's original analysis of computation, rather than from the consideration of digital computer architectures, although it was appropriate to introduce the ideas in that context. It is important to note in what follows that, in 1936, when Turing was thinking about computation, there were no electronic, digital computers. A *computer* was a person who carried out calculations, normally with pencil and paper. Turing was trying to understand the general nature, possibilities, and limitations of the processes in which one engages when carrying out routine calculations in that way. His reasons for being concerned with the process of calculation were connected with a fundamental problem in the foundations of mathematical logic. Interested readers might like to look at an excellent anthology (Herken, 1988) that was published to celebrate the 50th anniversary of the universal Turing machine concept. Turing's analysis of the process of computation involved an abstract machine that modeled the essential features of the process. His original description of the machine is both clear and informative:

> We may compare a man in the process of computing a real number to a machine which is only capable of a finite number of conditions $q_1, q_2, \ldots,$ $q_R$ which will be called "$m$-configurations". The machine is supplied with a "tape" (the analogue of paper) running through it, and divided into sections (called "squares") each capable of bearing a "symbol". At any moment there is just one square, say the $r$-th, bearing the symbol $S(r)$ which is "in the machine". We may call this square the "scanned square". The symbol

on the scanned square may be called the "scanned symbol". The "scanned symbol" is the only one of which the machine is, so to speak, "directly aware". However, by altering its $m$-configuration the machine can effectively remember some of the symbols which it has "seen" (scanned) previously. The possible behaviour of the machine at any moment is determined by the $m$-configuration $q_n$ and the scanned symbol $S(r)$. This pair $q_n$, $S(r)$ will be called the "configuration": thus the configuration determines the possible behaviour of the machine. In some of the configurations in which the scanned square is blank (*i.e.*, bears no symbol) the machine writes down a new symbol on the scanned square: in other configurations it erases the scanned symbol. The machine may also change the square which is being scanned, but only by shifting it one place to right or left. In addition to any of these operations the $m$-configuration may be changed. Some of the symbols written down will form the sequence of figures which is the decimal of the real number which is being computed. The others are just rough notes to "assist the memory". It will only be these rough notes which will be liable to erasure. It is my contention that these operations include all those which are used in the computation of a number. (Turing, 1936–1937, pp. 117–118)

The reader should be aware of two particular points about this definition of the Turing machine. The first is that Turing's analysis has stood the test of time. The Turing machine provides the theoretical foundation on which computer science rests, and it is accepted that a Turing machine can be specified to compute any of the computable functions. Therefore, we can confidently make use of the model when thinking about cognitive architecture. The second point is that the real-world system on which Turing based the machine model had two components: the mind of the human computer and the paper on which a calculation was worked. In the Turing machine model, these became the finite state control and the tape, respectively. This is a simple point, but it is fundamental to the adaptationist analysis of cognitive architecture. The finite state control is a model of the functional structure of the human mind, and the tape is a model of the external symbolic resources with which the mind interacts. Turing's clear distinction between these components is the basis for my proposal to treat the human mind in interaction with external symbol structures as a computer. The steps in Turing's analysis, and a pictorial representation of the resulting machine, are shown in Fig. 7.1.

Each Turing machine is a special-purpose mechanism that can be thought of as a logical blueprint for a physical machine that could be constructed. The finite state control is the blueprint for the processor of such a machine, and the tape is the blueprint for its symbol store. Turing took his analysis two further crucial steps beyond the special-purpose models thus far outlined. First, he showed that any Turing machine could be described as a sequence of symbols. Second, he showed how to con-

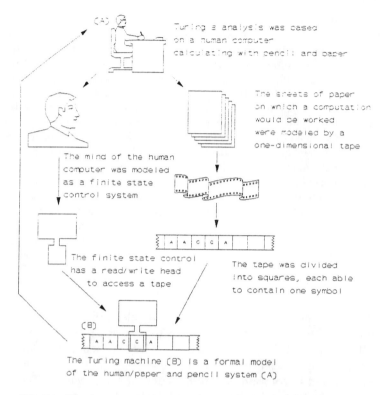

FIG. 7.1. The derivation of the Turing machine from the example of a human calculating with paper and pencil. The Turing machine is the abstract ancestor of the digital computer.

struct a Turing machine, which he called the *universal machine*, which could interpret the symbolic description of another Turing machine and act according to that description. The sequence of symbols describing a Turing machine is a program, and thus, Turing's universal machine was the first general-purpose programmable machine. Digital computers are direct descendants of the abstract universal machine. They incorporate substantial practical changes because, for example, the one-dimensional tape of the Turing machine is not suitable for high-speed computation. In essence, the processor of a computer is the physical realization of the finite state control of a universal Turing machine, and the memory of a computer is a two-dimensional physical realization of the tape of a universal Turing machine.

Given that computers are treated as formally equivalent to Turing machines, despite the many technological innovations that have altered the practical details of computer architecture out of all recognition, there can be no doubt that it is also appropriate to think of a human brain interacting with symbolic resources in the external environment as formally equivalent to a Turing machine because such a system was the basis for Turing's model.

A particularly promising aspect of the model is the way in which it focuses attention on the interaction between internal functional states and external symbols. There is an analogy here with an important point about adaptations, which is the intimacy of the connection between an adaptation and those recurrent features of the environment with respect to which it was selected:

> Adaptations evolve so that they mesh with the recurring structural features of the environment in such a way that reproduction is promoted in the organism or its kin. Like a key in a lock, adaptations and particular features of the world fit together tightly, to promote functional ends. (Tooby & Cosmides, 1992, p. 69)

The functional states of Turing machines are also tightly meshed with symbol structures on their tapes. Notice how different this is from the case of a programmable architecture, in which the modifiability of fit between the hardware and its environment is one of the principal virtues. It seems clear, in fact, that the adaptationist approach to cognitive architecture remains true to the spirit of Turing's analysis in a way in which the symbol systems approach, with its treatment of the tape of the Turing machine as a model for human memory, does not.

This observation shows how different the symbol systems and adaptationist approaches are, particularly in their understanding of the nature and function of human memory. In a symbol system, the primary requirement is for a large, general-purpose memory that can be used to store whatever programs and data are required. It is of the essence of such a memory that the storage should be erasable so that one program can be replaced by another as circumstances change. Newell (1990) explained the requirements on the memory medium: "the medium must have high stability so that what is processed can be retained. Yet, it must have low stability when it is being transformed, so that the transformation can be done at will" (p. 64). Size is also of primary importance because the processor in a symbol system interacts with representations of the external environment, rather than directly with that environment. The general-purpose memory needs to be as large as possible because a small memory would clearly limit the representational scope of the system. The role of the control system, or processor, is simply to manipulate representations that carry the bulk of the system's knowledge. The processor, therefore, will be as small as is compatible with its functions.

In an adaptationist architecture, by contrast, because symbol storage is primarily external rather than in the brain, the emphasis is different.

Adaptations interact directly with the world, rather than with representations of it. The bulk of the system's knowledge is stored in its adaptations, and it is plausible to think of them as hard-wired memories for behavioral sequences that were successful in ancestral environments. The fact that adaptations mesh with structural features of the environment suggests that they serve as memories and to initiate and control action. A good question to ask is whether this approach can give an adequate account of human long-term memory, which appears to have at least some of the characteristics of general-purpose computer memory and to serve some functions, such as remembering telephone numbers and computer passwords, which are quite clearly not solutions to adaptive problems. I think the way forward here is indicated by Sherry and Schacter (1987) in their paper on the evolution of multiple memory systems. They argued that memory systems that initially evolved to serve specific adaptive functions can come to serve more general functions as a result of processes such as exaptation (cf. Gould & Vrba, 1982) or the reduplication and sharing of circuitry as proposed by Rozin (1976).

An important related point that must also be made is that the human capacity to work with external symbol structures like books is almost certainly not based on adaptations for activities such as reading and writing. These accomplishments are simply too recent in evolutionary terms. It is much more plausible to suppose that symbolic activities of this kind also depend on the exaptation of adaptations that were originally selected for other purposes. It is not difficult to imagine the selective advantage that might have accrued to those individuals in ancestral environments who possessed the fine visual discrimination, motor control, and attention span that are required for reading and writing.

This point, however, has a further consequence. It seems to suggest that the Turing machine is, after all, an unsatisfactory model for cognitive architecture because Turing machines function only with alphanumeric symbols like 0 and 1, whereas minds interact with all sorts of other entities as well, with which the Turing machine model cannot deal. Furthermore, the symbol alphabet of a Turing machine is defined to be finite, whereas there appear to be indefinitely may different inputs that might impinge on the human organism. Thus, it appears that the Turing machine model can, at best, only explain how adaptations fulfill their exapted functions, and does not address the fit between adaptations and the nonsymbolic features of the environment with respect to which they were originally selected, and, in most cases presumably, are still functioning.

The first point to make in answer to this objection is historical. It is perfectly true that the Turing machine model was developed in the context of alphanumeric symbols. The reason for this is that Turing's concerns were mathematical, and therefore, logical and formal symbols were entirely appropriate. It does not follow from this, however, that other entities could not also serve perfectly well as inputs to Turing machines with appropriate functional states. The central requirement for a symbol is the property of type identity. For something to function as a symbol, any instance or token of it must be treated in the same way as any other token, and it must be discriminable from the tokens of any other symbol. For example, 0 and 1 demonstrate the property of type identity very clearly—0, 0, and 0 being quite clearly tokens of the same symbol and equally clearly distinct from 1, 1, and 1. The question, then, is whether entities other than alphanumeric symbols can be found that the perceptual systems of humans treat as tokens of specific types. In other words, are there innate classification principles subserving perception? The phenomenon of categorical perception (Harnad, 1987) suggests that there are. If such principles and classes of entities can be found, the problem of the potential infinity of inputs can also be overcome by postulating that complex symbols are composed from sequences or aggregates of simple symbols, as is the case with conventional Turing machines. A clear place to look is in the behavioral repertoires of neonates and young infants. If one were to observe systematic differences of response to specific classes of stimuli at ages sufficiently early to making learning an improbable explanation, there would be grounds for suggesting that these classes of stimuli function as basic symbols.

Recent research in child development strongly suggests that babies are equipped at, or very shortly after, birth with a range of distinct reactions to specific classes of stimuli. These results are in marked contrast to the prior Piagetian orthodoxy, which argued that, at birth, children were equipped only with very general sensory and discriminative capacities. Neonates are particularly responsive to auditory stimuli within the frequency range of the human voice, and they show special sensitivity to human speech sounds (Aslin, Pisoni, & Jusczyk, 1983; Eimas, Miller, & Jusczyk, 1987). Infants also appear to be specifically equipped to recognize human faces. By 2 to 3 months, when infants are sensitive to pattern structure, they prefer a schematic face to scrambled arrangements of features (Maurer, 1985). More recently, Johnson and Morton (1991) and Morton and Johnson (1991) showed that neonates preferentially attend to stimuli with a facelike arrangement of elements. Johnson and Morton hypothesized that two neural mechanisms underlie this performance. The first, which they call CONSPEC, is a subcortical mechanism that is functional at birth. The second, CONLERN, is a cortical mechanism that takes input from CONSPEC and controls face recognition from about the age of 2 months. Being able to reliably distinguish faces from nonfaces is logically the same sort of process as being able to distinguish 0s from 1s reliably, and there seems no reason to deny that faces can act as computational primitives given that binary digits can.

Prelinguistic infants also seem to be sensitive to a distinction between animate and inanimate objects based on the different ways in which they move (Mandler & Bauer, 1988). Premack (1991) argued that movement is the basis for a built-in capacity to distinguish intentionality from causality. He argued that infants are hard wired so as to divide objects into two classes: those that are self-propelled and those that are not. He suggested that the induced movements of nonself-propelled objects are the basis for perceptions of causality, and that the free movements of self-propelled objects are the basis of perceptions of intentionality. More generally, the infant's perception of objects appears to make use of a variety of built-in mechanisms that instantiate four principles: boundedness, rigidity, cohesion, and no action at a distance (Karmiloff-Smith, 1992; Spelke, 1990).

The famous visual cliff apparatus developed by Gibson and Walk (1960) also suggests that infants are sensitive to marked environmental discontinuities. The visual cliff was used to show that, by the time babies can crawl, they are sensitive to potentially dangerous drops and behave accordingly. Other types of studies (e.g., Arterberry & Yonas, 1988) indicate that kinetic depth perception is present at an even earlier stage, by 3 or 4 months of age. The perception of dangerous versus safe in terms of potential drops appears to have the logical qualities required for a primitive symbol. It appears, then, that the symbol notion is in fact quite broad enough to accommodate a wide range of organism–environment interactions in a recognizably computable fashion.

What the discussion of symbols suggests is that we should distinguish two superordinate classes of environmental symbol types, which might be called native and conventional. Native symbol types are those to which cognitive adaptations are tuned. They are types like human faces and speech sounds that have direct adaptive significance. Conventional symbol types, by contrast, are cultural products, such as alphabets and pictograms. The relation between a conventional symbol and what it represents is largely arbitrary. New conventional symbols can be created, and the signification of existing symbols can be changed over very short time scales, which are not possible for native symbols whose signification results from the workings of evolution. Conventional symbol systems such as the English alphabet, which have symbolic primitives and rules of combination, have unlimited representational capacity that native symbols lack, and it is conventional symbol systems that support computational universality. The point that the adaptationist approach to cognitive architecture makes, however, is that the representational power of these systems depends on the discriminative power of the machinery, which supports native symbol processing. Perhaps one of the most significant aspects of conventional symbol types is that they can be used to understand native symbol types and communicate that understanding.

Another possible objection to the adaptationist approach to cognitive architecture is that it loses one of the most valuable features of the symbol systems approach, which is the capacity to use symbolic models of the environment for thinking, planning, and predicting. If mental computation involves constant interaction with symbol structures in the environment, as the approach suggests, how is it ever possible for the mind to escape the "tyranny" of the immediate stimulus environment? There are two parts to the answer to this objection; the first is that finite state control systems do have the capacity for internal representational memory in which thinking, planning, and other reflective activities can take place; this is very clearly true of the processor of a computer that has a set of registers. The adaptationist approach to cognitive architecture does picture this memory as relatively limited, but this suggestion seems entirely appropriate given the psychological evidence about the limited capacity of human working memory within which thinking takes place (cf. Baddeley, 1986). The second part of the answer is that, even when thinking or planning, the human organism is still monitoring the state of the environment. Human minds are never isolated from their environments in the way in which computer "minds" usually are. The human mind, when deprived of environmental input, quickly starts to malfunction. Were this not so, sensory deprivation would not have the power it does as an instrument of interrogation. Thus, again, the connectedness to the environment that the adaptationist view of cognitive architecture proposes seems consonant with everyday experience.

A further possible objection to the Turing machine as a model of cognitive architecture is that Turing machines have no emotions, whereas human cognition and emotion are inseparable. The answer to this objection is again primarily historical and relates to Turing's purposes in developing the machine model, which were to elucidate the nature of formal computation. It is partly for this reason, and partly because of the developing technology of computers, that functional states are considered independently of affect, but there is no theoretical reason why this must be the case. It is perfectly feasible to give functional descriptions of behavioral sequences that involve emotions in an essential way. For example, the analysis of male sexual jealousy (Buss, 1994) is a clear case. The distinction between native and conventional symbol types may help to clarify these issues. Many native symbol types will elicit emotional reactions as part of their built-in signification. Conventional symbol types may or may not have emotional associations. For most people, the 0s and 1s of binary arithmetic do not, but conventional symbols such as national flags and other institutional emblems frequently do.

A more technical objection to the adaptationist proposal as outlined here is that adaptations can operate in parallel, whereas Turing machines are essentially serial. The short answer to this objection is that there is no conflict in principle between Turing computability and parallelism. A detailed formal analysis that shows how to incorporate parallelism has been done by Gandy (1980). Informally, we can get a feel for some of the issues by considering the example of a symphony orchestra in performance. An orchestra can be understood as a parallel system because there are many players playing at the same time, but also as a serial system when the performance is considered as a sequence of chords. Similarly, there is no reason, in principle, that we should not consider the implementation of the successive functional states of a Turing machine as states of a system of parallel components producing a serial output stream. Nevertheless, it is true that a more detailed model of the system of adaptations will need to be based on a formalism that explicitly incorporates parallel operations. Two approaches that have been developed in recent years are those of Hoare (1985) and Milner (1989). Either of these approaches might prove suitable for evolutionary modeling.

The primary architecture of the mind is a system of adaptations. This system is a collection of psychological mechanisms that were selected for their contributions to the solution of specific adaptive problems. Buss (1995) provided illustrative examples, for which there is some empirical evidence, of behavior patterns that may indicate underlying adaptations. Among them are fear of snakes; male sexual jealousy; preference for sweet and fatty foods; female mate preference for economic resources; male mate preferences for youth, attractiveness, and waist-to-hip ratio of about 0.7; natural language; cheat detection in social contract situations; and male desire for sexual variety. One of the issues that is not clearly understood is the extent to which the mechanisms underlying such disparate behavior patterns interact, and, if they do, whether their interactions are harmonious or discordant.

Leaving aside the precise details of the interactions among adaptations that will form an important area of future research in evolutionary psychology, we can think of the architecture as a confederation of semiautonomous mechanisms, which can be modeled as the finite state control of a Turing machine. These mechanisms are structured to interact with specific types of environmental cues (i.e., native symbol types, such as snakes, sexual rivals, foods, etc.). The hypothesis is that the set of adaptations constitutes a universal human nature in the sense that it is genetically specified in every human being. Variability in inputs exists in the different symbol tokens, different foods for example, and the different cultural traditions and resources to which individuals are exposed.

The primary functions of the set of adaptations that constitute the machinery of the individual mind were selected because they contributed to the reproductive success of their possessors in ancestral environments.

It is an open question that requires empirical research to determine whether our evolved psychological mechanisms remain adaptive in current environments. What the adaptationist approach argues is that some of these mechanisms, whether currently adaptive or not, are being used for the production and comprehension of conventional symbolic resources, such as drawings, paintings, and written materials. What Turing's analysis allows us to see is how a collection of special-purpose mechanisms, such as a set of adaptations or the instruction set of a computer processor, can interact with conventional symbol types to produce the representational power of a universal computer. Moreover, the use of permanent and durable external storage mechanisms for conventional symbolic resources both reduces the load on individual memory and enables the transmission of knowledge from one generation to the next.

Perhaps the most valuable feature of the adaptationist approach to cognitive architecture outlined and advocated in this chapter is the way it allows the differences between adaptations and external symbol structures to become manifest. The symbol systems approach blurs these differences because it insists on internal symbol structures. The extraordinary character of human intellectual life stems from the fact that it depends on the interaction between such different media as brains and books. As I sit at my desk, typing these remarks, I am surrounded by external symbol structures. There are several hundred volumes on the bookshelves in front of me. There is a jumble of papers on the desk, a pile of sheet music on the shelf to my right, a number of boxes of photographic slides, and a stack of music cassettes. Stored in these various media is a wealth of information about a wide range of subjects and events. The books were written over thousands of years. The insights and information contained in just my small share of the symbolic resources of the modern world are almost endless.

Without a brain to interact with them, however, these resources are just brute physical material. What of brains? The strange and remarkable truth is that brains were not originally developed to interact with conventional symbolic information at all. They were selected to solve the problems of living and reproducing. They are full of mechanisms that push and pull in different and often conflicting ways, mainly to do with other people. The most important influences in our lives are other humans. We need to cooperate and we have to compete. We are curious and lethargic by turns, active, fatigued, moody, exhilarated, mean, generous, inspired, and outraged, possibly all in the same day. We deceive others and ourselves, but are capable of insights into the structure of the universe and of understanding events that occurred at the dawn of time. Darwin furnished us with an understanding of ourselves as finite products of a blind, selective process, grinding away over the eons of evolutionary time.

Turing has furnished us with an understanding of the power of symbol systems to encode and represent an infinite amount of information. An adaptationist theory of cognitive architecture is an attempt to understand how brains and external symbol systems interact.

## SUMMARY AND CONCLUSIONS

The starting point of the chapter was the need to combine Darwin's theory of evolution by natural selection with Turing's theory of computation to provide a sound basis for a theory of cognitive architecture. Two central constraints on any such theory are that it must be compatible with evolution and that it must explain the remarkable behavioral flexibility of the cognitive system. A primary difficulty for any theory of cognitive architecture is that the evolutionary constraint and the universality constraint pull in different directions. One obvious candidate architecture on which human cognitive architecture might be modeled is the architecture of digital computers. The central property of computer architectures is programmability, which allows them to be used to implement arbitrary input–output functions. The internal representations that can be stored in a programmable memory and the independence of internal processing from the demands of the external environment provide a seemingly natural account of cognitive structures such as memory and of activities such as thinking and planning.

The symbol systems approach to cognitive architecture is based on the assumption that human cognitive architecture is indeed programmable and shares its essential features with computer architecture. This approach clearly meets the universality constraint, but, despite its explicit recognition of the evolutionary constraint, fails to meet it because programmability is incompatible with the evolutionary process. Current theorizing in evolutionary psychology, by contrast, treats the mind as a collection of adaptations that are special-purpose mechanisms selected for their success in ancestral environments. Evolutionary psychology clearly meets the evolutionary constraint, but has no clear account of the way in which a system of adaptations might meet the universality constraint. The adaptationist account described herein proposed that the Turing machine model provides a formal basis for the study of cognitive architecture. By separating adaptations from external symbolic resources, but making their interaction crucial for the capacities of the system as a whole, it is possible to see how a cognitive architecture can meet both the evolutionary constraint and the universality constraint. Identifying the adaptations that make up the finite control of the cognitive Turing machine and understanding how they interact with each other and with external symbol structures is a task on which work has only just begun.

## ACKNOWLEDGMENTS

I am particularly grateful to Charles Crawford for his encouragement and for inviting me to write the chapter. I would like to thank Dennis Krebs and Larry Fiddick, who provided very helpful comments on a draft of the chapter. It is also a pleasure to thank past and present colleagues in the working group on Darwinism at LSE, Christopher Badcock, Helena Cronin, Oliver Curry, Geoffrey Miller, Alex Monto, Valeria Mosini, Vana Papalois, Gemma Penn, Jennifer Scott, Colin Tudge, John Watkins, Richard Webb, Amanda Williams, and John Worrall for reading and discussing drafts of the chapter.

## REFERENCES

Arterberry, M. E., & Yonas, A. (1988). Infants' sensitivity to kinetic information for three-dimensional object shape. *Perception and Psychophysics, 44*, 1–6.

Aslin, R. N., Pisoni, D. B., & Jusczyk, P. W. (1983). Auditory development and speech perception in infancy. In M. M. Haith & J. J. Campos (Eds.), *Handbook of child psychology: Volume 2. Infancy and developmental psychology* (4th ed., pp. 573–687). New York: Wiley.

Baddeley, A. D. (1986). *Working memory.* Oxford, England: Oxford University Press.

Barkow, J. H., Cosmides, L., & Tooby, J. (1992). *The adapted mind. Evolutionary psychology and the generation of culture.* Oxford: Oxford University Press.

Brooks, R. A. (1991). Intelligence without representation. *Artificial Intelligence, 47*, 139–159.

Buss, D. M. (1994). *The evolution of desire. Strategies of human mating.* New York: Basic Books.

Buss, D. M. (1995). Evolutionary psychology: A new paradigm for psychological science. *Psychological inquiry, 6*(1), 1–30.

Conrad, M. (1985). On design principles for a molecular computer. *Communications of the Association for Computing Machinery, 28*(5), 464–480.

Conrad, M. (1988). The price of programmability. In R. Herken (Ed.), *The universal Turing machine. A half century survey* (pp. 285–307). Oxford, England: Oxford University Press.

Cosmides, L. (1989). The logic of social exchange: Has natural selection shaped how humans reason? Studies with the Wason selection task. *Cognition, 31*, 187–276.

Darwin, C. (1859). *On the origin of species.* A facsimile of the first edition with an introduction by Ernst Mayr (1964). Cambridge, MA: Harvard University Press.

Darwin, C. (1871). *The descent of man, and selection in relation to sex.* With an introduction by John Tyler Bonner and Robert M. May (1981). Princeton, NJ: Princeton University Press.

Dawkins, R. (1982). *The extended phenotype. The long reach of the gene.* Oxford, England: Oxford University Press.

Eimas, P. D., Miller, J. L., & Jusczyk, P. W. (1987). On infant speech perception and the acquisition of language. In S. Harnad (Ed.), *Categorical perception. The groundwork of cognition* (pp. 161–195). Cambridge, England: Cambridge University Press.

Gandy, R. (1980). Church's thesis and principles for mechanisms. In J. Barwise, H. J. Keisler, & K. Kunen (Eds.), *The Kleene symposium* (pp. 123–148). Amsterdam: North-Holland.

Gibson, E. J., & Walk, R. D. (1960). The "visual cliff." *Scientific American, 202*, 64–71.

Gould, S. J., & Vrba, E. S. (1982). Exaptation—A missing term in the science of form. *Paleobiology, 8*, 4–15.

Harnad, S. (Ed.). (1987). *Categorical perception. The groundwork of cognition.* Cambridge, England: Cambridge University Press.

Herken, R. (Ed.). (1988). *The universal Turing machine. A half-century survey.* Oxford, England: Oxford University Press.

Hoare, C. A. R. (1985). *Communicating sequential processes.* London: Prentice-Hall.

Hutchins, E. (1995). *Cognition in the wild.* Cambridge, MA: MIT Press.

Johnson, M. H., & Morton, J. (1991). *Biology and cognitive development: The case of face recognition.* Oxford, England: Basil Blackwell.

Karmiloff-Smith, A. (1992). *Beyond modularity. A developmental perspective on cognitive science.* Cambridge, MA: MIT Press.

Lewis, H. R., & Papadimitriou, C. H. (1981). *Elements of the theory of computation.* Englewood Cliffs, NJ: Prentice-Hall.

Mandler, J. M., & Bauer, P. J. (1988). The cradle of categorization: Is the basic level basic? *Cognitive Development, 3,* 247–264.

Maurer, D. (1985). Infants' perception of facedness. In T. Fields & N. Fox (Eds.), *Social perception in infants* (pp. 73–100). Norwood, NJ: Ablex.

Milner, R. (1989). *Communication and concurrency.* London: Prentice-Hall.

Minsky, M. L. (1967). *Computation: Finite and infinite machines.* Englewood Cliffs, NJ: Prentice-Hall.

Morse, S. (1982). *The 8086/8088 primer. An introduction to their architecture, system design, and programming.* Rochelle Park, NJ: Hayden Book Company.

Morton, J., & Johnson, M. H. (1991). CONSPEC and CONLERN: A two-process theory of infant face recognition. *Psychological Review, 98,* 164–181.

Newell, A. (1980). Physical symbol systems. *Cognitive Science, 4,* 135–183.

Newell, A. (1990). *Unified theories of cognition.* Cambridge, MA: Harvard University Press.

Newell, A., & Simon, H. A. (1972). *Human problem solving.* Englewood Cliffs, NJ: Prentice-Hall.

Newell, A., & Simon, H. A. (1976). Computer science as empirical inquiry: Symbols and search. *Communications of the Association for Computing Machinery, 19,* 113–126.

Norton, P. (1995). *Peter Norton's inside the PC* (6th ed.). Indianapolis, IN: Sams Publishing.

Pinker, S. (1994). *The language instinct. The new science of language and mind.* London: Allen Lane, The Penguin Press.

Premack, D. (1991). The infant's theory of self-propelled objects. In D. Frye & C. Moore (Eds.), *Children's theories of mind. Mental states and social understanding* (pp. 39–48). Hillsdale, NJ: Lawrence Erlbaum Associates.

Rozin, P. (1976). The evolution of intelligence and access to the cognitive unconscious. *Progress in Psychobiology and Physiological Psychology, 6,* 245–280.

Sherry, D. F., & Schacter, D. L. (1987). The evolution of multiple memory systems. *Psychological Review, 94*(4), 439–454.

Spelke, E. S. (1990). Principles of object perception. *Cognitive Science, 14,* 29–56.

Sterling, P. (1990). Retina. In G. M. Shepherd (Ed.), *The synaptic organization of the brain* (3rd ed.). Oxford, England: Oxford University Press.

Tooby, J., & Cosmides, L. (1990). On the universality of human nature and the uniqueness of the individual: The role of genetics and adaptation. *Journal of Personality, 58*(1), 17–67.

Tooby, J., & Cosmides, L. (1992). The psychological foundations of culture. In J. H. Barkow, L. Cosmides, & J. Tooby (Eds.), *The adapted mind. Evolutionary psychology and the generation of culture* (pp. 19–36). Oxford, England: Oxford University Press.

Turing, A. M. (1936–1937). On computable numbers, with an application to the Entscheidungs problem. *Proceedings of the London Mathematical Society, 42,* 230–265.

# 8

# Not Whether to Count Babies, but Which

Laura Betzig
*University of Michigan*

> *Of those which do survive, the best adapted individuals, supposing that there is any variability in a favourable direction, will tend to propagate their kind in larger numbers than the less well adapted.*
> —Darwin, *On the Origin of Species* (1859)

> *It will be observed that the principle of Natural Selection [refers] to the progressive modification of structure or function only in so far as variations in these are of advantage to the individual in respect to his chance of death or reproduction.*
> —Fisher, *The Genetical Theory of Natural Selection* (1958)

> *Adaptation would be a mechanism designed to promote the success of an individual organism, as measured by the extent to which it contributes genes to later generations.*
> —Williams, *Adaptation and Natural Selection* (1966)

Consider three possibilities.

We're primates (*Aegyptopithecus*? savannah baboons?) with culture.

We're hominids (*Homo erectus*? Kalahari !Kung?) with culture.

There's no such thing as culture.

The latest best guess is that your ancestors and mine spent the last 65 million years or so as some kind of primate. For those 65 million years, the problems they had to face—the selective pressures that shaped their actions and cognition—were something like the problems faced by modern prosimians, monkeys, and apes. That fact has inspired more than a few primatologists to look for the roots of human behavior in living primates. People, by their logic, are something like lemurs, baboons, or chimps. To understand human thought or behavior, they first try to understand what raised fitness in monkeys and apes, then they try to understand culture, and then they try to put them together (e.g., Washburn & DeVore, 1961; recent references include, among many others, Degler, 1991; Kinzey, 1997; Schubert & Masters, 1991).

Another best guess is that our ancestors spent on the order of the last 4 million years as pre-sapient hominids. For those 4 million years, the problems *they* had to face—the selective pressures that shaped *their* actions and cognition—were something like the problems faced by (AL) 288-1 ("Lucy") or KNM-ER 3733 (the Koobi Fora *Homo erectus*). That fact has inspired more than a few anthropologists to look for the roots of human behavior in Pleistocene woman and man—and in their supposed living analogues, the Kalahari !Kung. We moderns, by their logic, must be something like Koobi Fora or Botswana hunters and gatherers. The conclusions drawn are the same. Understanding modern human thought or behavior means understanding what raised fitness in foragers, then understanding culture, and then trying to put them together (e.g., Lee & DeVore, 1968; many recent examples include Barkow, Cosmides, & Tooby, 1992; Smith, 1992; Symons, 1979).

The third and last possibility is that the problems solved in the present are enough like the problems solved in the past that we still solve them. That *H. sapiens*—like baboons or bonobos, *Australopithecus* or *erectus*—continue to think and act adaptively. That people still maximize reproductive success (e.g., Alexander, 1979; Betzig, 1997; Betzig, Borgerhoff Mulder, & Turke, 1988; Reeve & Sherman, 1993).

## WHAT'S WRONG WITH THESE POSSIBILITIES?

One thing wrong with the baboons with culture idea is that 65 million years is a very long time. In it, a bewildering variety of prosimians, monkeys, and apes—with a bewildering variety of diets, group sizes and structures, mating systems, and so on—has evolved. In the 35 years that followed Washburn and DeVore's (1961) look at the "Social Behavior of Baboons and Early Man," living species have been found to vary enormously—to eat insects or leaves or fruits or hunted meat, to live solitarily or in families or in fission-fusion communities, and to mate monogamously or polyandrously or promiscuously or in harems (e.g., Dunbar, 1988; Smuts, Cheney, Seyfarth, Wrangham, & Struhsaker, 1987). Even African apes, which probably diverged from a common ancestor as recently as 6 million years ago, live in stable or variable groups, mate promiscuously or polygynously, and do or do not defend territories (Wrangham, 1987). Even chimpanzees—still, by consensus, our closest living primate kin—at Kibale, Mahale, Gombe, and other sites vary (Wrangham, McGrew, de Waal, & Heltne, 1994).

Another problem with the monkeys with culture idea is that every one of these living primates faces selective pressures different from its ancestors'. The array of fossil candidates for *the* common ancestors from which living primates diverged is large (e.g., Begun, Ward, & Rose, 1996). Even more recently, common ancestor candidates are many. Although just one hominid species survives, there are at least 9 known fossil hominids, and around 14 to 16 are guessed to have lived. Further back, the numbers increase: There are 183 species of living primate and more than 250 known species of fossil primate; an estimated 6,000 species of primate of modern aspect have lived since the Eocene (e.g., Foley, 1989). The more remote species are phylogenetically, the more trivial the similarities (Potts, 1987; Tooby & DeVore, 1987). Traits that make species interesting tend to be traits that make species unique.

The same sorts of things are wrong with the !Kung with culture possibility. Four million years, compared to 65 million, isn't much time. But it's enough to have left a great variety of fossils at a great variety of sites—with, again, a variety of possible diets (from seed eaters to meat eaters), group structures (with home bases or without), mating systems (suggested by varying degrees of sexual dimorphism), and so on. How important hunting, food sharing, and associated social activities have been to hominids, and for how long, remain debatable questions (e.g., Binford, 1981; Isaac, 1978). And a whole constellation of distinctly human characters—from language to art to much in human cognition—may be as recent as the human revolution of 40,000 to 60,000 years ago (e.g., Diamond, 1992; Mellars & Stringer, 1989). In short, neither primate evolution nor hominid evolution has been at all static (e.g., Foley, 1996; Irons, in press). Selective pressures have continued to change. And so have pelvises, cranial capacities, and teeth; subsistence strategies and diets; and family patterns, social interactions, and cognition.

Given all of which, no living foragers can be good models for our foraging ancestors (e.g., Kelly, 1995; Lee & DeVore, 1968). Not only are living hominids likely to differ significantly from dead hominids at any slice in selective time—from, say, 3½-foot-tall Lucy with her 400cc cranial capacity or the heavy-chewing, 850cc cranial capacity Koobi Fora *Homo erectus*. Living foragers also differ from one another. Lee and DeVore made that point in their classic "Man the Hunter" symposium; and it's been made ever since (Lee and DeVore, 1968; Kelly, 1995). For instance, Dobe !Kung get an estimated 67% of their calories from foods provided by women; but outside sub-Saharan Africa—where foragers have been pushed into particularly poor habitats—the range is from 51% (for the Venezuelan Hiwi) to just 2% (for the Canadian Inuit) (Betzig, 1992). Paternal care, measured in various ways, ranges from around 10 minutes a day among Paraguayan Aché to 88% of the day among African Aka Pygmies (Hewlett, 1992). Mating systems vary, fertility varies, and estimated homicide rates vary by at least a factor of five (Knauft, 1987). In short, if we want to reconstruct what selective pressures shaped *Homo sapiens'* behavioral adaptations by Pleistocene reconstruction (Tooby & Cosmides, 1992), where do we start? With which *Australopithecus*? With which *erectus*? With !Kung mongongo nut collecting or Hadza big game hunting? With Tiwi-type polygyny or Aché-type promiscuity? It isn't clear.

The obvious problem with the no such thing as culture idea is that people *do not* maximize reproductive success. Or do they? Studies of a variety of samples—from *Who's Who* to census data to detailed interviews on a representative group of Albuquerque men—have failed to show consistent correlations among wealth, education, rank, and various measures of reproductive success (e.g., Kaplan, Lancaster, & Johnson, 1995; Turke, 1990).

On the other hand, models with reproductive success, or other fitness proxies, as currency *have* successfully predicted a variety of behaviors in a variety of human societies. Some of these models have predicted age at maturity and interbirth intervals among living foragers (Blurton-Jones, 1986; Hill & Hurtado, 1996). Other models, tested on comparative samples ranging from Eskimo whale hunters to imperial Chinese, have predicted associations between polygyny and patrilateral inheritance, or between political and reproductive equality (Betzig, 1986; Cowlishaw & Mace, 1996; Hartung, 1982). Most recently, models tested on historical data from 13th-century Portugal to 17th-century England to 19th-century Sweden have predicted fertility and migration, and primogeniture and dowry with surprising elegance and accuracy (Bergstrom, 1994; Boone, 1986; Clarke & Low, 1992). Living people in a variety of places—from Peruvian forests to modern London—still do all sorts of things likely to spread their genes (e.g., review in Betzig, 1997).

## COUNTING BABIES IN THE PAST

Starting off with an assumption that most traits are vestiges—that they no longer raise fitness—makes it necessary to reconstruct their effects on fitness in the past. Obviously, it's much easier to measure fitness effects in the present. The trait itself, the context in which it's expressed, and its effect on fitness components like reproductive success can all be estimated much more accurately on living populations than on dead ones.

Whether evidence for adaptation is sought in the present or at some slice of time in the evolutionary past, an optimality model must be built (e.g.,

Parker & Maynard Smith, 1990). The selective pressures that shape or have shaped the trait—the parameters of diet, predation, and so on that constrain adaptation—must be taken into account. Over time, especially over evolutionary time, data are inevitably lost. As a result, selective pressures are much more precisely measured in the present than in the past.

After the model is built, it has to be tested. The only way that can be done—the only way a selective pressure molding an adaptation can be shown—is by demonstrating the effect of the trait in question on its bearers' reproduction. That is, testing the model requires measuring, or at least estimating, the trait's effects on its bearers' reproductive success (RS). *Fitness* itself—the rate of spread of a gene—is an immeasurable abstraction (Wright, 1968). Yet, there is a hierarchy of tractable proxies, including lifetime reproductive, mating, and foraging success, any of which is as good as our understanding of its effects on the spread of an individual's genes (e.g., Clutton-Brock, 1988). Again, testing these models—like building the models—is bound to be more precise on living populations than on dead ones.

Whether the models are built and tested on living populations or dead ones, the traits in question may not raise bearers' RS. If they do not, it may be because selection on earlier populations failed to produce such traits, or traits selected for in the past fail to develop or function as designed in environments that have rapidly changed. The first of these possibilities—that stochastic, historical, and other forces constrain "perfection" in evolution—has been discussed at length (e.g., Gould and Lewontin 1979; Travisano *et al.* 1995); the second possibility has often been taken for granted. Further *phylogenetic reconstruction* (Tinbergen, 1963)—a telescopic hunt for fitness effects in the more and more remote evolutionary past—may suggest whether traits in question were ever subject to selection in ancestral populations.

Where, on the other hand, traits *do* raise fitness in the living or dead population examined, the most likely reason is that related behaviors raised fitness—were naturally selected—in the past. Every other inference (that the trait was produced by random evolutionary forces, like drift; nonrandom evolutionary forces, like pleiotropy and other side effects of selection; random environmental forces, like learning errors; or nonrandom environmental forces, like culture) is relatively weak (Betzig, 1989).

Of the alternatives, "culture" is of course the one in which most stock has been put. But early, *sui generis* notions of cultural transmission failed to yield any predictive models (e.g., Durkheim, 1895; White, 1949). And though later dual-inheritance theories offered sophisticated models of distinct genetic and cultural change, they yielded few empirical results (e.g., Boyd & Richerson, 1986; Durham, 1991). On the other hand, models that dispense with "culture" altogether have predicted Aché age at maturity, English primogeniture and dowry, and so on, simply as individuals' means to spread genes.

## COUNTING BABIES IN THE PRESENT

Sometimes, fitness effects are sought for traits with a long evolutionary legacy. Pregnancy sickness would be one of these. Another might be gestational hypertension. A third may be men's tastes for symmetrical breasts. Recent work on each of these traits has made the case that they are adaptations, in part, by citing evidence of their fitness-enhancing effects. For instance, Profet (1992) strengthened her argument that pregnancy sickness evolved by natural selection by noting that "women who vomit or experience severe nausea during early pregnancy have lower risks of spontaneous abortion than women who experience only mild pregnancy sickness" (p. 327). Haig (1993) suggested that high blood pressure in pregnant mothers is an effect of conflict over fetus' supply of blood; he made his point, in part, by citing the fact that "gestational hypertension has a good fetal prognosis"—birthweight and survival have been positively correlated with maternal blood pressure (p. 515). And Møller, Soler, and Thornhill (1995) made the case that men are more attracted to women with symmetrical breasts by showing that women with more symmetrical breasts have higher reproductive success.

Sometimes, fitness effects are sought for relatively novel traits. Bride wealth is one example, and medieval canon law is another. Borgerhoff Mulder (1988) found bride wealth in one contemporary Kenyan society—the Kipsigis—to be paid out adaptively. Men and their families spent more on early maturing brides, and early maturing Kipsigis women gave birth to more children. In a look at an even more novel trait, medieval canon law was found to be adaptive as well. Younger sons in the church used canon law to keep their elder brothers—heirs to their fathers' estates—from raising heirs themselves. That put younger sons in a position to come into their fathers' estates by default and to father more children and grandchildren as a result (Betzig, 1995). For both of these groups—canon lawyers and Kipsigis grooms—a simple, fitness-maximizing model has made it possible to predict complex, novel acts. Each is undoubtedly made possible by a number of traits selected to do similar work in the past. How much novelty can an organism stand? When will adaptations cease to function? These are, and always have been, empirical questions.

## WHICH BABIES TO COUNT

When Washburn, DeVore, and others first looked for the biological roots of *H. sapiens'* behavior in their ancestors—and in those they took to be living ancestral analogues, like savannah baboons and Kalahari !Kung—they worked from the commendable assumption that people are, after all, like other animals. It's somewhat ironic that generations of their intellectual scions—the scores of field primatologists, fossil hunters, and hunter–gatherer ethnographers who followed their lead—have swung the pendulum the other way. They've shown how vastly primates, hominids, and humans vary among families, among genera, and among—even within—species. People are unmistakably vertebrates, mammals, primates, and hominids. But they're unmistakably unique. To look too hard for the roots of their behavior in other primates or even other hominids is to underestimate the power of natural selection to shape new families, genera, and species—with very new adaptations. And it may vastly underestimate the ability of those new families, genera, and species to use those adaptations, even under novel conditions, to behave in fitness-raising ways.

In short, counting *H. sapiens'* babies may tell us more about our behavior than counting baby baboons or bushmen, *Aegyptopithecus* or *erectus*, for at least two reasons. First, most comparisons underplay the power of selection. Living primates and foragers aren't necessarily good models for ancestral primates and foragers, and many of the most interesting traits are those that make *H. sapiens* unique. Second, living babies are easier to count than dead ones. Fossil demography is difficult at best; the traits in question, their effects on reproductive success, and the context in which they're expressed are all more precisely measured on the living than on the extinct.

In natural selection, babies are the only currency that count. Primate actions and cognitions should be those that reliably produced primate babies. Hominid actions and cognitions should have been those that reliably produced hominid babies. And *H. sapiens'* actions and cognitions should be those that reliably produce *H. sapiens'* babies. Until very recently, they seem to have been. And, more than most of us suspect, they may still be.

## REFERENCES

Alexander, R. D. (1979). Evolution and culture. In N. A. Chagnon & W. Irons (Eds.), *Evolutionary biology and human social behavior: An anthropological perspective* (pp. 59–78). North Scituate, MA: Duxbury.

Barkow, J., Cosmides, L., & Tooby, J. (Eds.). (1992). *The adapted mind.* New York: Oxford University Press.

Begun, D., Ward, C., & Rose, M. (Eds.). (1996). *Function, phylogeny, and fossils: Miocene hominoids and great ape and human origins.* New York: Plenum.

Bergstrom, T. (1994). *Primogeniture, monogamy, and reproductive value in a stratified society* (Working Paper No. 94-10). Ann Arbor: University of Michigan, Department of Economics.

Betzig, L. (1986). *Despotism and differential reproduction: A Darwinian view of history.* Hawthorne, NY: Aldine deGruyter.

Betzig, L. (1989). Rethinking human ethology: A response to some recent critiques. *Ethology and Sociobiology, 10,* 315–324.

Betzig, L. (1992). Of human bonding: Cooperation or exploitation? *Social Science Information, 31,* 611–642.

Betzig, L. (1995). Medieval monogamy. *Journal of Family History, 20,* 181–215.

Betzig, L. (1997). People are animals. In L. Betzig (Ed.), *Human nature: A critical reader* (pp. 1–17). New York: Oxford University Press.

Betzig, L., Borgerhoff Mulder, M., & Turke, P. (Eds.). (1988). *Human reproductive behavior: A Darwinian perspective.* New York: Cambridge University Press.

Binford, L. (1981). *Bones: Ancient men and modern myths.* New York: Academic Press.

Blurton-Jones, N. (1986). Bushman birth spacing: A test for optimal interbirth intervals. *Ethology and Sociobiology, 7,* 91–105.

Boone, J. (1986). Parental investment and elite family structure in preindustrial states: A case study of late medieval-early modern Portuguese genealogies. *American Anthropologist, 88,* 859–878.

Borgerhoff Mulder, M. (1988). Kipsigis bridewealth payments. In L. Betzig, M. Borgerhoff Mulder, & P. Turke (Eds.), *Human reproductive behaviour* (pp. 65–82). Cambridge, England: Cambridge University Press.

Boyd, R., & Richerson, P. (1986). *Culture and the evolutionary process.* Chicago: University of Chicago Press.

Clarke, A. L., & Low, B. S. (1992). Ecological correlates of human dispersal in 19th century Sweden. *Animal Behaviour, 44,* 677–693.

Clutton-Brock, T. (1988). Reproductive success. In T. Clutton-Brock (Ed.), *Reproductive success* (pp. 472–485). Chicago: University of Chicago Press.

Cowlishaw, G., & Mace, R. (1996). Cross-cultural patterns of marriage and inheritance: A phylogenetic approach. *Ethology and Sociobiology, 17,* 87–97.

Darwin, C. (1859). *On the origin of species.* New York: Modern Library Reprint Edition.

Degler, C. (1991). *In search of human nature: The decline and revival of Darwinism in American social thought.* New York: Oxford University Press.

Diamond, J. (1992). *The third chimpanzee.* New York: HarperCollins.

Dunbar, R. (1988). *Primate social systems.* Ithaca, NY: Comstock.

Durham, W. (1991). *Coevolution.* Palo Alto, CA: Stanford.

Durkheim, E. (1895). *The rules of sociological method.* New York: The Free Press.

Fisher, R. (1958). *The genetical theory of natural selection.* New York: Dover.

Foley, R. (1989). The evolution of hominid social behavior. In V. Standen & R. A. Foley (Eds.), *Comparative socioecology: The behavioural ecology of human and other mammals* (pp. 473–494). Oxford: Blackwell.

Foley, R. (1996). The adaptive legacy of human evolution: A search for the EEA. *Evolutionary Anthropology, 4,* 194–203.

Haig, D. (1993). Genetic conflicts in human pregnancy. *Quarterly Review of Biology, 68,* 495–532.

Hartung, J. (1982). Polygyny and the inheritance of wealth. *Current Anthropology, 23,* 1–12.

Hewlett, B. (1992). *Father–child relations.* Hawthorne, NY: Aldine deGruyter.

Hill, K., & Hurtado, M. (1996). *Ache life history.* Hawthorne, NY: Aldine deGruyter.

Irons, W. (in press). Adaptively relevant environments vs. the environment of evolutionary adaptedness. *Evolutionary Anthropology.*

Isaac, G. (1978). The food-sharing behavior of protohuman hominids. *Scientific American, 238,* 90–108.

Kaplan, H., Lancaster, J., & Johnson, S. (1995). Fertility and fitness among Albuquerque men: A competitive labour market theory. In R. Dunbar (Ed.), *Human reproductive decisions* (pp. 96–136). London: Macmillan.

Kelly, R. (1995). *The foraging spectrum.* Washington, DC: Smithsonian.

Kinzey, W. (Ed.). (1997). *The evolution of human behavior: Primate models.* Hawthorne, NY: Aldine deGruyter.

Knauft, B. (1987). Reconsidering violence in simple human societies. *Current Anthropology, 28,* 457–500.

Lee, R., & DeVore, I. (Eds.). (1968). *Man the hunter.* Chicago: Aldine.

Mellars, P., & Stringer, C. (Eds.). (1989). *The human revolution.* Edinburgh: Edinburgh University Press.

Møller, A. P., Soler, M., & Thornhill, R. (1995). Breast asymmetry, sexual selection, and human reproductive success. *Ethology and Sociobiology, 16,* 207–219.

Parker, G., & Maynard Smith, J. (1990). Optimality theory in evolutionary biology. *Nature, 348,* 27–33.

Potts, R. (1987). Reconstructions of early hominid socioecology: A critique of primate models. In W. G. Kinzey (Ed.), *The evolution of human behavior: Primate models* (pp. 28–47). Albany: SUNY Press.

Profet, M. (1992). Pregnancy sickness as adaptation: A deterrent to maternal ingestion of teratogens. In J. Barkow, L. Cosmides, & J. Tooby (Eds.), *The adapted mind* (pp. 327–365). New York: Oxford University Press.

Reeve, H. K., & Sherman, P. W. (1993). Adaption and the goals of evolutionary research. *Quarterly Review of Biology, 68,* 1–31.

Schubert, G., & Masters, R. (Eds.). (1991). *Primate politics.* Carbondale: Southern Illinois University Press.

Smith, E. A. (1992). Human behavioral ecology. *Evolutionary Anthropology, 1,* 20–25, 50–55.

Smuts, B., Cheney, D., Seyfarth, R., Wrangham, R., & Struhsaker, T. (Eds.). (1987). *Primate societies.* Chicago: University of Chicago Press.

Symons, D. (1979). *The evolution of human sexuality.* New York: Oxford University Press.

Tinbergen, N. (1963). On aims and methods of ethology. *Zeitschrift für Tierpsychologie, 20,* 410–433.

Tooby, J., & DeVore, I. (1987). The reconstruction of hominid behavioral evolution through strategic modeling. In W. G. Kinzey (Ed.), *The evolution of human behavior: Primate models* (pp. 183–237). Albany: SUNY Press.

Tooby, J., & Cosmides, L. (1992). The psychological foundations of culture. In J. Barkow, L. Cosmides, & J. Tooby (Eds.), *The adapted mind* (pp. 19–136). New York: Oxford University Press.

Travisano, M., Mongold, J., Bennett, A., & Lenski, R. (1995). Experimental tests of the roles of adaptation, chance, and history in evolution. *Science, 267,* 87–90.

Turke, P. (1990). Which humans behave adaptively, and why does it matter? *Ethology and Sociobiology, 11,* 305–339.

Washburn, S., & DeVore, I. (1961). Social behavior of baboons and early man. In S. Washburn (Ed.), *Social life of early man* (pp. 91–105). Chicago: Aldine-Atherton.

White, L. (1949). *The science of culture.* New York: Farrar, Straus & Giroux.

Williams, G. (1966). *Adaptation and natural selection: A critique of some current evolutionary thought.* Princeton, NJ: Princeton University Press.

Wrangham, R. (1987). The significance of African apes for reconstructing human social evolution. In W. G. Kinzey (Ed.), *The evolution of human behavior: Primate models* (pp. 51–71). Albany: SUNY Press.

Wrangham, R., McGrew, W., de Waal, F., & Heltne, P. (Eds.). (1994). *Chimpanzee cultures.* Cambridge, MA: Harvard University Press.

Wright, S. (1968). *Evolution and the genetics of populations.* Chicago: University of Chicago Press.

# 9

## Environments and Adaptations: Then and Now

Charles Crawford
*Simon Fraser University*

The world we live in is not what it was when our anatomy and physiology took their present form. If we compare our environments to those of modern hunter–gatherers (which may be more similar to our current environment than that of our Pleistocene ancestors), we find that population densities are greater; social, economic, and political structures are more complex; group sizes are larger; and the range of altitudes and latitudes inhabited is greater. Multinational corporations now dominate the production of goods and services. Industrial pollution is a serious problem in almost every part of the world. International conflicts seem to be a normal part of our lives. These, and a plethora of other differences, interact to produce a world that our Pleistocene ancestors would likely find strange and unnerving.

The supposed differences between ancestral and current environments often have been used to explain seemingly unusual or perplexing observations in both animals and humans. For example, they were used to explain the findings of male infanticide in a number of species of primates and cats (Hausfater & Hrdy, 1984). Power (1986) argued that Jane Goodall's findings of aggression in Gombe chimpanzees can be explained in terms of a habitat disturbed by banana feeding, rather than on the basis of evolved adaptations. Some scientists argue that several human psychological and societal malfunctions, as well as physical illnesses, can be caused by lifestyles differing from those we evolved to live (Bailey, 1987; Glantz & Pearce, 1989). Specifically, Coe and Steadman (1995) and Eaton et al. (1994) argued that some forms of women's reproductive cancer have their origin in environmental changes occurring in the last 30,000 or so years. The area of research concerned with how ancestral and current environments differ, and how this difference impacts on our current anatomy, physiology, and behavior, is known as *environmental mismatch theory* (Bailey, 1995).

Mismatch theorists are not the only researchers concerned about the differences between ancestral and current environments. In recent years, a dispute has developed between two groups of evolutionary scientists—Darwinian anthropologists and Evolutionary psychologists—over the appropriate methodology to use in studying the evolutionary significance of human behavior. One important difference between the approaches is that Evolutionary psychologists place much more emphasis on the differences between ancestral and current environments than do Darwinian anthropologists (Crawford, 1993; Symons, 1990); the former also argues that differences in reproductive fitness have little value in the evolutionary analysis of human behavior. If the most plausible hypothesis is that ancestral and current environments do not differ with respect to particular adaptations, then some of the methods animal behavioral ecologists have developed for the study of animal behavior, and that focus on reproductive success, may be useful in the study of human behavior. For a discussion of this point, see Sherman and Reeve (1997).

## ARGUMENTS FOR DIFFERENCE

Although the notion that differences between ancestral and current environments can be a source of stress and pathology for animals and humans has been around for more than a century, it was Bowlby's (1969) writing on the evolutionary significance of attachment that initiated much current thinking on the subject. He defined *adaptations* in terms of control theory and cybernetic mechanisms for adjusting an organism's physiology and behavior to environmental circumstances. For him, the *environment of evolutionary adaptedness* (EEA) referred to the environment in which a species evolved. He further recognized an environment for each system (adaptation) of a species, and defined the *system's EEA* as the ancestral environmental conditions an adaptation evolved to respond to. He identified the human EEA as the Pleistocene hunter–gatherer environment. Although Bowlby did not give a rigorous definition of the environment of evolutionary adaptedness, the term, and its abbreviation, EEA, has entered the language of most branches of evolutionary science.

Bowlby (1969) provided two arguments for his belief that ancestral and current human environments differ greatly. First, he observed that humans currently live in an enormous variety of environments. He believed this diversity is much greater than the diversity of the environments in which humans evolved, and hence, that many current humans must be living in less than natural environments. Second, and most important, he assumed that the speed at which human environments have diversified during the past few thousand years makes it likely that environmental change has outstripped adaptation change through natural selection, and therefore, that humans are no longer living in their environment of evolutionary adaptedness. Finally, it seemed obvious to Bowlby that if adaptations were defined in terms of control and cybernetic concepts for adjusting behavior to ancestral environmental contingencies, and if environments had changed greatly during the past 10,000 to 20,000 years, then there would be many instances when environmental change produced atypical, unusual, or pathological behavior. He wrote:

> We can therefore be fairly sure that none of the environments in which civilized, or even half-civilized, man lives today conforms to the environment in which man's environmentally stable behavioural systems were evolved and to which they are intrinsically adapted. (Bowlby, 1969, p. 86)

Clearly, Bowlby believed that the most plausible hypothesis is that ancestral and current environments differ in evolutionarily significant ways.

Bowlby is rarely quoted, but his reasoning has influenced the thinking of many scientists and scholars using the theory of evolution in their work. Although there is much wisdom in his thinking, a great deal of empirical and theoretical work on both the Theory of Evolution and the study of human behavior has occurred since Bowlby wrote in 1969. The purpose of this chapter is to consider the issue of whether ancestral and current environments differ, and to consider the kinds of evidence that might be used to determine whether they do differ. The chapter first reviews the notion of adaptation described in chap. 1. It then develops a definition of the EEA of an adaptation. These sections are followed by a set of arguments that the most plausible hypothesis is that ancestral and current environments do not differ vis-à-vis any particular adaptation. Finally, it discusses some of the kinds of data that might be used to reject the null hypothesis that ancestral and current environments do not differ vis-à-vis any particular adaptation. I hope my efforts may be of some value to mismatch theorists, Darwinian anthropologists, Evolutionary psychologists, and anyone interested in the difficult task of using the Theory of Evolution by Natural Selection in the study of human behavior.

This chapter uses the term *EEA* in two ways. It may refer to the environment where a particular adaptation is assumed to have evolved, or it may refer to the generalized Pleistocene environment where humans are assumed to have evolved. The context indicates which meaning is intended. Distinguishing between the EEA of an adaptation and the EEA of a species is important because it enables us to see that, although the environment of a species may have changed considerably in recent evolutionary time, the environment of any particular adaptation need not have changed.


## ADAPTATIONS AND ENVIRONMENTS: THEN AND NOW

### Adaptations

If we are to develop an evolutionary science that includes a conceptualization of the difference between ancestral and current environments, we must base it on the concept of adaptation. Wilson (1975) defined an *adaptation* as "any structure, physiological process, or behavior pattern that makes an organism more fit to survive and reproduce in comparison with other members of the same species" (p. 577). However, I would replace Wilson's word *makes* with the phrase *made an ancestral* to emphasize that adaptations came into being in an ancestral environment. This distinction is particularly important when considering human adaptations because the environment in which these adaptations are currently being expressed may differ from the environment in which they evolved; if it does, the functioning of these adaptations may be altered in both gross and subtle ways.

Although the beaks of Darwin's finches provide the classic example of an adaptation, consider two examples more relevant to the task at hand. Recently, Nesse and Williams (1994) reviewed the idea that the rise in body temperature that produces a fever may be an adaptation for fighting parasites that are invading the body. The notion is that many parasites have evolved to live at the normal body temperature of their hosts (Kluger, 1986). Hence, one way an organism can fight parasites is by determining when they are invading the body and then raising body temperature to help destroy them. There are obvious benefits to this adaptation, but it also has costs. Energy is required to raise body temperature to the appropriate level and hold it at that level until the invaders are destroyed. Moreover, if body temperature is raised too high or maintained at a high temperature too long, the body may be damaged. Consequently, the fever adaptation is the result of a compromise between its costs and benefits in the environments that shaped it. Some theorists would claim that it reflects an optimal compromise (Krebs & McCleery, 1984; Maynard-Smith,

1978). Thus, the fever adaptation, and indeed all adaptations, instantiate a cost–benefit analysis that may have provided optimal benefits in the environment in which the adaptation evolved.

The fever example is instructive because it emphasizes that adaptations do something for their possessors by enabling them to respond to contingencies in their environment; the operation of adaptations involves decision making; and the operation of adaptations reflects the costs and benefits that shaped them. These considerations lead to a conceptualization of an *adaptation* as a set of decision processes that enabled the cost–benefit analysis an ancestral organism carried out in response to a specific set of environmental contingencies, and that organized the effector processes for dealing with those contingencies so that the organism could survive and reproduce in competition with other members of its species.

Now let us consider a behavioral example—the courtship tactics of the male scorpionfly described in chap. 1. Males, depending on the level of male–male competition they encounter, use one of three tactics—dead insect, proteinaceous mass, and forced mating—for obtaining copulations. This adaptation reflects the ancestral cost–benefit structure that shaped its evolution. If the environment of a scorpionfly changed so that the adaptation no longer provided appropriate cost–benefit analyses of the situation, the scorpionfly might display nonadaptive behaviors. If a male scorpionfly were put in a laboratory and given false information, indicating it was encountering high levels of male–male competition, he might attempt to use the forced copulation tactic. Because this tactic is costly, in that only 50% of females who are forcibly mated have their eggs fertilized (Thornhill, 1980), it could be maladaptive in this situation if another tactic would result in the fertilization of more females. The assumption is that male scorpionflies have at least one specialized mechanism for choosing and implementing the appropriate courtship tactic.

Note that most evolutionary psychologists assume that, because mental adaptations evolved in response to specific ancestral conditions, the human mind is not a *tabula rasa*. For example, Symons (1987) wrote, "complex, specialized, species-typical brain/mind mechanisms are precisely what a Darwinian view of life should lead us to anticipate . . ." (p. 143). Just as the stomach could not have evolved to be a general digester because there are no general foods for natural selection to respond to, the psyche could not have evolved to be a *tabula rasa* because there are no general mental problems for natural selection to respond to. Thus, it follows that when we speak of the difference between current and ancestral environments, we must do so with respect to particular adaptations and the specific conditions to which they evolved to respond—about Bowlby's (1969) systems and his systems' environments of adaptedness.

## Adaptations and Environments

The environment of an adaptation includes all the internal and external conditions that impact on the reproduction of the genes mediating its development and functioning. In chap. 1, distinctions were made between innate and operational adaptations, between ancestral and current developmental and immediate environments, and between ancestral and current behavior. This chapter briefly reviews these distinctions in preparation for a discussion of the EEA (see Fig. 1.3 for help with this discussion).

The *innate adaptation* is the information encoded in the genes that mediates the development of the operational adaptation. The *operational adaptation* consists of the anatomical structures, physiological processes, and psychological processes that develop because of interactions with the environment, and that actually do the work of helping the organism survive and reproduce. For the male scorpionfly seeking a mate, the innate adaptation is the information in his genes that directs the development of the operational mating adaptation (i.e., the information-processing and effector processes enabling him to choose an appropriate mating tactic). For a child learning a language, the innate adaptation is the set of genes enabling the language to be acquired, and the operational adaptation is the language actually learned.

The *immediate environment* of an adaptation refers to the present environmental conditions, either ancestral or current, to which an operational adaptation responds. For the male scorpionfly seeking a mating, it is the level of male–male competition he is experiencing, as well as his internal states, such as energy levels and current physical strength, that produce his response in a particular time or place. For a child encountering a new word or grammatical form in a story told by a Pleistocene elder, or read by a teacher in a large urban school, it is the information in the environment that his or her sense organs are responding to, as well as his or her present level of language skills and other internal conditions influencing the response to the new information.

The *developmental environment* refers to the succession of immediate environments that have impinged on the formation of the operational adaptation in the individual to a particular point in time. An understanding of the developmental history of a male scorpionfly's courtship behavior is not necessary for predicting what he will do when confronting a particular instance of male–male competition because all adult males are capable of using all three mating tactics without previous experience (Thornhill, 1980). However, for understanding the language capability of a particular child learning a language, knowledge of the developmental history is crucial (Pinker, 1994). The tactics of the male scorpionfly are said to be *concurrently contingent* on environmental events because they depend only on the present state of the environment. In contrast, human language learning is said to be *developmentally contingent* on environmental conditions because present learning depends on previously acquired language skills (Crawford & Anderson, 1989).

Although most human evolutionists assume innate adaptations are unchanged across short intervals of evolutionary time, as did Bowlby (1969), both the developmental and immediate environments may differ in short time intervals. Hence, both ancestral and current operational adaptations and behavior may differ because of environmental changes that have occurred since an innate adaptation took its present form. It is these changes to which mismatch theorists refer when they claim that the current environment is problematic for humans, and that evolutionary psychologists claim are important to consider when studying the evolutionary significance of behavior.

## The Environment of Evolutionary Adaptedness

What is the EEA? Many anthropologists think of it as a selection environment acting on the adaptive traits of a lineage over time. They associate human EEA with a hunter–gatherer lifestyle (Foley, in press). However, the EEA is not a specific time or a specific place (Sherman & Reeve, 1997). The ancestral environments that influenced the evolution of bipedalism may have been separated in time by hundreds of thousands of years from those that shaped the language adaptation. One cannot use any extant population to delineate it; neither could one use data from any particular group from the past, even if one had such data. Selection pressures vary across both space and time, and they can even reverse at short intervals. We can think of the EEA as a multivariate and dynamic niche space that mathematically describes selection pressures on evolving humans (Mealey, e-mail communication, 1996). This space is made up of a host of only partially overlapping subenvironments because the particular part of the EEA that influenced the evolution of each adaptation may have existed in different times and spaces (Bowlby, 1969; Irons, in press).

Hence, we should not think of "the EEA," but instead of EEAs—one for each of our adaptations. Recently, Irons (in press) developed the notion of adaptively relevant environment of an evolved adaptation (ARE) as those features of the environment that the mechanisms must interact with to confer a reproductive advantage. However, it is difficult to compute the fitness of any particular adaptation because fitness normally refers to the fitness of an organism that is composed of a myriad of interacting adaptations. Therefore, the focus here is on the information inputs to, and the behavioral outputs from, the adaptation, rather than on fitness.

Therefore, the EEA of an adaptation is defined in terms of the features of the environment with which the mechanism must have interacted to produce the behavioral outputs that contributed to ancestral expected fitness. It is a statistical composite of the adaptation-relevant properties of the ancestral environment encountered by members of ancestral populations, weighted by their frequency and fitness consequences, and averaged across the time that it impacted on ancestral fitness (Tooby & Cosmides, 1990). For example, there are data suggesting that humans have an evolved mechanism for avoiding incest that involves the lack of sexual attraction to those with whom we had close contact during the first few years of life (Barkow, 1989; Shepher, 1971). What is the EEA—the niche space—of this putative adaptation? It consists of individuals of different genetic relatedness weighted by their frequency and their fitness consequences as mates, and averaged across the time humans and their ancestors lived in social situations where such matings might be likely.

Most important human activities may involve the interaction of a number of adaptations. For example, human mating choice is likely mediated by a number of adaptations. Thornhill and Gangestad (1993) provided evidence that the degree of fluctuating body asymmetry (FA) may provide important information about the quality of prospective mates, and that it may be an important factor in mate choice in both animals and humans. Singh's (1993) work on body image suggests that assessments of waist-to-hip ratio (WHR) may also be important in mate choice. What are the EEAs for these two putative adaptations? For FA, it is the degree of FA in individuals of the opposite sex, weighted by their frequency and the fitness consequences of choosing them as mates, and averaged over the period for which FA was important in mate choice. Because it is likely that FA is important in other species, the EEA for FA likely extends back in time before the evolution of *Homo sapiens*. The EEA for WHR could be similarly defined. However, because there is as yet no evidence suggesting WHR is important in nonhuman primate mating, its EEA likely does not extend back as far in time as that of FA. Although the EEAs for these two putative adaptations may overlap, it is unlikely that they evolved in exactly the same part of the EEA. When the concept of the EEA is used in the study of a particular adaptation, one does not have to reconstruct the entire EEA of the species.

Mismatches between ancestral and current EEAs specific to particular adaptations may cause an adaptation to malfunction. This malfunction may be caused by different immediate or different developmental environments. If an adaptation is malfunctioning because of adaptation–environment mismatch, it may be because the operational adaptation is in some way malformed or incompletely developed because of inadequate or inappropriate interactions during development. Those who argue that early menarche and the delay of first childbirth are possible causes of the increased incidence of breast cancer in the industrialized world because they impair the development of immune responses in the breast are making such a claim (Coe & Steadman, 1995; Eaton et al., 1994). To cite a behavioral example, we now know that, unless a child hears a language during the first few years of life, its language skills will be malformed and it will be unable to communicate using spoken language (Pinker, 1994).

Even if an operational adaptation is not malformed during development, it may still fail to function properly if it receives inputs outside its normal range of functioning. For example, adults who have been reared on an adequate diet may come to suffer from scurvy if their diet becomes deficient in vitamin C. Similarly, a child may have learned to speak its own language during the first few years of life, but may have difficulty learning a language it did not hear during that critical period, or its own language spoken with an unusual accent. Individuals who watch a great deal of violence on TV may interpret the world as more noxious than it actually is, and thus, act overly aggressively or fearfully. In this case, the environment is providing information that leads to inappropriate and possibly maladaptive behavior.

## A CLASSIFICATION OF ANCESTRAL AND CURRENT BEHAVIORS

Now that adaptations and the EEA have been discussed, it is possible to develop a classification of adaptive and nonadaptive behaviors in ancestral and current environments. Table 9.1 provides a classification of behaviors with respect to how the mechanisms producing them function in ancestral and current environments. The ancestral dimension in the table

TABLE 9.1
The Operation of Adaptations in Ancestral and Current Environments

| Adaptation | Current, Functional | Current, Dysfunctional |
|---|---|---|
| Ancestral, adaptive | Culturally variable, functionally invariant<br>courtship rituals<br>athletic sports<br>learning languages | Pseudopathologies<br>obesity<br>prostitution<br>wife abuse |
| Ancestral, maladaptive | Quasinormal behaviors<br>recreational sex<br>adoption<br>true altruism | True pathologies<br>Huntington's Chorea<br>phenylketonuria<br>serious brain damage |

is defined in terms of adaptive and maladaptive, where *adaptiveness* refers to expected reproductive fitness (Burian, 1983). The current dimension is defined in terms of functional and dysfunctional. However, functionality in the current environment is not defined in terms of reproductive fitness. It is defined in terms of malfunction of adaptations designed by natural selection to contribute to ancestral fitness. In many cases, current malfunction may detract from reproductive fitness. But there may be instances where a modern environment is particularly benign, and the malfunction of the adaptation may not detract from current fitness, and may even contribute to it. For example, the mechanisms for bonding to children may malfunction and result in a parent bonding to an adopted child. This bonding could contribute to the parent's fitness, if it contributes to the parent's ability to rear other children who share parental genes. The final section of this chapter argues that signs of physical stress, frequency in the ethnographic record, and disturbed reproductive patterns are sources of evidence that an adaptation may be malfunctioning in a current environment.

*True pathologies* are conditions that would detract from fitness in virtually any environment. They are due to serious genetic defects, such as Huntington's Chorea and phenylketoneuria, serious physiological damage, such as brain damage causing memory loss, or extreme cultural deprivation, such as the inability to speak caused by the absence of language experience during the early years of life. These conditions are pathological in any but the most benign of artificial environments.

*Pseudopathologies* are conditions or behaviors that are problematic in the current environment, although they may have their basis in evolved adaptations. Obesity due to our love for sugar and fat being expressed in environments rich in foods containing sugar and fat, prostitution due to the ancestral capacity to trade sex for resources being expressed in an industrial economy, and wife abuse due to exaggerated social cues suggesting infidelity come to mind. These and many other currently problematic conditions and behaviors may have their basis in adaptations that contributed to ancestral fitness.

*Quasinormal behaviors* are those that would have detracted from fitness in ancestral environments, but, because of changes in the environment and cultural standards, have become socially acceptable and even encouraged. Recreational sexual behavior due to modern methods of birth control, delayed childbearing, and short birth intervals caused by careers of modern women, adoption of genetically unrelated children due to the dearth of "substitute" children from extended family for childless couples, and "true altruism" caused by the failure of kin-recognition mechanisms to discriminate kin from nonkin in current environments are possible examples.

Finally, there are *culturally variable-functionally invariant behaviors*. These are behaviors that vary across time and space, but still serve their ancestral function. Learning of languages such as Esperanto is a good example. At a societal level, Murdock (1945; cited in Wilson, 1978) showed that there are a large number of traits, including age grading, athletic sports, bodily adornment, community organization, cooperative labor, courtship, division of labor, cleanliness training, gift giving, government, marriage, and penal sanctions that are characteristic of every known society. Although the form of expression of these traits may differ (i.e., the athletic sports that different societies engage in differ considerably), these apparently universal traits likely serve the same functions in all societies. The primary argument in this chapter is that many current human behaviors fall into this last group.

## THE MOST PLAUSIBLE HYPOTHESIS

The remainder of this chapter aims to do two things. The first is to argue that the most plausible hypothesis about EEA current environment differences is that ancestral and current environments do not differ vis-à-vis any particular adaptation, and that the proper course of action is to make a null hypothesis and then seek evidence that could reject it. The second is to say a bit about the kinds of evidence we need to falsify this hypothesis. I give three arguments for the proposition that the most plausible hypothesis is that ancestral and current environments do not differ vis-à-vis a particular adaptation.

### The Argument From Common Sense

We seem to live in a troubled world. War, famine, and disease exist in many parts of the planet. The global economy is changing the way we produce, earn, and consume goods and services. Cultural patterns that have existed for centuries are in a state of flux. Yet, throughout the world, most people are going about their business as much as they always have. People are finding mates, having babies, raising them relatively successfully, getting in disputes with their neighbors, settling those disputes, cooperating with their friends, cheating on social contracts when they get the chance, detecting the cheaters, and so on. The first argument for the most plausible hypothesis is based on common sense: Because most humans are going about their lives pretty much as usual, it does not make sense to claim that we are living in an environment that differs significantly from the environment of the EEA, the environment of evolutionary adaptedness. If we were, we would see many more signs of stress and pathology than we do see. Our species might even be threatened with extinction, as are many other species on the planet.

Let me expand the commonsense argument a bit. It is possible that most social environments, *qua* environment, may differ little from those in which our ancestors resided. Consider, for example, to what extent the social environment of a typical university academic department may differ from the group its members might have inhabited in the EEA. An average department will have a department chair, 35 or so faculty members, 15 support staff, and around 75 graduate students. Thus, it has a leader, or chief, a group of individuals, the faculty and staff, who are more or less permanent members of the social environment, and a group of graduate students who are preparing to disperse and join other permanent groups. How might the social environment of such a department differ from the sociality of the group the ancestors of its members might have inhabited 10,000 or 30,000 years ago?

The demography of the groups likely differs somewhat. The age structure and sex ratio may differ a bit. The reproductive value curve that describes the modern group is likely less peaked than the one for the EEA group because the infant mortality rate is much lower now than it was in the EEA. However, the new assistant professors are having babies. They all seem to have two children. How much does this family size differ from that of the EEA? Not much, if we can use the data of current hunter–gatherers to estimate ancestral family size (Betzig, Borgerhoff-Mulder, & Turke, 1988; Short, 1984).

The assistant professors in our department are struggling to establish themselves in the hierarchy of the department. The senior members of the department are attempting to maintain their positions as they age. The graduate students are working on acquiring the skills they need to disperse successfully. These are some of the tasks that all humans must accomplish if they are to live successful lives. Moreover, many of the consequences of the social interactions in the academic department, such as changes in status or gain or loss of wealth, may be similar to those produced on the basis of ancestral social interactions.

Our typical department is divided into lab groups, and most members of the department interact with only a small proportion of the whole department. Research shows that current social networks are surprisingly small. In a recent study, Dunbar and Spoors (1995) found that the mean of the distribution of individuals contacted on a monthly basis (the network) was 11.6, with a standard deviation of 5.64. Kinship accounted for 37.5% of the networks, and women had contact with more female friends and relatives, whereas males had contact with more male friends and relatives. The mean of the distribution of those the respondents relied on for advice and personal help (the support clique) was 4.72, with a standard deviation of 2.95. These data suggest the size of intimate human groups has changed little across evolutionary time.

The absence of genetic kin is probably the greatest difference between the department's social organization and that of a hunter–gatherer tribe. However, do the psychological processes involved in kin recognition (that may be assessing frequency of association, spatial distribution, phenotypic similarity, and genetic similarity—Alexander, 1979; Porter, 1987—as cues for treating individuals as kin) result in many of the department members treating each other as if they were genetic relatives?

The fact that the members of the department are all engaged in a variety of highly technical activities, using computers and other modern paraphernalia, may be irrelevant to the sociality of the situation. Our social adaptations may not even "see" this paraphernalia. In terms of the sociality of the situation, the way kinship, reciprocity, group size, resource distribution, and so on impact on social organization of a typical group, the sociality of a modern academic department may differ little from that of our Pleistocene ancestors. A similar argument could be made for many other social groupings in modern industrial societies. It can also be made for physiological processes such as digestion, and psychological adaptations such as language.

## Adaptation: More Than Residue of Environmental Forces

The second argument is more abstruse, and invokes notions associated with the concept of adaptation. To understand an adaptation, we must understand the specific ancestral selection pressures that built its genetic basis into its species. However, when we understand the operation of the proximate mechanisms of an adaptation in terms of the concepts of modern science (e.g., digestion in terms of the enzymes such as trypsin and pepsin, the language adaptation in terms of modern grammar), we can see that an adaptation is more than the residue of the environmental forces that produced it. When described in terms of the concepts of modern biochemistry, we can understand how the stomach can adaptively respond to foods that did not exist in the EEA. When we use concepts from modern linguistics, we can understand how the language adaptation can enable us to invent and use languages, such as Esperanto, that did not exist in the EEA.

*The English Baby Example.* First, let us consider an example to help with the argument. Suppose that several million years ago, a group of chimpanzee-like creatures swam the English Channel and settled down where London is now. Over time, they evolved into hominid creatures, and eventually they evolved the capacity to communicate using the

English language. One day they discovered people living across the channel who appeared to be quite like them, except that they spoke a rather strange language called French. With further exploration, they discovered a variety of people living in different parts of the world who, while they looked not too different from them, spoke quite different languages. They wondered if the genetic basis of the English language would enable them to learn these languages.

To find out, they had genetically English babies reared from conception in France, Tanzania, and Russia. They found that English babies reared in French, African, and Russian cultures learned these languages as easily as their parents had learned English. However, a considerable number of the French-reared babies became alcoholics as adults. The rate of skin cancer among the Tanzanian-reared babies was much higher than among native Africans. There was a problem with middle-aged obesity in the English children reared in the Russian homes.

Those English babies reared in French, Russian, and Tanzanian homes had not been reared in environments that differed from that of their English parents vis-à-vis their language adaptation. If they had been, they would not have been able to learn these languages as easily as their parents had learned English. Figure 9.1 illustrates the situation.

What appeared to be an adaptation to learn English turned out to be more than merely an adaptation to learn English. To do the things that the English language does required people to evolve the capacity for a system of symbolic communication. The adaptation to learn English was more than the residue of the linguistic experiences of those who evolved it. Thus, the EEA in which their English language adaptation evolved did not differ (via the language adaptation) from the current environment where the babies learned the other languages. The fact that different vocal movements were involved in communicating in the different languages was merely peripheral to the nature of the language adaptation. However, in this example, the environment of the Tanzanian-reared babies differed with respect to aspects of the environment related to sun-caused skin cancer. Similarly, aspects of the diet in France and Russia had a negative impact on the digestion adaptation of the English babies. For these traits, the current and ancestral environments differ with respect to the digestion adaptation.

The world is very different than it was when *Homo sapiens'* anatomy, physiology, and mind took their current form. The technology of the recent Gulf War differs greatly from that of the armies that fought in the Fertile Crescent 5,000 years ago. But if there are adaptations underlying human warfare, are they developing and being expressed in an environment that differs from our EEA with respect to the adaptations that make people go to war? If there are war adaptations, do they see the difference

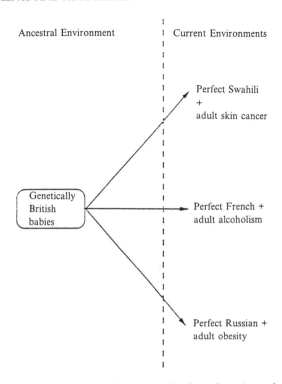

FIG. 9.1. Effects on language learning and other adaptations of rearing genetically British babies in various (current) environments.

between an obsidian spear and an AK-47? The argument here relates to the definitions of function and fortuitous effect that Williams (1966) made over 30 years ago.

*Adaptive Effects.* Let us review and expand on Williams' (1966) distinctions. Although adaptations came into being because they contributed to ancestral fitness, all traits that contribute to current fitness may not have done so in the past. A *beneficial effect* of an adaptation is an aspect of an adaptation that increases the probability that its carrier will have copies of its alleles represented in subsequent generations. A *function* is a beneficial effect of a trait that existed in an ancestral population, and hence that can be said to be a cause of the adaptation.

Because pizza, which contributes to fitness now, did not exist in the EEA, the ability to digest it is a beneficial effect of adaptations for digesting other foods. If we take a conservative view of adaptation (Gould & Lewontin, 1978), digesting pizza is not a function of the human digestive system because the digestive system did not respond to it while it was evolving. However, digesting fruit, which existed in the EEA and contributed to the evolution of our digestive system, is a function of the digestion adaptation. I claim it is being overly stringent to claim that digesting pizza is not a function of the human digestive system. Although it is true that specific foods in the ancestral environment posed problems for organisms, and it is reasonable to assume that the digestive system evolved to deal with these specific foods, it is incorrect to say that the digestion adaptation, *qua* adaptation, is merely a set of processes for digesting specific foods. Because all foods are constituted of certain basic components, such as sugars and proteins, an adaptation required to digest a set of foods sufficient to produce a nutritious diet may enable its possessor to digest a considerable variety of, but not all, foods that might be found in an environment inhabited by the possessor.

At the level of adaptation, the digestive system is a system of processes that can be described in terms of a set of decision rules for dealing with the substances that make up foods, such as sugars and proteins. Viewed from this perspective, the ability to digest pizza is as much the result of an adaptation as is the ability to digest molo nuts or any other food that existed in the EEA.

A beneficial effect of a trait is an aspect of the trait that increases the probability that its possessor's alleles are represented in subsequent generations. It is meaningful to define three types of beneficial effects: functions, adaptive effects, and fortuitous effects. If the effect regularly contributed to fitness in the EEA, it is a function of the trait. In addition to the distinction made by Williams (1966), an *adaptive effect* of a trait is one that contributes to current fitness because its efficacy depends on physiological or psychological processes that evolved in the EEA to carry out similar, but not identical, tasks. A *fortuitous effect* of a trait is one that contributes to current fitness, but does not call on physiological or psychological processes that, on the surface, appear to mediate it. Finally, although an effect may be a fortuitous effect of one adaptation, it may be a function or an adaptive effect of a different adaptation. Although the benefits of drinking Diet Coke or Diet Pepsi may not be an adaptive effect of the digestion adaptation, they may be an adaptive effect of a courtship adaptation. Polyandry, although it may not be a function or adaptive effect of a mating adaptation, may be an adaptive effect of adaptations for resource acquisition and control.

Now, let us return to the English baby example. Learning French, Russian, or Swahili is not a beneficial effect of the adaptation for learning English. Rather, it is an adaptive effect—an expression of the same adaptation in a slightly different environment—at least different from our limited perspective. The English language adaptation, although it evolved in an English EEA, is not an adaptation to learn English, but an adaptation consisting of a set of decision rules for processing symbolic information in particular ways. From this perspective, the ability to read and write is not a beneficial effect of the ability to use spoken language, but rather an expression of the adaptation to use symbolic communication. If there is order in the universe, and if that order can be expressed and communicated in symbolic form, then any communication system, such as English, that evolved to comprehend and communicate about that order may require the evolution of mental processes that enable its possessors to use a variety of transformations of the communication system (i.e., spoken or written French, Russian, or Swahili) to communicate about that order. In this context, it is interesting to note that deaf people who could not read have invented sign languages (Pinker, 1994), that people who only spoke a pidgin language have evolved creole languages within a generation (Bickerton, 1990), and that illiterate members of nonliterate groups have invented a written language for their group (Crystal, 1987).

Finally, although we must retain a historical conception of adaptation (Williams, 1966), in doing so our focus must be on the scientific description of how the adaptation works, rather than on the particular tasks it evolved to deal with in its EEA. If we describe the digestive system in terms of modern biochemistry, we can see that it is more than the residual of a digestive system that evolved to digest the foods present in its EEA. If we describe the language adaptation in terms of modern linguistic theory, we can see that it is more than a system for speaking a particular ancestral tongue. Finally, if we can develop an adequate human psychology, we will see that the mating system adaptations can help choose mates in a wide variety of past, present, and future circumstances. If we develop an adequate sociology and anthropology, we will discover an invariant system for understanding human social organization.

### Ancestralization: Maintaining the Pleistocene

Although the current world is different from the one in which we evolved, the two are not unrelated. To a considerable extent, we have created the changes that have occurred during the last 10,000 years. In doing so, we have designed our environment to reflect and accommodate our Paleolithic limitations and predilections. We live in a world designed for right-handers rather than left-handers. Much of the processing capacity of our computers is devoted to graphics and other devices that allow our Paleolithic brain to function effectively. Because we do not have genetically based adaptations to allow us to do so, we do not live in an environment designed for individuals who can fly, who choose mates indiscriminately, who have litters of offspring, who have fur to protect them from the cold, who make little investment in offspring once they are born, who do not mind being cheated on in a social contract, who do not value their close genetic relatives, and so on. There is considerable evidence that genetically innate mechanisms influence the development of the human psyche and behavior

(Barkow, Cosmides, & Tooby, 1992; Brown, 1991; Eibl-Eibesfeldt, 1989). For exmple, Ekman (1992, 1994) has shown that the facial expressions displaying fear, anger, disgust, loathing, and happiness are invariant across many cultures. Bickerton (1990) provided evidence to support the argument that deaf children and children reared in an impoverished language environment can reinvent a language. (For reviews of the role of genetic biases on a variety of behaviors, see Brown, 1991; Lumsden & Wilson, 1981, 1983.) Although our modern environment is different, our evolved perceptual, cognitive, and emotional mechanisms helped shape it in ways that are of evolutionary significance.

Although a variety of ecological pressures may move a culture away from its ancestral form, the existence of innate biases with respect to human behavior will produce a tendency for us to return to ancestral ways of behaving. This process is called *ancestralization*. It is the process whereby some aspects of a society return to a more ancestral form when ecological, political, religious, or cultural conditions liberalize. A society that had formerly been monogamous begins to tolerate polygyny, a culture that had been vegetarian begins to tolerate meat eating, a society that had forbidden teenagers to carry weapons allows them to do so, and so on. Such instances provide possible examples of ancestralization because it is likely that we are a mildly polygynous species, that meat was part of our ancestral diet, and that ancestral teenagers carried and used weapons.

Consider handedness as a model of ancestralization. Handedness is a trait that is affected quite strongly by genetic and other biological factors. About 12% of humans are left-handed. Societies that proscribe left-handed eating and writing, such as China, have few individuals who eat and write with their left hands. However, left-handed individuals in these societies, who have been trained to eat and write with their right hands, continue to perform other activities with their left hands (Wilson, 1978), which indicates that specific cultural training can have an important effect on handedness only for specific activities.

When handedness is no longer proscribed, the proportion of individuals using the left hand increases. In Taiwan, only .7% of students are left-handed, but in the United States the percentage of Chinese students who are left-handed is 6.5. In Australia and New Zealand, the proportion of individuals writing with their left hands has increased since the turn of the century. In 1900, about 2% wrote with their left hands. By the 1960s, about 13% wrote with their left hands. Although cultural pressures can have a strong influence on hand preferences, the proportion of left-handed individuals approaches 12% to 13% when individuals are allowed to develop their biologically preferred hand preference. For a discussion of handedness and the factors affecting it, see Corballis (1991).

What factors might cause ancestralization? Because of technological innovation, a society may be able to adopt a way of life more compatible with Pleistocene behavioral biases. A good example is provided by the Cheyenne and Arapaho Indians. In pre-Colombian times, they had developed agriculture to support their growing populations. However, when they obtained horses, their hunting became sufficiently efficient that they could return to a hunter–gatherer way of life (Lowie, 1963). The assumption here is that ecological and population pressures had forced them to adopt a somewhat unnatural way of life. When they obtained the technology that enabled them to do so, they returned to a more favored social organization.

The breakdown of power structures also may be a cause of ancestralization. An external political power may, in its own interest, impose on another group behaviors and/or social organizations that attenuate ancestral behavioral and social tendencies. For example, the Roman Empire, the British Empire, and the USSR imposed peace on large parts of the world. When these powers waned, tribal warfare began to break out. In addition, the breakdown of internal power structures that served the interests of special groups within a society may also lead to ancestralization. Powerful religious, political, and industrial organizations may impose unnatural behaviors or social organizations on a society. For example, it seems likely that humans are a mildly polygynous species (Buss, 1994; Daly & Wilson, 1983), but that a variety of economic, religious, or political circumstances can suppress the tendency (MacDonald, 1995). The waning of the power of the Christian church may be one of the factors leading to divorce and forms of sequential polygyny that are becoming increasingly common in Western society. To a large extent, the environment we inhabit is a creation of our own mental processes. Hence, we tend to recreate the Pleistocene in modern dress when given the opportunity.

We often hear that other cultures are adopting Western ways. More likely, what is happening is that these cultures, having diverged from ancestral ways because of ecological, social, and economic pressures, are liberalizing, just as the West has done during the past two centuries. People living in these Westernizing cultures are beginning to ancestralize some of their behaviors, just as we in the Western world did when liberated by the industrial, religious, and political revolutions of the 19th and early 20th centuries.

## Innocent Until Proven Guilty

In most areas of science, the null hypothesis is assumed. That is, it is assumed that population parameters describing important aspects of two populations do not differ, and that any observed differences are due to random sampling. The task of the scientist is to accumulate evidence that, in fact, the relevant population parameters do differ. A wide variety of statistical procedures are available to help scientists in this task. Similarly, in the Anglo-American system of justice, individuals are assumed innocent until proved guilty. The task of the prosecutor is to mount evidence that the not guilty assumption should be rejected. These procedures place the burden of proof on the scientist or prosecutor.

It may be some time before we will be able to do many, or even any, statistical tests of significance between population parameters of the EEA and the current environment of a putative adaptation. Until such methods are developed, a reasonable course of action would seem be to assume that ancestral and current environments do not differ with respect to an adaptation of interest, then attempt to accumulate evidence that they differ. The task of the evolutionary scientist is somewhat like that of a prosecutor in a civil trial, where responsibility is decided on the balance of probabilities. The concluding section of this chapter discusses some of the types of evidence that the scientists may use in rejecting what appears to be the most plausible hypothesis.

## DETERMINING IF ANCESTRAL AND CURRENT ENVIRONMENTS DIFFER

There may be a variety of sources of evidence for determining whether ancestral and current environments differ. Four are briefly discussed here: (a) direct comparisons of ancestral and current environments, (b) signs of stress and malfunction in the current environment, (c) frequency of behaviors in the ethnographic record, and (d) unusual reproductive patterns.

### Direct Comparisons of Ancestral and Current Environments

It may be possible to use ecological methods to make comparisons of ancestral and current environments. For example, we might estimate and compare population densities, group sizes, family structures, distribution of foods, food availability, altitudes, means and variances of temperatures, and so on of environments then and now. If we were to do this, we would find that they differ. It will always be possible to reject the hypothesis of no difference using this method. But such comparisons would tell us little because we have not considered the nature of the adaptations that respond to factors we are comparing. For example, humans cannot synthesize Vitamin C. If Vitamin C levels changed in the human environment, the change would impact on the functioning of human adaptations requiring

Vitamin C for their functioning. Members of species that can synthesize the vitamin would not be affected by the environmental change. In contrast, if ultrasound, ultraviolet light, or infrared light levels were to change in the human environment, our perceptual adaptations would not tell us about the change. The issue is whether the ancestral adaptation responds differently in the past and current environments.

### Signs of Stress and Malfunction

Ancestral adaptations were selected because they contributed to ancestral reproductive fitness by enabling their possessors to solve an important ancestral problem. However, no adaptation can respond to all possible values of the particular conditions with which it evolved to deal. The reaction norm is the range of environmental variation that an innate adaptation evolved to handle (Roff, 1992). The argument here is that adaptations evolved to respond to particular ranges of environmental variation, their reaction norms. Consequently, responding to conditions outside that range will cause physical stress and malfunction; if it did not, the reaction norm could not have evolved.

Adaptations vary in their specificity, the portion of the domain of problems to which they can respond adaptively. If an adaptation has a wide reaction norm, it can produce fitness-enhancing responses to a wide range of conditions. For example, the human omnivorous digestive system can deal with a wide variety of food stuffs. If an adaptation's reaction norm is very narrow, it can produce fitness-enhancing responses to only a very narrow range of conditions, as is the case for the digestion system of panda bears, which can respond adaptively only to bamboo. If the adaptation's reaction norm is very specific, it can function adaptively only in the specific environment in which it evolved. If the norm is very wide, it can function adaptively in the environment in which it evolved, or in a subset of that environment. In either case, it will malfunction if it encounters an environment outside that in which it evolved. If it did not, it could not have evolved through natural selection because variations in its functioning could not have contributed to differential ancestral reproductive fitness.

The failure of physiological adaptations causes physical stress and malfunction. Assuming that mental adaptations have a physical manifestation, their failure also should result in physical stress and malfunction. There is extensive evidence that mental stress has physiological manifestations (Sapolsky, 1993), and hence that the failure of mental adaptations results in at least some physical stress and malfunction. Finally, signs of physical stress and malfunction are one indication that an adaptation is attempting to function outside the environment in which it evolved to respond. However, particular instances of adaptation failure do not provide evidence for environmental changes because there would have been particular instances of adaptation failure in the EEA. No organism is perfectly adapted to its environment. To provide evidence for environmental mismatch, the researcher must show that there is a systematic relation between particular environmental circumstances and some type of anatomical, physiological, or psychological malfunction.

Determining whether an apparent instance of malfunction is the result of stress caused by life in a novel environment or the outcome of an adaptation functioning as it was designed to function, but merely appearing pathological because we do not know its function, can be very difficult. Expert opinion may be of value. A physician, veterinarian, or someone who has a detailed knowledge of the species in question and its habitat may be able to render an expert opinion. But there are at least two problems with expert opinion. First, the expert may not be sufficiently familiar with evolutionary theory to render a definitive opinion on whether an adaptation is malfunctioning. For example, there was considerable controversy over whether infanticide in Langur monkeys was a pathology due to a disturbed environment, or whether it was the result of an adaptation that evolved to contribute to male fitness (Hausfater & Hrdy, 1984). If one took a good-of-the-group perspective, the infanticide was clearly pathological. However, from either a good-of-the-genes or the good-of-the-individual perspective, it could be adaptive. Second, because moral standards change over time and place, an expert may be unduly influenced by current moral standards in making an expert judgment. Human infanticide, for example, is morally acceptable in some cultures and abhorrent in others. Those expressing an expert opinion must be conversant with contemporary evolutionary thinking, and must have a broad knowledge of how the adaptation responds in a variety of environments.

## Frequency in the Ethnographic Record

Cross-cultural studies can give some indication of whether an adaptation is operating outside the environment in which it evolved. If a behavior is very rare in the ethnographic record, then the particular conditions that produce it may be substantially different from those in which it evolved. For example, polyandry is very rare; only four cultures that display it are known (Daly & Wilson, 1983). Hence, it is likely that the conditions that produce it are sufficiently unusual that we can claim they differ from those under which the human mating system evolved. A harsh environment, characterized by scarcity of arable land and other resources needed for reproduction, may be one of the causes of polyandry. If we accept the concept of ancestralization, described earlier in the chapter, it seems likely that polyandry will revert to polygyny as ecological conditions moderate in those cultures where it is found. Because a trait that is rare in the ethnographic record may be the result of a genetic mutation peculiar to a particular population, it is necessary to identify the particular environmental conditions that produce the rare trait in the cultures where it does occur and that are absent in those where it does not occur.

## Disturbed Reproductive Functioning

There is much controversy over the use of fitness measures in the study of adaptation (Alexander, 1990; Irons, 1990; Reeve & Sherman, 1993; Sherman & Reeve, 1997; Symons, 1987, 1989, 1990; Tooby & Cosmides, 1990; Turke, 1990). There are those who argue that studies of differential fitness (i.e., fitness differences between different groups, such as high- and low-status men) should not be used in the study of adaptation. Their basic argument is that, because adaptations evolved in ancestral environments, potential differences between the ancestral and current environments attenuate the relationship between current function and fitness. Therefore, we cannot assume that, because a putative adaptation evolved because it made a greater contribution to lifetime reproductive fitness than some alternative adaptation, it serves to maximize, or even contribute to, current fitness.

Although these arguments may be valid, they do not obviate the use of reproductive data when considering whether a putative adaptation is functioning outside the environment in which it evolved. Adaptations evolved because they promoted their genetic basis better than alternative adaptations, by enhancing the reproductive success of their possessors, or of their possessor's genetic relatives, more than alternative adaptations (Tooby & Cosmides, 1990). If an adaptation malfunctions because it is systematically encountering environmental conditions different from those with which it evolved to deal, there should be some impact on expected reproductive success in the changed environment. If there were no impact on reproductive fitness when an adaptation encountered conditions different from those where it evolved, the adaptation could not have evolved through natural selection because it would not have contributed to ancestral differential reproductive fitness.

In many, but not all, cases, there will be a negative impact on expected fitness in comparison with ancestral expected fitness. This is because the cost–benefit structure associated with an adaptation will have evolved to respond to ancestral conditions in such a way that it contributed to ancestral fitness better than some alternative adaptation. Changes in the environmental conditions that the adaptation evolved to respond to are likely to impair its functioning in a way that detracts from fitness. However, changes in living conditions may short-circuit the cost–benefit structure. For example, the average number of live births for Canadian Hutterite women is 10.4 (Short, 1984). There are apparently two reasons for this high birth rate. First, Hutterite women nurse their babies on a very rigid pattern, once every 4 hours, which reduces the effectiveness of ancestral nursing adaptations for spacing children. Second, the Hutterite way of life provides the resources for rearing large families.

Thus, one indication that individuals are living in an environment different from that in which they evolved is unusual reproductive patterns. If a putative adaptation can be shown to be contributing to reproductive patterns that differ markedly from ancestral patterns, then we have evidence that ancestral and current environments differ with respect to that adaptation. There is considerable evidence that ancestral women had four to five children, spaced about 4 years apart, and that about half of them survived to maturity (Betzig, Borgerhoff-Mulder, & Turke, 1988). This suggests that the environment of Canadian Hutterite women differs from their ancestral environment with respect to the adaptations controlling birth spacing and number of children produced and reared. It is interesting to note that the birth rate in many Canadian Hutterite colonies has fallen from around 10 to 5 in the last few years because many Hutterite women are having hysterectomies (Karl Peter, personal communication, 1990). Apparently, when Hutterite women are given the option of acting on their reproductive preferences, they prefer to have about the same number of live births as our hunter–gatherer ancestors. This finding suggests that personal preferences may be another source of evidence that reproductive patterns differ from the ancestral norm.

A controversial example of an unusual reproductive pattern is Tibetan polyandry, studied by Crook and Crook (1988) as an example of adaptive behavior. They claimed that it was an instance of fitness maximization, given the conditions under which those who practiced it were living. Because polyandry is extremely rare in the ethnographic record, it seems likely that Tibetan polyandry is an anomalous mating system produced by the unique environmental conditions where it is seen. Although it may be adaptive in present circumstances, its presence is likely an indication that the Tibetan environment differs from the EEA where the human mating system evolved.

Most human behaviors are examples of functionally stable, culturally variable behaviors. Hence, it makes sense to assume that ancestral and current environments do not differ with respect to the functioning of many adaptations. Signs of stress and malfunction, frequency in the ethnographic record, and studies of reproductive function are three of the sources of information that can be used in rejecting this hypothesis. If there is little evidence that a behavior is systematically associated with stress and malfunction, if it is not rare in the ethnographic record, and if there is little evidence linking it with unusual reproductive consequences, then researchers may proceed assuming, with reasonable confidence, that detailed consideration of the EEA in the study of the functioning of particular adaptations is not necessary. However, if one of these sources of evidence indicates that there may be a difference between ancestral and current environments with respect to the behavior under considera- tion, then the researcher should use a research strategy that takes into consideration those properties of the EEA that may be relevant to the adaptation being studied.

## CONCLUSION

It was argued here that researchers should begin their research with the assumption that ancestral and current environments do not differ with respect to any particular adaptation. This is not to claim that, in general, ancestral and current environments do not differ. They obviously do differ. As mentioned in the introduction, it is possible for there to be a general difference between ancestral and current environments, and yet the environment of a number of adaptations may not differ significantly.

What are the implications of these arguments? First, perhaps they will put pressure on mismatch theorists to identify explicitly how the differ- ence between ancestral and current environments contributes to the par- ticular pathology they claim is caused by mismatch. This has been done in some cases. For example, Eaton et al. (1994) attempted to specify how changes in reproductive patterns occurring during the last 30,000 or so years may be the cause of some women's cancers.

Second, these arguments may broaden the range of acceptable method- ologies available to researchers working on the evolutionary significance of human behaviors. If there are plausible reasons for believing ancestral and current environments do not differ with respect to the functioning of an adaptation, more of the methods of animal behavioral ecology may be useful in the study of human behavior. (See Krebs & Davies, 1991, and its references for a discussion of the assumptions and methods of animal behavioral ecology. Smith & Winterhalder, 1992, provided an orientation to some of the methods and results of human behavioral ecology.)

## REFERENCES

Alexander, R. D. (1979). *Darwinism and human affairs.* Seattle: University of Washington Press.
Alexander, R. D. (1990). Epigenetic rules and Darwinian algorithms: The adaptive study of learning and development. *Ethology and Sociobiology, 11*(4/5), 241–304.

Bailey, K. (1987). *Human paleopsychology: Applications to aggression and pathological processes.* Hillsdale, NJ: Lawrence Erlbaum Associates.

Bailey, K. (1995). Mismatch theory and paleopsychopathology. In C. B. Crawford (Chair), *Human behavior and evolution society conference.* Symposium conducted at the meeting of Human Behavior and Evolution Society, Los Angeles, California.

Barkow, J. (1989). *Darwin, sex, and status: Biological approaches to mind and culture.* Toronto, Canada: University of Toronto Press.

Barkow, J., Cosmides, L., & Tooby, J. (1992). *The adapted mind: Evolutionary psychology and the generation of culture.* New York: Oxford University Press.

Betzig, L., Borgerhoff-Mulder, M., & Turke, P. (1988). *Human reproductive behavior.* Cambridge, England: Cambridge University Press.

Bickerton, D. (1990). *Language and species.* Chicago: University of Chicago Press.

Bowlby, J. (1969). *Attachment and loss: Volume 1. Attachment.* New York: Basic Books.

Brown, D. (1991). *Human universals.* New York: McGraw-Hill.

Burian, R. M. (1983). Adaptation. In M. Greene (Ed.), *Dimensions of Darwinism: Themes and counter themes in 20th century evolutionary thought* (pp. 287–314). Cambridge, England: Cambridge University Press.

Buss, D. (1994). *The evolution of desire: Strategies of human mating.* New York: Basic Books.

Coe, K., & Steadman, L. (1995). The human breast and ancestral reproductive cycle: A preliminary inquiry into breast cancer etiology. *Human Nature, 6,* 197–220.

Corballis, M. (1991). *The lopsided ape: The evolution of the generative mind.* Oxford, England: Oxford University Press.

Crawford, C. B. (1993). The future of sociobiology: Counting babies or studying proximate mechanisms? *Trends in Ecology and Evolution, 8*(5), 183–186.

Crawford, C. B., & Anderson, J. L. (1989). Sociobiology: An environmentalist discipline? *American Psychologist, 44,* 1449–1459.

Crook, J., & Crook, S. (1988). Tibetan polyandry: Problems of adaptation and fitness. In L. Betzig, M. Borgerhoff-Mulder, & P. Turke (Eds.), *Human reproductive behavior* (pp. 97–114). Cambridge, England: Cambridge University Press.

Crystal, D. (1987). *The Cambridge encyclopedia of language.* New York: Cambridge University Press.

Daly, M., & Wilson, M. (1983). *Sex, evolution and behavior* (2nd ed.). Boston: Willard Grant.

Dunbar, R., & Spoors, M. (1995). Social networks, support cliques, and kinship. *Human Nature, 6,* 273–290.

Eaton, S. B., Pike, M. C., Short, R. V., Lee, N. C., Trussell, J., Hatcher, R. A., Wood, J. W., Worthman, C. M., Blurton Jones, N. G., Konner, M. J., Hill, K. R., Bailey, R., & Hurtado, A. M. (1994). Women's reproductive cancers in evolutionary context. *The Quarterly Review of Biology, 69*(3), 353–367.

Eibl-Eibesfeldt, I. (1989). *Human ethology.* New York: Aldine deGruyter.

Ekman, P. (1992). Facial expressions of emotion. *Psychological Science, 3,* 34–38.

Ekman, P. (1994). Strong evidence for universals in facial expressions: A reply to Russell's mistaken critique. *Psychological Bulletin, 115,* 268–287.

Foley, R. (1996). The adaptive legacy of human evolution: A search for the EEA. *Evolutionary Anthropology, 4*(6), 194–203.

Glantz, K., & Pearce, J. (1989). *Exiles from Eden: Psychotherapy from an evolutionary perspective.* New York: Norton.

Gould, S., & Lewontin, R. (1978). The spandrels of San Marco and the Panglossian paradigm: A critique of the adaptationist programme. *Proceedings of the Royal Society. London, 205,* 581–598.

Hausfater, G., & Hrdy, S. (1984). *Infanticide: Comparative and evolutionary perspectives.* New York: Aldine.

Irons, W. (1990). Let's make our perspective broader rather than narrower: A comment on Turke's "Which humans behave adaptively, and why does it matter?" and on the so-called DA-DP debate. *Ethology and Sociobiology, 11*(4/5), 361–374.

Irons, W. (in press). Adaptively relevant environments versus the environment of evolutionary adaptedness. *Evolutionary Anthropology.*

Kellworth, P., Bernard, H., & McCarty, C. (1984). Measuring patterns of acquaintanceship. *Current Anthropology, 25*, 391–397.

Kluger, M. J. (1986). Is fever beneficial? *Yale Journal of Biological Medicine, 54*, 89–95.

Krebs, J. R., & Davies, N. B. (1991). *Behavioral ecology: An evolutionary approach.* Oxford, England: Blackwell.

Krebs, J. R., & McCleery, R. H. (1984). Optimization in behavioral ecology. In J. R. Krebs & N. B. Davies (Eds.), *Behavioral ecology: An evolutionary approach* (pp. 91–121). Oxford, England: Blackwell.

Lowie, R. H. (1963). *Indians of the plains.* New York: The Natural History Press.

Lumsden, C., & Wilson, E. (1981). *Genes, mind, and culture: The coevolutionary process.* Cambridge, MA: Harvard University Press.

Lumsden, C., & Wilson, E. (1983). *Promethean fire: Reflections on the origin of mind.* Cambridge, MA: Harvard University Press.

MacDonald, K. (1995). The establishment and maintenance of socially imposed monogamy in western Europe. *Politics and the Life Sciences, 14*, 3–23.

Maynard-Smith, J. (1978). Optimization theory and evolution. *Annual Review of Ecology and Systematics, 9*, 31–56.

Murdock, G. P. (1945). The common denominator of culture. In R. Linton (Ed.), *The science of man in the world crisis* (pp. 124–142). New York: Columbia University Press.

Nesse, R., & Williams, G. (1994). *Why we get sick: The new science of Darwinian medicine.* New York: Random House.

Pinker, S. (1994). *The language instinct.* New York: HarperCollins.

Porter, R. H. (1987). Kin recognition: Functions and mediating mechanisms. In C. Crawford, M. Smith, & D. Krebs (Eds.), *Sociobiology and psychology: Ideas, issues and applications* (pp. 175–204). Hillsdale, NJ: Lawrence Erlbaum Associates.

Power, M. (1986). The foraging adaptation of chimpanzees and the recent behaviors of the provisioned apes in Gombe and Mahale National Parks, Tanzania. *Human Evolution, 1*(3), 251–266.

Reeve, K., & Sherman, P. (1993). Adaptation and the goals of evolutionary research. *Quarterly Review of Biology, 68*, 1–32.

Roff, D. (1992). *The evolution of life histories: Theory and analysis.* New York: Chapman & Hall.

Sapolsky, M. (1993). Neuroendocrinology of the stress response. In J. Becker, S. Breedlove, & D. Craws (Eds.), *Behavioral endocrinology* (pp. 287–324). Cambridge, MA: MIT Press.

Shepher, J. (1971). Mate selection among second-generation Kibbutz adolescents and adults: Incest avoidance and negative imprinting. *Archives of Sexual Behavior, 1*, 293–307.

Sherman, P., & Reeve, K. (1997). Forward and backward: Alternative approaches to studying human social evolution. In L. Betzig (Ed.), *Human nature: A critical reader* (pp. 147–158). New York: Oxford University Press.

Short, R. (1984). Breast feeding. *Scientific American, 250*, 35–41.

Singh, D. (1993). Body shape and woman's attractiveness. *Human Nature, 4*, 297–321.

Smith, E. A., & Winterhalder, B. (Eds.). (1992). *Evolutionary ecology and human behavior.* New York: Aldine deGruyter.

Symons, D. (1987). If we're all Darwinians, what's the fuss about? In C. B. Crawford, M. Smith, & D. Krebs (Eds.), *Sociobiology and psychology: Ideas, issues, and applications* (pp. 121–146). Hillsdale, NJ: Lawrence Erlbaum Associates.

Symons, D. (1989). A critique of Darwinian Anthropology. *Ethology and Sociobiology, 10*(1–3), 131–144.

Symons, D. (1990). Adaptiveness and adaptation. *Ethology and Sociobiology, 11*(4/5), 427–444.

Thornhill, R. (1980). Rape in *Panorpa* scorpionflies and a general rape hypothesis. *Animal Behavior, 28,* 52–59.

Thornhill, R., & Gangestad, S. (1993). Human facial beauty: Averageness, symmetry, and parasite resistance. *Human Nature, 4,* 237–239.

Tooby, J., & Cosmides, C. (1990). The past explains the present: Adaptations and the structure of ancestral environments. *Ethology and Sociobiology, 4/5,* 375–424.

Turke, P. W. (1990). Which humans behave adaptively, and why does it matter? *Ethology and Sociobiology, 11*(4/5), 305–340.

Williams, G. (1966). *Adaptation and natural selection.* Princeton, NJ: Princeton University Press.

Wilson, E. (1975). *Sociobiology: The new synthesis.* Cambridge, MA: Harvard University Press.

Wilson, E. (1978). *On human nature.* Cambridge, MA: Harvard University Press.

# Testing Evolutionary Hypotheses

Harmon R. Holcomb III
*University of Kentucky*

Examination of such journals as *Ethology and Sociobiology,* renamed *Evolution and Human Behavior* in 1997, reveals that evolutionary psychology is progressing as a science due to improved hypothesis testing. Investigators make more imaginative uses of evolutionary theory and selection models to generate testable hypotheses. There are standard instruments to measure variables and parameters relevant to hypotheses. More extensive and detailed bodies of evidence have been developed to test hypotheses. A host of narrowly focused studies achieve statistically significant and replicable results that support evolutionary predictions. More powerful interpretive techniques connect local findings to cross-cultural and cross-species data. Conclusions are stated with greater caution.

The philosophy of hypothesis testing advocated here identifies some hidden units of scientific thought and patterns of scientific reasoning involved in deciding what conclusion(s) to draw from the test results. The principal theses clarify the nature of the argument leading to a conclusion as to which hypothesis should be chosen in the light of the test results. The chapter begins by briefly outlining the main general points about this argument. The body of the chapter exhibits their relevance to evolutionary psychology by using them to evaluate three deservedly influential studies in the following order: *Homicide* (1988) by Daly and Wilson, *The Evolution of Desire* (1994) by Buss, and *The Adapted Mind* (1992) by Barkow, Cosmides, and Tooby.

What important information about the deep structure of scientific thought should be contained in the premises? "Presuppositions in Hypothesis Testing" proposes that the premises should contain information about the presuppositions of the hypothesis. A hypothesis should be evaluated in the light of the test results in terms of its presuppositions, which span several levels of generality, termed *underlying theory, research programs,* and *conceptual frameworks.*

What sorts of inference are used to draw conclusions from such premises about the validity or invalidity of hypotheses? "Reasoning in Hypothesis Testing" contends that deductive and inductive inference have essential, but limited, roles in analyzing the test results, and that inference to the best explanation (abduction) is crucial for the final stage of validation. A hypothesis is validated as the best available explanation of the evidence among available alternative hypotheses. Building on the previous section, assessment of what counts as the best explanation should take into account the way its presuppositions involve multiple levels of analysis.

What difference does the status of rival hypotheses as evolutionary or nonevolutionary make for assessing whether the hypothesis better explains the test results than the alternatives? "Alternative Hypotheses" maintains that different sorts of arguments are appropriate to choosing an evolutionary hypothesis—as compared with a nonevolutionary (learning and culture) hypothesis rather than as compared with an evolutionary hypothesis—because the presuppositions of evolutionary and nonevolutionary hypotheses radically differ.

How does evaluation of past efforts at validating evolutionary hypotheses as superior to the alternatives contribute to scientific progress? "Implications for Scientific Progress" emphasizes the need for ongoing research projects to respond creatively to external challenges from researchers in nonevolutionary psychology, as well as to internal challenges from within evolutionary psychology. The hypothesis is tested against raw facts, which are then analyzed in terms of evolutionarily significant facts, as guided by theories, research programs, and conceptual frameworks.

## PRESUPPOSITIONS IN HYPOTHESIS TESTING

### Why Are Presuppositions Necessary?

Evolutionary hypotheses are validated in relation to a presupposed research context. Evolutionists aim to gather specific facts about behavior and to reach general conclusions about patterns of evolved behavioral predispositions. When general hypotheses are tested against specific facts, we rely on a set of guiding ideas to move back and forth between the general and the specific, using the cycles of induction, deduction, and abduction.

Roughly, constructing tests goes from the general to the specific; we deduce implications of general hypotheses for actual people at particular places and times. For each general evolutionary hypothesis, there are many possible implications we can draw from it to test it against the facts. Evaluating the evidence goes from the specific to the general: From specific facts we induce generalizations about the evolutionary significance of behaviors, which then form premises for further deductions. For each test outcome, there are many possible ways to evaluate its import for the general hypothesis tested. Using abduction, we choose the hypothesis that is the best among the alternatives for explaining the evidence.

Because we do not consciously explore this vast space of logical possibilities, we rely on presuppositions to do so. Cosmides and Tooby's (1992) arguments about the weakness of content-independent, domain-general behavioral mechanisms and the necessity of frames apply to any problem-solving computational system, even science. If scientific method were purely domain general—general for all science with no content particular to any one science—we would have no idea which possibilities hold promise, and our choices would be random. We need content-specific guidance on how to narrow down these sets of possibilities to find quick solutions to problems in evolutionary psychology. Information processing in hypothesis testing relies on an architecture of guiding ideas that regulates reasoning across levels of generality.

The hypothesis under test is the explicit object of attention, whereas the guiding ideas typically function as background information. The traditional image of science is impoverished, to use a visual analogy, in its focus on the figure (hypotheses) to the exclusion of the ground (presuppositions, background information). Neither the statement being tested nor the facts exist in isolation. As the physicist Duhem (1987) emphasized, the design and significance of the test involve the place of the statement in a whole group of statements. We need to turn from an atomistic view of a test to a holistic view, which makes the role of context explicit, identifying units of thought at multiple levels of generality that function as presuppositions.

Moving from general to specific, we differentiate the underlying theory (termed *theory*—e.g., various versions of evolutionary theory in general); various approaches for extending the underlying theory so that it applies to humans as a species having mind and culture (termed *research programs*—e.g., the program of extending evolutionary theory to homicide, mating, or cognition using a general model, such as the model of perceived conflicts of interest); and various conceptions of how to achieve relevance and consistency between the underlying theory applied using the research program and the specific topic of study (termed *conceptual frameworks*—e.g., the processing of raw facts in such domains as homicide, mating, or cognition into the form of evolutionarily significant facts so that they can be subsumed under evolutionary explanatory factors).

Test results have direct implications for the hypothesis and indirect implications for its presuppositions. An analysis gains depth from evaluating theoretical, programmatic, and conceptual prerequisites of hypotheses at their own levels of resolution in light of the data.

## How Is a Hypothesis Based on a Theory?

The standard image of science is that theoretical hypotheses should be both predictive, because theories are tested by testing predictions derived from them, and explanatory, because theories are systems of generalizations used to explain a wide variety of phenomena. A *hypothesis* is structurally defined as a claim, whereas a *prediction* and an *explanation* are functionally defined as uses of a claim or set of claims. Daly and Wilson (1988) portrayed the current state of knowledge as one in which, "We have only the most rudimentary scientific understanding of who is likely to kill whom and why" (p. ix). Their hypotheses are theoretical, designed to predict who is likely to kill whom and to explain why those who kill do so and why those who are killed are killed.

There is a good reason why evolutionists think in terms of hypothesis testing instead of theory testing. In evolutionary psychology, what is at issue is not evolutionary theory in general, but the way it is extended to explain the human psyche. This kind of research situation often occurs in science; an established underlying theory is extended to new domains. Thus, Daly and Wilson (1988) insisted, "We are not trying to 'test Darwinian theory,' but rather to use modern evolutionary ideas to generate new ideas about human social psychology and behavior" (p. 7). So, instead of talking about validating general theories, it is more appropriate to this type of research situation to talk about validating hypotheses and analyzing the criteria of their validity in terms of their basis in general theories.

A slightly different terminology is to call any set of related explanatory hypotheses a *theory*. Expressed in those terms, the point is to distinguish the lower level of generality of theories of the evolution of murder, mating, and cognition from the higher level of generality of the main tenets of neo-Darwinian evolutionary theory. A theory of the evolution of murder presupposes a whole body of theory of the existence, course, causes and results of evolutionary change, but not conversely; the latter is at a higher level of generality. The contrast between hypothesis and underlying theory captures this difference. A hypothesis has theoretical presuppositions.

The standard hypothetic-deductive (H-D) model of science posits that scientists deduce predictive and explanatory hypotheses from a theory and test the theory by checking these hypotheses (often termed *predictions*) against observed facts; if the theory fits the facts, the theory is confirmed; if not, the theory is disconfirmed. H-D advocates criticize *The Adapted Mind* for regarding evolutionary theory as a heuristic device for generating novel hypotheses, rather than as a testable theory that delivers falsifiable predictions.

This criticism arises from applying the H-D method beyond the boundaries of its usefulness. The H-D model is suitable for cases when the theory is not yet established. But in cases of the extension of an established theory (e.g., evolutionary theory) to a new domain (e.g., the behavior of organisms with minds and cultures), the issues turn on the way the theory is applied. To clarify these issues, we need to differentiate levels of resolution in applying the underlying, established theory.

### How Is a Hypothesis Based on a Research Program?

Recognizing which research Daly and Wilson are committed to is useful in understanding why, among all possible evolutionary hypotheses, they formulated some rather than others and subjected them to test. Daly and Wilson (1988) summarized the research program (paradigm) they use to narrow down the huge range of possible applications of evolutionary theory to the analysis of murder:

> Selection shapes behavioral control mechanisms—including the human psyche—so as to make behaving organisms effective reproductive competitors and nepotists. Species-typical motives have evolved to promote genetic posterity; it follows that our most basic human perceptions of self-interest are evolved tokens of the probable fitness consequences of alternative courses of action in historical environments. We therefore expect that two individuals will perceive themselves to be in conflict when the promotion of one's expected fitness entails the diminution of the other's. This, in brief, is the evolutionary psychological model that we have applied to the study of murder, and it has led us to a number of novel questions, hypotheses, and analyses. Although the research presented here is just a beginning, and although many of our ideas may prove wrong, we believe that the utility of the paradigm is established. (p. 293)

This is called the *Perceived Conflicts of Interest Program* (PCI). PCI contrasts with the Boyd–Richerson (1985) program, which emphasizes the interactions of human dual inheritance via both genetic and social transmission. PCI also differs from the Lumsden–Wilson (1981) program, which emphasized between-individual differential genetic propensities to acquire some cultural traits rather than others as part of their developmental (epigenetic) pathways. PCI is basically a modification of the Alexander (1979, 1987) program, which emphasized inclusive fitness and nepotism, as well as conflicts and confluences of interests among genetically similar organisms having mind and culture. However, the way Daly and Wilson (1988) articulated Alexander's program alludes to Symons' (1979) emphasis on adaptive design manifested in numerous, specific, complex psychological mechanisms, as opposed to particular behaviors or general mental abilities. Symons' thesis was developed into the Cosmides–Tooby (1992) program presented in *The Adapted Mind*, which views domain-specific psychological design in humans as adaptations to Pleistocene ecological and social conditions, rather than to present environments.

Daly and Wilson's (1988) commitment to the PCI program transforms their basic research question into an evolutionary problem. They started with a question common to nonevolutionary and evolutionary analyses: Who kills whom and why? Then they cited a traditional answer:

> The family is the most frequent single locus of all types of violence ranging from slaps, to beatings, to torture, to murder. Students of homicide are well aware that more murder victims are members of the same family than any other category of murder-victim relationship. (p. 19)

Kuhn (1987) noted that in normal science problems are treated as puzzles (i.e., the scientist's commitment to a research program [paradigm] guarantees that the problem has a solution and the scientist's job is to find it). Lakatos (1987) noted that research programs, from their inception to their end, confront a sea of anomalies (pp. 193–194). Thus, Daly and Wilson (1988) said, "This is all rather puzzling from the perspective of evolutionary theory . . . the fundamental commonality of interest among genetic relatives makes their killing one another seem especially anomalous, so we devoted much attention to such cases" (p. 293). The standard answer generates a problem, puzzle, or anomaly for evolutionary psychology guided by PCI, not for nonevolutionary psychology.

## How Is a Hypothesis Based on a Conceptual Framework?

Once the research program subsumes homicide under the domain of evolutionary theory, the phenomena associated with homicide must be reconceptualized by a conceptual framework so that their evolutionary significance is explicit. Any conceptual framework used in applying evolutionary theory to human behavior according to the perceived conflicts of interest program requires making genetic distinctions in the study of murder. *Homicide* processes facts about murder into facts that distinguish murders among family members that involve genetic relatives and those that do not. Recognizing which conceptual framework they are committed to helps us understand how they make data on homicide relevant to evolutionary theory in the first place. This is crucial because much debate over sociobiology or evolutionary psychology, as *The Adapted Mind* emphasized, is about whether, in what way, and to what extent evolution is relevant to human behavior.

Their Detroit data showed that, in fact, only 6.3% of homicides occur between genetic relatives. Part of the puzzle is solved, having presupposed a conceptual framework on which genetic distinctions are crucial for applying the underlying theory to the phenomena at hand. Evolutionists would say that evolutionary theory supplied the basis for questioning a common assumption (that murder is most frequent within families), which then proved to be false. Nonevolutionists would not agree that their thesis is false. Such disputes are quite common.

Disputes over facts often reflect differing concepts. According to evolutionary conceptual frameworks, a *family* is defined by genetic criteria for kinship. According to nonevolutionary conceptual frameworks, *family* is defined using cultural criteria for kinship, which need not imply shared genes identical by descent. Each side is right, given its own concepts. This episode illustrates how the meaning of a hypothesis and the import of its test depend on an implicit conceptual framework.

### How Should Hypotheses Be Evaluated?

The Multi-Unit Model (MUM) of science developed in *Sociobiology, Sex, and Science* (Holcomb, 1993) tells us to evaluate evolutionary hypotheses within their own research context—that is, at three levels of generality:

> The conclusions to be drawn from one or more tests of a hypothesis are justifiable only if they derive from premises informed by an accurate understanding of the way the hypothesis is based on one or more underlying theories, guiding research programs, and orienting conceptual frameworks. (pp. 9–14, 414–425)

MUM offers a principled basis for regarding the usual criticisms from outsiders as based on misinterpretations. Some misinterpret evolutionary psychology because they take its hypotheses out of context, and instead associate them with a different context (e.g., such typically, though not always, irrelevant ideologies as genetic or biological determinism, intelligence testing, social Darwinism, eugenics, etc.).

Daly and Wilson were not trying to explain exactly the same thing that nonevolutionary psychologists try to explain. What is being explained is not raw facts, but significant facts—behavioral facts (facts about homicide) whose significance is made determinate by an associated conceptual framework (genetic distinctions), research program (PCI), and theory (evolutionary theory). Crawford and Anderson (1989) invoked the concept of *evolutionary significance*, defining it as follows:

> We believe, however, that consideration of the evolutionary significance of a behavior—the ancestral conditions that may have evolved to render it adaptive, the mechanisms that may have evolved to produce that behavior, and how those putatively evolved mechanisms may function in current environments—will often provide insights that cannot be provided by any other theory of behavior. (p. 1458)

They emphasized that the usual criticisms of sociobiology involve misconceptions of evolutionary significance: "Therefore, the fact that a trait has evolutionary significance does not imply (a) that it cannot be affected by environmental conditions, (b) that it must have high heritability, or (c) that it must appear the same in all individuals" (Crawford & Anderson, 1981, p. 1449).

MUM diagnoses the usual criticisms as arising from false presuppositions—ones that ignore the role of current research programs and conceptual frameworks in determining the meaning and implications of evolutionary hypotheses. Daly and Wilson's (1988) evolutionary hypotheses explain species-typical psychologies (i.e., we behave as we do because of the evolved nature of our predispositions to form domain-specific psychological dispositions in the presence of environmental cues).

MUM identifies the source of the scope and limits of evolutionary psychology. A behavior has evolutionary significance if and only if it bears cause–effect relations to reproduction. Every human behavior is evolutionarily significant on this definition, thus, every human behavior is within the scope of evolutionary psychology. Those who do not care about a behavior's relation to reproduction, and prefer to study other features of behavioral patterns, study features beyond the limits of evolutionary psychology. We can knock the wind out of the debate between reductionists and antireductionists over whether social science reduces to sociobiology by recognizing two subtly different truths: For every human behavior, there is something about it that is evolutionarily significant; it is not the case that there is a human behavior such that everything about it is evolutionarily significant. Evolutionary and nonevolutionary hypotheses need not be incompatible once their domains of phenomena to be explained are distinguished.

MUM also enables us to differentiate various levels of generality in why evolutionists might not accept a hypothesis although it fits the test results. Consider, for instance, a hypothesis about parenting. Some might reject the particular way it incorporates evolutionary theory (e.g., they reject it because the underlying theory neglects nonadaptive change, fails to distinguish adaptations from by-products, or fails to do justice to differences between utility in ancestral environments and utility in current environments). Others might reject the program of Darwinian research it articulates (e.g., they reject it because it was arrived at by methods of behavioral ecology to study differences in lifetime reproductive success, and so fails to throw light on the naturally selected design of psychological mechanisms). Others might reject the conceptual framework in terms of which the phenomena to be explained are subsumed under evolutionary factors (e.g., they reject it because the prediction tested fails to logically connect the benefits of differential investment in sons and daughters to variation in parameters of health or status of the mother). Given the potential for criticism at all three levels of analysis, efforts toward validating evolutionary hypotheses using empirical tests should evaluate them at all three levels of analysis: "MUM's the word!"

## REASONING IN HYPOTHESIS TESTING

### How Should Conclusions Be Drawn From Tests?

It is argued here that validation crucially operates by means of inference to the hypothesis that best explains the evidence, called the method of hypothesis, inference to the best explanation, or abduction.

> In making this inference one infers, from the fact that a certain hypothesis would explain the evidence, to the truth of that hypothesis. In general, there will be several hypotheses which might explain the evidence, so one must be able to reject all such alternative hypotheses before one is warranted in making the inference. Thus one infers, from the premise that given hypothesis would provide a "better" explanation for the evidence than would any other hypothesis, to the conclusion that the given hypothesis is true. . . . Uses of the inference to the best explanation are manifold. When a detective puts the evidence together and decides that it must have been the butler, he is reasoning that no other explanation which accounts for all the facts is plausible enough or simple enough to be accepted. When a scientist infers the existence of atoms and subatomic particles, he is inferring the truth of an explanation for various data which he wishes to account for. (Harman, 1989, p. 324)

The received view of logical reasoning in science treats the logic of science as merely inductive (inductivism), merely deductive (deductivism), or both, thereby missing out on the crucial role of abduction. This chapter argues against the exclusivity of each inference form. Induction and deduction each have limited roles to play in hypothesis testing; the validation of hypotheses through inference to the best explanation is the only inference form that makes sense of how we can provide genuine support for theoretical hypotheses. Analysis of results and the drawing of conclusions in evolutionary psychology would benefit from thinking, as Daly and Wilson do, in those terms.

## What Is the Role of Induction?

Inductivism is a model of science in which scientific method basically consists in four phases: observation, classification, generalization, and prediction. Consider how this scheme applies to the previous refutation of the standard view that people usually kill family members.

Using official police records, Daly and Wilson (1988) tabulated all observed cases of homicide in Detroit during 1972. In 508 of 690 cases, the relationship between victim and offender was known, including 243 unrelated acquaintances (47.8%), 138 strangers (27.2%), and 127 relatives (25%). Nonevolutionary analyses classify both genetic and marital kin as family members, obscuring the evolutionary significance of the data. They reclassified relatives to include only genetic relatives, or 6.3% of the 508 usable cases.

By what reasoning can one justifiably generalize from the observed Detroit sample to a larger population? Straight induction is the rule of reasoning: (Induction) If m/n observed As are Bs, infer that m/n As are Bs, including those unobserved, assuming a suitable number have been observed over varied conditions.

Generality is related to issues over what counts as a well-designed test. Have a suitable number of cases been observed over varied conditions? Daly and Wilson argued that the proportions in these categories remain fairly constant in the FBI statistics for Americans. Indeed, similar proportions were documented in the 1994 Justice Department's Bureau of Justice Statistics from more than 8,000 homicides in 75 large urban counties during 1988. Hence, the data permit a reasonably good prediction to current Americans that murders of relatives are rare in comparison with murders of nonrelatives. To obtain a representative sample for making a good species-typical prediction, we need cross-cultural, cross-historical, cross-hominid, and cross-species data.

Generality is related to issues over standards of justification. One can prove an empirical hypothesis at the lowest level of generality, such as, "I hypothesize that the females in my sample will report less violence against their biological sons and daughters than the males in my sample." That is a hypothesis about the test results, and so it is proved by the test results without inductive generalization. One can confirm by induction, but not prove, a hypothesis that generalizes beyond the test results, such as, "I hypothesize that this gender difference holds for Americans in general," using many and varied tests. Tests have to be more numerous and varied to confirm hypotheses about our species-typical behavioral acts because confirmation by induction requires a prior argument for a representative sample.

Observability is related to issues over prediction and explanation. Daly and Wilson's (1988) predictive hypotheses concern facts about who kills whom. Given the observable rates in which murderers or the murdered are strangers, acquaintances, or family members, we can make predictions about what we should observe in new cases. Their explanatory hypotheses concern relations of conflicts of interests described in evolutionary terms. Why do normal people apparently reduce their fitnesses by murdering? Evolved psychological mechanisms that lead to murder are responding to conflicts of interests, in which people act as if they perceive their own fitnesses to be at serious risk.

Observability is also related to the scope of inductive inference; induction is silent about things we cannot observe. Because the rule of induction works only on observable types (the As and Bs), induction alone can never justify acceptance of theoretical hypotheses (i.e., hypotheses that refer to unobservable factors). We can neither prove nor confirm an explanatory hypothesis (at any level of generality) about people's evolved predispositions, the fitness strategies they reflect, and their evolutionary causes precisely because they are unobservable. Those doubtful that evolution is relevant to homicide can consistently accept the predictive generalized hypotheses about observable murder rates and reject the explanatory hypotheses about evolutionary causes, fitness strategies, and evolved predispositions.

**What Is the Role of Deduction?**

Deductivism (or the H-D method) is the model of science in which scientific method basically consists of four phases: conjecture, experimentation, deduction, and elimination. Daly and Wilson (1988) went on to test the basic evolutionary hypothesis that nepotism tempers interpersonal conflict. Their evolutionary conjecture is a deduction from their program for applying inclusive fitness theory to humans: Otherwise equivalent conflicts tend to be increasingly severe and dangerous as the principles become more distantly related. A competing hypothesis from standard psychology is that risk of violence is a matter of mutual access; violence within families happens so often because family members interact with each other so often.

The trick in using the comparative method in a natural experiment to justify a hypothesis is to locate the diversity required to randomize the effects of confusing variables. Daly and Wilson (1988) assumed that the requisite diversity was located by restricting attention to family members who were killed and comparing proportions of spouses, offspring, parents, and nonrelatives to the proportions killed. They compared an observed distribution of victim–killer relationships against expected distributions deduced from the inclusive fitness and availability hypotheses, finding that the observed distributions did not match availability (mutual access) but did match the inclusive fitness hypothesis ($p < .00001$).

Have they shown that the fitness hypothesis is consistent with the data and eliminated the availability hypothesis? Deductivism uses the rule of reasoning: (Modus Tollens) If the truth of a conjecture implies the truth of a consequence, then if the consequence turns out to be false, then the conjecture must be false.

Observability is related to issues over the possibility of justification. As Popper (1987) emphasized, deductivism views science as progressing by trial and error, conjecture, and refutation. There is no deductive rule of inference to justify saying, "The data fits the hypothesis, so the hypothesis is confirmed." If a hypothesis fits the data, that does not mean it is true. Rival hypotheses could predict the same data. We cannot deduce with validity the truth of explanatory evolutionary generalizations, which involve unobservables, from the observable data. Popper counseled not to conclude that the fitness hypothesis is confirmed (true, probably true, or otherwise justified), just corroborated (not yet falsified—that is, consistent with the data).

Generality is related to issues over standards of refutation. Can we say, "The data do not fit the hypothesis, so the hypothesis is eliminated?" Popper thought so, counseling to conclude that the availability hypothesis is *disconfirmed*. But if a hypothesis fails to fit the data, that does not mean it has been falsified (shown to be false, disproved). The test of the hypothesis might not be a good, appropriate test. Some statement assumed in applying the hypothesis to the data (auxiliary hypotheses, presuppositions at the three levels of generality identified in MUM), rather than the hypothesis being tested, might generate the false prediction.

Generality is also related to issues over what counts as a well-designed test. Modus Tollens is the valid inference schema: for statements P (the hypothesis being tested) and Q (the facts implied by the hypothesis), "if P, then Q, not-Q, therefore, not-P." Not only is P a conjecture, so is "If P, then Q." To rule out these possibilities is, in formal terms, the same as being sure that conditional "If P, then Q" is true. We have to rely on conditional statements to the effect that "If it is really true that we have such-and-such evolved predispositions that reflect such-and-such fitness strategies in general, then we should exhibit such-and-such behaviors in such-and-such a specific situation." Indeed, a good test of a hypothesis is one that produces replicable, independently verifiable data that should occur if the claim is true, but should not occur if the claim is false. Evolutionists need better arguments that they have good tests—that is, such true conditionals; otherwise refutations of competing hypotheses are illusory (Popper's view is subtle; see Holcomb, 1993).

## What Is the Role of Abduction?

Abductivism is the model of science on which the four basic phases of science are: puzzlement, speculation, mutual adjustment, and explanation. This method naturally underwrites the multilevel reasoning in *Homicide* as a whole, which integrates underlying theory, research programs, and conceptual frameworks. Daly and Wilson (1988) were puzzled by the apparent fitness-detracting behavior of homicide, given standard evolutionary theory. They speculated about how evolved psychological mechanisms may lead to homicide in extreme conditions of perceived risks to fitness; murders happen because people in fitness-threatening circumstances commit desperate deeds (the PCI research program). They developed new theoretical hypotheses and empirical data, extending and mutually adjusting data and theory until achieving a better fit, which required reconceptualizing the data using their evolutionary conceptual framework. Because their hypotheses best explained the data among the alternatives they considered, the data justified (confirmed) their hypotheses (i.e., giving good reasons to think that their hypotheses are true).

By what right may one accept a hypothesis as confirmed? Inference to the best explanation is the rule: (Abduction) Accept the hypothesis that provides the best explanation of the available evidence. If sufficient evidence is unavailable, the best explanation is accepted as preferable to alternative hypotheses. If sufficient evidence is available, the best explanation is accepted both as preferable and believable.

The previous discussions of induction and deduction raise an insoluble problem for inductivists and deductivists alike. If the inference from the evidence to hypothesis choice is inductive, because induction works only on observable predicates, one can make strong inferences to empirical (predictive) hypotheses about observable events, but can draw no conclusions about the truth or falsehood of theoretical (explanatory) hypotheses. If the inference is deductive, then, because one cannot deduce with validity a theoretical hypothesis from observation sentences, the deduction has to move from theory to observation via Modus Tollens, and so the test results allow us at best to eliminate theoretical hypotheses, but not to justify them. Neither form of reasoning gives us what we want—

namely, knowledge (true justified claims) about human evolution—because they cannot justify theoretical hypotheses.

Abductivism avoids the sources of difficulty in accounting for how theoretical hypotheses can be confirmed. Inductivist methods cannot confirm or disconfirm theoretical hypotheses, just observational ones, because the rule of induction does not work on theoretical predicates. By contrast, explanation typically invokes theoretical predicates, and so a rule to accept the best explanation gets theory into the inference from the start. Deductivist methods can disconfirm, but cannot confirm, theoretical hypotheses because no theoretical hypotheses are deductively entailed by observation sentences. By contrast, to explain the data is to make sense out of the data in relation to the puzzle that led to developing the data—an activity that involves postulating unobservables. Hence, the inference to the best explanation among the alternatives can justify theoretical hypotheses about the human evolution, thereby establishing evolutionary knowledge.

Daly and Wilson (1988) implicitly invoked abduction in drawing conclusions about killing kinfolk in chap. 2 of *Homicide*. From their research program for applying evolutionary theory, they develop the hypothesis (or prediction) that relatives tend to find common cause in murderous disputes, so that co-offenders should be more closely related on average than victim and offender. They tabulated data from contemporary America (Detroit, Miami), historical Europe (13th-century England), and other cultures (Bison-Horn Maria of India, Bhil, Munda, Oaon, Tzeltal Mayans, Gros Ventre). Using Wright's coefficient of genetic relatedness, $r$, they estimated average relatedness of victim and offender versus co-offenders, finding that people are indeed more likely to find common cause as consanguinity increases. They concluded that, "All the evidence in this chapter—and indeed all the evidence of which we are aware—confirms this fundamental prediction of a pervasive nepotism tempering inter-personal conflict" (p. 35). How do the data confirm this theoretical hypothesis? The best explanation of the data is the way of making the most sense of the totality of the evidence. The best explanation of the joint differential risks of relatives in being murdered and of kin in becoming murderers is not mutual access (availability), but rather genetic relationship.

Daly and Wilson (1988) explicitly invoked abduction in drawing conclusions about killing parents. They stated their conclusions:

> we showed the superiority of an evolutionary theoretical model of parent-offspring conflict to Freud's Oedipal theory. The evolutionary model predicts and explains detailed patterns in parent-offspring homicide data, and better accounts for the comparative and cross-cultural evidence, too. (p. 294)

What is important here about predictions is that they match the specificity of the data. Rather than say, "Choose the hypothesis that best explains and predicts the data," we say, "Choose the available hypothesis that best explains the data among the alternatives," when the goal is to account for the specificity of the data. Because scientific explanations have predictive implications (see Holcomb, 1993, pp. 39–43), inference to the best explanation takes predictive success into account.

## ALTERNATIVE HYPOTHESES

### Which Hypotheses Are Alternatives?

It is maintained here that progress in a new area of evolutionary psychology toward validated evolutionary hypotheses occurs in two phases: initially, when the field is immature, by means of tests between evolutionary and nonevolutionary hypotheses; and later, as the field matures, among alternative evolutionary hypotheses. Because most of our understanding of human psychology relied on claims that did not include an evolutionary perspective, critics adopt the conservative view that some nonevolutionary explanation will always provide the best explanation of the data. In responding to this intellectual milieu, evolutionary psychologists seek to show how evolutionary theory is relevant to our behavior by showing the superiority of evolutionary hypotheses over nonevolutionary hypotheses in explaining the data. Evolutionary theorists seek to turn behaviors that initially seem like counterexamples or exceptions to evolutionary principles into positive examples.

Thus, the sort of tests we find in *Homicide* are mainly those of the preliminary type, designed to legitimate using an evolutionary approach in contrast to a nonevolutionary approach, not of the mature type, designed to provide severe tests among evolutionary hypotheses. This is not a criticism because it makes sense to conduct tests of the mature type after the legitimacy of using an evolutionary approach has already been demonstrated for the behavior under study using tests of the preliminary type. However, if evolutionary psychology is to become a mature discipline, each topically defined area (the evolution of murder, mating, cognition, and so on) must move beyond sets of alternatives that oppose evolutionary and nonevolutionary hypotheses and toward sets that oppose more refined variants of evolutionary hypotheses.

Sometimes evolutionists identify an array of alternatives that include multiple evolutionary and nonevolutionary hypotheses. This is not wrong to do, but it complicates evaluating the implications of the test results. Differences between evolutionary and nonevolutionary conceptual frameworks are typically far greater than differences within evolutionary or nonevolutionary frameworks. Adherents of rival evolutionary hypotheses

usually agree that distinctions involving fitness, adaptation, natural selection, and genes are relevant to making sense of the test results, and go
on to discuss terminology within those categories. Adherents of rival
nonevolutionary hypotheses may deny the relevance of those categories
to human behavior altogether. To argue that an evolutionary hypothesis
is better than a nonevolutionary one, it helps to draw on the sorts of
conceptual arguments Cosmides and Tooby (1992) launched against the
Standard Social Science model in *The Adapted Mind*. To argue that one
evolutionary hypothesis is better than another, conceptual arguments of
that type are not needed, and the sorts of arguments used can presuppose
more shared basic commitments.

## The Best Explanation: Of What and Compared to What?

Behavior has various aspects; we can study its immediate causation, its
development, its function, and its evolution. Evolutionary theory does
not explain behavior per se; rather, it explains the evolution of behavior.
So the application of evolutionary theory to humans seeks to comprehend
the evolutionary significance of our behavior. One reason for the fruitless
clash between advocates and critics of evolutionary studies of human
behavior is that they do not realize observation is contoured by guiding
commitments. In evolutionary studies, the data are selected and conceptualized using evolutionary theory, concepts, and distinctions. If we have
done our work well, the evolutionary hypothesis under test will account
for the specificity of the data after they are processed by evolutionary
conceptual frameworks better than existing nonevolutionary hypotheses.

During the initial phase of testing, the hypothesis which best explains
the data is the best relative to a set of alternative hypotheses that include
both evolutionary and nonevolutionary hypotheses (typically in terms of
culture or learning divorced from the evolved predispositions that underlie them). Such tests show only that, given the evolutionary conceptual
framework at hand, nonevolutionary hypotheses are of the wrong kind
to account for the data so conceptualized.

For instance, Daly and Wilson's (1988) claims that selection thinking
better accounts for data on various categories of homicides than culture
thinking appears to work by sleight of hand. Of course it does; the game is
rigged in their favor. The facts about homicide are not expressed in any old
form, but expressed in a form relevant to evolutionary theory (e.g., facts
about murder are processed into facts that distinguish murders among
family members that involve genetic relatives and those that do not). It
appears that all that has been shown is that the data conceptualized using
culture thinking are better explained by culture hypotheses, and that data
conceptualized using selection thinking are better explained using selection

hypotheses. Recognition of conceptual frameworks is crucial to seeing what is going on beneath the surface of apparently positive test results.

For evolutionary hypotheses to be validated in the manner of a mature science, they must be tested against data using tests designed to draw the implications of competing evolutionary hypotheses. Rigorous hypothesis testing requires that the hypothesis to be accepted on the basis of the test results is the one that best explains the data, where they are drawn from a set of alternative evolutionary explanations. Evolutionary psychology has been in an immature phase, trying to legitimate the game of evolutionary theorizing about human psychology.

A conceptual framework, from the point of view of the anatomy of explanation, consists of the following items associated with an explanatory hypothesis: an implicit conception of explanatory problems addressed by the hypothesis, an implicit conception of the phenomena to be explained by the hypothesis, an implicit conception of the factors invoked by the hypothesis to do the explaining, and an implicit conception of the standards for assessing the hypothesis' performance in the test situation (Holcomb, 1993). The holistic nature of conceptual frameworks is the source of the seeming circularity, in which, for any domain, evolutionary hypotheses using evolutionary explanatory factors best meet standards for solving problems in that domain, and similarly for nonevolutionary studies. Consider the following example.

Chapter 3 of *Homicide* concerns killing children. First, the facts. How often does killing children occur? The Human Relations Area File (HRAF) provides sufficient data for a reliable cross-cultural comparison. Of the 60 societies in the sample, infanticide was mentioned in 39 societies. Second, why do parents kill their own children? The PCI program supplies three conditions when it may be in the fitness interests of an organism to kill its offspring: lack of paternity confidence, poor phenotypic quality, or low probability of survival for other reasons. The ethnographic record bore out this prediction: There was paternity uncertainty in 20 societies, concern over infant quality in 21 societies, concern over circumstances for childrearing in 56 societies, and other circumstances in 15 societies. This was said to confirm the hypothesis that infanticide would evolve so as to reflect evolved motives for allocating scarce resources, so that it would be practiced more often in these conditions than in other fitness-relevant conditions. However, that societies are concerned about paternity does not supply evidence that this concern caused infanticide. It is suggestive that seemingly counterexamples or exceptions (the 15 societies) occurred when coercion by third parties changed which parental allocations would enhance fitness.

So which hypothesis best explains the data? Daly and Wilson (1988) identified a competing hypothesis—culture. Culture could not account for

320                                                        HOLCOMB

the specificity of the data, which is not surprising because the data gathered were guided by evolutionary theory and the PCI program, whereas the nonevolutionary hypotheses were not. Daly and Wilson concluded that, "the risk factors suggested by selection thinking are demonstrably relevant" (p. 59). This victory was too easy. These risk factors are relevant because the data have been reconceptualized by selection thinking and because the parental allocation hypothesis was the only evolutionary hypothesis considered in explaining the data. Although the culture hypothesis was shown to be of the wrong type to explain the data, the test was not severe because it did not try to decide between rival evolutionary hypotheses.

Chapters 6, 7, and 8 of Daly and Wilson's book focus on the most frequent type of homicide in all cultures, in which rates of homicide are high—namely, murders of men by men. To test a hypothesis, one needs relevant evidence. Data gathered using a different theoretical approach needs to be reclassified under the guidance of an evolutionary research program so that its evolutionary significance is explicit.

For example, although Daly and Wilson (1988) state that Wolfgang's classic study found the motive in 35% of the cases studied to be "altercation of relatively trivial origin; insult, curse, jostling, etc.," they reclassified this motive category using selection thinking (pp. 170–174). Seemingly trivial conflicts are reclassified as situations of perceived risk to a male's fitness by potential actions of other males. The reclassification is predicated on reconceptualizing the data according to an evolutionary puzzle: "Why do men's minds work this way? Why would any creature place so much value on intangible social resources—on status, face, and honor—that he would risk his life pursuing them?" (Daly & Wilson, 1988, p. 131). The research program at hand guarantees an answer in terms of selection acting on the human psyche: "If selection has shaped this aspect of the human psyche, it would appear that the answer must somehow take the following form: Such social resources are (or formerly were) means to the end of fitness" (p. 131). Daly and Wilson cited statistical evidence to bear this out (e.g., Betzig's, 1985, cross-cultural data associating despotic power with extreme polygyny, but polygyny needs to be linked to these social resources for this confirmation to have much weight).

## Is the Test Procedure Well Designed?

Suppose we step inside the circle of evolutionary conceptual frameworks. Their holistic character does not make evolutionary hypotheses into self-validating pseudosuccesses. We can usually or always identify difficulties that need to be addressed to turn an evolutionary hypothesis shown to be better than nonevolutionary alternatives into one that is best among alternative evolutionary hypotheses. In a good test, the methods employed are effective in answering the research questions that drive the investigation. Should we regard questions at the level of generality (e.g., "Why do men's minds work this way?") as answered?

To decide whether a research method is effective for answering the questions addressed, one must know the level of specificity at which those questions are formulated. To see the hole in their conceptual framework, consider that their Detroit and Canadian samples are taken from murderers and victims only, not from a population that also contains nonmurderers and nonvictims. How can a sample taken from murderers (victims) tell whether someone is at risk of becoming a murderer (victim)? The data only tell, "If you are a murderer (victim), then you will probably fall into one of various categories," not "If you fall into one of various categories, then you have an increased risk of becoming a murderer (victim)."

Most people experience all the risk factors that Daly and Wilson (1988) invoked, but most people are neither killers nor victims. Because the evolutionary factors invoked do not discriminate the cases being explained from other cases, they do not explain what they are naively taken to explain. We need to compare murderers and nonmurderers, seeking some complex of psychological and environmental factors that differentiates them (e.g., as discussed in the abused become abusers literature).

Daly and Wilson's (1988) assumption that killers are normal people leads them to ignore such psychologically and/or environmentally differentiating factors. Consider men who kill their spouses after a personal history of abusing them. It is hard to believe that they are normal. A traditional psychological hypothesis for this case is obsession. Courtney Esposito (1994), an authority on spousal abuse at the Einstein Center for the Study of Violence, said, "at least 50 percent of the 3,000 abused women I've counseled have also been victims of an obsessive love, and that's a low estimate."

The person who becomes obsessed by love has an idealized view of the other person taking care of one's own needs. The obsessed man is childish, in the sense that his self-esteem depends on the other person loving him—relinquishing all control. Loving that other person to such extreme is tantamount to denying his self-worth, using love to facilitate abuse of power, insecurity, pathological jealousy, poor ability to control temper, tendency toward violence and lack of inhibitions to prevent violence when the impulse occurs, and deeper inadequacies in one's sense of self. The abusive husband typically blames the wife when she fails to do things his way, dogmatically requiring compliance with arbitrary demands. When the husband thinks he is about to lose the spouse, the cycle of demand–abuse–regret escalates toward the final act of killing her.

Obsession is a risk factor in the sense that, in the same circumstances, obsessive men are more likely to abuse and even kill their spouses than nonobsessive men. Sexual jealousy, fueled by lack of paternity confidence, is a risk factor in the sense that men are more likely to abuse and murder their spouses for reproductive security than are women. The former explains male–male differences, whereas the latter explains male–female differences. If we regard the obsession hypothesis as one about proximate causes, then we may ask why men, rather than women, are so often obsessed in ways that lead to abuse and murder. We can answer that ultimate question using the evolutionary hypothesis about paternity confidence and sexual jealousy.

Because Daly and Wilson (1988) echoed the refrain that proximate and ultimate explanations are complementary, it is misleading for them to pit their evolutionary explanations against nonevolutionary explanations. Why not combine both sorts of hypotheses to explain more of the variance? Daly and Wilson held that normal people murder because fitness-threatening situations activate evolved psychological mechanisms that lead to desperate acts. Instead, men abuse and even murder their spouses because they have normal evolved psychological mechanisms (e.g., specific to paternity confidence and sexual jealousy) activated by environmental cues; they have abnormal personalities (e.g., they are obsessive); and their evolved psychological mechanisms interact with their personality disorders to generate desperate acts (e.g., abuse and homicide).

A candidate for a better set of alternative hypotheses, both of which are evolutionary, would pit Daly and Wilson's hypothesis—that normal husbands murder their wives due to evolved psychological mechanisms specific to paternity confidence and sexual jealousy—against the hypothesis that abnormal husbands do so via an interaction of these mechanisms and, say, obsessive personality disorder, which has an evolutionary background. Progress in standards of validation requires more severe tests against data used to differentiate ever further refined sets of multiple evolutionary hypotheses.

## IMPLICATIONS FOR SCIENTIFIC PROGRESS

### How Does Progress Span Levels of Generality?

This section emphasizes the need to consciously design a temporal trajectory of hypothesis testing so as to meet the challenges posed by critics, being careful to assess the implications of our test results for what is directly being tested (a hypothesis) and for what is indirectly being tested (our guiding commitments to theory, research program, and conceptual framework). Let us turn to Buss' work in *The Evolution of Desire* (1994) and in *The Adapted Mind* (1992), and to the work of Cosmides and Tooby (1992) in *The Adapted Mind*.

Buss' ongoing research during the last decade, viewed at the highest level of generality, is driven by the opposition between standard (nonevolutionary) and evolutionary approaches to the study of human mating behavior. In *The Evolution of Desire*, Buss developed a unified evolutionary theory of human mating strategies that explain gender differences and gender conflicts in selecting, attracting, keeping, and replacing a mate. The significance of his test results is clear with respect to theory. His test results support his theory, but his theory was constructed to explain the body of test results he generated during the last decade, which other researchers have replicated.

His test results are unclear with respect to research programs. We could interpret what they mean in terms of either the Daly–Wilson program, which articulated the PCI model stated in *Homicide*, or the Cosmides–Tooby program, which articulated the *Integrated Causal Model* (ICM) stated in *The Adapted Mind*. In the acknowledgments of *The Evolution of Desire*, Buss gave credit to Cosmides and Tooby, Daly and Wilson, and Symons for their influence on his own thinking about human mating strategies, and hence, it can be interpreted as an articulation of both programs in tandem.

Cosmides and Tooby presented Buss' article in *The Adapted Mind* as a set of findings about domain-specific psychological mechanisms that evolved during the Pleistocene—the sort of mechanisms posited in their ICM. *The Evolution of Desire* is the culmination of a conception of social conflict between and within the genders that has been emerging over the years in Buss' research—one that makes use of the PCI model in relation to human mating. As Lakatos (1987) noted, research programs need not appear instantly, but may emerge during a lengthy gestation period (pp. 191–194).

For any test of hypotheses in evolutionary psychology, one can always come up with objections, regardless of whether the hypothesis fits the data. Evolutionists retain evolutionary hypotheses despite negative test results. Antievolutionists (antisociobiologists) remain suspicious of evolutionary hypotheses despite positive test results. This is a sign of deeper commitments. By making these deeper commitments explicit, we bring them within our control and make progress using abduction (Holcomb, 1996).

The problem of dealing with objections to evolutionary hypotheses from critics suspicious of applying evolutionary theory to human behavior plays a central role in *The Adapted Mind*. Cosmides and Tooby identified the deeper commitments that launch a million criticisms of evolutionary hypotheses in *The Adapted Mind*. They called it the *Standard Social Science Model* (SSSM)—a model that posits that all of the content of mind and behavior is supplied by socialization into one's culture, and so utilizes a "learning-plus-culture" conceptual framework. They launched a series of devastating objections against the SSSM, undermining the generalizations that function as the sources of the criticisms of evolutionary hypotheses.

Neutralizing the traditional learning-plus-culture alternative set of explanatory resources to evolutionary hypotheses makes for progress in two ways. First, we are not hostages to such basic commitments as arbitrary or dogmatic starting points because we can evaluate them at their own level of analysis. Second, it opens the way for evolutionists to free themselves from the need to test their hypotheses against nonevolutionary alternatives. We can simply refer to their conceptual arguments against the SSSM (assuming that their refutation is persuasive) and move into the heart of our evolutionary research problems, testing evolutionary hypotheses against more and more refined evolutionary hypotheses.

## How Are Tests Responses to Challenges?

The preceding themes have implications for the question of what constitutes genuine progress in evolutionary psychology. Science uses the general intellectual method of trying to defend a position against its most severe objections. This suggests a challenge–response model of scientific progress.

Among other things, Buss' chapter in *The Adapted Mind* on evolved mate preference mechanisms summarized his empirical findings on mate preferences, both within the United States and across 33 countries. To tell whether this work constitutes progress, we have to view it as a study within an ongoing research project, comparing work at successive time intervals. Buss' address at the sixth annual conference for Human Behavior and Evolution Society provides testimony that he designs his tests so that they meet the objections posed by critics.

Why do men pick young women so often as mates? A decade ago, it was thought that men did so because they were insecure, they needed to dominate women, and they found younger women easier to dominate than older women. Our culture imputes value to attractiveness in young women, and women are supposed to be submissive, whereas men are supposed to be dominant. More generally, how can we account for gender differences? Answers appealed to learning, culture, and patriarchy. The standard evolutionary thesis that men prefer women showing signs of fertility (e.g., youth, attractiveness, healthiness) and women prefer men showing signs of paternal investment of resources (e.g., willingness to commit wealth, status, and power to them) was rejected out of hand.

Buss constructed a prediction from the learning-plus-culture answer: The same pattern in United States culture would not be found in other cultures. In response, his cross-cultural data showed that standards of physical attractiveness are not so arbitrary and culture-bound as suspected. Predictions on how individuals of each sex value earning capacity, ambition-industriousness, youth, physical attractiveness, and chastity were tested using questionnaire data from 10,047 respondents in 33 countries. Demographic data were used to verify the validity of the questionnaire responses in 27 of these countries. This refutation was challenged on the grounds that his data were on desires, not actual behavior. In response, he developed further data showing that human mating behavior fits evolutionary hypotheses about selection pressures, mate preference mechanisms, and their outcomes for actual mate choice. Critics countered that the cause of gender differences is patriarchal culture, which is found throughout all these cultures.

Buss teased a prediction out of the patriarchy answer: If women could control resources, they would not need men with resources. In response, his data showed that successful women show stronger preferences for men with higher resources than less successful women. There is no correlation between economic inequality between the sexes and women marrying up in status, wealth, and power. Buss did not address the objection that evolutionary theory (adaptationism) and nonevolutionary theory (learning plus culture) each could be used to generate numerous different predictions about such matters. The prior discussion of deductivism emphasized the need for confidence that the theory really does imply the prediction under test. One might argue that women have been so thoroughly conditioned by patriarchy that, even when they have plenty of resources, they still want men with more resources. The moral is not that adaptationist and learning-plus-culture hypotheses are unfalsifiable, and hence unscientific; instead, we should not expect purely empirical falsification of such high-level generalizations, theories, or research programs. The number of hypotheses we can devise to apply an approach to the facts increases with the generality of the approach.

High-level progress is determined by the overall track record of successes and failures, not by the set of strengths and weaknesses at a given time. There is a double standard in method: Each side modifies their own predictions on refutation to save their own explanatory approach, but regards each falsified prediction on the other side as instantaneously refuting that approach. Instead, we should assess the track record of tests between evolutionary and standard accounts of patriarchy.

## How Are Domains Dependent
## on Conceptual Frameworks?

Buss joked that, whereas in the past the National Science Foundation (NSF) would not fund evolutionary research projects unless they could rule out all nonevolutionary explanations, now NSF will not fund nonevolutionary research projects unless they can rule out all evolutionary explanations. Is that progress? Yes, but the issue is subtle. Evolutionary and nonevolutionary hypotheses can be incompatible when they happen to posit incompatible proximate mechanisms, but not because of the type of fields they are.

Two explanations are incompatible only if they are explanations of the same facts. We have seen that the facts given evolutionary explanation are already classified (conceptualized) so that they are relevant to evolutionary theory (i.e., they are evolutionarily significant facts). The facts explained by nonevolutionary explanations are not so classified, and so are evolutionarily insignificant facts. Ironically, evolutionary and nonevolutionary explanations typically do try to explain the same phenomena, expressed in everyday theory-neutral language, but do not try to explain the same phenomena, expressed in scientific theory-laden language.

It becomes obvious, on identifying implicit conceptual frameworks, that evolutionary studies explain facts already processed for their relevance to evolutionary theory. For example, let us identify the conceptual framework Buss used in his chapter in *The Adapted Mind*. It specifies each of the following components of explanation: (a) the explanatory problem addressed (e.g., How tightly are inter- and intrasexual selection linked?); (b) the facts to be explained (e.g., Why do human females and males differ cross-culturally in their behavior in species-typical ways?); (c) the factors invoked to do the explaining (e.g., selection pressures and mate preference mechanisms in hunter–gatherers); and (d) the specific explanatory objectives in advancing inquiry (e.g., to show that the evolution of psychological mechanisms cannot be understood without identifying the class of acts generated by each psychological mechanism).

This conceptual framework is implicit in his methodology, which moves through the following sequences of steps: act nominations (e.g., name things people do to keep their mates), classification of acts into tactics (classify "He called her to see who she was with" as an act of vigilance), assess the frequency with which each act and tactic is performed, and evaluate the effectiveness of acts and tactics at performing the goal of mate retention. Here, acts are classified into tactics for carrying out evolved reproductive strategies.

To evaluate how well a competing hypothesis would explain the phenomena, we ask two questions. If it were true, how well would it succeed in explaining the puzzling or anomalous aspect of the phenomenon? Would it give a deeper understanding of the phenomenon, and not merely a truistic restatement of it?

We have seen that the meaning of Buss' hypotheses incorporates his own conceptual framework. In light of this context, learning, culture, and patriarchy are truistic restatements of what is to be explained. Evolutionary hypotheses take learning, culture, and so on into account as part of the phenomena to be explained, rather than as a rival set of explanatory factors. Following Tooby and Cosmides' (1992) program for applying evolutionary theory to organisms having mind and culture, Buss' theory explains human behavioral differences as individually, historically, and culturally variable mixes of behavioral acts and tactics that instantiate species-typical repertoires of domain-specific strategies.

## How Can We Learn From Discrepancies?

Genuine progress occurs when the cycle of constructing, revising, and abandoning evolutionary hypotheses leads to new ones that will better explain the totality of better evidence about evolutionarily significant features of behavior. Buss' investigation of discrepancies between his theoretical expectations about men's preference for virgins and empirical outcomes of his questionnaires led him toward new hypotheses and to a new theory of conflict elaborated in *The Evolution of Desire*. If we analyze progress as refinement, that is progress.

Another evolutionary prediction is that, due to the problem of paternity confidence, men are expected to value women's chastity more than women value men's chastity. Buss' data showed that chastity valuation shows greater cross-cultural variability than any other mate characteristic studied. So he abandoned the presumption that virginity per se is key, holding that men solve the problem of paternity confidence in other ways, as evident from the fact that men's number one desire for a long-term mate is fidelity. This move suggested that we should look at both short- and long-term mate preferences. Different reproductive problems apply to short- and long-term matings. But it had been supposed that women do not have short-term strategies because they want men with high paternal investment. Women would not pursue a strategy detrimental to their fitness. Hence, if women have short-term mates, they must have short-term strategies.

Here, new concepts are introduced to deal with discrepancies between theoretical expectation and observed facts that maintain as much of the basic approach as possible. This episode illustrates the conception of progress as refinement, whereby progress is made by working to optimize responses to challenges. The best response meets the challenge posed by discrepancies between theory and data in the most defensible manner, maximizing the severity of the challenge and minimizing revisions in the basic approach. To evaluate the progress-inducing effectiveness of a response, we ask three questions. Does the response treat the challenge in its most severe form, or does it underestimate the critical force of the challenge? Does the response minimize revision of what is being challenged, or does it give up too much of what is essential to one's research program and theory? Does the response meet the challenge in the most defensible way, or does it transform one difficulty into another without gain?

By exploring contexts in which desires shift, Buss' conceptual innovations lead to the beginning of a theory of social conflict—a further articulation of the PCI program. To understand social conflict between and within the sexes, one must examine: (a) men imposing fitness costs on men (e.g., Daly & Wilson's [1988] data on homicide, 70% or so of which is the murder of men by men as each strives to gain in relative status, wealth, and power); (b) men imposing fitness costs on women (e.g., Daly & Wilson's data on men abusing and killing their spouses as a result of motivation to gain access to or monopolize women's sexuality); (c) women imposing fitness costs on women (Buss' data on women derogating competitors' appearances as women try to control other women's sexuality); and (d) women imposing fitness costs on men (Buss' data on women manipulating their men toward sexual exclusivity or derogating their status).

Buss' (1994) *The Evolution of Desire* is the culmination of these developments, citing extensive empirical findings in support of his theory that conflict results from strategic interference and that negative emotions signal interference between the strategies of those involved. It is obvious that research on the evolution of desire has made holistic progress (i.e., following up discrepancies has refined hypotheses, theories, concepts, data, and methods, and gives us a better understanding). Studies of human mating continue to use Buss' methodology to good effect (e.g., Greenlees & McGrew, 1994; Walters & Crawford, 1994). This sort of development is a sign of scientific progress.

## How Are Research Programs Evaluated?

Evolutionary research programs can be evaluated for their external success, providing superior alternatives to contrary antievolutionary presuppositions at their own level of analysis.

Because traditional psychologists refuse to accept evolutionary hypotheses, although they fit the data, further data will not convert them. What is needed is to identify and undermine the source(s) of the objections. Tooby and Cosmides (1992) do this in *The Adapted Mind*, identifying the source in the SSSM and arguing for their alternative research program for applying evolutionary theory to humans, which they called the ICM. The SSSM states that no differences in human social behavior are biologically caused, all psychological mechanisms are general purpose and contain no content specificity, and all of the content of mind and behavior is supplied by socialization into one's culture. Someone who reasoned according to the SSSM would find evolution irrelevant to anything specific about human behavior, the fundamental issue between evolutionary psychologists and their critics. Tooby and Cosmides attacked the SSSM, a critique comparable to that made in Alexander's (1979) *Darwinism and Human Affairs*. One might evaluate their success here by addressing the open question of whether the attack really is devastating, whether the informed critics really are committed to the SSSM or merely criticized as if they are, or whether the SSSM is a caricature.

Refutation of the SSSM does not mean that the ICM is the best or even a plausible way to study evolution, mind, and culture. Evolutionary research programs can also be evaluated for their internal success, providing the basis for attaining well-reasoned and well-tested evolutionary hypotheses. It is argued here that they fail to acknowledge serious limitations and difficulties in the method inherent in the ICM, and in their direct evidence for content specificity in reasoning (Holcomb, 1994).

The theoretical core of the ICM states that the mind contains evolved information-processing mechanisms carried in the nervous systems, that these mechanisms are adaptations produced by natural selection in Pleistocene ancestral environments, that these adaptations are functionally specialized, and that the content of culture arises from content-dependent psychologies of individuals interacting in evolving populations (Tooby & Cosmides, 1992). The method advocated in the ICM consists in three phases. First, generate hypotheses about the types of physical and intellectual adaptive problems encountered by our ancestors living during the Pleistocene epoch. Second, generate hypotheses about the types of psychological adaptations that would have solved them. Third, test whether those psychological adaptations still exist, say, in the form of species-wide psychological bias or irrational behavior, distinguishing current effects from past adaptations.

Like other chapters in *The Adapted Mind*, Buss' failed to use this powerful new methodology to any great extent. It lapsed into reporting evidence that supports explanations of known facts without a detailed match between hypotheses and adaptive demands of Pleistocene conditions of human life. Instead, adaptation was identified by intuitive appreciation of complex design in a situation of ignorance of what our Pleistocene ancestors were doing. Such explanations are too ad hoc, speculative, and adaptationist to be valid.

In deciding whether to follow a research program, we ask: Would adopting it give us the simplest overall set of beliefs consistent with the observed facts? This question is vital to inference to the best explanation because simpler explanations are preferable to complex ones, other things being equal. However, too much simplicity in the wrong place obscures matters. For instance, paleoanthropology shows that different hominoid traits evolved at different times in different contexts in different ancestral populations and species. Rather than one ancestral environment, there are many. Different environmental variables and parameters are relevant to different evolved traits. In another instance, Tooby and Cosmides spoke as if for every adaptive problem there is a solution, for every solution there is a function, for every function there is a cognitive module, and for every module there is a special built-in content sensitivity. Such artificial, neat correspondence is hard to believe. Just how specific are our domain-specific mechanisms is a crucial question for which they give no method of study.

Further, although our psyches contain functionally specialized adaptations, and some of our psychological mechanisms may be content specific, these two facts do not logically imply that functionally specialized adaptations must be content specific. The link is motivated by prior commitment to computationalist cognitive psychology. Let us grant that we can write more realistic computer programs that simulate actual behavior by making content-specific assumptions in commands, thereby narrowing down the combinatorial explosion of logically possible behaviors to the small repertoire of witnessed behavior sequences. That may tell us more about computationalist functionalism than about organisms. Who makes assumptions that rule out combinatorial explosion, the organism or the scientist interpreting the organism? Content specificity may be an artifact of computation talk. The simplicity of philosophically naive realism blocks needed critical reflection.

Indeed, the concept of content dependence in computationalist psychology is so broad that it covers information processing in reasoning, emotion, motivation, and motor control, no matter whether they occur in humans, organisms without minds, or computers. The concept of content specificity here is not univocal, and its vague generality obscures differences that evolutionists would like to explain.

The only direct evidence for content specificity in reasoning given in *The Adapted Mind* is the Wason selection task (Cosmides & Tooby, 1992). Given the ICM program, it is postulated that increased logical capability during social exchange has been selected for in ancestral environments. Evolution brings about two design features: The human mind contains algorithms that produce and operate on cost–benefit representations of exchange interactions; it includes inferential procedures that use social exchange to enhance fitness. In the Wason task, subjects complete various tasks for which the logical answer is the same (P and not-Q, where P and Q are sentences). When topics and contents of P and Q are varied, the number of responses that match the logical answer also vary. This experimental result has been interpreted in terms of inference to the best explanation:

> Cosmides demonstrated that some content effects in performance on the Wason selection task can best be explained and predicted if the subject matter of the test is interpreted in terms of social exchange theory, which

analyses contracts between individuals, the consequences of cheating on the contracts, and methods of detecting cheaters. Cosmides therefore argued that the content-dependent error rate in reasoning may reflect the action of Darwinian algorithms that evolved in ancestral human beings to identify rapidly and accurately others who cheat on a social contract by accepting its benefits without paying its costs. (Crawford & Anderson, 1989, p. 1454)

They claimed that social exchange theory explains these content-dependent effects better than does deductive or inductive logic. This conclusion faces difficulties that go to the issue of whether we have a good test (Holcomb, 1994). It is not implied here that the theory is wrong, just that the argument for it is weak.

One alternative hypothesis is that we have a built-in deductive logic module responsible for these content effects. Logicians are quick to point out that their test is not a well-designed test of deductive logic. Cosmides and Tooby misused material conditionals of sentential deductive logic to symbolize such social contract claims as, "If anyone takes the benefit, then that person is obligated to pay the cost." Sentential deductive logic cannot adequately symbolize the reasoning employed here. Sentential logic can handle reasoning that turns on sentence connectives (in this sentence, "if . . . then"), but not predicates ("that person"), quantifers ("anyone"), or the modal operators necessarily and possibly ("obligated" and "permitted"). The appropriate deductive logic for symbolizing and assessing the reasoning here should be a quantified (modal) deontic logic (e.g., as found in Gensler, 1990). Cosmides and Tooby, in effect, ignored logical structure and then announced that we do not and/or should not reason logically. Their numerous blunders in translating English into logic and in understanding relations among formal systems means not only renders their test ill designed, but also indicates that their own theory of social exchanges misconceives essential elements in social contracts.

The test is indecisive because, to eliminate the deductive logic hypothesis, one would have to eliminate all forms of deductive logic (syllogistic, sentential, predicate, and modal forms of each) in all of their various versions, which are many.

The test is also inappropriate because deductive logic requires content-specific effects. Deductive logic cannot be used unless one translates natural language into its symbolic notation, and doing so correctly requires knowing the meanings of natural language sentences. Deductivists would posit two modules—a reasoning module in which the validity of inferences is content independent, and a translation module involving content specificity. The dichotomy presupposed by the test is confused.

Another alternative hypothesis is that we have a built-in inductive logic module responsible for content-dependent effects. Because whether an inductive inference is strong or weak depends on its content, this hypothesis deserves full exploration. The test is not a good test of the inductive logic hypothesis because a double standard is used to reject it. The experiments involve unfamiliar terms. The problem of how we reason about unfamiliar topics is a problem for both the Darwinian algorithm and the inductive logic hypothesis. Cosmides and Tooby permitted their own Darwinian algorithms, but not the inductive hypothesis, to operate in new contexts to structure new experiences.

Again, the test is not decisive because they do not consider all the sorts of inductive logic in all of their various versions. The rule of induction previously discussed can be interpreted by associationist psychology to relate the strength of association between A and B to their relative frequency as instances of types. Other nondeductive inference rules include the counterinductive rule, the a priori rule, the Bayesian inference rule, and the abductive rule advocated herein.

In addition, logicians have worked to deal with some sorts of content effects for years by developing relevance logics. These need to be taken into account, as well as pragmatic reasoning schemata. We could construct explanations for the evolution of any of these types of reasoning modules. Logicians have standard ways of dealing with content effects. Evolutionists jumped to a conclusion when they rallied behind the Cosmides–Tooby hypothesis without first clarifying how to construct alternative evolutionary and nonevolutionary hypotheses for a given logic, without surveying all the pertinent alternatives, and without giving them their due consideration in test design.

Stepping back from this sort of critique, we have to ask ourselves what conclusion can be drawn from a good criticism of a scientific study. This sort of critique, as levied in detail by Davies, Fetzer, and Foster (1995), leaves the impression that Cosmides and Tooby are ignorant of logic and get the logic all wrong, that their work is highly overrated, that their experiment provides no basis for drawing a justifiable conclusion about the evolutionary or deductive/inductive hypotheses, and that their social contract theory is not about genuine social contracts.

However, Gigerenzer and Hug (1992) set this critique within a more positive, constructive outlook. What counts as relevant logical structure depends on logical theory. There is a continuum between the poles of content dependence and content independence. The concept of a social contract should be disentangled from the concept of a cheater-detection algorithm, whose use turns on whether a person is cued into the perspective of a party who can be cheated. That pragmatic variable, not the perception of the rule as a social contract per se, is responsible for Cosmides and Tooby's results, which they replicated. They concluded, despite anticipating some of the points made by Davies, Fetzer, and Foster (1995), that the results indeed support the social contract hypothesis.

The moral is that good criticisms can be viewed in two ways: as devastating to a test of an evolutionary hypothesis or as something to be taken into account in future work on investigating that hypothesis. To decide what conclusions to draw from test results and whether the tests really advance research are often subtle matters indeed. They involve mechanical rules of method as well as something that brings the psychosocial dimensions of science into the heart of scientific method: both good sense and trained judgment (i.e., informed, good judgment).

## CONCLUSION

This chapter identified a number of serious issues that confront efforts to make evolutionary psychology as scientific as possible. To decide whether an evolutionary hypothesis is validated depends on whether it is the best among available evolutionary hypotheses for explaining the evolutionarily significant data. Conclusions drawn from a test of an hypothesis should be informed by insight into its presuppositions at multiple levels of generality. A test of a hypothesis has indirect import for the adequacy of its theoretical, programmatic, and conceptual presuppositions. Because tests show nothing by themselves, but function only within the context of argumentation, the name of the game is to work on improving evolutionary arguments. The question is not whether the deep structure of science enters into hypothesis testing, but whether evolutionary psychologists will use it to their advantage in constructing persuasive arguments.

## REFERENCES

Alexander, R. (1979). *Darwinism and human affairs.* Seattle, WA: University of Washington Press.

Alexander, R. (1987). *The biology of moral systems.* Hawthorne, NY: Aldine deGruyter.

Barkow, J., Cosmides, L., & Tooby, J. (1992). *The adapted mind: Evolutionary psychology and the generation of culture.* New York: Oxford University Press.

Betzig, L. L. (1985). *Despotism and differential reproduction: A Darwinian view of history.* Hawthorne, NY: Aldine deGruyter.

Boyd, R., & Richerson, P. J. (1985). *Culture and the evolutionary process.* Chicago: University of Chicago Press.

Buss, D. (1992). Mate preference mechanisms: Consequences for partner choice and intrasexual competition. In J. Barkow, L. Cosmides, & J. Tooby (Eds.), *The adapted mind: Evolutionary psychology and the generation of culture* (pp. 249–266). New York: Oxford University Press.

Buss, D. (1994). *The evolution of desire.* New York: Basic Books.

Cosmides, L., & Tooby, J. (1992). Cognitive adaptations for social exchange. In J. Barkow, L. Cosmides, & J. Tooby (Eds.), *The adapted mind: Evolutionary psychology and the generation of culture* (pp. 163–228). New York: Oxford University Press.

Crawford, C., & Anderson, J. (1989). Sociobiology: An environmentalist discipline? *American Psychologist, 44*(2), 1449–1459.

Daly, M., & Wilson, M. (1988). *Homicide.* New York: Aldine deGruyter.

Davies, P., Fetzer, H., & Foster, T. (1995). Logical reasoning and domain specificity: A critique of the social exchange theory of reasoning. *Biology and Philosophy, 10*(1), 1–37.

Duhem, P. (1987). Physical theory and experiment. In J. Kourany (Ed.), *Scientific knowledge: Basic issues in the philosophy of science* (pp. 158–169). Belmont, CA: Wadsworth.

Esposito, C. (1994, May). As quoted from live interview in the *Lexington Herald Leader* (Section A). Lexington, KY.

Gensler, H. (1990). *Symbolic logic: Classical and advanced systems.* Englewood Cliffs, NJ: Prentice-Hall.

Gigerenzer, G., & Hug, K. (1992). Domain-specific reasoning: Social contracts, cheating, and perspective change. *Cognition, 43,* 127–171.

Greenlees, I., & McGrew, W. (1994). Sex and age differences in preferences and tactics of mate attraction: Analysis of published advertisements. *Ethology and Sociobiology, 15,* 59–72.

Harman, G. (1989). The inference to the best explanation. In B. Brody & R. Grandy (Eds.), *Readings in the philosophy of science* (pp. 323–328). Englewood Cliffs, NJ: Prentice-Hall.

Holcomb, H. (1993). *Sociobiology, sex, and science.* Albany, NY: SUNY Press.

Holcomb, H. (1994). Evolved psychological mechanisms and content-specificity. *Anthropology of Consciousness, 5*(4), 19–23.

Holcomb, H. (1996). Just-so stories and inference to the best explanation in evolutionary psychology. *Minds and Machines, 6,* 525–540.

Kuhn, T. (1987). The function of dogma in scientific research. In J. Kourany (Ed.), *Scientific knowledge: Basic issues in the philosophy of science* (pp. 253–265). Belmont, CA: Wadsworth.

Lakatos, I. (1987). Falsification and the methodology of scientific research programs. In J. Kourany (Ed.), *Scientific knowledge: Basic issues in the philosophy of science* (pp. 170–196). Belmont, CA: Wadsworth.

Lumsden, C., & Wilson, E. O. (1981). *Genes, mind and culture.* Cambridge, MA: Harvard University Press.

Popper, K. (1987). Science: Conjecture and refutations. In J. Kourany (Ed.), *Scientific knowledge: Basic issues in the philosophy of science* (pp. 139–157). Belmont, CA: Wadsworth.

Symons, D. (1979). *The evolution of human sexuality.* New York: Oxford University Press.

Tooby, J., & Cosmides, L. (1992). The psychological foundations of culture. In J. Barkow, L. Cosmides, & J. Tooby (Eds.), *The adapted mind: Evolutionary psychology and the generation of culture* (pp. ). New York: Oxford University Press.

Walters, S., & Crawford, C. (1994). The importance of mate attraction for intrasexual competition in men and women. *Ethology and Sociobiology, 15,* 5–30.

# III

## APPLICATIONS

The 11 chapters in the final section of this book illustrate how a variety of researchers and scholars are currently using evolutionary thinking to explain psychological phenomena. This section opens with a chapter on the evolution of moral behavior (chap. 11), a topic that was of great concern to Darwin and that is currently receiving considerable attention from a variety of writers. Chapter 12 examines the field of developmental psychology from the perspective of evolutionary theory. It begins with an interesting analysis of the relationship between the fetus and its host, or mother, presents adolescence as the central transitional stage of development, and ends with an examination of evolutionary explanations of aging.

Chapter 13 supplies a review of evolutionary theory and the research it has inspired on mate selection, examining the strategies males and females use when they choose sexual and marital partners. In chapter 14, evolutionary theory is used as a framework for accounting for statistics on family violence, making and supporting predictions quite different from those made by traditional social scientists.

Charles Darwin and Sigmund Freud are two of the most important thinkers since the Renaissance. Chapter 15, entitled, "PsychoDarwinism: The New Synthesis of Darwin and Freud," attempts to integrate the theory of evolution and psychoanalysis.

Evolutionary psychology focuses on the architecture of the mind. Chapter 16 demonstrates how evolutionary theory can be used to help explain why people think and feel the way they do. Like chapter 14, chapter 17 uses evolutionary theory to explain aggression. In chapter 14, the focus is on murder; chapter 17 focuses on sexual aggression, especially rape. Research on nonhuman animals is used to help explain sexual aggression in humans. In a hopeful vein, evidence is presented that suggests rape is not a first choice strategy.

Evolutionary theory is commonly associated with sexual and aggressive behaviors, less so with the study of beauty. However, chapter 18 tackles the difficult problem of explaining how preferences for particular aesthetic tastes may have evolved. This task is difficult because it is not obvious how aesthetic preferences can enhance fitness. Chapter 19 employs evolutionary perspectives not only to examine the global environmental crisis we, as a species, are facing, but also to explain why we are doing so little about it.

Sex differences is one of the most controversial topics in contemporary psychology. Chapter 20 adduces strong and consistent evidence of sex differences in visual–spatial abilities and explains how these abilities may have been selected in our ancestral environment because they enhanced the ability of men and women to perform the task in which they specialized. Finally, employing findings from the development of pidgin and Creole languages in modern people, chapter 21 takes on the challenge of explaining how language could have evolved in the human species.

# 11

## The Evolution of Moral Behaviors

Dennis L. Krebs
*Simon Fraser University*

The goal of this chapter is to illustrate how evolutionary theory can help explain moral behaviors. There are three main models of morality in psychology: psychoanalytic, social learning, and cognitive-developmental. In the psychoanalytic model, infants are assumed to inherit powerful sexual and aggressive instincts that induce immoral desires. Parents oppose the satisfaction of these animal urges, which creates the classic Oedipal and Electra conflicts. Around 4 years of age, children resolve these conflicts by identifying with the parent of the opposite sex and introjecting his or her superego, or conscience. In psychoanalytic theory, behaving morally entails constraining instinctual, id-based, pleasure-seeking urges.

In the social learning model, infants are viewed as infinitely plastic—shaped by parents and other socializing agents to behave in moral or immoral ways. Social learning theorists emphasize the moralizing effects of modeling and vicarious reinforcement. In social learning theory, behaving morally equates to conforming to the norms of society and entails obeying the dictates of authorities.

For the past three decades, Kohlberg's (1984) cognitive-developmental model of morality has been regnant in psychology. According to Kohlberg, children become moral in stages as they develop the capacity to engage in increasingly sophisticated forms of moral reasoning. Kohlberg assumed that the cognitive structures people develop to solve moral problems are structures of the whole (i.e., they organize all moral thinking), and that later developing structures transpose and displace earlier structures. It follows that Kohlberg expected the structure of moral judgment to be highly consistent within people across varying content. In cognitive–developmental theory, behaving morally entails figuring out the most just solution to moral problems and acting accordingly.

Kohlberg's model of morality has been criticized by Gilligan (1982, 1988) and others for emphasizing what they consider to be the masculine, justice-based aspect of morality at the expense of the more feminine, care-based aspect. According to Gilligan (1982), females view moral issues in more care-based ways than males do. In Gilligan's model, behaving morally entails caring for others and assuming responsibility for their welfare.

Each psychological model of morality captures part of the process. Morality involves the self-control necessary to resist animal urges, conformity to social norms, deference to legitimate authorities, understanding why certain acts are right and wrong, and caring for others. However, each model also neglects important aspects of morality and emphasizes particular aspects at the expense of others. I believe evolutionary theory is equipped to integrate psychological approaches to morality, resolve many of their differences, and steer the study of morality in new, more productive directions.

## ON EVOLUTION AND MORALITY

When we think of biologically evolved dispositions, appetites such as gluttony, greed, envy, lust, sloth, pride, and anger (the seven deadly sins) come most readily to mind. Like psychoanalysts, most people assume that instincts we inherit are fundamentally immoral in nature. Like learning theorists, most people assume the source of morality is nurture: Children must be taught to behave morally. The idea that moral traits, dispositions, and behaviors can evolve biologically seems, on first glance, hopelessly misguided. If nature selects traits that enhance individuals' fitness, and if, by definition, moral traits induce individuals to resist the temptation to enhance their fitness at the expense of others, how could moral traits evolve?

The idea that moral dispositions and behaviors cannot evolve biologically is based on the fallacious assumption that moral traits constrain individuals from propagating their genes. This assumption is fallacious for two reasons. First, as Hamilton (1964) explained, individuals may sacrifice themselves to propagate replicas of their genes in their kin. Although such self-sacrificial behaviors are selfish genetically (i.e., they foster the propagation of the genes that induce them), they are altruistic at an individual level of analysis (Krebs, 1987).

Second, advancing one's interests at the expense of others may not be as effective a strategy as other, more moral alternatives. Imagine an original group of individuals. One of the strategies each individual could adopt—in some senses, the most basic strategy—is to pursue his or her interests individually with no regard for and, if resources were limited, at the expense of other members of the group. The problem with this uncompromisingly selfish strategy is that, as game theorists such as Axelrod and Hamilton (1981) have shown, it may not pay off (i.e., it may not enhance inclusive fitness) as well as less selfish strategies.

Game theorists have found that at least one cooperative strategy—tit-for-tat reciprocity—may pay off better than selfish individualism (Axelrod & Hamilton, 1981). I believe the principle that makes reciprocity such an effective strategy is the same principle that has mediated the evolution of morality: Individuals in social species may obtain more resources for themselves by cooperating with and by assisting some, but not all, members of their groups than by exploiting them or going it alone. In social species, it is in individuals' ultimate interest to make sacrifices to ensure the preservation of some members of their groups because individuals need others to propagate their genes (i.e., to survive, reproduce, and foster the fitness of their offspring or relatives). If genes that disposed our ancestors toward moral behaviors enhanced their inclusive fitness more than genes that disposed them toward immoral behaviors, genes for (cf. Bailey, chap. 6, this volume) such moral behaviors would have evolved.

The unconstrained pursuit of individual interests and the exploitation of others are ineffective interpersonal strategies for three main reasons. First, some resources are beyond the reach of individuals acting alone. Second, unconstrained selfishness may destroy the system of cooperation on which it feeds. Third, others are evolved to resist being exploited. In effect, individuals in cooperative groups agree to adopt moral strategies of interaction to maximize their mutual gain, although not necessarily consciously or explicitly. Moral rules uphold these strategies, defining the investments (e.g., duties) each individual is expected to make to obtain the returns (e.g., rights).

According to Damon and Hart (1992), "there have been three primary definitions of morality, each reflecting a certain philosophical tradition and leading to a focus on particular sorts of human behavior" (p. 445). Social learning theorists have defined morality in terms of respect for rules, which involves obedience to authority. Cognitive developmentalists such as Kohlberg (1984), as well as philosophers such as Rawls (1971), have defined morality in terms of justice, which involves rights, duties, contracts, and principles of fairness. Critics of Kohlberg's model of morality, such as Eisenberg (1986) and Gilligan (1982, 1986), have defined morality in terms of care, which involves altruism, devotion, and investments in relationships. I would add a fourth, psychoanalytic, definition based on resisting temptation.

The focus of this chapter is on the evolution of deferential, cooperative, caring, and temptation-resisting forms of behavior, often in nonhuman animals. This focus is different from that of cognitive-developmental psychologists, who seek to explain the ontogenetic development of moral judgment. Cognitive-developmental theorists such as Kohlberg would object to the notion that any form of behavior, especially in nonhuman animals, can be characterized as moral from the outside, in terms of its form or consequences. Indeed, Kohlberg (1984) argued that the only behaviors that qualify as moral are those that are guided by the intention to implement rational, moral decisions.

This issue is dealt with by aiming to explain how types of behavior that came to be labeled *moral* evolved. My theory on the relation between moral judgment and moral behavior is that the types of behavior that came to be labeled *right, wrong, good,* and *bad* evolved before the labels; moral labels evolved before articulated moral rules, and articulated moral rules evolved before the moral judgments people invoke to uphold them. I believe this sequence progressed phylogenetically in much the same way that Piaget (1932) suggested it progresses ontogenetically: Our ancestors, like the children Piaget observed, invoked moral judgments to uphold forms of behavior mediated by naturally selected dispositions. This chapter focuses mainly on the evolution of behaviors that came to be labeled moral, reserving the discussion of the evolution of moral rules and judgments for another forum.

Explaining how moral traits can evolve will open the door for the possibility that individuals—nonhuman and human alike—may be naturally good, or good by nature. This chapter offers evidence in support of this pleasant proposition, but ends up arguing that such goodness is, at best, only part of the story. All moral systems are potentially vulnerable to the temptation for individuals to maximize their gains by cheating, so all moral systems contain antidotes to cheating, which often involve moral sanctions. It is suggested here that the ability of individuals to detect cheating and their proclivity to punish it will vary in accordance with the costs and benefits of catching and punishing cheaters. All moral systems contain checks and balances, some more tenuous than others. What ends up evolving in individuals is the capacity to develop conditional strategies: to behave morally when it pays off, to cheat when one believes one can get away with it, and to catch and punish cheaters when it is to one's advantage.

The remainder of this chapter attempts to explain how behaviors that uphold authority, justice, and care can evolve biologically, and how these three aspects of morality may have evolved in the human species. It accounts for the evolution of respect for authority primarily in terms of the adaptive value of deference, the evolution of justice primarily in terms of the adaptive value of cooperation, and the evolution of care primarily in terms of the adaptive value of mating and assisting kin. Following this, it considers the possibility that moral traits have evolved through group selection, and then briefly discusses the evolution of cheating, antidotes to cheating, deception, and self-deception. Finally, it revisits the psychological theories outlined in the opening to see how they look from the perspective of evolutionary theory.

## THE EVOLUTION OF RESPECT FOR AUTHORITY

Two dogs confront one another. They bare their fangs, their fur bristles, they growl, and, perhaps, they engage in combat. Soon the smaller or weaker of the two turns and runs, or rolls over and bears its neck. Dominance has been established; from that point on, the weaker defers to the stronger. Dominance and subordination are organizing principles in most social species. The pecking order of chickens is a familiar example. Submissive individuals of many species groom more dominant individuals and beg favors from them in return. Dominant individuals frequently protect subordinates and serve a policing function, breaking up fights and maintaining order within the group.

The principle underlying the evolution of the deferential behavior of subordinates is simple: Faced with a Hobson's choice between the costs of deference and defiance, subordinate individuals minimize their losses by deferring to those who are more powerful than they. Individuals who defer to those who can harm them and ingratiate to those who can help them may be more likely than individuals who do not to survive and reproduce offspring who inherit the genes that induce such conditionally deferential dispositions.

Deference should be particularly adaptive in social species with dominance hierarchies and in polygynous species such as elephant seals and gorillas with intense male–male competition for females. Physical dimorphism may supply a rough index of the adaptive value of deference in a species. Physically small, weak individuals should, of course, be more deferential than larger, stronger individuals. Because individuals are both dominant to those below them in dominance hierarchies and subordinate to those above them, all individuals should inherit dispositions that mediate both dominant and submissive behaviors, and these dispositions should be activated by the relative power of others. In relatively large multimale, multifemale groups, such as those formed by chimpanzees, one would expect the ability to form coalitions to supersede the power of physical strength. In general, the prominence of deferential dispositions should decrease from infancy to adulthood, as individuals grow larger and less dependent. Deference should be a reluctant disposition activated by immediate threats of punishment from, or opportunities to ingratiate to, those in power.

## The Selection of Deference in the Human Species

As explained by Miller (chap. 3, this volume), our hominid ancestors probably evolved in multimale, multifemale groups with polygynous mating systems. The moderate sexual dimorphism of *Homo sapiens* is consistent with this supposition. As in chimpanzees and macaques, kin-based coalitions probably played an important role in defining dominance and status.

Human infants experience a longer period of dependency than do infants of any other species. Piaget (1932) and other developmental psychologists have characterized the social world of the child as involving unilateral respect for adults—"the respect felt by the small for the great" (p. 107). As put by Piaget (1932), this "Respect has its roots deep down in certain inborn feelings and is due to a *sui generis* mixture of fear and affection which develops as a function of the child's relation to his adult environment" (p. 375).

Dominance, status, social power, charismatic leaders, and hero worship are endemic to all human societies. Ethologically oriented psychologists have observed dominance hierarchies among school-age children (Strayer & Strayer, 1976). Religions demand deference to and supplication of powerful gods. The power of deferential dispositions in the human species is well demonstrated in Milgram's (1974) experiments on obedience to authority, and in cults such as Heaven's Gate and Jonestown that commit suicide on the command of their leaders (Campbell, 1965; Osherow, 1981).

## Implications for Morality

In large part, morality involves foregoing opportunities to satisfy one's own needs and deferring to the needs of others. Deference involves the restraint of selfish urges and the willingness to accommodate to others' needs. Deferential dispositions give rise to moral behaviors that involve obedience to and respect for the dictates, commandments, rules, and laws of authorities. Religious prescriptions direct God-fearing people to defer to the authority of God. In Colby and Kohlberg's (1987) classification of moral judgment, the moral value of deference is implicit in Element 1 (obeying persons or deity) and Norm 6 (Authority). Deference to "the supreme power of authorities," "obedience for its own sake," and "avoidance of punishment" (Colby & Kohlberg, 1987, p. 17) define Stage 1 moral judgment. At higher stages, deference takes the form of living up to what is expected by people close to you (Stage 3), upholding the law (Stage 4), and upholding the social contract (Stage 5).

## THE EVOLUTION OF JUSTICE

The moral value of deference varies across cultures. In the Western world, we tend to favor autonomy and justice. I believe principles of justice evolved to uphold systems of cooperation. There are many forms of cooperation, but two are especially important: mutualism and reciprocity.

### Mutualism

Felines and canines may prey on game that are many times larger than they, and much too large to be killed by any one member. For example, one lion may drive an antelope toward awaiting members of her pride, which then kills it. Following the kill, all members of the group share the spoils. In a similar vein, when individuals in some species, such as musk oxen, are vulnerable to predators, they may join together for mutual defense. The form of cooperation underlying group hunting and group defense—individuals behaving in ways that are mutually beneficial—is usually called *mutualism*, or *by-product mutualism* (Reeve, chap. 2, this volume). The adaptive principle underlying mutualism is simple: Individuals gain more for themselves by working together than by working alone.

As explained by Scheel and Packer (1991), mutualism usually evolves in hostile environments, in which individuals need assistance to survive and reproduce. The gains and losses of mutualism, and therefore the conditions regulating its evolution and activation, depend on factors such as the quantity and value of available resources, number of individuals required to obtain the resources, number of individuals with whom the resources must be shared, ability of individuals to obtain the resources themselves, and amount of effort or risk involved relative to other options.

*The Selection of Mutualism in the Human Species.* Our ancestors probably lived in relatively hostile environments containing predators much more ferocious than they. During the late Pleistocene, our ancestors began to hunt large game. For these reasons and others, experts on human evolution, such as Leakey and Lewin (1977), have concluded that mutualism was instrumental in the evolution of the human species:

Throughout our recent evolutionary history, particularly since the rise of a hunting way of life, there must have been extreme selective pressures in favor of our ability to cooperate as a group: organized food gathering and hunts are successful only if each member of the band knows his task and joins in with the activity of his fellows. The degree of selective pressure toward cooperation, group awareness and identification was so strong, and the period over which it operated was so extended, that it can hardly have failed to have become embedded to some degree in our genetic makeup. (p. 45)

Tooby and Devore (1987) identified 15 ways in which hominids diverged from other primates. At least two of these zoologically unique characteristics involve mutualism: far larger and more structural coalitions and a high degree of male coalitional intergroup aggression (war). Alexander (1987) suggested that the greatest threat to the welfare of our ancestors may have been coalitions of other hominids. Because the power of groups tends to increase with their size, there would have been selective pressure for increasingly large cooperative groups.

## Reciprocity

In addition to joining forces for mutual gain, individuals may cooperate by engaging in various forms of reciprocity. Consider vampire bats, *Desmodus rotundus*, for example. Members of this species venture out each night individually to forage for blood from cows, horses, and other large animals. If they fail to obtain blood within 60 hours of their last feeding, they starve to death. Female vampire bats are evolved to regurgitate blood for their offspring. As reported by Wilkinson (1984), vampire bats form cooperative groups of about 8 to 12 roostmates. When one member of a group is unsuccessful in obtaining blood, another member will regurgitate blood for her. Recipients may be related to donors (by blood), which has implications for kin selection (which is discussed later). However, vampire bats also regurgitate blood for friends with whom they have spent at least 60% of their time.

Wilkinson (1984) found that the mechanism mediating blood donation to nonrelatives is tit-for-tat reciprocity: Recipients repay donors when the donors are in need. The benefits donors receive exceed their costs because reciprocal donations enable them to survive and because donating blood does not threaten their lives. The adaptive principle underlying tit-for-tat reciprocity is that individuals can maximize their net gains by giving resources of relatively low value to them, but of relatively high value to recipients at one point in time in return for resources of greater value to them but lower cost to their recipients at some future date.

Axelrod and Hamilton (1981) modeled the evolution of cooperation in computer-simulated Prisoner's Dilemma games. These investigators found that if tit-for-tat reciprocity invades a system dominated by selfish individualism in sufficient strength, it can overrun it. The problem is that the initially altruistic overtures individuals must make to launch a system of tit-for-tat reciprocity would not, by definition, be reciprocated in a group of selfish individualists. For reciprocity to pay off, it must be directed toward reciprocators, which leaves the original question unanswered: How did reciprocators get there in the first place? This issue is revisited later. At this point, it is sufficient to point out that, as demonstrated in vampire bats, once a system of reciprocity is in place, it may pay off better than more selfish alternatives.

Reciprocity is dependent on repeated encounters between individuals with alternating opportunities to assist one another and on the ability to distinguish between those who repay assistance and those who do not. The multiple interactions necessary for reciprocity to flourish usually presume relatively stable groups. Trivers (1971) listed six conditions that favor the evolution of reciprocity: long life span, low rate of dispersal, high degree of mutual dependence, long parental care, ability to assist conspecifics in combat, and flexible dominance hierarchies. In addition, Trivers suggested that reciprocity should be favored in species capable of recognizing one another and remembering previous encounters.

*Indirect Reciprocity.* As explained by Alexander (1987), reciprocity may involve immediate or delayed payback, and it may be direct (individuals repaying those who helped them) or indirect (receiving repayment from a third party). The mechanism that sustains direct reciprocity involves the rewards individuals receive in future interactions from those they have assisted, but this mechanism could not sustain indirect reciprocity. What would induce a third party to repay a second party's debt? One mechanism might involve a circular system of exchange. If you owe me and a third person owes you, the third person could repay his or her debt to you and your debt to me by paying me. This arrangement would be beneficial when the third party possesses a resource the first party needs but the second party does not.

Systems of indirect reciprocity may be institutionalized in social roles as divisions of labor: One party may regularly give resources that he or she is specialized in acquiring to a second party, who may regularly give resources that he or she is specialized in acquiring to a third party, and so on, with each party receiving from other parties the resources he or she needs. In effect, people may implicitly negotiate deals in which they routinely make certain kinds of contributions to their groups in exchange for contributions others make to them. Such systems may be organized centrally: Individuals may give to a central distributor (e.g., Red Cross, financial institutions, insurance agencies) that then redistributes the resources to those who have contributed when they are in need. Legal tender, which in effect verifies that an individual has made a contribution to the group and therefore is owed some compensation, would have facilitated such exchanges.

Alexander (1987) identified three additional ways in which indirect reciprocity may pay off. First, and most important, altruistic-appearing individuals may be viewed by observers as desirable partners in reciprocal exchanges, thereby reaping the benefits of invitational overtures from others. Conversely, "to be judged harshly because of failure to deliver small social benefits indiscriminately in appropriate situations may lead to formidable disadvantages because of either direct penalties or lost opportunities in subsequent reciprocal interactions" (Alexander, 1987, p. 100). Second, beneficent individuals may be given rewards by their groups for their beneficent behaviors (e.g., medals for heroism) because such individuals uphold the interests of others in the groups. Finally, the success of the group's beneficent individuals' help may contribute to the fitness of their kin.

According to Alexander (1987), systems of indirect reciprocity may mediate a modicum of indiscriminate altruism if individuals' genetic interests correspond closely to the interests of their groups. This might occur when groups are composed mainly of kin and when external forces threaten to destroy entire groups.

*The Selection of Reciprocity in the Human Species.* As concluded by Trivers (1985):

> During the Pleistocene, and probably before, a hominid species would have met the preconditions for the evolution of reciprocal altruism; for example, long life span, low dispersal rate, life in small, mutually dependent and stable social groups, and a long period of parental care leading to extensive contacts with close relatives over may years. (p. 386)

Our ancestors undoubtedly accumulated resources that could be traded. The acquisition of weapons would have helped equalize dominance relations. Tools would have made divisions of labor increasingly adaptive as individuals specialized in tasks. In Tooby and Devore's (1987) list of 15 unique hominid characteristics, four are based in reciprocity: (a) "unprecedented development in the frequency and degree of reciprocity and the variety of its manifestation"; (b) "unparalleled degree of negotiation, intercontingent behavior, and social exchange"; (c) "an increased division of labor between the sexes"; and (d) "mating negotiation and exchange, probably consisting of wife exchange among groups" (pp. 207–208).

Alexander (1987) believed the human species is the only species in which indirect reciprocity has evolved, although he allowed that it may turn out to have evolved in chimpanzees, canines, and felines. Alexander speculated that indirect reciprocity leading to indiscriminate altruism may have evolved in the human species in four stages. In early stages, hominids lived in small bands and invested most of their social effort in their mates and offspring. As the size of social groups increased (mainly to defend against other groups of hominids), our ancestors invested increasingly large amounts of social effort in discriminate reciprocity and then indiscriminate reciprocity.

If reciprocity were as important in the evolution of the human species as many theorists assume, we would expect dispositions supporting it to be reflected in the structure of the human brain and in the structure of human behavior. Reciprocity seems to be a universal norm (Gouldner, 1960). Trivers (1985) suggested that emotions such as affection, gratitude, sympathy, and guilt evolved to regulate systems of reciprocity. It is possible that the adaptive value of mental abilities underlying increasingly complex forms of reciprocity and other types of cooperation (e.g., mental abilities such as keeping track of debts, computing equitable exchanges, remembering debtors, taking the perspective of exchange partners, negotiating, and forming cooperative alliances) contributed in no small way to the evolution of the human brain.

*Implications for Morality.* The idea that the primary function of morality is to uphold systems of cooperation has been espoused by many scholars. The philosopher Rawls (1971) suggested that the function of justice is to solve the fundamental social problem created when "social cooperation makes possible a better life for all than any would have if each were to live solely by his own efforts . . . [but each individual] prefer[s] a larger to a lesser share" (p. 4). Trivers (1985) concluded "a sense of justice has evolved in human beings as the standard against which to measure the behavior of other people, so as to guard against cheating in reciprocal relationships" (p. 388). Piaget (1932) depicted morality as "the equilibrium of individuals in society, as individuals reciprocating with other individuals according to rules that balance the benefits and burdens of cooperation" (cited in Rest, 1983, pp. 572–573).

Upholding systems of cooperation also figures prominently in Kohlberg's (1984) theory of moral development. As characterized by Rest (1983), Kohlberg's hierarchy of moral development is based on a "progressive understanding of the various possibilities of cooperative relationships" (p. 580). For example, as described by Colby and Kohlberg

(1987), at Stage 2, "right is . . . an equal exchange, a deal, an agreement"; at Stage 3, right is "keeping mutual relationships," "loyalty," and ensuring that "agreements and expectations . . . take primacy over individual interests"; at Stage 4, right is "fulfilling the actual duties to which you have agreed . . . contributing to society, the group, or institution"; and Stage 5 involves "a sense of obligation to law because of one's social contract to make and abide by laws for the welfare of all" (pp. 18–20).

Mutualistic cooperation and reciprocity involve the sorts of balance between inputs and outputs, rights and duties, and give and take intrinsic in conceptions of distributive justice. Reciprocity is based on trust that one's investments will be repaid. Reciprocal agreements involve implicit or explicit contracts. The "eye for an eye" code of Hammurabi is based in tit-for-tat reciprocity, and the Golden Rule is based in ideal reciprocity.

Alexander (1987) believed "moral systems are systems of indirect reciprocity" (p. 77). According to Alexander, the moral ideal involves all members of a group behaving in indiscriminately beneficent or altruistic ways to all other members of the group, which would promote the greatest good for the greatest number, as espoused in Kohlberg's Stage 5 structures of moral judgment. According to Alexander, the function of moral rules is to induce individuals to resist the temptation to exploit the implicit contracts they make when they reap the benefits of indirect reciprocity (i.e., assistance from group members whom they have not assisted). Moral rules exhort individuals to assist other members of their groups, contribute their fair share to the groups, and take only what they deserve. The role of indirect reciprocity in morality is reflected in Kohlbergian Elements 4 (*having a duty*), 5 (*having a right*), 9 (*good group consequences*), 12 (*upholding social ideal or harmony*), 15 (*reciprocity or positive desert*), 16 (*maintaining procedural fairness*), and 17 (*maintaining social contract*).

## THE EVOLUTION OF CARE

Several contributors to this volume (e.g., Crawford, chap. 1; Miller, chap. 3; Malamuth & Heilmann, chap. 17) discuss the mating habits of Panorpa scorpionflies. The males from this species viciously compete against one another for dead insects to present to females as nuptial gifts, and the females show a preference for the males who present the most savory gifts. This combination of behaviors—male–male power-based competition for resources and female choice for males able to provision them and their offspring—is characteristic of many species. Helpers at the nest are perhaps the most familiar example. Although sex-for-provisions types of exchanges may seem to involve simple reciprocity, they also are based in another form of cooperation—the alliance between partners' genes in their offspring.

The most direct way in which individuals propagate their genes is through survival and reproduction. Nature (including conspecifics) determines which individuals survive. In many species, members of the opposite sex play the decisive role in determining who reproduces. Inasmuch as individuals exert choice over the types of individuals with whom they mate, females would have selected the qualities that evolved in males, and males would have selected the qualities that evolved in females. As explained by Miller (chap. 3, this volume), characteristics selected by the opposite sex are passed onto offspring of both sexes (although in some cases more strongly in one sex than in the other). Females tend to be more choosy than males about their mates because females generate fewer and larger gametes and usually invest more in their offspring. Males tend to be more promiscuous and more competitive than females, and to exert more courtship effort.

As explained by Miller, all kinds of weird and wonderful characteristics may evolve through sexual selection, especially when runaway mechanisms become engaged. However, as exemplified by scorpionflies and birds, two types of characteristics are particularly important—those that reflect power (size, health, strength, ferociousness, vigor, possession of resources, status, dominance) and those that reflect devotion (provisioning, protectiveness, altruism, fidelity, loyalty, love). In general, we would expect females to seek mates who are both powerful and devoted—those who are willing and able to serve, protect, and produce fecund offspring. In some species, such as the scorpionflies discussed earlier, power (the ability to obtain a nuptial gift) and devotion (the willingness to give the gift) go together, but these qualities need not necessarily covary. For example, in polygynous species with dominance hierarchies, all eligible females may prefer the Alpha male, and less powerful males may compensate for their relative lack of power through increases in devotion.

Devotion should evolve through sexual selection when individuals are able to exert considerable choice over those with whom they mate; when the need for (ongoing) assistance, especially during pregnancy and/or in provisioning offspring, is high; and when such assistance is not supplied by members of the same sex. In general, these conditions also are conducive to the evolution of monogamous mating systems.

## The Selection of Devotion in the Human Species

Human infants are born altricial; they require more care than the infants of any other species. The immaturity of human infants at birth appears to be an evolutionary solution to the problem created by the conflicting adaptive values of bipedalism in mothers (which requires a constricted birth canal) and large brains in infants (which require a large birth canal). Whatever the source, the extreme dependency of human infants was clearly an important selective pressure in the evolution of devotion.

Lovejoy (1981) published a model of the evolution of the human species that featured the adaptive value of devotion. Lovejoy suggested that, in the ecological conditions of our ancestors, survival was enhanced through a division of labor, in which females maintained a home base where they reared dependent offspring and males provisioned them. According to Lovejoy, pair bonding and monogamy were more adaptive than other mating strategies, so dispositions supporting love and devotion were selected. Females selected males who would provision them and their offspring. Males selected faithful females so the offspring in whom they invested possessed their genes.

As pointed out by several critics, one of the problems with Lovejoy's model is that human males are significantly larger than human females. As explained by Miller (chap. 3, this volume), "our moderate size dimorphism is consistent with our species having evolved under a moderately polygynous mating system, with more intense sexual competition between males than between females (Fleagle, Kay, & Simons, 1980; Martin, Willner, & Dettling, 1994)" (p. 110).

A survey of human mating systems suggests that we are neither completely monogamous nor completely polygynous. Humans are evolved to invoke whatever mating strategy pays off best for them in the environments in which they make their choices. As suggested by Miller (chap. 3, this volume),

> Each sex probably evolved a multitude of flexible strategies . . . [that] might depend on his or her personal attributes (e.g., age, health, attractiveness, parenting skills, social skills, and seduction skills), the state of his or her kin network and social network (e.g., number of dependable child-care helpers), and various ecological conditions (e.g., reliability and patchiness of resources, foraging costs, and dangers) and demographic conditions (e.g., operational sex ratio). (p. 109)

Flexibility in mating strategies, and therefore variability in devotion, is not unique to humans. Even Panorpa scorpionflies have fall-back strategies: Males who fail to obtain dead insects as nuptial gifts may offer a nutritious salivary mass in their place; failing that, they may attempt forced copulation. In some cases, humans engage in promiscuous, exploitative, and uncaring behaviors; in other cases, they fall in love with, are faithful to, and worship their mates. Although some individuals might be more strongly disposed to one alternative than to the other, all individuals inherit the capacity for both. The central task in explaining the evolution of human devotion is to identify the factors that regulate these dispositions. This task is complicated in the human species for a variety of reasons, not the least of which is mutual choice.

Mutual choice complicates sexual selection because each partner selects qualities in the other, and a match must be found before mating occurs. To put it in rather crass economic terms, each partner has a package of goods to trade and is motivated to get the best deal in return. The value of the package is based on the perceived potential for an individual to enhance his or her partner's welfare, make a good genetic contribution to his or her share in offspring, and contribute to the welfare of the offspring after they are born. (Note how reciprocity regulates mate choice at different levels of selection.) Although there are many potential partners in circulation, most people cannot, in effect, afford them: They do not have enough to offer in return. As a result, people tend to end up with those who are similar to them in perceived worth.

Romantic love is among the most powerful prosocial emotions; it gives rise to caring, altruistic behaviors. Although many factors undoubtedly are involved in the regulation of romantic love, I believe one of the most powerful factors is the perception that a potential partner is of relatively high reproductive value, compared with oneself. The altered state of people in love is not that different from the frenzied acquisitiveness of some shoppers. One implication of this principle is that the perception that one is of relatively high value relative to one's partner will tend to diminish feelings of devotion. As noted by Miller (chap. 3, this volume), it is the case in many species of birds that the more attractive partner does less work, copulates more with other partners, and forms more short-term unions.

*Implications for Morality.* Colby and Kohlberg's (1987) classification of morality includes two moral norms that relate to devotion: affiliation (Norm 4) and erotic love (Norm 5). As suggested by Gilligan (1982), care-based moral judgments are particularly prominent at Stage 3 in Kohlberg's hierarchy of moral development. At Stage 3, *right* is defined in terms of "showing concern for others," "keeping mutual relationships," and "caring for others" (p. 18).

According to Gilligan (1982, 1988), justice upholds individual rights; as such, it is based in independence and autonomy. In contrast, care upholds relationships; as such, it is based in the affective bonds that connect people. As pointed out by Nunner-Winkler (1984), the morality of care involves upholding imperfect duties—thou shalts—whereas the morality of justice involves upholding perfect duties—thou shalt nots.

There are two problems with the morality of sexually selected dispositions to care for others. First, they are inherently discriminatory. It would not have been in our ancestors' interest to select dispositions in their mates that mediated indiscriminate caring. Rather, it would have been in their interest to select partners disposed to care only for them, their offspring, and their relatives. (It is conceivable that eligible mates who are disposed to care indiscriminately could, through such behaviors, elevate their status, and therefore their attractiveness as mates, but the fitness losses to the partner incurred by a mate's extrafamilial caring would virtually always seem to outweigh the gains.) The good side of sexually selected caring is that it is an antidote to selfishness. The bad side is that it is directed to only a narrow range of recipients—one's immediate family. Although a moral virtue, fidelity is inherently discriminatory: It entails allocating one's erotic love to just one recipient. Sexual selection does not supply a good explanation of caring for friends.

The moral problem of imperfect duties pertains to the allocation of care. Kohlberg (1984) argued that, to qualify as moral, care-based behaviors must be regulated by justice: individuals have a moral obligation to allocate their caring behaviors equitably, in accordance with an overriding principle of justice, such as promoting the greatest good for the greatest number. In Kohlberg's theory, moral judgments that advocate assisting one's wife if one does not love her and helping strangers as much as friends are considered more moral than more discriminatory moral judgments.

The second problem with the morality of sexually selected devotion is that it may be regulated by intrinsically amoral or immoral factors. People may be evolved to be only as devoted as they have to be to mate and rear fecund offspring. As suggested earlier, the more desirable a partner is, compared with his or her mate, the less devoted he or she may be inclined to be. A rather unfortunate consequence of this process is that people may be most inclined to devote themselves to those who need it the least. Hero worship and infatuation with celebrities are extreme cases in point.

There is good evidence that sexually selected devotion is a fickle disposition in the human species. The gifts with which men shower women during courtship become increasingly rare after marriage. Typically, the passion of being in love is transient. In most societies, the bonds of marriage must be reinforced through a social contract. People have extramarital affairs. Wives are abandoned when children come of age. Husbands are dumped when richer men of higher status come along. It is perhaps fortunate that caring behaviors can evolve through mechanisms other than sexual selection. Let us turn to one of them now.

## THE EVOLUTION OF ALTRUISM

The primary recipients of blood regurgitated from the vampire bats discussed earlier are their offspring, who are the primary recipients of altruism in most sexually reproducing species. The open mouths of nestlings, nursing mammals, distraction displays of ground-nesting birds, and the protective behavior of parents of many species come readily to mind. Such self-sacrificially altruistic behaviors do not seem particularly surprising or moral. However, as put by Tiger (1979),

> When all is said and done, the act of being a parent involves a set of radically unselfish and often incomprehensibly inconvenient activities. Two adults who could otherwise employ their time and resources in pleasurable activities of various kinds elect to [indulge] completely dependent organisms. . . . (p. 96)

The theory of evolution supplies an easy explanation for the altruistic behavior of parents: They are simply doing what they must to propagate their genes. Genetically speaking, they are helping themselves.

In addition to helping their offspring, vampire bats, lions, and many other species frequently make sacrifices to enhance the welfare of relatives other than their offspring. Indeed, social insects such as ants and bees readily sacrifice their lives for their sisters. The principle underlying such altruism is simple, but its implications are profound. As stated by Hamilton (1964), "a gene may receive positive selection even though disadvantageous to its bearers if it causes them to confer sufficiently large advantages on relatives" (p. 17).

Hamilton (1964) offered a formula: Altruism should evolve through kin selection when $k > 1/r$, where $k$ is the ratio of recipient benefit to altruist cost, and $r$ is the coefficient of genetic relatedness between altruist and recipient. The factor $r$, which represents the probability of sharing an allele, is centrally important in kin selection. All else equal, dispositions to assist kin should decline with degree of genetic relatedness. All else equal, individuals should be most inclined to assist themselves (100% probability of sharing an allele), then their offspring, siblings, and parents (50% probability of sharing an allele), then their nieces, nephews, aunts, uncles, and grandparents (25% probability), and so on. Among relatives, individuals should favor those with the greatest promise of fecundity (e.g., nieces and nephews over aunts and uncles, and aunts and uncles over grandparents).

In short, individuals become increasingly likely to invest in others as the others become increasingly similar to them genetically. Observations of species such as white-fronted bee eaters (Emlem & Wrege, 1988) and Belding's ground squirrels (Holmes & Sherman, 1983) have revealed that the probability of individuals provisioning conspecifics, issuing alarm calls when a predator is near, and coming to others' aid in defense increases in relation to their degree of genetic relatedness. The extreme self-sacrificial altruism of social insects makes sense in terms of the unusually high degree of genetic relatedness (75%) among sisters of the species.

It is a fortunate quirk of nature that genes cannot evolve to recognize replicas of themselves (Dawkins, 1989; Krebs, 1989; Porter, 1987). Individuals must rely on cues to genetic relatedness such as phenotypic similarity, association, and location. The reason that this may be fortunate is because it may enlarge the circle of recipients of kin-selected altruism. People may be disposed to help nonrelatives who share the characteristics that distinguished relatives from nonrelatives in ancestral environments.

## The Selection of Altruism in the Human Species

There is good reason to believe that kin selection played an important role in the evolution of individual altruism in the human species. Our ancestors probably lived in groups composed of extended families. As any anthropology textbook can verify, concerns about kinship are salient in all societies, although kinship need not necessarily correspond to biological relatedness (Chagnon & Irons, 1979; van den Berghe, 1983). Kinship was undoubtedly an important principle of coalition formation, as exemplified by the gangs formed by brothers such as the James, Clantons, and Earps in the Old West. Rushton (1989) adduced a great deal of evidence in support of the proposition that individuals show preferences for those who are genetically similar to them. Following a review of the literature, Krebs (1987) concluded,

> Several strands of social psychological research are consistent with the idea that humans are genetically predisposed to enhance the fitness of unrelated individuals who possess the types of characteristics that were associated with kinship in our evolutionary past, even though this anachronistic disposition may not pay off in their present environment. (p. 102)

*Implications for Human Morality.*  Dispositions that induce people to help relatives can be considered moral because they induce people to moderate their selfishness and to behave benevolently toward others. In this sense, such dispositions uphold the ethics of care. However, like sexually selected, care-based dispositions, such dispositions raise problems for justice. Kin-selected altruistic dispositions are intrinsically nepotistic. Although, as explained earlier, such dispositions may be generalized to nonrelatives who look, live, and act like kin, and although such generalized dispositions may give rise to genuinely (i.e., genetically) altruistic behaviors (Krebs, 1987), they are nonetheless limited to kinlike recipients, or members of ingroups (Krebs & Denton, 1997). The other side of kin-selected altruism is discrimination, ethnocentrism, and xenophobia, which are all too evident in human interactions.

## CAN MORAL BEHAVIORS EVOLVE THROUGH GROUP SELECTION?

Queens from the harvester ant species *Messor pergandei* team up to form cooperative colonies, which then compete against one another for brood. At the end of the competition, only one colony of cooperative queens remains (Rissing & Pollock, 1986). Mesterton and Dugatkin (1992) suggested that dispositions that induce such ants to work together for the good of their colonies may have evolved through group selection. The principle underlying group selection has appealed to many social scientists (see Wilson & Sober, 1994): Dispositions that induce individuals to make sacrifices for their groups have evolved because groups containing members willing to sacrifice their own interests for the sake of the group fare better than more selfish groups in intergroup competition.

As explained by many theorists (e.g., Williams, 1966), a potentially powerful countervailing force must be overcome before group-upholding traits can evolve—the force of individual selfishness within cooperative groups. Assuming the disposition to sacrifice oneself for the sake of one's group varies among individuals within groups, those who are relatively disinclined to sacrifice themselves will fare better than their more altruistic cohorts. Thus, all else equal, the group will become increasingly selfish in nature. The latent power of such within-group selfishness is demonstrated in the harvester ants: After prevailing in between-group competitions, the cooperating queens in victorious colonies compete against one another until only one of them survives.

Although between-group selection of altruistic dispositions is a theoretical possibility, most biologists believe that few, if any, species have met the conditions necessary for group selection. For altruism to evolve through group selection, groups composed of individuals inclined to sacrifice themselves for the sake of their groups must prevail over groups containing more selfish individuals (which may occur when the costs of individual altruism to the fitness of members of altruistic groups are relatively low and the gains to the group are high). Between-group selection for altruism must occur at a faster rate than within-group selection for selfishness. The probability of selfish individuals infiltrating altruistic groups must be low. Altruistic members of altruistic groups must reproduce fast enough to leave altruistic offspring before they perish, and the interests of individuals in groups must correspond to the interests of the groups as a whole.

### Group Selection of Altruism in the Human Species

In 1871, Darwin wrote, "although a high standard of morality gives but a slight or no advantage to each individual man and his children over the other men of his tribe, yet that an increase in the number of well-endowed men and advancement in the standard of morality will certainly give an immense advantage to one tribe over another" (p. 500). The idea that a form of group selection that advances the interests of groups at the expense of individual members has produced human morality is popular in the social sciences, but a close reading of Darwin reveals he did not fully endorse this idea. The key difference between Darwin's version of group selection and versions popular in the social sciences can be detected in the phrase *a slight or no advantage*. To evolve through group selection, traits must benefit the individuals who inherit them. As Alexander (1987) explained, this means the interests of individuals and groups must coincide.

Alexander and Borgia (1978) suggested that two characteristics of hominid groups would have favored group selection: rapid increases in group differences in adaptiveness caused by cultural innovations such as the invention of weapons, and the ability and incentive for groups to function as effective units, both by constraining within-group selfishness and dissent and fostering collective action. As discussed earlier, our ancestors probably formed cooperative groups to enhance hunting and defense; these groups may have competed against one another in war, thereby increasing their susceptibility to rapid extinction. Groups with high levels of solidarity may have defeated groups with high levels of individualistic selfishness at relatively little cost, and high-solidarity groups may have weeded out their selfish individualists by killing them off or ostracizing them.

As Alexander (1987), Axelrod and Hamilton (1981), and other theorists have emphasized, the costs of investment in groups may be mitigated considerably when the groups are composed of kin. However, social-psychological research on group formation (e.g., Tajfel, 1982) has found that humans form coalitions on the basis of virtually any commonality of interest, and they change alliances quickly when interests diverge. Krebs and Denton (1997) adduced evidence that cognitive structures have evolved in humans that induce them to categorize others as members of ingroups or outgroups (Devine, 1989), and to process information about ingroup members in systematically more favorable ways than they process information about outgroup members (Linville, Fischer, & Salovey, 1989).

*Implications for Morality.* Among Kohlberg's elements of morality, Element 9, good group consequences, and Element 12, serving social ideal and harmony, reflect the moral value of group-upholding behaviors. These elements are most prevalent at Kohlberg's Stage 4, at which conceptions of right are based on "contributing to society, the group, or institution" (Colby & Kohlberg, 1987, p. 18). In effect, the moral judgments that define Stage 4 in Kohlberg's sequence prescribe behaving in ways that uphold the mechanisms of group selection.

The problem with group-upholding conceptions of morality is that they only pertain to members of ingroups. Thus, sexual selection, kin selection, and group selection all give rise to discriminatory behaviors. As demonstrated during wars, moral norms do not generally apply to relations between ingroups and outgroups (see Krebs, 1987, for a review of psychological research supporting this conclusion; Alexander, 1987, for a discussion of its frightening implications).

## THE INTERACTION AMONG MECHANISMS OF SELECTION

I have been acting as if each type of moral behavior explained here evolved by way of a particular mechanism of selection. It is now time to acknowledge that evolution is much more complicated than that. Forms of selection interact with each other; sometimes one augments the effects of another, and sometimes it exerts counteracting effects.

When we calculate the evolutionary benefits of a type of behavior, we need to determine its net contribution to fitness, which entails adding the benefits and subtracting the costs across all forms of selection. For example, it has been suggested that deferential behaviors enhance individual fitness by subverting the wrath of the powerful. Deferential behaviors also might enhance fitness by supporting a hierarchically based system of cooperation, ingratiating members of the opposite sex, enhancing the fitness of powerful kin, and contributing to the success of groups. Similarly, in addition to fostering one's inclusive fitness by fostering the fitness of relatives, altruistic behaviors could enhance fitness by initiating reciprocal exchanges, enhancing sexual attractiveness, and contributing to the benefits one receives through membership in a group. To a great extent, the characteristics individuals desire in their mates (e.g., health, power, status, nurturance) are characteristics that foster the fitness of those who possess them through other mechanisms.

Investigators who have attempted to explain the genetic benefits of mutualism have been forced to posit supplementary benefits from kin selection. For example, Caraco and Wolf (1975) found that, although two lions hunting together generally obtained more net nutrition than each hunting alone, three or more lions did not. It is only when the supplementary benefits of other factors, such as kin selection, are added to those of mutualism that group hunting pays off.

In a similar vein, systems of reciprocity may have needed the benefits of kin selection to kick start them. As discussed earlier, although systems of tit-for-tat reciprocity are evolutionarily stable once entrenched, someone must make an altruistic overture to start the process. Axelrod and Hamilton (1981) suggested that, for systems of tit-for-tat reciprocity to invade systems of selfish individualism, they need some assistance from kin selection: "recalculation of the payoff matrix in such a way that an individual has a part interest in the partner's gain (that is, reckoning payoffs in terms of inclusive fitness) can often eliminate the inequalities [of reciprocity]" (p. 1399).

To complicate matters more, different mechanisms of selection do not always support one another; they may exert opposing influences. For example, deferential behaviors could increase the probability of surviving, but lower the probability of reproducing. Altruistic behaviors might enhance the fitness of kin or the group at costs to the reproductive fitness of the altruist, which certainly is the case with the self-sacrificial behavior of social insects (Trivers & Hare, 1976).

To understand how moral dispositions evolved in the human species, we must understand how all mechanisms of selection interacted in the social and physical environments of our ancestors. It is not unreasonable to expect there to have been a great deal of mutual support from complementary mechanisms in the evolution of moral behaviors. If our ancestors lived in groups that included relatively high proportions of kin, and if such groups lived in hostile environments that created a convergence between individual and group interests, reciprocity, kin selection, and group selection all would have supported the evolution of altruistic and cooperative dispositions. Alexander and Borgia (1978) and Alexander (1987) argued that kin selection and reciprocity were closely connected in our evolutionary history. In effect, our ancestors covered the bets they made in reciprocity by directing it toward kin. Reeve (chap. 2, this volume) proves that reciprocity and kin selection are based in the same evolutionary (and algebraic) logic.

However, it is unlikely that our ancestors met the conditions necessary for the evolution of an ideal moral system, in which all individuals promote the interests of all other individuals equally. To meet this condition, the correspondence between individual and group interests would have had to have been so strong that helping others paid off as much as helping oneself. There are only two ways to meet this condition: when all individuals in a group are clones, and when the environment is organized in a way that induces a perfect commonality of interests. Humans are not clones. Although they have pursued the second option, they have not been able to overcome the powerful countervailing forces intrinsic in the process. It is time now to deal with this issue.

## THE EVOLUTION OF CHEATING

The main goal in this chapter has been to offer an account of how naturally good, moral dispositions could have evolved in the human species. However, this story would not be complete without a somewhat darker epilogue. It is useful and appropriate to view the forms of moral behavior that have evolved in the human species as strategies—means to the end of increasing inclusive fitness in ancestral environments. By behaving in ways we now consider moral, our ancestors sacrificed opportunities to enhance their immediate, individual fitness to reap greater net genetic gains in the final summation. If moral strategies paid off better than immoral strategies, they would have evolved. That is the good news. However, the bad news is that it is quite clear our ancestors often could have maximized their net gains through immoral strategies, such as those that involve appearing more moral than they actually were and cheating when they could get away with it.

All mechanisms of morality are susceptible to cheating. Individuals may show respect for authority only when Big Brother is watching, pull less than their weight in group endeavors (which is well documented in research on social loafing), and return less than they receive. Spouses may commit adultery. Nonrelatives may act like kin. Individuals are evolved to avail themselves of these forms of cheating when they pay off better than behaving in fairer and more beneficent ways.

It would not, of course, have been in our ancestors' interest to be cheated by others, so adaptations that enabled them to guard against being cheated should have evolved. Indeed, if such antidotes did not evolve, cheating would have consumed the system of morality on which it preyed. Hardin's (1968) account of the tragedy of the commons demonstrated the potentially self-defeating and destructive effects of unabated individual selfishness: sheep owners seeking more than their share of a common land ultimately destroyed it through overgrazing.

Antidotes to cheating come in two main varieties. The first is preventive. Examples would include giving with one hand and receiving with the other, checking the value of the resources one receives, mating with males who have demonstrated their power over other males, demanding nuptial gifts in advance, and guarding against adultery through the use of chastity belts. The second is reactive. Reactive antidotes equate to moral sanctions (Kohlberg's Norm 12), and come in four main forms: punishment (Element 7), retribution (Element 3), bad reputation (Element 6), and ostracism. One of the reasons tit-for-tat reciprocity is such a robust strategy is because it contains both preventive and reactive measures. In effect, cheaters are expelled from the system until they reform: cheat me once, shame on you; cheat me twice, shame on me.

As Cosmides (1989) demonstrated, cognitive mechanisms have evolved in humans to detect deception. Krebs and Denton (1997) called such mechanisms *deception detectors*. Trivers (1985) suggested moralistic aggression evolved in humans to control cheating. Alexander (1987) suggested cheating is controlled in systems of indirect reciprocity in two main ways: (a) the adverse consequences to cheaters of a bad reputation, and (b) the adverse consequences to the system of morality that upholds the group that benefits the individual.

## The Evolution of Deception

Individuals respond to others in terms of their cognitive representations, beliefs, and interpretations of others' appearance and behavior, which may or may not correspond to the reality of what others are, what they have done, or what they intend to do. It is in individuals' interest to induce others to form images (cognitive representations) of them that foster their fitness. When the images that individuals induce others to form of them depart from reality, the images involve deception, whether intentional or *de facto*. Many species manipulate others into believing (or at least behaving toward them as if) they possess qualities they do not (Mitchell & Thompson, 1986). Camouflage, mimicry, and bluffing are prevalent examples in the animal kingdom (Trivers, 1985).

Humans form exceptionally elaborate cognitive representations of their worlds. As a result, humans avail themselves of more forms of deception than any other species. As Goffman (1959) so eloquently illustrated, the world is like a stage to humans, and social life is like a play. People are actors who employ costumes, makeup, and various props to put on acts that induce others to treat them in beneficial ways. "Face lifts, tummy tucks, fancy clothes, wigs, BMWs, Rolex watches, and other status symbols are the stock in trade of self-presentation" (Krebs & Denton, 1997, p. 37).

In moral systems, individuals' decisions about whether they owe others and, if so, how much are governed by whether they believe others have given to them, and, if so, how much, as opposed to whether in fact others have given to them. It follows that it pays for individuals to foster the appearance of giving a lot and receiving a little, while in fact giving a little and receiving a lot. It is in individuals' interest to exploit moral systems by inducing others to believe they are more righteous than they are.

All mechanisms of evolution are susceptible to exploitation through deception. Individuals may act respectfully in the presence of authorities, but show disrespect behind their backs. People may inflate the value of their contributions to reciprocal exchanges. In systems of indirect reciprocity, "individuals gain from portraying themselves as indiscriminate altruists, and from thereby inducing indiscriminate beneficence in others" (Alexander, 1987, p. 102). Nowhere perhaps is the manipulation of appearance more prevalent than in courting behavior.

Alexander (1987) summarized the implications of deception in the evolution of indirect reciprocity:

> The long-term existence of complex patterns of indirect reciprocity, then, seems to favor the evolution of keen abilities to (1) make one's self seem

more beneficent than is the case; and (2) influence others to be beneficent in such fashions as to be deleterious to themselves and beneficial to the moralizer, e.g., to lead others to (a) invest too much, (b) invest wrongly in the moralizer or his relatives and friends, or (c) invest indiscriminately on a larger scale than would otherwise be the case . . . [People] may be expected to locate and exploit social interactions mimicking genetic relatedness leading to nepotistic flows of benefits (e.g., to insinuate themselves deceptively into the role of relative or reciprocator so as to receive the benefits therefrom). (p. 103)

Alexander went on to suggest that individuals may engage in self-deception to reduce the probability their cheating will be detected.

## The Evolution of Self-Deception

In the same way adaptations that induced our ancestors to deceive others would have evolved if they paid off, so also would adaptations that induced our ancestors to deceive themselves (Krebs & Denton, 1997; Krebs, Denton, & Higgins, 1988; Lockard & Paulhus, 1988). One adaptive function of self-deception is to facilitate the deception of others.

With powers to deceive and to spot deception being improved by natural selection, a new kind of deception may be favored: self-deception. Self-deception renders the deception being practiced unconscious to the practitioner, thereby hiding from other individuals the subtle signs of self-knowledge that may give away the deception being practiced. (Trivers, 1985, p. 395)

Ghiselin (1974) suggested humans are evolved to resist the truth when the consequences of facing the truth jeopardize inclusive fitness:

We are anything but a mechanism set up to perceive the truth for its own sake. Rather, we have evolved a nervous system that acts in the interest of our gonads. . . . If ignorance aids in obtaining a mate, then men and women will tend to be ignorant. (p. 126)

Goleman (1985), Lockard and Paulhus (1988), Krebs and Denton (1997), Martin (1985), and Taylor (1989) reviewed evidence that humans are disposed to process information about themselves and others in systematically biased ways. For example, when dividing resources and reckoning debt, people are prone to believe they deserve more than their share, overvalue their contributions, and devalue the contributions of others (Brown, 1985; Fiske & Taylor, 1991; Miller & Porter, 1988). People are amazingly adept at excusing and justifying their misdeeds (Laird & Krebs, 1993; Snyder & Higgins, 1988), often blaming them on others (Baumeister,

Wotman, & Stillwell, 1993). Virtually everyone believes he or she is more moral than the average person—a phenomenon labeled the *self-righteous bias* in moral attribution (Krebs, Vermeulen, Carpendale, & Denton, 1991). All these self-deceptive tendencies may support deception and cheating.

*Differentially Sensitive Deception Detectors.* Given adaptations that increase the adaptiveness of deception, one would expect more sensitive antidotes to evolve. Alexander (1987) suggested that variability in conditions that affect the security of groups, and therefore the value of assisting others, would be expected to affect the evolution of the ability to detect beneficence-inducing deceptions. More generally, evolutionary theory leads us to infer that the capacity and proclivity to detect deception will evolve only when it pays off (Krebs & Denton, 1997).

When individuals share interests with others through kinship, reciprocity, or coalition, it may be in their genetic interest to overlook or minimize others' deceptions. Indeed, it may sometimes be in individuals' best interest to be deceived by their friends and relatives. The capacity of parents and people in love to repress and deny evidence that they have been deceived by their children and partners sometimes seems unbounded. Mutual deception may be based in reciprocity, producing "a benign *folie a deux*—a subtle and largely unconscious conspiracy between two (or more) people to support their misconceptions of themselves" (Krebs & Denton, 1997, emphasis added). Indeed, Alexander (1987) suggested that, as members of the human species, we all collaborate in positive illusions about human nature. The portrait of human social interaction that follows from this analysis is one in which individuals interact mainly on the basis of mutually beneficial shared illusions, including the illusion that they and their friends are more moral than they actually are.

This completes this sketch of the evolution of systems of moral behavior. In closing, the chapter returns to the psychological approaches to morality outlined earlier, and examines them briefly from the perspective of evolutionary theory.

## PSYCHOLOGICAL MODELS OF MORALITY REVISITED

The evolutionary model of morality outlined here is consistent with Freud's general notion that other people—parents and society—seek to constrain inherited sexual and aggressive dispositions, but not, as Freud sometimes implied, for the sake of society per se (cf. Badcock, chap. 15, this volume). Viewed from an evolutionary perspective, the parent–child conflict, which leads to the formation of the superego, is the first significant experience children have with the costs of unconstrained selfishness and the adaptive functions of deference. Surely, fear—the basis of deference—is as important in human interaction as is aggression. Identification with the aggressor (the same-gender parent) may involve the activation of kin-selected mechanisms. The central difference between psychoanalytic and evolutionary models of morality is that Freud viewed all biologically based dispositions (instincts) as fundamentally immoral (operating in terms of the Pleasure Principle), whereas evolutionary theory allows for the selection of conditionally moral dispositions.

There is no question that moral behavior can be shaped through conditioning in much the same ways that pets can be trained to be obedient (Aronfreed, 1968). The basic principle of operant conditioning—that behavior is controlled by its consequences—parallels at a proximate level the basic principle of evolution. The fundamental question left unanswered in operant conditioning is what makes some consequences rewarding and others punishing—as Barash (1977) asked, "What makes sugar sweet?" Evolutionary theory is the only theory equipped to supply a plausible answer to this question. From the perspective of evolution, operant conditioning is based on the evolved conditional strategy, increase the behaviors that worked at enhancing your ancestors' fitness; decrease the behaviors that did not.

Learning theorists such as Breland and Breland (1951) demonstrated that different species are prepared to learn different types of behavior. This chapter has argued that social species are prepared to learn to defer to authority, cooperate, care for their mates, and make sacrifices for their relatives and members of ingroups.

The social learning principles intrinsic in modeling and vicarious reinforcement are viewed from the perspective of evolution as evolved strategies for enhancing fitness. Through vicarious reinforcement, individuals are able to get a sneak preview of the fitness-enhancing or fitness-diminishing consequences of their behavior by observing how the behaviors affect the fitness of others, without suffering the consequences of trial and error. Evolutionary theory also supplies a basis for explaining where the rules social learning theorists assume define moral behavior came from, although this issue is not pursued in this chapter.

Cognitive-developmental theorists such as Kohlberg focus on the ontogenetic development of moral judgment. Evolutionary theory leads us to question two of the main assumptions of Kohlberg's theory—that individuals develop cognitive "structures of the whole" that organize their moral judgments across domains, and that old structures are transformed and displaced by new structures. As explained by Tooby and Cosmides (1990), evolutionary theory expects cognition to be more domain specific than Kohlberg postulated. In particular, there is little reason to expect moral judgments about following rules, cooperating, and caring for others to develop in concert and be organized in the same cognitive structure. Indeed, many of our most difficult moral conflicts may involve conflicts between domain-specific inductions, such as obeying authority versus treating others fairly or helping those we love versus treating all people equally. Damon (1977), Krebs et al. (1991), and Rest (1983) have found that moral judgment develops in an additive-inclusive way—people retain their old cognitive structures after they develop new ones—and that moral judgment is more context specific than Kohlberg assumed.

In place of the constructivistic approach of cognitive-developmental theory, evolutionary theory offers a life-history perspective that is more interactional in nature. As young children, the children of our ancestors, like children today, made Stage 1 moral judgments because they were small and weak compared with the adults in their environments. Obeying authority and avoiding physical punishment are adaptive strategies for children and for adults in childlike roles. As explained by Piaget (1932), older children make Stage 2 types of moral judgment to uphold systems of cooperation that advance their mutual interests. Care-based moral judgments are salient at Stage 3 because it is the stage at which adolescents bond in enduring friendships and romantic relations. The moral judgments people make reflect not only their level of cognitive sophistication, as Kohlberg has shown, but also the salient issues in their social worlds, as emphasized by other theorists (Aronfreed, 1968; Erikson, 1963; Higgins & Eccles-Parson, 1983; Krebs & Van Hesteren, 1994; Wark & Krebs, 1996).

Kohlberg (1984) argued that moral judgment gives rise to moral behavior. Evolutionary models of morality imply the opposite: moral behavior gave rise to moral judgment. Interestingly, Piaget (1932), who was trained as a biologist, also believed behavior precedes judgment. To understand why the form of moral judgment undergoes systematic changes with development, evolutionary theory directs us to attend to its functions; this, more than anything, is what is missing in cognitive-developmental models of moral development (Krebs, Wark, & Krebs, 1995).

It is only by attending to the fitness-enhancing functions of moral judgment in ancestral environments that we will be able to explain why it varies across contexts (Carpendale & Krebs, 1995), why there is a tension between care and justice (Wark & Krebs, 1996), why it is biased in "self-serving" and group-enhancing ways (Laird & Krebs, 1993), why it is as often employed to excuse immoral behavior as it is to uphold moral norms (Denton & Krebs, 1990), and why it is prominent in gossip as a form of social control (Sabini & Silver, 1982). The value of evolutionary theory is that it supplies a framework—perhaps the broadest framework—for organizing, revising, and resolving the inconsistencies among more proximally based psychological approaches to morality.

## ACKNOWLEDGMENTS

The research in this chapter was supported by Social Science and Humanities Research Council of Canada, Grant # 410-94-0345.

## REFERENCES

Alexander, R. D. (1987). *The biology of moral systems*. New York: Aldine deGruyter.

Alexander, R. D., & Borgia, G. (1978). On the origin and basis of the male–female phenomenon. In M. F. Blum & N. Blum (Eds.), *Sexual selection and reproductive competition in insects* (pp. 417–440). New York: Academic Press.

Aronfreed, J. (1968). *Conduct and conscience*. New York: Academic Press.

Axelrod, R., & Hamilton, W. D. (1981). The evolution of cooperation. *Science, 211*, 1390–1396.

Barash, D. P. (1977). *Sociology and behavior*. New York: Elsevier.

Baumeister, R. F., Wotman, S. R., & Stillwell A. (1993). Unrequited love: On heartbreak, anger, guilt, scriptlessness and humiliation. *Journal of Personality and Social Psychology, 64*, 377–394.

Breland, K., & Breland, M. (1951). A field of applied animal psychology. *American Psychologist, 6*, 202–204.

Brown, R. (1985). *Social psychology* (2nd ed.). New York: The Free Press.

Campbell, D. T. (1965). Ethnocentric and other altruistic motives. In D. Levine (Ed.), *Nebraska symposium on motivation* (pp. 283–311). Lincoln, NE: University of Nebraska Press.

Caraco, T., & Wolf, L. L. (1975). Ecological determinants of group sizes of foraging lions. *American Naturalist, 109*, 343–352.

Carpendale, J., & Krebs, D. L. (1995). Variations in moral judgment as a function of type of dilemma and moral choice. *Journal of Personality, 63*, 289–313.

Chagnon, N. A., & Irons, W. I. (Eds.). (1979). *Evolutionary biology and human social behavior: An anthropological perspective*. North Scituate, MA: Duxbury.

Colby, A., & Kohlberg, L. (1987). *The measurement of moral judgment* (Vols. 1–2). Cambridge, England: Cambridge University Press.

Cosmides, L. (1989). The logic of social exchange: Has natural selection shaped how humans reason? Studies with the Wason selection task. *Cognition, 31*, 187–276.

Damon, W. (1977). *The social world of the child*. San Francisco: Jossey-Bass.

Damon, W., & Hart, D. (1992). Self understanding and its role in social and moral development. In M. H. Bornstein & E. M. Lamb (Eds.), *Developmental psychology: An advanced textbook* (2nd ed., pp. 421–465). Hillsdale, NJ: Lawrence Erlbaum Associates.

Darwin, C. (1871). *The descent of man and selection in relation to sex* (2 vols.). New York: Appleton-Century-Crofts.

Dawkins, R. (1989). *The selfish gene*. Oxford: Oxford University Press.

Denton, K., & Krebs, D. (1990). From the scene to the crime: The effect of alcohol and social context on moral judgment. *Journal of Personality and Social Psychology, 59*, 242–248.

Devine, P. G. (1989). Stereotypes and prejudice: Their automatic and controlled components. *Journal of Personality and Social Psychology, 56*, 5–18.

Eisenberg, N. (1986). *Altruistic emotion, cognition, and behavior*. Hillsdale, NJ: Lawrence Erlbaum Associates.

Emlem, S. T., & Wrege, P. H. (1988). The role of kinship in helping decisions among white-fronted bee-eaters. *Behavioral Ecology and Sociobiology, 23*, 305–315.

Erikson, E. H. (1963). *Childhood and society* (2nd ed.). New York: Norton.

Fiske, S. T., & Taylor, S. E. (1991). *Social cognition*. New York: Random House.

Fleagle, J. G., Kay, R. F., & Simons, E. L. (1980). Sexual dimorphism in early anthropods. *Nature (London), 287,* 328–330.

Gangestead, S. W., & Thornhill, R. (1994, July). *Sexual selection and the nature of relationships: Trade offs between partner quality and exclusivity.* Talk presented at the 1994 Human Behavior and Evolution Society conference, University of Michigan, Ann Arbor, MI.

Ghiselin, M. T. (1974). *The economy of nature and the evolution of sex.* Berkeley, CA: University of California Press.

Gilligan, C. (1982). *In a different voice: Psychological theory and women's development.* Cambridge, MA: Harvard University Press.

Gilligan, C. (1988). Adolescent development reconsidered. In C. Gilligan, J. V. Ward, & J. M. Taylor (Eds.), *Mapping the moral domain: A contribution of women's thinking to psychological theory and education* (pp. vii–xxxix). Cambridge, MA: Harvard University Press.

Goffman, E. (1959). *The presentation of self in everyday life.* New York: Anchor Books.

Goleman, D. (1985). *Vital lies, simple truths: The psychology of self-deception.* New York: Simon & Schuster.

Gouldner, A. W. (1960). The norm of reciprocity: A preliminary statement. *American Sociological Review, 25,* 161–178.

Hamilton, W. D. (1964). The evolution of social behavior. *Journal of Theoretical Biology, 7,* 1–52.

Hardin, G. (1968). The tragedy of the commons. *Science, 162,* 1243–1248.

Holmes, W. G., & Sherman, P. W. (1983). Kin recognition in animals. *Journal of American Science, 71,* 46–55.

Kohlberg, L. (1984). *Essays on moral development: Vol. 2. The psychology of moral development.* San Francisco: Harper & Row.

Krebs, D. L. (1987). The challenge of altruism in biology and psychology. In C. Crawford, M. Smith, & D. Krebs (Eds.), *Sociobiology and psychology: Ideas, issues, and applications* (pp. 81–118). Hillsdale, NJ: Lawrence Erlbaum Associates.

Krebs, D. L. (1989). Detecting genetic similarity without detecting genetic similarity. *Behavior and Brain Sciences, 12,* 533–534.

Krebs, D. L., & Denton, K. (1997). Social illusions and self-deception: The evolution of biases in person perception. In J. A. Simpson & D. T. Kenrick (Eds.), *Evolutionary social psychology.* Mahwah, NJ: Lawrence Erlbaum Associates.

Krebs, D., Denton, K., & Higgins, N. (1988). On the evolution of self-knowledge and self-deception. In K. McDonald (Ed.), *Sociobiological perspectives on human behavior* (pp. 103–139). New York: Springer-Verlag.

Krebs, D., & Van Hesteren, F. (1992). The development of altruistic personality. In P. Oliner, S. Oliner, L. Baron, L. Blum, D. Krebs, & Z. Smolenska (Eds.), *Embracing the other: Philosophical, psychological, and historical perspectives on altruism* (pp. 142–169). New York: New York University Press.

Krebs, D. L., & Van Hesteren, F. (1994). The development of altruism: Toward an integrative model. *Developmental Review, 14,* 1–56.

Krebs, D. L., Vermeulen, S. C., Carpendale, J. I., & Denton, K. (1991). Structural and situational influences on moral judgment: The interaction between stage and dilemma. In W. Kurtines & J. Gewirtz (Eds.), *Handbook of moral behavior and development: Theory, research, and application* (pp. 139–169). Hillsdale, NJ: Lawrence Erlbaum Associates.

Krebs, D. L., Vermeulen, S., Denton, K., & Carpendale, J. (1994). Gender and perspective differences in moral judgment and moral orientation. *Journal of Moral Education, 23,* 17–26.

Krebs, D. L., Wark, G., & Krebs, D. L. (1995). Lessons from life: Toward a functional model of morality. *Moral Education Forum, 20,* 22–29.

Laird, P., & Krebs, D. L. (1993, June). *Self-serving bias in attributions about moral transgressions.* Paper presented at the 1993 annual convention of the Canadian Psychological Association, Montreal, Quebec.

Leakey, R. E., & Lewin, R. (1977). *Origins.* New York: Dutton.

Linville, P. W., Fischer, G. W., & Salovey, P. (1989). Perceived distributions of the characteristics of in-group and out-group members: Empirical evidence and a computer simulation. *Journal of Personality and Social Psychology, 57,* 165–188.

Lockard, J. S., & Paulhus, D. L. (Eds.). (1988). *Self-deception: An adaptive mechanism?* Englewood Cliffs, NJ: Prentice-Hall.

Lovejoy, C. O. (1981). The origin of man. *Science, 211,* 341–350.

Martin, M. W. (Ed.). (1985). *Self-deception and self-understanding.* Lawrence, KS: University Press of Kansas.

Martin, R. D., Willner, L. A., & Dettling, A. (1994). The evolution of sexual size dimorphism in primates. In R. V. Short & E. Balaban (Eds.), *The differences between the sexes* (pp. 159–200). Cambridge, England: Cambridge University Press.

Mesterton-Gibbons, M., & Dugatkin, L. A. (1992). Cooperation among unrelated individuals: Evolutionary factors. *Quarterly Review of Biology, 67,* 267–281.

Milgram, S. (1974). *Obedience to authority.* New York: Harper & Row.

Miller, D. T., & Porter, C. A. (1988). Errors and biases in the attribution process. In L. Y. Abramson (Ed.), *Social cognition and clinical psychology: A synthesis* (pp. 3–32). New York: Guilford.

Mitchell, R. W., & Thompson, N. S. (Eds.). (1986). *Deception: Perspectives on human and non-human deceit.* Albany, NY: State University of New York Press.

Nunner-Winkler, G. (1984). Two moralities: A critical discussion of an ethic of care and responsibility versus an ethic of rights and justice. In W. Kurtines & J. Gewirtz (Eds.), *Morality, moral behavior, and moral development* (pp. 348–361). New York: Wiley.

Osherow, N. (1981). Making sense of the nonsensical: An analysis of Jonestown. In E. Aronson (Ed.), *Readings about the social animal* (7th ed., pp. 68–86). San Francisco: Freeman.

Parker, G. A. (1984). Evolutionarily stable strategies. In J. R. Krebs & N. B. Davies (Eds.), *Behavioral ecology: An evolutionary approach* (2nd ed., pp. 30–61). London: Blackwell.

Piaget, J. (1932). *The moral judgment of the child.* London: Routledge & Kegan Paul.

Porter, R. H. (1987). Kin recognition: Functions and mediating mechanisms. In C. B. Crawford & D. Krebs (Eds.), *Sociobiology and psychology: Ideas, issues and applications* (pp. 175–205). Hillsdale, NJ: Lawrence Erlbaum Associates.

Rawls, J. (1971). *A theory of justice.* Cambridge, MA: Harvard University Press.

Rest, J. F. (1983). Morality. In J. H. Flavell & E. M. Markman (Eds.), *Handbook of child psychology: Vol. 3. Cognitive development* (4th ed., pp. 556–629). New York: Wiley.

Rissing, S., & Pollock, G. (1986). Social interaction among pleometric queens of *Veromessor pergandei* during colony foundation. *Animal Behavior, 34,* 226–234.

Rushton, J. P. (1989). Genetic similarity, human altruism and group selection. *Behavior and Brain Sciences, 12,* 503–559.

Sabini, J., & Silver, M. (1982). *Moralities of everyday life.* Oxford, England: Oxford University Press.

Scheel, D., & Packer, C. (1991). Group hunting behavior of lions: A search for cooperation. *Animal Behavior, 41,* 711–722.

Snyder, C. R., & Higgins, R. L. (1988). Excuses: Their effective role in the negotiation of reality. *Psychological Bulletin, 104,* 23–35.

Strayer, F. F., & Strayer, J. (1976). An ethological analysis of social agonism and dominance relations among preschool children. *Child Development, 47,* 980–989.

Tajfel, H. (1982). *Social identify and intergroup relations.* Cambridge, England: Cambridge University Press.

Taylor, S. E. (1989). *Positive illusions: Creative self-deception and the healthy mind.* New York: Basic Books.

Tiger, L. (1979). *Optimism: The biology of hope.* New York: Simon & Schuster.

Tooby, J., & Cosmides, L. (1990). The past explains the present: Emotional adaptions and the structure of ancestral environments. *Ethology and Sociobiology, 11*(4/5), 375–424.

Tooby, J., & Devore, I. (1987). The reconstruction of hominid behavioral evolution through strategic modeling. In W. G. Kinzey (Ed.), *The evolution of human behavior: Primate models* (pp. 183–237). Albany, NY: SUNY Press.

Trivers, R. L. (1971). The evolution of reciprocal altruism. *Quarterly Review of Biology, 46,* 35–57.

Trivers, R. (1985). *Social evolution.* Menlo Park, CA: Benjamin/Cummings.

Trivers, R. L., & Hare, H. (1976). Haplodiploidy and the evolution of the social insects. *Science, 191,* 249–263.

van den Berghe, P. (1983). Human inbreeding avoidance: Culture in nature. *The Behavior and Brain Sciences, 6,* 91–125.

Wark, G., & Krebs, D. L. (1996). Gender and dilemma differences in real-life moral judgment. *Developmental Psychology, 32,* 220–230.

Wilkinson, G. S. (1984). Reciprocal food sharing in the vampire bat. *Nature, 308,* 181–184.

Williams, G. C. (1966). *Adaptation and natural selection: A critique of some current evolutionary thought.* Princeton, NJ: Princeton University Press.

Wilson, D. S., & Sober, E. (1994). Re-introducing group selection to the human behavioral sciences. *Behavior and Brain Sciences, 17,* 585–608.

# Developmental Psychology and Modern Darwinism

Michele K. Surbey
*Mount Allison University*

> Development and embryology. *This is one of the most important subjects in the whole round of natural history.*
>
> —Darwin (1888)

The immature organism does not merely careen along a developmental landscape coincidentally avoiding blind alleys and pitfalls, rebounding randomly from perturbations, haphazardly skimming experience from extrusions arising along the way, and then come to a great screeching halt at adulthood. Ontogeny is not a random walk or fitful rollercoaster ride along an unexpected course that mysteriously reaches its apex in the adult form. An organism's development has been shaped by a long process of selection acting on individual ontogenies resulting in a particular *life history*. In contrast to the variegated life histories of other inhabitants of our planet, such as the insects, the human life history is relatively unelaborate, punctuated by perhaps only one metamorphosis, with all remaining transitions fairly gradual and superficially unremarkable. Comparatively speaking, we are a species that is developmentally unadorned. Yet we human beings, uniquely capable of scientific inquiry, remain so transfixed by our own phenomenological experiences of development that we have been unable to fully consider human ontogeny through the dispassionate eye of selection theory. Although admittedly the earliest attempts to incorporate evolutionary approaches into developmental theory fell short, the theoretical groundwork has now been fully laid for the proper re-acquaintance of developmental psychology with modern Darwinism.

## HISTORICAL ALLIANCES BETWEEN EVOLUTIONARY THEORY AND DEVELOPMENTAL PSYCHOLOGY

Philosophical and scientific communities have long held the assumption that ontogeny (individual development) contains the secret to understanding phylogeny (evolution of species), and that, in turn, phyletic information must reside or be expressed in the development of individuals. In other words, one underlying historical precept is that the processes of ontogeny and phylogeny feed into, and thus inform, one another.

As portrayed in the quote at the beginning of this chapter from his most famous work, Darwin promoted this line of thinking in his time by suggesting that the study of individual development could lend great insight into the phylogenetic development of species. As a result of his emphasis on the importance of understanding development and the methods he devised for the careful documentation of growth and development in his own child, Darwin is among those individuals commonly considered to have laid the early foundation for the systematic study of child development (e.g., Bukatko & Daehler, 1992). However, Darwin was not able to codify the complex nature of the relationship between individual development and phylogeny in terms of his greatest contribution toward the understanding of the process of evolution: the theory of natural selection. Therefore, other than developing means for documenting child development and shifting the focus toward the study of childhood, Darwin's concrete conceptual impact on developmental psychology in terms of his greatest theoretical advance was relatively small (Charlesworth, 1992). In addition, although greatly impressed by Darwin's theory of natural selection, the earliest developmentalists dabbled in and drew from evolutionary perspectives that were generally *non-Darwinian*, most of which were eventually discredited.

One of the most notable attempts to draw non-Darwinian evolutionary processes into explanations of development involved the incorporation of the law of recapitulation or the biogenetic law, heralded by Haeckel (1866; see also Gould, 1977, for a scholarly discussion of this theory). Haeckel, noticing commonalities in embryonic forms of "higher" organisms with the adult forms of "lower" organisms, suggested that each embryo goes through a succession of stages that reveal the evolutionary history of its lineage. Haeckel suggested that ontogeny is an abbreviated repetition of phylogeny, or that "ontogeny recapitulates phylogeny." The doctrine of recapitulation had an enormous impact on biology and psychology, and was perhaps only second to natural selection in terms of its influence (Gould, 1977). The notion of recapitulation lent itself particularly well to the stage theories of Freud, Hall, and Piaget. Freud's fascination with human antiquity was reflected in his personal collection of ancient objects and in his thesis that human history is "recapitulated" during personality development. In a discussion of the regressive nature of dreams, he stated, "in so far as each individual repeats in some abbreviated fashion during childhood the whole course of development of the human race, the reference is phylogenetic" (Freud, 1924/1967, p. 209). Similarly, Hall (1904) formulated a psychological theory of recapitulation, in which he described how individuals retrace the psychological history of humanity by passing through the developmental stages of animal-like primitivism, savagery, and barbarism, finally entering maturity, a stage akin to modern civilization. Furthermore, Piaget's exposure to the biogenetic law during his early training as a biologist is evident in his belief that human intellectual prehistory repeats itself during individual cognitive development—a notion that underlies his concept of genetic epistemology (see Piaget, 1971).

Like many of their contemporaries, Freud and Piaget were additionally influenced by Lamarck's (1809) theory of the inheritance of acquired characteristics (see Hooker, 1994; Nesse & Lloyd, 1992), an evolutionary perspective generally considered outmoded and unworkable in its original formulation. Lamarck's theory gained popularity, in part, because of its seemingly optimistic view that the positive results of individual lives could be passed on through generations in a cumulative fashion, thus driving the evolution of species. The notion that species' characteristics could be altered through their use or disuse in individuals was one of the most compelling cases made for the feedback between ontogeny and phylogeny, influencing even Darwin, although he remained somewhat skeptical of its veracity (see Darwin, 1871, Vol. 1, p. 112; Darwin, 1888, p. 108). However, with the discovery of Mendel's work, suggesting that only copies of genes were passed from generation to generation, not acquired phenotypic traits, Lamarck's theory quickly lost credibility. Nevertheless, Lamarck's basic postulate maintains its intuitive appeal even today. It has resurfaced in the work of other theorists including Waddington (1957), whose concept of genetic assimilation suggests how ontogenetic processes might affect changes in gene frequencies, the modern definition of *evolution*.

The discovery of genes and the particulate nature of inheritance demolished the biogenetic law, as it did Lamarckianism, by suggesting that species did not develop from one another, forming a hierarchical ladder of life through the addition of adult characteristics because phenotypic characteristics could just not be "added on" to a species' genome at the end of individual ontogenies. The biogenetic law had already been severely shaken by discoveries in embryology, suggesting that embryonic features did not necessarily develop in an order that consistently recapitulated the phyletic history of a species, and that the mature forms of some organisms, including *Homo sapiens*, exhibit the juvenile features of ancestral species rather than the adult features (see de Beer, 1958; Gould, 1977). For example, the facial features of human adults more closely resemble those of the young of our primate cousins (e.g., baboons) than those of the adults. With the fall of the biogenetic law and Lamarckianism, many psychologists turned away from biological and evolutionary explanations of human behavior and embraced Watson's new behaviorism. This led to decades of adherence to a focus on the influence of experiential factors, eventually culminating in the nature–nurture controversy when the role of innate dispositions once again came into the foreground in the work of the ethologists. In general, it was not until the resolution of this controversy that developmentalists were again prepared to entertain phylogenetic views of ontogeny (Oppenheim, 1982).

With the nature–nurture controversy purportedly decades behind us, many developmental psychologists nonetheless remain somewhat skeptical of the adaptationist perspective. In the first edition of this volume, Smith (1987) outlined some of the obstacles that developmental psychologists face in attempting to incorporate modern Darwinism into developmental theory. These include ideological and theoretical obstacles, such as the feeling that evolutionary perspectives are deterministic and pessimistic; that purportedly nonevolved factors, such as learning, cognition, and culture are more important in shaping human development than evolved dispositions; that evolution can explain simple, reflexive behaviors, but not complex behaviors and cognition; and that a consideration of past selective pressures has little to tell us about contemporary human development (Smith, 1987). A further obstacle, not discussed by Smith (1987) is that many developmental psychologists have not been adequately apprised of modern Darwinian concepts to successfully apply this approach to their work, and therefore have been appropriately hesitant. This hesitancy may be lessened by access to an exponentially growing literature, including two compendia addressing the application of modern Darwinism to developmental psychology appearing in the year after Smith's chapter was published (MacDonald, 1988a, 1988b).

Another, more practical, reason why developmentalists have resisted the adaptationist perspective is that reputable developmental studies have and will continue to be successfully completed without employing an evolutionary level of analysis. Developmental phenomena may be explicated at many levels: phenomenological, physiological, sociocultural, behavior genetic, and evolutionary. These varied levels of analysis focus on qualitatively different types of explanations, including proximate, more immediate explanations to distal or evolutionary explanations, and are therefore neither competing nor mutually exclusive. Like the parable of the blindfolded men and the elephant, this suggests that employing multiple levels of analysis will yield the most complete picture of developmental phenomena. Therefore, the goal of this chapter is not to admonish developmental psychologists for not being evolutionists, but rather to demonstrate how an up-to-date Darwinian perspective both complements and promises interesting extensions of the existing literature in the modern field of developmental psychology.

## NEO-DARWINIAN PERSPECTIVES ON DEVELOPMENT

Although influential, Darwin's theory of evolution by natural selection was not extensively or exclusively employed by those individuals whose theories laid the groundwork for the emergence of the modern field of developmental psychology. The reason that Darwin's theory was not widely utilized is that, aside from describing how general behaviors may increase an individual's probability of survival or reproduction, Darwin's definition of fitness was not easily applied in a sophisticated manner to complex human behavior patterns or psychological processes. According to Darwin, over time, natural selection results in an increased frequency of the fittest types of characteristics or individuals in a given population, as measured by those who contribute the greatest number of surviving offspring to the following generation. The modern synthetic view of evolution combines population genetics with natural selection theory and depicts evolution purely as a numbers game, where those genes producing the fittest phenotypes eventually overwhelm alternative alleles in a population by sheer numbers, resulting in a change in gene frequencies.

The concept of *inclusive fitness* (Hamilton, 1964) extends the synthetic view one step further, and is a measure of individual fitness that includes the number of copies of one's genes passed on through surviving offspring, as well as those copies found in descendent collateral kin. Therefore, an individual's inclusive fitness can be increased by behavioral strategies, such as aiding kin, and psychological strategies, such as preferring kin. The concept of inclusive fitness is revolutionary: It explains the seeming paradox of altruism directed toward individuals other than offspring, and it permits the analysis of behavioral and psychological adaptations in ways not afforded by Darwin's conception of fitness. In addition to the physiological chains of events influencing morphology, complicated strings of behavior or psychological processes can now be readily considered as adaptations or strategies (unconscious acts that enable organisms not just to survive, but to leave behind the greatest number of gene copies). Because aiding kin may increase an individual's inclusive fitness, *kin investment*, which includes anything an individual does to help raise a relative's personal fitness, is a basic strategy of many organisms.

A special form of kin investment is *parental investment*, or any investment a parent puts into an offspring at the cost of investing in other offspring (Trivers, 1972). Parental investment may include behaviors involved in the maintenance and training of offspring, as well as a variety of energetic expenditures that increase an offspring's fitness, such as those involved in lactation and gestation. Not surprisingly, offspring have been selected to attempt to garner maximal investment from parents, but because parent and offspring share only 50% of their genes, the possibility of conflict arises with regard to their respective fitness interests. Parental resources are not limitless. Because of this, parental investment has evolved to be conditional and apportioned depending on a number of factors, including environmental conditions, number of dependent offspring, and offspring's *reproductive value*—expected reproductive output during its remaining life. Parents have been selected to withdraw investment in one offspring and invest in another when the fitness payoffs for diverting investment are greater than the costs. Insofar as the offspring's own fitness is best served by producing offspring itself, rather than through the reproduction of siblings, the offspring may resist the withdrawal of parental investment. The situation whereby the fitness interests of the offspring and parent result in a conflict over the duration or amount of parental investment has been termed *parent–offspring conflict*. Genetic conflicts of interest between parents and young are reflected in parent–offspring interactions at a number of developmental stages, including the behavioral conflict occurring at weaning (Trivers, 1974).

Parent–offspring conflict ends when the fitness benefits of offspring continuing to seek investment for themselves are outweighed by the cost to the offspring in terms of the fitness lost by reducing the parent's investment in siblings who share, on average, 50% of the offspring's genes. Before this point is reached, however, offspring may engage in behaviors to encourage further investment. However, parent and offspring are generally not equally matched, and parents may respond to such continued attempts in ways that result in the subjugation of the fitness interests of the offspring to parental interests—a phenomenon referred to as *parental manipulation* (Alexander, 1974). Insofar as the minimum parental investment in offspring differs for male and female parents, the sexes have evolved to partition reproductive effort differently. These *reproductive strategies* reveal themselves typically in adults, although male and female strategies may diverge at earlier developmental stages. Sexually dimorphic reproductive strategies may result from natural selection or the selective pressures resulting from competition for mates—termed *sexual selection*.

Taken together, the neo-Darwinian concepts of inclusive fitness, parental investment, and parent–offspring conflict may be applied to our understanding of the life spans of organisms, including humans, portraying them not as random sequences of events controlled only at the level of immediate experience, but rather as evolved strategies that have been selected because of their long-term consequences on individual fitness. This selection has created a unique complement of genes for each species, whose expression varies over time, resulting in that species' particular *life history strategy*. For the neo-Darwinian, ontogeny involves the passage of individuals through a series of stages, all of which are adapted in some sense to the environmental and social circumstances at that point in the life span. For example, for individuals to become adults and reproduce, they must survive prenatal development, infancy, childhood, and adolescence. Initially synonymous with child psychology, developmental psychology's more recent adherence to a life-span approach therefore increases its compatibility with an adaptationist perspective. From a modern Darwinian view, adulthood is not the only competent stage of the species, but rather each stage displays its own forms of competence, and this is witnessed in the behavior and physiology displayed at each stage.

This chapter traces the stages of human development, applying an adaptationist perspective to phenomena and issues commonly associated with each of these stages in the traditional psychological literature. It begins by considering how the conceptus—a partially foreign cell—has evolved to inhabit its mother's body, when this squatting may at times benefit a mother's fitness and conflict with it at others. The adaptive features with which newborns are equipped are then discussed as mechanisms to both garner parental investment and by which parents assess the reproductive value of offspring. The extended juvenile phase in human beings is described as functional, in that it provides time for the learning of survival skills and the socialization of children, which is dependent on the maturation of particular mental processes. Adolescence is a crossroads—a stage involving a virtual metamorphosis, whereby childhood strategies shift toward those of the reproductive phase of life. Evolved sex differences in mate selection and later life behaviors, discriminative parental solicitude, and senescence and its physiological and behavioral sequelae highlight how adults and seniors play out the final acts in the human life history.

## CONFLUENCE AND CONFLICTS OF INTEREST
## IN THE PRENATAL MOTHER–OFFSPRING
## RELATIONSHIP

Once a mysterious process, prenatal development is disclosed in glossy photos in modern developmental texts and described in matter-of-fact chronological detail. With few exceptions (e.g., Smith & Cowie, 1991), evolutionary considerations and questions concerning such developmental phenomena rarely appear in modern texts. For example, *how* and *why* the human conceptus, a foreign tissue containing only one half of the maternal genotype, like the zygotes of all sexually reproducing species, not only survives but thrives in the maternal environment are questions not typically pondered. The answer is that, along the road to viviparity (production of living offspring that develop within the mother), numerous maternal and embryonic adaptations co-evolved, allowing foreign cells access to and lodging in a mother's body. The conceptus evolved to infiltrate the mother's tissues, manipulate her physiology to its own benefit, and extract resources. The resulting changes in physiology and behavior that serve to differentiate the sexes are examples of *gestation-driven selection* (GDS)—selection pressures exerted on a female by the presence of internally gestating young. Mothers have also been subject to external selective pressures, such as availability of resources, and have been selected to apportion prenatal investment according to both environmental conditions and the reproductive value of offspring. Fetal fitness interests in extracting maternal resources may at times conflict with a mother's fitness as a consequence of providing these resources. Although often discussed in the context of the postnatal parent–offspring relationship, Trivers (1974) suggested that the notion of parent–offspring conflict may apply equally to the prenatal mother–child relationship. Does the normal human experience of pregnancy and prenatal development conform to a parent–offspring conflict model, revealing the adaptations driven by selection pressures operating on this early stage of development?

Because the human conceptus is an allograft, containing only half of its mother's genes and half of its father's, the maternal genome should recognize the conceptus as an incomplete copy of itself, and it should be at great risk of immunological rejection. Most organisms evolved defense mechanisms against the invasion of parasites, and overcoming such immunological rejection was a milestone in the evolution of viviparity. The embryos of egg-laying (oviparous) species do not face this same problem because they are encased in various membranes and shells of maternal origin, and are thus protected from the maternal immune system until ejected (Sharman, 1976).

In this sense, laying an egg is just a female's way of ridding herself of a foreign cell. During the evolution of placental mammals, embryos devised means of avoiding immunological rejection, as their membranes became specialized to make contact with the maternal environment for the purposes of drawing resources. Presumably the costs of overcoming immunological rejection for mother and embryo alike were less than the benefits afforded by viviparity, hence placentation has evolved independently in a number of animal lineages (Trevathan, 1987). Internal gestation enables a female to both identify and invest solely in young who carry copies of a high proportion of her genes (50%). Moreover, it constrains the production of offspring to times when resources are plentiful and female parental investment maximal, by conferring direct control over the number of offspring produced and the timing of reproduction through the alteration of ovulation rates and spontaneous abortion. From the point of view of the offspring, viviparity provides a buffer from environmental perturbations and a manipulable host from whom resources can be drawn and behaviors elicited.

Although overcoming maternal immunological rejection is one ability that has clearly evolved in the embryos of placental mammals, the particular mechanisms by which this occurs are not fully elucidated, nor is this a perfect system. There is some evidence that, as the conceptus attaches to the uterine lining, it emits hormones that effectively suppress the maternal immune response at the site of implantation (Smart, Roberts, Clancy, & Cripps, 1981), and that the placenta acts as a barrier to the entry of maternal cells and antibodies to the fetus (Wegmann, 1983). Furthermore, the obstetrical literature is rife with other examples demonstrating that the conceptus is more than just a passive hitchhiker in its mother's body; actively invading maternal tissues, it eventually alters maternal physiology to meet its own metabolic needs. For example, as the rapidly dividing fertilized egg approaches the site of implantation, it secretes enzymes that in effect alter cells in the uterine lining, allowing it to attach (Begley, Firth, & Hoult, 1980). Once implanted, the suppression of the menstrual cycle necessary for continued development is achieved by the the secretion of human chorionic gonadatropin (hCG) by the trophoblast (exterior layer of the developing fertilized ovum) into the uterine vessels. The secretion of hCG prevents the involution of the corpus luteum, thus maintaining progesterone and estradiol secretion. Because menstruation is dependent on the withdrawal of these two hormones, menstruation is effectively suppressed. During later stages of development, pregnancy is maintained by the secretion of steroids (e.g., progesterone) from the trophoblast. If the placental tissues should fail to secrete such steroids, there is a breakdown in the endometrium and pregnancy is terminated (Begley, Firth, & Hoult, 1980).

Once pregnancy is established, female physiology undergoes sometimes rapid and dramatic changes. As described in any current text on human reproduction, most major systems (e.g., cardiovascular-renal, pulmonary, endocrine, and gastrointestinal) are affected. In humans, alteration of such systems often creates symptoms that, to a certain degree, are recognized by medical practitioners as normal complications of pregnancy because they occur in a significant proportion of women. Such complications may arise as a direct result of trophoblastic secretions affecting target organs, indirectly as a result of suppression or alteration of normal maternal functioning, or as a response of female systems to the presence of fetal hormones. In sharp contrast to the traditional medical model, Haig (1993) recently described in impressive detail how medical complications of pregnancy may be expressions of genetic conflicts between a fetus and mother, whereby, as a result of the fetus being selected to extract more resources from the mother than the mother has evolved to impart, a wavering compromise has been struck.

For example, pregnancy has often been referred to as a diabetogenic state (Huff, 1979). Carbohydrate metabolism and normal pancreatic function are altered markedly in the pregnant woman. These changes, which often result in diabetic symptoms, are related to human placental lactogen, which has antiinsulin properties. It appears that energy metabolism in pregnant women utilizes fatty acids, rather than carbohydrates, so that carbohydrates are then spared for the use of the fetus. Diversion of carbohydrate utilization for the use of the fetus then interrupts the mother's own metabolic function, and sometimes results in a diabetic-like state. The maternal respiratory system also undergoes changes to allow the optimum environment for fetal respiratory exchange. These changes contribute to the hyperventilation typical of pregnancy, which is often associated with complaints of breathlessness in 60% to 70% of women. To accommodate the fetus' needs, the arterial partial pressure of $CO_2$ is lowered, resulting in hyperventilation and an increase of oxygen uptake by 20% in the mother (Hayashi, 1979). Iron deficiency anemia often occurs in pregnancy because most healthy women do not have enough iron in storage to meet the demands of pregnancy. The fetus demands 800 mg of iron, and iron passes preferentially across the placenta to aid in the formation of fetal blood cells, despite maternal deficiencies (Hayashi, 1979). Thus, the fetus of a mother with iron deficiency is rarely anemic itself, and the preferential crossing of iron to the fetus from the mother can have detrimental effects on the mother's health.

Pregnancy sickness, including nausea and vomiting, is a very common, but ill-explained, symptom of pregnancy. One proximal explanation relates it to the secretion of gonadotropic hormone produced by the trophoblast early in pregnancy, and suggests that degree of vulnerability to pregnancy sickness is loosely tied to circulating levels of this hormone (Jacobs & Janovich, 1975). But why didn't natural selection eliminate this rather nasty symptom of pregnancy? Profet (1992) convincingly argued that the heightened sensitivity to the odiforous and gustatory qualities of food underlying pregnancy sickness is an adaptation that has arisen to protect the fetus from exposure to naturally occurring toxins in the Pleistocene diet. She maintained that the primary symptoms of nausea and vomiting represent proximate mechanisms to deter maternal ingestion of foods that may have teratogenic (defect-inducing) effects on the developing fetus. She provided evidence substantiating that pregnancy sickness is at its peak during organogenesis, the most vulnerable stage of embryonic development, and that the most violent reactions occur to foodstuffs having bitter or pungent flavors—flavors that tend to be associated with the presence of toxins. Therefore, pregnancy sickness serves to enhance embryonic fitness, and thus maternal fitness, by protecting the embryo from exposure to teratogens.

Pregnancy sickness may protect the vulnerable fetus from exposure to teratogens and enhance maternal and fetal fitness, but this begs the question as to why the fetus is so vulnerable in the first place. Should not fetal defense mechanisms have evolved to render it invulnerable to environmental perturbations? The answer is apparently no. A totally invulnerable fetus could develop at the complete expense of the mother. Extreme insensitivity to the maternal environment could result in a dead or spent mother with the fetus not likely to survive much beyond this period of invulnerability. An optimal level of vulnerability presumably has been selected because, under some conditions, a fetus who gives up its life (e.g., is vulnerable), resulting in parental investment being more appropriately diverted elsewhere, may have a higher level of inclusive fitness than one that is completely invulnerable. Although fetal vulnerability may select for maternal avoidance of toxins, it is also a necessary precondition for prenatal suicide or sibling altruism and maternal termination of pregnancy, in which fetal inclusive fitness is enhanced through the increased fitness of siblings at the expense of fetal survival.

The early termination of pregnancy by a mother is a strategy invoked to end parental investment when the costs of reproducing at that time are too high (Wasser & Barash, 1983). Indicants of poor maternal environmental conditions, such as undernutrition, physical trauma, and emotional distress, have been related to increased rates of spontaneous abortion. Presumably, terminating parental investment under these conditions and waiting for more auspicious times have enhanced female fitness. Bernds and Barash (1979) suggested that along with the evolution of relatively high levels of parental investment should have evolved mechanisms to facilitate the early termination of parental investment in offspring that represent a poor future investment. In humans, spontaneous abortion occurs at a high rate and represents one means of eliminating offspring of low reproductive value at little cost to the mother. A high percentage of aborted fetuses have genetic or morphological anomalies; presumably, inappropriate signals emanating from them may fail to suppress the maternal immune system, leading to immunological rejection, or fail to adequately manipulate maternal physiology to sustain development. Therefore, there seem to be two types of spontaneous abortions: those that involve the abortion of defective zygotes in a good maternal environment, and those that involve abortion of a nondefective zygote in a less than optimal maternal environment.

If genetic conflicts of interest are endemic to the prenatal mother–offspring relationship, as described by Haig (1993), we might expect natural selection to have produced adaptations serving to mediate such conflicts between mother and fetus, according to internal and external conditions. In an ingenious article, Mackey (1984) suggested that the placenta has evolved to fulfill this role. Mackey likened the placenta to an identical twin of the fetus. It has the identical gene complement and its own metabolism and life span, it can live even after the fetus has died, and it is generally less dependent on the fetus than the fetus is on it. However, the placenta cannot reproduce; like the infertile workers in eusocial insect species, it must depend on other means by which to maximize fitness. What is the best way for the placenta to increase its own fitness? One way is to support the life and growth of its fertile sibling. When the benefits of supporting the development of its fertile twin are outweighed by the costs to maternal fitness, then we might expect the placenta to shift its investment. If the mother dies, so do both the placenta and fetus. Therefore, although the placenta is usually seen as an organ whose main function is to nourish and sustain the fetus, selection pressures would limit the extent of this benevolent energy flow.

Under some conditions (e.g., low reproductive value of fetus, scarcity of resources threatening the life of the mother), we might expect the placenta to cut its investment in the fetus entirely, resulting in the death and spontaneous abortion or resorption of the fetus. The evidence in support of this bias toward maternal fitness interests is overwhelming. When conditions are not conducive to the successful gestation of a child, it is generally the fetus who succumbs rather than the mother. In an analysis of data from the U.S. National Center for Health Statistics, Mackey (1984) showed how fetal death rates are consistently higher than maternal death rates. In Mackey's words, the placenta is essentially a "celibate sibling" who referees the contest between maternal and fetal interests, acting to minimize maternal deaths at the expense of fetal deaths. The placenta, while representing a biological necessity in the evolution of viviparity, also has theoretical importance in the role it plays in parent–offspring conflict. The placenta, which displays great differentiation between lineages and has evolved numerous times within lineages (Trevathan, 1987), exists primarily as a result of internal selective pressures ensuing from maternal–fetal genetic conflict.

In addition to the complications arising during pregnancy, the timing of parturition and the related phenomenon of birth weight may also be interpreted in light of parent–offspring conflict. In most mammals, parturition appears to be at least partially under the control of the fetus, and in many the timing and onset of parturition appears to be an autonomous function of the fetus. For example, in the ewe, increased levels of cortisol in the fetal circulation precipitate a fall in progesterone secretion, which in turn stimulates the onset of labor (Liggins, 1969). Some fetal control of parturition makes sense because both late and early termination of gestation are associated with increased neonatal mortality. Nevertheless, alterations in gestational length should also be associated with costs and benefits for the mother. In this light, Blurton Jones (1978) offered a prescient reinterpretation of the common finding that the average birth weight of human infants is somewhat lower than the weight associated with the lowest risk of perinatal mortality (e.g., Karn & Penrose, 1952).

This finding had been long considered a counterexample of the potency of natural selection because one would assume that natural selection would result in a birth weight associated with maximum robustness. Indeed, from the point of view of the offspring, the longer it remains in utero and the greater its size, the higher the probability of survival following birth and the greater its personal fitness. However, from the point of view of the mother, an offspring who remains in utero too long, growing too large, will not only increase the hazards associated with childbirth, including maternal mortality, but even if birthed successfully may reduce a mother's future ability to produce or invest in subsequent offspring. Under these conditions, selection would have resulted in offspring ceasing to extract maternal resources when the costs (high probability of a caregiver dying or shared genes lost in existing or potential siblings) outweigh the benefits (increased personal fitness through the production of additional offspring). Therefore, the timing of human birth and the weight accrued up to that point in time represent a compromise between offspring and maternal personal fitness interests.

## THE COMPETENT INFANT

Selection for larger brain size and plasticity in brain development in the hominid line are reflected in the human neonate making its entry into the world as a seemingly helpless creature whose brain does not reach maturity until many years after birth. Presumably, the size of the hominid birth canal and bipedalism constrained brain size at birth, resulting in a major portion of brain development occurring outside the womb under the relatively direct influence of the environment (Trevathan, 1987). Compared with the precocious offspring of other mammalian species, such as guinea pigs, human infants are immature and incapable of survival by themselves. Yet, over five decades of developmental research have shown that human neonates are by no means totally helpless and passive. They come into the world with numerous abilities that may be considered adaptations to this dependent stage of life, and are active participants in their own development. At birth, the offspring of viviparous species must shift strategies because it is no longer capable of altering its environment (its mother) through cellular manipulation, as does the embryo or fetus. Other properties of the individual, such as behavior, become important in negotiating the neonatal stage of development.

The human infant is born with a set of useful motor reflexes (e.g., sucking, rooting, palmar) that precede and temporarily fill in for voluntary motor movements that will develop later. Interestingly, these reflexes occur as a result of the spinal cord maturing before the primary motor cortex, in a developmental sequence opposite to the usual trajectory of physical maturation, which proceeds in a cephalocaudal direction (Kalat, 1992). In addition, the newborn infant is capable of perceiving and organizing complex information, selectively attending to particular stimuli such as human faces and voices, imitating, and learning (Butterfield & Siperstein, 1974; Johnson, Dziurawiec, Ellis, & Morton, 1991). Lorenz (1971) noted that the young of many species also tend to possess physical features that elicit nurturing and parental feelings. Human babies have a distinctive odor that appears to play a role in recognition and attraction, and thereby consolidation of the emotional bond between parent and infant (Fabes & Filsinger, 1988; Fleming, Corter, Franks, Surbey, Schneider, & Steiner, 1993; Porter, Cernoch, & McLaughlin, 1983; Russell, Mendelson, & Peeke, 1983). Most important, the newborn is capable of communication, social exchange, and behaviors promoting attachment between itself and a caregiver.

Bowlby's (1969) influential theory of attachment incorporated an ethological view into traditional psychoanalytic theory and emphasized that infants were predisposed to form attachments. In a pivotal extension of this ethological tradition, Goldberg (1977) described how infants participate in reciprocal contingencies with their caregivers that revolve around mutual feelings of efficacy. According to Goldberg, parental feelings of efficacy are produced when parental behaviors result in desirable infant responses. Increased feelings of parental efficacy serve to both reinforce the behaviors that produced them and enhance attachment. Similarly, feelings of efficacy instilled in an infant by appropriate parental responses to infant behaviors reinforce the repetition of those behaviors, but also facilitate development by promoting increased exploration and the rehearsal of new skills. The infant's capacity to engage in reciprocal exchanges, thereby increasing parental feelings of efficacy, are affected by its ability to clearly communicate its needs, or its *readability*, the *predictability* of its responses, and its *responsiveness* or production of appropriate responses with relatively short latencies (Goldberg, 1977). The behaviors of infants lacking these capabilities, due to physical or mental handicaps, for example, may lead to reduced feelings of parental efficacy and increased levels of frustration, although heightened parental sensitivity and motivation may compensate for such infant incompetencies. Underlying Goldberg's model of infant attachment is the implicit suggestion that maternal feelings, being somewhat labile after birth, are presumably influenced both by characteristics of the infant and maternal condition and motivation. The qualities of the infant, whether it is capable of sending the appropriate cues to the parent and responding in a way that builds parental efficacy, interact with maternal factors to either promote or attenuate attachment.

This notion crystallizes in Daly and Wilson's (1988) functional perspective on the development of the mother–infant bond after birth. In an original and important evolutionary treatise on human homicide, these authors suggested that a period of *assessment* occurs immediately after birth, where both the condition of the infant and a mother's present circumstances influence the quality of the emotional bond. Maternal indifference and ambivalence toward infants is not uncommon at this stage. Daly and Wilson considered the initial lability after birth an adaptive mechanism, allowing a parent to terminate investment when the costs of investing in an infant are too great or when the infant is of low reproductive value. For example, when maternal circumstances are not conducive to childrearing, a period of flattened affect may facilitate abandonment or neglect of a child and increase the likelihood of infanticide, hence enabling a mother to forego childrearing until more favorable times. Ambivalence following birth may also be functional in that it serves to reduce the psychological pain of the early death of a defective infant or increase the likelihood of a mother giving up a child who is likely to die, and redirecting investment into other existing or future offspring.

A 2 × 2 table (Fig. 12.1), where the condition or reproductive value of a child is crossed with the condition or circumstances of the mother, enables the formation of predictions about the quality of mother–child attachment consistent with Daly and Wilson's logic. Each cell in the figure represents a different combination of circumstances that are associated with different costs and benefits for maternal provisioning and infant solicitation of investment, which together result in different outcomes for

## Infant's Reproductive Value

|  | LOW | HIGH |
|---|---|---|
| **POOR** | Poor attachment, low parental investment, highest rate of infanticide & neglect | Intermediate attachment, parental investment (<C) & neglect |
|  | **A** | **B** |
|  | **C** | **D** |
| **GOOD** | Intermediate attachment, parental investment, maternal compensation for infant deficits | High level of attachment, parental investment, mutual feelings of efficacy |

*Maternal Conditions* (vertical label on left axis)

FIG. 12.1. The predicted level of attachment, parental investment, and parental and nonparental behaviors when an offspring is of low or high reproductive value and the mother is in poor or good condition.

parent–infant attachment. When a child is atypical in a way that lowers its reproductive value or is unable to produce the cues that elicit parental solicitude, and its mother is in poor physical or emotional condition or environmental circumstances (Cell A), one would expect the mother–infant bond to be the poorest. When an infant is in good condition, but the mother is not (Cell B), mother–infant attachment will be better, but reduced compared with the situation where the infant is of low reproductive value and the mother is otherwise in good condition (Cell C), because we would expect parent–offspring conflict to result in a bias toward the mother's fitness interests.

A comparison between these two cells would include a comparison of the attachment process in highly motivated secure mothers of premature infants compared with attachment between poor unprepared mothers living in stressful conditions without family or community support who have essentially normal children at birth. The situation in which both maternal conditions and a child's reproductive value are high (Cell D) should lead to the highest level of mother–infant attachment. Although fairly simplistic predictions can be derived from this model (e.g., the quality of mother–infant attachment and parental investment in each of the four cells will follow the order: A < B < C < D), more variables, such as maternal age and child's age or birth order, can be added to create more specific, perhaps somewhat counterintuitive, hypotheses.

Although most extant studies do not include all four conditions described in Fig. 12.1, there is empirical evidence in support of the main effects and some of the pairwise comparisons predicted therein. In a cross-cultural study, Daly and Wilson (1984, 1988) examined the patterns of infanticide in a sample of 60 societies drawn from the Human Relations Area Files. Presumably, infanticide represents both a failure in the parent–offspring bond and the most extreme and final form of withdrawal of parental investment. Daly and Wilson suggested that if parental psychology has been shaped by selection to make adaptive decisions about when to invest in offspring, one might expect reluctance to invest in offspring (a) when there is some doubt that the putative offspring is indeed the parent's genetic offspring, (b) if a child is abnormal or nonviable and unlikely to contribute to parental fitness even if nurtured, and (c) if childrearing attempts in a parent's current circumstances are likely to be futile (e.g., under conditions of food scarcity). Daly and Wilson noted 112 infanticidal circumstances in their sample, along with the purported rationale for these acts. In 20 societies, circumstances suggesting the infant was probably not or clearly not the child of the woman's husband were described. In some of these cases, a mother's decision to kill the infant was related to her husband's overt or implicit reluctance to nurture another man's child. Characteristics indicative of low reproductive value, such as physical deformities and serious illness, were reasons given for the infanticide and abandonment of infants in 21 societies. Situations suggesting that the fitness costs associated with childrearing may outweigh the benefits because of a mother's circumstances were reported in 56 societies. These included the killing of one in a set of twins, of an infant born too soon after another child or into a family already considered too large, or the killing of infants where the mother was unwed, lacked male support, or was facing economic hardship. In this study, then, maternal circumstances were most often cited in the decision to kill infants—a prediction corresponding to the main effect of maternal conditions in Fig. 12.1.

Daly and Wilson focused on the stated reasons for withdrawing investment or killing a child, whereas Mann (1992) explored some of the factors involved in maternal decisions to care for high-risk offspring. Mann suggested that when parents are faced with a high-risk child, they can either cut their investment and minimize their cost or increase their investment to meet the child's heightened needs. She examined maternal behavior directed toward seven pairs of extremely low birth weight (ELBW) twins who were discordant in health status. She recorded the behavioral interactions between a mother and the healthy twin, compared with the unhealthy twin. She found that more positive parental behaviors (e.g., holding, soothing, mutual gazing) were directed toward the healthy twin versus the sicker twin, and that this was not affected by differences in exposure to the twins related to different discharge dates. She concluded that when presented with both a healthy and unhealthy twin, mothers biased their investment toward the healthy twin. These results are consistent with the main effect for infants' reproductive value predicted in Fig. 12.1, whereby, everything else being equal, mothers should invest more readily in a healthy than a sick child. In addition, although Mann's sample was too small to examine socioeconomic effects, she predicted that mothers of higher economic status may have invested more in the sicker twin than mothers with fewer resources. These expectations are consistent with the interaction between infant reproductive value and maternal conditions predicted in Fig. 12.1.

## ADAPTATIONS OF CHILDHOOD EXISTENCE

Although infants depend on the skills of their parents or guardians for survival, children must begin the long process of acquiring these skills for themselves. Humans have an extended childhood or juvenile stage compared with other mammals (Tanner, 1962), during which the best strategy for a child involves accruing the highest level of parental investment (resources, nurturing, love) and learning skills from the parent that will enable the successful negotiation of adulthood. In addition to acquiring information relevant to basic survival, the goals of childhood include the internalization of social rules and the development of social skills necessary for the formation of social networks on which all social animals depend. As described by Charlesworth (1988), "The main goal of socialization is to ensure the child's later adaptation and reproductive success" (p. 53). Because parents are the main agents of socialization, Slavin (1985) suggested that such goals necessitate a child's conformity with parental desires, although parental fitness interests are not identical with those of the child. Such parent–offspring conflict is just one particular type of conflict of interest in which most social organisms find themselves.

To the extent that any organism is social and depends on social networks, it is inherently conflicted, caught in a balancing act between its own needs and the needs of others in the social landscape. Clearly, under some conditions, self-interested behavior has evolved to predominate, and this may entail outward conflict as well as deceptive ploys. Trivers (1985) and Alexander (1975) suggested that, among social species where individuals mutually benefit from reciprocity, there has been selection to detect deception. The evolution of mechanisms to spot deception has in turn selected for self-deception and other psychological mechanisms, allowing the deceiver to be unconscious of his or her own motivations, thereby being better able to conceal deception. In addition to facilitating deception, however, self-deception may allow individuals to repress and disguise their own needs to reduce internal conflict and avoid conscious recognition of the selfish motives of others to facilitate long-term social relationships (Nesse & Lloyd, 1992).

A number of fascinating attempts to integrate psychodynamic theory with evolutionary thought (e.g., Badcock, 1986; Nesse & Lloyd, 1992; Slavin, 1985) reflect the notion that the function of psychological development during childhood goes beyond producing individuals capable of integrating experience with abstract reasoning skills and performing competently in the human environment to maintaining the crucial social relationship between parent and child. In a compelling argument, Slavin (1985) suggested that repression during childhood, broadly defined, represents an adaptive mechanism regulating parent–offspring conflict, thus playing a fundamental role in the maintenance of the parent–child relationship during the extended juvenile stage of development. Cognitive mechanisms, such as those manifested in the *self-serving biases*, rendering particular types of information about oneself or others more or less accessible, are not unique to childhood or to children, and also appear to play a functional role in adult social relationships (see Krebs, Denton, & Higgins, 1988). Further to this point, Nesse and Lloyd (1992) suggested that the ego defense mechanisms, as described by Freud, have been shaped by natural selection and "appear to be related to the tasks faced at each phase of life" (p. 601).

Over two decades ago, Trivers (1974) suggested that regression, a highly observable defense mechanism, played a role in moderating parent–offspring conflict. Although it is also displayed at other life stages, Trivers suggested that regression is a psychological tactic engaged in by children to extend the period of parental investment during a time of parent–offspring conflict. Regression involves older children exhibiting behaviors typical of younger children and infants, thus appearing more dependent than they actually are; it is often observed when a new child is born into the family. To the extent that this unusual behavior captures parental attention, an offspring who engages in it may be successful in resisting the complete diversion of parental investment toward a new sibling.

In addition to regression, identification and introjection may be important mechanisms for garnering investment, reducing parent–offspring conflict, and in the intergenerational transmission of culture and social rules. These defense mechanisms result in children taking on the values and characteristics of their parents and the internalization of social norms and beliefs. In particular, identification aligns parental and offspring views, thus reducing conflict, but it may also be very useful to a child in accruing parental investment through favoritism. There is a tendency for parents to feel closer to children who are most like them and, as discussed in a later section, to grieve more intensely for them than for children who are dissimilar (Littlefield & Rushton, 1986).

The parent–child relationship and other kin relationships tend to be the most important long-term relationships formed in *Homo sapiens*, and in this sense repression and the defense mechanisms may have evolved via kin selection. Maintaining long-term bonds with kin, such as those that develop between child and parent, may necessitate the suppression of self-interests of one or the other party for prescribed periods of time. This way a child's self-interest can be submerged during the period of dependence, yet remain intact and accessible for guiding behavior in later stages of life when parental investment is no longer crucial to offspring fitness. This is why Slavin (1985) suggested that failures of repression occur during adolescence (the initiation of the reproductive life), and it may also be why repressed childhood experiences and wishes are often revealed in adulthood, when we would expect the mechanisms of repression to let up somewhat.

Hence, while the placenta acts as a referee in the biological contest arising out of parent–offspring conflict in utero, repression acts as a psychological arbitrator maintaining a tenuous equilibrium between the fitness interests of parent and offspring during an extended childhood. According to Slavin (1985), childhood wishes and motivations that are acceptable to the parent and maintain family cohesiveness remain in a child's consciousness, whereas those that are not congruent with parental views are repressed and exist primarily at the level of the unconscious. At adolescence, the individual's self-interest begins to emerge again as it gains independence and, as a sexually mature organism, is able to pursue its own fitness interests through the production of its own offspring. This self-interest, however, remains constrained by the need to maintain and build social support networks with both kin and nonkin.

## ADOLESCENCE AND PHYLOGENY

Imagine the human life history as a fiber-optic bundle of waning and emerging adaptations winding itself from conception into senescence. If we were to slice the human life history at any particular point and examine the fibers of our ontogenetic past and future, it is the point at which the reproductive life begins—adolescence—in which the greatest numbers of fibers would be revealed. Charlesworth (1988) partitioned the human life history into two general phases: prereproductive and reproductive. At the end of the prereproductive phase, a child must transform from a dependent organism, incapable of reproduction and self-sustenance, into an autonomous, reproductively mature individual capable of dealing with a wide variety of environmental exigencies (Charlesworth, 1988). Adolescence approximates this period of transformation. In becoming autonomous, reproductively mature individuals, adolescents' fitness interests begin to diverge distinctly from the interests of parents. According to the concept of parent–offspring conflict, we would expect heightened manifestations of conflict at points in the life span when parental investment decreases, or when the (repressed) self-interests of offspring emerge. Adolescence is precisely one of these points in the life span. Interestingly, one of Hall's (1904) contributions to the study of adolescence was the notion that adolescence was necessarily a time of storm and stress; he attributed this in part to the underlying biological changes occurring at puberty. Although this perspective is consistent with a parent–offspring conflict model, it has been hotly disputed in both the psychological and anthropological literatures, with anthropologist Margaret Mead (1928) being one of the most notable critics of this position.

Weisfeld and Billings (1988) authored what is still the most comprehensive overview of human adolescence from an evolutionary perspective. A "must-read" for anyone interested in adolescence, this review includes detailed discussions and functional analyses of topics including: comparative maturation rates in primates, the social-psychological sequelae of early and late puberty in girls and boys, and intergenerational conflict. If one has not yet come to this realization, it becomes readily apparent that adolescence entails the only true metamorphosis in the human life span. Prior to puberty, girls and boys have similar body shapes and distributions of fat, but at puberty these morphological traits undergo rapid transformation and divergence. The physical changes at puberty that result in the acquisition of secondary sexual characteristics are accompanied by behavioral and psychological changes, such as increased aggressiveness in boys, higher levels of nurturance in girls, and changes in attractiveness and dominance (Weisfeld & Billings, 1988). Therefore, the metamorphosis at adolescence includes dramatic morphological changes, as well as psychological and behavioral changes that call out for explanation beyond the proximal level. How has the human life history come to contain this highly apparent stage with these particular characteristics? Why do girls mature (at least outwardly) earlier than boys? Why does the onset of gametogenesis (the production of sperm and ova) occur relatively early in the sequence of pubertal events in boys, but late in girls? Why is early maturity socially disadvantageous for girls, but advantageous for boys?

*Homo sapiens* exhibit sexual dimorphism in maturation rate, with girls beginning the sequence of pubertal changes, including the height spurt, approximately 2 years earlier than boys (Tanner, 1962). Due to the cessation of menstruation at menopause, the length of the reproductive life span in female humans is truncated compared with males. Presumably the fitness of female mammals is affected more by the length of the reproductive life span than is male fitness; if an earlier onset of puberty serves to lengthen the reproductive life span, then it should have been selected. Therefore, selective pressures driving the age of female puberty downward may account for human sexual bimaturism. Although girls begin to go through puberty earlier than boys, they do not experience menarche until relatively late in the sequence of pubertal events. In contrast, boys produce sperm early in the sequence of events, even when they do not yet possess the mature morphological features necessary to successfully compete for mates. Therefore, girls possess the outward signs of reproductive maturity before they can conceive, but the opposite is true for boys.

This suggests that there may have been different selective pressures acting on the timing of external morphological changes and gametogenesis in boys and girls. Late puberty in males may reduce competition with older males, and the accompanying small size may protect a young male from aggression by older males. Nevertheless, such an underdeveloped juvenile male could theoretically fertilize a female should the opportunity arise, so the early production of sperm may have been favored by selection. For girls, appearing more mature than they are may be advantageous if it aids in the choice of the best possible mate and further preparation for childrearing. Because human infants require extensive parental care, females should have been selected to choose mates who will invest both behaviorally and economically in children. The early physical changes at puberty (e.g., breast development) tend to attract male attention and may allow for more careful selection of a mate before conception, either through the observation of male–male competition or the prolonged assessment of potential mates.

Weisfeld and Billings (1988) also noted that the long juvenile growth period typical of humans provides time for learning about child care. Based on extant hunter–gatherer populations, such as the !Kung San (Howell, 1979), it would appear that the prototypic human girl usually reaches menarche at 16 to 17 years of age. Because of a period of adolescent subfertility, first births do not usually occur until 19 to 20 years of age. This suggests that, throughout much of human history, most females had approximately two decades to acquire cognitive, survival, and parenting skills before becoming a parent.

In many modern societies, there has been an uncoupling of reproductive development from cognitive and social development because the age at menarche has declined considerably over the last century (Tanner, 1962). Most North American girls now achieve menarche between 12 and 13 years of age, on average, and are able to become pregnant shortly after the first decade of life. The babies of teenage mothers are at greater risk of abuse, are unlikely to receive assistance from fathers, and have more health problems due to poor prenatal care than the babies of older mothers (see Konner & Shostak, 1986). Early reproduction, which tends to preclude the careful selection of a mate and adequate social and emotional preparation, is not only atypical of ancestral *Homo sapiens,* but appears to be disadvantageous for many modern girls and their babies. As aptly stated by Weisfeld and Billings (1988), "American adolescents' bodies, then, are prepared for parenthood very early, but their minds seem not to have kept pace" (p. 211). The costs of early puberty and reproduction are borne primarily by girls. As reviewed by Weisfeld and Billings (1988), early maturity in boys tends to be advantageous. Early maturing boys are larger and more developed than peers and are considered more attractive and mature by peers and adults. They are more likely to excel at sports, more often chosen as leaders, and, in ethological terms, hold higher positions on the male dominance hierarchy.

The secular decline in menarche has been attributed to changes in health care and nutrition, exposure to artificial light, and socioenvironmental factors (Johnston, 1974; Surbey, 1990). Because mammalian females invest so heavily in offspring and reproductive mistakes are costly, female reproductive function should be more highly sensitive to bodily and environmental conditions than it is in males. Human females, like other mammalian females, appear to possess mechanisms to both delay and accelerate puberty and reproduction when warranted by environmental conditions (Anderson & Crawford, 1992; Surbey, 1987a; Wasser & Barash, 1983). In the mid-1980s, Surbey (1988, 1990) tested three hypotheses regarding the relationship between girls' exposure to family members, stress (as measured by a life events index), and timing of menarche based on these two assumptions. These hypotheses included the inbreeding avoidance hypothesis, which suggests girls may delay menarche in the presence of a related adult male (a biological father), the possibility that girls may adaptively adjust developmental trajectories and employ alternative reproductive strategies in different rearing environments (Draper & Harpending, 1982), and the hypothesis that physical maturation may be accelerated in stressful environments due to a compensatory response.

Among her most interesting results, Surbey reported that age of menarche was earlier in girls who reported experiencing high levels of stress and the absence of their biological fathers, compared with those girls experiencing little stress and growing up continuously with both biological parents (Surbey, 1987b, 1988, 1990). The mothers of father-absent girls were also early maturers, and this accounted for the effect of father absence, but not for the acceleration of puberty under stressful conditions. Some of Surbey's results have since been replicated by others (e.g., Graber, Brooks-Gunn, & Warren, 1995; Mekos, Hetherington, Clingempeel, & Reiss, 1995; Moffitt, Caspi, Belsky, & Silva, 1992). In 1991,

Belsky, Steinberg, and Draper extended Draper and Harpending's (1982) hypothesis, suggesting that father-absent and father-present children employ alternative reproductive strategies, and predicted the relationship among stress, father absence, and menarche previously reported by Surbey (1987b, 1988, 1990).

Although Surbey's results were consistent with the Draper and Harpending hypothesis, they also could have been explained, in large part, by a simple behavior-genetic effect, without drawing on the problematic notion of alternative reproductive strategies (Surbey, 1988, 1990). That is, women who have matured, married, and had children at an early age are more likely to divorce and produce father-absent daughters who have experienced high levels of stress than are later maturers (Surbey, 1990). Because the timing of menarche is moderately heritable, the early menarche observed in father-absent girls is due, in part, to the inheritance of an early age at puberty from their mothers and to the acceleratory effects of exposure to stress. Early puberty and reduced parental supervision puts such girls at risk for early pregnancy, and thus the cycle of father absence, economic and social disadvantage, and early pregnancy continues. Therefore, the different trajectories experienced by father-absent and father-present girls in modern societies may be consistent with, but are not necessarily equivalent to, evolved alternative reproductive strategies.

Surbey (1993) was unable to replicate her findings in a male sample, and her results may be indicative of an evolved, sex-specific sensitivity to environmental events, resulting in either the delay or acceleration of puberty. In particular, Surbey (1988, 1990) suggested that mechanisms that compensate for the reproductive delays caused by stress or illness may have been particularly selected in females because their fitness is more dependent on the length of the reproductive life span than is male fitness. Her findings of a relationship between childhood stress and early menarche provide support for the counterintuitive proposition that stress may have an acceleratory, rather than a retarding, effect on development. In addition, Surbey's results may be particularly useful in targeting girls at risk for early puberty and, therefore, early pregnancy, which, as discussed in an earlier section, tends to be associated with poor outcomes for mother and child. In this sense, evolutionary considerations of both the causes and consequences of pubertal timing may have practical value and serve to place modern situations into perspective. The problems experienced by modern, early maturing, teenage mothers and their children would have been rare among our relatively late-maturing, Pleistocene ancestors, and are further testimony to the inherent difficulties associated with unusually early reproduction in *Homo sapiens*.

Trivers (1974) suggested that, insofar as offspring reproductive success affects parental fitness, parents should have an interest in the reproductive behavior of their offspring. In those species where female investment in offspring is substantially greater than male investment, parents should be particularly directive to daughters because their errors in mate choice will be more costly to parental fitness than a son's. In human families, it is common for parents to constrain a daughter's reproductive behavior and choices more so than a son's, and the onset of menarche appears to act as a trigger for increased parental vigilance and chaperonage of daughters. Hill, Holmbeck, Marlow, Green, and Lynch (1985) examined familial adaptation to menarche and found that the occurrence of menarche was generally followed by perturbations in a girl's relationship with her parents. Mothers were perceived as less accepting and parents as more controlling and less egalitarian 6 months after the occurrence of menarche. Such perturbations in parent–daughter relationships were generally temporary, but persisted to a greater degree in families with early maturing girls.

Interestingly, early menarche is an important risk factor in early pregnancy. In this study, employing the traditional methodology of developmental psychologists, Hill and his colleagues described the underlying psychology of a phenomenon referred to as daughter guarding in the evolutionary literature. For example, Flinn (1988), an anthropologist, observed fathers' behavior toward their daughters and potential suitors in a small Caribbean village. Using an instantaneous scan sampling procedure to record behavioral observations, Flinn found that fathers had a high rate of interaction with their daughters. A peak in agonistic father–daughter interactions occurred in families with daughters between 11 and 15 years of age, compared with those with prepubertal or older daughters. Fathers with daughters between 10 and 25 years of age were also observed to have more agonistic interactions with unrelated males than fathers without daughters in that age range. In addition, teenage girls with resident fathers were more likely to be observed at home than daughters without resident fathers or brothers.

Flinn considered these results substantial evidence that fathers were guarding their daughters to control their reproductive behavior. Although daughter guarding would not need to be a conscious act to increase parental fitness, Flinn found that villagers were aware that such parental behaviors could increase a daughter's chances of achieving a stable mating relationship with a wealthy man. In addition, Flinn's results suggest that girls with resident fathers did achieve more stable marriages than those without resident fathers. To the extent that a woman in a stable relationship might be more successful at raising children, daughter guarding would ultimately benefit her father's fitness.

Conflicts over a child's reproductive behavior represent just one manifestation of parent–offspring conflict during adolescence. Although parent–offspring conflict may be mitigated during childhood by psychological mechanisms, including repression, its winding down at adolescence may be reflected in the changes in identity development that occur at this time. In his comprehensive evolutionary analysis of social and personality development, MacDonald (1988a) noted that the psychological sequelae of adolescence and puberty not surprisingly include changes in identity formation. Basing his observations on Erickson's (1968) influential theory of life-span development, which follows an epigenetic principle, Marcia (1966) described four classes of adolescent identity status. These classes vary in terms of adolescents' identification with parental values or their commitment to their own personal values discovered following a period of crisis or searching. Whereas *identity-diffused* adolescents have not yet resolved the crisis or committed to a system of values, those in *foreclosure* have accepted parental values without question. Those individuals in *moratorium* have begun to question parental values and are in a state of crisis, whereas those who are *identity-achieved* have resolved their crises and have become committed to a new set of values. The redefinition of one's identity, as separate from that of one's parents, represents the undoing of the process of identification occurring during childhood, and is the psychological equivalent of achieving fitness independence. At adolescence, an individual's fitness no longer heavily depends on the investment and fitness of a parent, and the adaptive value of psychological identification with a parent wanes. The search for and achievement of an individual identity during adolescence may signify the end of the last major manifestation of parent–offspring conflict.

## ADULTHOOD AND THE MAKING OF FUTURE GENERATIONS

Two of the primary tasks of human adulthood are the procurement of mates and the rearing of offspring. Because the fitness outcomes of engaging in these two activities are unquestionable, it would be difficult to imagine that the way human adults go about these activities has not been touched by natural selection. Studies of human mate selection are founded on the assumptions that the human psyche has evolved through natural selection in overcoming the various survival and reproductive problems faced by early hominids, and that differential selection pressures have operated on human male and female psychologies, resulting in the employment of sexually dimorphic mate-selection strategies (Symons, 1979). Sex differences in the psychology and behaviors associated with mate selection presumably arose as a function of the initial disparity in parental investment (Bateman, 1948; Trivers, 1972). In species where minimum male investment in offspring is negligible compared with a female's investment in gestation and lactation, including most mammals, males have been selected to maximize copulations with fertile partners. Therefore, we might expect human male reproductive strategies to be biased toward the seeking of high numbers of partners who display signs of fertility or high reproductive value.

In humans, the evidence is quite consistent: Men tend to have more partners and are more likely to engage in casual sex, short-term mating, or one-night stands, than are women (e.g., Symons & Ellis, 1989). In addition, when choosing partners, men focus on the physical attributes of women, such as a healthy appearance or general physical attractiveness, youth, and bodily proportions, such as small waist-to-hip ratio (e.g., Buss, 1989; Singh, 1993; Symons, 1979)—characteristics that are all positively correlated with fertility and fecundity. In contrast, females, the high-investment sex whose fitness is not greatly incremented by copulating with high numbers of partners (Bateman, 1948), have been under greater selective pressures to choose mates who, either by possessing "good" genes or contributing resources or parental care, increase the fitness of offspring. The processes by which men and women choose one another for short- or long-term relationships have been studied fairly extensively by social psychologists, but the pioneering work of Buss has contributed much to an evolutionary perspective in the literature (e.g., Buss, 1985, 1989, 1994; Buss & Schmitt, 1993; Buss, chap. 13, this volume).

When it comes to parental behavior and its underlying psychology, parents have evolved to apportion their investment nonrandomly—a phenomenon referred to as *discriminative parental solicitude* (Daly & Wilson, 1980). According to Daly (1989):

> If offspring are the goal of striving and the currency of success, then a selfless parental solicitude might seem to follow. But parents are not selfless, nor does Darwinian theory suggest that they should be. Not all offspring are equally capable of utilizing parental nurture to promote the long-term survival of parental genetic materials, and it follows that selection favours *mechanisms of discriminative parental solicitude*, which in effect assess the probable fitness consequences *for the parent* of alternative ways of allocating parental effort. (p. 29)

From adherence to inclusive fitness theory, one would predict that parental solicitude would be selected in such a way as to result in the maximum number of parental genes being passed into the first and second filial generations. As discussed in an earlier section, considerable evidence in support of this view suggests that parents have inherited a psychology shaped by selection that generally results in biases toward investing in their own offspring versus unrelated children, children with whom they are unlikely to share genes, older children versus younger children, or children of high reproductive value versus those of low reproductive value. Putting aside the initial lability of human maternal feelings, human mothers always invest more in offspring than fathers. The evolution of viviparity has virtually guaranteed mothers 100% maternity confidence (offspring born to any female are genetically related with 100% certainty), whereas the possibility of cuckoldry reduces the certainty that a male's putative off-spring are genetically related to him. The inherent reduced level of certainty of parenthood in males, deemed *paternal uncertainty*, has apparently shaped the behavior of both fathers and mothers. In a unique report, Daly and Wilson (1982) noted that, following the birth of a child, the utterances of new parents, their friends, and relatives more often focus on the baby's resemblance to the father than to the mother. This interesting postpartum behavior is interpreted as an attempt to assure the male of his parentage.

Discriminative parental solicitude is evidenced in observable failures of parental investment, and through an examination of the underlying psychology and phenomenology of parental behavior, such as feelings of grief following the death of a child. In a cross-cultural study employing the HRAF files, described previously, Daly and Wilson (1984, 1988) found that, in 20 of 112 cases of infanticide, a child was killed by the mother if the child was either known not to be or suspected not to be the child of a potential or current partner. In addition, Wilson, Daly, and Weghorst (1980) reported that a child under 3 years of age living with a stepparent and one natural parent is 6.9 times as likely to be abused than a child living in a household with two natural parents. In 1985, Daly and Wilson reported that preschoolers living with one natural and one stepparent were 40 times more likely to be abused than peers living with both natural parents, and this could not be accounted for by socioeconomic status, family size, or maternal age.

Risk of homicide at the hands of parents is also a declining function of children's age (Daly & Wilson, 1988), age being positively correlated with reproductive value. Working under the assumption that level of bereavement is a reflection of the strength of parental feelings and attach-ment, Littlefield and Rushton (1986) investigated grief intensity of be-reaved parents. Findings that provide evidence for the discriminative grief of parents, and that were in accord with their hypotheses, include: Mothers grieved more than fathers, healthy children were grieved for more than unhealthy children, and children phenotypically similar to parents were grieved for more than dissimilar children. In an extension of this study, Crawford, Salter, and Jang (1989) asked individuals to predict parental grief after the hypothetical loss of two children described in vignettes to be of the same sex but of differing reproductive value. In line with the notion of parental solicitude, they found that parents were expected to grieve more for children of higher reproductive value than for those of lower reproductive value.

## SENESCENCE AND BEQUEATHMENT

Gerontology has become a burgeoning field in response to an aging population and the realization of the paucity of research on the final stage in the human life span. Many proximate theories of senescence exist, including the notion that senescence is the inevitable outcome of the deterioration of physiological systems over time. Yet, as product manufacturers could theoretically produce products that never wear out, so could natural selection have produced an organism that does not senesce. Williams (1957) suggested that senescence may be the outcome of selection for pleitropic genes with positive effects on fitness in the reproductive years and negative effects later on. For example, selection for characteristics such as high levels of testosterone in young males, which could have positive effects on a male's reproductive success, may have negative effects on survival later on in life, and thus contribute to the aging process. The potency of natural selection in shaping characteristics associated with the postreproductive portion of the life span may be considerably reduced because characteristics expressed at this stage of the life span generally have little effect on an individual's fitness. However, if we assume that some elderly humans did survive in the Pleistocene (although there is considerable debate about this), it is possible that some traits exhibited at this point in the life span, although not having direct effects on an individual's fitness through the production of offspring, may have had indirect effects through kin selection because of their effects on relatives such as grandchildren.

Gaulin (1980) pondered the existence of sexual dimorphism in the human postreproductive life span, and suggested that the postreproductive period may have evolved in humans because of the high level of parental care required by human offspring. He suggested that the postreproductive period may be more abrupt in females because they contribute a greater amount of parental investment compared with males. Because of their high degree of physiological investment in reproduction, at some point in their lives, the physiological costs become too great, and selection may have favored the cessation of menstruation along with the diversion of investment toward kin that could offset the cost of menopause. Because males invest less in offspring and face lower physiological costs, they may continue to partition their investment between the production of offspring and aiding other kin throughout most of their later adult life. Alington-MacKinnon and Troll (1981) suggested that menopause reduces a woman's exposure to endogenous estrogen, prolonged exposure of which is associated with an increased risk of certain cancers, such as endometrial and breast cancer. If menopause results in women remaining healthy and continuing to invest in kin during the nonreproductive phase of life, then the apparent paradox of menopause becomes explicable in adaptationist terms.

Smith (1988) suggested that if the postreproductive period exists, in part, because of the increased investment it affords developing children, one should expect grandparental behavior to exhibit characteristics consistent with kin investment theory. For example, he suggested that, because grandfathers are still capable of producing children and because of the uncertain genetic link between males and their offspring (paternal uncertainty), grandmothers should spend more time with or invest more in grandchildren than grandfathers. In addition, grandparents might be expected to invest more in their daughters' children than their sons' because of an increased probability of being related to their daughters' children. Overall, grandparents should be expected to apportion their investment in the following order: maternal grandmothers > maternal grandfathers and paternal grandmothers > paternal grandfathers. Smith tested these predictions by surveying 587 grandparents and recording the amount of time spent with grandchildren as a measure of investment. He found that grandmothers spent more time with their grandchildren than did grandfathers, but this difference was not statistically significant. He also found, as predicted, that maternal grandmothers spent almost twice as much time with their grandchildren than paternal grandfathers, and that the other two groups were intermediate.

In another interesting study of postreproductive behavior, Smith, Kish, and Crawford (1987) considered the inheritance of wealth as a uniquely human form of kin investment. These authors suggested that, if fitness-enhancing dispositions influence will makers, beneficiaries should be favored according to their reproductive value and degree of relatedness to the deceased. They predicted that: (a) decedents would bequeath more to kin compared with nonkin, (b) close relatives should receive higher proportions of an estate compared with more distant relatives, (c) with close relatives of equal relatedness, decedents should bequeath more to those with the highest reproductive value, and (d) according to the Trivers and Willard (1973) hypothesis, wealthier decedents should leave more to their sons and poorer decedents should leave more to their daughters. An analysis of 1,000 probated wills confirmed all four of these predictions. Therefore, one of the final acts in which a human being can engage—that of bequeathing resources—also appears to reflect a psychology shaped by natural selection.

## CONCLUDING REMARKS

Organisms evolved in a developmental landscape, and their life histories reveal the unavoidable tracks of ancestral selection pressures fluctuating over individual lifetimes. This chapter supplied selective coverage of the growing interface between developmental and Darwinian psychology, hopefully capturing some of the flavor and richness that results when traditional developmental studies are complemented by an adaptationist approach. Earlier attempts to unite evolutionary perspectives with the study of human development were unsuccessful because evolutionary theory was not sufficiently equipped to elucidate complex behavioral and ontogenetic patterns. From an examination of the more recent works of several authors (e.g., Charlesworth, 1992; Chisholm, 1988; MacDonald 1988a, 1988b; Weisfeld & Billings, 1988), it is now patently clear that the theoretical groundwork has been laid for the productive re-acquaintance of developmental psychology with evolutionary thought.

Some caution and skepticism is warranted, however, to avoid both panglossian adaptationism or the inappropriate use of evolutionary concepts, such as that resulting in a backlash against adaptationist approaches in the early part of this century. Since then, the adaptationist perspective has matured in conjunction with the careful documentation of developmental phenomena occurring over the last 50 years. In this sense, a reconsideration of the phylogeny of development has benefited considerably from the volumes of work focusing on proximate analyses of individual ontogenies. The converse is not necessarily true: Respectable studies employing a proximate level of analysis have and will continue to be conducted without referring to or being informed by an adaptationist perspective. However, scholarship, like evolving organisms, seems compelled to seek out new, uninhabited niches, and attempts to apply modern Darwinism to developmental theory promise extensive new horizons.

## ACKNOWLEDGMENTS

This chapter was written in memory of my mother, F. A. Surbey, with whom, happily, both proximate and ultimate conflicts of interest were resolved during our individual ontogenies. I thank those who have contributed to this chapter through interesting published and verbal discussions, and apologize to those given short shrift for lack of space. In addition, I thank B. Slugoski and the editors of this volume for helpful comments on the manuscript. This chapter was prepared with the support of a standard research grant from the Social Sciences and Humanities Research Council of Canada.

## REFERENCES

Alexander, R. D. (1974). The evolution of social behavior. *Annual Review of Ecology and Systematics, 5*, 325–384.

Alington-MacKinnon, D., & Troll, L. E. (1981). The adaptive function of the menopause: A devil's advocate position. *Journal of the American Geriatrics Society, 29*, 349–353.

Anderson, J. L., & Crawford, C. B. (1992). Modeling costs and benefits of adolescent weight control as a mechanism for reproductive suppression. *Human Nature, 3,* 299–334.

Badcock, C. R. (1986). *The problem of altruism.* Oxford, England: Basil Blackwell.

Bateman, A. J. (1948). Intra-sexual selection in *Drosophila. Heredity, 2,* 349–368.

Begley, D. J., Firth, J. A., & Hoult, J. R. S. (1980). *Human reproduction and developmental biology.* Bristol, England: J. W. Arrowsmith.

Belsky, J., Steinberg, L., & Draper, P. (1991). Childhood experience, interpersonal development, and reproductive strategy: An evolutionary theory of socialization. *Child Development, 62,* 647–670.

Bernds, W. P., & Barash, D. P. (1979). Early termination of parental investment in mammals, including humans. In N. A. Chagnon & W. Irons (Eds.), *Evolutionary biology and human social behavior: An anthropological perspective* (pp. 487–506). North Scituate, MA: Duxbury.

Blurton Jones, N. (1978). Natural selection and birthweight. *Annals of Human Biology, 5,* 487–489.

Bowlby, J. (1969). *Attachment and loss: Vol. 1. Attachment.* London: Hogarth.

Bukatko, D., & Daehler, M. W. (1992). *Child development: A topical approach.* Boston: Houghton Mifflin.

Buss, D. M. (1985). Human mate selection. *American Scientist, 73,* 47–51.

Buss, D. M. (1989). Sex differences in human mate preferences: Evolutionary hypotheses tested in 37 cultures. *Behavioral and Brain Sciences, 12,* 1–14.

Buss, D. M. (1994). *The evolution of desire.* New York: Basic Books.

Buss, D. M., & Schmitt, D. P. (1993). Sexual strategies theory: An evolutionary perspective on human mating. *Psychological Review, 100,* 204–232.

Butterfield, E. C., & Siperstein, G. N. (1974). Influence of contingent auditory stimulation upon non-nutritional suckle. *Proceedings of third symposium on oral sensations and perception: The mouth of the infant.* Springfield, IL: Thomas.

Charlesworth, W. R. (1988). Resources and resource acquisition during ontogeny. In K. B. MacDonald (Ed.), *Sociobiological perspectives on human development* (pp. 24–77). New York: Springer-Verlag.

Charlesworth, W. R. (1992). Darwin and developmental psychology: Past and present. *Developmental Psychology, 28,* 5–16.

Chisholm, J. S. (1988). Toward a developmental evolutionary ecology of humans. In K. B. MacDonald (Ed.), *Sociobiological perspectives on human development* (pp. 78–102). New York: Springer-Verlag.

Crawford, C. B., Salter, B., & Jang, K. L. (1989). Human grief: Is its intensity related to the reproductive value of the deceased? *Ethology and Sociobiology, 10,* 297–307.

Daly, M. (1989). Parent–offspring conflict and violence in evolutionary perspective. In R. W. Bell & N. J. Bell (Eds.), *Sociobiology and the social sciences* (pp. 25–43). Lubbock: Texas University Press.

Daly, M., & Wilson, M. (1980). Discriminative parental solicitude: A biological perspective. *Journal of Marriage and the Family, 42,* 277–288.

Daly, M., & Wilson, M. (1982). Whom are newborn babies said to resemble? *Ethology and Sociobiology, 3,* 69–78.

Daly, M., & Wilson, M. (1984). A sociobiological analysis of human infanticide. In G. Hausfater & S. B. Hrdy (Eds.), *Infanticide: Comparative and evolutionary perspectives* (pp. 487–502). New York: Aldine.

Daly, M., & Wilson, M. (1985). Child abuse and other risks of not living with both parents. *Ethology & Sociobiology, 6,* 197–210.

Daly, M., & Wilson, M. (1988). *Homicide.* New York: Aldine.

Darwin, C. (1871). *The descent of man* (Vols. I & II). New York: Appleton-Century-Crofts.

Darwin, C. (1888). *The origin of species* (6th ed.). London: John Murray.

de Beer, G. (1958). *Embryos and ancestors* (3rd ed.). Oxford, England: Clarendon.

Draper, P., & Harpending, H. (1982). Father absence and reproductive strategy: An evolutionary perspective. *Journal of Anthropological Research, 38*, 255–273.

Erickson, E. H. (1968). *Identity: Youth and crisis.* New York: Norton.

Fabes, R. A., & Filsinger, E. E. (1988). Odor communication in parent–child interaction. In E. E. Filsinger (Ed.), *Biosocial perspectives on the family* (pp. 93–118). Newbury Park, CA: Sage.

Fleming, A. S., Corter, C., Franks, P., Surbey, M. K., Schneider, B., & Steiner, M. (1993). Postpartum factors related to mothers' attraction to newborn infant odors. *Developmental Psychobiology, 26*, 115–132.

Flinn, M. V. (1988). Parent–offspring interactions in a Caribbean village: Daughter guarding. In L. Betzig, M. Mulder, & P. Turke (Eds.), *Human reproductive behavior* (pp. 189–200). London: Cambridge University Press.

Freud, S. (1924/1967). *A general introduction to psychoanalysis.* New York: Washington Square.

Gaulin, S. J. C. (1980). Sexual dimorphism in the human post-reproductive life-span: Possible causes. *Journal of Human Evolution, 9*, 227–232.

Goldberg, S. (1977). Social competence in infancy: A model of parent–infant interactions. *Merrill-Palmer Quarterly, 23*, 163–177.

Gould, S. J. (1977). *Ontogeny and phylogeny.* Cambridge, MA: Harvard University Press.

Graber, J. A., Brooks-Gunn, J., & Warren, M. P. (1995). The antecedents of menarcheal age: Heredity, family environment and stressful life events. *Child Development, 66*, 346–359.

Haeckel, E. (1866). *Generelle morphologie der organismen: Allgemeine Grundzuge der organischen Formen-Weissenschaft, mechanisch bergrundet durche die von Charles Darwin reformirte Descendenz-Theorie.* Berlin: George Reimer.

Haig, D. (1993). Genetic conflicts in human pregnancy. *The Quarterly Review of Biology, 68*, 495–532.

Hall, G. S. (1904). *Adolescence* (Vols. 1 & 2). New York: Appleton-Century-Crofts.

Hamilton, W. D. (1964). The genetical evolution of social behaviour: I and II. *Journal of Theoretical Biology, 7*, 1–52.

Hayashi, R. H. (1979). Physiological adjustments in pregnancy. In R. W. Huff & C. J. Pauerstein (Eds.), *Human reproduction: Physiology and pathophysiology* (pp. 310–331). New York: Wiley.

Hill, J. P., Holmbeck, G. N., Marlow, L., Green, T. M., & Lynch, M. E. (1985). Menarcheal status and parent–child relations in families of seventh-grade girls. *Journal of Youth and Adolescence, 14*, 301–316.

Hooker, C. A. (1994). Regulatory constructivism: On the relation between evolutionary epistemology and Piaget's genetic epistemology. *Biology and Philosophy, 9*, 197–244.

Howell, N. (1979). *Demography of the dobe !Kung.* New York: Academic Press.

Huff, R. W. (1979). Medical problems in pregnancy. In R. W. Huff & C. J. Pauerstein (Eds.), *Human reproduction: Physiology and pathophysiology* (pp. 365–388). New York: Wiley.

Jacobs, R. W., & Janowitz, P. (1975). The digestive tract. In J. J. Rovinsky & A. F. Guttmacher (Eds.), *Medical, surgical and gynecologic complications of pregnancy* (pp. 177–199). Baltimore: Williams & Wilkins.

Johnson, M. H., Dziurawiec, S., Ellis, H., & Morton, J. (1991). Newborns' preferential tracking of face-like stimuli and its subsequent decline. *Cognition, 40*, 1–19.

Johnston, F. E. (1974). Control of the age of menarche. *Human Biology, 46*, 159–171.

Kalat, J. W. (1992). *Biological psychology* (4th ed.). Pacific Grove, CA: Brooks/Cole.

Karn, M. N., & Penrose, L. S. (1952). Birthweight and gestational time in relation to maternal age, parity and infant survival. *Annals of Eugenics, 16*, 147–164.

Konner, M., & Shostak, M. (1986). Adolescent pregnancy and childbearing: An anthropological perspective. In J. B. Lancaster & B. A. Hamburg (Eds.), *School-age pregnancy and parenthood: Biosocial dimensions* (pp. 325–345) New York: Aldine deGruyter.

Krebs, D., Denton, K., & Higgins, N. (1988). On the evolution of self-knowledge and self-deception. In K. B. MacDonald (Ed.), *Sociobiological perspectives on human development* (pp. 103–139). New York: Springer-Verlag.

Lamarck, J.-B. de. (1809). *Philosophie zoologique* (2 vols.). Paris: Dentu.

Liggins, G. C. (1969). The foetal role in the initiation of parturition in the ewe. In G. E. W. Wolstenholme & M. O'Connor (Eds.), *Foetal autonomy* (pp. 219–228). London: Churchill.

Littlefield, C. H., & Rushton, J. P. (1986). When a child dies: The sociobiology of bereavement. *Journal of Personality and Social Psychology, 51,* 797–802.

Lorenz, K. (1971). *Studies in animal behavior* (Vol. 3). London: Methuen.

MacDonald, K. B. (1988a). *Social and personality development: An evolutionary synthesis.* New York: Plenum.

MacDonald, K. B. (Ed.). (1988b). *Sociobiological perspectives on human development.* New York: Springer-Verlag.

Mackey, W. C. (1984). The placenta: The celibate sibling. *Journal of Human Evolution, 13,* 449–455.

Mann, J. (1992). Nurturance or negligence: Maternal psychology and behavioral preference among preterm twins. In J. Barkow, L. Cosmides, & J. Tooby (Eds.), *The adapted mind: Evolutionary psychology and the generation of culture* (pp. 367–390). New York: Oxford University Press.

Marcia, J. E. (1966). Development and validation of ego-identity status. *Journal of Personality and Social Psychology, 20,* 551–558.

Mead, M. (1928). *Coming of age in Samoa.* New York: William Morrow.

Mekos, D., Hetherington, E. M., Clingempeel, W. G., & Reiss, D. (1995). *Psychosocial influences on the rate and timing of pubertal development.* Unpublished manuscript, University of North Carolina, Carolina Population Center, Chapel Hill.

Moffitt, T. E., Caspi, A., Belsky, J., & Silva, P. A. (1992). Childhood experience and the onset of menarche: A test of a sociobiological hypothesis. *Child Development, 63,* 47–58.

Nesse, R. M., & Lloyd, A. T. (1992). The evolution of psychodynamic mechanisms. In J. Barkow, L. Cosmides, & J. Tooby (Eds.), *The adapted mind: Evolutionary psychology and the generation of culture* (pp. 602–624). New York: Oxford University Press.

Oppenheim, R. W. (1982). Preformation and epigenesis in the origins of the nervous system and behavior: Issues, concepts and their history. In P. P. G. Bateson & P. H. Klopfer (Eds.), *Perspectives in ethology: Vol. 5. Ontogeny.* New York: Plenum.

Piaget, J. (1971). *Biology and knowledge.* Chicago: University of Chicago Press.

Porter, R. H., Cernoch, J. M., & McLaughlin, F. J. (1983). Maternal recognition of neonates through olfactory cues. *Physiology & Behaviour, 30,* 151–154.

Profet, M. (1992). Pregnancy sickness as adaptation: A deterrent to maternal ingestion of teratogens. In J. Barkow, L. Cosmides, & J. Tooby (Eds.), *The adapted mind: Evolutionary psychology and the generation of culture* (pp. 327–365). New York: Oxford University Press.

Russell, M. J., Mendelson, T., & Peeke, H. V. S. (1983). Mother's identification of their infant's odors. *Ethology and Sociobiology, 4,* 29–31.

Sharman, G. B. (1976). Evolution of viviparity in mammals. In C. R. Austin & R. V. Short (Eds.), *Reproduction in mammals: Book 6. The evolution of reproduction* (pp. 32–70). Cambridge, England: Cambridge University Press.

Singh, D. (1993). Adaptive significance of female physical attractiveness: Role of waist-to-hip ratio. *Journal of Personality and Social Psychology, 85,* 293–307.

Slavin, M. O. (1985). The origins of psychic conflict and the adaptive functions of repression: An evolutionary biological view. *Psychoanalysis and Contemporary Thought, 8,* 407–440.

Smart, Y. C., Roberts, T. K., Clancy, R. L., & Cripps, A. W. (1981). Early pregnancy factor: Its role in mammalian reproduction-research review. *Fertility and Sterility, 35,* 397.

Smith, M. S. (1987). Evolution and developmental psychology: Toward a sociobiology of human development. In C. B. Crawford, M. S. Smith, & D. Krebs (Eds.), *Sociobiology and psychology: Ideas, issues and applications* (pp. 225–252). Hillsdale, NJ: Lawrence Erlbaum Associates.

Smith, M. S. (1988). Research in developmental sociobiology: Parenting and family behavior. In K. B. MacDonald (Ed.), *Sociobiological perspectives on human development* (pp. 271–292). New York: Springer-Verlag.

Smith, M. S., Kish, B. J., & Crawford, C. B. (1987). Inheritance of wealth as human kin investment. *Ethology and Sociobiology, 8,* 171–182.

Smith, P. K., & Cowie, H. (1991). *Understanding children's development* (2nd ed.). Cambridge, MA: Basil Blackwell.

Surbey, M. K. (1987a). Anorexia nervosa, amenorrhea, and adaptation. *Ethology and Sociobiology, 8,* 47S–61S.

Surbey, M. K. (1987b). Family composition and the timing of human menarche. *International Journal of Primatology, 8,* 455. (Abstracts of the Annual Meeting of the International Primatological Society)

Surbey, M. K. (1988). *The timing of human menarche.* Unpublished doctoral dissertation, McMaster University, Hamilton, Ontario, Canada.

Surbey, M. K. (1990). Family composition, stress, and human menarche. In T. E. Ziegler & F. B. Bercovitch (Eds.), *The socioendocrinology of primate reproduction* (pp. 11–32). New York: Wiley.

Surbey, M. K. (1993). Predicting environmental correlates of pubertal timing from Darwinian theory. *Canadian Psychology, 34*(2a), 473. (Abstracts of the Annual Convention of the Canadian Psychological Association)

Symons, D. (1979). *The evolution of human sexuality.* Oxford, England: Oxford University Press.

Symons, D., & Ellis, B. (1989). Human male-female differences in sexual desire. In A. E. Rasa, C. Vogel, & E. Voland (Eds.), *The sociobiology of sexual and reproductive strategies* (pp. 131–146). London: Chapman & Hall.

Tanner, J. M. (1962). *Growth at adolescence* (2nd ed.). Oxford: Blackwell.

Trevathan, W. R. (1987). *Human birth: An evolutionary perspective.* New York: Aldine.

Trivers, R. L. (1972). Parental investment and sexual selection. In B. Campbell (Ed.), *Sexual selection and the descent of man 1871–1971* (pp. 136–179). Chicago: Aldine.

Trivers, R. L. (1974). Parent-offspring conflict. *American Zoologist, 14,* 247–262.

Trivers, R. L. (1985). *Social evolution.* Menlo Park, CA: Benjamin/Cummings.

Trivers, R. L., & Willard, D. E. (1983). Natural selection of parental ability to vary the sex ratio of offspring. *Science, 179,* 90–92.

Waddington, C. H. (1957). *The strategy of the genes: A discussion of some aspects of theoretical biology.* New York: Macmillan.

Wasser, S. K., & Barash, D. P. (1983). Reproductive suppression among female mammals: Implications for biomedicine and sexual selection theory. *The Quarterly Review of Biology, 58,* 513–538.

Wegmann, T. G. (1983). The placental immunological barrier. In S. Isojima & W. D. Billington (Eds.), *Reproductive immunology 1983* (pp. 67–78). Amsterdam, The Netherlands: Elsevier.

Weisfeld, G. E., & Billings, R. (1988). Observations on adolescence. In K. B. MacDonald (Ed.), *Sociobiological perspectives on human development* (pp. 207–233). New York: Springer-Verlag.

Williams, G. C. (1957). Pleiotrophy, natural selection and the evolution of senescence. *Evolution, 11,* 398–411.

Wilson, M., Daly, M., & Weghorst, S. J. (1980). Household composition and the risk of child abuse and neglect. *Journal of Biosocial Science, 12,* 333–340.

# 13

## The Psychology of Human Mate Selection: Exploring the Complexity of the Strategic Repertoire

David M. Buss
*University of Michigan*

Imagine a world in which people had no mate preferences. Mate selection would be random. Each person would have a equal probability of mating with everyone else, and no one would suffer discrimination on the mating market. People riddled with disease, open sores, and lesions would be desired as mates as often as people brimming with robust good health. Pimply faced adolescent boys and arthritic senior citizens would be desired as often as successful athletes, CEOs, artists, and orators. Graying grandmothers covered with liver spots and lacking real teeth would be desired as much as 20-year-old women with clear skin, white teeth, and firm muscle tone.

This is not the world in which we live. Few things are more obvious than the fact that people have strong preferences about who they mate with. There are powerful evolutionary reasons why this is so. Imagine living as our ancestors did long ago—struggling to keep warm by the fire; hunting meat for our kin; gathering nuts, berries, and herbs; and avoiding dangerous animals and hostile humans. If we were to select a mate who failed to deliver the resources promised, who had affairs, who was lazy, who lacked hunting skills, or who heaped physical abuse on us, our survival would be tenuous, our reproduction at risk. In contrast, a mate who provided abundant resources, who protected us and our children, and who devoted time, energy, and effort to our family would be a great asset. As a result of the powerful survival and reproductive advantages that were reaped by those of our ancestors who chose a mate wisely, clear desires in a mate evolved. As descendants of those people, we carry their desires with us today.


## SEXUAL SELECTION

More than a century ago, Darwin (1871) offered a revolutionary explanation for the mysteries of mating. He became intrigued by the puzzling development in animals of characteristics that would appear to impair their chances of survival. The elaborate plumage, large antlers, and other conspicuous features displayed by many species seem costly in the currency of survival. He wondered how the brilliant plumage of peacocks could evolve, or increase in frequency over time, when it poses such an obvious threat to survival, acting as an open lure to predators. Darwin's answer was that these displays evolved because they led to reproductive success, providing an advantage over competitors in obtaining a desirable mate and continuing that peacock's genetic line. The evolution of these characteristics because of their reproductive benefits, and not their survival benefits, is known as sexual selection.

According to Darwin, sexual selection takes two forms. In one case, members of the same sex compete with each other, and the outcome of their contest gives the winner greater sexual access to members of the opposite sex. Two stags locking horns in combat is the prototypical image of this intrasexual competition. The characteristics that lead to success in contests of this kind, such as greater strength, intelligence, or attractiveness to allies, evolve because the victors are able to mate more often, and hence pass on more genes. This is known as sexual selection through intrasexual competition.

In the other type of sexual selection, members of one sex choose a mate based on their preferences for particular qualities in that mate. These characteristics evolve in the other sex because animals possessing them are chosen more often as mates, and their genes thrive. Animals lacking the desired characteristics are excluded from mating, and their genes perish. Because peahens prefer peacocks with plumage that flashes and glitters, dull-feathered males get left in the evolutionary dust. The reason that peacocks today possess brilliant plumage is because of a long evolutionary history of peahens preferring to mate with dazzling and colorful males. This type of sexual selection is referred to as *intersexual selection*, to emphasize evolution due to the desires of one sex affecting the evolution of characteristics in the other sex.

Darwin's theory of sexual selection begins to explain mating behavior by identifying two key processes by which evolutionary change can occur—preferences for a mate and competition for a mate. Yet, it was vigorously resisted by male scientists for over a century, in part because the active choosing of mates seemed to grant too much power to females, who were thought to remain more passive in the mating process. Sexual selection was also resisted by mainstream social scientists because it implied a portrait of human nature that seemed too instinct-like to account for the uniqueness and flexibility of humans. Culture and consciousness were presumed to free us from evolutionary forces. The breakthrough in applying sexual selection to humans came in the late 1970s and 1980s in the form of theoretical advances initiated by my colleagues and myself in the fields of psychology and anthropology. We shifted the focus to trying to identify underlying psychological mechanisms that were also the products of evolution—mechanisms that help to explain both the extraordinary flexibility of human behavior and the active mating strategies pursued by women and men. This new discipline is called *evolutionary psychology*.

## THE EMPIRICAL SCIENCE OF HUMAN MATING

When I began work in the field in the early 1980s, little concrete knowledge was available about actual human mating behavior. There was a frustrating lack of scientific evidence on mating in the broad array of human populations, and practically no documented support for grand evolutionary theorizing applied to humans. No one knew whether some mating desires are universal, whether certain sex differences are characteristic of all people in all cultures, or whether culture exerts so powerful an influence as to override any evolved preferences that might happen to be there. So I departed from the traditional path of mainstream psychology to explore possible characteristics of our mating behavior that should follow if evolutionary principles were correct. In the beginning, I simply wanted to verify a few of the most obvious evolutionary predictions about differences between the desires of the sexes, such as discovering whether men desire youth and physical attractiveness in a mate, and whether women desire status and economic security as suggested by evolutionary theory. Toward that end, I interviewed and administered questionnaires to 186 married individuals and 100 college students within the United States.

The next critical step was to verify whether the psychological phenomena uncovered by this study were species-wide. If mating desires and other features of human psychology are products of our evolutionary history, they should be found universally, not just in the United States. So I initiated an international study to explore how mates are selected in other cultures, starting with a few European countries, such as Germany and the Netherlands. However, I soon realized that, because these cultures share many features of Western civilization, they do not provide the most rigorous test for evolutionary psychology.

Over the next 5 years, I expanded the study to include 50 collaborators from 37 cultures located on six continents and five islands, from Australia to Zambia. Local residents of each culture administered the questionnaire about mating desires in the native language. We sampled large urban cities, such as Rio de Janeiro and São Paulo in Brazil, Shanghai in China, Bangalore and Amadebad in India, Jerusalem and Tel Aviv in Israel, and Tehran in Iran. We also sampled rural peoples, such as Gujarati Indians and the South African Zulus. We covered the educated and the less educated. We included every age from 14 through 70, as well as the entire range of political systems from capitalist to communist and socialist. All major racial, religious, and ethnic groups were represented. In all, we surveyed 10,047 individuals worldwide.

This study, the most massive ever undertaken on human mating desires, was merely the beginning. The findings had implications that reached into every sphere of human mating life, from dating to marriage, extramarital affairs, and divorce. They were also relevant to major social issues, such as sexual harassment, domestic abuse, pornography, and patriarchy (see Buss & Malamuth, 1996). To explore as many of these far-flung mating domains as possible, I launched over 50 new studies, involving thousands of individuals. Included in these studies were men and women on the search for a mate in singles bars and on college campuses, dating couples at various stages of commitment, newlywed couples in the first 5 years of marriage, and couples who ended up divorced.

The findings from all of these studies caused controversy and confusion among my colleagues because, in many respects, they flew in the face of conventional thinking. They required a radical shift from the standard view of men's and women's sexual psychology. Much of what I discovered about human mating is not nice. For example, in the ruthless pursuit of sexual goals, men and women derogate their rivals, deceive members of the opposite sex, and even subvert their own mates. These discoveries are disturbing to me; I would prefer that the competitive, conflictual, and manipulative aspects of human mating did not exist, but it is not a scientist's obligation to like what he or she finds. Ultimately, the disturbing side of human mating must be confronted if its harsh consequences are ever to be ameliorated.

## THE EVOLUTIONARY PSYCHOLOGY
## OF SEXUAL STRATEGIES

*Strategies* are methods for accomplishing goals, the means for solving problems. The term is typically used in military settings, so it may seem odd to view human mating, romance, sex, and love as inherently strategic.

But we never choose mates at random. We do not attract mates indiscriminately. We do not derogate our competitors out of sheer boredom. Our mating is strategic, and our strategies are specifically designed to solve particular problems required for successful mating. Understanding how people solve those problems requires an analysis of sexual strategies. If that sounds military or mercenary, so be it. Strategies are essential for our survival on the mating battlefield.

Adaptations are our evolved solutions to the problems posed by survival and reproduction. Over millions of years of human evolution, natural selection has produced in us hunger mechanisms to solve the problem of providing nutrients to the organism; taste buds that are sensitive to fat and sugar to solve the problem of what to put into our mouths (nuts and berries, but not dirt or gravel); sweat glands and shivering mechanisms to solve the problems of extreme hot and cold; emotions such as fear and rage that motivate flight and fight to combat predators or aggressive competitors; and a complex immune system to combat diseases and parasites. These adaptations are human solutions to the problems of existence posed by the hostile forces of nature—they are our survival strategies. Those who failed to develop these characteristics failed to survive.

Correspondingly, sexual strategies are our adaptive solutions to mating problems. Those in our evolutionary past who failed to mate successfully failed to become our ancestors. All of us descend from a long and unbroken line of ancestors who competed successfully for desirable mates, attracted mates who were reproductively valuable, retained mates long enough to reproduce, fended off interested rivals, and solved the problems that could have impeded reproductive success. We carry with us the sexual strategies of those success stories.

Each sexual strategy is tailored to a specific adaptive problem, such as identifying a desirable mate or besting competitors in attracting a mate. Underlying each sexual strategy are psychological mechanisms, such as preferences for a particular mate, feelings of love, desire for sex, or jealousy. Each psychological mechanism is sensitive to information or cues from the external world, such as physical features, signs of sexual interest, or hints of potential infidelity. Our psychological mechanisms are also sensitive to information about ourselves, such as the ability to attract a mate who has a certain degree of desirability. My goal has been to peel back the layers of adaptive problems that men and women have faced in the course of mating and uncover the complex sexual strategies they have evolved for solving them.

Although the term *sexual strategies* provides a useful metaphor for thinking about solutions to mating problems, it is misleading in the sense of connoting conscious intent. Sexual strategies do not require conscious planning or awareness. Our sweat glands are "strategies" for accomplishing the goal of thermal regulation, but they require neither conscious planning nor awareness of the goal. Indeed, just as a piano player's sudden awareness of her hands may impede performance, human sexual strategies are often best carried out without conscious knowledge by the actor.

## MEN AND WOMEN: WHY DO THEY DIFFER?

Our current psychology of mating is the end product of a long evolutionary history, in which our ancestors confronted recurrent adaptive problems. As end products of this long history of selection, our mating mechanisms should bear the marks or design features of solutions to those adaptive problems. Indeed, given that differential reproduction is the engine that drives the evolutionary process, our psychology of human mating should show clearly sculpted evidence of design because mating is so close and so consequential for reproduction.

Evolutionary psychology provides a precise metatheory for the domains in which men and women are predicted to be similar and those in which they are predicted to be different. Specifically, men and women are expected to be similar in all those domains in which they have faced essentially the same (or similar) adaptive problems. Both have sweat glands and shivering mechanisms because both have faced similar problems of thermal regulation. Both have food preferences for fat, sugar, salt, and protein because both have faced similar food consumption problems.

Only in domains where the sexes have faced different adaptive problems recurrently over evolutionary history does an evolutionary psychologist expect to find sex differences. One example is in the domain of obligatory parental investment—the amount of energy and effort required as a minimum to produce a single offspring. In the case of women, the minimum obligatory parental investment is 9 months of internal fertilization, gestation, and placentation. Women also incur the costs of breastfeeding, which in tribal societies can last for several years. In contrast, men need not invest much at all to produce a child. At a minimum, a single act of sex on their part may be enough. Although men typically invest more than the minimum, the key point is that men and women differ substantially in the minimum obligatory parental investment.

According to Trivers' (1972) theory of parental investment, these sex differences should select over evolutionary time for sex differences in mating strategies. Specifically, Trivers proposed that the sex investing less in offspring (typically, but not always, the female) should be more selective, discriminating, or choosy about whom they mate with. This is because the high-investing sex has more to lose by making a poor mate choice, and more to gain by being discriminating. A woman who chose poorly—perhaps by selecting a man who would abandon her and fail to help protect and invest in her and her children—would suffer in reproductive currencies compared with the woman who chose wisely (e.g., by selecting a man who would stick around and invest in her and her children).

Compare this with the costs and benefits to the less investing sex—in this case, men. Men who made a poor choice and had sex with the wrong women could leave without losing much. They do not bear the burdens of pregnancy. On the other side of the coin, the benefits of being relatively unchoosy might be great in reproductive currencies. The low level of minimum obligatory investment allows men to fertilize a large number of women, in principle, and so gain a great advantage by pursuing a short-term, relatively indiscriminate mating strategy. One constraint, of course, is that highly discriminating women limit men's pursuit of such a short-term strategy.

Parental investment theory also predicts that the sex that invests less in offspring should be more competitive with one another for access to the high-investing sex. In the human case, a person who carries your child for 9 months, with all the investment entailed by internal gestation, is a tremendously valuable reproductive resource. Therefore, competition is keen for access to these valuable resources.

In short, parental investment theory provides a set of predictions about the relative strength of the two forms of sexual selection. Intersexual selection—driven by preferential mate choice—should operate most strongly in the high-investing sex discriminating among potential partners of the less-investing sex. Intrasexual competition, in contrast, should be strongest among the sex that invests less in offspring.

One of the key features of parental investment theory is that it is not sex (maleness and femaleness) per se that is important. Rather, it is the relative amounts of investment. In the human case, for example, the theory would predict that men should be highly choosy and discriminating in contexts where they invest a lot, and less discriminating in contexts where they invest little. This leads us to the dual mating strategies of humans—long- and short-term mating.

## LONG- AND SHORT-TERM MATING: CORE COMPONENTS OF THE HUMAN STRATEGIC REPERTOIRE

One must be wary of any casual comparisons between humans and other animals. Nonetheless, the mating strategies of other animals sometimes provide insight into the sorts of adaptive problems commonly faced and the wide range of potential evolved solutions to these problems.

For example, many other species have evolved mate preferences. The African village weaverbird provides a vivid illustration. When a female weaverbird arrives in the vicinity of a male, he displays his recently built nest by suspending himself upside down from the bottom and vigorously flapping his wings. If the male passes this test, the female approaches the nest, enters it, and examines the nest materials, poking and pulling them for as long as 10 minutes. During this inspection, the male sings to her from nearby the nest. At any point in this sequence, she may decide that the nest does not meet her standards and depart to inspect another male's nest. A male whose nest is rejected by several females will often break it down and rebuild another from scratch. By exerting a preference for males capable of building a superior nest, the female weaverbird solves the problems of protecting and provisioning her chicks. Her preferences have evolved because they bestowed a reproductive advantage over other weaverbirds who had no preferences and who mated with any random males who happened along.

Women, like weaverbirds, also prefer men with "nests" of various kinds. Consider one of the problems that women in evolutionary history had to face: selecting a man who would be willing to commit to a long-term relationship. A woman in our evolutionary past who chose to mate with a man who was flighty, impulsive, philandering, or unable to sustain relationships found herself raising her children alone, without benefit of the resources, aid, and protection that another man might have offered. A woman who preferred to mate with a reliable man willing to commit to her likely had children who survived and thrived. Over thousands of generations, a preference for men who showed signs of being willing and able to commit to them evolved in women, just as preferences for mates with adequate nests evolved in weaverbirds. This preference solved key reproductive problems, just as food preferences solved key survival problems.

People do not always desire the commitment required of long-term mating. Men and women sometimes deliberately seek a short-term fling, a temporary liaison, or a brief affair. When they do, their preferences shift, sometimes dramatically. Therefore, one of the key problems for humans in selecting a mate is to decide whether they are seeking a short-term mate or a long-term partner. The sexual strategies pursued hinge on this crucial decision. This chapter documents the universal preferences that men and women display for particular characteristics in a mate, reveals the evolutionary logic behind the different desires of each sex, and explores the changes that occur when people shift their goal from casual sex to a committed relationship.

## Men's Short-Term Mating Psychology

The ingredients needed for the successful pursuit of short-term mating differ from those needed for successful long-term mating. They differ for each sex across these two contexts (see Table 13.1). Consider first the

TABLE 13.1
Mate Selection Problems Men and Women Confront
in Short-Term and Long-Term Mating Contexts

| Type of Mating | Men | Women |
|---|---|---|
| Short term | 1. Problem of partner number<br>2 Problem of identifying which women are sexually accessible<br>3. Problem of minimizing cost, risk, and commitment<br>4. Problem of fertility | 1. Problem of immediate resource extraction<br>2. Problem of evaluating short-term mates as possible long-term mates<br>3. Problem of gene quality<br>4. Problem of mate switching, mate expulsion, or mate back-up |
| Long term | 1. Problem of paternity confidence<br>2. Problem of female reproductive value<br>3. Problem of commitment<br>4. Problem of good parenting skills<br>5. Problem of gene quality | 1. Problem of identifying men who are able to invest<br>2. Problem of identifying men who are willing to invest<br>3. Problem of physical protection<br>4. Problem of commitment<br>5. Problem of good parenting skills<br>6. Problem of gene quality |

*Note.* This table represents a task analysis of some of the major adaptive problems that men and women would have confronted over human evolutionary history when pursuing short-term and long-term mating. From "Sexual Strategies Theory: An Evolutionary Perspective on Human Mating," by D. M. Buss and D. P. Schmitt, 1993, *Psychological Review, 100*, p. 207. Copyright © 1993 by the American Psychological Association. Reprinted with permission.

problems men face in pursuing a short-term mating strategy. To be successful, men must solve the problem of partner number—gaining sexual access to a number of women. One first-line solution to the problem of number is expected in desire: Over human evolutionary history, men may have evolved a powerful desire for sexual access to a variety of women (Symons, 1979).

A second specialized adaptation expected on theoretical grounds would be a relaxation of standards imposed for acceptable short-term partners. Elevated standards, by definition, preclude a large number of women from exceeding them. The relaxation of standards should apply to a wide range of characteristics, such as a woman's age, intelligence, personality traits, and special circumstances—such as whether she is already involved with someone else.

A third specialized feature of men's evolved strategy of short-term mating should be to impose minimum time constraints in knowing a prospective mate before seeking sexual intercourse. The less time that is permitted to elapse before obtaining sexual intercourse, the larger the number of women a man can gain sexual access to. Prolonged time delays, by absorbing more of a man's mating effort, interfere with solving the problem of partner number.

A similar kind of task analysis can be made of the other adaptive problems men confront when pursuing a short-term mating strategy. Such men must be able to identify women who are sexually accessible. Wasting time on women for whom sexual access is unlikely would interfere with the successful pursuit of a short-term mating strategy. Men also must be able to minimize the cost and commitment to each women because the more absorbed by one women the less available for the pursuit of other. Each of these adaptive problems generates specific predictions about the underlying psychology of men's short-term mating.

## Men's Long-Term Mating Psychology

Consider the adaptive problems men face when pursuing long-term committed mating. When men pursue a long-term mating strategy—one of heavy investment in a woman and children—their standards should go up. They should be highly discriminating and choosy because making a poor choice in the context of high investment can be costly in the currency of reproduction. But on which attributes should they be choosy?

First, they should select a woman capable of bearing children—a women of high reproductive value. Reproductive value may be defined in units of expected future reproduction—the extent to which the woman will contribute, on average, to the ancestry of future generations (Fisher, 1930). Female reproductive value can be expected to increase as sexual maturity approaches, and to decrease as the reproductive years pass. For example, a 35-year-old woman has a lower reproductive value than a 25-year-old woman because the average number of future offspring is lower for the older woman. Reproductive value may be distinguished from *fertility*, which refers to age-specific birth rate, and *fecundity*, which refers to the probability of conception per act of intercourse.

In humans, two strong cues to reproductive capacity are age and health (Symons, 1979; Williams, 1975). In our evolutionary past prior to the development of counting systems, age was not a characteristic that could be evaluated directly. Instead, cues that correlate with age and health could be used to identify reproductively capable women. Physical appearance probably provides the strongest set of cues—features such as clear, smooth, and unblemished skin; lustrous hair; white teeth; clear eyes; and full lips (Symons, 1979). Behavioral cues such as a sprightly gain and high energy level also provide cues to youth.

According to this line of reasoning, men should come to value and view as attractive the physical and behavioral features that signal reproductive value. Men failing to prefer women possessing these attributes would, on average, mate with less reproductively valuable women. Consequently, such men would tend to leave fewer offspring, and would be selected against. In summary, men's long-term mate preferences and standards of female beauty are predicted to evolve to reflect the physical and behavioral cues that signify high female reproductive value, as shown in Fig. 13.1.

Another adaptive problem that men face in long-term mating is the problem of paternity uncertainty. Because fertilization occurs internally within women, women are always 100% certain that they are the mothers of their children. No woman ever gave birth and wondered whether the baby that came out of her body was her own. In contrast, men can never

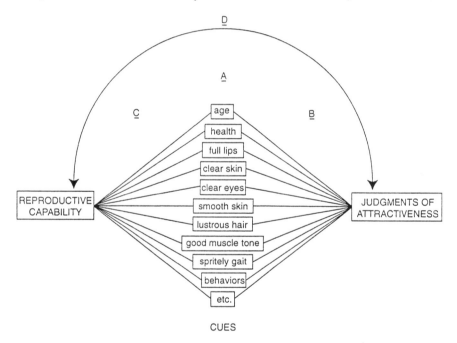

A = Relations between cues, especially between physical cues and age and health.

B = Relations between cues and judgments of female attractiveness.

C = Relations between cues and reproductive capability.

D = Relation between judgments of attractiveness and female reproductive capability.

FIG. 13.1. Hypothesized links among female attractiveness, cues, and reproductive capability. This figure depicts the hypothesized relations among observable cues such as a woman's clear skin and full lips, judgments of attractiveness, and her reproductive capacity.

be sure. In a short-term mating context, the problem of paternity certainty is less relevant because the investment is so small. When men invest tremendously in the children, however, including feeding, protection, and provisioning them for years or decades, the problem of paternity uncertainty looms large. Men who invested in other men's children for this length of time may gain our admiration for their altruism. But men who acted to ensure that the children were their own would have been more reproductively successful. Men's psychological mechanisms—such as preferring women likely to be sexually faithful to them and being sensitive to cues of potential infidelity—should bear the marks of solutions to the problem of paternity uncertainty.

These two problems—identifying women of high reproductive value and ensuring paternity certainty—may be the most important adaptive problems men confront in long-term mating, but they are not the only ones. Other problems include selecting women likely to commit to them, identifying women who will be good mothers, and perhaps even identifying women with good genes (this latter suggestion is, at the current time, highly speculative).

### Women's Long-Term Mating Psychology

Men can provide many resources to women over the long run. Men may provide women with food, find and defend territories and shelters, and defend women and their children against predators and aggressive humans. Men also may teach children skills; transfer status, power, or resources; and aid them in forming reciprocal alliances later in life.

In addition to these direct benefits to the children, women are especially vulnerable when pregnant and lactating. A lone woman in ancestral environments may have been susceptible to food deprivation. She may also become a target for aggressive men (Smuts, 1992). Thus, a long-term mate can provide protection and sustenance to the woman, in addition to the parental investment he devotes to her children.

These reproductive advantages all garnered by women through long-term mating can be summarized by three categories: immediate material advantage to the woman and her children, enhanced reproductive advantage for her children through acquired social and economic benefits, and genetic reproductive advantage for her children if variations in the qualities that lead to resource acquisition are partly heritable. Women should seek long-term mates who can provide these benefits, and their mate preferences should embody solutions to these adaptive problems.

Figure 13.2 graphically depicts the hypothesized links among observable cues, judgments of a man's attractiveness as a long-term mate, and his ability to devote resources to a particular woman. A woman is pro-

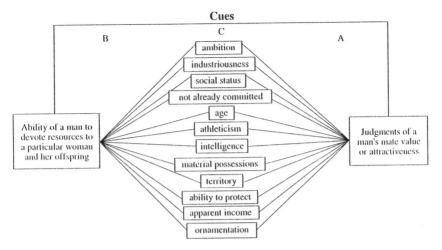

FIG. 13.2.   This figure depicts the hypothesized relations among observable or inferable cues such as a man's ambition and athleticism, judgments of his mate value or attractiveness, and his ability to devote resources to a specific woman and her children. From "Sexual Strategies Theory: An Evolutionary Perspective on Human Mating" by D. M. Buss and D. P. Schmitt, 1993, *Psychological Review, 100*, p. 223. Copyright © 1993 by American Psychological Association. Reprinted by permission.

posed to judge a man's attractiveness or mate value, in part, on the basis of her observations of his ambition, industriousness, status, lack of existing commitments, and apparent income (A). These observable cues, in turn, are known to be closely linked with a man's overall ability to devote resources to her (B). Judgments of a man's attractiveness as a long-term mate should be linked with his overall ability to provide resources.

## Women's Short-Term Mating Psychology

Given all the advantages to women of choosing a long-term mate, why would women ever pursue a short-term mating strategy? In principle, there are several classes of benefits women could derive from short-term mating, depending heavily on context and condition.

First, women could obtain immediate resources in exchange for short-term copulations. In many societies, men are expected to bring gifts such as food or jewelry to their mistresses, and women may decline to engage in sex if these gifts are not presented (Malinowski, 1929; Shostak, 1981). Thus, women who pursue short-term mating might be expected to desire mate characteristics that signal men's ability and willingness to provide immediate resources, and should disfavor men with characteristics, such as frugality or stinginess, that signal such resources will not be forthcoming.

Second, women could gain genetic advantages, in principle, through short-term mating. If a woman is able to mate in the short term with a man who has better genes than her long-term mate, she might be able to produce children of higher genetic quality. A variant on the better genes hypothesis is the diverse genes hypothesis (Smith, 1984). Women might benefit by having children fathered by different men, perhaps as a hedge against environmental change. These genetic hypotheses are highly speculative, of course, and difficult to test with the methods currently available.

Women might also benefit by mating short term as a means of mate switching (Greiling & Buss, submitted) or mate insurance (Buss, 1994). A short-term mating might make it easier for a woman to get rid of a bad long-term mate and switch to another mate of higher quality. Short-term mating might give a woman back-up mating insurance, in the event that her regular mate becomes injured, deserts her, or dies—events that happened recurrently in ancestral times, and often happen in modern times as well.

Women might also be able to develop mating skills through short-term mating. A woman might be able to get a more accurate assessment of her mate value, hone her skills of attraction and seduction, or clarify more precisely the characteristics she desires in a long-term mate.

In summary, although short-term mating is expected to be generally more advantageous for men, there are certain conditions in which women can benefit from it.

## COSTS AND CONTEXTS OF MATING STRATEGIES

All mating strategies carry costs. Over evolutionary time, the reproductive benefits of a mating strategy must outweigh the costs if it is to evolve. For example, short-term mating might carry reputational costs—damage to one's reputation if word gets around that one is promiscuous. Long-term mating also carries costs, such as the opportunity costs of mating opportunities lost while embedded within a long-term relationship.

Ultimately, the relative costs and benefits of each mating strategy hinge on the circumstances of the individual. An imbalanced sex-ratio—such as a surplus of women relative to men—might make it more beneficial for men to pursue short- rather than long-term mating because of the greater opportunities for doing so. However, a surplus of men might render short-term mating extremely difficult to pursue for men due to a shortage of willing women.

A woman living in a large city with a husband who is frequently absent might have opportunities to engage in short-term mating without incurring the costs of discovery. In contrast, a women living in a small community and surrounded by her husband's kin might make it nearly impossible to engage in short-term mating without incurring the costs of discovery.

Another context likely to affect choice of mating strategy is mate value. A man with high mate value, other things being equal, is more able to pursue short-term matings, in addition to whatever long-term mating he engages in. A woman with high mate value may be able to pursue her strategy of choice, such as attracting a high-status, heavily investing man as a long-term mate, thus rendering the potential benefits of short-term mating superfluous.

Other contextual factors are likely to affect the choice of mating strategy: one's network of family and alliances, the degree to which parents and other kin affect mating decisions, cultural norms about the status and prestige associated with each mating strategy, and individual successes or failures in the pursuit of each strategy. The key point is that humans have a complex repertoire of mating strategies; which components of this repertoire are activated is likely to depend heavily on context.

## EMPIRICAL FINDINGS ABOUT MATE PREFERENCES

This section presents some of the highlights of the empirical findings about human mate preferences in long- and short-term contexts. It starts with the study of 37 cultures, the largest study of long-term mate preferences yet conducted (Buss, 1989). This study found three major clusters of results: universal mate preferences essentially the same for both sexes; universal sex differences in mate preferences, and cultural variation in mate preferences.

### Universal Long-Term Mate Preferences

Table 13.2 shows a list of characteristics that are highly desired by both sexes in a long-term mate, with little or no evidence that one sex places greater value than the other. Both sexes desire mates who are kind, understanding, intelligent, dependable, healthy, and creative. Neither sex likes long-term mates who are cruel, stupid, undependable, riddled with diseases, or boring. Furthermore, both sexes place a premium on love and mutual attraction in a long-term mate.

Precisely why these characteristics are universally desired is a matter for future research. However, a few speculations are in order. Both sexes may value love and mutual attraction because these signal the depth of a person's commitment. Specifically, some studies have found that love signals the commitment of a host of reproductively valuable resources:

TABLE 13.2
Characteristics Commonly Sought in a Mate

| Rank | Characteristics Preferred by Males | Characteristics Preferred by Females |
|------|-----------------------------------|--------------------------------------|
| 1 | Kindness and understanding | Kindness and understanding |
| 2 | Intelligence | Intelligence |
| 3 | *Physical attractiveness** | Exciting personality |
| 4 | Exciting personality | Good health |
| 5 | Good health | Adaptability |
| 6 | Adaptability | *Physical attractiveness* |
| 7 | Creativity | Creativity |
| 8 | Desire for children | *Good earning capacity* |
| 9 | College graduate | College graduate |
| 10 | Good heredity | Desire for children |
| 11 | *Good earning capacity* | Good heredity |
| 12 | Good housekeeper | Good housekeeper |
| 13 | Religious orientation | Religious orientation |

*Note.* These characteristics were ranked according to their desirability in a long-term mate or marriage partner using a scale of 1 (*most desirable*) to 13 (*least desirable*).

*The sex differences in ranking are significant beyond the 0.001 level ($n = 162$) for characteristics in italics.

economic (e.g., gifts, food), physical (e.g., protection), sexual, psychological (e.g., helping mate when he or she is down), and reproductive (e.g., such as having children together).

The adaptive reason for placing a premium on health may be obvious. By selecting an unhealthy mate, a person might risk contracting a communicable disease. An unhealthy mate is more likely to be unable to provide an array of resources; an unhealthy mate is more likely to die. An unhealthy mate may pass on genes for unhealthiness to offspring, if there is a heritable basis to individual differences in health. Selecting a healthy mate lowers the odds of incurring these multiple costs.

A dependable mate may be a more reliable provisioner than a mate who is erratic or lazy. Furthermore, recent research has found that people low on the personality trait of dependability are more likely to have extramarital affairs (Buss & Shackelford, in press). Furthermore, a dependable mate may make a better parent, thus aiding the children in their growth, survival, and eventual reproduction.

A mate who is kind and understanding may be more prone to engage in the long-term reciprocity typically required of committed mating. People low on kindness tend to be more selfish and uncooperative (Buss, 1991). Furthermore, unkind people are more likely to inflict a variety of costs, such as physical and verbal abuse (Buss, 1991). Unkind people also may make lousy parents, inflicting costs on children.

These speculations have some basis in known research, but clearly require further empirical examination. The key point to note is that men and women worldwide have many of the same desires in a long-term mate. These universal desires provide the broader context within which to examine sex differences.

## Universal Sex Differences in Long-Term Mate Preferences

As noted earlier, men and women are predicted to differ only in the domains in which they have faced recurrently different adaptive problems over the long expanse of human evolutionary history. The study of 37 cultures revealed two clusters of universal or near-universal sex differences.

*What Women Desire More.* As predicted, women universally desire men with good financial prospects. A sample of the findings is shown in Fig. 13.3. Across all 37 cultures, women place a greater premium on a man's income than men do on a woman's income. Women also tend to

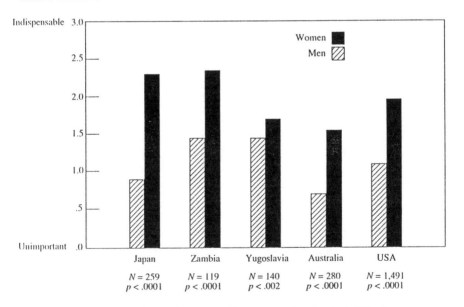

FIG. 13.3. Good financial prospect. This was rated on its desirability in a long-term mate or marriage partner, using a scale of *0* (*irrelevant* or *unimportant*) to *3* (*indispensable*). Under each country is the sample size, followed by the statistical significance of the sex difference in value placed on the characteristic. From "Sexual Strategies Theory: An Evolutionary Perspective on Human Mating," by D. M. Buss and D. P. Schmitt, 1993, *Psychological Review, 100,* p. 224. Copyright © 1993 by the American Psychological Association. Reprinted with permission.

desire characteristics in men that lead to resources over time. Thus, women in most cultures place a premium on a man's social status, his ambition and industriousness, and his older age—qualities known to be linked with resource acquisition.

*What Men Desire More.* The study of 37 cultures found only two qualities that men universally desired more than women: youth and physical attractiveness (see Figs. 13.4 and 13.5). Not a single culture showed a reversal of this trend or even an equal valuation of these qualities.

As described earlier, these findings support the prediction that men place a premium on cues to a women's reproductive value in a long-term mate. Youth is a known correlate of reproductive value because women's reproductive value declines sharply with increasing age.

Furthermore, a large number of studies conducted over the past decade have shown that beauty is in the adaptations of the beholder (Symons,

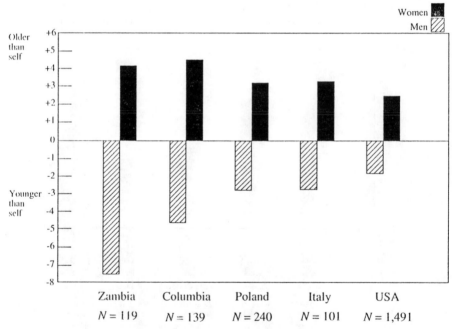

FIG. 13.4. Age difference preferred between self and spouse. This figure shows that men universally desire long-term mates or marriage partners who are younger than they are, as indicated in years. Thus, a –4 would indicate that a man wanted a partner who was 4 years younger than himself. Women universally desire men who are older than they are. From "Sexual Strategies Theory: An Evolutionary Perspective on Human Mating," by D. M. Buss and D. P. Schmitt, 1993, *Psychological Review, 100*, p. 220. Copyright © 1993 by the American Psychological Association. Reprinted with permission.

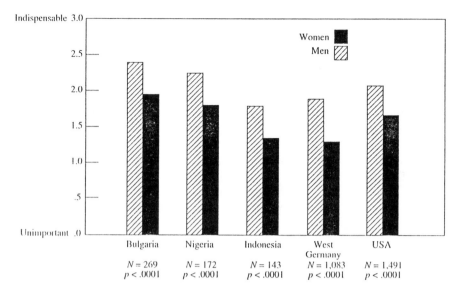

FIG. 13.5. Physical attractiveness. This figure shows that men across cultures place a greater premium than do women on long-term mates who are physically attractive. Subjects used a rating scale from *0* (*irrelevant* or *unimportant*) to *3* (*indispensable*). From "Sexual Strategies Theory: An Evolutionary Perspective on Human Mating," by D. M. Buss and D. P. Schmitt, 1993, *Psychological Review, 100*, p. 218. Copyright © 1993 by the American Psychological Association. Reprinted with permission.

1995). Specifically, there is evidence that men's standards of beauty are highly uniform across cultures (Cunningham, Roberts, Barbee, Druen, & Wu, 1995); linked with cues such as smooth skin, clear skin, and a youthful appearance (Symons, 1979); linked with a low waist-to-hips ratio, which signals fertility (Singh, 1993); and linked with symmetrical features, which signals health and youth (Gangestad, Thornhill, & Yeo, 1994). Thus, the premium that men place on physical attractiveness is a proxy for a premium that men place on youth and health, and hence high reproductive value.

## What Men Want in Short-Term Mating

Many studies show that men's standards generally plummet in short-term mating as contrasted with long-term mating. Men are willing to accept lower levels on a host of mate characteristics, such as intelligence, kindness, dependability, and emotional stability (Buss & Schmitt, 1993; Kenrick, Sadalla, Groth, & Trost, 1990).

Within this context, it is especially striking that there are a few reversals of this trend—qualities that men desire more in the short-term than in the long-term mating context. The first is physical attractiveness. Men value physical attractiveness more in a short-term mate than in a long-term mate—a finding that has been replicated across several studies by independent investigators (Buss & Schmitt, 1993; Kenrick et al., 1990).

Second, men place a greater premium on sex appeal and sexual experience in the short-term than in the long-term mating context. This could be a solution to the problem of sexual accessibility. Women who are sexually experienced may be more easily accessible than women who lack sexual experience. This elevation in preference could facilitate men's solution to the problem of sexual access.

Further support for this notion is found in the finding that men are not at all turned off by promiscuity in a short-term mate, whereas they find promiscuity terribly repugnant in a long-term mate. Again, a woman who shows signs of promiscuity may be more sexually accessible than women who do not.

Men dislike in a short-term mate, more than in a long-term mate, women who want a commitment, have a low sex drive, are prudish, lack sexual experience, and are physically unattractive. These dislikes appear to function to solve some of the problems men encounter in short-term mating—the problems of increasing sexual accessibility and minimizing commitment.

Further studies are underway to examine a larger array of men's desires and dislikes in short-term, as contrasted with long-term, mating contexts. The available evidence points to an evolved psychology of short-term mating, in which the design features of that psychology—the specific desires and dislikes—correspond precisely with the specific adaptive problems men confront in short-term mating contexts.

### What Women Want in Short-Term Mating

Only a few studies have been devoted to exploring women's desires in a short-term mate (e.g., Buss & Schmitt, 1993; Greiling & Buss, submitted; Kenrick et al., 1990). Several findings are clear. First, women maintain high standards in the short-term mating context, in contrast to men, whose standards plummet.

Second, women place a greater premium on physical attractiveness in a short-term mate compared with a long-term mate (Buss & Schmitt, 1993; Gangestad & Simpson, 1990; Kenrick et al., 1990). This finding is consistent with the hypothesis that women may be seeking good genes from a short-term mate (Fisher, 1930; Gangestad & Simpson, 1990).

Women also elevate the importance they attach to immediate resources in short-term mating contexts (Buss & Schmitt, 1993). They desire men who spend a lot of money on them early on, who give them gifts early on, and who have an extravagant lifestyle. Women also dislike men who are stingy early on. These findings are consistent with the hypothesis that women seek immediate resources in the short-term mating context.

In summary, the hidden side of women's mating—their pursuit of short-term partners—reveals a set of preferences with specific design features. Thus far, the design features support the hypothesis that women benefit from short-term mating in the form of immediate access to resources and possibly better genes. However, many of the other hypothesized benefits of short-term mating remain to be tested (see Greiling & Buss, submitted). Future research can be expected to reveal other design features of women's short-term mating—a strategy clearly present in women's mating repertoire.

## Cultural Variation in Mating Strategies

Cultures vary in the value they place on certain mate characteristics. Conventional dogma within the social sciences holds that the discovery of cultural variation falsifies evolutionary accounts. According to this social science view, evolution and culture are in some sort of causal competition, where it is thought that the greater influence of one, the less of the other (see Tooby & Cosmides, 1992). Because the discovery of cultural variation was thought to contradict evolutionary accounts, they were triumphantly celebrated as proof that humans had shuffled off their evolutionary coil.

Recent formulations in evolutionary psychology show that this traditional social science dogma is simply wrong. Evolutionary psychology provides a truly interactionist position. To account for cultural variation in the thickness and distribution of calluses on the skin of humans, one needs to invoke the existence of species-typical universal callous-producing mechanisms, and variation in the environmental friction of individuals in different cultures. The existence of cultural variation in calluses does not falsify or in any way contradict the notion that humans everywhere have essentially the same evolved callous-producing mechanisms.

Evolutionary psychologists expect that selection has fashioned psychological mating mechanisms that are highly sensitive to context and circumstance. Two examples will be used to illustrate this point—one involving cultural variation in the importance of physical attractiveness, and one involving cultural variation in the pursuit of short-term versus long-term mating strategies.

Although the sexes differ universally in the value they place on physical attractiveness in a long-term mate, it is also clear that cultures differ substantially in the value they place on attractiveness. What accounts for this cultural variability? Recent work in evolutionary biology has stressed the importance of parasite for physical appearance (Hamilton & Zuk, 1982). For example, it has long been a mystery precisely why peahens place such a premium on the brilliant plumage of the peacocks. Hamilton and Zuk (1980) proposed that the brilliant plumage might signal a low parasite load, and hence be a powerful cue to the health of the peacock. Subsequent work has confirmed that the prevalence of parasite degrades physical appearance, and especially the luminescence of the feathers of certain birds. Thus, peahens appear to place a premium on the peacock's brilliant plumage because it signals low parasite load, and hence health.

Humans, as long-lived organisms, also play host to hundreds of parasites. However, too many parasites can be extremely dangerous to health and longevity. My colleague Steve Gangestad and I reasoned that, in cultures in ecologies containing many parasites, people might shift their preferences to place a greater value on physical attractiveness. By placing a greater premium on attractiveness in parasite-prevalent cultures, individuals would partially solve the adaptive problems of: contracting communicable parasites, exposing their children to communicable parasites, and risking the possibility of early death or ill health of their mate. In cultures in which parasites are far less prevalent, the importance of these adaptive problems is not as severe, and so individuals might adjust down the importance they place on physical attractiveness.

To test this hypothesis, data were obtained on the prevalence of six major classes of parasites in each of 29 countries (Gangestad & Buss, 1993). Then we correlated the prevalence of parasites with average value placed on physical appearance in the culture. After applying appropriate statistical controls for possible confounds, the correlation was .72, which is highly significant. Thus, we were able to account for an astonishing 50% of the cultural variation in the premium placed on appearance by ecological variation in parasite prevalence.

Although further research clearly needs to explore this link, this example highlights an important feature of the scientific discipline of evolutionary psychology: Cultural variation, far from falsifying evolutionary accounts, provides important phenomena that can sometimes be explained by evolutionary accounts.

Another cultural variation in mating is the prevalence of short-term versus long-term mating. Some cultures are characterized by stable marriages, high levels of monogamy, little extramarital sex, and few casual sexual relationships. Other cultures are characterized by high levels of promiscuity, unstable marriages, and numerous affairs. How can this cultural variability be explained?

One evolutionary psychological explanation invokes the sex ratio—the ratio of men to women in the eligible mating pool. According to the sex ratio hypothesis, cultures in which there is a surplus of women should be characterized by a shift to short-term mating. The rationale is this. Men, more than women, have a desire for sexual variety or a large number of sex partners. When there is a surplus of women relative to men, they are better able to act on that desire. On the flip side of the coin, women have a great desire for long-term mating. In contexts where there are not enough men to go around, however, some women have to shift to a short-term mating strategy or forego mating altogether.

The presence of women willing to engage in short-term mating causes men to be more reluctant to commit to long-term mating; when they do, there are more frequent opportunities for affairs. Furthermore, should they tire of their mate, there are plenty of women to take their place, and so one source of impediment to divorce is lacking when there is a surplus of women.

In contexts characterized by a surplus of men, in contrast, both sexes are predicted to shift to a long-term mating strategy. Women are better able to pursue their desire for men who commit, and men fortunate enough to attract women go to great lengths to fulfill their desires to retain them. Thus, both sexes shift to stable long-term mating.

Although extensive tests of the sex ratio hypothesis have not been conducted, there is already some cross-cultural evidence to support it. In South America, there are two Indian groups characterized by different sex ratios. The Ache tribe has a sex ratio of 1.5 women for every man, whereas the Hiwi tribe shows a surplus of men (Hill & Hurtado, 1996). In many ways, the groups are similar in their mode of subsistence and nature of ecology. However, the Ache and Hiwi differ considerably in the nature of their mating, precisely as predicted by the sex ratio hypothesis. Among the Ache, short-term mating is common, extramarital affairs are rampant, and marriages are highly unstable. The average Ache gets married and divorced 12 times by the age of 40. Among the Hiwi, in contrast, marriages are highly stable and affairs are far less frequent. Evidence from other cultures, and from our own culture over time, supports the sex ratio hypothesis (Guttentag & Secord, 1983; Pedersen, 1991).

The sex ratio hypothesis illustrates a second way in which evolutionary psychology can explain cultural variation in a principled way. Cultural variation is real, it is important, and it must be explained. Traditional social science simply pointed to the existence of cultural variation, and attributed it to culture—a circular nonexplanation. We now have some of the conceptual tools needed to explain cultural variation in a principled way. Evolutionary psychology provides those tools.

## CONCLUSION

Standard social science theories of human mating historically have been astonishingly simplistic. These theories typically invoked a single factor to explain all of human mating. Some invoked the desire for others who are similar. Others invoked the notion of opposite attraction or complementary mating. Still others invoked the notion that people seek in mates those who have an equivalent market value. Although containing elements of truth, none of these theories could account for sex differences, preference shifts across contexts, cultural variation, or the domain specificity of desire.

We now know that human mating is extraordinarily complex. Humans have a repertoire of mating strategies that are pursued by different people at the same time, by the same people at different times, and that differ by sex. Furthermore, which strategy gets pursued is highly sensitive to context—the context of parasite prevalence, the context of sex ratio, the context of personal mate value, and undoubtedly many more. It is the entire repertoire of human mating strategies—the ways in which they are sex differentiated, and the ways in which they are differentially pursued according to personal and social context—that requires explanation.

Today we have a deeper understanding of the evolutionary psychology of human mating. Adaptation is best seen in evidence for special design—features of organic life that are tailored to specific adaptive problems (Williams, 1966). The evidence summarized in this chapter shows strong evidence of special design in the form of domain-specific mate preferences that shift according to sex and temporal context.

Even this account will eventually turn out to be a simplified version of the actual complexity of human mating psychology. Given the tremendous importance of mating for reproduction, our psychology of mating has been specially targeted by selection. Our psychology of mating has been grooved and scored with intricate design by sexual selection operating over the millions of years of human evolution. Although we now have some of the larger landmarks of that design, future research and theorizing should reveal many markings that have been missed in our search for a deeper understanding of the mysteries of human mating.

## REFERENCES

Buss, D. M. (1989). Sex differences in human mate preferences: Evolutionary hypotheses tested in 37 cultures. *Behavioral and Brain Sciences, 12,* 1–49.

Buss, D. M. (1991). Conflict in married couples: Personality predictors of anger and upset. *Journal of Personality, 59,* 663–688.

Buss, D. M. (1994). *The evolution of desire: Strategies of human mating.* New York: Basic Books.

Buss, D. M., & Malamuth, N. (Eds.). (1996). *Sex, power, conflict: Evolutionary and feminist perspectives.* New York: Oxford University Press.

Buss, D. M., & Schmitt, D. P. (1993). Sexual strategies theory: An evolutionary perspective on human mating. *Psychological Review, 100,* 204–232.

Buss, D. M., & Shackelford, T. K. (in press). Susceptibility to infidelity in the first year of marriage. *Journal of Research in Personality.*

Cunningham, M., Roberts, A. R., Barbee, A. P., Druen, P. B., & Wu, C. (1995). "Their ideas of beauty are, on the whole, the same as ours": Consistency and variability in cross-cultural perception of female physical attractiveness. *Journal of Personality and Social Psychology, 68*, 261–279.

Darwin, C. (1871). *The descent of man and selection in relation to sex.* London: Murray.

Fisher, R. A. (1930). *The genetical theory of natural selection.* Oxford, England: Clarendon.

Gangestad, S. W., & Buss, D. M. (1993). Pathogen prevalence and human mate preferences. *Ethology and Sociobiology, 14*, 89–96.

Gangestad, S. W., & Simpson, J. A. (1990). Toward an evolutionary history of female sociosexual variation. *Journal of Personality, 58*, 69–96.

Gangestad, S. W., Thornhill, R., & Yeo, R. A. (1994). Facial attractiveness, developmental stability, and fluctuating asymmetry. *Ethology and Sociobiology, 15*, 73–85.

Greiling, H., & Buss, D. M. (submitted). *Women's sexual strategies: The hidden dimension of short-term extra-pair mating.*

Guttentag, M., & Secord, P. (1983). *Too many women?* Beverly Hills, CA: Sage.

Hamilton, W. D., & Zuk, M. (1982). Heritable true fitness and bright birds: A role for parasites? *Science, 218*, 384–387.

Hill, K., & Hurtado, M. (1996). *Demographic/life history of Ache foragers.* Hawthorne, NY: Aldine deGruyter.

Kenrick, D. T., Sadalla, E. K., Groth, G., & Trost, M. R. (1990). Evolution, traits, and the stages of human courtship: Qualifying the parental investment model. *Journal of Personality, 58*, 97–116.

Malinowski, B. (1929). *The sexual life of savages in North-Western Melanesia.* London: Routledge.

Pedersen, F. A. (1991). Secular trends in human sex ratios: Their influence on individual and family behavior. *Human Nature, 3*, 271–291.

Shostak, M. (1981). Nisa: The life and words of a !Kung woman. Cambridge, MA: Harvard University Press.

Singh, D. (1993). Adaptive significance of female attractiveness: Role of waist-to-hip ratio. *Journal of Personality and Social Psychology, 65*, 293–307.

Smith, R. L. (1984). Human sperm competition. In R. L. Smith (Ed.), *Sperm competition and the evolution of mating systems* (pp. 601–659). New York: Academic Press.

Smuts, B. (1992). Male aggression against women: An evolutionary perspective. *Human Nature, 3*, 1–44.

Symons, D. (1979). *The evolution of human sexuality.* New York: Oxford University Press.

Symons, D. (1995). Beauty is in the adaptations of the beholder. In P. R. Abramson & S. D. Pinkerton (Eds.), *Sexual nature, sexual culture* (pp. 80–118). Chicago: University of Chicago Press.

Tooby, J., & Cosmides, L. (1992). Psychological foundations of culture. In J. Barkow, L. Cosmides, & J. Tooby (Eds.), *The adapted mind* (pp. 19–136). New York: Oxford University Press.

Trivers, R. (1972). Parental investment and sexual selection. In B. Campbell (Ed.), *Sexual selection and the descent of man: 1871–1971* (pp. 136–179). New York: Aldine deGruyter.

Williams, G. C. (1966). *Adaptation and natural selection.* Princeton, NJ: Princeton University Press.

Williams, G. C. (1975). *Sex and evolution.* Princeton, NJ: Princeton University Press.

# 14

## The Evolutionary Social Psychology of Family Violence

Martin Daly
Margo Wilson
*McMaster University*

Psychological science is in large measure a quest to characterize perceptual and cognitive processes, motives, emotions, and so forth at a level of abstraction that transcends such local particularities as cultural differences and historical influences. This is true regardless of whether one's pet constructs are things like selective attention or self-esteem, social norms or Hebbian cell assemblies. Psychologists are interested in variability, to be sure, but they generally try to account for variability as the contingent outputs of more universal psychological phenomena. If persuaded by the anthropological record that Oedipal conflict occurs in some but not other societies, for example, a psychoanalytic theorist must find a fall-back position that will describe human nature in terms of more universal psychodynamic constructs. If theorists of social cognition were to become convinced that exotic peoples do not indulge in attributions or social comparisons, they too would have to seek a more universal level of abstraction.

Thus, we would suggest that most scientists interested in human psychology implicitly assume the existence of a complexly functional, panhuman psychological nature (Tooby & Cosmides, 1992). If such a human nature exists, there is no alternative to the proposition that it evolved by selection. It follows that a shared objective of psychological scientists is the discovery and elucidation of evolved psychological adaptations—a subset of evolved biological adaptations. Evolutionary psychologists, then, are those who take explicit note of the fact that the objects of their interest are evolved adaptations, and who find it useful to pay some attention to theory and knowledge about how the evolutionary process works.

Evolutionary biology's specific conception of adaptive function has practical relevance for the pursuit of psychological science. Had Freud better understood Darwin, for example, we might all have been spared the confusion engendered by his bizarre misconstrual of parent–offspring conflict as an instance of sexual rivalry (Daly & Wilson, 1990a). Psychologists necessarily work in the shadow of their assumptions about the functional organization of the mind, assumptions of which they are often scarcely aware, and without the rigorous criterion of functionality provided by evolutionary theory, their assumptions are often faulty. Selection does not design organisms to be happy or homeostatic or even long-lived, for example, except insofar as these achievements contribute to a more basic criterion of success: outreproducing same-sex members of one's species. More precisely, any functionally integrated, complex, biological entity such as the human psyche may be presumed to be organized in such a way as to promote fitness (i.e., to contribute to the relative replicative success of the focal individual's genes in competition with their alleles).

Social psychologists, too, have always made the broad, basic objectives of an hypothesized panhuman social-psychological nature the centerpieces of their theories, and so they should, but unfortunately, like Freud, they have typically formulated their notions of what those psychological objectives might be without reference to the adaptive problems that the social psyche must solve to promote fitness. The result has been a series of apparently arbitrary conceptions of what the psyche is designed to do—to maintain Heiderian balance, seek self-actualization, eliminate cognitive dissonance, and so forth—conceptions that have simply fallen from fashion and been replaced by equally arbitrary successors, rather than becoming the validated building blocks of a cumulative understanding. Meanwhile, evolutionists have made rapid, cumulative progress in understanding social phenomena in animals (and plants) by organizing their inquiries around the adaptive problems that social life presents: problems like mate choice, the assessment of the prowess and intentions of rivals, kin recognition, and the allocation of parental resources among one's young. By paying explicit attention to adaptive significance and selective forces, behavioral ecologists and sociobiologists attained well-founded expectations about which proximate causal cues are likely to affect animals, and about what sorts of contingencies, priorities, and combinatorial information-processing algorithms are likely to be instantiated in the architecture of the psyche (e.g., Krebs & Davies, 1987; Trivers, 1985).

It must be stressed that Darwinism is not a psychological theory, nor does it directly imply any single such theory. A common error is to suppose that an evolutionarily informed psychology will identify fitness as the "goal" toward which people and other animals strive. In fact, fitness plays a quite different role in evolutionary theory from the role that self-esteem or a target level of blood glucose or some other goal plays in a psychological theory. When the fitness consequences of behavior are invoked to explain it, they are invoked not as direct objectives or motivators, but as explanations of why particular more proximal objectives and motivators have evolved to play their particular roles in the causal control of behavior, with particular domains of relevance, and why they are calibrated as they are. This crucial point is consistently misunderstood by those social scientists who point to modern novelties such as vasectomies or adoptions of unrelated strangers as evidence against evolutionary ideas. Ironically, as Symons (1990) and Tooby and Cosmides (1990) discussed, it has been misunderstood by some evolutionists too. Selection has equipped us with psychological machinery that is specifically designed to solve only those particular adaptive problems that challenged many generations of our ancestors.

It is sometimes useful to visualize a hierarchy of adaptive functions with fitness at its summit. The idea of functional hierarchy is already second nature to psychologists. Lateral inhibition in the retina is understood as a means to the end of edge detection, which is a means to the end of object recognition, which is a means to the ends of foraging and predator avoidance, which are means to the ends of energy accrual and survival. However, the idea that fitness is the summit of this hierarchy is less familiar, and its implications may be counterintuitive to psychologists.

One such implication is that animals do not treat homeostasis and survival as irreducible ends, but as means to the end of genetic posterity. Can we assume, for example, that the evolved mechanisms of "hunger" will be organized in such a way as to motivate action to avert starvation? Not when feeding behavior's predictable side effects on reproductive success are sufficiently negative. This insight has led to the discovery and investigation of a variety of adaptive anorexias, unsuspected by researchers unaccustomed to selectional thinking (Mrosovsky & Sherry, 1980). Nor is the functional primacy of reproduction the end of the matter. Can we assume that the evolved mechanisms of maternal–fetal interaction will be organized in such a way as to promote fetal well-being with minimal wastage? Not if reproduction is sexual, so that maternal and fetal fitnesses are disjunct (Trivers, 1974). This insight has illuminated a host of otherwise puzzling phenomena in human pregnancy (Haig, 1993). In general, then, selectional thinking is an invaluable aid to psychological theory and research by providing functional descriptions of the sorts of adaptations that are likely to have evolved, and are therefore worth seeking in the proximate causal machinery that generates behavior.

## SELF-INTEREST, CONFLICT, AND VIOLENCE

Sweet tastes evolved to be appealing because they are cues to the presence of nutrients that are means to the end of fitness. Infidelity of one's mate is aversive because of the threats to fitness that it has entailed. Although it is a mistake to imagine that fitness is directly instantiated in the psyche, there is certainly a sense in which one's perceptions of where one's interests lie may be said to constitute tokens of expected fitness consequences in ancestral environments. The phrase "perceptions of where one's interests lie" should be interpreted broadly. Our immune systems and cell membranes operate outside our awareness, for example, but they participate in perceiving and defending our interests nonetheless.

The postulate that expected fitness is the bedrock of perceived self-interest entails an implicit theory about where interests intersect and where they diverge. You and I are likely to perceive our interests as consonant, and hence to experience our relationship as harmonious, to the degree that the exigencies that raise your expected fitness raise mine too. Conversely, we are likely to perceive our interests as discordant, and hence to experience conflict, to the degree that the exigencies that raise your expected fitness diminish mine. Insofar as interpersonal violence is a response to apprehended conflict, this theory has implications about who is likely to use violence against whom, and about the circumstances that will exacerbate or mitigate the risk of violence in particular relationship categories (Daly & Wilson, 1988c). That has been the unifying idea behind our evolutionary psychological hypotheses about family violence.

## NEPOTISTIC RESTRAINT?

The proposition that social motives have evolved by selection suggests that there will be psychological adaptations tending to soften potentially costly conflicts among genetic relatives. If my rival in a contest for a limited resource is my brother, for example, it makes less difference to my fitness who wins than if the rival were unrelated, and the potential costs of using dangerous competitive tactics are higher in the case of fraternal rivalry because injury to either party hurts the fitness of both. Hamilton's (1964) theory of inclusive fitness, formalizing and generalizing this "nepotistic" logic, was perhaps the single most important stimulus to recent selectionist theorizing and research on social behavior, and hence to the emergence of an evolutionary social psychology. By extending the concept of fitness to include the actor's effects on the expected reproduction of collateral as well as descendant kin, Hamilton solved the problem of accounting for the evolution of "altruistic" actions that reduce the actor's expected reproductive success while enhancing someone else's.

Inclusive fitness theory replaced the classical Darwinian conception of organisms as evolved reproductive strategists with the notion that they have evolved to be nepotistic strategists.

An interesting example is provided by Hamilton's (1979) own comparative study of male weaponry in fig wasps and other insects. Hamilton focused on taxa in which wingless males never move far between the egg stage and death, leaving it up to the winged females to disperse. Within each of several such insect groups, there are some species in which females lay eggs singly as they move about, with the result that the males who hatch out at any one site and then compete for mating opportunities are typically unrelated; there are other species in which females lay clusters of eggs, with the result that competing males are often brothers. Hamilton found that the unrelated competitors of the former group are often heavily armed and fight to the death, whereas males of those species in which one's rival is likely to be one's brother lack specialized weaponry and do not fight. Close kinship among male competitors has tipped the selective balance away from confrontational violence in male–male competition and toward a pacifistic scramble competition instead.

Hamilton's analysis of male sexual competition in fig wasps exemplifies the possibility of a nepotistic restraint of dangerous competitive tactics without anything that would ordinarily be thought of as kin recognition. The restraint in the fraternally aggregated species is morphological, behavioral, and obligate: The species-typical expected degree of relatedness between male competitors has been a factor in the evolution of competitive tactics that are then employed against all, and nepotistic adaptation is evident only when different species are compared. However, many animals (including insects) also exhibit discriminative social behavior within species, in relation to a variety of cues indicative of relatedness (Hepper, 1991). Hamilton's theory implies that we may expect evolved social psychologies to function in such a way as to effectuate discriminative favoritism toward kin when information permits, and a large body of research on nonhuman animals has confirmed this expectation.

There is no apparent reason to doubt the applicability of this proposition to human beings. So when evolutionary biologists inspired by Hamilton turned their attentions to the human sciences, it came as no surprise that anthropologists had already identified kinship as both a human preoccupation and the central principle by which our societies are organized. In the words of Leach (1966, p. 41), "Human beings, wherever we meet them, display an almost obsessional interest in matters of sex and kinship" (p. 41). It was initially in anthropology that sociobiologists found data of relevance to their theories (e.g., Alexander, 1974, 1979), as well as converts ready to apply a Hamiltonian perspective in their research (e.g., Chagnon & Irons, 1979).

Social psychology, as noted earlier, has been slower to recognize and exploit the recent theoretical work on social evolution, and there is an irony in this reticence. The individualistic focus of psychology is in general much more compatible with evolutionary analyses than is anthropology's emphasis on group-level entities like "society" and "culture." Natural selection's capacity to generate and maintain complexly functional organization is overwhelmingly a matter of the differential survival and reproductive success of individual organismic designs, and that is why most evolutionary biologists consider the individual to be the highest level in life's hierarchy at which we may expect to find functionally integrated, complex adaptations (Dawkins, 1986; Williams, 1966). A corollary is this: If nepotistic Hamiltonian adaptations await discovery, they are likely to be primarily adaptations of the individual social psyche, rather than emergent properties of societies, families, or other collectivities, and the science that will elucidate their structure and functioning will be psychological in its focus.

In this light, it is remarkable that social-psychological textbooks and treatises remain almost completely devoid of reference to kinship or family relations. Anthropology's obsession with these matters did not await the impetus of Hamilton's inclusive fitness theory, so why has kinship never commanded the attention of social psychologists? There appear to be at least two major reasons for this unfortunate neglect. The first has more to do with convenience than with conceptualization: The academic research tradition of social psychology has been largely limited to the study of readily available, captive undergraduates interacting with one another or with the experimenters' confederates. It is simply a lot less trouble to assemble a subject group of strangers than a group of relatives, or even acquaintances, and this is surely the main reason that mainstream social psychology remains overwhelmingly a social psychology of stranger interactions. Yet, there is a more conceptual reason, too, and that is social psychology's lingering attachment to a behaviorist legacy of "parsimony" in construct formation (Tooby & Cosmides, 1992). In such an atmosphere, the evolutionary psychological hypothesis that each person may possess qualitatively distinct social-psychological modules appropriate to the several sorts of basic social relationships could hardly be entertained.

The study of the relationships among family members in modern industrialized society has thus been left mainly to social workers and others with applied interests. Not surprisingly, the resultant family relations literature places great emphasis on such topics as developmental disadvantage and delinquency, marital (un)happiness and divorce, and family violence. Nor perhaps is it surprising that specialists in the study of family violence regularly maintain that it is a more pervasive problem than is generally recognized. According to the heads of the most prominent family violence research program in the United States, for example, violence is "at least as typical of family relations as is love" (Gelles & Straus, 1979, p. 188). More specifically:

> With the exception of the police and the military, the family is perhaps the most violent social group, and the home the most violent social setting, in our society. A person is more likely to be hit or killed in his or her home by another family member than anywhere else or by anyone else. (Gelles & Straus, 1985, p. 88)

## HOMICIDE AS A CONFLICT ASSAY

How can such remarkable claims about the ubiquity of family violence be squared with Hamilton's compelling theoretical argument for the ubiquity of nepotistic social motives? The first challenge is to assess the validity of the family violence researchers' claims. What evidence warrants the conclusion that the family is an exceptionally violent social milieu? How has violence been measured? In the case of Straus and Gelles' own research, the answer is by the self-reports of interviewees contacted at random, and the data are highly suspect (Dobash, Dobash, Wilson, & Daly, 1992). But even where more convincing measures such as assault charges and emergency room admissions have been employed, studies of interpersonal violence are plagued by problems of biased detection and reportage. It is probable, for example, that assaults on wives are greatly underestimated by such methods, relative to comparably severe assaults on neighbors or strangers, which are more likely to be reported to the police.

Our solution to these methodological problems has been to confine analysis to the most extreme interpersonal violence—namely, the lethal instances, for which biases of reporting and detection should be minimal (Daly & Wilson, 1988b, 1988c). The presumption behind this strategy is that homicide is the tip of the iceberg of normal violence. But we must remain alert to the possibility that this presumption could be false: The motivational, demographic, and other factors affecting the likelihood of a murder may not always be the same as those affecting the likelihood of a nonlethal assault. Therefore, our strategy in this chapter and in our research is to treat homicide as the primary test of hypotheses about factors exacerbating or mitigating interpersonal conflict, and hence violence, but also to assess, where possible, whether the available evidence is consistent with the proposition that homicide risk factors have parallel effects on the incidence of nonlethal violence.

It is important to stress that this use of homicide cases as a sort of "window" on violence, and hence as the material for tests of evolutionary psychological hypotheses about conflict, does not presuppose that killing per se is (or indeed ever was) adaptive, neither on average nor even occasionally. Insofar as killings represent the extreme tail of a distribution—rare products of psychological processes and behavior whose more usual, nonlethal manifestations have useful effects like successful resource expropriation, deterrence of infidelity, coercion, and intimidation—then factors that raise the likelihood of violence in the pursuit of these valuable social outcomes may be expected to raise the risk of homicide too. It is quite possible that actually killing one's antagonist is more often than not an overreactive *mistake*—an act with negative consequences both for the killer's net hedonic utility and for the actual expected fitness of which that utility is an evolved token. Indeed, it seems likely that killing is on average maladaptive in this way in contemporary state societies, and it may have been maladaptive in the unpoliced face-to-face societies of our ancestors too. Or maybe not. In either case, homicide can provide a sort of conflict assay.

## HOMICIDE RISK AND RELATEDNESS

So what do the facts about homicide imply about the applicability of Hamiltonian theory to human families? Are Gelles and Straus (1979) correct in claiming that family relationships are exceptionally violent relationships, or is there a pervasive nepotistic restraint of conflict and violence, as theory and research on other animals might lead us to expect?

At first glance, homicides seem to belie the notion of kin solidarity. People indeed kill relatives, and in certain societies, such cases can constitute a substantial proportion of all killings. But substantial compared to what? The notion of restraint in the use of violence is implicitly relative, and the question is whether kinship mitigates the risk of violent conflict, all else equal. Of course all else is never equal, and it is far from obvious how to compute what fraction of homicides we should expect to be intrafamilial if kinship were irrelevant.

One way of tackling the problem of computing a statistically expected distribution of victim–killer relationships is to confine analysis to a tractable limited domain, such as those cases in which the two parties were members of the same household. Information on the living arrangements of the population-at-large can then be used to specify the universe of potential victim–killer pairs, and relationship-specific rates can be computed. Daly and Wilson (1982) performed such an analysis of homicides in the city of Detroit (the results are portrayed in Fig. 14.1).

Several facets of these results are worth noting. One is that family homicide consists primarily of spousal homicide. Mates are not genetic relatives, and their distinct relationship has its own sources of conflict, as

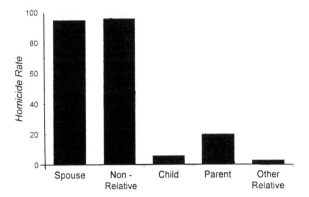

FIG. 14.1. Relationship-specific homicide rates (homicides per million coresiding potential victims) among members of the same household in Detroit in 1972. All persons 14 years of age or older are treated as potential killers.

is considered at length in the following text. Thus, deadly conflict between marriage partners does not speak to the issue of nepotistic restraint, except insofar as it provides a point of comparison against the much lower levels of lethal violence between blood kin. A second noteworthy aspect of the Detroit data is that people who lived in the same household, but were not genetic relatives, experienced a homicide rate more than 11 times greater than coresiding blood kin, and that this much greater level of violence was just as true of other unrelated dyads (mainly roommates and boarders) as it was true of marriage partners. Thus, one cannot simply interpret the relative rarity of lethal violence among blood kin as a misdirected description of the marital relationship's exceptionally high capacity for violence. A third noteworthy point is that, although the data conflate step- and in-law relationships with genetic relationships (because population-at-large data were inadequate for making these distinctions), stepfathers were implicated in fully half of the cases in which children were killed by "parents"; this, too, is a topic to which we return. In general, then, the data from the Detroit analysis are entirely consistent with the Hamiltonian proposition that genetic relationship is associated with a reduction in conflict and violence, and there is no reason to believe that Detroit is unusual in this regard. People are much less likely to be killed by a close relative than by a nonrelative living in comparable proximity.

Other sorts of analyses support the same conclusion. For example, another way to operationalize the null hypothesis concerning the relationship between kinship and violence is to propose that the distribution of relationships between persons collaborating in a homicide should be similar to the distribution of relationships between victims and their killers (Daly & Wilson, 1988c). The logic is this: If relationship distributions in homicide cases were due merely to opportunity differences in the frequency and intimacy of interactions, rather than to qualitative distinctions among relationships, then such opportunity variables should affect cooperative and conflictual interactions in parallel. This null hypothesis is no straw man: Differential opportunity of just this sort has been the dominant criminological explanation for patterns of victimization. However, the null hypothesis can be emphatically rejected for every relevant data set we have found, including anthropological and historical materials from a wide range of societies (Daly & Wilson, 1988c). Close genetic relationships are far more prevalent among collaborators in violence than among victim and killer, everywhere (whereas the reverse is true about in-laws). Even in patrilineal social systems, in which brothers are one another's principal rivals for familial lands and titles, there is evidence that close genealogical relationship softens otherwise equivalent conflicts and reduces the incidence of violence (Daly & Wilson, 1988c). Familial solidarity cannot be reduced to a mere consequence of proximity and familiarity.

## SUBSTITUTE PARENTHOOD AND VIOLENCE

It was noted earlier that stepfathers were implicated in several family homicides in Detroit, and there is again nothing unusual about Detroit in this regard. An obvious hypothesis from a Darwinian–Hamiltonian perspective on sociality is that substitute parenthood is a risky proposition. Parenting is a costly investment (Trivers, 1972) of time and resources, and selection favors parental psychologies that allocate parental efforts to yield the greatest expected fitness. A predictable consequence is the evolution of subtle psychological mechanisms of discriminative parental solicitude, and this prediction has been abundantly and diversely verified in studies of nonhuman animals (Daly & Wilson, 1988a, 1995; Wilson & Daly, 1994). One important issue in such discrimination is whether the youngster is really the putative parent's own.

The evolved psychologies of animals are sensitive to a variety of species-appropriate cues that help parents avoid misdirecting resources to nonrelatives. Nevertheless, parents can be deceived, especially because selection is also acting on those unrelated usurpers to evolve means of bypassing parental defences. More puzzling than such deception are instances in which adults take on parental duties despite possessing reliable cues of nonparenthood. The principal such circumstance is that in which one establishes a new mateship with someone who already has dependent young (Rohwer, 1986). In many species, such young are likely to be killed (Parmigiani & vom Saal, 1994), but in species in which the single parent has some leverage, the replacement mate may assume the role of stepparent, with varying degrees of effort and enthusiasm (Daly & Wilson, 1994b; Rohwer, 1986). And *Homo sapiens* is clearly such a species: New mates make pseudoparental investments in their predecessors' children as part of the reciprocal exchange involved in courting and establishing a relationship with the widowed or divorced parent.

Human stepparents invest considerable effort and may even come to love their wards, but it would be surprising if the psychology of genetic parenthood were fully engaged with full commitment. It is adaptive and normal for genetic parents to accept nontrivial risks to their own lives in caring for their young, but selection presumably favors much lower thresholds of tolerable cost in stepparenting. Stepchildren are seldom or never so valuable to one's expected fitness as one's own offspring would be, and those parental psyches that are easily parasitized by just any appealing youngster must always have incurred a selective disadvantage. Little wonder, then, that the exploitation and mistreatment of stepchildren is a thematic staple of folk tales all around the world (Daly & Wilson, 1994b; Wilson & Daly, 1987). Little wonder, too, that stepparental obligation generally enters into remarriage decisions as a cost, not a benefit, with dependent children from past unions both detracting from the single parent's marriage market value and raising the chance that the remarriage will fail (Daly, Singh, & Wilson, 1993; White & Booth, 1985; Wilson & Daly, 1987).

In light of these considerations, it may seem that familiarity with evolutionary thinking should scarcely have been necessary to alert child abuse researchers to the necessity of assessing the risks in stepfamilies. Nevertheless, just as with social psychology's neglect of kinship, those lacking an evolutionary perspective did not in fact think to pursue this question. Wilson, Daly, and Weghorst (1980) were the first to assess whether stepparenthood was associated with child abuse, in a study of the epidemiology of cases reported to the American Humane Association, and we found it to be a hugely important risk factor.

It is an initially plausible hypothesis that the disproportionately frequent discovery of child abuse in stepfamilies might be an artifact of biased detection or reporting. However, analysis of homicide cases indicates that the differences are genuine and massive (Fig. 14.2). The youngest children rarely have stepparents, but when they do, studies in Canada, Britain, and the United States indicate that their risk of being fatally abused is on the order of 50 to 100 times higher than risk at the hands of a genetic parent (Daly & Wilson, 1988b, 1988c, 1994a). Having a stepparent has turned out to be the single most powerful predictor of severe child maltreatment yet discovered.

Perhaps surprisingly, these differentials tend to be smaller in studies of nonlethal abuse, despite the fact that these are the very cases in which

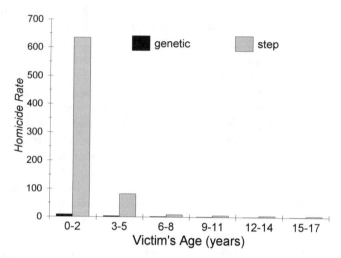

FIG. 14.2. Age-specific rates of homicide incurred by Canadian children at the hands of stepparents versus (putative) genetic parents in 1974–1990. Homicide rate = homicides per million coresiding "parent–child" dyads per annum.

detection or reporting biases may exaggerate the overrepresentation of stepparents. But in any event, excess risk at the hands of stepparents remains substantial in all studies in which abuse measures were in any way validated. Precise epidemiological comparisons have not been made for non-Western countries, but there is considerable evidence that more or less the same differential risk occurs in quite different societies too (e.g., Flinn, 1988b; Hill & Kaplan, 1988; Voland, 1988). We hypothesize that substantially elevated risk of child maltreatment at the hands of stepparents is cross-culturally universal, and we are aware of no contrary evidence.

Of course, demonstrations of differential risk do not prove that steprelationship per se is the relevant risk factor. It might instead be an incidental correlate of some more directly relevant factor. To date, however, all such hypotheses have failed. There are good evolutionary psychological grounds for predicting that both poverty and maternal youth might be risk factors for child maltreatment, for example, and indeed they are, but they are distinct risk factors whose effects do not account for the stepparent effect (Daly & Wilson, 1985, 1988c; Wilson & Daly, 1987; Wilson et al., 1980). Neither can the effect be accounted for by an overrepresentation of generally violent personalities among remarried persons because abusive stepparents are discriminative, sparing their own children within the same household (Daly & Wilson, 1985; Lightcap, Kurland, & Burgess, 1982).

Stepparental abuse is overwhelmingly perpetrated by men, not because stepmothers are benign, but because many more small children live with stepfathers than with stepmothers. Homicides perpetrated by stepfathers differ from those by genetic fathers not just in their incidence, but in qualitative attributes. A substantial proportion of the children killed by genetic parents, but virtually none of those killed by stepparents, are slain in the context of a suicide (Daly & Wilson, 1994a), and the distraught parent may even construe the homicide as a rescue (Wilson, Daly, & Daniele, 1995). Steppaternal cases are especially likely to involve a violent, assaultive rage reaction: Most small children killed by stepfathers are beaten to death, whereas genetic fathers are relatively likely to have disposed of the child by gunshot or asphyxiation (Daly & Wilson, 1994a).

Infants cry and defecate and otherwise tax the patience of parents. Potentially damaging, angry responses are inhibited by *child-specific parental love*—an evolved psychological adaptation that makes the efforts of childrearing tolerable and even delightful. Assuredly, stepparents vary in their degrees of personalized affection for the children, as do genetic parents, but it is equally sure that the average stepparent loves the child less (Wilson & Daly, 1987). As we would anticipate from the argument that excess risk derives ultimately from a lesser commitment to that individual child's welfare, stepparents are overrepresented in all forms of child maltreatment—in neglectful and assaultive cases, as well as sexual misuse (Daly & Wilson, 1991). Thus, the higher rates of neglect, exploitation, assault, and murder incurred by stepchildren are the most dramatic, but by no means the only, consequences of a difference in the distributions of parental and stepparental affection.

## DISCRIMINATIVE PARENTAL SOLICITUDE AND FILICIDE RISK

Even genetic parents abuse and sometimes kill their children, albeit rarely, and these cases seem especially challenging. Our children are our primary vehicles of fitness and typically ought to be cherished. What can evolutionary psychology make of parentally perpetrated abuse and filicide?

We reiterate that it is not necessarily the case that an adaptationist analysis of these phenomena must find them to be adaptive. Lenington (1981) and others have assumed that to seek a selectionist explanation of child abuse is to hypothesize that abuse per se promotes the abuser's fitness, or did so in our evolutionary past. This assumption is unfounded. As argued earlier with respect to the use of homicides as a conflict assay, extreme categories of behavior that represent the tail of some motivational distribution and/or have a chance element in their definitional criteria (as does any category delimited by lethality) need not be adaptations for a selectionist analysis to be illuminating. Even unequivocally pathological manifestations can be interpreted as the predictable by-products of adaptations, especially when interests conflict, and selection-minded analysis may then permit prediction of additional aspects of the pathologies and systematic variations in their incidence (Williams & Nesse, 1991). Haig's (1993) analysis of the reasons for various pathologies of human pregnancy provides several examples, including detailed interpretations of preeclampsia as a by-product of an evolutionary "arms race" between mother and fetus over control of the maternal blood flow, and of pregnant diabetes as a by-product of a parallel arms race over the control of maternal glucose levels.

The criterion of adaptation is functional design for the promotion of fitness (Williams, 1966). By this criterion, "child abuse" is certainly not an adaptation, for it surely diminishes the fitness prospects of the victim while being spectacularly ill suited to provide any compensatory benefit to parental fitness (Daly & Wilson, 1981, 1985). Indeed, by intermittently inflicting damage on a child, abusers commonly raise their own investment costs. Nevertheless, child abuse risk can be treated as a "reverse assay" of discriminative parental solicitude, which *is* an adaptation (Daly & Wilson, 1988a, 1995). If a theory suggests that some particular demographic or other attribute should be a partial determinant of parental willingness to invest in a given offspring, then it should also be a predictor of lapses in parental solicitude, including violent lapses. The epidemiology of child abuse can therefore provide tests of adaptationist hypotheses, although the abuse itself is maladaptive.

It is actually more plausible that there is specific psychological adaptation for committing infanticide than that there is specific psychological adaptation for committing child abuse. A discrete act of infanticide (including abandonment) at least entails a discrete termination of parental investment. Moreover, the ethnographic record is fairly clear in indicating that the dominant circumstances eliciting (and justifying) infanticide in face-to-face, nonstate societies have been material or social circumstances in which attempts to raise a baby are likely to fail, so that infanticidal parents may well have been making the fittest available choice (Daly & Wilson, 1984). Pregnant women's consciously felt inclinations to abort appear to reflect the same strategic logic, responding to the same predictor variables as does infanticide (e.g., David et al., 1988).

Possible psychological adaptations enabling mothers in bad circumstances to terminate lost causes include the flat affect of postpartum "depression," and the fact that intense feelings of individualized love and commitment toward the baby commonly develop over a period of days, rather than immediately (e.g., Robson & Kumar, 1980). Moreover, it is noteworthy that conspicuous defects are common grounds for infanticide in nonstate societies (Daly & Wilson, 1984), and are also elicitors of parental shock and rejection in our own society (e.g., Fletcher, 1974); they are also associated with subsequent abuse risk when social norms do not permit infanticide or abandonment (Daly & Wilson, 1981).

Neonaticide may often represent an adaptive parental allocation of reproductive effort, then, at least in premodern circumstances. The hypothesis that people possess psychological adaptations with the specific function of facilitating optimal neonaticidal decisions is not easily dismissed. It seems much less plausible, however, that filicides of older children are something that the human psyche is in any sense designed to effectuate. Indeed, the risk of such filicide plummets beyond early infancy, as well as being relatively often the act of parents who are suicidal or insane (Daly & Wilson, 1988b, 1994a). But again, regardless of whether filicides are adaptive, their variable rates of occurrence can be treated as a conflict assay and/or as a reverse assay of parental solicitude in tests of hypotheses concerning the sources of variation in these more abstract psychological quantities.

A child's expected contribution to its parents' fitness is directly related to the child's *reproductive value*—its own expected future fitness, given its phenotype and circumstances. So if parental psychology has evolved to cherish individual offspring in relation to their expected contributions to parental fitness, then the variable parental valuation of children that is manifested as child-specific love may be expected to be sensitive to ancestral cues of reproductive value. Reproductive value generally increases steadily from birth until at least puberty, simply because the likelihood of surviving to reproduce increases. Where age-specific mortality and fertility are similar to the levels that must have prevailed for most of human evolutionary history, this prepubertal increase in reproductive value is substantial. Therefore, one may predict that parental feelings would have evolved such that parents will seem to value offspring increasingly with age, a prediction that jibes with both nonhuman and human evidence (e.g., Montgomerie & Weatherhead, 1988; Wilson & Daly, 1994).

It follows that we might then expect to see an age-related decrease in the likelihood of lapses of parental solicitude, and if child abuse and filicide are extreme instances of such lapses, this line of reasoning suggests that the risk of such violence at the hands of parents should diminish with age. This prediction has been confirmed (Daly & Wilson, 1985, 1988b, 1988c; Wilson, Daly, & Weghorst, 1983). In Canada, for example, lethal assaults by parents have been found to decline monotonically from infancy, becoming virtually nonexistent as children approach their maximal reproductive value in young adulthood (Fig. 14.3). This increasing immunity from severe parental violence is especially striking when one considers teenagers' burgeoning involvement in conflictual interactions with nonrelatives; while the likelihood of being killed by parents continues to fall, the overall likelihood of becoming a homicide victim (or a perpetrator) is rising rapidly.

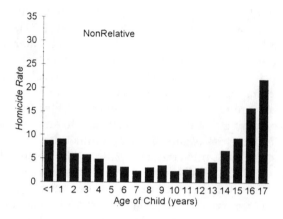

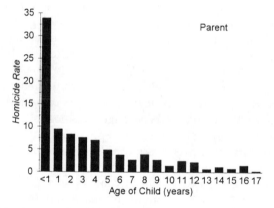

FIG. 14.3. Age-specific rates of homicide incurred by Canadian children at the hands of parents versus unrelated killers in 1974–1990. Homicide rate = homicides per million children per annum.

The specific schedule of age-related decline in filicide risk mirrors the age-related schedule of increasing reproductive value in foraging societies (Daly & Wilson, 1988b), lending support to the idea that it represents a reverse assay of age-related changes in parental solicitude. The observed steep decline in risk from the first to the second year of the child's life was predicted both because the lion's share of the prepubertal increase in reproductive value in ancestral humans occurred within the first year, and because, insofar as parental disinclination reflects a "strategic" assessment of the reproductive episode, an evolved assessment mechanism should be such as to terminate hopeless ventures as early as possible.

Many of the variables that are relevant to changes in maternal solicitude (and lapses therein) can be expected to have similar relevance for fathers. However, the paternal case is different in at least three significant ways. One is that women's reproductive life span ends before men's, so the utility of alternative reproductive efforts declines more steeply with age for women than for men. A second noteworthy difference is that dependent children impose different opportunity costs on mothers and fathers; a nursing infant constrains a mother's immediate alternative reproductive prospects much more than a father's, for example, and the magnitude of this differential impact on mother versus father diminishes as the child grows older. Third, phenotypic and other evidence of paternity may surface after infancy and may be expected to influence paternal solicitude. Each of these three considerations provides a reason to expect that a mother's valuation of a child relative to her valuation of herself is likely to rise more steeply with time since the child's birth than is the corresponding quantity for the father. Hence, if filicides constitute a sort of reverse assay of parental solicitude, it follows that filicides by mothers should exhibit a steeper age-related decline than filicides by fathers. This prediction, too, has been upheld (Daly & Wilson, 1988b; Wilson & Daly, 1994).

In general, then, although parentally perpetrated filicide is severely damaging to parental fitness, its epidemiology can be predicted in considerable detail from an evolutionary adaptationist model. Rather like the physiologist who elucidates the normal functioning of a complex adaptive system by examining its failures, we gain a window on the contingent control of parental solicitude when it collapses.

## FACTORS AFFECTING SPOUSAL VIOLENCE AND HOMICIDE

As noted earlier, the primary victims of family homicide are spouses rather than children. More specifically, most are wives (with the interesting exception of certain samples from U.S. cities; see Wilson & Daly, 1992b). Spouses are not genetic relatives, but they are reproductive partners who have intersecting fitness interests in the welfare of their joint offspring. From this perspective, marital violence presents a challenge to the evolutionary psychologist no less interesting than that provided by violence against blood kin. Why inflict damage on your mate?

The marital relationship is a special one from an evolutionary theoretical perspective (Daly & Wilson, 1996). Because the well-being of a child contributes similarly to the fitness of both its parents, the resource allocations and other states of affairs that appeal to one parent are likely to have appeal for the other, too. In fact, insofar as reproduction rather than collateral nepotism is the dominant means by which individuals promote their fitness, the fitness linkage, and hence the solidarity of mated couples, is likely to exceed that of blood kin (Alexander, 1987). However, the marital relationship is more fragile than genetic relationships because the correlation between the partners' expected fitnesses can be diminished, or even abolished, if either party becomes less committed to their joint venture.

One challenge to that joint commitment comes from the demands of other family members. Marriage partners have separate kindreds, and each may resent the other's continued nepotistic investment of time, attention, and material resources in collateral kin. This is the evolutionary theoretical gloss on a cross-culturally ubiquitous and widely recognized source of marital friction—in-laws. The in-law problem and others deriving from the marriage partners' separate agendas, such as conflicts over the husband's resource expenditures in the pursuit of extramarital matings, are potentially serious because both partners accrue expected fitness from either's investments in the welfare of their joint offspring, so that each faces temptations to parasitize the other's efforts. As might be expected, conflicts over both domestic work and contributions to household income are prevalent in cases of marital violence (e.g., Dobash & Dobash, 1979), which usually means violence against wives (Dobash et al., 1992), and wife beaters often complain of their wives' excessive attention to collateral kin. However, these are not the issues that seem to be of central motivational importance in most cases of marital violence, and especially not in the lethal ones. By far the most important motive in spousal homicides is male sexual proprietariness (Wilson & Daly, 1992a, 1993b).

Case descriptions of spousal homicide exist in the form of court reports, police investigative files, narratives of witnesses and acquaintances, and killers' own accounts. According to all these sources, the principal motivating factor in a substantial majority of the cases is the husband's discovery or suspicion of his wife's infidelity and/or her intention to desert the marriage (Campbell, 1992; Chimbos, 1978; Daly & Wilson, 1988c; Polk, 1994; Wilson & Daly, 1992a, 1993a, 1993b). Even when the husband is the eventual victim, it seems that he was usually the initial assailant, and that his motives were the same. In studies of nonlethal wife assault, too, the husband's jealousy has emerged as the leading motive, according to both the women (e.g., Dobash & Dobash, 1979) and the men (e.g., Brisson, 1983), although it is not quite so consistently the dominant issue as it is in the homicides.

There is considerable evidence that the human male mind construes marriage in large measure as a matter of entitlement to monopolize a woman, and perhaps especially to monopolize her sexuality (Wilson & Daly, 1992a). There is an obvious adaptive rationale for the existence of this proprietary mind-set. As long as we have been a biparentally investing species, wifely infidelity has been an especially potent threat to a husband's fitness because it entails risk that he will be *cuckolded*—that he will invest unwittingly in the upbringing of unrelated children. The asymmetry of this threat is presumably of evolutionary relevance to the fact that the jealousy of men is more focused on the copulatory act than is that of women (Buss et al., 1992; Daly, Wilson, & Weghorst, 1982; Teismann & Mosher, 1978). Moreover, female infidelity is universally recognized as a uniquely potent stimulus to violence on the part of normal men (Daly & Wilson, 1988c; Wilson & Daly, 1992a), and there is again an obvious functional explanation for a rage reaction (at least if it stops short of lethality, as, of course, it usually does): A predictably violent response presumably has some chilling effect on the adulterous ardor of both wives and their lovers.

The psychological linkage between proprietary jealousy and rage does not always succeed in generating effective coercion, however, and when it does not, the violence of spurned men often appears to be dysfunctionally spiteful. The stalking and sometimes suicidal ex-husband who has vowed, "If I can't have her, no-one will" is an unnervingly recurrent figure in homicide archives. In fact, a woman who has recently left her husband has a much higher statistical risk of being killed by him than does a coresiding wife (Wilson & Daly, 1993a; Wilson, Daly, & Wright, 1993). This contrast could of course reflect a correlational artifact because those husbands whose wives leave them are probably a much more violent group of men, on average, than those whose wives stay, and the leavers may therefore have been at high risk whether they left or not. However, detailed case descriptions indicate that the murder was often a response to the separation itself: The husband who stalks and kills has often gone on record with threats to do just that, should his wife ever leave him, and he often proclaims his act to be a justified or irresistible response to the intolerable stimulus of the wife's departure (Campbell, 1992; Wallace, 1986; Wilson, 1989; Wilson & Daly, 1993b).

We propose that such homicides are the dysfunctionally extreme by-products of those same violent inclinations whose much more typical effects are successful deterrence and coercion. Uxoricide may seldom serve the interests of the killer, but it is far from clear that the same can be said of nonlethal assaults and threats to kill; for every woman actually slain, hundreds are subjected to such coercive violence (Wilson, Johnson, & Daly, 1995). A credible threat of violent death is a valuable social tool, and credibility may only be attainable at the cost of some sincere willingness to accept costs in order to punish transgressors. The theoretical issue here extends beyond violence in the family to deterrence, threat, and vengeance in general. Why is the human psyche ever so spiteful as to follow through on threats once deterrence has failed and that which was being protected is lost? But, then, what good is a threat unless its audience believes that the threatener will indeed follow through? These considerations suggest that signals of sincerity in threat may have evolved to be hard to fake ("honest advertisements") under the selection pressure of skeptical audiences, as has been argued for other signals such as in courtship, with the result that only those who really will follow through with spiteful violence can enjoy a threat's deterrent and coercive benefits. These notions suggest the need for careful studies of deceit, of emotional leakage, and of how (and how well) people judge sincerity in others.

If uxoricides are largely to be understood as the maladaptive by-products of motives whose function resides in nonlethal coercion, and if men's coercive inclinations are most strongly aroused when they perceive the greatest threat to their monopoly and when they value their wives relatively highly, then some rather odd patterns of risk begin to make sense. One is the seemingly paradoxical phenomenon of men killing estranged wives because they could not stand to lose them. Another is the tendency for women of the greatest reproductive value to incur the greatest risk.

A woman's reproductive value is maximal soon after puberty, and begins to decline steeply in her 30s. As one would then expect, youth is a major determinant of women's sexual and marital attractiveness. Young women are therefore likely to have more (and superior) opportunities for both clandestine extramarital liaisons and mate replacements than older women, and the husbands of young women are likely to be especially jealous, proprietary, and coercive to their wives (Daly & Wilson, 1988c; Flinn, 1988a; Wilson & Daly, 1992a, 1993b). It turns out that uxoricide risk is indeed maximal for the youngest wives (Daly & Wilson, 1988b, 1988c; Mercy & Saltzman, 1989; Wilson, Daly, & Wright, 1993). The direct relevance of wife's youth to husband's violence is still uncertain, however, because many other variables are confounded with age, including parity, childlessness, and duration of the union. Moreover, because young men are the most violent age–sex class generally (Daly & Wilson, 1990b), an obvious hypothesis is that the husband's youth is the relevant risk factor rather than the wife's. This seems not to be the case, however, because the wife's age is a more consistent predictor of risk than the husband's (Wilson, Daly, & Scheib, 1997), and a young woman is actually increasingly likely to be killed by her husband the *older* he is (Wilson, Daly, & Wright, 1993). This result, too, seems best understood in terms of predictable elicitors of male sexual proprietariness.

A final demographic factor of great relevance to marital homicide risk is the distinction between registered and de facto marital unions. The latter sort of union is less secure, both in legal and social recognition, and in its likelihood of having produced any joint offspring. It is also commonly associated with greater financial stresses, a greater incidence of stepchildren, and perhaps a greater incidence of adultery. Not surprisingly, de facto unions also entail much higher risks of lethal assault than registered unions, for both partners and at all ages (Daly & Wilson, 1988c; Wilson, Daly, & Wright, 1993). Somewhat more surprising, however, is the fact that risk is a quite different function of the wife's age in de facto unions, peaking in middle age rather than in youth. Unpublished evidence indicates that an exceptionally high incidence of steprelationships is to be found in de facto unions of middle-aged people, and we suggest that this could account for the remarkably high levels of spouse killing in this relatively rare demographic group.

To an evolutionist, the hypothesis that the presence of stepchildren will be a risk factor for violence against wives seems almost as obvious (at least in retrospect) as the hypothesis of risks to the stepchildren themselves. For one thing, the genetic parent must often be motivated to counter stepparental mistreatment, but exacerbation of marital conflict is not likely to be limited to abusive families. Any child of one partner to a marriage who is not the other's child is likely to induce some disparity in the partners' notions of how their joint resources should be allocated.

The hypothesis that children of former unions are sources of marital strife gains support both from divorce data and from studies in which married people have been asked directly about their conflicts (Daly & Wilson, 1996). So is the presence of stepchildren also associated with elevated risk of marital violence? Remarkably, as with the question of risk to stepchildren, this hypothesis seems never to have occurred to researchers lacking a Darwinian perspective. For example, Hotaling and Sugarman (1986) listed 97 proposed risk markers for violence against wives without mentioning stepchildren.

Daly and Wilson (1988c) first raised this issue and reviewed the fragmentary but suggestive evidence from studies of homicide. Several monographs have presented brief case synopses for samples of spousal homicides, and stepchildren appear in these scenarios with uncanny frequency (Chimbos, 1978; Lundsgaarde, 1977; Polk, 1994). However, differential spousal homicide risk in relation to family composition has not yet been quantified anywhere; the necessary data are missing for the homicide cases or for the relevant population-at-large, or both. Daly, Singh, and Wilson (1993) finally addressed the question of whether violence against wives is elevated in families with stepchildren in a study of women seeking refuge from assaultive husbands in a Canadian city. Wives with children from former unions used this service at a five times higher per capita rate than those whose children were all sired by the current husband.

Homicide, as noted earlier, is a manifestation of conflict and violence that is relatively free from biases of detection and reportage, but it constitutes a good test arena for hypotheses about the demographic and circumstantial determinants of violence in general, only if its risk factors are much the same as those for "ordinary," nonlethal violence. Thus far, the evidence is largely in favor of this assumption of similar causes. As noted earlier, for example, male sexual proprietariness is the dominant ostensible motivating factor in both wife beating and uxoricide, and the existence of stepchildren is apparently relevant to both sorts of risk, too. Other risk patterns discussed earlier also appear to be similar, with female youth and de facto marital status having parallel associations with uxoricide and wives' reports of assault victimization (Wilson, Johnson, & Daly, 1995).

## CONCLUDING REMARKS

The incidence of homicide exhibits great cross-cultural and cross-national variability, both within families and in total (Daly & Wilson, 1989), proving that the terrible toll of violence can be alleviated. An evolutionary psychological understanding of violent passions will contribute to our capacity for effective, collective response. Wilson and Daly (1993b) argued that such an understanding is crucial for predicting and explaining how cross-cultural variations in violence are the intelligible consequences of other societal differences, and proposed a series of predictions about the ways in which violence against wives is likely to vary with social and ecological variables if our evolutionary psychological hypotheses about its sources are sound.

One thing that is already certain is that a sophisticated understanding of violence cannot be achieved without the recognition that there are several fundamental kinds of interpersonal relationships, which have distinct characteristics including distinct sources of conflict. Sexual infidelity is a potent betrayal of the marital relationship, for example, but friendships are threatened mainly by failures of reciprocity. Conflicts between parent and offspring have their own calculus (Haig, 1993; Trivers, 1974), distinguishing them from conflicts between affinal relatives and steprelatives, conflicts between sexual rivals, or conflicts between friends. Marital solidarity can be utterly destroyed, but no act of betrayal can abolish the residual commonality of interests among blood kin. These basic human relationships—and their characteristic conflicts—exhibit an impressive consistency across the gamut of societal diversity, and it is likely that we possess social-psychological adaptations peculiar to each of them. Certainly, each has its own patterns of risk, and evolutionary psychological reasoning has contributed to the discovery of several such patterns. We expect that it will be an invaluable aid to further discoveries.

## ACKNOWLEDGMENTS

We thank the following agencies for funding our research on family violence: the Arts & Humanities Research Board of McMaster University, the Harry Frank Guggenheim Foundation, Health & Welfare Canada, the John Simon Guggenheim Memorial Foundation, the Natural Sciences & Engineering Research Council of Canada, the North Atlantic Treaty Organization, and the Social Sciences & Humanities Research Council of Canada.

## REFERENCES

Alexander, R. D. (1974). The evolution of social behavior. *Annual Review of Ecology & Systematics, 5*, 325–383.

Alexander, R. D. (1979). *Darwinism and human affairs.* Seattle: University of Washington Press.

Alexander, R. D. (1987). *The biology of moral systems.* Hawthorne, NY: Aldine deGruyter.

Brisson, N. J. (1983). Battering husbands: A survey of abusive men. *Victimology, 6*, 338–344.

Buss, D. M., Larsen, R. J., Westen, D., & Semmelroth, J. (1992). Sex differences in jealousy: Evolution, physiology, and psychology. *Psychological Science, 3*, 251–255.

Campbell, J. C. (1992). If I can't have you, no one can: Issues of power and control in homicide of female partners. In J. Radford & D. E. H. Russell (Eds.), *Femicide* (pp. 99–113). New York: Twayne.

Chagnon, N. A., & Irons, W. (Eds.). (1979). *Evolutionary biology and human social behavior.* North Scituate, MA: Duxbury.

Chimbos, P. D. (1978). *Marital violence: A study of interspouse homicide.* San Francisco: R & E Research Associates.

Daly, M., Singh, L. S., & Wilson, M. I. (1993). Children fathered by previous partners: A risk factor for violence against women. *Canadian Journal of Public Health, 84*, 209–210.

Daly, M., & Wilson, M. I. (1981). Abuse and neglect of children in evolutionary perspective. In R. D. Alexander & D. W. Tinkle (Eds.), *Natural selection and social behavior* (pp. 405–416). New York: Chiron.

Daly, M., & Wilson, M. I. (1982). Homicide and kinship. *American Anthropologist, 84*, 372–378.

Daly, M., & Wilson, M. I. (1984). A sociobiological analysis of human infanticide. In G. Hausfater & S. B. Hrdy (Eds.), *Infanticide: Comparative and evolutionary perspectives* (pp. 487–502). New York: Aldine deGruyter.

Daly, M., & Wilson, M. I. (1985). Child abuse and other risks of not living with both parents. *Ethology and Sociobiology, 6*, 197–210.

Daly, M., & Wilson, M. I. (1988a). The Darwinian psychology of discriminative parental solicitude. *Nebraska Symposium on Motivation, 35*, 91–144.

Daly, M., & Wilson, M. I. (1988b). Evolutionary social psychology and family homicide. *Science, 242*, 519–524.

Daly, M., & Wilson, M. I. (1988c). *Homicide.* New York: Aldine deGruyter.

Daly, M., & Wilson, M. I. (1989). Homicide and cultural evolution. *Ethology and Sociobiology, 10*, 99–110.

Daly, M., & Wilson, M. I. (1990a). Is parent-offspring conflict sex-linked? Freudian and Darwinian models. *Journal of Personality, 58*, 163–189.

Daly, M., & Wilson, M. I. (1990b). Killing the competition. *Human Nature, 1*, 83–109.

Daly, M., & Wilson, M. I. (1991). A reply to Gelles: Stepchildren *are* disproportionately abused, and diverse forms of violence can share causal factors. *Human Nature, 2,* 419–426.

Daly, M., & Wilson, M. I. (1994a). Some differential attributes of lethal assaults on small children by stepfathers versus genetic fathers. *Ethology and Sociobiology, 15,* 207–217.

Daly, M., & Wilson, M. I. (1994b). Stepparenthood and the evolved psychology of discriminative parental solicitude. In S. Parmigiami & F. S. vom Saal (Eds.), *Infanticide and parental care* (pp. 121–134). Chur, Switzerland: Harwood.

Daly, M., & Wilson, M. I. (1995). Discriminative parental solicitude and the relevance of evolutionary models to the analysis of motivational systems. In M. Gazzaniga (Ed.), *The cognitive neurosciences* (pp. 1269–1286). Cambridge, MA: MIT Press.

Daly, M., & Wilson, M. I. (1996). Evolutionary psychology and marital conflict: The relevance of stepchildren. In D. M. Buss & N. Malamuth (Eds.), *Sex, power, conflict: Feminist and evolutionary perspectives* (pp. 9–28). New York: Oxford University Press.

Daly, M., Wilson, M. I., & Weghorst, S. J. (1982). Male sexual jealousy. *Ethology and Sociobiology, 3,* 11–27.

David, H. P., Dytrych, Z., Matejcek, Z., & Schüller, V. (1988). *Born unwanted: Developmental effects of denied abortion.* New York: Springer.

Dawkins, R. (1986). *The blind watchmaker.* Harlow, England: Longman.

Dobash, R. E., & Dobash, R. P. (1979). *Violence against wives.* New York: The Free Press.

Dobash, R. P., Dobash, R. E., Wilson, M. I., & Daly, M. (1992). The myth of sexual symmetry in marital violence. *Social Problems, 39,* 71–91.

Fletcher, J. (1974). Attitudes toward defective newborns. *Hastings Center Studies, 2,* 21–32.

Flinn, M. V. (1988a). Mate guarding in a Caribbean village. *Ethology and Sociobiology, 9,* 1–28.

Flinn, M.V. (1988b). Step- and genetic parent/offspring relationships in a Caribbean village. *Ethology & Sociobiology, 9,* 335–369.

Gelles, R. J., & Straus, M. A. (1979). Family experience and public support for the death penalty. In R. J. Gelles (Ed.), *Family violence* (pp. 181–203). Beverly Hills, CA: Sage.

Gelles, R. J., & Straus, M. A. (1985). Violence in the American family. In A. J. Lincoln & M. A. Straus (Eds.), *Crime and the family* (pp. 88–110). Springfield, IL: Thomas.

Haig, D. (1993). Genetic conflicts in human pregnancy. *Quarterly Review of Biology, 68,* 495–532.

Hamilton, W. D. (1964). The genetical evolution of social behaviour: I and II. *Journal of Theoretical Biology, 7,* 1–52.

Hamilton, W. D. (1979). Wingless and fighting males in fig wasps and other insects. In M. S. Blum & N. A. Blum (Eds.), *Sexual selection and reproductive competition in insects* (pp. 167–220). New York: Academic Press.

Hepper, P. G. (Ed.). (1991). *Kin recognition.* Cambridge, England: Cambridge University Press.

Hill, K., & Kaplan, H. (1988). Tradeoffs in male and female reproductive strategies among the Ache: Part 2. In L. Betzig, M. Borgerhoff Mulder, & P. Turke (Eds.), *Human reproductive behavior* (pp. 277–305). Cambridge, England: Cambridge University Press.

Hotaling, G. T., & Sugarman, D. B. (1986). An analysis of risk markers in husband to wife violence: The current state of knowledge. *Violence & Victims, 2,* 101–124.

Krebs, J. R., & Davies, N. B. (1987). *An introduction to behavioural ecology* (2nd ed.). Oxford, England: Blackwell.

Leach, E. (1966). Virgin birth. *Proceedings of the Royal Anthropological Institute of Great Britain & Ireland for 1966,* 39–49.

Lenington, S. (1981). Child abuse: The limits of sociobiology. *Ethology and Sociobiology, 2,* 17–29.

Lightcap, J. L., Kurland, J. A., & Burgess, R. L. (1982). Child abuse: A test of some predictions from evolutionary biology. *Ethology and Sociobiology, 3,* 61–67.

Lundsgaarde, H. P. (1977). *Murder in space city.* New York: Oxford University Press.

Mercy, J. A., & Saltzman, L. E. (1989). Fatal violence among spouses in the United States, 1976–85. *American Journal of Public Health, 79,* 595–599.

Montgomerie, R. D., & Weatherhead, P. J. (1988). Risks and rewards of nest defence by parent birds. *Quarterly Review of Biology, 63,* 167–187.

Mrosovsky, N., & Sherry, D. F. (1980). Animal anorexias. *Science, 207,* 837–842.

Parmigiani, S., & vom Saal, F. S. (Eds.). (1994). *Infanticide and parental care.* Chur, Switzerland: Harwood.

Polk, K. (1994). *When men kill: Scenarios of masculine violence.* Cambridge, England: Cambridge University Press.

Robson, K. M., & Kumar, R. (1980). Delayed onset of maternal affection after childbirth. *British Journal of Psychiatry, 136,* 347–353.

Rohwer, S. (1986). Selection for adoption versus infanticide by replacement "mates" in birds. *Current Ornithology, 3,* 353–395.

Symons, D. (1990). Adaptiveness and adaptation. *Ethology and Sociobiology, 11,* 427–444.

Teismann, M. W., & Mosher, D. L. (1978). Jealous conflict in dating couples. *Psychological Reports, 42,* 1211–1216.

Tooby, J., & Cosmides, L. (1990). The past explains the present: Emotional adaptations and the structure of ancestral environments. *Ethology and Sociobiology, 11,* 375–424.

Tooby, J., & Cosmides, L. (1992). The psychological foundations of culture. In J. H. Barkow, L. Cosmides, & J. Tooby (Eds.), *The adapted mind* (pp. 19–136). New York: Oxford University Press.

Trivers, R. L. (1972). Parental investment and sexual selection. In B. Campbell (Ed.), *Sexual selection and the descent of man 1871–1971* (pp. 136–179). Chicago: Aldine deGruyter.

Trivers, R. L. (1974). Parent–offspring conflict. *American Zoologist, 14,* 249–264.

Trivers, R. L. (1985). *Social evolution.* Menlo Park, CA: Benjamin/Cummings.

Voland, E. (1988). Differential infant and child mortality in evolutionary perspective: Data from late 17th to 19th century Ostfriesland. In L. Betzig, M. Borgerhoff Mulder, & P. Turke (Eds.), *Human reproductive behavior* (pp. 253–276). Cambridge, England: Cambridge University Press.

Wallace, A. (1986). *Homicide: The social reality.* Sydney: New South Wales Bureau of Crime Statistics & Research.

White, L. K., & Booth, A. (1985). The quality and stability of remarriages: The role of stepchildren. *American Sociological Review, 50,* 689–698.

Williams, G. C. (1966). *Adaptation and natural selection.* Princeton, NJ: Princeton University Press.

Williams, G. C., & Nesse, R. M. (1991). The dawn of Darwinian medicine. *Quarterly Review of Biology, 66,* 1–22.

Wilson, M. I. (1989). Marital conflict and violence in evolutionary perspective. In R. W. Bell & N. J. Bell (Eds.), *Sociobiology and the social sciences* (pp. 45–62). Lubbock, TX: Texas Tech University Press.

Wilson, M. I., & Daly, M. (1987). Risk of maltreatment of children living with stepparents. In R. J. Gelles & J. B. Lancaster (Eds.), *Child abuse and neglect: Biosocial dimensions* (pp. 215–232). New York: Aldine deGruyter.

Wilson, M. I., & Daly, M. (1992a). The man who mistook his wife for a chattel. In J. H. Barkow, L. Cosmides, & J. Tooby (Eds.), *The adapted mind* (pp. 289–322). New York: Oxford University Press.

Wilson, M. I., & Daly, M. (1992b). Who kills whom in spouse killings? On the exceptional sex ratio of spousal homicides in the United States. *Criminology, 30,* 189–215.

Wilson, M. I., & Daly, M. (1993a). Spousal homicide risk and estrangement. *Violence & Victims, 8,* 3–16.

Wilson, M. I., & Daly, M. (1993b). An evolutionary psychological perspective on male sexual proprietariness and violence against wives. *Violence & Victims, 8,* 271–294.

Wilson, M. I., & Daly, M. (1994). The psychology of parenting in evolutionary perspective and the case of human filicide. In S. Parmigiami & F. S. vom Saal (Eds.), *Infanticide and parental care* (pp. 73–104). Chur, Switzerland: Harwood.

Wilson, M. I., Daly, M., & Daniele, A. (1995). Familicide: The killing of spouse and children. *Aggressive Behavior, 21*, 331–361.

Wilson, M. I., Daly, M., & Scheib, J. (1997). Femicide: An evolutionary psychological perspective. In P. A. Gowaty (Ed.), *Feminism and evolutionary biology* (pp. 431–465). New York: Chapman Hall.

Wilson, M. I., Daly, M., & Weghorst, S. J. (1980). Household composition and the risk of child abuse and neglect. *Journal of Biosocial Science, 12*, 333–340.

Wilson, M. I., Daly, M., & Weghorst, S. J. (1983). Differential maltreatment of girls and boys. *Victimology, 6*, 249–261.

Wilson, M. I., Daly, M., & Wright, C. (1993). Uxoricide in Canada: Demographic risk patterns. *Canadian Journal of Criminology, 35*, 263–291.

Wilson, M. I., Johnson, H., & Daly, M. (1995). Lethal and nonlethal violence against wives. *Canadian Journal of Criminology, 37*, 331–361.

# 15

## PsychoDarwinism: The New Synthesis of Darwin and Freud

Christopher R. Badcock
*London School of Economics*

In recent years, an increasing number of authors have begun to discuss the possibility of reconciling Darwin and Freud (e.g., Badcock, 1986, 1990a, 1990b, 1991, 1992, 1994; Bischof, 1985; Edelman, 1992; Fox, 1980; Grubrich-Simitis, 1985; Leak & Christopher, 1982; Lloyd, 1990; Lloyd & Nesse, 1992; Nesse, 1990a, 1990b; Rancour-Laferriere, 1981, 1985; Ritvo, 1990; Slavin, 1990; Slavin & Kriegman, 1992; Sulloway, 1979; Wenegrat, 1984, 1990a, 1990b; Wilson, 1977; Wright, 1994). As long ago as 1962, Dobzhansky expressed the opinion that, "the discoveries of Freud and his successors are probably amenable to interpretation in agreement with concepts of modern genetics" (cited in Rancour-Laferriere, 1981, p. 441). Wilson declared that, "psychoanalytic theory appears to be exceptionally compatible with sociobiological theory" (cited in Rancour-Laferriere, 1981, p. 435), and Barash (1979) was among the first to explore the extensive overlap between Freud's discoveries and modern Darwinism.

An initial difficulty is the fact that Freud was a self-confessed Lamarckian—in other words, he believed in the inheritance of acquired characteristics. To our modern way of thinking, this makes Lamarckism antithetical to Darwinism, which now stands on a secure Mendelian genetic foundation (Dawkins, 1986). Nevertheless, we tend to forget that Darwin was a Lamarckian to the extent that he too believed in the inheritance of acquired characteristics, and that it was not until the last decade of Freud's life that the modern synthesis of Mendelian genetics and Darwinism was complete. Only then did it begin to be generally accepted that inheritance of acquired characteristics was impossible (Ritvo, 1990). However, we shall see here that, notwithstanding sharing what was at the time an almost universal error about inheritance, Freud very much anticipated the modern, selfish gene view in reporting some of his most controversial findings. Indeed, it is the argument here that, whatever his own misconceptions may have been, Freud's findings can only be understood in terms of advances in genetics and evolution that were not to take place until he had been dead for some decades (Badcock, 1994).

Another difficulty is that, although modern Darwinists have been aware of the shortcomings of the so-called Standard Social Science Model (SSSM; Tooby & Cosmides, 1992), they have been more reluctant to challenge the SSSM's interpretation of Freud. The SSSM has been highly selective in its approach to Freud, and has tended to deemphasize or even ignore the very features that Darwinists might find most promising, such as Freud's biological thinking and emphasis on basic instincts (Badcock, 1992). There has been little protest from psychoanalysts, who have generally shared the SSSM's de-biologized view of Freud to the extent that object relations theory has replaced drive theory in modern psychoanalysis (Slavin & Kriegman, 1992). Yet, in his own day, Freud was as critical of the cultural-determinist orthodoxy that was to typify the SSSM as any modern Darwinist has been, denouncing those who "have picked out a few cultural overtones from the symphony of life and have once more failed to hear the mighty and primordial melody of the instincts" (Freud, 1914b, p. 62).

The SSSM has portrayed Freud as a Hobbesian social thinker who thought that social order had to be imposed on a recalcitrant human nature, just as many sociologists believe (Wright, 1994). However, a careful reading of key texts like *Civilization and Its Discontents* (1930) shows that Freud did not find that guilt and neurosis were caused by society, as the SSSM suggests. On the contrary, Freud found that society and neurosis were based on preexisting guilt. Furthermore, he insisted that the guilt in question originated in the conflict of basic biological drives and had an evolutionary dimension. Again, although the SSSM treated Freud's developmental psychology as a socialization theory, Trivers (1985) credited Freud with coming on "sexual overtones in parent–offspring conflict" (pp. 146–147), and suggested an evolutionary rationale for Freudian findings, such as regression and repression (Trivers, 1981).

## REPRESSION AND SELF-DECEPTION

Freud's basic discovery was that there existed beneath conscious awareness a repressed unconscious. This had two principal characteristics: first, the unconscious was *topographical* in the sense that it represented a psychological region of the mind inaccessible to consciousness. Second, the unconscious was *dynamic* in the sense that its contents were actively excluded from consciousness by the force of *repression* (Badcock, 1986).

Modern Darwinists invoke the unconscious almost as frequently as Freudians do because of their assumption that natural selection will shape behavior to maximize reproductive success at the genetic level (Wright, 1994). This does not require selective forces to inform consciousness of their ultimate intention. On the contrary, Alexander, Barash, Trivers, and others have suggested that natural selection may have shaped human consciousness to prevent such awareness reaching consciousness. They proposed an arms race between deception and detection-of-deception in human psychology, particularly over critical issues like cooperation. Research by Ekman (one of the few modern psychologists to follow Darwin's lead in studying the expression of the emotions) showed that tone of voice, facial expression, and body language can frequently reveal evidence of conscious deception (Ekman, 1985). Consequently, natural selection may have rewarded deceivers who did not know that they were deceiving, and thereby were less likely to give away clues of their deceit. The most effective liars would be those who had convinced themselves that their lies were in fact the truth. Having achieved that feat of self-deception, duping others would be all the more easy. Now, they could lie in total sincerity (Alexander, 1979; Barash, 1979; Trivers, 1981).

Although experiments on self-deception are difficult to devise and carry out, one particularly elegant one has been performed. The experiment measured galvanic skin response (GSR) to voices. It established that GSR is heightened on hearing your own voice by contrast to hearing someone else's, and that GSR to your own voice increases with time, rather than declining, as it does in the case of someone else's voice. The experiment compared experimental subjects' GSR to the sound of voices with their conscious awareness of whose voices they were hearing, and found discrepancies in perception. The experiment showed that, of those individuals who failed to recognize their own voice, GSR was a much more reliable indicator of the truth than was their conscious awareness. As Trivers (1985) commented, "for most mistakes, the part of the brain controlling speech got it wrong, while the part controlling arousal got it right" (p. 417). This finding establishes that unconscious perception can occur while consciousness remains ignorant of it—in other words, consciousness is topographical, with discrepant pieces of information existing in different places.

However, to demonstrate the dynamic aspect of the Freudian unconscious, we would need to show that unawareness was motivated, and not just a random error or failure of conscious perception. To test this aspect of the situation, a second experiment was carried out, in which subjects' self-perception was manipulated prior to a repetition of the first voice-recognition experiment. It is a common finding that we draw more attention to ourselves when we have something to be proud of than when we are ashamed of ourselves, and previous experimental work had established that subjects with high self-esteem are more ready to recognize their own voice than those with low self-esteem. The repetition of the experiment after manipulation of the subjects' self-regard by means of telling them how well or badly they had done at a verbal aptitude test showed that self-deception where voice recognition was concerned was indeed motivated. Those who were made to feel good about themselves by being told that they scored well on the test were much more likely to recognize their own voices, and indeed even to attribute their own voice to others. Those whose self-esteem had been lowered by being told that they had done badly, however, showed the opposite response: a tendency to avoid themselves and deny their own voices. Furthermore, when questioned after the experiment, those with lowered self-esteem reported enjoying hearing their own voice less and rated their own voices as less pleasant than did the successful group. This demonstrates that repression is both motivated and dynamic in the sense that the subjects had a reason for becoming unconscious of their own voices and showed an ability to employ repression facultatively as a result (Gur & Sacheim, 1979). It also illustrates the authentic Freudian conception of repression as a defensive measure carried out by the individual to avoid anxiety, rather than the SSSM's view of repression as a social force acting against the individual (Badcock, 1992).

## THE LIBIDO AND THE SELFISH GENE

Modern, selfish-gene (Dawkins, 1989; Williams, 1966) Darwinism differs from earlier Darwinism in a number of important ways. One is its repudiation of group selection (Hamilton, 1975; Trivers, 1981, 1985). Group selection made the error of believing that the benefit to the family, group, or species could explain why individuals would incur the costs involved. The result was that self-sacrifice in the interests of others seemed self-explanatory, and sexual behavior was assumed to benefit the species, rather than the individual. As a result, Darwin's insight into sexual selection was widely ridiculed and rejected because it saw sex in terms of its costs and benefits to individuals, rather than the species (Cronin, 1991). From the beginning, Freud was far too well informed about the real motives and feelings of people to fail to notice that there was often considerable conflict between the interests of the individual and those of others where sex and self-sacrifice were concerned. "It does not seem as though any influence could induce a man to change his nature into a termite's," remarked Freud, adding, "he will always defend his claim to individual liberty against the will of the group" (Freud, 1930, p. 96). This is the major theme of *Civilization and Its Discontents*. Although Freud occasionally spoke of the sexual drive as existing to reproduce the species, he did not think that sex is an intrinsically prosocial force as both group selectionists and the SSSM believe (Lévi-Strauss, 1969). On the contrary, his actual findings left him in no doubt that "Sexual needs are not capable of uniting men in the same way as are the demands of self-preservation. Sexual satisfaction is essentially a private affair of each individual" (Freud, 1913, p. 74).

Social Darwinism owed more to Herbert Spencer than to Darwin; it was Spencer, not Darwin, who coined the notorious slogan, *survival of the fittest*. This suggests that evolution by natural selection is a mechanism aimed at perfecting the health, strength, and survival of organisms. It overlooks the all-important fact that health, strength, and survival are all means to the end of reproductive success, rather than ends in themselves (Badcock, 1994; Dawkins, 1982). Had Freud been influenced by the correct view of Darwinism in his own day, he probably would have emphasized aggression, rather than sex. This is because survival of the fittest Darwinism put the emphasis on the struggle for survival, rather than on reproductive success as we do today. The fact that Freud emphasized the sexual over all other drives in motivating human behavior suggests not only that his views were shaped much more by his findings than by contemporary prejudices, but also that his findings were correct. As Barash (1979) put it in one of the earliest contributions to PsychoDarwinism: "much of being human consists of contributing to the success of our genes. . . . Freud was right: much of our behavior has to do with sex" (p. 40).

The problem of explaining altruism without recourse to group selection was definitively solved by Hamilton in the early 1960s (Hamilton, 1964). Here, *altruism* is defined as a benefit to the reproductive success of the recipient at a cost to that of the altruist. Because natural selection is ultimately a question of reproductive success, it follows that altruism as defined earlier seemingly cannot evolve. But Hamilton proved that altruism could evolve by natural selection wherever $Br > C$, where $B$ was the benefit to the gene for altruism in the recipient, $C$ was the cost to an identical copy of the same gene in the altruist, and $r$ was the degree of genetic relatedness (Fig. 15.1). This insight is fundamental to the modern selfish-gene view of evolution acting at the level of the individual gene (Dawkins, 1989). It leads to a view of the organism as existing for the benefit of its genes, rather than vice versa, and reveals the errors of both group selection and survival of the fittest social Darwinism.

Despite the belief in Lamarckian inheritance of acquired characteristics that Freud shared with most of his contemporaries, his psychological findings revealed a much more modern insight. As early as 1914, when

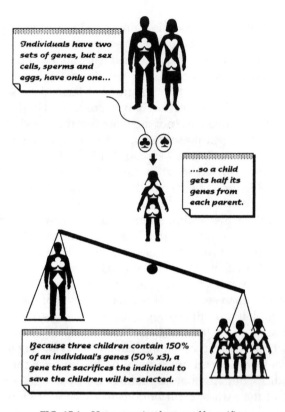

FIG. 15.1.  How genetics favors self-sacrifice.

Weismann's insistence that only the germ line was inherited was still highly controversial, Freud (1914a) reported that:

> The individual himself regards sexuality as one of his own ends; whereas from another point of view he is an appendage to his germ-plasm, at whose disposal he puts his energies in return for a bonus of pleasure. He is the mortal vehicle of a (possibly) immortal substance—like the inheritor of an entailed property, who is only the temporary holder of an estate that survives him. (p. 78).

It is notable that Freud's English translators use the very term *vehicle*, which Richard Dawkins, author of *The Selfish Gene*, was to adopt 60-odd years later, to describe the view of the organism as little more than the temporary repository of its DNA. The words of Freud previously quoted are strong grounds for thinking that, had he been alive today, he would have adopted the modern Darwinian view of evolution advocated here and regarded the organism as existing for the benefit of its genes, rather than the converse.

If we allow ourselves to adopt a wider, less narrowly and genitally focused view of sex, we can distinguish between what Freud termed ego libido and object libido. *Object libido* is libido directed toward outside objects—normally, but not exclusively (thanks to the concept of libido), the opposite sex. The clear reproductive function of the latter raises no difficulties, at least insofar as its objects are members of the opposite sex. But the other category, *ego libido* is different. It describes libido reserved for the self and is one of the prime discoveries of Freud and the essence of what he came to call *narcissism*.

At first sight, this seems to blatantly contradict our expectations about sex from an evolutionary point of view. This is because reproductive success appears to demand only object libido, if we insist on calling it that, and even then only if the object in question is a member of the opposite sex. But a moment's reflection shows that there is a sense in which natural selection does indeed select for survival, rather than reproductive success. This is because an organism has to reach reproductive age before it can have any reproductive success. Up to that point, selection will act on the individual's survival capacity, rather than on its reproductive potential, because it has to exist and mature sexually before it can have any direct reproductive success of its own. So survival does matter as a means to the end of individual reproductive success, even if survival of the organism can never be an end in itself as far as evolution is concerned.

If this is so, we can begin to discern an unsuspected logic in Freud's otherwise strange finding that the libido—understood as a generalized, defocused sexuality—could relate to the individual's own self, as well as to the outside objects on which the organism relies for its reproduction. We could begin to see how genes whose ultimate goal is reproductive success would have a self-interest in the organism itself prior to the age of sexual potency simply because such genes could not have any reproductive success until that time. Rather than appearing as a biological absurdity, ego libido would now appear to be an emotion that expressed the interests of the genes in their vehicle—the individual's mind and body.

If this were true, we could predict that, if what Freud called narcissism is a finding reflecting the value of the organism to its genes, then ego libido should begin at a high level, but decline, especially after sexual maturity, to be replaced by or transformed into object libido. This is exactly what Freud reported. Furthermore, this transformation of libido seemed to be a continuous process right up to the end of life, as if the declining value of the organism to its genes was directly reflected in the level of ego libido remaining (Freud, 1914a).

A second prediction we might make if we believed that narcissism expressed the value of the organism to its genes would be that the sexes normally should show some differences. This is because a woman's bodily well-being and general health are more critical to her reproductive success than are a man's for two reasons. First, worldwide studies of mating preferences show that, with no exceptions, good looks are more critical to women than to men (Buss, 1994). Second, a woman's health is more important to her reproductive success than is a man's because, whereas he only has to perform the act of insemination, she has to face 9 months of demanding pregnancy followed by dangerous childbirth. Freud reported that women tend to be more narcissistic than men. If we take expenditure on cosmetics and beauty products as an index of narcissism, there is ample reason to believe him. Another measure of sex differences in narcissism can be found in studies of risk taking. Clearly, a readiness to take risks is inversely related to narcissism because the more you value something, the less likely are you to hazard it. If the self is highly valued, the self should not be risked. Numerous studies of risk taking in many different contexts consistently and reliably indicate a marked difference between the sexes (Daly & Wilson, 1985). With few, if any, exceptions, women are much less likely to indulge in behavior that risks life and limb in comparison with men. Indeed, a recent study showed that the predicted differences in risk-taking behavior could still be found in Kibbutznics after three generations of socialization aimed at eliminating sex-role differences (Lampert & Yassour, 1992).

However, the same study showed that there was one respect where women were ready to take greater risks than men—in defense of their own children. If narcissism is about the self-interest of genes in the preservation of their vehicles, and if women truly are more narcissistic than men, we can immediately understand why risk taking on behalf of children is the exception where women are concerned. We can also see why Freud found that narcissism should include love of one's children, but not normally of unrelated individuals. "At the most touchy point in the narcissistic system, the immortality of the ego . . . security is achieved by taking refuge in the child"—or, in other words, in the fact that, if individual organisms age and die, their DNA can in principle go on for ever. "Parental love," Freud concluded, "which is so moving and at bottom so childish, is nothing but the parents' narcissism born again" (Freud, 1914a, p. 91).

## ALTRUISM AND IDENTIFICATION

If narcissism is indeed the emotional expression of genes' self-interest in the survival of their vehicles, such narcissistic feelings should extend to near kin, as well as to the self and to children. Freud's finding was that this comes about by the process he called *identification*. Identification describes a subjective feeling of similarity with another person or thing and underlies much cooperation, as many other writers have also noted:

> We actively seek out people whom we perceive as being similar to ourselves, and interact preferentially with them when we find them. In many cases these people are our biological relatives. In others . . . unrelated people are, in fact, treated as "honourary kin." (Wells, 1987, p. 412)

Specifically, Freud found that members of groups identify the leader with some aspect of their superego, and then form a secondary identification with one another. However, the parents are the models for the superego. This means that the leader is often seen unconsciously as a parent, with the implication that all the followers are the leader's children (Freud, 1921; see Fig. 15.2).

Individuals with the same parents are likely to share the same genes for altruism, at least to a 50% probability. In the primal hunter–gatherer societies in which our ancestors evolved, most groups to which you might belong almost certainly would center on relatives—perhaps most likely actual parents—given the small-scale, kin-based nature of such societies. Hence, feeling that you had the same parent—or ego identification—as someone else would mean that you were likely to be their kin. Identifi-

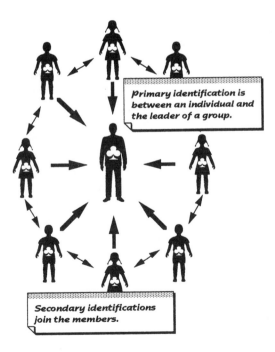

FIG. 15.2. Freud's model of group psychology.

cation with the parental leader, then, would be identification of kin, solving the recognition problem by comparison, not merely with the self, but, more important, with the common parent. This would be the human, psychological equivalent of the phenotypic matching that is commonly the means of kin identification in other animals (Badcock, 1986, 1990b, 1991). Nor is it one limited to identification of parents: "one can tentatively conclude that early visual recognition of neonates by their mothers may be mediated through the interaction of rapid familiarization and matching facial features with those of other known relatives, or of the mother herself (i.e., self-matching)" (Porter, 1987, p. 194).

The fact that Freud found identification with the father to be particularly important may simply reflect that paternity is uncertain by comparison with maternity. For example, a child living with full siblings ($r = \frac{1}{2}$) is selected to direct twice as much altruism to them as compared with one living with half siblings ($r = \frac{1}{4}$). Even today, half siblings in a coresident family are more likely to share a common mother than a common father, and this presumably would have been even more true in primal societies. Phenotypic matching with a sibling also reveals genes shared through the mother, but self-comparison with a putative father reveals genes shared only with him, critically predicting the level of altruism to be shown toward siblings (see Fig. 15.2, but now interpret it as representing genes shared by children with a common father). If this line of reasoning is correct, it casts a striking new evolutionary light on the widely reported finding that children without fathers show deviations from the norm in both cooperative behavior and sex role (Dennis & Erdos, 1992; Lamb, 1981)—both aspects of the personality found by Freud to be strongly influenced by identification and to reflect characteristics of the superego (Badcock, 1990b, 1994).

However, kin altruism is not the only fundamental form of altruism. Altruism can also evolve on a reciprocal basis between organisms that are totally unrelated, even members of different species (Trivers, 1971). Identification may also play a role here, and may explain why abstract principles or values can provide the focus of shared ego ideals in some psychological groups. Such ideals are also an aspect of the superego, and usually represent values and aspirations that ultimately influence cooperation among those who share them in common. This explains why religious and political ideals are often prime focuses of groups. However, if this were to be true, identification would also have to be able to motivate noncooperation because cooperation based on reciprocity demands that both cooperation and defection be reciprocated. This results in tit-for-tat strategies of cooperation, in which cooperators protect themselves from the exploitation of noncooperators by cooperating with cooperation, but defecting against defection (Axelrod, 1984). This may explain so-called *identification with the aggressor*, especially because the identification is "not with the person of the aggressor, but with his aggression" (Freud, 1968, p. 112). Identification with the aggressor shows that the fundamental mechanism of identification can repay both cooperation and defection in this case (Badcock, 1991).

Contrary to the SSSM's view of the Freudian superego as principally a product of socialization, these considerations suggest that it may be more fruitfully seen as a psychological agent, evolved principally to modulate both kin and reciprocal altruism. As Trivers (1981, 1983) pointed out, the evolution of reciprocal altruism also might select for an innate sense of fairness, guilt, and conscience. Moralistic aggression and self-righteous indignation would be important emotions in punishing offenses against reciprocity. Values, guilt, and conscience are prime elements of the Freudian superego, and they do not have to be seen as evolving to serve the interests of others. They can just as well be seen as agencies that warn the ego of the consequences of its actions and police it accordingly. Again, the fact that Freud could not account for the severity of individuals' superegos in terms of their socialization (Freud, 1930, p. 130) and stubbornly insisted on an evolutionary heritage for the sense of guilt (Freud, 1913, 1930, 1939) shows how close his view was to a modern evolutionary one.

## INFANTILE SEXUALITY AND PARENT–OFFSPRING CONFLICT

The concept of infantile sexuality seems biologically preposterous because children can have no reproductive success as children, and therefore, appear to have no need of sexuality. Nevertheless, where physical development is concerned, we would be seriously in error if we observed that, because human embryos have tails and gill slits and human adults do not, the facts of embryonic development could not be true. In a similar way, Freud's findings about child development conceived of it in distinct stages that did not appear to directly correspond to adult psychology, but nevertheless prepared the way for it.

The first phase of infantile sexuality discovered by Freud is known as the oral stage. He observed that young children will suck for sucking's sake, even when they are not hungry, and that they will use fingers, thumbs, comforters, or whatever in so doing (Freud, 1905). Recent research shows that oral behavior—sucking without being hungry—has important consequences for the mother in primal or Third World conditions (Blurton Jones & da Costa, 1987). If the baby is kept constantly with the mother, and can have unrestricted access to her breasts, the effect of oral behavior is to make the baby suck its mother's nipples very frequently and for long periods of time (often playing with the other nipple while doing so). Persistent stimulation of the mother's nipples by the baby inhibits her sexual cycles for something over 3 years after giving birth (Short, 1987). However, children will eventually begin to eat solid food, and mothers' sensitivity to nipple stimulation begins to decline after approximately 3 years. Given that it may take a few months for a woman's sexual cycles to become reestablished and for her to conceive, succeeded by 9 months of pregnancy, it follows that the contraceptive effect of oral behavior on women tends to result in births being spaced approximately 4 years apart—a prediction confirmed by studies of birth spacing among the !Kung, for example (Howell, 1979).

Freud was aware of the contraceptive effect of breastfeeding, which has been known to science since Aristotle, and was correctly informed about its duration in traditional cultures (Freud, 1931). However, he never could have realized its full significance, which only becomes apparent in relation to the finding that, in Third World conditions, the birth of a child within the first 4 to 5 years of the life of an existing child is the greatest single threat to the older child's life. Indeed, in West Africa, a term has been coined to describe *the disease of the displaced one*—gross protein deficiency in a child peremptorily weaned because of the birth of a sibling (Thapa, Short, & Potts, 1988). If such conditions are a guide to those that existed for the greater part of our evolutionary history, it may explain reports that Australian aborigines traditionally would allow newborn babies to starve to death, rather than displace existing children at the breast (Róheim, 1932). Such behavior makes considerable sense if the alternative were to be the death of the older child. A mother who gave birth at short intervals and prematurely weaned an existing child would probably find very few of her children surviving to any later age if premature weaning usually meant death for the weaned child.

It begins to look very much as if oral behavior could be a Darwinian adaptation, by means of which young children attempt to postpone the life-threatening birth of competitors for their mother's care and attention. Given that the birth of a sibling within the first 4 years of an existing child's life is such a critical factor for the existing child's survival, we can see that oral behavior makes a great deal of sense when we look at it from the point of view of the child whose life is likely to be threatened (Badcock, 1990b). If this is so, we can see that Freud's oral stage corresponds to a facet of development that has only recently been fully appreciated—parent–offspring conflict over parental investment (Trivers, 1974).

Precedents for this can be found in recent research into parent–offspring conflict. A gene from the mother has a 50% chance of being in any other child that she may have, and so has a vested interest in her reproductive future. An example is Prader–Willi syndrome. It is caused by a maternal gene that lacks a corresponding paternal copy, and results in poor suckling, a weak cry, inactivity, and sleepiness. Presumably this is because the mother's genes are selected to make the baby as undemanding as possible. However, a gene from the father has no necessary chance of being in another offspring of the same mother, and so can be expected to make much greater demands on her. This is what seems to happen in Angelman syndrome children, who are characteristically hyperactive, wakeful, and given to prolonged suckling. Angelman is caused by a single paternal gene that lacks a maternal copy to counteract it, and sets a precedent for the prior argument about oral behavior (Haig, 1993).

*Parental investment* is defined as any contribution to the reproductive success of an offspring at a cost to the remaining reproductive success of the parent (Trivers, 1972). Trivers pointed out that crying is an expression of distress that young children can employ to solicit parental attention of all kinds, along with the investment that may follow from it, whether in the form of food, protection, emotional reassurance, or whatever. However, Trivers added that, having once established the signal, there is nothing to stop a child from employing it more intensively or more frequently than the parent might think fit. If the result of amplified or prolonged crying was to attract marginally more parental investment, it would be selected (recall that parental investment was defined in terms of contributions to an offspring's reproductive success). The result would be an arms race, in which infants would amplify the crying signal to maximize the parental investment it might bring them, but parents would become desensitized to it by seeing the behavior as normal in children. Consequently, adults show a double standard of sensitivity to crying. Relative indifference is shown to children, who are expected to cry for the slightest reason. Yet, in the case of adults, crying is usually taken to be a significant expression of disturbed emotions and is taken much more seriously (Badcock, 1990b).

If it paid infants to amplify distress signals, then the amplification of more positive signals might pay even more if the result were to secure enhanced parental investment from the mother. A smile that expressed liking might be serviceable in this respect, but a fond look of love might be more serviceable still. Indeed, if the infant showed that it loved the mother passionately, and reinforced the message not merely with facial expressions of its love, but with embraces, kisses, and verbal expressions, the likelihood is that the benefit to its ultimate reproductive success by enhanced parental investment in it would be even greater.

This may be at the bottom of one of Freud's most controversial findings, what might be called *Oedipal behavior*. By this I mean powerful feelings of love and affection for the mother and a tendency to see the father as a rival for the mother's affections. If my interpretation of Oedipal behavior is correct, this would simply be an amplification of the expression of the positive response to the mother that is first found in smiling. It would amplify pleasure, gratitude, and liking into a deep love for the mother that would show itself in all manner of ways and be expressed in every aspect of the child's relationship with her.

We could explain this by appeal to the fact that, in primal conditions, and indeed in all human societies up to the present, the mother is the chief and often the sole agent of parental investment in the first few years of life. It is she who breastfeeds the infant (as we have seen, usually for 3 or more years), and it is she who cares for it throughout most of the early period of childhood. Traditionally the father has little or nothing to do with day-to-day child care, and seldom if ever carries out any significant tasks in this respect while children are very young. This would explain why the mother is the target of early Oedipal behavior and why the father is not. Indeed, it might also explain why the father tends to be seen as something of a rival by the child. Even in our own, less traditionally sex-stereotyped societies, fathers often see newborn babies as competitors for the mother's attention; clearly, if the father can see it this way, so too can the child. In claiming the maximum of its mother's time, care, attention, love, and resources available for investment in itself, the child will almost certainly sometimes find itself in competition with its father. The father, for his part, is bound to notice that the child is effectively attempting to monopolize the mother, and to resent it, making the Oedipal picture of him as a jealous rival to some extent inevitably correct.

However, if this is the right interpretation, we can immediately see that both sexes should show Oedipal behavior, at least in early childhood. This is because the mother remains the prime source of parental investment in primal conditions, irrespective of the child's sex. Although Freud originally tended to think that the Oedipus complexes of the sexes were symmetrical, with both girls and boys feeling love for the opposite-sex parent and rivalry with the parent of the same sex, he later abandoned that view. Further observation convinced him of something about which Anna Freud was adamant: that little girls too have an Oedipus complex centering on the mother as a love object, at least in early childhood (Freud, 1931). Indeed, Anna Freud often pointed out that some little girls (although certainly not all) go through a definite stage of tomboy behavior, and act toward their mothers as if they were boys themselves, rather than girls (personal communication, 1981).

Another prediction of this interpretation of Oedipal behavior in early childhood is that children overprovided with parental investment should not need to show much of it. Although no direct studies have been made to the best of my knowledge, reports of so-called *transsexuals* by Stoller (1986) establish that they are normally overwhelmed with solicitude by the opposite-sex parent, and that evidence of Oedipal conflict is lacking.

The fact that the father becomes the target for Oedipal behavior in girls at a slightly later age may result from the fact that fathers are more critical agents of parental investment in later childhood (Flinn, 1988). Again, by its very nature, Oedipal behavior may prove more effective with the parent of the opposite sex, especially as little girls get older. Furthermore, there may be special factors that boys can exploit in their relationship with their mothers that little girls never can.

## SEXUAL SELECTION IN INFANCY

One of most important consequences of the fundamental asymmetry between the size and number of the sex cells is that, with millions of sperm at his disposal and no further necessary parental investment to contribute, a man's reproductive success is only limited by the number of women he can fertilize. A woman, by contrast, can only have one pregnancy at a time. Assuming 10 children per woman, a man with 10 wives has an order of magnitude more children than a woman with 10 husbands (Fig. 15.3).

Darwin clearly realized that if one male could in principle fertilize large numbers of females, other males might not fertilize any at all. The result would be that successful males would have many offspring, whereas less successful males would have few or none. The successful males would have been selected thanks to whatever it was that ensured their reproductive success. One possibility might be conflict between males for access to females. However, another mechanism of sexual selection might be *female choice*: the possibility that some males might appeal to females more than others, and therefore have greater reproductive success than those less preferred (Darwin, 1871). Darwin did not hesitate to draw a parallel between human and animal psychology in this respect: "In regard to sexual selection. A girl sees a handsome man, and . . . admires his appearance and says she will marry him. So, I suppose with the peahen . . . ." (cited in Cronin, 1991, p. 171.) It was probably this subjective, psychological basis for female choice—not to mention the attribution of such selective power over males to females—that made the concept appear so ridiculous to Darwin's critics.

As far as Darwin was concerned, female choice was a matter of observation that had to be accepted. There seemed little point in asking why peahens like peacocks' tails. However, it remained a mystery what was in the peacock's tail for the individual female, particularly in view of the enormous cost of it to males, an individual female's own male offspring included. It was not until 1915 that a solution was found. Fisher (1915) suggested that if a female chose a mate who appealed to her, for whatever

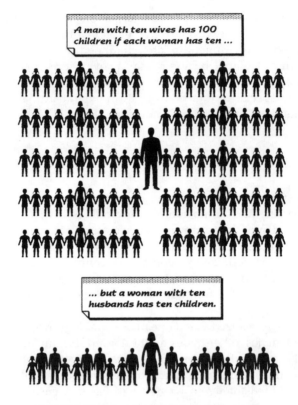

FIG. 15.3.  Male and female reproductive success.

reason that might be, the chances were that her own male offspring would inherit some of the attractive traits of their father. If female tastes were also heritable, as they probably would be, a female choosing a mate who appealed to her would effectively be choosing genes for her sons, which would make them appealing to the next generation of females. In other words, if sons shared genes for attractiveness with their fathers in the way that other females might share genes for being attracted to them with those sons' mothers, the mother's reproductive success would be maximized by her mating with the most attractive male she could find. This immediately made female choice look more comprehensible because it showed how ostensibly absurd tastes in male decoration like peacocks' tails could promote the reproductive success of the females who favored them. Furthermore, once started, the cycle of females choosing attractive mates and having more attractive sons as a result could run away with itself, producing the extremes that are so often seen in sexual selection.

In 1973, Trivers and Willard considered the consequences of sexual selection theory for differential parental investment in relation to sex of offspring. They predicted that, all other things being equal, where off-spring were likely to be more than averagely reproductively successful, parents should invest more in males, and more in females in the contrary circumstance. Today there is a considerable amount of data, from both animal and human studies, in support of this proposition (for a discussion, see Gaulin & Robbins, 1991). Furthermore, a recent study of American coots demonstrated that, if given a choice, parents invested preferentially in chicks with characteristic colorful plumage (Lyon, Eadie, & Hamilton, 1994). Coot chicks do not beg for food vocally, but by displaying in competition with others in the clutch. This looks strikingly like sexual selection by female choice in the sense that gaudy plumage appears to be the factor that influences parental preference. Hamilton and Zuk (1989) proposed that bright colors in adult birds might have evolved to advertise general health and resistance to pathogens, and a similar argument may apply to American coot chicks, although other explanations are possible (Pagel, 1994).

In any event, American coot chicks provide a precedent for one possible evolutionary interpretation of the male Oedipus complex, which analysts generally regard as more pronounced than the female one. It may simply be that amorous displays by the son toward the mother and sisters, along with expressions of rivalry and jealousy toward the father, serve to advertise a son's future reproductive success. At the very least, it could be interpreted as confirming the Fisher effect: that a little boy really had inherited the traits that made her father attractive to her mother by showing similar traits in childhood.

It is important to recall that *parental investment* was defined as promoting reproductive success, rather than reducing it (all other things being equal). This means that extra parental investment directed toward a son who showed signs of reproductive promise in childhood would probably add to his mother's reproductive success more than it might if directed to a daughter. This is because, even allowing for the fact that he only copies half his mother's genes, a son with 10 wives can have vastly greater reproductive success than a mother with 10 husbands (Fig. 15.3). By this means, infantile sexuality in little boys could evolve as a precocious expression of their sexual prowess that tended to attract parental investment from their mothers. This would certainly seem to explain Anna Freud's observation that what 5-year-old boys demand above all is the mother's admiration of their masculinity (Freud, 1969, p. 254).

What of little girls? How does their behavior evolve in a setting that seems so satisfactory for sons? In his original article on parent–offspring conflict, Trivers (1974) remarked that, "in many species sex is irreversibly determined early on . . . and the offspring is expected at the very beginning to be able to discern its own sex and hence the predicted pattern of investment it will receive" (p. 257). If parental investment is likely to be biased toward one sex rather than the other, as Trivers and Willard predicted it could be, then offspring might also be expected to be able to determine the sex of its siblings, along with that of itself. In childhood, secondary sexual characteristics of the kind that adults often use to determine sex, such as depth of voice, facial appearance, or figure, have not yet developed. Only the primary sex differences are present, and, of these, the presence of the male genital is almost always much easier to determine than the female one, thanks to the effects of the evolution of upright posture on our species, and to the fact that the penis protrudes from the body in a prominent position. So if a little girl needed reliably to diagnose her own sex and that of others—particularly in primal societies, where children even more than adults usually go naked—she would need to do no more than look for a penis and assume that anything with one was male and anything without one was female. Such a child should have some way of diagnosing its own sex and that of its siblings independent of parental ideology, and if it discovers that it is female, should expect to be discriminated against.

In childhood, envy might certainly be expected in rivalry between siblings; if it were unconsciously associated with ideas about how to diagnose sex, Freud's strange finding of penis envy would follow naturally. Essentially, penis envy would be an emotion that evolved to motivate little girls to compete with their brothers for preferential parental investment allocated according to sex. In the light of this interpretation, it is worth pointing out that Freud remarked that penis envy often expresses itself as a reproach against the mother, who is somehow assumed to be responsible for the daughter's lack of a penis. He added, however, that this is often followed by "A second reproach," which Freud (1931) found to be "a rather surprising one. It is that her mother did not give her enough milk, did not suckle her long enough . . . that she did not feed her sufficiently" (p. 234). Although this additional complaint may have surprised Freud, it is exactly as it should be if my suggestion about the evolutionary basis of penis envy is correct. Furthermore, data on breastfeeding rates and birth separations in modern North American households suggest that the complaint is often justified (Gaulin & Robbins, 1991).

## THE QUESTION OF INCEST

Thanks to the way the SSSM has interpreted it, Freud's Oedipus complex suggests to many an instinct for incest in childhood, which is only "repressed" by socialization. If, as argued earlier, precocious sexuality directed toward the mother by so-called sexy sons were all about securing preferential parental investment, rather than actual incest, one major difficulty would have been removed. If I am right, it now begins to look as if the incestuous element is only illusory, and that what is at issue in Oedipal behavior is personal reproductive success in adult life.

Yet most people still think that Freud's view was that the incestuous tendencies of the Oedipal period were repressed by outside pressure that went against the grain of human nature. According to this view, incest was natural. Its avoidance was cultural and the result, not of nature, but of nurture. As late as 1924, Freud was still expressing doubt about what brings about the dissolution of the Oedipus complex. Although he reported that analyses give the impression that "the Œdipus complex would go to its destruction from its lack of success, from the effects of its internal impossibility," he immediately added a further consideration:

> Another view is that the Œdipus complex must collapse because the time has come for its disintegration, just as the milk-teeth fall out when the permanent ones begin to grow. Although the majority of human beings go through the Œdipus complex as an individual experience, it is nevertheless a phenomenon which is determined and laid down by heredity and which is bound to pass away according to programme when the next preordained phase of development sets in. This being so, it is of no great importance what the occasions are which allow this to happen, or, indeed, whether any such occasions can be discovered at all (Freud, 1924, pp. 173–174)

If we add the point that he made a few pages on that the dissolution of the Oedipus complex also constitutes the basis of the prohibition against incest, we can clearly see that the preceding quotation refutes those who have interpreted Freud as a believer in a purely environmental, acquired mechanism of incest avoidance. On the contrary, in his work of 1913, *Totem and Taboo*, Freud went out of his way to insist on an evolved, inherited basis for guilt about incest and violence against relatives. The exact scenario Freud suggested is Lamarckian, and therefore, unacceptable to modern Darwinism, but it is an evolutionary argument nevertheless.

This suggests that Freud's most notorious finding—the Oedipus complex—should be seen as yet another episode in psychological epigenesis, rather than the way it has tended to be seen up until now—that is, as the natural, if repressed, basis of human nature. Here it is important to note that Freud insisted that "the process we have described is more than a repression. It is equivalent, if it is ideally carried out, to a destruction and an abolition of the complex" (Freud, 1924, p. 177). "In boys . . . the complex is not simply repressed, it is literally smashed to pieces . . . in ideal cases, the Œdipus complex exists no longer, even in the unconscious" (Freud, 1925, p. 257). Indeed, "If the ego has in fact not achieved much more than a repression of the complex, the latter persists in an unconscious state in the id and will later manifest its pathogenic effect" (Freud, 1924, p. 177).

As far as adult psychology was concerned, what Freud reported was that adults were ambivalent about incest, and that powerful feelings flowed in the unconscious both for and against it. Freud was adamant that social taboos against incest were the product of this fundamental ambivalence, rather than the ambivalence being the product of the taboo (Freud, 1913, 1930). However, this finding has not found favor with self-styled Darwinists in the 20th century, who have followed Westermarck (1925) in his belief that, "The home is kept pure from incestuous defilement, neither by laws, nor by customs, nor by education, but by instinct which under normal circumstances makes sexual love between the nearest kin a psychical impossibility" (pp. 478–479). According to Lumsden and Wilson (1983), "when children are raised together in close domestic proximity during the first six years of life, they are automatically inhibited from full sexual activity at maturity" (p. 133). Consequently, "It is natural—in the full, biological sense—for people to be opposed to brother-sister incest" (p. 176).

*Self-styled Darwinists* is used here because Darwin held that, "it has been clearly shown . . . that there is no instinctive feeling in man against incest" (cited in Ritvo, 1990, p. 106), and proved it by marrying his first cousin (a criminally incestuous act in some jurisdictions today). Recent research into first cousin marriages in the Third World suggests that fatalities and congenital abnormalities do increase, but have less effect on the overall reproductive success of such marriages than do the advantages of marrying a cousin. These advantages are earlier marriage and more pregnancies (Bittles, Mason, Greene, & Rao, 1991).

Freud's finding that individuals are typically ambivalent about incest may reflect that inbreeding and outbreeding both carry costs and convey benefits. The benefits of inbreeding appear to be primarily social and mean that parents with shared genes are predisposed to kin altruism toward each other and higher degrees of relatedness to their offspring (i.e., driving up $r$ where $Br > C$). Indeed, this is the explanation of eusociality among diploid species such as naked mole rats, where DNA fingerprinting has shown 80% identity of genes in colonies where 85% of matings are between siblings or parents and their offspring. The cost of inbreeding appears to be reduced disease resistance and viability, thanks to greater homozygosity (Hamilton & Zuk, 1989), again illustrated by the tendency for entire colonies of mole rats to be wiped out by single infections (Sherman, Jarvis, & Braude, 1992). If cost–benefit ratios of inbreeding versus outbreeding vary from person to person in a species with a wide range of adaptive behavior, the result could easily be the innate ambivalence reported by Freud. Finally, this would explain why women have been found to prefer the odor of men whose major histo-compatibility complex is different from their own, but to prefer the odor of men whose MHC is similar if they are taking the contraceptive pill. Here the explanation could be that the contraceptive pill mimics pregnancy so that women taking it are looking for helpers, rather than mates, and so prefer genetically similar partners (Wedekind, Seebeck, Bettens, & Paepke, 1995).

## CONCLUSION

Ambivalence relating to inbreeding and outbreeding illustrates one last aspect of Freudian psychology that is in many ways the most important. This is its view of the mind as fundamentally in conflict. Not merely the conscious and unconscious, but instincts and other repressed elements were found to be irremediably in contention with one another by Freud. For example, Freud traced the unconscious guilt on which both civilization and neurosis were built to antithetical life and death instincts. In the past, the death instinct has been seen as biological nonsense, but the recent discovery of *apoptosis* (programmed cell death) suggests that Freud's concept may not have been completely absurd (Raff, 1992). Again, recent interest in intragenomic conflict aroused by the discovery of parental imprinting of genes (Haig & Moore, 1991; Maynard Smith & Szathmáry, 1995; Sapienza, 1990) has caused some leading Darwinists to question the assumption that mental harmony, rather than conflict, is either normal or adaptive. The fact that sex chromosomes are subject to differing selection pressure thanks to X chromosomes spending two thirds of their time in female bodies, but the Y chromosome only ever being present in male ones, is another occasion for potential intragenomic conflict. However, that both X and Y chromosomes are found in males and that one of a female's Xs must always have come from the father raises the prospect of genetic conflict concerning sex within the individual (W. D. Hamilton, 1967).

Psychologically, this has long been known to Freudian psychology as *bisexuality*, and yet it is another discovery of Freud's that has previously seemed biologically implausible. It was already pointed out that Haig's insights into genetic conflict between maternal and paternal genomes within the developing child may be continued much further into childhood than so far suspected, and that this may be the genetic basis of some of the psychological conflicts uncovered by Freud. Whether these recent developments will vindicate or refute Freud remains to be seen. One thing is certain: In his discovery of the repressed unconscious as a form of self-deception, in seeing the individual as serving the gene rather than contrariwise, in discovering parent–offspring conflict, and in isolating the ambivalence that may reflect intragenomic conflict over inbreeding, out-breeding, and other aspects of behavior, Freud found much that should give modern Darwinians serious cause for thought.

This is all the more significant because recent evolutionary psychology shows three major shortcomings, all of which could be remedied by some attention to Freud. First, as Wright (1994) noted in his recent book reviewing the field, there is no developmental evolutionary psychology worth mentioning. If my reinterpretations earlier and elsewhere of Freud's findings regarding so-called infantile sexuality are even vaguely correct, they suggest that psychoanalysis may have something to offer here. Certainly, no one can deny that Freud's theory of child development took biological factors very seriously and deserves some consideration on those grounds alone.

Wright observed that, "evolutionary analysis often lets us figure out the role of genes without worrying about the nuts and bolts of their influence" (p. 244). Faced with having to explain instances of remembering and forgetting, the evolutionary psychologist "can relax and come up with different explanations for each one" (Wright, 1994, p. 320). This begins to sound like complacency, and ignores that forgetting is what Freud called *repression*—a mechanism that he found was fundamental to the topography of consciousness. Simply inventing a new instinct or mental module every time another adaptive explanation is proposed is neither sound science nor credible psychology.

Darwin himself proposed a much more general principle: "An animal may be led to pursue that course of action which is most beneficial . . . by suffering . . . or by pleasure"; he added that, "Hence . . . all sentient beings have been developed in such a manner, through natural selection, that pleasurable sensations serve as their habitual guides" (Darwin, 1958, p. 89). This is what Freud later called the pleasure–unpleasure principle. Today it would be seen as a prime epigenetic rule, and probably the principal means by which genes latent in what Freud would have called the *id* could manifest themselves as action mediated through what he termed the *ego*. When we add the superego to this model of the mind, what emerges is not merely intrapsychic conflict, but a psychological structure that promises a realistic solution to the problem of how genes influence human behavior.

Finally, evolutionary psychology has to confront the problem of seemingly maladaptive, unnatural, nonevolved, and cultural behavior. The best we have been offered so far is the so-called elastic leash model of how genes control behavior, with the elasticity explaining these deviations and discrepancies (Lumsden & Wilson, 1981). The example of sexual aberration immediately shows that a Freudian approach might have much to offer, given that the Freudian model of the mind bases the greater part of it on the instinctual drives, but also takes developmental influences very seriously. If the intrapsychic conflict that Freud discovered is, in part, the expression of intragenomic conflicts, as suggested here, the Freudian model of the mind would be the natural one for evolutionary psychology to adopt, albeit suitably modified. Rather than a simple, linear elastic leash, we would have a complex, nonlinear interaction of at least three psychological agencies contributing to a chaotic system (Badcock, 1994).

Indeed, a stunning discovery about the role that imprinted genes play in building the brain suggests that the Freudian model of mental conflict may be much more relevant to the evolution of human psychology than anyone could have guessed. Recently, it was discovered that the limbic system, or *emotional brain*, is built exclusively by paternal alleles, and that the neocortex, or *executive brain*, is constructed only by maternal ones (Allen et al., 1995; Keverne, Fundele, Narasimha, Barton, & Surani, 1996; Keverne, Martel, & Nevison, 1996). The limbic system is primarily concerned with motivation expressed through emotions, drives, and instincts. The neocortex supports functions such as consciousness, speech, and reason, and has the ability to restrain, repress, and redirect demands addressed to it from the limbic system.

The precedent set by Angelman and Prader–Willi syndromes discussed earlier leads us to expect paternal, limbic brain-building alleles to lack the concern for the mother and her other offspring. Such concern can be assumed in maternal genes, thanks to the latter's 50% representation in all of a mother's children. Again, the fact that the mother is normally present to influence her children's development, thanks to her role as prime nurturer, means that her genes do not merely build and pay for the neocortical brain during pregnancy and lactation, but have a strategic advantage in programming it. However, because the father makes no necessary contribution to a child beyond his genes, those genes may have to rely on themselves alone to influence the child's growth, development, and behavior through their exclusive contribution to the limbic brain, and its notoriously incorrigible drives, instincts, and emotions.

This raises the possibility that the Freudian id could be seen as a psychological agency primarily representing the much more selfish, demanding interests of paternal genes expressed in the limbic brain. Correspondingly, the ego could be understood as the opposing agency entrusted with more prosocial, cooperative, maternal genetic interests expressed by the neocortex. If so, the endemic psychological conflict between id and ego described by Freud becomes immediately transparent and appears to be founded on a fundamental genetic conflict comparable to the one suggested earlier between sex chromosome genes. Indeed, it is possible that conflict between maternal and paternal genes for control of development and behavior has driven the exponential growth of the human brain and triggered an evolutionary arms race that has inflated the human psyche to the extent that it believes culture and consciousness to have finally freed it from natural constraints (Badcock, in press). If this is so, the fate of Freud's findings—not to mention Darwin's—appears to be largely determined by the extent to which a mind born of internal conflict can come to terms with the forces that created it.

## ACKNOWLEDGMENTS

I must thank Charles Crawford and Dennis Krebs for their many helpful comments and suggestions on this chapter, not to mention honoring me by asking me to contribute to this volume.

## REFERENCES

Alexander, R. D. (1979). *Darwinism and human affairs*. WA: University of Washington Press.
Allen, N. D., Logan, K., Lally, G., Drage, J. D., Norris, M. L., & Keverne, B. (1995). Distribution of parthenogenetic cells in the mouse brain and their influence on brain development and behavior. *Proceedings of the National Academy of Sciences, USA, 92*, 10782–10786.
Axelrod, R. (1984). *The evolution of cooperation*. New York: Basic Books.
Badcock, C. (1986). *The problem of altruism: Freudian-Darwinian solutions*. Oxford, England: Blackwell.
Badcock, C. (1990a). Is the Oedipus complex a Darwinian adaptation? *The Journal of the American Academy of Psychoanalysis, 18*(2), 368–377.
Badcock, C. R. (1990b). *Oedipus in evolution: A new theory of sex*. Cambridge, MA: Basil Blackwell.
Badcock, C. R. (1991). *Evolution and individual behavior: An introduction to human sociobiology*. Cambridge, MA: Basil Blackwell.
Badcock, C. R. (1992). *Essential Freud: An introduction to classical psychoanalysis* (2nd ed.). Cambridge, MA: Basil Blackwell.
Badcock, C. (1994). *PsychoDarwinism: The new synthesis of Darwin and Freud*. London: HarperCollins.
Badcock, C. R. (in press). *The maternal brain and the battle of the sexes in the mind*. Munich: Carl Hanser Verlag.
Barash, D. (1979). *Sociobiology: The whisperings within*. London: Souvenir.
Bischof, N. (1985). *Das Rätsel Ödipus: Die Biologischen Wurzeln des Urkonfliktes von Intimität und Autonomie*. Munich: Piper.
Bittles, A., Mason, W., Greene, J., & Rao, N. (1991). Reproductive behavior and health in consanguineous marriages. *Science, 252*, 789–794.
Blurton Jones, N., & da Costa, E. (1987). A suggested adaptive value of toddler night waking: Delaying the birth of the next sibling. *Ethology and Sociobiology, 8*, 135–142.
Buss, D. (1994). *The evolution of desire: Strategies of human mating*. New York: Basic Books.
Cronin, H. (1991). *The ant and the peacock: Altruism and sexual selection from Darwin to today*. Cambridge, England: Cambridge University Press.
Daly, M., & Wilson, M. (1985). Competitiveness, risk taking and violence: The young male syndrome. *Ethology and Sociobiology, 6*, 59–73.

Darwin, C. (1871). *The descent of man, and selection in relation to sex* (facsimile reproduction of first edition with an introduction by John Tyler Bonner & Robert M. May, Princeton University Press, Princeton, 1981 ed.). London: John Murray.

Darwin, C. (1958). *The autobiography of Charles Darwin* (with original omissions restored. Edited with Appendix and Notes by his granddaughter, Nora Barlow). London: HarperCollins.

Dawkins, R. (1982). *The extended phenotype.* Oxford, England: Oxford University Press.

Dawkins, R. (1986). *The blind watchmaker.* Essex, England: Longman.

Dawkins, R. (1989). *The selfish gene* (2nd ed.). Oxford, England: Oxford University Press.

Dennis, N., & Erdos, G. (1992). *Families without fatherhood.* London: Institute of Economic Affairs.

Edelman, G. (1992). *Bright air, brilliant fire: On the matter of the mind.* London: Allen Lane.

Ekman, P. (1985). *Telling lies: Clues to deceit in the marketplace, politics, and marriage.* New York: Norton.

Fisher, R. A. (1915). The evolution of sexual preference. *Eugenics Review, 7,* 184–192.

Flinn, M. (1988). Parent–offspring interactions in a Caribbean village: Daughter guarding. In L. Betzig, M. Borgerhoff Mulder, & P. Turke (Eds.), *Human reproductive behavior* (pp. 189–200). Cambridge, England: Cambridge University Press.

Fox, R. (1980). *The red lamp of incest.* New York: Dutton.

Freud, A. (1968). *The ego and the mechanisms of defense* (rev. ed.). London: Hogarth Press and Institute of Psychoanalysis.

Freud, A. (1969). Studies in passivity. In *Indications for child analysis* (pp. 245–259). London: Hogarth Press and Institute of Psychoanalysis.

Freud, S. (1905). Three essays on the theory of sexuality. In J. Strachey, A. Freud, A. Strachey, & A. Tyson (Eds.), *The complete psychological works of Sigmund Freud* (Vol. 7, pp. 1–243). London: Hogarth Press and Institute of Psychoanalysis.

Freud, S. (1913). Totem and taboo. In J. Strachey, A. Freud, A. Strachey, & A. Tyson (Eds.), *The complete psychological works of Sigmund Freud* (Vol. 13, pp. 1–161). London: Hogarth Press and Institute of Psychoanalysis.

Freud, S. (1914a). On narcissism: An introduction. In J. Strachey, A. Freud, A. Strachey, & A. Tyson (Eds.), *The standard edition of the complete psychological works of Sigmund Freud* (Vol. 14, pp. 69–102). London: Hogarth Press and Institute of Psychoanalysis.

Freud, S. (1914b). On the history of the psychoanalytic movement. In J. Strachey, A. Freud, A. Strachey, & A. Tyson (Eds.), *The standard edition of the complete psychological works of Sigmund Freud* (Vol. 14, pp. 1–66). London: Hogarth Press and Institute of Psychoanalysis.

Freud, S. (1921). Group psychology and the analysis of the ego. In J. Strachey, A. Freud, A. Strachey, & A. Tyson (Eds.), *The standard edition of the complete psychological works of Sigmund Freud* (Vol. 18, pp. 1–143). London: Hogarth Press and Institute of Psychoanalysis.

Freud, S. (1924). The dissolution of the Oedipus complex. In J. Strachey, A. Freud, A. Strachey, & A. Tyson (Eds.), *The complete psychological works of Sigmund Freud* (Vol. 19, pp. 173–179). London: Hogarth Press and Institute of Psychoanalysis.

Freud, S. (1925). Some psychical consequences of the anatomical distinction between the sexes. In J. Strachey, A. Freud, A. Strachey, & A. Tyson (Eds.), *The complete psychological works of Sigmund Freud* (Vol. 19, pp. 248–258). London: Hogarth Press and Institute of Psychoanalysis.

Freud, S. (1930). Civilization and its discontents. In J. Strachey, A. Freud, A. Strachey, & A. Tyson (Eds.), *The standard edition of the complete psychological works of Sigmund Freud* (Vol. 21, pp. 59–148). London: Hogarth Press and Institute of Psychoanalysis.

Freud, S. (1931). Female sexuality. In J. Strachey, A. Freud, A. Strachey, & A. Tyson (Eds.), *The standard edition of the complete psychological works of Sigmund Freud* (Vol. 21, pp. 223–243). London: Hogarth Press and Institute of Psychoanalysis.

Freud, S. (1939). Moses and monotheism. In J. Strachey, A. Freud, A. Strachey, & A. Tyson (Eds.), *The complete psychological works of Sigmund Freud* (Vol. 23, pp. 1–138). London: Hogarth Press and Institute of Psychoanalysis.

Gaulin, S., & Robbins, C. (1991). Trivers-Willard effect in contemporary North American society. *American Journal of Physical Anthropology, 85,* 61–69.

Grubrich-Simitis, I. (1985). Metapsychology and metabiology. In I. Grubrich-Simitis (Ed.), *A phylogenetic fantasy: Overview of the transference neuroses by Sigmund Freud* (pp. 75–107). Cambridge, MA: Harvard University Press.

Gur, R., & Sacheim, H. (1979). Self-deception: A concept in search of a phenomenon. *Journal of Personality and Social Psychology, 37*(2), 147–169.

Haig, D. (1993). Genetic conflicts in human pregnancy. *The Quarterly Review of Biology, 68*(4), 495–523.

Haig, D., & Moore, T. (1991). Genomic imprinting in mammalian development: A parental tug-of-war. *Trends in Genetics, 7*(2), 45–49.

Hamilton, W. (1975). Innate social aptitudes of man: An approach from evolutionary genetics. In R. Fox (Ed.), *Biosocial anthropology* (pp. 133–153). London: Souvenir.

Hamilton, W. D. (1964). The genetical evolution of social behaviour. *Journal of Theoretical Biology, 7,* 1–16, 17–52.

Hamilton, W. D. (1967). Extraordinary sex ratios. *Science, 156,* 477–488.

Hamilton, W. D., & Zuk, M. (1989). Parasites and sexual selection. *Nature, 341,* 289–290.

Howell, N. (1979). *A demography of the Dobe !Kung.* New York: Academic Press.

Keverne, E. B., Fundele, R., Narasimha, M., Barton, S. C., & Surani, M. A. (1996). Genomic imprinting and the differential roles of parental genomes in brain development. *Developmental Brain Research, 92,* 91–100.

Keverne, E. B., Martel, F. L., & Nevison, C. M. (1996). Primate brain evolution: Genetic and functional considerations. *Proceedings of the Royal Society of London, B, 262,* 689–696.

Lamb, M. (Ed.). (1981). *The role of the father in child development* (2nd ed.). New York: Wiley.

Lampert, A., & Yassour, J. (1992). Parental investment and risk taking in simulated family situations. *Journal of Economic Psychology, 13*(3), 499–507.

Leak, G., & Christopher, S. (1982). Freudian psychoanalysis and sociobiology. *American Psychologist, 37,* 313.

Lévi-Strauss, C. (1969). *The elementary structures of kinship.* Boston: Beacon.

Lloyd, A. (1990). Implications of an evolutionary metapsychology for clinical psychoanalysis. *The Journal of the American Academy of Psychoanalysis, 18*(2), 286–306.

Lloyd, A., & Nesse, R. (1992). The evolution of dynamic mechanisms. In J. Barkow, L. Cosmides, & J. Tooby (Eds.), *The adapted mind: Evolutionary psychology and the generation of culture* (pp. 601–624). Oxford, England: Oxford University Press.

Lumsden, C. J., & Wilson, E. O. (1981). *Genes, mind, and culture: The coevolutionary process.* Cambridge, MA: Harvard University Press.

Lumsden, C. J., & Wilson, E. O. (1983). *Promethean fire: Reflections on the origin of mind.* Cambridge, MA: Harvard University Press.

Lyon, B., Eadie, J., & Hamilton, L. (1994). Parental choice selects for ornamental plumage in American coot chicks. *Nature, 371,* 240–243.

Maynard Smith, J., & Szathmáry, E. (1995). *The major transitions in evolution.* Oxford, England: Freeman.

Nesse, R. (1990a). Evolutionary explanations of the emotions. *Human Nature, 1*(3), 261–289.

Nesse, R. (1990b). The evolutionary functions of repression and the ego defenses. *The Journal of the American Academy of Psychoanalysis, 18*(2), 260–285.

Pagel, M. (1994). Parents prefer pretty plumage. *Nature, 371,* 200.

Porter, H. (1987). Kin recognition: Functions and mediating mechanisms. In C. Crawford, M. Smith, & D. Krebs (Eds.), *Sociobiology and psychology: Ideas, issues and applications* (pp. 175–203). Hillsdale, NJ: Lawrence Erlbaum Associates.

Raff, M. (1992). Social controls on cell survival and cell death. *Nature, 356,* 387–399.

Rancour-Laferriere, D. (1981). Sociobiology and psychoanalysis: Interdisciplinary remarks on the most imitative animal. *Psychoanalysis and Contemporary Thought,* 4(4), 435–526.

Rancour-Laferriere, D. (1985). *Signs of the flesh: An essay on the evolution of hominid sexuality.* Bloomington: Indiana University Press.

Ritvo, L. (1990). *Darwin's influence on Freud: A tale of two sciences.* New Haven, CT: Yale University Press.

Róheim, G. (1932). Psycho-analysis of primitive cultural types. *International Journal of Psycho-Analysis, 13,* 1–221.

Sapienza, C. (1990). Parental imprinting of genes. *Scientific American, 263*(4), 26–32.

Sherman, P., Jarvis, U., & Braude, S. (1992). Naked mole rats. *Scientific American, 267*(2), 42–48.

Short, R. (1987). The biological basis for the contraceptive effects of breast feeding. *International Journal of Gynæcology and Obstetrics,* 25(x), 207–217.

Slavin, M. (1990). The dual meaning of repression and the adaptive design of the human psyche. *Journal of the American Academy of Psychoanalysis,* 18(2), 307–341.

Slavin, M., & Kriegman, D. (1992). *The adaptive design of the human psyche: Psychoanalysis, evolutionary biology and the therapeutic process.* New York: Guilford.

Stoller, R. (1986). *Presentations of gender.* New Haven, CT: Yale University Press.

Sulloway, F. (1979). *Freud: Biologist of the mind.* New York: Basic Books.

Thapa, S., Short, R. V., & Potts, M. (1988). Breast feeding, birth spacing and their effects on child survival. *Nature, 335,* 679.

Tooby, J., & Cosmides, L. (1992). The psychological foundations of culture. In J. Barkow, L. Cosmides, & J. Tooby (Eds.), *The adapted mind: Evolutionary psychology and the generation of culture* (pp. xxx–xxx). Oxford, England: Oxford University Press.

Trivers, R. (1974). Parent-offspring conflict. *American Zoologist, 14,* 249–264.

Trivers, R. (1981). Sociobiology and politics. In E. White (Ed.), *Sociobiology and human politics.* Lexington, MA: Lexington.

Trivers, R. (1983). The evolution of a sense of fairness, absolute values and the creation of the new world. *Proceedings of the Eleventh International Conference on the Unity of the Sciences,* 2 (pp. 1189–1208). New York: International Cultural Foundation Press.

Trivers, R. (1985). *Social evolution.* Menlo Park, CA: Benjamin/Cummings.

Trivers, R., & Burt, A. (in press). *Intragenomic conflict.*

Trivers, R. L. (1971). The evolution of reciprocal altruism. *Quarterly Review of Biology, 46,* 35–57.

Trivers, R. L. (1972). Parental investment and sexual selection. In B. Campbell (Ed.), *Sexual selection and the descent of man 1871–1971* (pp. 136–179). London: Heinemann.

Wedekind, C., Seebeck, J., Bettens, F., & Paepke, A. (1995). MHC-dependent mate preferences in humans. *Proceedings of the Royal Society B, 260,* 245–249.

Wells, P. (1987). Kin recognition in humans. In D. Fletcher & C. Michener (Eds.), *Kin recognition in animals* (pp. 395–415). New York: Wiley.

Wenegrat, B. (1984). *Sociobiology and mental disorder.* Menlo Park, CA: Addison-Wesley.

Wenegrat, B. (1990a). *The divine archetype: The sociobiology and psychology of religion.* Lexington, MA: Lexington.

Wenegrat, B. (1990b). *Sociobiological psychiatry: Normal behavior and psychopathology.* Lexington, MA: Lexington.

Westermarck, E. (1925). *The history of human marriage.* London: Macmillan.

Williams, G. C. (1966). *Adaptation and natural selection: A critique of some current evolutionary thought.* Princeton, NJ: Princeton University Press.

Wilson, E. O. (1977). Biology and the social sciences. *Dædalus, 106,* 127–140.

Wright, R. (1994). *The moral animal: The new science of evolutionary psychology.* New York: Pantheon.

# Evolutionary Cognitive Psychology: The Missing Heart of Modern Cognitive Science

Douglas T. Kenrick
Edward K. Sadalla
*Arizona State University*

Richard C. Keefe
*Scottsdale College*

> *Several months ago one of our graduate students . . . asked if I knew anything about the impact of Darwin's theory of evolution on cognitive psychology. I . . . suggested that he talk to one of the faculty in our department who is an expert in cognition and who also knows a fair bit about the theory of evolution. The expert in cognition told him that as far as he knew the theory of evolution had no impact on the field of cognition.*
> —Charles Crawford (personal communication, April 11, 1994)

Although the previous quote may slightly overstate the case, traditional cognitive psychology has, for the most part, proceeded as if it were possible to understand human thought processes without asking, "What is the human brain ultimately designed to do?" The field has also been biased toward an excessive preoccupation with the processes involved in comprehending written language. In the introductory chapter of a popular text on cognition, Glass and Holyoak (1986) justified this emphasis with the argument that reading printed words "calls into play virtually every aspect of . . . cognitive processes" (p. 15). Implicit in this assumption is a commitment to a view of cognition based on domain-general processes that can explain thoughts about topics ranging from the perception of simple shapes and words to complex social relationships (e.g., Markus & Zajonc, 1985; Wyer & Srull, 1986).

Evolutionary approaches to cognition, in contrast, reject these arguments for two reasons. First, many of the central problems that humans have been designed to solve are shared with our mammalian ancestors, and thus antedate the development of language. Evolutionary psychologists assume that, to understand the operation of the human mind, it is important to ask what functions it was designed to perform, including not only those functions unique to our species (such as language), but also those we share with other related species (e.g., Buss, 1994; Tooby & Cosmides, 1992). Second, cognition is assumed to be mediated by domain-specific or content-specific mechanisms, rather than a general central processor that is used for processing both linguistic and nonlinguistic information. Although it might be possible that the human brain was designed as a general processor of information, and that linguistic analysis is involved in all information processing, there are both theoretical and empirical reasons to assume otherwise (e.g., Lumsden & Wilson, 1981; Pinker, 1994; Sherry & Schacter, 1987; Tooby & Cosmides, 1992).

With a few notable exceptions (e.g., Tooby & Cosmides, 1992), the converse of the opening quote is also true—just as cognitive psychologists have tended to benefit little from developments in evolutionary theory, evolutionary psychologists have benefited little from developments in cognitive science. The independence of these two interdisciplines is unfortunate because they are both concerned with similar questions about the ultimate structure and function of the human mind. Like evolutionary psychology, cognitive psychology also makes bridges outside the field of psychology, being itself a central part of the other great modern indisciplinary synthesis—cognitive science—which fuses the field of psychology with computer science, linguistics, anthropology, and the neurosciences. The findings of cognitive science contain exciting insights about the structure and function of the human mind (e.g., Gardner, 1985; Martindale, 1991; Pinker, 1994). An awareness of these findings is important to anyone interested in an understanding of the unique adaptations of *Homo sapiens*.

## BASIC ASSUMPTIONS OF EVOLUTIONARY COGNITIVE PSYCHOLOGY

Evolutionary psychologists rely on a number of common assumptions (see, e.g., Buss, 1994; Crawford & Anderson, 1989; Daly & Wilson, 1983, 1988; Kenrick, 1994; Kenrick & Hogan, 1991; Kenrick & Trost, 1989; Tooby & Cosmides, 1992). Three main assumptions that provide a foundation for our later discussion include:

1. The pressures of natural selection have sculpted not only the physical bodies of living organisms, but also the behavioral and cognitive programs used to operate those bodies.

2. Natural selection and sexual selection have favored universal species-typical solutions for dealing with those features of the social and physical environments that were constant for our ancestors (such as the need to become aroused under threat, or the necessity to avoid eating poisonous foods).

3. The processes of sexual selection and differential parental investment have sculpted different behavioral and cognitive strategies in the two sexes. For example, because of initially higher levels of parental investment, and lesser potential payoffs for multiple mates, human females will tend to be more selective in choosing mates and less attentive to opportunities for additional mates, whereas males will compete with one another for the opportunity to gain access to females and will tend to be more promiscuous than will females. These behavioral differences will, in turn, have their cognitive counterparts.

An evolutionary approach assumes fundamental cognitive categories. The search for such categories is guided by the question, "What would our ancestors have needed for cognitive equipment in the environment of evolutionary adaptedness (i.e., the social and physical ecology within which mankind evolved)?" This question is addressed in the next section.

### What Problems Were the Human Mind Functionally Designed to Solve?

Many of the problems of human life are simply particular extensions of the problems of primate social life. For instance, the ability to recognize specific features of other people's faces is a particular extension of the ability to recognize group members. Indeed, research suggests that the human brain has features designed to assist in facial recognition. Infants begin to attend to facial arrays shortly after birth, for instance, and adults with one specific type of brain damage suffer from a specific inability to recognize faces. In this disorder, called *prosopagnosia*, individuals are able to identify the specific features of faces (noses, eyes, etc.), to identify individuals by their voices, to distinguish female and male faces, and so on. However, they are unable to recognize a face, even their own (Damasio, 1985). Other problems are even more particular to our species. One is the need to understand complex spoken language. Indeed, a great deal of evidence suggests that humans are born with a brain predesigned to rapidly learn language (Chomsky, 1972; Pinker, 1994).

The hierarchical nature of all human groups would lead one to expect that humans will think about, and their words will reflect, behaviors involving dominance versus submissiveness. The interdependent nature of human groups leads to a similar expectation regarding terms for agreeableness versus disagreeableness. Indeed, factor analytic studies of personality reliably find these two dimensions to be foremost among the social categories used in social relationships (Goldberg, 1981; McCrae & John, 1992). Research done with American and Canadian college students reveals that those two dimensions are the main axes of a circumplex of interpersonal terms (Wiggins & Broughton, 1985). Cross-cultural research reveals that those same two dimensions are found in studies of trait adjectives in other cultures (White, 1980), and the same dimensions apply to people's common problems with others (Gurtman, 1992). From an evolutionary perspective, the tendency to think about other people in terms of dominance and agreeableness is thus fundamental to human cognition.

Many problems faced by humans were also faced by our nonhuman ancestors. For instance, all social mammals would have benefited from the ability to understand their own position in a social group (Hogan, 1982; Lancaster, 1976), and to recognize threats and other signs of emotion in others (Darwin, 1872; Ekman, 1992; Hansen & Hansen, 1988; Plutchik, 1980). In line with the notion of differential parental investment mentioned earlier, males and females would have been designed to have different mechanisms for evaluating mates, and for evaluating and responding to potential infidelities by their partners (Buss, 1994; Daly & Wilson, 1988; Kenrick & Keefe, 1992). Because of the centrality of reproduction to evolutionary design, these issues, along with relevant empirical data, are considered in detail in a later section.

## HOW AN EVOLUTIONARY APPROACH DIFFERS FROM TRADITIONAL COGNITIVE PSYCHOLOGY

It is a rare social scientist these days who would argue that human beings are not products of natural selection (cf. Symons, 1987). However, there are important differences of emphasis between those who explicitly adopt an evolutionary perspective on the human mind and those who do not. From an evolutionary perspective, traditional cognitive psychologists are wrong to consider cognitive processes without considering what content is being processed. The evolutionary emphasis on cognitive content over disembodied process stems from an assumption of independent domain-specific cognitive modules, as opposed to domain-general cognitive processes (e.g., Tooby & Cosmides, 1992). Further, evolutionary psychologists presume that cognitive modules are designed not for cool rationality, but for hot cognition, to respond to crucial events related to survival and reproduction. As such, evolutionary theorists assume natural interconnections between affect and cognition. Consistent with the focus on function, evolutionary psychologists have tended to emphasize how cognitive modules are designed to solve real problems posed by objective reality. This is in opposition to the tacit, but widely held, assumption that cognition consists of arbitrary constructions. Finally, whereas conscious verbal processing has been the hub of traditional cognitive psychology, evolutionary psychologists have questioned whether cognition necessarily involves either verbal processing or conscious awareness. The rationale for each of these points is reviewed in turn.

**Content Versus Process**

Traditional textbooks on cognitive psychology are arranged in terms of processes, such as attention, encoding, retrieval, and complex problem solving. As noted earlier, it has been assumed that the same general processes apply across different content domains—from letter recognition to person perception. However, there is evidence that even similar stimuli are processed somewhat differently depending on their content. For instance, DeSoto, Hamilton, and Taylor (1985) found that the semantic associates of identical words were different when subjects believed those words referred to objects as opposed to people. For instance, the word *warm* is associated with *sweet*, but not *hot*, if it is being considered as a personality attribute, but the reverse is true if it is being considered as an attribute of an inanimate object. In the more complex domain of logical reasoning, Cosmides and Tooby (1989) found that subjects were very good at solving the normally difficult Wason task if it was presented in terms of a cheater-detection problem. Subsequent research indicated that the better solution of the cheater-detection problem could not be explained in terms of obvious confounds such as the greater familiarity with certain classes of stimuli (Cosmides, 1994; Cosmides & Tooby, 1989).

As mentioned earlier, White (1980) found that linguistic terms used to describe personality universally fit a basic two-dimensional circumplex. White argued that the selection pressures of living in hominid groups have designed the human mind to be particularly attentive to the dominance and agreeableness of other people. Other research on social cognition, although not conducted from an evolutionary perspective, consistently finds that experimental subjects spontaneously attend to and encode certain dimensions of others. At the top of the list of spontaneously attention-grabbing dimensions are gender, status, and age (Brewer & Lui, 1989; Hastie & Park, 1986).

There is evidence for specific mechanisms designed to detect anger. Research on social perception indicates that people are especially attentive to evidence of hostility in another person. For instance, Hansen and Hansen (1988) found that angry faces were especially likely to pop out of crowds. Subjects were much more accurate at correctly identifying discrepant angry faces in happy crowds than in identifying happy faces in angry crowds.

Further, although the tendency for happy faces to pop out of an array was affected by increases in the size of the crowd, angry faces popped out regardless of the size of the array. Other evidence of a particular sensitivity to hostility comes from research on social inference, where it is found that negative information about another person carries seemingly inordinate weight in impression formation (Pratto & John, 1991).

There is evidence to suggest that the amount, complexity, or depth of information processing depends on the content of the information being processed. In line with the general notion that people are cognitive misers, who will not expend cognitive effort unless it is necessary, research on social cognition indicates that people generally avoid engaging in complex attributional processes when others do what is expected (Fiske & Neuberg, 1990). Likewise, research on the processing of attitude-relevant information indicates that when information is deemed "irrelevant" to one's central concerns, it is processed in a shallow way, but when it has personally relevant implications, it receives more thoughtful processing (Chaiken, Liberman, & Eagly, 1989; Petty & Cacioppo, 1986; Trost, Maass, & Kenrick, 1992).

It is of interest that researchers have not systematically studied which topics are deemed especially relevant and worthy of central processing. From an evolutionary perspective, it would be expected that people would be especially likely to engage in complex attributional processes under particular circumstances, as when there is a possibility of mating, of a change in one's status or one's coalitions, or when an event has implications for one's offspring. We would also expect that, in line with differential parental investment and sexual-selection notions, cognitive processing of mating relevant stimuli will differ for males and females (Kenrick, Neuberg, Zierk, & Krones, 1994). Research relevant to this expectation is discussed later. The emphasis on specific content over general process is closely related to the next distinction discussed—the differential emphasis on domain-general versus modular cognitive mechanisms.

**Modules Versus Domain-General Mechanisms**

Traditional experimental psychology has been strongly influenced by the equipotentiality theory of the prominent neurophysiologist Carl Lashley (1929). Lashley found that when increasingly larger areas of a rat's cortex were destroyed, there was gradually greater disruption of memory, and that other areas could sometimes take over function for the damaged area. The alternative notion, that brain functions can be localized, may have been tainted by a perceived association with phrenology, despite the early support for localization provided by findings such as Broca's observation that aphasics all had damage to the left frontal lobe. An even more important historical influence on experimental psychology has been the centrality of domain-general learning theories. The most prominent theories of learning have assumed that all behaviors, regardless not only of content-domain, but even of the species manifesting them, could be explained in terms of one or a few simple domain-general mechanisms (e.g., Skinner, 1953).

Evolutionary approaches to cognition have generally favored an alternative view—that organisms' brains are composed of some number of relatively independent modular mechanisms, designed to deal specifically with particular cognitive problems confronting particular species. It is possible to marshall a number of arguments that the human brain could have evolved into a general learning device. For instance, the assumption of a general learning mechanism that operates according to a few general-purpose learning rules (such as the Law of Effect, contiguity, etc.) is more parsimonious than the assumption of domain-specific mechanisms. Indeed, principles such as classical and operant conditioning do have a wide range of applicability, and it would be a mistake to assume that every cognitive module must be completely independent of the others, or that the processes used by different modules are nonoverlapping. However, there are clearly instances in which a parsimonious general-purpose mechanism will fail to optimize learning. Sherry and Schacter (1987) noted that some types of memory tasks are functionally incompatible. For instance, song learning in birds often occurs during a very restricted period, in which the bird is sensitive to the songs it hears. Several months may pass before the bird actively produces the song, and learning of new songs is closed after the critical period. However, memory for food caches involves continually updated memory for novel locations—with food being stored in many places each day, and no repetition of sites over time. A common memory process for these two types of learning would be highly inefficient, and each system is in fact associated with particular neural structures. In humans, there is also evidence of qualitatively different memory systems, particularly a distinction between procedural and episodic memory. Patients who are completely amnesiac for learning episodes (such as the famous H. M.), for instance, can learn new habits or nonverbal skills in a normal fashion, although they are unaware of having learned them (Sherry & Schacter, 1987). Sherry and Schacter (1987) were conservative in proposing modules, arguing that different systems may evolve only when the demands of one system are incompatible with another. It is also quite feasible that cognitive modules may be incompatible in certain ways, yet share some general processing mechanisms with other modules for certain subtasks.

Gardner (1985) reviewed a number of lines of evidence for modularity in human cognition in proposing his concept of multiple intelligences.

He argued that several lines of evidence were inconsistent with the notion of a single processor overseeing all aspects of human intelligence, and he proposed relatively autonomous processing for several categories of information: linguistic, musical, logical-mathematical, spatial, bodily-kinesthetic, and interpersonal. Gardner's general arguments for autonomy stemmed from several types of evidence. For one, certain individuals occasionally demonstrate prodigious performance in one area, with poor performance in other areas (the classical example is the *idiot savant* who is highly capable in dealing with numerical problems, but is otherwise intellectually retarded). For another, studies of brain-damaged patients indicate that certain of these abilities can be destroyed while the others are left relatively intact, as in classical cases of Wernicke's and Broca's syndrome patients.

Although it is not necessary to assume that modular mechanisms are narrowly localized, empirical evidence since Broca indicates that at least some of them are. For instance, H. M.'s specific memory disability was linked to a hippocampal lesion. Other studies of brain damage also indicate that specific cognitive abilities can be destroyed by localized lesions, although general learning and cognitive capacities remain otherwise normal. One example, discussed earlier, is prosopagnosia, which is linked to a particular pattern of bilateral damage (Damasio, 1985).

Beyond the empirical justifications for assuming modularity, evolutionary cognitive psychologists believe there are compelling theoretical reasons. Tooby and Cosmides (1992) noted that evolution generally favors specific organs designed to solve particular tasks. Rather than having a general "sense organ," for instance, we have special organs designed to process sound waves, light waves, touch, smell, taste, and temperature. At the neurological level, recent investigations support this reasoning, indicating distinct brain mechanisms for analyzing visual input, color, shape, movement, depth, and other complex features of visual stimuli (Livingstone & Hubel, 1988). Likewise, completely separate mechanisms analyze different features of auditory input, whereas others are designed for understanding spoken words, still others are designed for producing spoken words, and so on.

Cosmides (1994) used the metaphor of the mind as a Swiss army knife. A picnic would be difficult if one were permitted to bring only a single knife blade to serve all purposes: opening the wine, cutting the bread and cheese, tightening the loose screw, filing a rough edge on the picnic basket, removing a splinter, and so on. The Swiss army knife contains separate tools better designed to perform each task effectively. With regard to behavior, the brain also appears to come pre-equipped with cognitive tools designed to carry out specific functions.

**What Is a Module?**

Although evolutionary psychologists are in some general agreement about the modularity of cognition, they are not always clear about what they mean by a module. Cognitive psychologists have offered a number of suggestions. For instance, in referring to memory modules, Sherry and Shacter (1987) suggested that modules are separate systems with their "own acquisition, retention, and retrieval processes" and separate "rules of operation" (p. 440). They suggested the possibility of different processors or modules for facial, linguistic, and/or spatial information. Matlin and Foley (1992) suggested a similar definition of a module, and offered echolocation in bats as an example.

In a recent book on the innate features of human language, Pinker (1994) dedicated a chapter to mind design. In that chapter, he considered the concept of a module in some detail. He suggested some negative examples, doubting that we have modules for bicycling or matching ties with shirts. He also suggested four criteria for a module, including:

1. Functional engineering. We can ask what a system would need, in principle, to perform its normal functions.
2. Biological anthropology. We can ask what our ancestors would have needed to do in their everyday lives.
3. Developmental psychology. Pinker suggested that modules might be evidenced by findings that children solve certain problems readily, as compared with other problems where the learning curve is long and hard.
4. Neurology. If a module exists, there should be evidence of a related neural architecture, circuitry, or subsystem.

Pinker provided his own list of possible modules of the human mind, including: intuitive mechanics, biology, number, large map territories, habitat selection rules, danger, food, contamination, monitoring well-being (emotion, mood), intuitive psychology (predicting others' behavior from their beliefs and desires), a mental Rolodex (for categorizing other people in terms of kinship, status, history of favors, inherent skills and strengths, criteria to evaluate each trait), self-concept (for appraising our value to others), justice, kinship (nepotism, parental effort), and mating (including sexual attraction, love, intentions of fidelity and desertion).

One can think of modules at different levels of complexity, or as dedicated units in hierarchically designed subsystems. At the simplest level, modules might perform tasks such as feature analysis. These simple units may subserve one or more complex analyzers. Prototypical examples of simple modules would be the specialized bug detector units discovered in frogs' brains by Lettvin, Maturana, McCulloch, and Pitts (1959). Hubel and Wiesel's (1959, 1962, 1979) research on simple, complex, and hyper-complex cells is also relevant to simple modular processing. They found that simple cells in a cat's visual cortex only responded to stimuli such as bars of light moving at particular angles, whereas hypercomplex cells responded to specific stimulus patterns, such as moving angles or corners, or lines at particular orientations moving across the retina in specific directions. By building from simple to more and more complex feature detectors, it is quite feasible to imagine not only cortical systems dedicated to recognizing faces, but also systems specialized to recognize facial arrays signifying particular emotions.

Evolutionary psychologists interested in cognitive mechanisms and their function would benefit from exposure to modern research on neural networks. In particular, Martindale's (1980, 1991) neural network ap-proach to cognition makes extensive use of the notion of modular processing to explain how simple feature analyzers interact to build up to more and more complex modules, which, at the highest level, he called *subselves*. The notion of subselves is consistent with research on state-dependent memory: Memories are more accessible when one is in the same physiological state as when the memory was formed. Martindale suggested that different executive systems may likewise have special access to particular memories and behavioral repertoires. The notion of subselves also helps understand phenomena such as dissociation, which occurs in extreme form in amnesia and multiple personality disorder, and in minor form in normal individuals. As James (1890) noted:

> Many a youth who is demure enough before his parents and teachers, swears and swaggers like a pirate among his "tough" young friends. We do not show ourselves to our children as to our club-companions, to our customers as to the laborers we employ, to our masters and employers as to our intimate friends. (p. 294)

Considered in light of Martindale's notions of lateral inhibition and state-dependent learning, the concept of modules could be expanded to understand the discontinuity between people's behavior in situations where they are angry or sexually aroused, at which times they may act like more like Mr. Hyde than their Dr. Jekyll subself could have ever predicted in moments of cooler analysis.

To argue for modularity does not commit one to a completely localized view of the brain or to a view that there are no commonly shared proc-esses. The whole brain may be involved in most activities, and modules may be viewed in terms of patterns of activity across different areas, as opposed to spatially localized activity. As noted earlier, existing evidence suggests at least some localization of certain functions. It is simply not necessary that such localization apply to all modular activity.

It is not necessary to assume that all cognitive activities studied by cognitive psychologists, such as mathematics, abstract reasoning, reading, or puzzle solving, are directly related to the problems most often encountered in the African veldt. It could be argued that such general abilities might have grown out of other abilities, or might emerge from skills designed to solve more specific classes or problems. The requirements of spatial navigation during hunting–gathering, for example, may underpin the spatial abilities involved in some types of mathematics.

### Instincts and Epigenetic Rules Versus a Tabula Rasa

Implicit in the notion of cognitive modules is the assumption of mechanisms designed to perform specific adaptive functions. There is an accompanying assumption among evolutionary psychologists that many important modules are species-wide and innate, as in the case of universals in color perception or the recognition of emotional expression (Darwin, 1872; Ekman, 1992; Rosch, 1974).

The evolutionary position is explicitly contrary to the constructivist position that local culture or language determines the way information is processed. The case of color perception is representative of this controversy. Cognitive psychologists arguing from the position of linguistic relativity have suggested that the perception of color will be strongly influenced by the classification system imposed by an individual's language. From this perspective, languages that are well differentiated for a particular color region will allow a person to detect subtleties of color that a person with a less well-differentiated language could not detect. However, recent empirical work does not support the contention that language plays a major role in color perception. For example, Rosch found that even groups with sparse color vocabularies, such as the Dani of New Guinea, categorized color chips into the same basic color categories as did those in cultures with rich color vocabularies. Likewise, colors that posed categorization difficulties in one culture (such as aquamarine) also posed problems in other cultures (even those with fine color distinctions in the language).

In a similar vein, facial expressions related to basic emotions such as anger, fear, and happiness are similarly categorized by people in widely divergent linguistic communities—even those that are quite isolated, such as the Fore of New Guinea (Ekman & Friesen, 1971).

Lumsden and Wilson (1981) suggested that organisms inherit epigenetic rules, or genetically encoded biases, to preferentially attend to, encode, learn, and remember particular associations between stimuli and responses. They argued any bias that predisposes an adaptive decision will be subject to strong selection pressure if it avoids costly mistakes of a *tabula rasa* machine.

Although modern evolutionary psychologists prefer to avoid the term, Pinker (1994) recently suggested that, at least with regard to the concept of language, psychologists might do well to revive the concept of instinct. He argued that this term "conveys the idea that people know how to talk in more or less the sense that spiders know how to spin webs" (p. 18). Among psychologists, the term *instinct* has come to mean an inflexible pattern of behavior that is "wired in" at birth and manifests itself full blown in infancy, or at the first available opportunity. Critics of early evolutionary psychologists such as James (1890) and McDougall (1908) claimed that they invented human instincts on an ad hoc basis to explain any observed pattern of behavior, and that humans were viewed as responding robotically to these multifarious instincts. However, if one actually goes back to read the positions advanced by James and McDougall, one finds a much more reasonable view. Both, like Darwin before them, viewed human instincts more in terms that we would call drives today, and both believed that human instincts were subject to inhibition by higher faculties, as well as modification by learning.

In his often caricatured *Social Psychology*, for instance, McDougall (1908) proposed seven instincts—(flight, repulsion, curiosity, pugnacity, self-abasement, self-assertion, and the parental instinct). Like James, he viewed these instincts as analogous to hunger. According to McDougall, instinctive tendencies cause us to pay attention to certain events in the environment, feel certain emotions when we notice those important events in the environment, and act in particular ways in response to those feelings. As an example, the instinct of *pugnacity* (which we would today call *aggression*) predisposes a person to feel angry and prepare to fight when another person obstructs the satisfaction of his or her other needs. McDougall believed that the angry reaction was automatically activated, but that people can and do learn to control and suppress its expression.

An advantage of the concept of instinct is that it captures the notion of a complete system of perceptual, affective, and behavioral mechanisms designed to perform specific adaptive functions. Modern research on animal behavior indicates that, "instincts are not purely genetic and learning is not purely environmental" (Alcock, 1993, p. 34). Instinctive behavior shows an interplay of environmental inputs, internal physiological states, and behaviors that unfolds in complex ways over time and between organisms (e.g., Gross, 1984; Lehrman, 1966). To ignore this useful concept because of outmoded preconceptions is self-handicapping for psychologists interested in a full understanding of affect, cognition, and behavior.

Although it is not generally advertised as dealing with instinctive behavior, modern research on emotion, which is discussed in the next section, is actually quite reminiscent of McDougall's early work. From an evolutionary perspective, it makes no sense to consider cognitive processes independently of other processes such as motivation, emotion, or behavior; all are interrelated parts of adaptive systems designed to deal with functional problems.

## The Interplay of Affect and Cognition: Adaptive Emotion Systems

Although researchers studying human emotion are not completely unanimous in all details, they have come to some agreement that there are a small number of basic human emotions (e.g., Izard, 1971; Plutchik, 1980). Plutchik's model of emotion has a number of similarities to McDougall's concept of basic human instincts. According to Plutchik (1980), an emotion consists of a stimulus event (such as a bear) that elicits a cognition (I am in danger) that leads, in turn, to a feeling state (fear) that instigates particular behaviors (such as running) designed to produce an adaptive effect (in this case, self-protection). Table 16.1 summarizes Plutchik's model of emotion.

One can quibble with the specifics of Plutchik's model, and it is important not to assume that inferred cognition means processing in terms of verbal labels (similar inference processes are no doubt involved in motivated decisions made by other animals). However, Plutchik's model nicely illustrates the general point that emotional reactions work hand-in-hand with cognitions and behaviors as interrelated parts of functionally designed systems. Scott (1980) developed a model that is compatible to Plutchik's, except that it goes a step further toward integrating different processes. Scott's model includes other internal states, such as hunger

TABLE 16.1
Plutchik's Evolutionary Model of Emotional Systems

| Stimulus Event | Inferred Cognition | Feeling | Behavior | Effect |
|---|---|---|---|---|
| Threat | Danger | Fear, terror | Running away | Protection |
| Obstacle | Enemy | Anger, rage | Biting, hitting | Destruction |
| Potential mate | Possess | Joy, ecstasy | Courting, mating | Reproduction |
| Loss of valued person | Isolation | Sadness, grief | Crying for help | Reintegration |
| Group member | Friend | Acceptance, trust | Grooming, sharing | Affiliation |
| Gruesome object | Poison | Disgust, loathing | Vomiting, pushing away | Rejection |
| New territory | What's out there? | Anticipation | Examining, mapping | Exploration |
| Sudden novel object | What is it? | Surprise | Stopping, alerting | Orientation |

and sexual arousal (normally distinguished as drives), within the same framework with emotions, such as fear and anger. According to Scott's approach, hunger, thirst, love, fear, and anger are all innate motivational systems that have different functions—each is designed to respond to a particular combination of environmental stimuli and internal needs, and to carry out a particular set of adaptive functions.

The evolutionary view of affect and cognition contrasts sharply with the model proposed by Shacter and Singer (1962). Their simple two-factor model assumed one general-purpose emotion (Factor 1), to which a person (often mistakenly) attaches arbitrary situational labels (Factor 2). For instance, fear may be mistakenly labeled as *romantic attraction* (Dutton & Aron, 1974). This model of one general-purpose emotional state has enjoyed wide acceptance within cognitive and social psychology, despite evidence against it (Allen, Kenrick, Linder, & McCall, 1989; Reisenzein, 1983). Although different emotional states may share certain aspects of their physiological patterns, an evolutionary perspective assumes an adaptive interplay between specific environmental problems, cognitions, affective states, and behaviors. Although arbitrary mistakes may happen in making attributions about one's arousal state, those are assumed to be potentially costly exceptions to the rule. The issue of arbitrariness in cognition relates to the next point of contention between evolutionary approaches and other views.

## Arbitrary Construction Versus Problem-Constrained Discovery

Evolutionary models of cognition have historically been differentiated from constructivist models. Among many differences in basic premises, a central distinction between these two approaches has to do with assumptions concerning the ontological status of events. Evolutionary theorists assume a world of extant phenomena that a given cognitive system is obliged to deal with and, to some extent, understand. Constructivist accounts emphasize that there are always alternative ways to cognize the environment, and that the structure of events—the to-be-explained phenomena—is dependent on the cognitive system that is developed.

From an evolutionary perspective, the members of a given species remain viable through the development of cognitive, perceptual, and behavioral skills, which adequately take into account contingencies inherent in their ecological surroundings. Cognitive processes may be regarded as means of adaptation to the environment. Perception and cognition are regarded as instrumental acts that allow the members of a species to come to terms with the resources and dangers in a physical or social environment. Implicit in this approach is the assumption that the environment consists of a structured arrangement of objects, events, and relationships. Environmental elements have an ontological status independent of any particular observer; and those elements may be described as preperceptual, objective, and independent.

In their classical ecological models, Tolman and Brunswick (1935) suggested that the environment be conceptualized as a causal texture, in which different events are regularly dependent on each other. To deal with relevant, remote, or distal objects, organisms must develop both a model of the distal ecology as well as a knowledge of cue–event relationships. The adequacy of any particular perceptual–cognitive system is evaluated with respect to the degree to which it achieves a representation of that structure.

For example, it is assumed that, over an evolutionary time scale, members of a species that could quickly detect predators would live longer and leave more offspring than would those who were deficient at this task. Predator detection and avoidance is a complex cognitive skill that involves vigilance, memory, and reasoning, as well as the ability to plan alternative courses of action. More to the point of our later discussion, it may also be assumed that members of a species who were capable of selecting high-quality mates (mates with sufficient fertility or resources to contribute to offspring viability) would have a selective advantage over individuals who made poor choices.

The assumption here is that there are contingencies in the environment that cannot be reconstrued, reinterpreted, or ignored without affecting an individual's fitness. An alternative way of phrasing this is that individuals who more accurately model environmental contingencies will survive and reproduce more successfully than will individuals who have deficient models. The causal texture of the environment must, to some degree, affect an individual's model of the world, as well as that individual's cognitive skills, emotional responses, and preferences.

This view may be contrasted with the constructivist position that emphasizes that an individual's model of the world tends to be more of an invention than a discovery of real ecological structure, and that such inventions are highly variable depending on local language, history, and custom. For example, Hare-Mustin and Marecek (1990) argued:

> Constructivism asserts that we do not discover reality, we invent it. Our experience does not directly reflect what is out there but is a selecting, ordering, and organizing of it. . . . Representations of reality are shared meaning that derive from shared language, history, and culture . . . the "realities" of social life are products of language and agreed-on meanings. (p. 27)

It should be noted that an evolutionary perspective does not deny that cognition is an active, rather than a passive, process. Human knowledge involves selective attention, encoding systems that transform sensory data into linguistic or visual representational formats, and categorization systems that organize and give meaning to events. It is undeniable that humans actively construct the meanings that frame and organize our experience. Evolutionary approaches also do not deny that the human understanding of social and physical events involves maps, models, or representations that invariably contain error. However, evolutionary approaches assume that there are some classes of problems (related to survival and reproduction) that have endured over an evolutionary time scale and that impose strong constraints on our construction of the environment. Evolutionary approaches further assume that individuals who more accurately understood these problems survived and reproduced more successfully than did those who did not.

## Evolved Mechanisms Are Functional
## Over the Long Haul, but Are Not Omniscient

There is a misconception sometimes attributed to evolutionary models—that individuals are selected to think, feel, and act in ways that are generally adaptive. A generally adaptive organism is somehow presumed to be omniscient: to have prior knowledge about the particular genetic advantages likely to be gained from using each mechanism in each particular set of circumstances. The fallacy inherent in this assumption can be demonstrated by considering a few mechanisms that have evolved because of their past adaptive consequences. For instance, our ancestors were selected to have a general preference for sweet-tasting foods presumably because of the association of sweetness with ripeness in fruit (Lumsden & Wilson, 1981). In contrast, carnivorous cats have no particular preference for sweet substances. The mechanism underlying the human preference for sweet tastes operates even in a modern social context, in which technology has made available superabundant supplies of sugary substances. Although the sweet-preference mechanism now sometimes leads to obesity and diabetes, and is seemingly irrational in the context of modern society, it was selected under circumstances where it had, on average, a strong positive effect on survival.

Another example of the seemingly irrational operation of modular mechanisms comes from the arena of sexual attraction. Shepher (1971) found evidence that strongly contradicted the normal propinquity effect on attraction among children raised in the kibbutz. On reaching maturity, unrelated children raised in the same familylike kibbutz pods showed a decided lack of sexual and romantic attraction in later years. Although they did show the usual tendency to marry those raised nearby, the propinquity–attraction link seemed to stop just outside their own door-step, although it was not in any way discouraged by societal norms, and pod mates tended to become lifelong friends. Shepher argued that the unusual conditions of raising these children together had somehow triggered a mechanism designed to dampen strong romantic attraction between siblings, which generally would have lowered the probability of incest (which increases the danger of deleterious recessive gene combinations). Like the sugar-preference mechanism, then, the incest mechanism's operation seems irrational if considered in isolation in a novel modern context.

## Conscious Verbal Processing
## Versus Nonconscious Automaticity

Evolutionary explanations of behavior sometimes seem to run contrary to phenomenological experience. For instance, those who do not understand the perspective sometimes protest that they personally have no interest in reproducing, that they spend little or no time calculating the adaptive benefits of their behaviors, or that they do not even like their kin. The confusion here may arise because evolutionary theorists do indeed assume that cognitive processes and cognitive abilities were selected because of their adaptive consequences. However, this assumption does not mean that the functions of cognitive and behavioral strategies are available to consciousness. For example, individuals who prefer sugar-laden desserts are unlikely to cite functional reasons for their preferences; rather, they are most likely to say simply that sugar tastes good to them. From an evolutionary perspective, it was not necessary for our ancestors to understand the ultimate reason for why they liked sugar. The simple phenomenological experience, "I like it," was proximate mechanism enough to lead them to eat calorie-rich substances.

In some cases, it may indeed be adaptive for humans to be unaware of the functional basis of their behavior (Lockard, 1988; Trivers, 1985). For instance, human females have evolved to be unaware of their own ovulation. Alexander and Noonan (1979) suggested that it was adaptive for females to conceal their periods of ovulation from others, and that self-awareness on their part would involve more costs than it was worth. For instance, a female who knowingly concealed ovulation would betray the trust of a partner, and risk the dangers of potential retaliation if she inadvertently slipped in her deceit, and so on. Because no useful function is served by self-awareness in this instance, it is arguably better for the female simply not to consciously know when she is ovulating.

In the area of mating behaviors in general, one might expect a great deal of self-deception. For instance, women tend to choose older partners, and to be relatively selective about engaging in casual sexual liaisons, whereas men are attracted to women in their years of maximum fertility, and are willing to lower their criteria if a partner is willing to have a casual sexual liaison (Kenrick, Groth, Trost, & Sadalla, 1993; Kenrick & Keefe, 1992; Kenrick, Sadalla, Groth, & Trost, 1990). It is not necessary to assume that men say to themselves, "I am attracted to this woman because she is in the years of maximum fertility, and if I mate with her, preferably on a short-term basis, it will optimize my chances of replicating my genes," or that females say, "In order to maximize my reproductive potential, I will withhold sexual favors from younger resource-poor men, and demand extensive resource investment before copulating with older men." Indeed, individuals who were self-aware of such ultimate mechanisms might be expected to be less skillful at developing socially appropriate affectionate relationships.

Gazzaniga (1985) reviewed evidence from split-brain studies to indicate the disparity between people's explanations of their behavior and their self-awareness of the antecedents of that behavior. For instance, split-brain patients who are shown an emotion-inducing stimulus to the (relatively less verbal) right brain will often produce an explanation (that they apparently believe) for the feelings, but which is completely wrong. One woman who was shown a fear-producing slide attributed her fear to the researcher, claiming he had an intimidating appearance. There are no doubt differences between those with split brains and normal individuals whose two hemispheres communicate. However, Gazzaniga argued that a tendency to create erroneous explanations stems from the fact that the brain module that explains our behavior is naturally somewhat limited in its sources of relevant information, even in people with intact brains. Consistent with this reasoning, Nisbett and Wilson (1977) reviewed evidence that normal subjects in experiments often fabricate explanations for their behavior that are incorrect, but they nevertheless believe.

Cognitive psychologists distinguish between automatic and controlled processing (e.g., Chaiken, Liberman, & Eagly, 1989; Petty & Cacioppo, 1986; Shiffrin & Schneider, 1977). The general model is that automatic processing occurs when a decision is low in importance or highly familiar, and hence does not require extensive thoughful analysis. From an evolutionary perspective, it would be assumed that many processes are *automatic* because they solve perennial problems faced by our ancestors, or because conscious consideration would interfere with appropriate social performances. As noted earlier, an evolutionary perspective can tell us which topics are likely to be important—those that relate to the recurring problems faced by our ancestors. It also suggests that what is personally relevant should, in some instances, be different for the two sexes.

Consistent with the central concern with lexical decision making, traditional cognitive models have tended to view the mind as organized in terms of semantic networks. Concepts are represented as semantic nodes, which are linked with other concepts through similarities of meaning or pronunciation. Wyer and Srull (1986) developed a model of social cognition very much along these lines, in which memories of other people are represented as verbal codes whose accessibility to consciousness will depend on procedures such as semantic priming. For instance, judgments about another person's risky behavior will depend on recent exposure to words such as *foolhardy* or *adventuresome*.

From an evolutionary perspective, it would be expected that much of cognition will be nonverbal. As compared with the notion of a brain made up of networks of verbally coded nodes, a mind made up of Jungian archetypes might make more sense. Jung conceptualized archetypes as powerful emotion-laden images, such as images of mothers, heroes, and marauding villains. He and his followers explored worldwide myth systems and children's dreams for such images. Even across species, there is evidence that animals inherit emotion-laden cognitive images. Chimps, for instance, show an instinctive response to snake forms.

## SOME PRELIMINARY STUDIES OF EVOLUTION-BASED GENDER DIFFERENCES IN COGNITION

As indicated earlier, certain human gender differences are presumed to follow from common features of mammalian mating patterns. Mating strategies tend to be sex differentiated because, among all mammals, females invest more biological energy in reproduction than do males. Because of this high initial parental investment, females are generally more selective in their choice of mates. Consistent with these assumptions, a number of researchers studying human behavior find that females are less willing to take advantage of an opportunity for a casual sexual liaison (Buss & Schmitt, 1993; Clark & Hatfield, 1989), and that females, compared with males, insist on much higher mate value before considering such liaisons (Kenrick et al., 1990; Kenrick et al., 1993). Females also show the common mammalian tendency to place more emphasis on a potential mate's position in a status hierarchy (Buss, 1989; Sadalla, Kenrick, & Vershure, 1987; Townsend & Levy, 1990). In contrast, males place relatively more emphasis on youth and physical attractiveness, which are presumably associated with fertility (e.g., Buss, 1989; Kenrick & Keefe, 1992). Researchers interested in these topics have tacitly assumed that the gender differences are mainly based on differential motivational processes in the two sexes, and thus, have not explored how the two sexes might differ in processes such as perception and memory. Do the notions of differential parental investment and sexual selection, which have been so profitable in examining mating choices, have implications for cognitive processes such as attention, encoding, categorization, and retrieval? We consider several preliminary attempts to address these questions by ourselves and our colleagues.

## Perceptual Contrast and Mate Judgments

One well-known cognitive phenomenon is called a *contrast effect*—or a shift in judgment of one stimulus following exposure to extreme stimuli on the dimension being judged. The classic demonstration used in general psychology is to have students place one hand in a bucket of cold water and another in a bucket of hot water. Following a short period during which the hands adapt to the extreme temperatures, both hands are removed and placed in a bucket of lukewarm water. The result is that the hand from the hot bucket registers the lukewarm water as cold, whereas the hand from the icewater registers the same lukewarm water as hot. Contrast effects are generally thought to be domain-general—to apply similarly to temperature, weight, decisions about crime severity, physical attractiveness, and so on. For instance, average looking people are judged as less attractive after exposure to highly physically attractive individuals of the same sex (Kenrick & Gutierres, 1980).

In one series of investigations, judgments of cohabiting romantic partners were found to be adversely influenced by exposure to attractive centerfolds (Kenrick, Gutierres, & Goldberg, 1989). Men exposed to beautiful female centerfolds showed more of a contrast effect than did women exposed to highly attractive male centerfolds. One possible explanation for the sex difference fits with the findings reviewed earlier—perhaps women's register for partner satisfaction is not as closely linked with judgments of physical attractiveness. Instead, perhaps women would be more subject to contrast effects after being exposed to socially dominant versus physically attractive men. Indeed, an experiment in which subjects were exposed to opposite-sex individuals who varied in both physical attractiveness and social dominance revealed that women were uninfluenced by physical attractiveness, but reported lower commitment to their partners after exposure to socially dominant individuals. Conversely, men's commitment to their partners was directly affected by the physical attractiveness of the alternatives to which they were exposed, and social dominance had no main effect (but interacted with attractiveness, such that men were least committed after viewing nondominant beautiful women; Kenrick, Neuberg, Zierk, & Krones, 1994).

## Self-Evaluation Processes

An evolutionary perspective may also have implications for how people think about themselves. Social psychologists have extensively studied processes of self-concept formation and self-esteem, but not generally considered such processes in evolutionary terms. Indeed, the general tendency has been to assume that high self-esteem is an end in itself because it feels good. Leary and his colleagues (1994) suggested that these approaches have been analogous to an alien psychologist's observing earthling driving behavior, and concluding that there is a drive to keep the fuel gauge from touching E. Based on evolutionary considerations, Leary argued that the more important question is, "Why?"

Just as people's motivation to keep the gas gauge from reaching E is not an end in itself, so people's desire to avoid low self-esteem is not an end in itself. Leary viewed self-esteem as a gauge of one's acceptance in the social group, and presented evidence to support such a view. We would add that position in the group is, in large part, an index of mate value. Given the prior reasoning, self-evaluation processes as mates would not be expected to be the same for the two sexes. In judging their own mate value, men should be more likely to show contrast effects following exposure to socially dominant as opposed to physically attractive members of their sex. Women's judgments of their own mate value, conversely, should be more influenced by physical attractiveness versus social dominance of members of their sex.

In another recent study, Gutierres, Kenrick, and Partch (1994) exposed subjects to same-sex individuals who varied in physical attractiveness and social status. The results of that study were the converse of the Kenrick et al. (1994) findings. Men rated their own value as a marriage partner lower after they were exposed to high-status men, and were relatively unaffected by the other men's physical attractiveness. However, women's judgments of their own value as a marriage partner were significantly affected by the other women's physical attractiveness, but not by other women's social status. These findings suggest that men and women are not different in their possession of attractiveness-evaluation mechanisms, but that they differ instead in how those mechanisms are linked to self- and mate-evaluation processes.

Examining another aspect of self-evaluation, Kenrick, Groth, Trost, and Sadalla (1993) examined the correlations between self-ratings and criteria for a mate. Consistent with general social-psychological models of economic exchange, it was found that, generally, the more a subject thought of him or herself on a given dimension, the more he or she demanded in a mate. The two sexes showed virtually identical patterns of correlation between self-rating and mate criteria when considering marriage partners (a relationship in which both sexes make a high investment). This exchange process broke down, however, when males were considering partners for one-night stands, at which point their self-ratings were not significantly connected to their criteria. Females considering short-term sexual partners, however, showed the same strong correlations between self-worth and mate criteria that they had shown for a marriage partner. Consistent with more general evolutionary models, casual sexual liaisons trigger important self-evaluation questions for females, but lead males to disengage comparison-shopping concerns.

## Naturalistic Cognitions About Homicide

The behavior of animals in the constraining environment of a cage in New York's Central Park Zoo is of limited value in inferring natural behavior on the African plains or in the jungles of South America. Likewise, the cognitions of subjects in laboratory experiments may not tell us much about what people think about normally. Laboratory subjects are constrained to respond to whatever stimuli the experimenter has provided. Although everyday concerns may occasionally impinge, the experimenter is unlikely to record them. A number of techniques are now available for obtaining naturalistic measurements of ongoing cognition. For instance, a number of researchers are now using beepers that randomly signal subjects to record whatever concerns are on their minds as they go about their daily activities. As far as we are aware, none of the findings from such studies have been subjected to evolutionary analysis.

Another way to get at natural cognition is to ask subjects about their fantasies. What thoughts commonly pop into people's minds when they go off-line? Are there any sex differences in such thoughts that would fit with the research and theory discussed earlier? Kenrick and Sheets (1994) conducted a pair of studies examining fantasies in a more focused way, asking whether subjects had ever experienced a homicidal fantasy, how recent the last one was, how frequently such fantasies occurred, how detailed they were, who the imagined victims were, and so on. Consistent with evolutionary views of aggression (Daly & Wilson, 1988), it was found that males were more likely to report such fantasies. The differences in ever having had a fantasy were not as large as one would have expected on the basis of actual homicide data, however. Whereas the ratio actual homicides has never, in any examined society, been less than 80:20 for male versus female homicides; the incidence for fantasies were approximately 75% for males and 60% for females. Closer examination revealed a number of other differences, however. Males had more frequent, longer, and more detailed fantasies. Males were also more likely to include weapons in their fantasies. Hence, the overall topography of males' fantasies was more consistent with the observed differences in violent behavior. Similarly, for those subjects who had spent considerable time around stepparents, fantasies about killing them were substantially higher than fantasies about biological parents (although all had spent even more time with biological parents).

## Modularity and Attraction

The reinforcement-affect model has been one of the more influential models of interpersonal attraction, and is a classic domain-general explanation (Byrne, 1971; Byrne & Clore, 1970). The model presumes that reactions to other people are a simple function of classically conditioned positive and negative affect. Liking for physically attractive persons, for instance, was explained in terms of the state of positive affect that physical attractiveness elicited in the observer (Byrne, London, & Reeves, 1968; Lott & Lott, 1974). Recent research suggests that interpersonal judgments are more complex than was suggested by the reinforcement-affect model.

In one study, it was found that subjects exposed to attractive photos of either the same or opposite sex showed perceptual effects of the sort previously described (i.e., a subsequently rated average photo was seen as relatively less attractive than in control conditions). However, an examination of mood effects indicated a completely different pattern. Exposure to attractive members of one's own sex seemed to lower mood, whereas breaking the series with an average looking person provided a mood boost. Just the reverse occurred with exposure to members of the opposite sex. These findings suggest that perceptual judgments of another person's physical attractiveness and affective reactions to those judgments are potentially independent processes (Kenrick, Montello, Gutierres, & Trost, 1993). A judgment of another person's attractiveness has different affective consequences when the relevant adaptation problem is appraisal of one's own relative standing, as compared with appraisal of a potential mate.

The modularity perspective may also shed some light on mating choices made by homosexuals. It is sometimes assumed that homosexual orientation is outside the realm of evolutionary explanation because it is not immediately obvious how natural selection could have directly favored a preference pattern that would undermine reproductive behavior (as would be the case for exclusive homosexuality). However, a number of findings make the biological status of homosexuality seem even more puzzling. For one, behavior genetic research indicates substantial support for the existence of inherited variation in the predisposition to homosexuality (e.g., Bailey & Pillard, 1991; Whitam, Diamond, & Martin, 1993). For another, physiological research indicates some involvement of hormones and neural structures in homosexuality (Ellis & Ames, 1987; LeVay, 1993). Hence, homosexuality poses an interesting puzzle for biological models of human behavior. It seems to involve biological mechanisms that are carried along via sexual reproduction, yet the behavior is not obviously adaptive in itself.

Ostensibly enigmatic behaviors are, on more careful observation, often illuminating about general processes. The case of altruism is an excellent example of a seemingly nonadaptive strategy, which, on careful examination, proved to be quite informative regarding generally selfish evolutionary mechanisms, such as kin selection and reciprocity (e.g., Burnstein, Kitayama, & Crandall, 1994; Hamilton, 1964; Trivers, 1985). Although we cannot offer the answer to the question of the genesis of homosexuality, we have collected some data on homosexual choice, which, in combination with other available data sets, indicates that homosexual mate preferences may illustrate the operation of independently evolved modules, as well as the lack of any conscious rationality in the expression of those modules.

In a study of age preferences among homosexuals, we found that homosexual males showed the same pattern of life-span changes found in heterosexual males (Kenrick, Keefe, Bryan, Barr, & Brown, 1994). Homosexual males in their 20s were, like heterosexual males, interested in partners older as well as younger than themselves; whereas homosexual males in their 40s and older, like older heterosexual males, expressed an interest in partners considerably younger than themselves. The two life-span patterns were, in fact, nearly identical, except that older homosexual males showed a slightly stronger interest in younger partners than did heterosexual males. If the similar life-span pattern is due to a common mechanism, it is clearly not a conscious desire to reproduce (which would be irrelevant to homosexual males).

It is also the case that older homosexuals' choices are irrational, from the perspective of either sex ratios or the economic marketplace perspectives often used to explain mate choice. Although older heterosexual males have a reasonable chance of attracting a younger partner, older homosexual males are searching for partners who are not interested in them. Other research conducted by Bailey, Gaulin, Agyei, and Gladue (1994) indicate that homosexual men are similar to heterosexual men in other ways (e.g., they place high value on physical attractiveness and low value on social status and resources). However, they are different in their levels of jealousy and, of course, in the direction of their preferences.

Although these data on mate choice do not tell us what specific proximate or ultimate mechanisms are responsible for homosexuality, they do tell us that there is no single global mechanism underlying mate choice. Homosexuals do not behave according to some simple rule of sex-role reversal, and they do not simply have one physiological switch thrown. Indeed, many of the switches appear to be set in the *default* settings—settings that make sense for heterosexual reproduction, although they make no apparent sense in an individual with a homosexual orientation. Given the central importance of reproduction to evolution, and given the complexity of tasks involved in reproducing, it would be surprising if the human brain had a single mechanism that controlled reproducing like a male versus reproducing like a female. It would also be surprising if evolutionary pressures had left the development of reproductive mechanisms up to some simple and random process of conditioning, such as doing what feels good. Reproduction involves a series of very different tasks, including choosing a mate (weighing the relative importance of such things as physical health, status, beauty, and faithfulness), evaluating one's own chances of attracting different mates, making oneself attractive to a potential mate, competing with members of one's own sex for that mate, establishing an ongoing relationship, and so on (Buss, 1994; Kenrick & Trost, 1989).

## CONCLUSION

The separate branches of the field of psychology have frequently proceeded as if the different structures and functions of the human organism could be studied in isolation, developing separate subdisciplines with separate minitheories to deal with cognition, neurophysiology, treatment of disordered behavior, and social behavior, among others. The central theories used by cognitive psychologists studying word recognition overlap little with the theories advanced by physiological psychologists studying brain responses to opiates, clinical psychologists studying treatments for depression, or social psychologists studying human mate selection. Within a subdiscipline, researchers further subdivide themselves, so that social psychologists studying mate selection use different theories than social psychologists studying group processes or social psychologists studying attitude formation or social psychologists studying aggression. Such intellectual anarchy may flow from one part of scientific reasoning—the analytic tendency to draw lines that were not visible before. It is also consistent with a focus on microscopic-resolution methodological skills. However, it leaves unsated the other goal of scientific pursuit—synthesis. A good scientific theory not only provides a finely textured route map for getting from Point a to Point b, but it also provides a system of coordinates that tells us where Points a and b are in relation to Points c and d and the rest of the atlas.

Evolutionary psychologists forsake the traditional nested assumptions that the social sciences have nothing to do with living matter, that anthropology has nothing to with psychology and sociology, that cognitive psychology has nothing to do with social psychology, and that the study of social relationships has nothing to do with the study of social perception, ad absurdiam. Part of the appeal of evolutionary psychology is that it is founded on the most powerful synthetic theory in the life sciences, and that it assumes that that theory applies to all domains of life—from the simplest patch of algae passively photosynthesizing on the ocean floor to the most complex behaviors of humans actively negotiating on the dance floor, Senate floor, or living room rug (all of which, as the prior discussion suggests, are connected). Hence, an understanding of evolutionary principles is an essential and central part of the emerging synthetic paradigm, which will reunite the behavioral and natural sciences.

## REFERENCES

Alcock, J. (1993). *Animal behavior* (5th ed.). Sunderland, MA: Sinauer.

Alexander, R. D., & Noonan, K. N. (1979). Concealment of ovulation, parental care, and human social evolution. In N. A. Chagnon & W. Irons (Eds.), *Evolutionary biology and human social behavior* (pp. 436–453). North Scituate, MA: Duxbury.

Allen, J. B., Kenrick, D. T., Linder, D. E., & McCall, M. A. (1989). Arousal and attraction: A response facilitation alternative to misattribution and negative reinforcement models. *Journal of Personality and Social Psychology, 57,* 261–270.

Bailey, J. M., Gaulin, S., Agyei, Y., & Gladue, B. A. (1994). Effects of gender and sexual orientation on evolutionarily relevant aspects of human mating psychology. *Journal of Personality and Social Psychology, 66,* 1081–1093.

Bailey, J. M., & Pillard, R. C. (1991). A genetic study of male sexual orientation. *Archives of General Psychiatry, 48,* 1089–1096.

Brewer, M. B., & Lui, L. N. (1989). The primacy of age and sex in the structure of person categories. *Social Cognition, 3,* 262–274.

Burnstein, E., Kitayama, S., & Crandall, C. (1994). *Journal of Personality and Social Psychology, 67,* 773–789.

Buss, D. M. (1989). Sex differences in human mate preferences: Evolutionary hypotheses tested in 37 cultures. *Behavioral and Brain Sciences, 12,* 1–49.

Buss, D. M. (1994). Evolutionary psychology: A new paradigm for psychological science. *Psychological Inquiry.*

Buss, D. M., & Schmitt, D. P. (1993). Sexual strategies theory: An evolutionary perspective on human mating. *Psychological Review, 100,* 204–232.

Byrne, D. (1971). *The attraction paradigm.* New York: Academic Press.

Byrne, D., & Clore, G. L. (1970). A reinforcement-affect model of evaluative responses. *Personality: An International Journal, 1,* 103–128.

Byrne, D., London, O., & Reeves, K. (1968). The effects of physical attractiveness, sex, and attitude similarity on interpersonal attraction. *Journal of Personality, 36,* 259–271.

Chaiken, S., Liberman, A., & Eagly, A. H. (1989). Heuristic and systematic information processing within and beyond the persuasion context. In J. S. Uleman & J. A. Bargh (Eds.), *Unintended thought* (pp. 212–252). New York: Guilford.

Chomsky, N. (1972). *Language and mind.* New York: Harcourt Brace.

Clark, R. D., & Hatfield, E. (1989). Gender differences in receptivity to sexual offers. *Journal of Psychology and Human Sexuality, 2,* 39–55.

Cosmides, L. (1994, August). *Emergence of evolutionary psychology.* Distinguished early career address, American Psychological Association, Los Angeles, CA.

Cosmides, L., & Tooby, J. (1989). Evolutionary psychology and the generation of culture: Part II. A computational theory of social exchange. *Ethology and Sociobiology, 10,* 51–97.

Crawford, C. B., & Anderson, J. L. (1989). Sociobiology: An environmentalist discipline. *American Psychologist, 44,* 1449–1459.

Daly, M., & Wilson, M. (1983). *Sex, evolution, and behavior* (2nd ed.), New York: Willard Grant Press.

Daly, M., & Wilson, M. (1988). *Homicide.* New York: Aldine deGruyter.

Damasio, A. R. (1985). Prosopagnosia. *Trends in Neuroscience, 8,* 132–135.

Darwin, C. (1872). *The expression of emotions in man and animals.* London: Murray.

DeSoto, C. B., Hamilton, M. M., & Taylor, R. B. (1985). Words, people, and implicit personality theory. *Social Cognition, 3,* 369–382.

Dutton, A., & Aron, A. (1974). Some evidence for heightened sexual attraction under conditions of high anxiety. *Journal of Personality and Social Psychology, 30,* 510–517.

Ekman, P. (1992). An argument for basic emotions. *Cognition and Emotion, 6,* 169–200.

Ekman, P., & Friesen, W. V. (1971). Constants across cultures in the face and emotion. *Journal of Personality and Social Psychology, 17,* 124–129.

Ellis, L., & Ames, M. A. (1987). Neurohormonal functioning and sexual orientation: A theory of homosexuality–heterosexuality. *Psychological Bulletin, 101,* 233–258.

Fiske, S. T., & Neuberg, S. L. (1990). A continuum of impression formation, from category-based to individuating processes: Influences of information and motivation on attention and interpretation. In M. P. Zanna (Ed.), *Advances in experimental social psychology* (Vol. 23, pp. 1–74). New York: Academic Press.

Gardner, H. (1985). *The mind's new science: A history of the cognitive revolution.* New York: Basic Books.

Gazzaniga, M. S. (1985). *The social brain: Discovering the networks of the mind.* New York: Basic Books.

Glass, A. L., & Holyoak, K. J. (1986). *Cognition* (2nd ed.). New York: Random House.

Goldberg, L. R. (1981). Language and individual differences: The search for universals in personality lexicons. In L. Wheeler (Ed.), *Personality and social psychology review* (Vol. 2, pp. 100–141). Beverly Hills, CA: Sage.

Gross, M. (1984). Sunfish, salmon, and the evolution of alternative reproductive strategies and tactics in fishes. In G. Potts & R. Wootton (Eds.), *Fish reproduction: Strategies and tactics* (pp. 55–75). New York: Academic Press.

Gurtman, M. B. (1992). Trust, distrust, and interpersonal problems: A circumplex analysis. *Journal of Personality and Social Psychology, 62,* 989–1002.

Gutierres, S. E., Kenrick, D. T., & Partch, J. (1994). *Effects of others' dominance and attractiveness on self-ratings.* Unpublished manuscript.

Hamilton, W. D. (1964). The genetical evolution of social behavior: I & II. *Journal of Theoretical Biology, 7,* 1–32.

Hansen, C. H., & Hansen, R. D. (1988). Finding faces in the crowd: An anger superiority effect. *Journal of Personality and Social Psychology, 54,* 917–924.

Hare-Mustin, R. T., & Marecek, J. (1990). *Making a difference: Psychology and the construction of gender.* New Haven, CT: Yale University Press.

Hastie, R., & Park, B. (1986). The relationship between memory and judgment depends on whether the judgment task is memory based or on-line. *Psychological Review, 93,* 258–268.

Hogan, R. (1982). A socioanalytic theory of personality. In M. Page (Ed.), *Nebraska symposium on motivation* (pp. 55–89). Lincoln: University of Nebraska Press.

Hubel, D. H., & Wiesel, T. N. (1959). Receptive fields of single neurons in the cat's striate cortex. *Journal of Physiology, 148,* 574–591.

Hubel, D. H., & Wiesel, T. N. (1962). Receptive fields, binocular interaction and functional architecture in the cat's visual cortex. *Journal of Physiology, 160,* 106–154.

Hubel, D. H., & Wiesel, T. N. (1979). Brain mechanisms in vision. *Scientific American, 241,* 250–263.

Izard, C. E. (1971). *The face of emotion.* New York: Appleton-Century-Crofts.

James, W. (1890). *The principles of psychology.* New York: Holt.

Kenrick, D. T. (1994). Evolutionary social psychology: From sexual selection to social cognition. In M. P. Zanna (Ed.), *Advances in experimental social psychology* (Vol. 26, pp. 75–122). San Diego, CA: Academic Press.

Kenrick, D. T., Gabrielidis, C., Keefe, R. C., & Cornelius, J. S. (1996). Adolescents' age preferences for dating partners: Support for an evolutionary life-history model of life-history strategies. *Child Development, 67,* 1499–1511.

Kenrick, D. T., Groth, G. E., Trost, M. R., & Sadalla, E. K. (1993). Integrating evolutionary and social exchange perspectives on relationships: Effects of gender, self-appraisal, and involvement level on mate selection criteria. *Journal of Personality and Social Psychology, 64,* 951–969.

Kenrick, D. T., & Gutierres, S. E. (1980). Contrast effects and judgments of physical attractiveness: When beauty becomes a social problem. *Journal of Personality and Social Psychology, 38,* 131–140.

Kenrick, D. T., Gutierres, S. E., & Goldberg, L. (1989). Influence of popular erotica on judgments of strangers and mates. *Journal of Experimental Social Psychology, 25,* 159–167.

Kenrick, D. T., & Hogan, R. (1991). Cognitive psychology. In M. Maxwell (Ed.), *The sociobiological imagination* (pp. 171–186). Albany, NY: SUNY Press.

Kenrick, D. T., & Keefe, R. C. (1992). Age preferences in mates reflect sex differences in human reproductive strategies. *Behavioral and Brain Sciences, 15,* 75–133.

Kenrick, D. T., Keefe, R. C., Bryan, A., Barr, A., & Brown, S. (1995). Age preferences and mate choice among homosexuals and heterosexuals: A case for modular psychological mechanisms. *Journal of Personality and Social Psychology, 69,* 1166–1172.

Kenrick, D. T., Montello, D. R., Gutierres, S. E., & Trost, M. R. (1993). Effects of physical attractiveness on affect and perceptual judgments: When social comparison overrides social reinforcement. *Personality and Social Psychology Bulletin, 19,* 195–199.

Kenrick, D. T., Neuberg, S. L., Zierk, K. L., & Krones, J. M. (1994). Evolution and social cognition: Contrast effects as a function of sex, dominance, and physical attractiveness. *Personality and Social Psychology Bulletin, 20,* 210–217.

Kenrick, D. T., Sadalla, E. K., Groth, G., & Trost, M. R. (1990) Evolution, traits, and the stages of human courtship: Qualifying the parental investment model. *Journal of Personality, 58,* 97–117.

Kenrick, D. T., & Sheets, V. (1994). Homicidal fantasies. *Ethology and Sociobiology, 14,* 231–246.

Kenrick, D. T., & Trost, M. R. (1989). A reproductive exchange model of heterosexual relationships: Putting proximate economics in ultimate perspective. In C. Hendrick (Ed.), *Review of personality and social psychology, 10. Close relationships* (pp. 92–118). Newbury Park, CA: Sage.

Lancaster, J. B. (1976). *Primate behavior and the emergence of human culture.* New York: Holt.

Lashley, K. S. (1929). *Brain mechanisms and intelligence.* Chicago: University of Chicago Press.

Leary, M. R., Tambor, E. S., Terdal, S. K., & Downs, D. L. (1995). Self-esteem as an interpersonal monitor: The sociometer hypothesis. *Journal of Personality and Social Psychology, 68,* 518–530.

Lehrman, D. S. (1966). The reproductive behavior of ring doves. In S. Coopersmith (Ed.), *Frontiers of psychological research* (pp. 18–24). San Francisco: Freeman.

Lettvin, J. Y., Maturana, H. R., McCulloch, W. S., & Pitts, W. H. (1959). What the frog's eye tells the frog's brain. *Proceedings of the Institute of Radio Engineers, 47*, 1940–1951.

LeVay, S. (1993). *The sexual brain.* Cambridge, MA: MIT Press.

Livingstone, M., & Hubel, D. (1988). Segregation of form, color, movement, and depth: Anatomy, physiology, and perception. *Science, 240*, 740–749.

Lockard, J. S. (1988). Origins of self-deception: Is lying to oneself uniquely human? In J. S. Lockard & D. L. Paulhus (Eds.), *Self-deception: An adaptive mechanism?* (pp. 14–39). Englewood Cliffs, NJ: Prentice-Hall.

Lott, A. J., & Lott, B. E. (1974). The role of reward in the formation of positive interpersonal attitudes. In T. L. Huston (Ed.), *Foundations of interpersonal attraction* (pp. 171–192). New York: Academic Press.

Lumsden, C. J., & Wilson, E. O. (1981). *Genes, mind, and culture: The coevolutionary process.* Cambridge, MA: Harvard University Press.

Markus, H., & Zajonc, R. B. (1985). The cognitive perspective in social psychology. In G. Lindzey & E. Aronson (Eds.), *Handbook of social psychology* (Vol. 1, pp. 137–230). New York: Random House.

Martindale, C. (1980). Subselves. In L. Wheeler (Ed.), *Review of personality and social psychology* (pp. 193–218). Beverly Hills, CA: Sage.

Martindale, C. (1991). *Cognitive psychology: A neural-network approach.* Pacific Grove, CA: Brooks/Cole.

Matlin, M. W., & Foley, H. J. (1992). *Sensation and perception* (3rd ed.). Boston: Allyn & Bacon.

McCrae, R. R., & John, O. P. (1992). An introduction to the five-factor model and its applications. *Journal of Personality, 60*, 175–216.

McDougall, W. (1908). *Social psychology: An introduction.* London: Methuen.

Nisbett, R. E., & Wilson, T. (1977). Telling more than we know: Verbal reports on mental processes. *Psychological Review, 84*, 231–259.

Petty, R. E., & Cacioppo, J. T. (1986). The elaboration likelihood model of persuasion. In L. Berkowitz (Ed.), *Advances in experimental social psychology* (Vol. 19, pp. 123–205). New York: Academic Press.

Pinker, S. (1994). *The language instinct.* New York: William Morrow.

Plutchik, R. (1980). A general psychoevolutionary theory of emotion. In R. Plutchik, & H. Kellerman (Eds.), *Emotion: Theory, research, and experience* (Vol. 1, pp. 3–32). New York: Academic Press.

Pratto, F., & John, O. P. (1991). Automatic vigilance: The attention-grabbing power of negative social information. *Journal of Personality and Social Psychology, 61*, 380–391.

Reisenzein, R. (1983). The Shacter theory of emotion: Two decades later. *Psychological Bulletin, 94*, 239–264.

Rosch, E. (1974). Linguistic relativity. In A. Silverstein (Ed.), *Human communication: Theoretical perspectives* (pp. 95–112). New York: Halsted.

Sadalla, E. K., Kenrick, D. T., & Vershure, B. (1987). Dominance and heterosexual attraction. *Journal of Personality and Social Psychology, 52*, 730–738.

Schachter, S., & Singer, J. E. (1962). Cognitive, social, and physiological determinants of emotional state. *Psychological Review, 69*, 379–399.

Scott, J. P. (1980). The function of emotions in behavioral systems: A systems theory analysis. In R. Plutchik & H. Kellerman (Eds.), *Emotion: Theory, research, and experience* (Vol. 1, pp. 35–56). New York: Academic Press.

Shepher, J. (1971). Mate selection among second generation kibbutz adolescents and adults: Incest avoidance and negative imprinting. *Archives of Sexual Behavior, 1*, 293–307.

Sherry, D. F., & Schacter, D. L. (1987). The evolution of multiple memory systems. *Psychological Review, 94*, 439–454.

Shiffrin, R. M., & Schneider, W. (1977). Controlled and automatic human information processing: II. Perceptual learning, automatic attending, and a general theory. *Psychological Review, 84,* 127–190.

Skinner, B. F. (1953). *Science and human behavior.* New York: The Free Press.

Symons, D. (1987). If we're all Darwinians, what's the fuss about? In C. B. Crawford, M. F. Smith, & D. L. Krebs (Eds.), *Sociobiology and psychology: Ideas, issues, and applications* (pp. 121–146). Hillsdale, NJ: Lawrence Erlbaum Associates.

Tolman, E. C., & Brunswick, E. (1935). The organism and the causal texture of the environment. *Psychological Review, 42,* 43–77.

Tooby, J., & Cosmides, L. (1992). The psychological foundations of culture. In J. H. Barkow, L. Cosmides, & J. Tooby (Eds.), *The adapted mind: Evolutionary psychology and the generation of culture* (pp. 19–136). New York: Oxford University Press.

Townsend, J. M., & Levy, G. D. (1990). Effects of potential partner's costume and physical attractiveness on sexuality and partner selection: Sex differences in reported preferences of university students. *Journal of Psychology, 124,* 371–376.

Trivers, R. L. (1985). *Social evolution.* Menlo Park, CA: Benjamin/Cummings.

Trost, M. R., Maass, A., & Kenrick, D. T. (1992). Minority influence: Personal relevance biases cognitive processes and reverses private acceptance. *Journal of Experimental Social Psychology, 28,* 234–254.

Whitam, F. L., Diamond, M., & Martin, J. (1993). Homosexual orientation in twins: A report on 61 pairs and three triplet sets. *Archives of Sexual Behavior, 22,* 187–206.

White, G. M. (1980). Conceptual universals in interpersonal language. *American Anthropologist, 82,* 759–781.

Wiggins, J. S., & Broughton, R. (1985). The interpersonal circle: A structural model for the integration of personality research. In R. Hogan & W. H. Jones (Eds.), *Perspectives in personality* (Vol. 1, pp. 1–48). Greenwich, CT: JAI.

Wyer, R. S., & Srull, T. K. (1986). Human cognition in its social context. *Psychological Review, 93,* 322–359.

# 17

## Evolutionary Psychology and Sexual Aggression

Neil M. Malamuth
Mario F. Heilmann
*University of California, Los Angeles*

The evolutionary history of our species has provided an important framework for understanding sexual coercion (Crawford, 1989; Shields & Shields, 1983; Thornhill & Thornhill, 1983). Such coercion is not unique to the human species and is found in a wide range of other species, including those most similar to us (Clutton-Brock & Parker, 1995; Smuts, 1992). The evolutionary approach generally places coercive sexuality within the framework of various strategies involving self-interested manipulative and dishonest strategies that would have, directly or indirectly, increased reproductive success in Pleistocene environments.

Whenever two individuals have divergent interests, tactics such as violence and/or deceit often occur. Human sexual coercion is typically perpetrated by males. Acts such as rape circumvent a female's choice by forcing her to copulate with a male she would have otherwise not chosen to mate with. Female sexual choice is also commonly restricted by fathers, brothers, husbands, other females' jealousy, and even laws. Although such restrictions may not be considered comparable to coerced sex, the important point is that they are also examples of others' self-interest restricting female sexual choices.

The present chapter presents an overview of general evolutionary theory directly relevant to the topic of sexual aggression. It includes in this section brief discussions of evolutionary psychology's approach to studying individual and gender differences. Next, it considers the literature regarding forced copulation in other species. Finally, it proposes an

515

evolutionarily based model of the characteristics of human sexual aggressors and examines recent data pertaining to this model.

## EVOLUTIONARY PSYCHOLOGY

Evolutionary psychology applies current knowledge of evolutionary processes to understanding the human mind[1] and behavior. Darwin's evolutionary theory posits that living organisms are formed by natural selection. Evolution is a continuous process of differential reproductive success, whereby certain design differences are transmitted to subsequent generations. Within the past two to three decades, considerable strides have been made within this field that enable better understanding of humans and their social interactions (Buss, 1995; Crawford, 1989).

As noted earlier, the basic underlying force that designed the human mind is natural selection (i.e., reproductive success, or *fitness*). According to evolutionary psychology, to understand the human mind today, it is essential to analyze the psychological mechanisms (i.e., information-processing algorithms or decision rules) that evolved in ancestral environments.[2] These mechanisms continue to guide our reactions (i.e., emotions, thoughts, behaviors) in contemporary environments. According to the version of evolutionary psychology emphasized here, the mind is composed of many domain-specific[3] mechanisms, rather than general mechanisms relevant to many domains (Buss, 1995; Cosmides & Tooby, 1987). Although under ancestral environments these mechanisms contributed to reproductive success and were therefore transmitted to subsequent generations, in current environments they may or may not contribute to any type of success. Although the mind was designed by natural selection processes operating in ancestral environments to promote fitness, people are not presumed to consciously strive to achieve the goal of fitness. In

---

[1]The brain describes the physiological entity, whereas the mind is denominated as the psychological entity.

[2]Current environments in modern technological societies are radically different in many respects from the type of environments that were a relatively stable feature during most of human evolutionary development. Although evolutionary processes continue, of course, in current environments, the processes of natural selection typically take many generations to significantly change features of the human mind. Therefore, evolutionary psychology contends that it is particularly important to historically contextualize the development of the mind within ancestral environments, sometimes referred to as environment of evolutionary adaptedness (EEA).

[3]A *domain* refers to an area where a problem occurs that requires some adaptive solution. Examples of domains include problems of how to regulate body heat, how to differentiate allies from enemies, how to detect cheaters, how to fight parasites, how to obtain mates, how to obtain food, and so on.

other words, people do not consciously choose their actions to promote fitness. Rather, the types of mind mechanisms that evolved in ancestral environments, and that can be activated in current environments, were naturally selected because, in those earlier environments, they had fitness-favoring consequences.

Adaptations are responses that were naturally selected for (i.e., increased reproductive success) in the evolutionary history of our species. Human responses may be adaptations, by-products of adaptations, or noise (e.g., mutations, genetic drift, etc.). Much effort is directed within this approach to understanding which of these three possibilities particular behaviors represent by formulating testable hypotheses (Buss, 1995). Because a behavior may have been adaptive in evolutionary environments, and therefore, contributed to the current structure of the mind, does not mean that such a behavior is desirable, moral, or inevitable.

One of the fallacies about this approach is that it suggests that humans are hard wired or do not make choices. On the contrary, evolutionary approaches focus on the interaction between organisms and their environments, and how organisms change their behavior in different environments (Crawford & Anderson, 1989). In humans, behavior is viewed as highly flexible, in that the mind is very much attuned to situational information and can take a variety of forms precisely because we have complex, situation-contingent psychological mechanisms. In our species, social interactions are a crucial part of the environment. Cultures that humans create reflect characteristics of the human mind and also shape the behaviors that are elicited in social environments.

It is important to note that the question is not whether evolutionary principles apply to human behavior and the psychology underlying it, but which evolutionary model is more accurate (Symons, 1992). The only alternatives offered to the theory that humans evolved by the same principles as other species is the belief that God created us or that we were planted here by some extraterrestrial beings (Buss, 1990). No other viable scientific theory currently exists regarding the origins of life and of the human mind. Within the evolutionary framework, however, there are various alternatives. One difference in evolutionary-based models is between those conceptualizing the human mind as a general information processor and those emphasizing specific mechanisms relevant to particular domains. Similarly, there may be various competing minitheories to explain any particular phenomenon, all derived from the evolutionary metatheory. These are then tested empirically to evaluate which best fits the data. Theories emphasizing the role of learning or culture are not alternatives to theories encompassing the role of evolutionary processes because what can be learned and how learning takes place are determined by the characteristics of the evolved mind of a species. Rather, learning theories are focusing on one aspect of a more comprehensive model of human nature and its interaction with the environment. Such a comprehensive theory needs to incorporate understanding of the "design" of the mind, as formed by evolutionary processes, as it interacts with the physical and social environment, including the cultures created by those minds (Buss, 1990, 1995).[4]

## Emphasis on Function

According to evolutionary psychology, therefore, to understand our reactions (i.e., emotions, thoughts, behaviors) in contemporary environments, it is essential to analyze the function of the psychological mechanisms that evolved in ancestral environments and continue to guide our behavior today. The mechanisms and what type of environmental input they can process and are responsive to are the result of evolutionary processes. In other words, they are not two separable causal processes, but rather elements of the same evolved package (Tooby & Cosmides, 1990). The function of psychological mechanisms cannot be understood just in terms of current environments. Human psychological mechanisms, comprising the complex architecture of the mind, developed to their present form in ancestral environments, and have undergone only minor changes since then (Cosmides & Tooby, 1987).

All theories of human behavior and the workings of the mind, including those that focus only on the impact of the environment, assume the existence of psychological mechanisms, although this is often not explicitly recognized (Quine, 1981). Moreover, researching the reasons for the particular design or architecture of the mind within the framework of the problems they were a solution to provides an understanding of the features of the mind that are not likely be understood without asking the question "Why would that design have been selected for rather than the other one?" (Cosmides & Tooby, 1996, p. 10).

## Individual Differences

Evolutionary psychologists have generally focused on species-typical mechanisms because evolutionary selective pressures[5] have been essen-

---

[4]Using the analogy of a computer program, it is only possible to understand how the input to the program affects the output by understanding the underlying rules of the program governing how input may be processed.

[5]The term *selective pressures* refers to natural selection favoring particular characteristics. For example, if females choose relatively intelligent males as mates, thereby resulting in a correlation between males' intelligence levels and their reproductive success, then there are selective pressures for more intelligent males.

tially the same for all humans in most domains where problem-solving adaptations occurred (e.g., how to regulate heat, how to detect cheaters, etc.; Tooby & Cosmides, 1990). However, the behavioral manifestations of these mechanisms are not invariant or fixed. Such mechanisms process environmental information (e.g., the likely consequences of various behaviors). Their expression (in behavior) is expected to vary with the nature of the environment, both developmentally and contemporarily. To understand individual differences, evolutionary psychologists therefore generally focus on ontogenetic experiences and ongoing environmental variation (Buss, 1990, 1991). In addition, they may consider the role of genetic differences, including their interaction with environmental factors.

Although a discussion of genetic variability that might contribute to individual differences in sexual aggression is beyond the scope of the present chapter, this chapter considers the role of some ontogenetic experiences, as well as ongoing environmental variation or long-term role occupancy. Illustrations of the latter concept may be needed. Consider the example of a man who is married to a woman who gets a great deal of attention from other men. He may be frequently showing jealousy, as compared with a man whose wife seldom receives much attention. Both, however, may have the same underlying jealousy mechanisms (Buss, 1991). A man who is frequently rejected by women may appear to be habitually feeling rejected, as compared with one who is seldom rejected. Individual differences in feeling rejected are not necessarily due to inherited or developmental differences (although these can directly or indirectly be contributors as well), but to being frequently in recurring environmental conditions that activate the relevant mechanisms. However, the threshold for activation of the mechanisms may become adjusted or recalibrated. In the prior example, the man may become relatively prone to perceiving rejection or being suspicious of women's intentions, so that he indeed feels rejected in circumstances that would not elicit that reaction in other men (Malamuth & Brown, 1994).

## Sex Differences

One important class of individual differences is sex differences. Females and males are expected to have the same psychological mechanisms in those domains where natural selection processes favored the same solutions to adaptive problems for all humans, regardless of their gender. Correspondingly, in some domains, the problems faced in evolutionary history by males were not identical to those faced by females. In this case, mechanisms are expected to have evolved differently because the identical solution or strategy for the different sexes would not be optimal for dissimilar problems (Buss, 1994). One of these areas is sexuality, where the differing natural selection processes for males and females resulted in sexual dimorphism in relevant psychological mechanisms (Buss & Schmitt, 1993).

## Evolutionary Psychology and Aggression

Before turning to specifically focus on the topic of sexual aggression, it is important to briefly consider an evolutionary-based perspective on aggression generally. Other models have often conceptualized aggression as a form of pathology because of the terrible harm and suffering that it can cause. From an evolutionary model, pathological behavior involves the failure of a set of mechanisms to function in the way they were designed by evolutionary forces, due to such factors as decay or subversion by competitive forms of life (e.g., viruses). Aggressive behavior generally does not reveal such characteristics, nor does it seem to be a by-product of other adaptations. Instead, aggression shows characteristics of functional design, revealing an evolved adaptation that resulted in fitness-promoting consequences for the aggressing individuals, at least in some recurring ancestral environments (Daly & Wilson, 1994).[6]

## RAPE IN OTHER SPECIES

This section illustrates various patterns in sexual coercion across differing species. Sexual dimorphism in physiological mechanisms is very frequent in nature. In many species, including the human species, males possess, on average, greater strength, size, and fighting abilities than females of the same species. These and other characteristics create in a male a capacity for coercion, which may be used to his reproductive advantage. Not only can he aggress against other males to restrict their sexual choices, but he can also restrict female sexual choice by preventing her from copulating with other males of her choosing or by forcing her to copulate with him, even if she would otherwise not choose to do so. As an example of the former, high-ranking chimpanzees routinely interfere in sex acts of females with lower ranking males (Smuts, 1992). The latter—male use of forced copulation—has been observed in a number of species.[7] In some

---

[6]The evolutionary analysis of the functions of aggression might be compared to pain. In terms of ultimate causes, the ability to experience pain clearly has been naturally selected for in our species. Yet, many individuals suffer greatly from pain in various situations that do not appear to have anything to do with increased fitness or even increased likelihood of survival.

[7]*Forced copulation* is a term used by biologists. It is preferred by some scholars because it does not have the legal and emotional connotations of the word *rape* (Palmer, 1989). The present chapter interchangeably uses terms such as *coercive sex, rape, forced sex,* and *sexual aggression.*

species, the data support the view that forced copulation is an adaptation for males. In others, the data are more consistent with forced copulation being a by-product of a general hypersexuality of males. Yet in other species, some researchers have argued that forced copulation might even be an adaptation for females. It seems that, in the majority of species, forced copulations do not occur.

### Rape as a Male Adaptation

Proving the existence of a specialized psychological mechanism for rape is very difficult. In many species, it cannot be clearly determined whether rape is an adaptation or a by-product of other mechanisms. The Panorpa scorpionfly is easier to categorize because the male has a physiological adaptation—a dorsal clamp—that seems to serve the sole purpose of holding onto a reluctant female and raping her. Experimental inactivation of the clamp inhibits the completion of rape, but no other functions (Thornhill, 1980; Thornhill & Thornhill, 1987). Panorpa males use rape only as a mating strategy of last resort. Females successfully escape most of these attempts. Even after completed forced copulations, reproductive success is low because only 50% of the females become fertilized. These lay fewer eggs and return to sexual receptivity earlier than after consensual copulations. This is partly because a female without the nuptial food offering is not as well nourished. Additionally, low fertility and faster receptivity to new fertilization may be a female counterstrategy to rape, thus making it the male's least preferred strategy. Interference, which occurs in species such as ducks, may consist of males attempting to block rapes of their female partners. It is probably another important factor that renders forced copulations more costly and less beneficial, and thus less likely. It is probable that in species where rape does not occur at all, the counterstrategies of the female and of her mate reliably prevent rape or even prevented it from ever evolving as a mechanism in that species (see Clutton-Brock & Parker's, 1995, mathematical model of the costs and benefits of animal rape or harassment attempts and of female resistance).

Panorpa females prefer males who can offer a dead insect to her as a nuptial gift, and typically choose to mate with such males. Males compete viciously for dead insects, and consequently, they have greater mortality than females. They not only risk injury in fighting, but also risk being caught in spider webs while seeking the nuptial offering. Alternatively, males who possess no insect, but are well nourished, may secrete a nutritious salivary mass as an offer to the female. Both these nutrient offerings increase female reproductive fitness. As a third alternative, Panorpa scorpionfly males attempt forced copulation. A later section discusses the type of algorithm or program that may guide human males in terms of coercive sexual behavior. The algorithm underlying the Panorpa scorpionfly's behavior is an environmentally contingent one and quite complicated. It might be organized as follows: (a) If the physical environment, male competition, and your prowess allow, get an insect offering; (b) If this is not possible, try to get well nourished and secrete a salivary mass to attract females; and (c) Only as a last resort, if neither is possible, attempt to copulate by force. Cosmides and Tooby (1987) presented an excellent discussion of the importance of analyzing cognitive programs within an evolutionary framework.

### Rape as By-Product of Other Mechanisms

Interspecies rapes are reported among some marine mammals. Copulation with a female of the wrong species cannot be an adaptation that contributed to anyone's reproductive success because no pregnancy can result.[8] Rather, such acts appear to clearly constitute side effects, probably a by-product of the low threshold of male sexual arousal that is calibrated to ensure that opportunities with potential mates are not missed (see Palmer, 1989, for more examples and a fuller discussion of this issue).

### Rape as a Female Selection Device

In elephant seals, much protest on the part of the female seems to be a species-typical precopulatory behavior. In this species, rape is the most common type of copulation. Cox and LeBoeuf (1977) considered rape to be a reproductive tactic of these females. The delay and commotion caused by her whipping her hindquarters from side to side and trying to escape calls the attention of other males. A lower ranking bull would be disturbed and displaced by a higher ranking one. Only the highest ranking bull around can proceed without interference.

### Species Without Coerced Sexuality

Although the majority of species do not appear to use forced copulations, the relevant literature seldom discusses such cases. Typically, researchers do not focus on nonevents like absence of rape. An exception is the article by McKinney, Derrickson, and Mineau (1983), who, in the context of reporting on duck species where forced copulations are rampant, also

---

[8]Similarly, homosexual rape among humans obviously does not lead to immediate reproductive advantage. Homosexual rape is mostly perpetrated by males, particularly in unusual environments, such as prisons. Its occurrence might be due to dominance mechanisms or an unintended side effect of other mechanisms. The evolutionary literature focusing on the potential causes of homosexuality (e.g., Bailey, Gaulin, Agyei, & Gladue, 1994; Dickemann, 1993; Weinrich, 1987) might be relevant to this issue as well.

discussed closely related duck species where forced copulation does not seem to occur. It also seems to be absent in swans and most geese.

The issue of absence of rape is further complicated because, on the one hand, female coyness and male aggressiveness are found in many species, and, on the other hand, what looks like consensual sex may have some coercive elements. For example, chimpanzees rarely use aggression during the sexual act, but often use "a fair amount of brutality" to intimidate estrous females (Goodall, 1986, p. 453). A female that seems to follow willingly on a sexual foray into the forest might have been punished by the male when she resisted previously. If resistance is obviously fruitless or too costly, selection could favor females yielding to such a male without any resistance. Cost can also be inflicted on offspring. For example, a female snow goose will not resist a forced copulation while she sits on her fragile eggs (Mineau & Cooke, 1979).

### Forced Copulation in Animals as a Model for Human Rape?

General evolutionary theory deduces that rape may evolve in a species when the reproductive advantage to the perpetrator is greater than his cost, and when the parties who suffer reproductive disadvantage—namely, the female and her mate—did not evolve a highly effective counterstrategy.

Crawford and Galdikas (1986) suggest some relevant factors that make rape more likely. Heavy male parental investment, like the Panorpa nuptial gift or parental care in ducks, yields a reproductive advantage to the forced copulator who avoids the costly investment. Male size and aggressiveness, as well as female social isolation (e.g., in orangutans) also facilitate rape. Nevertheless, so far, no comprehensive model has been developed that can explain or predict in which species rape will or will not occur. Only a comparative model that "could uncover the ecological factor(s) associated with the presence and absence of rape-specific male and female (counter-rape) adaptation across species" would be relevant for the understanding of human rape (Thornhill & Thornhill, 1992, p. 415). Moreover, theory about human rape must be guided by studies on humans.

## AN EVOLUTIONARY-BASED MODEL OF HUMAN SEXUAL AGGRESSORS

This section attempts to outline an evolutionary-based model of the characteristics of sexual coercers. Although various ideas are drawn from the writings of other researchers, the model presented contains some new elements not described elsewhere.

Thornhill and Thornhill (1987) proposed that human rape can be considered an evolved behavior that "is employed by men who are unable to compete for resources and status necessary to attract and reproduce successfully with desirable mates" (p. 275). It appears quite clear that a literal interpretation of this assertion, which might be labeled the simple *rapist as loser hypothesis*, is incorrect. For example, there are a variety of studies (e.g., Kanin, 1977, 1984; Malamuth, Sockloskie, Koss, & Tanaka, 1991) that show that, in comparison with their less aggressive counterparts, sexually aggressive men often begin to have sexual intercourse earlier in life, have more sexual partners throughout the life course, and may consider themselves no less successful in their ability to attract females. Although the underlying logic of the prior mating hypothesis may have some merit, it is clear that it requires some additional development to account for much of the available data in this area.

It is suggested here that three types of mechanisms may be directly relevant to male use of aggression or coercion against females in the sexual domain. These are the mechanisms underlying sexuality, mechanisms guiding coercion, and those underlying dominance of the opposite gender.[9] The first class of mechanisms is largely independent from the other two, which are hypothesized to be interrelated to one another and are discussed together here using the label *dominance/hostility mechanisms*.

## Mechanisms Underlying Sexuality

The psychological mechanisms governing male sexuality are not the same as those guiding female sexuality, due to the different reproductive consequences for the two genders, in ancestral environments, of sexual behavior. These created differences in which type of "mating strategies" were most adaptive for each gender (Symons, 1979).

These differences in mating strategies can be traced to the minimum parental investment required to produce an offspring (Trivers, 1972). In our species, the parental investment required to produce offspring is much greater for females (i.e., 9 months vs. 9 minutes). Given that females can only produce a maximum of about 20 offspring in a lifetime, having sex with a relatively large number of males is unlikely to have adaptive advantages. It is generally far better to invest more in each offspring by carefully selecting a mate with good genes who will participate in the raising of the offspring. In contrast, for males, having intercourse with a larger number of fertile females is likely to be correlated with reproductive

---

[9]Independently of the line of research described later, Ellis (1989) also proposed that rape is motivated by "the sex drive and the drive to possess and control (especially in regard to sex partners)" (p. 104). There are several important differences between the model developed here and that of Ellis. A discussion of the similarities and differences is beyond the scope of this chapter.

success because, in ancestral environments, contraceptive devices were not available, and the upper limit for siring offspring is in the thousands.[10] Therefore, even totally uninvested sex may have favorable reproductive consequences (Buss, 1994).

In light of these differences, men and women differ considerably in their orientation to "impersonal sexuality" (i.e., sex not associated with affection and bonding, which typically characterize long-term relationships; Symons, 1979). Although males are capable of "personal sex" involving "bonding" emotions such as love, the psychological mechanisms underlying their sexual behavior also foster impersonal sex to a greater degree than females. Similarly, although females are capable of impersonal sexuality, their psychological mechanisms are relatively more consonant with personal sex.

If male sexuality were unconstrained by other mechanisms processing information regarding real-life exigencies, such as competition and threats from other men, rejection by females, and limited resources, the mechanisms governing this domain would result in sex with many more fertile women. Such desires are indeed revealed in the type of sexually explicit mass media men prefer, as compared with women. Just as candy created by a modern company is capitalizing on the evolutionary-based mechanisms of taste, so is the mass media capitalizing on the evolutionary-based male and female mechanisms of sexuality (Ellis & Symons, 1990; Malamuth, 1996b).

Although men's sexuality mechanisms may be relatively primed to take advantage of both short- and long-term mating opportunities, and women's mechanisms are relatively more oriented to take advantage of the latter, individual differences within each gender are certainly expected. Particularly relevant here, as suggested later, are certain ontogenetic experiences that may result among men in differing degrees of relatively short- (i.e., impersonal) versus long-term mating strategies.

## Sexuality Mechanisms and Sexual Coercion

It may be said that the sexuality mechanisms in the minds of men "set the stage" for the occurrence of coercive sexuality, although an impersonal sexual orientation is by no means necessarily associated with forced sex. Because of their greater capacity for impersonal sex, men can be fully sexually functional in the face of an unwilling sexual partner who has no

---

[10]These generalizations are, of course, oversimplifying some complexities. For example, females may prefer to mate with males who show signs of willingness to commit to monogamous relationships. Therefore, a man who develops a reputation for being highly promiscuous may not be chosen as a mate by some females, thereby creating a selection pressure for males who are not taking advantage of every mating opportunity.

emotional desire for or bonds with the male (e.g., Malamuth & Check, 1983). Under certain circumstances, if the risk of punishment or loss of reputation is low, the progeny of such sex could contribute to the man's reproductive success, in addition to the reproductive success he might have through intercourse with willing partners. In speculating about the potential reproductive costs and benefits in ancestral environments, we might note that the reproductive loss could be very high if aggressing sexually were followed by retribution, such as the killing of the rapist by the woman or her relatives. Paul Abramson (personal communication, on August 5, 1995) suggests that, in contrast, the reproductive benefits of a single act of rape are likely to be low because a single instance of consenting sexual intercourse has only a slight chance of resulting in pregnancy. Considering that the environment is not very conducive to the survival of a child conceived by rape, this would predict that the average male would resort to rape only when the chances of detection and punishment are small. The reproductive benefit is much higher in the case of repeated rape, as it might occur in the rape abductions mentioned in Chagnon (1994).

The male potential for coercive sex is not simply a function of body differences, such as physical strength or anatomical ability to penetrate, as emphasized by some feminists (e.g., Brownmiller, 1975). It may be just as feasible for a woman to coerce a man to engage in oral sex by threatening him with a gun as for a man to similarly coerce a woman. There is also a crucial difference of minds. Even in situations where the potential for females to coerce males is as high as for males to coerce females, it is expected that gender differences will occur even if males and females were raised in the identical environments. This is particularly true when environmental conditions are conducive to coercive sex. War time is a good example (Brownmiller, 1975). For instance, in the recent conflict in Bosnia, many men raped women, but it is doubtful that many women coerced men. These men were, in most cases, probably unlikely to commit such atrocities under peace-time conditions. Similarly, in Japan, a country where the known rate of rape is very low under peacetime conditions, during World War II, very large numbers of men had coercive sex with Korean women.

Overall, the evolutionary approach suggests that the highly controversial assertion made by some feminists that "all men are real or potential rapists" (Clark & Lewis, 1977, p. 140) has some validity, although individual differences among men in activation of the relevant mechanisms would clearly be important. This approach provides a theoretical basis for explaining the huge gender differences that exist in sexual aggression by consideration of the "functional design" of the mind resulting from fitness consequences in ancestral environments. In some environmental conditions, "fitness benefits" may have accrued for males who might sexually coerce females, but the fitness benefits to females using such coercion against males would be relatively rare.

Individual differences among men in their proneness to impersonal sexuality would be expected to help predict their likelihood of engaging in coercion, particularly in the context of an environment that discourages such acts. In such an environment, the role of other mechanisms that interact with the sexuality mechanisms may be particularly important.

## Mechanisms Underlying Dominance/Hostility

Conflict often occurs in the context of human interactions. From the perspective of evolutionary psychology, conflict between individuals is related to the degree to which their reproductive interests are at odds (e.g., Alexander, 1979; Hamilton, 1964). Coercion is one of the tactics that may be used to deal with conflict. Coercion typically involves using force to attain one's interests at the expense of others. The human system appears to include an interrelated network of responses (Berkowitz, 1993), including emotions (e.g., anger, hostility, jealousy, and so on), attitudes (e.g., acceptance of the use of violence), and motor tendencies (e.g., impulsivity) that may be mobilized to activate coercive tactics, such as violence that may be used to overcome blocked goals.

Buss (1989) studied one important aspect of such a hypothesized network of responses. His work focused on the sources of male and female anger and upset as part of analyzing conflict between the sexes. He provided support for the hypothesis that both sexes will be angered by aspects of the other sex's evolutionary-based reproductive strategy that conflict with their own sex's reproductive strategy. In the case of males, these include females' selectively withholding of sex from them. Negative emotions such as anger are hypothesized to serve as signals that cause people to act in ways that reduce others' interference with their own reproductive strategies. When such negative emotions occur recurrently and/or at critical stages in one's development, they may lead to a relatively fixed hostile personality. Such a personality, calibrated to respond relatively violently to even mild provocations, can be adaptive within the context of certain threatening environments, although it can obviously be counterproductive when individuals are no longer in such environments.

Within the evolutionary framework, one important source of potential conflict between male and female interests stems from male uncertainty of parenthood. Because only females give birth to children, a male may be uncertain that a child being born was conceived by him, whereas the woman can be certain that the child she is giving birth to was conceived

by her. Consequently, natural selection operated on those male characteristics that served to increase the likelihood that the men are investing
in their own offspring. If a man had intercourse with more than one
woman prior to each becoming pregnant, it did not affect the maternity
certainty of each woman. However, if a woman had intercourse with
more than one man prior to her becoming pregnant, it reduced the
paternal certainty of each of the men. This resulted in the evolution within
the male mind of a psychology with greater proprietary feelings. Men are
predicted to be more likely to dominate, monopolize, and control the
sexuality of women. The extent to which men try to accomplish this and
the methods they use differ, depending on social conditions, but the
underlying psychological mechanisms are universal in male minds (Daly
& Wilson, 1987; Symons, 1979; Wilson & Daly, 1992).

### Dominance/Hostility Mechanisms and Sexual Coercion

Although males may be motivated to dominate the sexual behavior of
women directly, they may also be motivated to control other facets of
women's lives, such as who women interact with, because this increases
their ability to control the women's sexual behavior.

As indicated earlier, an interrelated network of characteristics (Berkowitz, 1993) may be mobilized when a man perceives blocked access to a
desired female or impediments to dominating her.[11] These may be become
relatively fixed or characterological (i.e., occupancy of role) if such perceived experiences occur at critical periods in one's development and are
sufficiently recurrent. Such responses may have had reproductive consequences for some men in ancestral environments by limiting female
choice, just as rage that energized violence in response to a perceived
threat by a competitor may have also had improved fitness in these
environments.

### Integrating Different Mechanisms

Evolutionary psychologists have sought to determine whether mechanisms affecting sexual coercion are the result of the direct consequences
of rape on fitness (i.e., an adaptation) or incidental by-products (i.e., side
effects) of other mechanisms that relate to general sexual or coercive
strategies designed to promote benefits and reduce costs. The question
has been addressed by focusing on both perpetrators (Thornhill & Thornhill, 1992) and victims (Thornhill & Thornhill, 1990). It is also essential to

---

[11]The emphasis here is on a person's perceptions or feelings, rather than on the objective
situation. Thus, a man who feels relatively entitled to be desired by various women may
feel more rejected in the same situation than a man who does not have a feeling of entitlement.

consider whether the integration or interaction of different mechanisms may have their own fitness consequences. It may be that natural selection processes operate at the level of specific mechanisms. However, they may also operate at the level of the interaction or integration of different mechanisms, conferring on each a further fitness benefit. Consider, as an analogy, the modularity of the brain in the area of vision. It has been well established that there is a high level of specialization of modules for perception (e.g., form, color, movement, and so on) and comprehension—processes that occur simultaneously (Zeki, 1992). Each of these mechanisms is controlled by different areas in the brain. The functioning of each mechanism may be impaired independently of the mechanisms with which it integrates (Restak, 1994). Fitness advantages are likely to occur at the level of the integrated act, which combines activities of the separate units involved in vision as well as at the level of individual mechanisms (Malamuth, 1996a).

With respect to rape, researchers continue to debate whether such coercion was likely to have had direct fitness consequences in ancestral environments. Some evolutionary psychologists posit on reasons why such consequences may not have occurred (e.g., Symons, 1979). However, it is useful to consider more complex models that include algorithms, which allow for flexibility and take into account men's alternative strategies in the face of different environmental experiences or input. For example, in discussing why rape may not have fitness consequences, Symons (1979) indicated that a female's best choice is often a male who succeeds in competition with other males, and successful males are most likely to be her suitors. He suggested a linear correlation between opportunities to mate with females and being successful in fitness terms without resorting to the use of force against females. Such a model does not incorporate nonlinear relationships, whereby for males who were relatively unsuccessful in attracting females (perhaps at critical stages relatively early in life), the algorithms affecting sexual arousal and other processes may be altered more in favor of coercive sex because for them such a strategy may indeed have had better fitness consequences in ancestral environments.[12] Similarly, men may benefit from using "mixed" mating strategies. These could include having mutually consenting sex with some women, such as members of one's own tribe, and having coercive sex with other women, such as those abducted from neighboring groups. Such abduction seems to have been quite common in our species' evolutionary history (Chagnon, 1994).

---

[12]Research by Yates, Barbaree, and Marshall (1984) supports the view that, in contemporary environments, when men are angered by being put down by a woman, they become more sexually aroused to coercive sex.

## Human Algorithm Controlling Coercive Sex

The algorithm controlling coercive sex in human males may be illustrated, in a somewhat oversimplistic manner of course, as follows: (a) If there are extremely low chances of negative consequences to yourself (e.g., external punishments or internalized prohibitions) and female is attractive sexually, then have sex with her regardless whether she desires you. (b) If there are potential negative consequences to yourself, then weigh the costs and do not engage in coercive sex if costs are potentially serious relative to benefits. In the same objective circumstances, calculation of costs–benefits would differ for various individuals. Such calculation may be calibrated based on various dimensions, including the man's personal history of perceived female rejection versus receptivity. Such calibration may occur at certain critical periods in one's development, and may set a relatively fixed personality profile that affects the threshold for engaging in coercive sexual behavior.

## A MODEL RELEVANT TO THE PROPOSED ALGORITHM: THE CONFLUENCE MODEL OF SEXUAL AGGRESSION

The evolutionary approach has been interpreted here as stressing both sexuality mechanisms (i.e., impersonal sexual orientation) and incorporating dominance/hostility mechanisms, which may be mobilized in response to blocked goals. The research described next empirically tests the role of both sets of mechanisms as contributors to sexual aggression. Although some of the research was not initially designed to directly test an evolutionary-based model, the findings support predictions derived from such an approach.

Malamuth, Sockloskie, Koss, and Tanaka (1991) proposed a model of the ontogenetic and current characteristics of aggressors. This approach may be described as the *cumulative-conditional-probability* model (e.g., Wickens, 1982), which suggests two interrelated aspects. First, the probability of the occurrence of certain factors is affected by the presence or absence of other factors. However, each antecedent does not constitute a necessary condition for the next factor to occur in a hypothesized sequence, nor is any factor always necessary for the final outcome to occur. Second, when a combination of certain antecedent conditions in a sequence of factors exists, the probability of a particular outcome is greater than when only some of these antecedent conditions exist. Although each antecedent condition independently contributes to a higher probability of the outcome, some "synergistic" effect is also predicted, such that a combination of certain antecedents has more than a simple additive effect on the likelihood of the outcome.

The Malamuth et al. model suggests that coercive sex may be conceptualized as resulting from the convergence of two sets of characteristics or paths. The first consists of relatively high levels of promiscuous/impersonal sex and the second of hostile, dominating characteristics (also see Malamuth, Heavey, & Linz, 1993). In terms of the first path, the model proposes that certain harsh early environments, such as those in the home, are likely to lead to various acting out behaviors as the individual matures, leading to a relatively high orientation to casual, promiscuous, or impersonal sex.

Belsky, Steinberg, and Draper (1991) independently published a model of reproductive strategies that has clear parallels to this constellation of promiscuous/impersonal sex characteristics. Those investigators presented a more explicit delineation of the evolutionary basis for this aspect of the model. Both models emphasize aspects of the early family or home environment as contributors to later development via the mediation of cognitive and emotional attachment mechanisms. Belsky et al. suggested that early experience may serve as a switch or trigger at a critical formative period (i.e., the first 5–7 years of life), which will shape an enduring reproductive strategy (also see Draper & Harpending, 1982). The environmental input at this critical stage informs the developing child of the extent to which the physical environment (e.g., the availability of resources) and the social environment (e.g., the trustworthiness of others and the enduringness of close personal relationships) are relatively benign or harsh.[13] Evolutionary pressures would be expected to select for differing reproductive strategies, with more benign environments favoring a long-term quality strategy that involves high investment in relatively few offspring versus harsh environments that favor a short-term orientation, high quantity of offspring, and relatively little investment in each. Particularly relevant to the present focus on the development of a more promiscuous or impersonal sexual orientation[14] are harsh familial contex-

---

[13]Such information would, from the evolutionary framework, be important if the environments in our ancestral history varied considerably from one geographical area to the other, but were quite stable for any particular person over his or her life course.

[14]This impersonal sex construct is similar to the concept used by evolutionary psychologists in the context of studying *sociosexuality*, which refers to individual differences in the willingness to engage in sexual relations without closeness or commitment (Gangestad & Simpson, 1990; Simpson & Gangestad, 1991). Unrestricted sexuality individuals report having sex earlier in relationships, more than one concurrent sexual relationship, many one-time partners in the past, and sex with partners on only one occasion, and they foresee many partners in the future. In contrast, restricted individuals tend to insist on the development of closeness and commitment before engaging in sex, and they possess the opposite set of behavioral characteristics. Simpson and Gangestad (1991) supported the prior profiles with research that gathered independent reports provided by people's sexual partners.

tual stressors, such as marital discord and rejecting, violent, or abusive parenting behaviors.

Both models also propose that such harsh early childhood environments may lead to problem behavior patterns involving nonconformity, impulsivity, and antisocial behaviors (labeled *delinquency* in one model and *externaling symptoms* in the other). Belsky et al. suggested that this oppositional behavior, via some yet unspecified biological mechanism that may involve androgenic activity, stimulates earlier biological maturation that also fosters among boys indiscriminate and opportunistic sexuality, increasing the likelihood of becoming fathers before other men.[15] Malamuth et al. also hypothesized that such nonconforming behaviors are likely to be expressed in various forms of early sexual acting out involving short-term, promiscuous relations. Belsky et al. noted that in harsh environments such a high-quantity orientation would make biological sense because it would be more likely to result in successful reproduction than a strategy involving quality long-term investment.[16]

Although the Belsky et al. model did not address the topic of sexual coercion, Malamuth et al. argued that such a promiscuity or impersonal sex orientation (or reproductive strategy) is much more likely to actually be expressed in sexually aggressive behaviors when a man possesses another set of characterological factors. Malamuth et al. labeled these as the *hostile masculinity path*, which includes hostility toward women (e.g., feelings of rejection, hurt, anger), gratification from dominating them (e.g., sexual arousal to having power over women), and attitudes accepting of aggression toward women. As suggested earlier, from an evolutionary framework, the mobilization of the type of attitudes and emotions encompassed in this path may increase the likelihood and effectiveness of aggressive behaviors used in a sexual context. These characteristics may operate via several processes. First, they may decrease the impact of internal inhibitions and anxiety. For example, hostility may reduce sympathy for the victim and make the woman seem less powerful by denigrating her. Attitudes accepting of violence may nullify prohibitions against using aggression. Second, such characteristics may reduce the strength of external barriers or inhibitions. For instance, anger accompanying the hostility may increase the likelihood of overcoming a woman's resistance due to the vigor with which

---

[15]In other species, there are examples of how environmental conditions may set the future biological life course. In some lizards, turtles, and crocodilians, the sex of the offspring is determined by the environmental temperature the eggs experience (Trivers, 1985). Of course, the life-course effects that may be set in humans by childhood experience and attachment history are less rigidly determined.

[16]A prudent investor in a stable economy may invest for a long-term return in the distant future. In contrast, in a war zone, the best business strategy may be to seek short-term gains because the future is uncertain. Other species (e.g., those that suffer low predation rates, such as elephants or lions) can afford to invest heavily in just a few offspring.

the act is carried out. Third, the sexual arousal and gratification derived from dominating women may make highly hostile masculine men less anxious about women's potential rejection of them (Malamuth, Feshbach, & Jaffe, 1977), and may reinforce the use of aggressive behaviors. In certain ancestral environments, such aggression may have increased some males' fitness by reducing women's choice and enabling sex with a woman who otherwise would have rejected the man.

## EMPIRICAL TESTING OF THE MODEL

Considerable data exist to support various portions of the model of the characteristics of sexually aggressive men described by Malamuth et al., which are reviewed in that article and elsewhere (e.g., Malamuth, Heavey, & Linz, 1993; Malamuth, Linz, Heavey, Barnes, & Acker, 1995). Although Belsky et al. (1991) did not consider sexual aggression, they also reviewed much data supporting the links described in the sexual promiscuity/impersonal sex path. In addition to studies that have supported particular segments of the model, there have been studies that have tested the full model using latent-variable structural equation modeling. Such modeling may be described as combining techniques similar to factor and path analyses. The former technique enables extraction of the common variance among several assessments of the same construct, whereas the latter technique examines the links among the constructs. The results indicate the success of the overall hypothesized model in accounting for the patterning of the data observed, as well as supporting the specific hypothesized relationships among constructs.

An example of correlated data consistent with the model are shown in Table 17.1, taken from Malamuth, Linz, Heavey, Barnes, and Acker (1995). These are cross-sectional data with 64 men who provided information regarding the degree to which violence and abuse had occurred in their early childhood, the extent to which they had engaged in various delinquent or antisocial behaviors during adolescence, their sexual maturation and experience, attitudes supporting violence against

TABLE 17.1
Correlations for Variables Used in the Model

| Measure | 1 | 2 | 3 | 4 | 5 | 6 |
|---|---|---|---|---|---|---|
| 1. Early family violence and abuse | — | | | | | |
| 2. Delinquency | .50*** | — | | | | |
| 3. Early sex experience | .28* | 34** | — | | | |
| 4. Attitudes supporting violence | .20 | .07 | .00 | — | | |
| 5. Hostile masculinity | .04 | .05 | .11 | .50*** | — | |
| 6. Sexual aggression | .46*** | .39*** | .44*** | .32*** | .42*** | — |

$*p < .05.$ $**p < .01.$ $***p < .001.$

women, hostile masculinity (i.e., hostility toward women and gratification from sexual dominance), and the extent to which they had been sexually aggressive. These correlations show the basic two-path structure of the model, with the first three measures forming a highly intercorrelated cluster, the next two measures forming a second independent cluster, and the variables in both clusters correlating with sexual aggression.

An example of structural equation models can be found in Malamuth et al. (1991), who tested the model based on the theoretical framework described earlier and shown in Fig. 17.1. Data from a large, nationally representative sample of about 3,000 males enrolled in any form of post-high school education were used. In this study, subjects' data were based only on their self-reports, and the findings concerning earlier experiences were based on their recollections.

Although the development of this model was guided by the theory outlined previously, the initial model was refined using half of the available sample and then cross-validated using the second half of the sample. This model fit the data well in both sample halves, supporting both the links among each of the constructs and the overall fit of the model.[17] As depicted by the percentage in the small circle, 78% of the latent variance of coerciveness against women was accounted for by the sexual promiscuity and hostile masculinity paths.[18]

## The Interaction of the Two Paths

Malamuth et al. (1991) hypothesized that the degree to which a person possesses characteristics of the hostile path will determine whether a

---

[17]In their original model, Malamuth et al. predicted that early home experiences in relatively harsh environments and delinquency (i.e., acting out experiences during adolescence) would also contribute to attitudes supporting violence against women, and therefore to characteristics of the hostile masculinity path. This link was not well supported, being significant and quite weak in only one of the sample halves. This finding and later data suggest that the hostile masculinity and sexual promiscuity sets of characteristics are independent, although their combination characterizes many sexual aggressors. This is surprising not only because experiences such as observing violence in the home may be expected to affect attitudes regarding violence, but because it might also be expected that a promiscuous sexual orientation would create a high likelihood of rejection experiences, even for men who are quite successful in attracting female partners. Such experiences may contribute to the development of the emotional pattern associated with hostile masculinity. Perhaps more refined analyses, such as those focusing on curvilinear relationships between home experiences and attitudes toward violence, those considering desired number of sexual partners relative to the number actually achieved (e.g., distinctions between successful vs. unsuccessful promiscuous men), may be more likely to identify the conditions under which there are links between the promiscuous/impersonal sex and the hostile masculinity paths.

[18]As a word of caution, it must be remembered that latent variables are hypothetical constructs that are supposed to be error-free. Due to measuring error, correlations between and variances explained by actually measured variables are considerably lower.

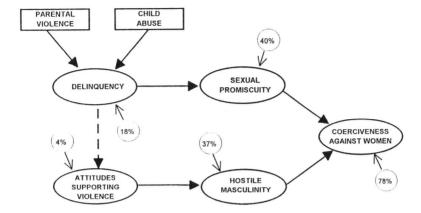

FIG. 17.1. Structural model of the characteristics of sexual aggressors supported by the findings of Malamuth et al. (1991). Percentage in small circles indicates amount of variance of the latent variable that was successfully accounted for by the preceding variables that have arrows pointing toward it. Broken line indicates hypothesized connection that received only weak support and was later dropped from model. Coerciveness against women included assessment of both sexual and nonsexual aggression. (Adapted from Malamuth et al., 1991.)

promiscuous sexual orientation leads to sexual aggression. As expected, an analysis of variance (ANOVA) revealed a significant interaction between sexual promiscuity and hostile masculinity when predicting sexual aggression (see Fig. 17.2), and no interaction when predicting nonsexual aggression against women. To further explore this interaction, subjects were divided into three groups based on their level of hostile masculinity and sexual promiscuity. The group that was high on both sexual promiscuity and hostile masculinity reported higher levels of sexual aggression than all other groups. High promiscuity alone, without hostile masculinity, or high hostile masculinity alone, without high levels of promiscuity, do not strongly predict sexual aggression.

## REPLICATING AND EXTENDING THE CONFLUENCE MODEL

Recently, Malamuth et al. followed up 150 men who had participated in several of the studies conducted 10 years earlier. Four primary outcome measures were used to assess behaviors occurring during the 10 years subsequent to the subjects' initial participation: sexual aggression, non-sexual physical and verbal aggression, and general relationship quality and distress. Support for the validity of the measures was obtained by

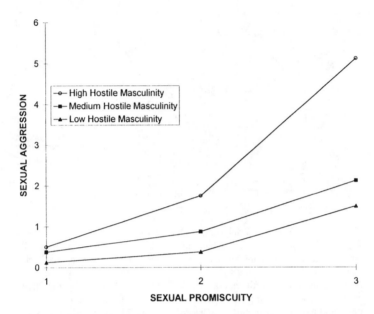

FIG. 17.2.   Mean levels of sexual aggression as a function of levels of hostile masculinity and sexual promiscuity (Malamuth et al., 1991).

the men's self-reports, and the investigators also obtained reports from many of the men's partners and videotaped some of the couples.

First using cross-sectional data, these researchers were able to successfully replicate the findings of Malamuth et al. (1991) with a different sample. Next, they tested an extended model adding the longitudinal data. They hypothesized that the same two-path causal structure used in cross-sectional analyses would be useful for the longitudinal prediction of sexual aggression. The predictions were borne out, and this model generally fit the data well.

Having established the usefulness of the model for longitudinal prediction of conflict with women, Malamuth et al. (1995) attempted to refine several aspects of the model. For example, the investigators sought to further explore the role of sex drive in sexual aggression, and to examine the role of general hostility in aggression. Various theorists have argued that more sexually aggressive men have a higher sex drive (e.g., Ellis, 1989). In the Malamuth et al. model, in contrast, it is a particular orientation to sexuality or a particular "mating strategy" that characterizes sexual aggressors, rather than heightened sex drive. Therefore, Malamuth et al. (1995) hypothesized that indicators of "impersonal sex" would be associated with increased sexual aggression, but that other sex drive indicators would not. Analyses supported this contention. The findings show that sexual aggression earlier in adult life was predictive later in life of impersonal

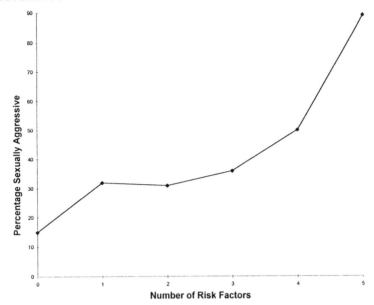

FIG. 17.3.  Percentage of subjects who reported engaging in some form of sexual aggression, as a function of the number of risk variables on which participants scored relatively high (based on Malamuth et al., 1995).

sexual relations in such forms as sexual arousal when looking at attractive unknown women and having more extrarelationship affairs. By contrast, early sexual aggression did not predict responses reflective of sex drive generally, such as the degree of pleasure derived from sex, the frequency of sex with a woman, or the number of orgasms per week.

Finally, these investigators performed a risk analysis using cross-sectional data with five factors used in a version of the confluence model. The investigators computed for each subject whether he scored relatively high (in the upper third of the sample distribution) on each risk factor. Figure 17.3 shows that 89% of men who scored high on all five of these risk factors reported having engaged in some sexual aggression, compared with only 15% of those who did not score high on any one of the factors. These data are consistent with the "conditional probability" formulation of the model mentioned earlier in suggesting increased risk of sexual aggression as a result of the convergence of several factors.

## OTHER RECENT REPLICATIONS AND EXTENSIONS

Two recent studies have provided additional evidence highlighting the utility of the confluence model of sexual aggression. In the work by Malamuth and associates, the characteristics comprising the hostile masculinity path included assessment of feelings of rejection and hurt within larger scales assessing several related characteristics. For example, the Hostility Toward Women scale (Check, 1985; Check, Malamuth, Elias, & Barton, 1985) used consistently in this line of research (e.g., Malamuth, 1986; Malamuth et al., 1991) includes items such as, "I have been rejected by too many women in my life" and "I am sure that I get a raw deal from the women in my life." Similarly, Lisak and Roth (1988) found that sexually aggressive men were more likely to perceive themselves as having been hurt by women, including perceptions of being deceived, betrayed, and manipulated. They also found that variables assessing such hurt correlated highly with items assessing anger toward women and a desire to dominate them.

However, in these studies, the variable of perceived rejection or negative experiences in relationships with women was not explicitly included as a separate construct within a structural equation model. Such assessment was recently reported by Christopher, Owens, and Stecker (1993), who successfully replicated the two-path model suggested by Malamuth et al (1991). This construct of negative relationships was found to have a strong link with the other elements of the characteristics comprising the hostile masculinity path, and it had a significant impact on sexually aggressive behavior. It is not clear at this stage whether such hurt feelings represent some degree of objective reality, with the more aggressive men having experienced more rejection, and/or whether they are hypersensitive to the same type of experiences as nonaggressive men.

## SUMMARY AND CONCLUSIONS

According to evolutionary theory, human psychological mechanisms evolved in ancestral times. The genes responsible for them were maintained and spread if they conferred reproductive advantages, and their carriers outreproduced those who did not have the mechanisms. Human mechanisms are not inflexible to environmental inputs. Rather, they are often activated according to environmental conditions and calibrated during critical developmental periods, thus adapting the individual's life strategies to maximize (at least in ancestral environments) reproductive success in his or her specific life circumstances.

An evolutionary framework suggests that one's lifetime mating strategy is affected by early childhood experiences that activate a mechanism that channels the individual to a relatively high-quantity or high-quality mating strategy. Relatively harsh conditions, such as conflict and abuse in the home, increase the likelihood of the more promiscuous or high-quantity strategy. This mating strategy is more likely to be expressed in sexually aggressive behavior when the individual has also become hostile to women, derives gratification from dominating them, and believes that the use of aggression is justified. The evolutionary framework explains the role of such a constellation of characteristics by suggesting that it may result from feelings of having been blocked from mating opportunities (e.g., been rejected by many women). Its function may be to mobilize an interrelated network of attitudes and emotions that could have increased the likelihood of effectively using aggression to overcome a woman's resistance, and thereby reduce her choice. In certain ancestral conditions, such sexual aggression may have increased some men's reproductive success.

Considerable data support the accuracy of a model consistent with such an evolutionary framework. We particularly emphasized a set of both cross-sectional and longitudinal studies, which reveal that men who are sexually aggressive show both a promiscuous, impersonal mating strategy that is associated with having been brought up in relatively harsh early environments, and hostile-dominant personality characteristics that are correlated with feelings of having been rejected by many women.

Although such a model provides an evolutionary framework for understanding the existence of male sexual aggression against women, it in no way minimizes the outrage that such behaviors should elicit, nor does it minimize the importance of strategies designed to minimize such acts. Just as recognizing that being able to kill under some circumstances probably contributed to reproductive success in our species, sexual coercion under some circumstances may also have increased fitness.

We believe that to adequately understand the causes of sexual coercion, it is necessary to develop a comprehensive, vertically integrated model that includes multilevel complementary explanations of ultimate and proximate causes (Barkow, 1989). In developing such a model of the characteristics of sexual aggressors, it is important to consider the following: (a) specieswide mechanisms resulting from natural selection that mediate between environmental stimuli and the person's behavior; (b) genderwide differences in certain psychological mechanisms; (c) cultural and subcultural differences in ideology, social climate, and so on; and (d) individual variability within males (e.g., genetic, hormonal, experiential, and so on). In a research area focusing on such a critical problem as sexual coercion, it will be particularly important to demonstrate that this integrated model not only serves heuristic purposes, but that it performs well in such areas as predicting the likelihood that a person will aggress, generating new hypotheses that otherwise would not have been made, and guiding more effective prevention and treatment programs.

## ACKNOWLEDGMENTS

The research summarized here was supported by a grant from the National Institute of Mental Health to Neil Malamuth.

## REFERENCES

Alexander, R. D. (1979). *Darwinism and human behavior*. Seattle: Washington University Press.
Bailey, J. M., Gaulin, S., Agyei, Y., & Gladue, B. A. (1994). Effects of gender and sexual orientation on evolutionarily relevant aspects of human mating psychology. *Journal of Personality and Social Psychology, 66*(6), 1081–1093.
Barkow, J. H. (1989). *Darwin, sex, and status: Biological approaches to mind and culture*. Toronto, Canada: University of Toronto Press.
Belsky, J., Steinberg, L., & Draper, P. (1991). Childhood experience, interpersonal development, and reproductive strategy: An evolutionary theory of socialization. *Child Development, 62*, 647–670.
Berkowitz, L. (1993). Towards a general theory of anger and emotional aggression: Implications of the cognitive-neoassociationistic perspective for the analysis of anger and other emotions. In R. S. Wyer & T. K. Srull (Eds.), *Perspectives on anger and emotion. Advances in social cognition* (Vol. 6, pp. 1–46). Hillsdale, NJ: Lawrence Erlbaum Associates.
Brownmiller, S. (1975). *Against our will: Men, women and rape*. New York: Simon & Schuster.
Buss, D. M. (1989). Conflict between the sexes: Strategic interference and the evocation of anger and upset. *Journal of Personality and Social Psychology, 56*, 735–747.
Buss, D. M. (1990). Evolutionary social psychology: Prospects and pitfalls. *Motivation and Emotion, 14*, 265–286.
Buss, D. M. (1991). Evolutionary personality psychology. *Annual Review of Psychology, 42*, 459–491.
Buss, D. M. (1994). *The evolution of desire: Strategies of human mating*. New York: Basic Books.
Buss, D. M. (1995). Evolutionary psychology. *Psychological Inquiry, 6*, 1–30.
Buss, D. M., & Schmitt, D. P. (1993). Sexual strategies theory: An evolutionary perspective on human mating. *Psychological Review, 100*, 204–232.
Chagnon, N. A. (August, 1994). How important was "marriage by capture" as a mating strategy in the EEA? *Human Behavior and Evolution Society Newsletter, 3*(3), 1–2.
Check, J., Malamuth, N., Elias, B., & Barton, S. (1985). On hostile ground. *Psychology Today, 19*, 56–61.
Check, J. V. P. (1985). *The hostility towards women scale*. Unpublished doctoral dissertation, University of Manitoba, Winnipeg, Canada.
Christopher, F. S., Owens, L. A., & Stecker, H. L. (1993). Exploring the dark side of courtship: A test of a model of premarital sexual aggressiveness. *Journal of Marriage and the Family, 55*, 469–479.
Clark, L., & Lewis, D. (1977). *Rape: The price of coercive sexuality*. Toronto, Canada: The Women's Press.
Clutton-Brock, T. H., & Parker, G. A. (1995). Sexual coercion in animal societies. *Animal Behaviour, 49*, 1345–1365.
Cosmides, L., & Tooby, J. (1987). From evolution to behavior: Evolutionary psychology as the missing link. In J. Dupre (Ed.), *The latest on the best: Essays on evolution and optimality* (pp. 277–306). Cambridge, MA: MIT Press.
Cosmides, L., & Tooby, J. (1996). Are humans good intuitive statisticians after all? Rethinking some conclusions from the literature on judgment under uncertainty. *Cognition, 58*, 1–73.

Cox, C. R., & LeBoeuf, B. J. (1977). Female incitation of male competition: A mechanism in sexual selection. *American Naturalist, 111*, 317–335.

Crawford, C. B. (1989). The theory of evolution: Of what value to psychology? *Journal of Comparative Psychology, 103*, 4–22.

Crawford, C. B., & Anderson, J. L. (1989). Sociobiology: An environmentalist discipline? *American Psychologist, 44*, 1449–1459.

Crawford, C. B., & Galdikas, B. (1986). Rape in non-human animals. *Canadian Psychology, 27*, 215–230.

Daly, M., & Wilson, M. (1987). *Homicide.* New York: Aldine deGruyter.

Daly, M., & Wilson, M. (1994). Evolutionary psychology of male violence. In J. Archer (Ed.), *Male violence* (pp. 253–288). London: Routledge & Kegan Paul.

Dickemann, M. (1993). Reproductive strategies and gender construction: An evolutionary view of homosexualities. Homosexuality, which homosexuality? Conference (1987, Amsterdam, Netherlands). *Journal of Homosexuality, 24*, 55–71.

Draper, P., & Harpending, H. (1982). Father absence and reproductive strategy: An evolutionary perspective. *Journal of Anthropological Research, 38*, 255–273.

Ellis, B., & Symons, D. (1990). Sex differences in sexual fantasy. *Journal of Sex Research, 27*, 527–555.

Ellis, L. (1989). *Theories of rape.* New York: Hemisphere.

Gangestad, S. W., & Simpson, J. A. (1990). Toward an evolutionary history of female sociosexual variation. *Journal of Personality, 58*, 69–96.

Goodall, J. (1986). *The chimpanzees of Gombe: Patterns of behavior.* Cambridge, MA: Harvard University Press.

Hamilton, W. D. (1964). The genetical theory of social behavior (I and II). *Journal of Theoretical Biology, 7*, 1–16, 17–32.

Kanin, E. J. (1977). Sexual aggression: A second look at the offended female. *Archives of Sexual Behavior, 6*, 67–76.

Kanin, E. J. (1984). Date rape: Unofficial criminals and victims. *Victimology: An International Journal, 9*, 95–108.

Lisak, D., & Roth, S. (1988). Motivational factors in nonincarcerated sexually aggressive men. *Journal of Personality and Social Psychology, 55*, 795–802.

Malamuth, N. M. (1986). Predictors of naturalistic sexual aggression. *Journal of Personality and Social Psychology, 50*, 953–962.

Malamuth, N. (1996a). Evolutionary psychology and the confluence model of sexual aggression. In D. Buss & N. Malamuth (Eds.), *Sex, power and conflict: Evolutionary and feminist perspectives* (pp. 269–295). Oxford: Oxford University Press.

Malamuth, N. M. (1996b). Sexually explicit media, gender differences, and evolutionary theory. *Journal of Communication, 46*(3), 8–31.

Malamuth, N. M., & Brown, L. M. (1994). Sexually aggressive men's perceptions of women's communications: Testing three explanations. *Journal of Personality and Social Psychology, 67*, 699–712.

Malamuth, N., & Check, J. (1983). Sexual arousal to rape depictions: Individual differences. *Journal of Abnormal Psychology, 92*, 55–67.

Malamuth, N., Feshbach, S., & Jaffe, Y. (1977). Sexual arousal and aggression: Recent experiments and theoretical issues. *Journal of Social Issues, 33*, 110–133.

Malamuth, N. M., Heavey, C., & Linz, D. (1993). Predicting men's antisocial behavior against women: The "interaction model" of sexual aggression. In G. N. Hall, R. Hirschmann, J. R. Graham, & M. S. Zaragoza (Eds.), *Sexual aggression: Issues in etiology and assessment, and treatment* (pp. 63–97). New York: Hemisphere.

Malamuth, N. M., Linz, D., Heavey, C. L., Barnes, G., & Acker, M. (1995). *Journal of Personality and Social Psychology, 69*, 353–369.

Malamuth, N. M., Sockloskie, R., Koss, M. P., & Tanaka, J. (1991). The characteristics of aggressors against women: Testing a model using a national sample of college students. *Journal of Consulting and Clinical Psychology, 59,* 670–681.

McKinney, F., Derrickson, S. R., & Mineau, P. (1983). Forced copulation in waterfowl. *Behaviour, 86,* 250–294.

Mineau, P., & Cooke, F. (1979). Rape in the lesser snow goose. *Behaviour, 70,* 280–291.

Palmer, C. T. (1989). Rape in nonhuman animal species: Definitions, evidence, and implications. *Journal of Sex Research, 26*(3), 355–374.

Quine, W. V. (1981). *Theories and things.* Cambridge, MA: Harvard University Press.

Restak, R. M. (1994). *The modular brain.* New York: Macmillan.

Shields, W., & Shields, L. M. (1983). Forcible rape: An evolutionary perspective. *Ethology and Sociobiology, 4,* 137–173.

Simpson, J. A., & Gangestad, S. W. (1991). Individual differences in sociosexuality: Evidence for convergent and discriminant validity. *Journal of Personality and Social Psychology, 60,* 870–883.

Smuts, B. B. (1992). Male aggression against women: An evolutionary perspective. *Human Nature, 3,* 1–44.

Symons, D. (1979). *The evolution of human sexuality.* New York: Oxford University Press.

Symons, D. (1992). On the use and misuse of Darwinism in the study of human behavior. In J. Barkow, L. Cosmides, & J. Tooby (Eds.), *The adapted mind* (pp. 137–162). New York: Oxford University Press.

Thornhill, R. (1980). Rape in Panorpa scorpionflies and a general rape hypothesis. *Animal Behaviour, 28,* 52–59.

Thornhill, R., & Thornhill, N. W.(1983). Human rape: An evolutionary analysis. *Ethology and Sociobiology, 4,* 1–74.

Thornhill, R., & Thornhill, N. W. (1987). Human rape: The strengths of the evolutionary perspective. In C. Crawford, M. Smith, & D. Krebs (Eds.), *Sociobiology and psychology: Ideas, issues and applications* (pp. 269–291). Hillsdale, NJ: Lawrence Erlbaum Associates.

Thornhill, N. W., & Thornhill, R. (1990). An evolutionary analysis of psychological pain following rape: 1. The effects of victim's age and marital status. *Ethology and Sociobiology, 11,* 155–176.

Thornhill, R., & Thornhill, N. W. (1992). The evolutionary psychology of men's coercive sexuality. *Behavioral and Brain Sciences, 15,* 363–421.

Tooby, J., & Cosmides, L. (1990). On the universality of human nature and the uniqueness of the individual. The role of genetics and adaptation. *Journal of Personality, 58,* 17–68.

Tooby, J., & Cosmides, L. (1992). The psychological foundations of culture. In J. Barkow, L. Cosmides, & J. Tooby, (Eds.), *The adapted mind* (pp. 19–136). New York: Oxford University Press.

Trivers, R. (1985). *Social evolution.* Menlo Park, CA: Benjamin/Cummings.

Trivers, R. L. (1972). Parental investment and sexual selection. In B. Campbell (Ed.), *Sexual selection and the descent of man* (pp. 1871–1971). Chicago: Aldine.

Weinrich, J. D. (1987). A new sociobiological theory of homosexuality applicable to societies with universal marriage. *Ethology and Sociobiology, 8,* 37–47.

Wickens, T. D. (1982). *Models for behavior: Stochastic processes in psychology.* San Francisco: Freeman.

Wilson, M., & Daly, M. (1992). The man who mistook his wife for a chattel. In J. H. Barkow, L. Cosmides, & J. Tooby (Eds.), *The adapted mind: Evolutionary psychology and the generation of culture* (pp. 289–322). New York: Oxford University Press.

Yates, E., Barbaree, H. E., & Marshall, W. L. (1984). Anger and deviant sexual arousal. *Behavior Therapy, 15,* 287–294.

Zeki, S. (1992, September). The visual image in mind and brain. *Scientific American, 6.*

# 18

## Darwinian Aesthetics

Randy Thornhill
*University of New Mexico*

This chapter treats the topics that have been of long interest to aestheticians. Traditional aesthetics (i.e., aesthetics in philosophy) is broad and diverse, including such topics as the beauty of ideas, body form, natural landscapes, and so on. Some readers of this chapter suggested that I provide a succinct definition of *aesthetics*. It is not possible, however, to provide an objective definition based on Darwinian theory. As D. Symons (personal communication, in April 1995) concisely put it:

> The whole notion of "aesthetics," as a "natural" domain, i.e., as a domain that carves nature at a joint, is misguided. . . . All adaptations are aesthetic adaptations, because all adaptations interact in some way with the environment, external or internal, and prefer certain states to others. An adaptation that instantiates the rule, "prefer productive habitats" is no more or less aesthetic than an adaptation that instantiates the rule, "prefer a particular blood pressure."

Although there is no way to objectively define the aesthetic domain, there is value in treating the various topics of traditional aesthetics in a modern, Darwinian–adaptationist framework.

The Darwinian theory of brain design, whether human or nonhuman, is that of many functionally specific psychological adaptations. Just as human blood pressure regulation and habitat selection are guided by different, functionally specific psychological adaptations, the traditional topics of aesthetics each arise from fundamentally different psychological adaptations. It is the many psychological adaptations that underlie the diversity of aesthetic experiences of interest to aestheticians that I address. Darwinian aesthetics has great promise for elucidating the design of the psychological adaptations involved in these experiences.

The starting point for the Darwinian theory of aesthetics I offer is as follows. Beauty experiences are unconsciously realized avenues to high fitness in human evolutionary history. Ugliness defines just the reverse. Greenough (1958), in reference to architectural structures, defined *beauty* as the promise of function. The Darwinian theory of human aesthetic value is that beauty is promise of function in the environments in which humans evolved (i.e., of high likelihood of survival and reproductive success in the environments of human evolutionary history). *Ugliness* is the promise of low survival and reproductive failure. Human aesthetic value is a scale of reproductive success and failure in human evolutionary history (i.e., over the last few million years—the Pleistocene).

First, the chapter briefly lists the experiential domain of interest to academic aestheticians. It then discusses the adaptationist program and how it applies to these experiences in a general way. Next, it resolves some dilemmas in traditional aesthetics using the adaptationist perspective. Finally, it gives a taxonomy of the psychological adaptations underlying the diverse experiences of interest to aestheticians.

## AESTHETICS: THE TOPICS OF INTEREST

The study of beauty is a major endeavor in academia. Intellectual beauty is the beauty that scholars in all academic disciplines find in scholarship. Intellectual beauty is the most noble goal of academic pursuit, and is a sublime reward of the pursuit. Also, the academic discipline of aesthetics, a part of philosophy, is concerned with the rhetorical meaning of beauty and ugliness. Aesthetics apparently first became a distinct discipline within philosophy with Baumgarten's *Aesthetica*, published in 1750. But as documented by the historical aesthetician Kovach (1974), speculation about aesthetics by scholars has been going on in the Western world at least since the sixth-century BC in Greece. In addition, the arts and other areas of the humanities are fundamentally concerned with beauty. The humanities are focused on competition in heightening sensation in general and in generating beauty experiences in the minds of people in particular. Beauty may be generated in the mind by poetry, literature, paintings, dance, oral or written rhetoric, and so on. When humanists contemplate beauty and analyze its meaning, they present their views rhetorically, again striving to generate the effect of beauty.

Whereas the arts and humanities compete in creating the effect of beauty in human minds, scientific aestheticians use the scientific method to understand how the effect arises and why it exists. Scientific aestheticians, then, are concerned with proximate causes (the how—physiology, development, cues or stimuli, and information processing) and/or ultimate causes (the why—evolutionary history). Scientific aesthetics is a diverse discipline that includes aesthetic valuations by nonhuman animals.

Since Darwin and Wallace, biologists have studied natural beauty's meaning in terms of the evolved signal content of striking phenotypic features, such as showy flowers, the peacock's tail, and elaborate courtship behavior. Hypotheses to explain the existence of these kinds of extravagant features, in ultimate or evolutionary functional terms, have ranged from species or sexual identity to advertisement of phenotypic quality (i.e., an organism's advertisement of its ability to deal effectively with adverse environmental agents that impact survival and reproduction). This form of biological aesthetics has become a major research area in the last 20 years, as a result of theoretical treatments validating the idea that elaborate features can evolve to honestly signal phenotypic quality, as first suggested for secondary sexual traits by A.R. Wallace (see Cronin, 1991) and explicitly treated first by Zahavi (1975).

For extravagant sexual traits such as the peacock's tail, some biologists ally with Darwin's and R. Fisher's formulation about the evolution of beauty and aesthetic preference, which was that the beauty of the peacock's tail merely signals sexual attractiveness to females, not viability or phenotypic and underlying genotypic quality. The preference for the elaborate tail evolved because it yields attractive and thus sexually preferred sons, not offspring with high viability (for discussion of recent theory, see Cronin, 1991; Ridley, 1993). There is total agreement that sexual selection is the biological process that has made extravagant features such as the peacock's tail. Many sexual-selection aestheticians now are engaged in efforts to determine the exact nature of the process of sexual selection responsible for the features (i.e., advertisement of and preference for phenotypic quality, or for sexual attractiveness only). The general consensus is that mate choice is focused on phenotypic (and often genotypic) quality, and sexual advertisement is basically about displaying phenotypic quality (for useful reviews, see Cronin, 1991; Ridley, 1993). This same conclusion seems to best fit the human data of mate choice and sexual display involving physical bodily features (reviewed in Gangestad & Thornhill, 1997; Symons, 1995; Thornhill & Gangestad, 1996). The scientific study of human sexual attraction and attractiveness is carried out by human sexual-selection aestheticians.

Biophilia is another branch of scientific aesthetics. Wilson (1984) coined the term *biophilia* to describe the innately emotional affiliation of human beings to natural phenomena such as animals, plants, and habitats. Wilson emphasized that aesthetic judgments are central to biophilia. Considerable recent and current research is clarifying human aesthetic feelings toward habitats, animals, and plants (see review in Kellert & Wilson, 1993).

The final branch of scientific aesthetics has been called *experimental aesthetics* by those in this field. Experimental aesthetics is a branch of experimental psychology dating back to about the mid-19th century. It focuses on the aesthetic value of shapes and patterns (for review, see Berlyne, 1971; Solso, 1994).

When a scientific aesthetician discovers the scientific meaning of beauty, he or she may generate beauty in the same way that the artist or other humanist does. Any significant scientific discovery may generate the effect of beauty in the mind of the discoverer and the minds of scientists in general.

## ADAPTATIONISM

In this chapter, and in theoretical (evolutionary) biology in general, *adaptation* refers to goal-directed (i.e., functionally designed), phenotypic features (e.g., Symons, 1992; Thornhill, 1990; Williams, 1992). As Williams (1992) put it, an adaptation is the material effect of response to selection. Four natural processes are known to cause evolution or changes in gene frequencies of populations, but selection is the only one that can create an adaptation. The other three—mutation, drift, and gene flow—lack the necessary creativity because their action is random relative to individuals' environmental problems. Selection is not a random process. It consists of differential survival and reproduction by individuals because of differences in their phenotypic design for the environment. Thus, *selection* is concisely defined as nonrandom differential reproduction of individuals. The nonrandomness of selection is a result of individual differences in fitness (i.e., ability to cope with environmental problems). This nonrandomness has differential reproductive consequences. When design differences among individuals reflect genetic differences, selection accumulates genes in subsequent generations, which lead (through ontogeny) to an increased fit of individuals to their environment. An *adaptation*, then, is a phenotypic solution to a past environmental problem that persistently impinged on individuals for long periods of evolutionary time, and thereby caused cumulative directional selection, which in turn caused cumulative directional change in the gene pool. Evolution by selection is not a purposeful process, but gradually incorporates ever more refined and focused purpose into its products (adaptations) by persistent effects.

Each adaptation is the archive of data of the selection that made it. These data are in the functional design of the adaptation. Said differently, to discover the purposeful design of an adaptation is to discover the kind of selection that made the adaptation. This is why the study of adaptation is fundamental to understanding the evolution of life. Adaptations are our *sole* source of information about the forces of selection that actually were effective in designing phenotypes over the course of evolutionary history.

Note that the data encoded in the design of an adaptation concern the environmental features that caused differences in individual reproductive success during the evolution of the adaptation. This is just another way of saying that adaptations have stamped in their functional designs the selective forces that made them. Thus, the way to discover the environmental forces (i.e., the selective forces) that made human adaptations is by deciphering the functional design of human adaptations. Contrary to the belief of some (e.g., Hrdy, 1981), the selective forces that designed humans cannot be elucidated directly by the study of nonhuman primates (see Symons, 1982, for a detailed critique of Hrdy's inference about people based on nonhuman primates).

The aim of the adaptationist program is to identify adaptations and characterize their functional designs. An adaptation is a phenotypic feature that is so precisely organized for some apparent purpose that chance cannot be the explanation for the feature's existence. Thus, the feature cannot merely be the chance by-product or incidental effect of an adaptation or the product of random genetic drift. The feature has to be the product of long-term evolution by directional selection. Once a true adaptation is recognized and its apparent purpose perceived, the next step is to examine in detail and fully characterize the functional design of the adaptation to determine the adaptation's actual evolutionary purpose. To discover an adaptation's evolutionary purpose entails describing specifically how the adaptation contributed to reproduction of individuals during its evolution, or, put differently, detailing the precise relationship between a phenotypic trait and selection during the trait's evolution into an adaptation (for a full discussion of the study of adaptation, see Symons, 1992; Thornhill, 1990; Williams, 1992).

Adaptationist studies do not typically include analysis of the evolutionary origin of adaptations (i.e., the phenotypic precursors that were modified by directional selection over long-term evolution into complex features with identifiable purposeful designs). Instead, the focus is on the understanding of phenotypic design, and thus the forces of selection responsible for adaptation. Both the origin and selection history of an adaptation are useful to understand, but origin and selection history are different questions; the two types of questions deal with different historical causes. Thus, the evolutionary purpose/function of an adaptation can be studied productively without any reference to or understanding of the adaptation's origin.

Evolutionary psychology is the discipline of applying the adaptationist program to discover psychological design of animals. Psychological adaptation causally underlies *all* human feelings, emotion, arousal, creativity, learning, and behavior (Cosmides & Tooby, 1987; Symons, 1987); this is undisputable. Behavior and psychological change are each the product of the processing of environmental information by psychological mechanisms. In turn, psychological mechanisms are psychological structure/design. Thus, aesthetic judgments are manifestations of psychological adaptation. As Symons (1995) put it:

> Pleasure, like all experiences, is the product of brain mechanisms, and brain mechanisms are the products of evolution by . . . selection. The question is not whether this view of pleasure is *correct*—as there is no known or suspected scientific alternative—but whether it is useful. (p. 80)

Symons meant *scientifically* useful. That is, can the view guide researchers to empirical understanding of aesthetic judgments? An unequivocal "yes" was his answer.

Human psychological adaptations are information-processing mechanisms providing solutions to information-processing problems that influenced the survival and reproductive performance of individuals during our species' evolutionary history. Human psychological adaptations are engineered to process environmental information and to guide feelings, emotions, learning, and behavior toward ends that were maximally reproductive in human evolutionary history. Psychological adaptations are characterized in functional evolutionary terms (i.e., by the kinds of information they are designed by selection to process, rather than by neurophysiology or neuroanatomy; see also Cosmides & Tooby, 1987; Tooby & Cosmides, 1989).

Knowledge of human habitat aesthetics illustrates the purposeful design of psychological adaptation. Heerwagen, Kaplan, and Orians, in a series of articles (see Heerwagen & Orians, 1993; Kaplan, 1992, for reviews), provided considerable evidence for the existence of a number of *ancestral* cues to productive habitats in human evolutionary history. These are the cues processed by human habitat aesthetics adaptations. In human evolution, individuals with the psychological ability to use these specific cues solved the problem of choosing a habitat that was safe and fruitful. For example, humans like savanna features, specifically those that provide evidence of productive and safe habitats. People even distinguish the branching patterns of trees and leaf shapes, and prefer those that connote rich over impoverished savanna habitats. Also, people prefer tree-trunk branching patterns that would have allowed climbing and escaping from terrestrial predators. These preferences have been documented cross-culturally in people who have never been in a savanna.

As is the case with all human aesthetic judgments, habitat aesthetic judgments are associated with feelings. The feelings arise from the processing of information, specifically ancestral cues to habitable and unhabitable environments, by the human habitat aesthetics adaptation. These feelings guided our ancestors toward productive and safe habitats and away from unproductive, hostile habitats. In aesthetic adaptation resides not only the data of the environmental features that generated the selection that made the adaptation, but also the data of the feelings of our ancestors about those features.

Hence, one can conclude with great confidence that beauty and ugliness were important feelings in the lives of the evolutionary ancestors of humans (i.e., those individuals who outreproduced others in human evolutionary history). The existence of human aesthetic adaptation demonstrates that human feelings about aesthetic value distinguished our evolutionary ancestors from the other individuals present in human evolutionary history who failed to reproduce or reproduced less. A beautiful idea of evolutionary psychology is that the discipline allows discovery of how human ancestors felt about various aspects of their environments; the discipline allows discovery of our emotional roots.

## CHARACTERISTICS OF ADAPTATIONS

In addition to possessing purposeful design, which is the evidence of the selection that created the design, adaptations have the following characteristics.

### Adaptations Are Species Typical

Adaptations are possessed by all members of the species. Of course, an adaptation may be sex-specific and species-typical. It may be present in only one sex (e.g., the human penis) or show different design between the sexes (e.g., sexual jealousy is cued by sex-specific environmental stimuli in men and women; see review in Buss, 1994). Similarly, adult and juvenile humans are differently designed in many regards; in this case, the adaptations are age-specific and species-typical. Evolutionary psychology emphasizes the universality of human nature, the collection of psychological adaptations that characterize the entire human species, some of which are age- and sex-specific.

Darwinian aesthetics leads to the hypothesis that the adaptations of aesthetic judgment are present in the brains of essentially all people; all people are aesthetes. Accordingly, the psychological inability to experience beauty is extremely rare in people. The absence of the psychological structure involved is as rare as the absence of a liver. Only occasionally would a human be born without beauty psychology. Indeed, the themes of beauty and ugliness seem to be universal among human cultures (Arnheim, 1988; also others discussed in Brown, 1991). For example, this is seen in humans who everywhere structure their homes to increase positive aesthetic experience. In technologically advanced societies, offices, vacations, spare time, reading, and TV watching are so structured as well. Moreover, there is much evidence that humans strive to structure their social relationships to enhance aesthetic experience: Attractiveness is a desirable feature in one's mates and friends (for reviews, see Alley & Hildebrandt, 1988; Eagley, Ashmore, Makhijani, & Longo, 1991; Hatfield & Sprecher, 1986; Jackson, 1992; Thornhill & Gangestad, 1993). Many aesthetic judgments are made every day by each human being.

## Adaptations Show Little or No Heritability

Obviously, adaptations are *inherited* (i.e., they are passed between generations from parent to offspring), but they are not *heritable* (Crawford & Anderson, 1989; Symons, 1992; Thornhill, 1990; Tooby & Cosmides, 1990). *Heritability* is a term that describes the extent to which the variation *among* individuals in a phenotypic trait (e.g., jaw size) is caused by genetic, as opposed to environmental, variation among individuals. The term *heritability* does not apply to the traits of any single individual, and, as mentioned, the dichotomy of genetic versus environmental cannot be applied to the features of an individual. Directional selection for function (e.g., to recognize mates of high reproductive value) fixes the genes involved in making (through ontogeny) a mate aesthetic value adaptation.

That Darwinism applies only to heritable traits (e.g., Lewontin, Rose, & Kamin, 1984) is an erroneous, but not uncommon, view. For an adaptation to come into existence, there must, in the evolutionary past, have been genetic variation among individuals underlying the phenotypic variation in the feature. For example, the human psychological adaptation underlying habitat aesthetics demonstrates by its existence that there was heritable variation in feelings about habitats in human evolutionary history.

Research on the heritability of aesthetic judgments is in a very elementary stage. The heritability issue is central to some researchers. For example, Wilson (1993) saw significant heritability as central in verifying notions that humans have adaptations to natural history, such as aesthetic habitat adaptation. Soulé (1992) felt the same way, and even suggested that to show heritability is the way to elucidate the genetic mechanism of human biophilic adaptation. Other researchers working on aesthetics (e.g., Heerwagen & Orians, 1993; Symons, 1995) emphasized correctly that human variation in aesthetic judgments will primarily arise not from genetic differences, but from differing conditions affecting species-typical psychological adaptation (i.e., from environmental, condition-dependent ancestral experiences). The experience may involve the past, as in a person's ontogeny or upbringing, or it may be solely due to cues of the moment. Heerwagen and Orians (1993) explained the adaptation-based, condition-dependent view of individual variation in aesthetic valuation of landscape as follows:

> Unlike many current approaches to landscape aesthetics, we do not assume that everyone will respond similarly to a certain environment. . . . Variability in people's preferences and assessments is expected, but that variability is not random. Rather, it is a function of such biologically relevant factors as age, gender, familiarity, physical condition, and presence of others. . . . [P]eople's preferences for spatial enclosure should move back and forth along a prospect [open spaces]-refuge continuum in accordance with their social, physical and emotional feelings of vulnerability. Thus, children and elderly people, as well as those who are physically ill or depressed, should prefer spaces offering refuge rather than open spaces where they can be readily seen by others. (p. 165)

Heerwagen and Orians said that a species-typical adaptation for judging the value of prospect and refuge in landscapes will be sensitive to conditions, which include such subtle things as the perceiver's physical condition. This species-typical psychological adaptation, the one all humans have, is designed to evaluate the openness and refuge features of landscapes and to value these features (i.e., feel about them) based on circumstances that were consistently present and significantly influenced differential reproduction of individuals during human evolution.

Knowing the heritability of a trait in no sense implies direct knowledge of the genetic mechanism for the trait or of a causal genetic effect on the trait (see Watson & Thornhill, 1994). Health is typically heritable because of the nature of the co-evolutionary arms race between hosts and disease organisms (see Tooby & Cosmides, 1990). Prospect-refuge valuation may show heritability because health is heritable and individuals adopt prospect-refuge behavior based on personal condition, not because of heritability in the adaptation for judging prospect-refuge. The heritability of *agoraphobia* (fear of being in open or public places) is considerable (0.4, i.e., 40% of individual variation arises from genetic differences; Ulrich, 1993). Such a finding does not detract from Heerwagen and Orians' hypothesis that valuation of openness and refuge in habitats arises from psychological design that is universal in people's brains. For the most part, heritability is useful primarily in artificial selection of desirable features in domesticated plants and animals. Studies of heritability in evolutionary biology must be carefully framed and interpreted (see Thornhill, 1990).

## Adaptations Are Special-Purpose, Not General-Purpose, in Functional Design

As Symons (1987) emphasized, environmental problems bringing about selection are specific and not general problems. Thus, it is expected that phenotypic solutions to environmental problems—that is, adaptations—will be special purpose in design because a general-purpose mechanism cannot solve a specific problem (see also Tooby & Cosmides, 1989). Beyond this theoretical understanding of adaptation is the vast body of empirical data showing that adaptations in plants and animals are indeed special purpose in their functional design.

Thinking of adaptations as general purpose, rather than special purpose, is widespread in the biological literature. This general-adaptation concept stems, in large part, from superficial thinking about functional level. If one concludes that the human heart's evolutionary function is to pump blood, it is not difficult to imagine that any general pump design will work. But if the adaptive problem to be solved by selection is framed more specifically and appropriately as the need for a pump that will work in a human body (not a generalized primate or baboon body), the general-adaptation concept is unreasonable. The same conclusion is reached by substituting habitat or mate for heart in the example. Choosing a human mate of high reproductive value or a human habitat that is safe and productive are highly specific adaptive problems, each requiring a specialized psychological adaptation.

It is often assumed in the social sciences that the human mind consists of a *tabula rasa*, or only a few general-purpose learning adaptations (Symons, 1987). However, given current knowledge of the functional specificity of the vast numbers of nonpsychological adaptations whose design is understood (e.g., the human heart is specially designed to pump blood in a human body), the vast numbers of psychological adaptations of humans and nonhuman animals whose design has been elucidated, as well as theoretical understanding of how selection works in molding adaptations (they are specific solutions to specific environmental problems), it is most likely that the human brain is composed of only highly specialized adaptations. The ontogeny of some of these adaptations is influenced by experiences most would refer to as learning. Yet, these, like other psychological adaptations, are designed to process specific information—namely, the ancestral cues that guided learning toward adaptive ends in human evolutionary history (see Symons, 1987, for a detailed critique of the idea that human psychology consists of only a few general-purpose adaptations).

The special-purpose design of human psychological adaptations forces rejection of the common view in aesthetics that there is one or a few principles of beauty that will work equally well for landscapes, human bodily form, ideas, and so on. Such principles as symmetry, harmony, truth, unity, order, femininity or woman, and so on, have been suggested (Kovach, 1974). Choosing a habitat, mate, and belief system are different information-processing problems. Each domain of aesthetic judgment is expected to coincide with special-purpose aesthetic adaptation. Turner (1991) called these specialized pieces of human psychological machinery *neurocharms,* which emphasizes their output of pleasure when viewing beauty. Of course, each neurocharm has a strong negative output as well when perceiving ugliness in the domain in which it is designed to assess aesthetic value.

Evolutionarily sophisticated scholars yawn at the debate among biologists in Darwin's time and after (see Bajema, 1984) as to whether nonhuman animals have aesthetic preferences. However, the general position in philosophical aesthetics is unambiguous: Only humans have aesthetic experiences (Kovach, 1974). Darwin (1874) first demonstrated that animals in general—insects, birds, mammals, and so on—have tastes expressed as mate preferences. For example, female barn swallows have an aesthetic preference for male tail feathers that are symmetrical (Møller, 1992). Female scorpionflies, moths, and wasps perceive the scent of symmetrical males as more attractive than the scent of asymmetrical males. Also, mobile animals face environments that present variation in the habitat features impacting survival and reproduction. As Orians (1980) pointed out, such species will have evolved faculties that judge habitats in terms of cues to survival and motivate them to settle in suitable habitat. All mobile animals from amoebae to primates are environmental aestheticians. Humans and other animals that depend on foods that were limited in evolutionary history are culinary aestheticians.

This is not to say that humans, scorpionflies, flatworms, barn swallows, or chimps make the same aesthetic judgments. Adaptationism says that they definitely do not. Each species has species-specific psychological machinery designed for aesthetic appreciation of species-specific features of the environment that impacted reproductive fitness in each species' evolutionary history. Indeed, the machinery will frequently be sex-specific in its design or function as well. Also, it is not to say that nonhuman animals feel their aesthetic preferences (i.e., are consciously aware of their mental activity surrounding aesthetic judgments). It is not necessary to feel preferences for the judgments to guide motivation and behavioral action in adaptive directions.

## An Adaptation Need Not Be Currently Adaptive

An adaptation's current form or expression need not positively affect survival or offspring production. An adaptation was necessarily adaptive in the environments of its evolution to the state of being an adaptation.

Current adaptiveness is not a legitimate theoretical expectation for any adaptation. The relationship between an adaptation and current reproduction depends on the similarity between the environment in which the adaptation is expressed currently and the environmental features that generated the selection that designed the adaptation. Often this correlation no longer exists for contemporary organisms (perhaps especially for humans, who now may all live in environments, social and nonsocial, that are significantly different from the environments of evolutionary adaptedness). As a result, adaptations are not distinguished from nonadaptations by their effects on current reproduction. A phenotypic trait can influence current reproduction negatively, but still be an adaptation—a product of long-term directional selection for a solution to a fitness-related ecological problem—and a trait can influence current reproduction positively and not be an adaptation. In addition, the effect of an adaptation on current reproduction does not identify the evolutionary function of the adaptation (only the adaptation's functional design does this) because the current environment may differ from the evolutionary environment that generated the selection that designed the adaptation (for detailed discussions, see Symons, 1992; Thornhill, 1990; Williams, 1992).

Behavioral ecologists frequently study current adaptiveness (see Crawford, 1993; Symons, 1992; Thornhill, 1990). This emphasis on current adaptiveness arises, in part, from the erroneous belief that a trait is only interesting evolutionarily if it is currently adaptive (for a discussion, see Symons, 1992; Thornhill, 1990). Some behavioral ecologists advocate defining an adaptation as any feature that is currently adaptive (Reeve & Sherman, 1993). This perspective of behavioral ecologists fails to appreciate the central significance of the adaptationist program: It is *the* method of discovery of the selective forces that mattered in the evolutionary history of life (i.e., those that actually produced phenotypic design).

Data on the current offspring-producing consequences of aesthetic judgment are totally irrelevant to the Darwinian approach to understanding aesthetic judgments discussed herein. With regard to aesthetics of ideas, one could ask questions such as, do individuals who adopt politically correct ideology have more children than those who do not? There are some interesting questions about the beauty of ideas, but they do not include how variation in beliefs covary currently with reproductive success. Instead, they pertain to the design of our ideological neurocharm. One could ask also, do more symmetrical Western men have more grandchildren than asymmetrical men? It is doubtful because of contraception use and so on. More symmetrical men are more sexually successful than asymmetrical men. They have more sex partners in a lifetime, and engage in more extra-pair copulations, achieve copulation earlier in relationships, and their mates have more orgasms of the type that retain sperm

(Gangestad & Thornhill, 1997; Thornhill & Gangestad, 1994; Thornhill, Gangestad, & Comer, 1995). These findings on male symmetry and sexual behavior imply that women find symmetrical men more aesthetically pleasing. Such men are rated more attractive (see review in Gangestad & Thornhill, 1997). Male symmetry may be positively or negatively correlated, or not correlated, with offspring production in any given human society. Regardless, there seems to be a bias in women's sexual aesthetic judgment machinery that gives symmetrical males an edge in sexual competition.

## THE PERPETUAL PROBLEMS OF TRADITIONAL AESTHETICS

Philosophical aesthetics yields a list of unresolved issues that aestheticians through the ages have attempted to treat (e.g., Kovach, 1974). Darwinian aesthetics accounts for the central place of these issues in the minds of aestheticians and helps resolve them.

### Strong Feelings

One perpetual concern has been why aesthetic judgments often involve strong feelings, which range from sublime ecstasy when beauty is perceived to deep repugnance when ugliness is perceived. Visualize a human body covered with oozing sores or, better yet, view a picture of one in a book on skin diseases. Contrast the feeling that arises with the feeling felt when you view a healthy, professional model of the sex that you prefer for sexual intercourse. Similarly, contrast your feelings when you have listened to the cacophony of a jackhammer in operation with your feelings when listening to your favorite music or viewing a rich, natural habitat with lush vegetation, a crystal-clear stream, abundant flowers, ripe fruit, and game animals. Contrast that feeling with your feelings when you view a rat-infested city dump or a polluted pond with dead fish afloat. Viewing oozing sores or nonproductive habitats or hearing jackhammers and untestable, discovery-stifling ideas cause aesthetically negative mental experiences. Viewing a model's looks or productive habitats, or hearing a favorite tune or a scientifically meaningful idea lead to aesthetically pleasant mental experiences.

Aesthetic experience is affective (i.e., immediate, intuitive, and creative of response and mood that may be profound; e.g., Kaplan, 1992; Orians & Heerwagen, 1992). The immediate affective response to the aesthetic value of a thing, when positive, can generate subsequent imagination and fantasy (e.g., when one views a beautiful landscape or hears a beautiful idea). The strength of aesthetic feelings identifies the importance of such feelings in human evolutionary history. By importance I mean that the feelings covaried with and promoted adaptive judgments in human evolutionary history.

Feelings may have evolved in humans to promote immediate and focused interest in ancestral cues and the gathering of information for use in assessing alternatives. Most human mentation is not felt. For instance, mental activity associated with digestion, respiration, and blood circulation is continuous, but all this mental activity has been delegated by selection to unconscious and subconscious components of the human brain. The beauty experience is the physiological reward for having processed ancestral cues of promised evolutionary function, and promotes further acquisition of information about the habitat, potential mate, or idea that may then be cross-referenced with stored knowledge and decision rules to assess appropriate courses of action. Aversive feelings are the physiological punishment for having encountered ancestral cues of poor circumstances for survival and reproduction; they are designed o promote avoidance and the pursuit of better circumstances.

Mystery in landscapes, whether real or in landscape art, promotes gathering more information (Kaplan, 1992). Mystery involves such items as a winding road that ends at the top of a hill, distant trees that appear to be bearing fruit, distant and vague savanna habitat features, distant people, or distant flowers that may yield fruit or otherwise imply good habitat. Mystery is the promise of more information, and the mental inference of mystery draws us into the scenario for more information gathering. Mystery plays a role in domains of aesthetics other than habitat judgments (Kaplan, 1992). For example, certain features of a stranger's physique or voice may promote closer inspection to gain further information about mate value or danger. Also, the mystery of a new idea can focus our thoughts and divert them from other channels.

Always with habitats, potential mates, other social allies, and ideas, our information processing about aesthetic value coincides with the existence of alternative courses of action. There are other habitats, potential mates, social allies, and ideas to evaluate in relation to evolutionary historical effects on personal survival and reproduction. The ancestral aesthetic cues guide us intuitively via our feelings about them.

## Essence of Beauty

Another long-standing issue in aesthetics is the elusiveness of the essence of beauty (Kovach, 1974). Said differently, why has it been so difficult to define beauty? The elusiveness of beauty led many aestheticians to the conclusion that beauty cannot be defined. Some of this sentiment arises from theological aesthetics: God alone knoweth the principle of beauty. But aestheticians of many varieties have rejected the possibility of understanding beauty. After all, they did not grasp it, and all noted philosophers of recorded history have failed to comprehend the essence of beauty. In part, the elusiveness of beauty is paramount throughout aesthetic literature as a result of the strong feelings associated with beauty judgment. These strong feelings implied, to many aestheticians, that personal introspection of aesthetic experience should uncover the essence of beauty (Kovach, 1974).

Aesthetic value assessment is inaccessible to introspection. Kant may have appreciated this given his definition of a beautiful thing—something that gives the viewer pleasure that does not arise from any knowledge of principles, proportions, causes, or the usefulness of the object (see Kovach, 1974). As Kaplan (1992) pointed out for landscape preferences, the preferences are made rapidly and easily, but study subjects' explanations of their choices have no relationship to the differences that consistently are associated with preferred and nonpreferred landscapes. *Fine art* is defined as "art produced or intended primarily for beauty alone rather than utility" (Morris, 1976). I believe that the utility in art is subliminal, but present to the extent that it is judged as beautiful. The analysis of famous architectural structures, which provide evolutionarily historical cues to refuge, ease of exit from refuge and monitoring the outside environment (Hildebrand, 1991), and the analysis of paintings (Appleton, 1975; Heerwagen & Orians, 1993), strongly supports that art has unconsciously perceived cues to utility in human evolutionary history (see Heerwagen & Orians, 1993, for a review).

Feelings are evolved designs for guiding human motivation and behavior, and arise from ancestral cue processing by the mind. For the most part, humans are not designed to consciously comprehend the ancestral cues, nor are they designed to perceive the evolutionary function of an aesthetic preference. A beautiful thing is one that has high personal, evolutionarily historical reproductive value, but this value is totally out of reach of introspection. Only the scientific method can identify the cues involved in aesthetic judgment and the evolutionary function of the judgment.

Many aestheticians have struggled with the matter of where beauty resides—in the object, the beholder's mind, or the interrelationship of object with mind. Symons (1995) put it succinctly: "Beauty is in the adaptations of the beholder" (p. 80). Beauty is the moving experience associated with information processing by aesthetic judgment adaptations when they perceive information of evolutionarily historical promise of high reproductive success.

## Beauty Principles: General or Individually Variable?

As mentioned earlier, aestheticians have frequently sought a single general principle, or a few general principles, that will explain all aesthetic judgments regardless of the thing perceived. Darwinian aesthetics leads to the conclusion that there will be many aesthetic rules, and they will be highly specialized in application. This follows from the modern understanding of adaptations, including psychological adaptations such as aesthetic value detectors, as special purpose in design.

Although many traditional aestheticians searched for a general principle of beauty, many others have emphasized the absence of generality as implied by a lack of consensus among people of what constitutes aesthetic value in a given domain. The diversity of individual tastes is one of the central unresolved issues of aesthetics (e.g., Humphrey, 1980; Kovach, 1974). Darwinism may resolve the apparent contradiction between universal beauty and wide diversity of tastes between and within societies. Cross-cultural and individual variation in aesthetic value that arises from species-typical psychological adaptations for aesthetic valuation is expected to occur in all aesthetic domains. For example, although there is evidence of a universal preference for savanna habitat cues, there are individual habitat preferences as well, which may modify, but not eliminate, the universal preference (Kaplan, 1992; Orians & Heerwagen, 1992). Humans often feel positive about features of habitats of their upbringing, which is probably a manifestation of human design for learning the rearing environment so as to increase success in that environment (see Orians & Heerwagen, 1992). Individual variation in valuation of open spaces and refuge was discussed earlier in Darwinian terms. As a final example, people are designed to learn their cultural environment, which varies across and within societies, and thereby generates variation in intellectual beauty.

## The Truth in Beauty

Is beauty truth? This question is central to classical aesthetics analysis (Kovach, 1974). Much of the discussion of beauty as truth in the mainstream aesthetics literature arises from the view that beauty is morally good and ugly is morally bad. To argue that beauty is goodness or is our guide to goodness, commits the so-called naturalist fallacy. The fallacious reasoning is the conclusion that what is actually true (determined by scientific procedure to be true), natural (occurs in nature or is the product of a natural process such as Darwinian selection), or intepreted as the way of nature is therefore good or morally correct. It seems to be a fact that human physical beauty is a health certification. What is, is, and that is the end of it. No normative implications reside in this fact or arise automatically from it. The same can be said about any other scientific fact. Of course, for personal gain, humans often ascribe ideologically based values to scientific facts or to their view of what is natural (for reasons discussed later).

The naturalist fallacy, applied to human physical attractiveness, has repeatedly led to oppressive and inhumane social policies, including the human breeding programs widely implemented under Nazism. The many eugenic programs of history have defined human beauty in ways that meet the political aspirations of the powerful. The programs view eliminating the ugly and attaining greater beauty as a moral obligation of civilized society. In these programs, the standard for attractiveness is set by interpretations based on mythology (e.g., the features of mythological Aryan heroes or the desires of a spirit) and by contorted interpretations of what is optimal under natural processes, including natural selection. Nose form, body shape, head size, various facial and body proportions, and skin and hair color have been used in discrimination and the establishment of human reproductive goals. Also, asymmetries of face and body commonly are listed as undesirable in the eugenics programs of history, some of which give detailed accounts of body features that are to be eliminated (see Hersey, 1996, for an excellent historical account).

People strongly favor attractive others (for reviews, see Alley & Hildebrandt, 1988; Hatfield & Sprecher, 1986; Herman, Zanna, & Tory Higgins, 1986; Jackson, 1992). The literature just cited leads to the conclusion that there is probably more prejudice in the context of physical attractiveness per se than on the basis of ethnic group and sex combined. Darwinism gives scientific insight into the beauty bias, but has nothing at all to say about the bias being right or wrong. A useful discussion of the naturalist fallacy can be found in Symons (1979).

Beauty is truth in a number of ways. The signaling traits of animals, from the peacock's tail to the waist of women (Singh, 1993), appear to be truthful indicators of phenotypic quality. In this formulation, beauty is truth and so is ugliness. It is suggested later that great art is a record of the design of human aesthetic adaptations, and thus artistic beauty may contain scientific truth about the nature of the human mind. Also, a beautiful idea to a person is truthful in the sense that its beauty is in how the idea can promote the perceiver's status, ability to affiliate with a desired group or individual, or other social gain. A beautiful idea is one that identifies the most important path for pursuit of personal gain. The idea that a spirit created humans is scientifically unsupported, but it is the ideological truth of many people. Aesthetic judgments of ideas are based on the data of personal social experience that arises from holding a belief or from observation of the social success of others with the belief, and in this sense beautiful ideas are truthful. The data of experience make truthful to the theist the spiritual origin of humanity.

The aesthetic value of ideas varies cross-culturally, and often there is considerable variation in ideology among individuals in a culture. All people are immersed in attempts to have personal ideas viewed as beautiful—whether one is a teacher trying to convince students, a parent trying to persuade children, a scientist trying to persuade colleagues, or a politician trying to gain political support. People are immersed in sifting through the diversity of ideas presented by others, and this sifting is done by psychological information-processing machinery that is specifically designed for assessing the value to self (technically, to self's reproductive success in evolutionary historical environments) that alternative ideas can convey, in essence, an evolved intellectual beauty detector.

According to *The American Heritage Dictionary* (1976), *ideology* means "The body of ideas reflecting the social needs and aspirations of an individual, group, class, or culture." Thus, a person's ideology is a significant component of its social strategy (i.e., how it presents itself, pursues social status, and accesses social groups, friends, and mates). It is argued here that intellectual aesthetic value represents a functionally based way of dealing with a cultural environment that is full of diverse ideas. In this perspective, cultural learning of values is not arbitrary. Learning mechanisms, in conjunction with feeling mechanisms and mechanisms of self-awareness that allow us to test how our ideas and behaviors are perceived by others, guide us through a maze of ideas toward intellectual beauty. Appropriate values will often differ between societies and within societies between social strata and among individuals.

The greatest resistance in teaching the Darwinian view of human nature to students arises when it is applied to human values (i.e., to intellectual beauty). This is as predicted: One's ideology is sacred because it is truth in the sense of a data-based conclusion as to how to proceed in one's social competition.

Traditional aestheticians have given humanity a voluminous literature containing a rich description of their interpretations, but they have not done as much as they could have. In general, the literature of aesthetics views arbitrary cultural experience as the complete explanation of aesthetic preference. This is the mainstream theory of traditional aesthetics. Thus, aestheticians have contributed to the widespread image of humans as having brains that are equally likely to learn anything through cultural conditioning; this image erroneously assumes that the human mind consists of a *tabula rasa* or a few general-purpose learning mechanisms (Symons, 1987). Fox (1989) called this scientifically inaccurate view of mind in our time "the whole secular social ideology" (p. 24). Certainly, it is the typical view of mind in the social environment in which I work and live, and it is fundamental to thinking in social sciences and humanities (see also Brown, 1991; Degler, 1991; Symons, 1987; Tooby & Cosmides, 1992).

The evolutionarily psychological view on the issue of culture creating human aesthetic pleasures is that causally the matter is fundamentally the other way around; there exists a complex and diverse set of psychological adaptations that comprise the human nature of pleasure seeking. As emphasized here, when culture plays a causal role, as is the case for individual and group differences in aesthetic preference, arbitrariness is not involved. Thus, there is no inconsistency between universal design for aesthetic valuation and cross-cultural and individual variation in the valuations.

## PSYCHOLOGICAL ADAPTATIONS OF AESTHETICS

This section attempts to dissect the aspect of the human mind that is responsible for the traditional topics of interest to aestheticians into a number of distinct aesthetic valuation adaptations using the principles of evolutionary psychology already mentioned. One proceeds as follows: First, envision an information-processing problem to have been solved in human evolutionary history—for example, choice of a mate of high mate value (e.g., mature, developmentally sound, hormonally healthy, and possessing disease resistance). Clearly, mate choice is a distinct domain in which special-purpose adaptation should exist (Symons, 1995; Thornhill & Gangestad, 1993). Then, one attempts to deduce the cues or stimuli that would have reliably provided the information needed to solve the adaptive problem in human evolutionary history. For example, it appears that body and face symmetry are cues to high-quality development, and probably genetic quality. Also the development of certain facial and body features is facilitated by sex hormones (testosterone and estrogen), and thus, the features may cue hormonal health and immunocompetence. Sex hormone-facilitated traits appear to be honest indicators of immunocompetence because they are immunosuppressors (see review in Thornhill & Gangestad, 1996). Obviously, mate choosers in human evolutionary history could not directly evaluate a potential mate's genetic quality, immunocompetence, or ability to resist environmental insults during development; they used reliable indicators of these traits. The deductions about hypothetical cues are the predictions that can be tested. When a prediction receives support, an ancestral cue is potentially identified. When a prediction is false, other potential cues are examined. Cross-cultural work is used to test universality (see Brown, 1991).

Other researchers have addressed psychological adaptations of aesthetic judgment. Turner's (1991) discussion of various neurocharms is the broadest treatment of the topic (see also Dissanayake, 1988; Rentschler, Herzberger, & Epstein, 1988). Wilson (1993) pointed out that biophilia arises from numerous evolved rules. Grammer (1993), Singh (1993), and Thornhill and Gangestad (1993) treated psychological adaptations of aesthetic valuation of human bodily form. The psychological adaptations associated with valuations of facial attractiveness have been treated by Grammer and Thornhill (1994), Johnston and Franklin (1993), Perret, May, and Yoskikawa (1994), Symons (1995), and Thornhill and Gangestad (1993). Research on environmental aesthetics deals with psychological adaptations associated with habitat assessments (reviewed in Heerwagen & Orians, 1993; Kaplan, 1992; Orians & Heerwagen, 1992; Ulrich, 1993) and with assessment of potential dangers (e.g., predators), weather, and season (Heerwagen & Orians, 1993; Orians & Heerwagen, 1992; Ulrich, 1993).

Before a taxonomy of aesthetic adaptations can be discussed, it is important to mention again that there is no objective way to delimit the aesthetic domain in Darwinian terms. Historical precedent in the field of aesthetics is the criterion for defining the types of experiences to which beauty is applied. It is assumed that when aestheticians show great interest in a domain of experience, it is because of the power of aesthetic feelings in the domain. All 10 categories that follow have been considered in philosophical aesthetics throughout its history (e.g., Kovach, 1974).

*1. Adaptations for Aesthetic Valuation of Landscape Features.* Beauty is hypothesized to be the perception of ancestral cues to productive and safe habitats in the environments of human evolutionary history. Candidate ancestral cues that have received considerable empirical support are mountains, water sources, oasis, flowers, ripe fruits, savanna (open forests that give easy visual access), growth and leaf patterns of healthy savanna trees, closed forest canopy (shelter), caves (with easy access to outside landscape), and mountains. Considerable cross-cultural research has been done on some of these landscape cues (for reviews, see Kaplan, 1992; Heerwagen & Orians, 1993; Orians & Heerwagen, 1992). Given the distinctiveness of many of the cues to suitable Pleistocene habitat, it is likely that there are numerous special-purpose adaptations involved. To my knowledge, habitat scents have not been studied. I suggest that habitat scents become perfumes when the scents are ancestral cues to promised survival in human evolutionary history.

*2. Adaptations for Aesthetic Valuation of Nonhuman Animals.* Beauty is hypothesized to be the perception of ancestral cues to available animal food and safety from predators as revealed in the behavior of nonhuman animals in one's environment. Animal food cues might be fish, large or small ungulates, certain rodents, and birds (see Heerwagen & Orians, 1993, for evidence for the cue of ungulates). Observing ungulates grazing (e.g., antelopes or cattle) without showing any alarm (not showing vigilance toward possible predators) can be very aesthetically pleasing, perhaps because it is a cue to a predator-safe habitat (see Heerwagen & Orians, 1993, for evidence). Another similar candidate cue may be the presence of active, unalarmed birds. I predict that the behavioral actions (excluding the vocalizations) of startled or nervous ungulates or birds will generate interest, apprehension, and even alarm in humans (see also Orians & Heerwagen, 1992). Aesthetic value in this domain could be studied further by having subjects self-report their feelings toward movies and still pictures. This could be coupled with recordings of physiological responses of subjects to stimuli predicted to be attractive or unattractive (see Ulrich, 1993, for methods).

3. *Adaptations for Aesthetic Valuation of the Acoustical Behavior of Nonhuman Animals.* Productive habitats have a more diverse bird and acoustic insect fauna than impoverished habitats. I predict that the sounds of these animals will often give rise to positive aesthetic experiences. Death and alarm calls of mammals and birds, buzzing noises (like those produced by bees), and growls are expected to result in cautious attention, apprehension, and anxiety. This domain could be studied by having subjects judge different natural sounds and/or by measuring subjects' physiological responses.

4. *Adaptations for Aesthetic Judgments Arising From Daily or Seasonal Environmental Cues That Signal a Need to Change Behavior.* Orians and Heerwagen (1992) predicted that reliable environmental cues to the need to change behavior are responsible for certain strong emotional reactions that people show toward both the environment and landscape paintings. Weather events such as clouds may alert one to the need to seek shelter or indicate that there is time to move about before the weather changes. Long shadows in the afternoon indicate approaching darkness, and thus the need to change behavior. Sunsets reliably indicate approaching darkness as well. Light features after the clearing of storms, such as rainbows, have aesthetic appeal. They, like sunrise light, indicate opportunities to explore the habitat. The painter Maxfield Parrish appreciated the power of light effects indicative of diurnal light rhythms on human emotions (e.g., see his paintings *Sunrise, Daybreak,* and *Puss in Boots*). Portrayals indicative of seasonal shifts are, like weather and light effects, important ingredients in landscape art. The ancestral seasonal cues are predicted to be those environmental cues that were reliably correlated with seasonal resource changes in human evolutionary history (see Orians & Heerwagen, 1992). Cues in this domain could be studied further using methods suggested for the previously discussed domains.

Categories 1 through 4 above constitute the topics discussed under biophilia (Kellert & Wilson, 1993). However, there are other domains of aesthetic valuation that arise from ancestral hominids' evolutionary historical interactions with life in the form of conspecifics (i.e., the domains of human biophilia). These are outlined in the remaining categories.

5. *Adaptations for Aesthetic Valuation of Human Bodily Form.* Beauty is the perception of cues to high reproductive potential in the body features of others. The others may be relatives, potential mates, or potential partners in nonmateship forms of social alliances. There is considerable evidence that physical attractiveness in adult humans is positively correlated with conditions that would have covaried with the bearer's reproductive potential during human evolutionary history (in women, youth; in men and women, sound development [bilateral symmetry], disease resistance, hormonal health, and overall health; for reviews see Gangestad & Thornhill, 1997; Singh, 1993; Symons, 1995; Thornhill & Gangestad, 1993, 1996). These reviews and numerous other works show that physical attraction to adults correlates positively with sexual interest and interest in romantic involvement (e.g., Hatfield & Sprecher, 1986; Jackson, 1992). Furthermore, there is some evidence that physical attractiveness positively affects the nepotism children receive (see Thornhill & Gangestad, 1993), and considerable evidence that physical attractiveness affects the number of friends one has and one's social success in general (e.g., popularity, job opportunities, salary; see reviews in Alley & Hildebrandt, 1988; Eagley et al., 1991; Hatfield & Sprecher, 1986; Herman et al., 1986; Jackson, 1992). Social success, to an important extent, arises out of evalution by others that one is a useful partner in social reciprocity (see Thornhill & Gangestad, 1993).

To my knowledge, no research has examined the physiological responses of people when viewing attractive versus unattractive others. Research along these lines modeled after the studies of physiological reactions to habitats or to phobic cues (see Ulrich, 1993) may yield strong effects. Also, research that examines self-reported feelings of well-being might be illuminating in this domain, as it has been in the domain of habitat preference. In comparison to when nonpreferred habitat features are viewed, when preferred habitats are viewed, subjects report more positive emotional states (Ulrich, 1993). Even nature posters cue the mechanisms to the point that viewers feel better when the posters are visible (Heerwagen & Orians, 1993; Ulrich, 1993). I suggest that one reason for people's preference for attractive human forms in pictures in their environment is that the pictures affect a state of well-being arising from the perception that they are amid healthy conspecifics.

6. *Adaptations for Aesthetic Valuation of Status Cues.* Humans almost constantly seek to possess, control, or be associated with status markers. Markers of social rank are of many types: accents, music, ideology, education, friends, mates, pets, automobiles, homes, cellular telephones, recreation, clothes, and so on. In general, status markers confer status

because they reliably indicate social rank by their rarity, expense, or difficulty by which they are achieved or obtained. Ascription of aesthetic value occurs with each type of status marker. Beauty here is the perception of cues to increased status.

People seem to have species-typical adaptations for identifying and adopting status markers (Alexander, 1979; Barkow, 1989, 1992; Brown, 1988; Flinn & Alexander, 1982). This special-purpose machinery will interact with other special-purpose adaptations to yield preference. As an example, attractive people are judged to be of higher status than unattractive people, and association with attractive others is perceived as status enhancing (for review, see Jackson, 1992). Our status-pursuit machinery apparently motivates us to pursue attractive others based on information processing by the psychological adaptation for valuation of physical attractiveness as phenotypic quality. Ideological preferences seem to work similarly. Humans pay more attention to and more readily adopt the views of people of social rank, compared with the views of lower ranking individuals (e.g., Wright, 1994). The psychological mechanism of intellectual beauty evaluation assesses ideas for their effects on personal interests, including personal status. This adaptation uses inferential information provided by the status-pursuit machinery.

*7. Adaptations for Aesthetic Valuation of Social Scenarios.* In technological societies, social scenarios are commonly provided by literature, theater, movies, TV, music, and everyday life. Although much human interest in this domain involves status pursuit, there is aesthetic judgment independent of pursuit of rank involved. *Beauty* is the perception of information that gives solutions to social problems. Human interest in social scenarios, both real and acted, seems to function in allowing people to practice thinking about relevant social scenarios (Alexander, 1989; Barkow, 1992; Brown, 1988). Romance novels and soap operas may provide women with information pertaining to problems of sexual competition faced by our adult female evolutionary ancestors, such as the benefits and costs of sexual infidelity and how to secure and keep male investment and commitment. Scenarios involving male–male competition or group competition (sports and warfare) may provide men with information that was central to success in male sexual competition in human evolutionary history.

*8. Adaptations for Aesthetic Valuations Based on Skill.* Brown (1991) pointed out that appreciation of tool making and language skill can evoke positive aesthetic experiences. Athletic skills, including the postural and coordinational skills of dance, and musical skills also provide pleasure to people. Skill is aesthetically pleasing when it would have positively covaried in human evolutionary history with phenotypic quality, especially neural and non-neural physical development. Because assessing skill in language, athletics, music, and tool making requires the successful processing of distinct information, it is likely that human nature contains numerous functionally specialized psychological skill detectors. Turner (1991) proposed that both a language evaluator neurocharm and a dance neurocharm exist. The aesthetic judgments of dance are outputs of a detector designed to assess athletic skill. Aesthetic experience with poetry arises from information processing by the human language skill assessment mechanism, and is not due to, as suggested by Turner (1991), a distinct, functionally specialized poetry beauty detector. Duration of phrases (three seconds in poetry) and repetition or rhyme seem as important in speech as in poetry (see Turner & Pöppel, 1988, for an analysis of universal poetic elements).

   *9. Adaptations for Aesthetic Judgments of Food.* Humans are predicted to make emotional judgments of foods based on their nutritional value (see also Rozin, 1988; Turner, 1991). *Beauty* is the perception of cues of high nutritional value in human evolutionary history (e.g., foods containing sugar, salt, and fat).

   *10. Adaptations for Aesthetic Judgments of Ideas.* It was mentioned earlier that hypothetical design features of the intellectual beauty detector are important.

   Undoubtedly, this list of categories of human aesthetic valuation adaptations that may underlie the typical topics of interest to aestheticians is incomplete and needs refinement as knowledge of the relevant beauty detectors increases. For example, the subject matter of experimental aesthetics, the aesthetics of shapes and patterns, is not covered in the prior taxonomy. Humphrey (1980) attempted to deal with experimental aesthetics in Darwinian terms. He argued that human aesthetic pleasure happens on viewing shapes and patterns when solutions are seen to classifying objects in our environment, because "an activity as vital as classification was bound to evolve to be a source of pleasure" (p. 64). There is no reason to expect all vital activities to be tied to aesthetic feelings. Digestion is vital, but not consciously experienced. Also, classification is what perception entails—that is, perception is the active psychological process by which we seek order. Clarity in perception (i.e., classification) does not automatically lead to aesthetic pleasure.

   The truth that Humphrey touches on is that the inability to classify generates the design inference of mystery when certain cues of historical reproductive significance appear to be present. The relevance of mystery in human aesthetic feelings was previously discussed. Experimental aestheticians have shown the importance of features such as novelty, complexity, surprise, ambiguity, asymmetry, and incongruity in shapes and patterns to viewers' interest, arousal, and curiosity (Berlyne, 1971; Solso, 1994). However, it is not these features per se that generate mystery. Instead, mystery arises when these features are used to confuse the perception of ancestral cues. Rubin's cup is a good example of how patterns can give the inference of mystery: The viewer is motivated to discern the lateral profiles of two human faces facing and in close proximity to one another from the background of a prominent cup that delimits the fronts of the faces. The mystery arises from the need to discern the presence of conspecifics that may be in an intimate interaction, negative or positive. Possibly another factor promoting mystery in Rubin's cup is that the faces are intersexes. The eyebrow region of the faces is projected outward as in adult males, whereas the chins and lower faces are short as in adult females and children (see Symons, 1995, for a discussion of sex differences in facial traits). Artists' use of various filtering techniques and artifical distortions in visual art has effects when they create mystery in the human mind. These ideas are largely consistent with the interpretation of such alterations of shape and pattern by Rentschler, Caelli, and Maffei (1988). Mystery generated by incongruity may be the reason for the prominence of Modigliani's art, in which there is exaggeration of the asymmetry in faces of people who were otherwise above average in attractiveness (e.g., *Chaim Soutine Seated at a Table*). Modigliani also painted a large lower jaw on an otherwise beautiful female body form (e.g., *Seated Nude*). Small lower jaw is attractive in the adult female face (Johnston & Franklin, 1993; Perret et al., 1994; Symons, 1995). Dali's *The Enigma of William Tell* is the epitome of incongruity in phenotypic quality: highly asymmetrical buttocks depicted on a man of otherwise above-average body attractiveness. These ideas could be examined empirically by manipulating features in visual art. Self-report evaluations, as well as physiological responses, would be appropriate dependent variables.

Turner (1991) listed a number of candidate aesthetic adaptations not discussed here, but that can be accounted for by adaptations in the previous 10 categories, with the possible exception of the music neurocharm(s). For example, human aesthetic valuations of colors probably arise from special-purpose adaptations for assessing colors in relation to Pleistocene adaptive problems, such as the ripeness of fruit and suitability of vegetables (see Zollinger, 1988). These pieces of mind are components of design in Categories 1, 2, and 9. Music appreciation is a human universal (Brown, 1991), but it is unclear whether there are ancestral cues contained in music that are independent of the status, ideology, and skill considerations discussed here.

## CONCLUDING REMARKS

Darwinian aesthetics has much to offer the scientific study of aesthetic value. Two groups of scholars are most likely to advance scientific understanding of aesthetics. First, evolutionary psychologists may figure importantly because they are most interested in strong emotions, which are the most easily studied in terms of large empirical effects. Also, evolutionary psychologists assume the special-purpose design of psychological machinery—an assumption necessary for identifying the appropriate experiments and observations for analyzing the design of each beauty detector. Second, in general, the arts and humanities will play a crucial role in the scientific study of aesthetics. The criterion that distinguishes significant art and humanistic rhetorical scholarship from the vulgar and ordinary in these fields is the profundity of emotional effect in the former. Thus, great art—in the broad sense of art—is hypothesized to be one important record of the design of our aesthetic adaptations. Darwinian aesthetics is the method to determine the cues in great art that make it great (i.e., determine the actual information that human aesthetic mechanisms process during aesthetic valuation of art).

There will be strong opposition to Darwinian aesthetics. In part, the opposition will arise from the widespread ideology in academia that sees beauty arising from a human psychology created by arbitrary learning. This opposition will include strong elements of mainstream aesthetics. As Turner (1991) pointed out, most Modernist and post-Modernist aestheticians advocate that beauty is only a social construction, not a reality. Feminist aestheticians show some diversity of opinion: Some agree with the modernist's view that beauty has no meaning, some emphasize arbitrary cultural conditioning and the absence of general or universal laws pertaining to aesthetic values, and some argue that there exists a female ascription of value that is different from the male value ascription (see Hein & Korsmeyer, 1993). The view that male and female humans have certain sex-specific aesthetic preferences is the only scientifically defensible opinion of the three just given, and it is strongly supported empirically.

## ACKNOWLEDGMENTS

This chapter is dedicated to the major sources of beauty experiences in my life: Joy and my children, Aubri, Margo, and Patrick. Joy has critiqued my views on aesthetics over the last few years, and has assisted me in the culling of the ugly. Any erroneous or ugly ideas that remain are solely due to my own poor aesthetic judgment. Anne Rice's assistance with manuscript preparation is greatly appreciated. I thank Richard Alexander, Rob Brooks, Don Brown, Joseph Carroll, Chuck Crawford, George Hersey, Dennis Krebs, Kurt McKean, Don Symons, and Paul Watson for helpful comments on the manuscript.

# REFERENCES

Alexander, R. D. (1979). *Darwinism and human affairs*. Seattle: University of Washington Press.

Alexander, R. D. (1989). The evolution of the human psyche. In P. Mellars & C. Stringer (Eds.), *The human revolution* (pp. 456–512). Edinburgh, Scotland: University of Edinburgh Press.

Alley, T. R., & Hildebrandt, K. A. (1988). Determinants and consequences of facial aesthetics. In T. R. Alley (Ed.), *Social and applied aspects of perceiving faces* (pp. 101–140). Hillsdale, NJ: Lawrence Erlbaum Associates.

Appleton, J. (1975). *The experience of landscape*. New York: Wiley.

Arnheim, R. (1988). Universals in the arts. *Journal of Social and Biological Structures, 11*, 60–65.

Bajema, C. J. (Ed.). (1984). *Evolution by sexual selection theory prior to 1900*. New York: Van Nostrand.

Barkow, J. H. (1989). *Darwin, sex and status: Biological approaches to mind and culture*. Toronto, Canada: University of Toronto Press.

Barkow, J. H. (1992). Beneath new culture is old psychology: Gossip and social stratification. In J. H. Barkow, L. Cosmides, & J. Tooby (Eds.), *The adapted mind: Evolutionary psychology and the generation of culture* (pp. 627–638). Oxford, England: Oxford University Press.

Baumgarten, A. G. (1750). *Aesthetica*. Francofurti cis Viadrum, Italy: J. C. Kleyb.

Berlyne, D. E. (1971). *Aesthetics and psychobiology*. New York: Appleton-Century-Crofts.

Brown, D. (1988). *Hierarchy, history and human nature: The social origins of historical consciousness*. Tucson: University of Arizona Press.

Brown, D. (1991). *Human universals*. New York: McGraw-Hill.

Buss, D. M. (1994). *The evolution of desire: Strategies of human mating*. New York: Basis Books.

Cosmides, L., & Tooby, J. (1987). From evolution to behavior: Evolutionary psychology as the missing link. In J. Dupre (Ed.), *The latest on the best: Essays on evolution and optimality* (pp. 277–306). Cambridge, MA: MIT Press.

Crawford, C., & Anderson, J. (1989). Sociobiology: An environmentalist discipline? *American Psychologist, 44*, 1449–1459.

Crawford, C. B. (1993). The future of sociobiology: Counting babies or studying proximate mechanisms. *Trends in Ecology and Evolution, 8*, 183–186.

Cronin, D. (1991). *The ant and the peacock: Altruism and sexual selection from Darwin to today*. New York: Cambridge University Press.

Darwin, C. (1874). *The descent of man and selection in relation to sex*. Chicago: Rand McNally.

Degler, C. N. (1991). *In search of human nature: The decline and revival of Darwinism in American social thought*. Oxford, England: Oxford University Press.

Dissanayake, E. (1988). *What is art for?* Seattle: University of Washington Press.

Eagley, A. H., Ashmore, R. D., Makhijani, M. G., & Longo, L. C. (1991). What is beautiful is good, but . . . : A meta-analysis review of research on the physical attractiveness stereotype. *Psychological Bulletin, 110*, 109–128.

Flinn, M. V., & Alexander, R. D. (1982). Culture theory: The developing synthesis from biology. *Human Ecology, 10*, 383–400.

Fox, R. (1989). *The search for society: Quest for a biosocial science and morality*. New Brunswick, NJ: Rutgers University Press.

Gangestad, S. W., & Thornhill, R. (1997). Human sexual selection and developmental stability. In J.A. Simpson & D.T. Kenrick (Eds.), *Evolutionary social psychology* (pp. 169–195). Hillsdale, NJ: Lawrence Erlbaum Associates.

Grammer, K. (1993). *Signale der liebe: Die biologischen gesetze der partnerschaft* [Signals of love: The biology of partnership]. Hamburg: Hoffmann and Campe.

Grammer, K., & Thornhill, R. (1994). Human (*Homo sapiens*) facial attractiveness and sexual selection: The role of symmetry and averageness. *Journal of Comparative Psychology, 108,* 233–243.

Greenough, H. (1958). *Form and function: Remarks on art, design and architecture.* Berkeley: University of California Press.

Hatfield, E., & Sprecher, S. (1986). *Mirror, mirror . . . : The importance of looks in everyday life.* Albany, NY: SUNY Press.

Heerwagen, J. H., & Orians, G. H. (1993). Humans, habitats and aesthetics. In S. R. Kellert & E. O. Wilson (Eds.), *The biophilia hypothesis* (pp. 138–172). Washington, DC: Island Press.

Hein, H., & Korsmeyer, C. (Eds.). (1993). *Aesthetics in feminist perspective.* Bloomington: Indiana University Press.

Herman, C. P., Zanna, M. P., & Tory Higgins, E. (Eds.). (1986). *Physical appearance, stigma and social behavior.* Hillsdale, NJ: Lawrence Erlbaum Associates.

Hersey, G. L. (1996). *The evolution of allure: Art and sexual selection from Aphrodite to the Incredible Hulk.* Cambridge, MA: MIT Press.

Hildebrand, G. (1991). *The Wright space.* Seattle: Washington University Press.

Hrdy, S. (1981). *The woman that never evolved.* Cambridge, MA: Harvard University Press.

Humphrey, N. K. (1980). Natural aesthetics. In B. Mikellides (Ed)., *Architecture for people* (pp. 59–73). London: Studis Vista.

Jackson, L. A. (1992). *Physical appearance and gender: Sociobiological and sociocultural perspective.* Albany, NY: SUNY Press.

Johnston, V. S., & Franklin, W. M. (1993). Is beauty in the eye of the beholder? *Ethology and Sociobiology, 14,* 183–199.

Kaplan, S. (1992). Environmental preference in a knowledge-seeking, knowledge-using organism. In J. Barkow, L. Cosmides, & J. Tooby (Eds.), *The adapted mind: Evolutionary psychology and the generation of culture* (pp. 581–600). Oxford, England: Oxford University Press.

Kellert, S. R., & Wilson, E. O. (Eds.). (1993). *The biophilia hypothesis.* Washington, DC: Island Press.

Kovach, F. J. (1974). *Philosophy of beauty.* Norman: University of Oklahoma Press.

Lewontin, R. C., Rose, S., & Kamin, L. J. (1984). *Not in our genes: Biology, ideology and human nature.* New York: Pantheon.

Møller, A. P. (1992). Female swallow preference for symmetrical male sexual ornaments. *Nature, 357,* 238–240.

Morris, W. (Ed.). (1976). *The American heritage dictionary.* Boston: Houghton-Mifflin.

Orians, G. H. (1980). Habitat selection: General theory and applications to human behavior. In J. S. Lockard (Ed.), *The evolution of human social behavior* (pp. 49–66). Chicago: Elsevier.

Orians, G. H., & Heerwagen, J. H. (1992). Evolved responses to landscapes. In J. Barkow, L. Cosmides, & J. Tooby (Eds.), *The adapted mind: Evolutionary psychology and the generation of culture* (pp. 555–580). Oxford, England: Oxford University Press.

Perret, D. I., May, K. A., & Yoshikawa, S. (1994). Facial shape and judgments of facial attractiveness. *Nature, 368,* 239–242.

Reeve, H. K., & Sherman, P. W. (1993). Adaptation and the goals of evolutionary research. *Quarterly Review of Biology, 68,* 1–32.

Rentschler, I., Caelli, T., & Maffei, L. (1988). Focusing in on art. In I. Rentschler, B. Herzberger, & D. Epstein (Eds.), *Beauty and the brain: Biological aspects of aesthetics* (pp. 181–218). Berlin: Birkhäuser Verlag.

Rentschler, I., Herzberger, B., & Epstein, D. (Eds.). (1988). *Beauty and the brain: Biological aspects of aesthetics.* Berlin: Birkhäuser Verlag.

Ridley, M. (1993). *The red queen: Sex and the evolution of human nature.* New York: Macmillan.

Rozin, E. (1988). Aesthetics and cuisine—mind over matter. In I. Rentschler, B. Herzberger, & D. Epstein (Eds.), *Beauty and the brain: Biological aspects of aesthetics* (pp. 315–326). Berlin: Birkhäuser Verlag.

Singh, D. (1993). Adaptive significance of female physical attractiveness: Role of waist-to-hip ratio. *Journal of Personality and Social Psychology, 65,* 293–307.

Solso, R. L. (1994). *Cognition and the visual arts.* Cambridge, MA: MIT Press.

Soulé, M. E. (1992). Biophilia: Unanswered questions. In S. R. Kellert & E. O. Wilson (Eds.), *The biophilia hypothesis* (pp. 441–455). Washington, DC: Island Press.

Symons, D. (1979). *The evolution of human sexuality.* Oxford, England: Oxford University Press.

Symons, D. (1982). Another woman that never evolved. *Quarterly Review of Biology, 57,* 297–300.

Symons, D. (1987). If we're all Darwinians, what's the fuss about? In C. Crawford, M. Smith, & D. Krebs (Eds.), *Sociobiology and psychology: Ideas, issues and applications* (pp. 121–146). Hillsdale, NJ: Lawrence Erlbaum Associates.

Symons, D. (1992). On the use and misuse of Darwinism in the study of human behavior. In J. Barkow, L. Cosmides, & J. Tooby (Eds.), *The adapted mind: Evolutionary psychology and the generation of culture* (pp. 137–162). Oxford, England: Oxford University Press.

Symons, D. (1995). Beauty is in the adaptations of the beholder: The evolutionary psychology of human female sexual attractiveness. In P. R. Abramson & S. D. Pinkerton (Eds.), *Sexual nature/sexual culture* (pp. 80–118). Chicago: University of Chicago Press.

Thornhill, R. (1990). The study of adaptation. In M. Bekoff & D. Jamieson (Eds.), *Interpretation and explanation in the study of animal behavior* (Vol. 2, pp. 31–61). Boulder, CO: Westview.

Thornhill, R., & Gangestad, S. W. (1993). Human facial beauty: Averageness, symmetry and parasite resistance. *Human Nature, 4,* 237–269.

Thornhill, R., & Gangestad, S. W. (1994). Human fluctuating asymmetry and sexual behavior. *Psychological Science, 5,* 297–302.

Thornhill, R., & Gangestad, S. W. (1996). The evolution of human sexuality. *Trends in Ecology and Evolution, 11,* 98–102.

Thornhill, R., Gangestad, S. W., & Comer, R. (1995). Human female orgasm and mate fluctuating asymmetry. *Animal Behaviour, 50,* 1601–1615.

Tooby, J., & Cosmides, L. (1989). Evolutionary psychology and the generation of culture: Part I. Theoretical considerations. *Ethology and Sociobiology, 10,* 29–50.

Tooby, J., & Cosmides, L. (1990). On the universality of human nature and the uniqueness of the individual: The role of genetics and adaptation. *The Journal of Personality, 58,* 17–67.

Tooby, J., & Cosmides, L. (1992). The psychological foundations of culture. In J. H. Barkow, L. Cosmides, & J. Tooby (Eds.), *The adapted mind: Evolutionary psychology and the generation of culture* (pp. 19–136). Oxford, England: Oxford University Press.

Turner, F. (1991). *Beauty: The value of values.* Charlottesville: University of Virginia Press.

Turner, F., & Pöppel, E. (1988). Metered poetry, the brain and time. In I. Rentschler, B. Herzberger, & D. Epstein (Eds.), *Beauty and the brain: Biological aspects of aesthetics* (pp. 71–90). Berlin: Birkhäuser Verlag.

Ulrich, R. S. (1993). Biophilia, biophobia and natural landscapes. In S. R. Kellert & E. O. Wilson (Eds.), *The biophilia hypothesis* (pp. 73–137). Washington, DC: Island Press.

Watson, P. W., & Thornhill, R. (1994). Fluctuating asymmetry and sexual selection. *Trends in Ecology and Evolution, 9,* 21–24.

Williams, G. C. (1992). *Natural selection: Domains, levels and challenges.* Oxford, England: Oxford University Press.

Wilson, E. O. (1984). *Biophilia.* Cambridge, MA: Harvard University Press.

Wilson, E. O. (1993). Biophilia and the conservative ethic. In S. R. Kellert & E. O. Wilson (Eds.), *The biophilia hypothesis* (pp. 31–41). Washington, DC: Island Press.

Wright, R. (1994). *The moral animal. Why we are the way we are: The new science of evolutionary psychology.* New York: Pantheon.

Zahavi, A. (1975). Mate selection—a selection for a handicap. *Journal of Theoretical Biology, 53,* 205–214.

Zollinger, H. (1988). Biological aspects of color naming. In I. Rentschler, B. Herzberger, & D. Epstein (Eds.), *Beauty and the brain: Biological aspects of aesthetics* (pp. 149–164). Berlin: Birkhäuser Verlag.

# 19

## The Global Environmental Crisis and State Behavior: An Evolutionary Perspective*

Yuwa Hedrick-Wong
*Horizon Pacific International, Vancouver*

Global warming, ozone depletion, deforestation, soil erosion, the poisoning of the seas and rivers, the loss of biodiversity, and species extinction have become the all too familiar litany of warnings that environmental scientists have been telling us. A consensus has emerged over the past decade among the scientific community that large-scale atmospheric, terrestrial, and aquatic environmental changes are becoming increasing probable if nothing is done, and done effectively, to check the degradation of the environment. Many of these changes could mean potentially catastrophic trends that threaten to destroy the earth's capacity to sustain life. As the Worldwatch Institute recently stated: "The environmental era now dawning is distinguished by problems truly global in scale" (Brown, Flavin, & Postel, 1989; Gordon & Suzuki, 1991; see also World Commission on Environment and Development, 1987).

This specter of environmental destruction is the latest addition to a long list of threats and dangers that have come to characterize our late 20th-century existence. It is well known that the nuclear arms race mortgaged the future of humanity to the maintaining of the balance of power between the superpowers. It is also well known that a fraction of what we spend annually on armaments would suffice in eradicating famine

*Previously published in *Politics and the Life Sciences*, 13(1), 3–14, 1994, as "Impotence and Intransigence: State Behaviour in the Throes of Deepening Global Crisis." Revised and updated in February 1995.

and disease in some of the poorest countries. There is little doubt that insidious and continuous proliferation of nuclear weapons, particularly in more unstable and war-prone regions, may pose a far greater threat of nuclear war than the arms race between the superpowers once had.

More recently, it has become apparent that environmental degradation and conflict potential is closely linked, especially when competition for dwindling essential resources becomes desperate. One estimate indicates that about 40% of the world's population depends on the 214 major river systems shared by two or more countries for drinking water, irrigation, and hydropower. Twelve water basins of these river systems, where some of the most fertile lands are located, are shared by five or more countries (Renner, 1989). It does not take an active imagination to see how a rise of water level or contamination of these water sources would lead to boundary disputes and open hostilities. Homer-Dixon (1991) developed a conceptual framework linking types of environmental change and their impact on the social system with specific kinds of acute conflict. The economic and political consequences of the environmental crisis may well exceed those of the natural kind (Gleick, 1993; Hampson, 1988; Ophuls & Boyan, 1992; Stern, Young, & Druckman, 1992; Wirick, 1989).

Why have we put up with these dangerous developments for so long? The answer is simple. To deal effectively with problems posed by these developments, genuine international cooperation is required. It is precisely genuine international cooperation that we do not have. As the environmental crisis threatens the fate of humanity as a whole, humanity must act in concert to avert disasters. Strangely enough, even in the face of such disasters, humanity remains divided.

Leading scholars have meticulously worked out systems and institutional structures through which genuine international cooperation might be fostered. These scholars are aware of the egoistic nature and self-centered orientation of sovereign states. Yet, they believe that, given a recognition of mutual interests, coupled with appropriate international institutions, states could be made to cooperate in pursuit of common good (Axelrod & Keohane, 1985; Beitz, 1979; Keohane, 1984).[1] Many international institutions, particularly those within United Nations (U.N.) organizations, have been consciously modeled in accordance with some of these theoretical principles intended to promote international morality and cosmopolitanism in state behavior. Yet the reality has been sadly disappointing. Keenly aware of the impending perils ahead, political scientist

---

[1]The potential for applying Axelrod's (1984) intriguing reciprocity model of cooperation is limited in this context because it requires genuine altruism on the part of some of the players for the protection of the global commons. Reciprocity simply could not be maintained in all cases.

Deutsch (1986) suggested that sovereign states in the future must become what he called adaptive-learning states, capable of abandoning self-interest in favor of new global priorities. He also conceded that the adaptive-learning state remains a speculative construction.

The problem is not that we do not know what we must do—the writing is on the wall. We know we must cooperate and make sacrifices when necessary to save the environment and improve the welfare of the global poor. There is no lack of visionaries who can vividly describe far better alternatives than what we face today. Indeed, the World Commission on Environment and Development's authoritative text on the environmental crisis, *Our Common Future* (1987), is eloquent and passionate on the need for international cooperation, yet it is also awkwardly silent on how it can be accomplished. It is as if something built into the nature of the state renders it *impotent* in pursuing genuine cooperation and *intransigent* in upholding national interests, even when these interests are at the expense of global welfare.

## IMPOTENCE

As essayist Cousins (1987) pointed out, "the self-determination of one nation is the anarchy of all" (p. 37). Nowhere is the situation of anarchy more vividly demonstrated than in issues involving the environment. Each country has its own priorities regarding development and economic growth that are formulated quite independently from those of other countries, let alone priorities of humanity as a whole. These national priorities typically supersede concerns about the environment, especially when such concerns are perceived as occurring outside one's territory. Even when serious environmental damages occur within one's territory, the immediate benefits almost always take priority over future consequences.

In such an anarchic system, sovereign states appear to be impotent in attempting genuine cooperation. The state's ability to project its military power remains the ultimate means to exert influence and settle disputes (Puchala, 1971; Tilly, 1979). Collective action can occur only on the basis of great power agreement, or when a block of countries share a common interest in opposition against another power or block of countries (Finkelstein & Finkelstein, 1966). NATO and the Warsaw Pact were perfect examples in the era of superpower confrontation. As the Cold War has come to pass, new alliances are forming while old ones are dissolving. The power vacuum left behind by the former USSR is either being filled by regional powers, or is resulting in unbalance, uncertainties, and regional upheavals. Global anarchy is now worsening, not improving, in the era of postsuperpower confrontation.[2]


## INTRANSIGENCE


In such an anarchic international arena, the most important concern for a sovereign state is the integrity of its territory. This "hard shell," which provides a state's ultimate identification, is typically seen as more important than other factors such as language, customs, law, and politics (Herz, 1957). Political scientist Ted Robert Gurr (1986) concisely captured this aspect of the state. He observed that: "The essence of the state, past and present, is a bureaucratically institutionalized pattern of authority whose rulers claim to exercise sovereign (ultimate) control over the inhabitants of a territory, and who demonstrate enduring capacity to enforce that claim" (p. 11).

Therefore, for the sovereign state the protection and preservation of territorial integrity is the ultimate national interest. From this stems their intransigent persistence in setting national priorities above global ones. Indeed, many international orders have been established explicitly to preserve member states' territorial integrity. Among weak and inefficient states, such as those in sub-Sahara Africa, for example, interstate organizations such as the Organization for African Unity have been created to help maintain the existing state boundaries, and to preserve the independence and survival of member states. This is so even when it is clear that most of the existing state boundaries in sub-Saharan Africa today are inherited from past colonial administrations, and bear virtually no resemblances to the continent's ethnic and cultural divisions (Jackson & Rosenberg, 1982).

Consequently, many governments in the Third World have resisted international efforts in environmental conservation not only because these efforts would slow economic development, but because they are also seen as an encroachment on sovereignty. In many countries, both rich and poor, environmental activists are routinely accused of being traitors and

---

[2]The dissolution of the USSR also means that the world is now more distinctively divided into the wealthy industrialized North versus the underdeveloped South. Krasner (1985) observed that the North–South conflict will be an enduring one in the international arena. The North will continue to preserve the status quo in international transactions that largely favor the North. The South will staunchly defend its sovereignty against foreign encroachment and internal dismemberment, and consequently resist international efforts in areas like population control, human rights, basic human needs, and environmental conservation, which it perceives as the state's internal affairs in dealing with its own subjects.

unpatriotic.[3] Former Brazilian president Jose Sarney, when faced with the rising barrage of international criticism over the destruction of the Amazon rain forests, replied that: "Brazil is ours. The Amazonia is ours. Nature there is ours and it is our duty to defend it. We are free" (*The Global and Mail*, September 16, 1988, p. A7). Thus, every state clings to its sovereignty, like a lead lifesaver in a sea of looming global disasters. As each hides behind its own zealously guarded hard shell, blind to the plight of the global commons, the lament of the World Commission on Environment and Development, that the earth is one but the world is not rings truer than ever.

Given this state of affairs, a terrible dilemma confronts genuine transnational cooperation. On the one hand, global anarchy reigns if the sovereignty of the state is upheld as the constitutive principle of the international system. In lieu of a miraculous mass transformation of priorities and behavior everywhere, the alternative is some form of hegemony, led by either a global or regional power, that can temporarily overcome the anarchy that hinders collective action. Unfortunately, this would be collective action in the service of the hegemonic power, rather than genuine transnational cooperation for the common good. Neither anarchy or hegemony is desirable.

## AN EVOLUTIONARY PERSPECTIVE

To better understand the impotence and intransigence of sovereign state, this chapter explores the origin of today's sovereign state from a perspective that is largely foreign to mainstream political science—an evolutionary perspective. I believe such shackles on state behavior are but the tip of an iceberg, their evolutionary base hidden from view. Their foundation lies in behavioral and psychological patterns that have been shaped throughout 99% of humanity's evolutionary history.

The development of such an evolutionary perspective is spurred by the consideration of two puzzles. First, why did large-scale societies evolve from small bands of extended families that had been the prevalent form of human social structure for millions of years? Large-scale societies came into being only a few thousand years ago. How did this abrupt transformation come about, and what are some of its consequences? Second, how are the cohesion and stability of large-scale societies, such as today's sovereign states, maintained? Given their lack of any obvious biological evolutionary basis, how have these states managed to bring together hundreds of thousands, even millions, of biologically unrelated

---

[3]For example, see "The Environment Special Report," *Maclean's*, September 17, 1990.

individuals to share a common identity, to develop a sense of loyalty to the state, to the extent that some would even sacrifice their lives in times of war? These two puzzles guide this inquiry. Resolving them casts new light on the impotence and intransigence of sovereign states to fully effect international environmental development and cooperation required today. It also offers possible clues on a way out.

## THE EVOLUTION OF THE STATE

Living in a society with a centralized government and bureaucracy seems normal. From an evolutionary perspective, however, the existence of centralized states is neither natural nor easily explained. Roger Masters, a political scientist who has devoted his scholarship to bridging the gap between political theory and the theory of evolution, pointed out that: "Humans survived and flourished for millennia in face-to-face social groups or tribes that did not need the institution of a state; . . . the origin of the state must be shown to have adaptive benefits for competing individuals who did not need to cooperate with strangers or support governments in order to survive and reproduce" (Masters, 1989, p. 151).

What were those early human groups, and why had they survived for such an extended time period? The remarkable stability of early human groups, prior to the recent emergence of centralized states, stems from the fact that they were actually extended families. Group members, numbering a hundred or so individuals at most, were related by birth. It was within these early human groups, over millennia, that humans evolved to care and protect not only themselves, but also their genetic relatives. In their hunter–gatherer existence, cooperation and sharing between members of these groups were easily accomplished, and self-sacrificial behavior in defense of the group came naturally.[4]

The stability of these groups also meant strong resistance to group expansion. To group members, group expansion means accepting biologically unrelated strangers into their midst. This entails tremendous risk. Strangers may take advantage of the group, they may cheat, or they may alter or complicate the existing hierarchical structure of the group, consequently weakening its solidarity. Why then would the early human

---

[4]William Hamilton, the Oxford biologist, coined the term *inclusive fitness* to describe this phenomenon of mutual aid and assistance between genetic relatives. Under certain conditions, an individual may sacrifice him- or herself for the protection of his genetic relatives, with the result that his or her inclusive fitness is increased even if he or she perishes in doing so. As a reproductive strategy that is favored by evolution, inclusive fitness has far-reaching consequences in affecting human social behavior, including the evolution of our altruistic preferences, group identity, and sense of belonging (Hamilton, 1963, 1964).

bands expand in the face of such risks? There must have been powerful factors that drove groups to expand despite these risks.

## Balance of Power Hypothesis

One factor consistently identified by scholars is group competition and warfare. The central role of intergroup conflict in spurring the process of group expansion has been formulated as the *balance of power hypothesis* (Alexander, 1971, 1975, 1979). It postulates a process in which the expansion of one group and its consequent competitive advantages in warfare would lead to other groups attempting to expand in response. Those groups that failed to expand and evolve increasingly more complex and efficient social structures would have been eliminated over evolutionary time. Thus, the balance of power hypothesis suggests that, once the process of intergroup competition started, the extended family-based bands became inadequate and obsolete. The ultimate incentive for group expansion was the need to avoid paying the ultimate price—conquest and destruction by rival bands.

Available evidence on the emergence and demise of prehistoric societies is remarkably consistent with the balance of power hypothesis. All point to the central role of intergroup competition and conflict, and how it may have interacted with population growth, discoveries of new technologies, production of surplus, and new social organizations that launched the process of group expansion (Adams, 1975; Bigelow, 1971; Claessen & ven de Velde, 1987; Dumond, 1972; Sahlins, 1968; Service, 1971, 1975; Strate, 1982; Wittfogel, 1957).

Environmental factors also played a role. For example, Joyce (1989) argued convincingly that environmental changes during the Holocene period accelerated the process of intergroup competition and expansion. The most significant change was the extinction of large mammals and the subsequent proliferation and concentration of many seasonally available tropical plants and animals in "strategic areas." A shift toward reliance on these resources would have compelled early human bands to settle in and defend regions where these resources were abundant, thereby intensifying intergroup competition and conflict.

## Group Expansion

As group size increased, social organization became correspondingly more complex. Elite and centralized organizations emerged. The absorption of conquered populations into the group further increased the complexity of the hierarchical structures of the society (Carneiro, 1970). These developments, to the extent they were successful, in turn rendered the society yet more efficient in mobilizing its resources and manpower, and thus more successful in warfare. This resulted in a process of expansion from band to tribe, to chiefdom, to centralized state (Willhoite, 1986). Scholars have documented how, throughout history, chiefdoms have eventually been united into states, and states have gone to war to create larger states. They also confirm that preindustrial political systems that evolved into complex formations were almost always accompanied by military conquest or defense against equally large external groups (Carneiro, 1978; Lewellen, 1983). This process, driven by technological change and political competition, constitutes much of what is called *cultural evolution* (Phillips, 1992).

The emergence of contemporary states in the past few hundred years has, to a large extent, followed this pattern. For example, one estimate reports that, by 1900, there were around 20 times fewer independent polities in Europe than there had been in 1500. Most of these did not disappear peacefully, but were losers in a protracted period of incessant warfare (Cohen, Brown, & Organski, 1981). Examination of data from the United States, Great Britain, France, and Japan also shows that success in warfare tends to have positive impacts on consolidating and expanding state power. The more intensive and extensive the wars, the more powerful the impacts (Rasler & Thompson, 1985). A substantial body of empirical literature has also identified, in cross-cultural and historical contexts, the intimate relationship between war making and state making, leaving little doubt that the *raison d'être* for the existence of the state is to protect its subjects against predation from other states (Ames & Rapp, 1977; Anderson, 1974; Bean, 1973; Gilpin, 1981; McNeill, 1982; Modelski, 1978; Shaw & Wong, 1989; Tilly, 1979).

## STABILITY AND COHESION: THE PRICE OF SUCCESS

The victors that emerged from the process of intergroup conflict and competition were those with the savvy to form larger, more cohesive groups through conquest, absorption, or alliance. The outcome of this process is that the small early human bands, where face-to-face contact was the basis of social relations among members related by birth, were inexorably wiped off the face of the earth.[5] The norm today is that most of humanity lives in societies hundreds of thousand times larger than the individuals' respective extended families—hence, the second puzzle posed earlier: How are cohesion and stability maintained in these societies,

---

[5]The few exceptions are the !Kung bushmen of the Kalahari desert, the Australian aborigines, and the Inuits.

within which, from an evolutionary perspective, humanity has not really been equipped to live in?

## Coercion

One school of thought emphasizes the role of coercion in the maintenance of cohesion and stability in large-scale societies. Individuals are seen as coerced to live in their given society most of the time, sometimes violently against their wishes as in the extreme case of slavery. Elites that emerged as ruling clans, hereditary chiefdoms, dynastic orders, or aristocracy exercised coercion and control. The ruling elite may base their claim of superiority on the basis of ethnicity, religion, language, divine ordination, or, more frequently, some convenient combination of these (van den Berghe, 1981).

Irrespective of the basis of their claims, the ruling elite can succeed in superior status and disproportionate shares of wealth only if they can also succeed in monopolizing political power. Historical and anthropological data show that the cultural evolution of complex society has always been paralleled by the establishment of political domination, centralized government, and formal law. As such, effective use of political power is a prerequisite for stable, large-scale societies. Centralized political power, at least potentially, means the capacity for violent enforcement of social behavior in an impersonal context, and is most suitable for mass manipulation and persuasion (Geiger, 1988).

The structures of the society and the relationship between the ruler and the ruled may have changed, often radically, in the past few thousand years, but the monopoly of political power has remained an essential requisite for a viable society. It is no different in the liberal democratic states of today. Max Weber characterized contemporary states in terms of their features of legitimacy and the monopoly of the means of coercion (Gerth & Mills, 1946). In this context, the only distinction between liberal democratic states and various forms of dictatorship, personal rule, and despotism is that, in the former, political power is monopolized by the institutions of the state, whereas, in the latter, power is typically in the hands of ruling individuals.

Given such a monopoly of political power, whether by individuals or impersonal institutions, its abuse is inevitable. Indeed, recorded history is abundant with episodes of such abuse, the most extreme being genocide—premeditated large-scale murder of certain groups of people, whose existence is perceived as dangerous to the society by those in control of the state machinery of violence and coercion. It is by no means a rare occurrence. Political scientist Ted Gurr, for example, estimated that racially and ethnically motivated genocide has claimed between 7 and 16 million lives since World War II (Gurr & Harff, 1988). Contemporary examples include the Jewish Holocaust, the Bengalis in Bangladesh (1971), Southern Sudanese by Northern Sudanese (1950–1970), Tibetans by communist Chinese (1959–present), Kurds by Iraqis (1960–present), Burundi (1972), Cambodia (1975–1979), and East Timor (1975; Harff, 1986; Kuper, 1981). More recently, the ethnic cleansing in the former Yugoslavia, which is going on despite the presence of the U.N.'s peace-keeping forces and worldwide condemnation.

Even more disturbing are claims made by social scientists who have examined genocide in depth—that no society is immune from genocidal tendencies. It is somehow built into the institution of the sovereign state (Charny, 1982; Horowitz, 1980). Sociologist Leo Kuper (1981) put the matter precisely and bluntly: "the sovereign territorial state claims, as an integral part of its sovereignty, the right to commit genocide, or engage in genocidal massacres, against peoples under its rule, and that the United Nations, for all practical purposes, defends this right" (p. 21).

However, unmitigated coercion on its own has not always been effective in maintaining the cohesion and stability of the society. Indeed, history often shows that brutal repression may keep the lid on for the short term, only for it to explode with disastrous consequences later. Two recent examples illustrate the limitation of unrestrained use of coercion in maintaining societal cohesion.

When the revolutionary Khmer Rouge took over Cambodia in 1975, it unleashed a reign of terror. Khmer Rouge cadres systematically eliminated certain social classes deemed unfit for the new Cambodia they were building. Traditional family structures were uprooted, to be replaced by scientific socialism in the form of communes (labor camps). In the 5 years of Khmer Rouge's rule, millions of Cambodians perished—many were summarily executed in the "killing fields." Such a regime of terror, however, weakened the society so much so that when the Vietnamese invaded in 1979, the Khmer Rouge could not rally the people to put up an effective resistance, and was toppled in a matter of months.[6]

Events in the former USSR present a different aspect of the limitation of coercion. The USSR, a society composed of over 100 nationalities, had been incorporated by the Russian majority by force, first under the Czar and then under Stalin. During the past 70 years, an elaborate system of coercion and control had been established to smother any nationalistic dissent or sentiments. Whole nationalities have been uprooted and exiled, others dispersed or otherwise silenced. Yet the explosive fragmentation of the former USSR into myriad new independent states powerfully demonstrates that aspiration for independence and self-determination had

---

[6]For a detailed description of life under the Khmer Rouge, see Becker (1986).

been alive and well even during those years of brutal suppression. As Brzezinski (1989/1990) put it: "whereas Marx once described the Tsarist Russian empire as the prison of nations, and Stalin turned it into the graveyard of nations, under Gorbachev the Soviet empire is rapidly becoming the volcano of nations" (p. 2; see also Shaw & Wong, 1989). The volcano exploded.

Coercion may be an effective means to maintain societal cohesion and stability in the short term, but unrestrained use of brutality and repression frequently leads to the disintegration of the society. Therefore, coercion on its own is insufficient in holding large-scale societies together in the long term. It is only one side of the coin. The other side, and every bit as important as coercion, is loyalty.

## Loyalty

Individuals' heartfelt loyalty to their countries is unquestionably an important factor that makes many large-scale societies viable. No amount of coercion can explain why individuals routinely sacrifice themselves in warfare, often with the knowledge of certain death. Such self-sacrificial behavior, although easily understood when parents protect their children or relatives band together in defense of their clans, is puzzling when found among individuals in groups of hundreds of thousands of unrelated members. How does a large-scale society mobilize individuals for its defense, and successfully exact a loyalty strong enough to inspire self-sacrificial behavior?

The answer is this: For all societies to mobilize successfully, they must return to what humanity knows best—over hundreds of thousands of years of mutual assistance and solidarity in bands of extended families. Although societies today are enormously large from the standpoint of the family, they are often made to bear as much resemblance to the family unit as possible. It begins with the label.

All sovereign states today would like to be known as nation-states, although they rarely are. The implication of being a nation-state is that all members of the state are supposed to belong to a nation. What then is a nation? Anthony Smith (1981, 1984, 1988, 1989), a leading scholar in this field, described a *nation* as a community that displays characteristics of sharing a set of myths of common origin and descent, a common historic territory or homeland, and common language, religion, customs, and cultural traditions—factors that contribute critically to a sense of solidarity among members of the so-called nation.

From this point of view, the essence of a nation is its psychological bond that joins its members together and instills a notion that they are somehow different from all other people (Connor, 1978). It has been argued that the social solidarity of a nation is ultimately based on the subtle belief that it is a suprafamily (see Shaw & Wong, 1989). Thus, when a sovereign state labels itself as a *nation-state*, its intention is clear: It would like its members to believe they all share a common descent and belong to a vast, extended family. Witness familial labels such as *fatherland, mother country*, and *Uncle Sam*, which harness a sense of loyalty that comes with being a member of an extended family, something to which humanity has been conditioned during its evolutionary past (Hinde, 1989; Johnson, 1986, 1989).

Not all sovereign states succeed, however, in convincingmembers it is a nation-state. In fact, the vast majority of the states today are not nation-states. Most of them are what we would call *multiethnic states*. In other words, they are sovereign states composed of groups of people distinguishable by their respective ethnic and cultural characteristics, including their different beliefs of common descent. They have ended up as members of the same sovereign state because of historical conquest, migration, absorption, slavery, and, more recently, immigration. To sort out these complexities, and to ascertain how effectively loyalty can be instilled in these different contexts, a model known as the *identification mechanism* has been formulated.

Five variables, known as *recognition markers*, are singled out by the model as most critical in transferring group allegiance from small extended family-based bands to tribes, to chiefdoms, to centralized states. They are language, religion, phenotype, homeland, and the myth of common descent. The more these five recognition markers converge in the same group, the easier it is for group members to feel that they belong together, and that the group resembles a suprafamily. When all five recognition markers are forcefully present in the same group, the group is ethnically homogenous and qualifies as a true nation.[7] Group mobilization utilizing a convergence of these recognition markers tends to be extremely powerful. A historical analysis of the English, French, Russian, and Chinese revolutions, for example, shows that these drastic regime changes were accompanied by effective nationalistic mobilization at the grassroots level involving the five recognition markers. As a result, the new regimes all exhibited renewed military prowess and capability (Adelman, 1985).

However, not all societies can tap the potential strength conveyed by the recognition markers. The ultimate test for true "nation" status, as

---

[7]For a detailed discussion of the model of the identification mechanism, see Shaw and Wong (1989). A prime example of a true nation-state is Japan. Its extraordinary cohesion, sense of ethnocentrism and xenophobia, and particularly the people's willingness for self-sacrifice, both in times of war and national reconstruction, can be explained in terms of the similarity between national and family affairs (see Shaw & Wong, 1989).

specified by the identification mechanism model, is whether the society in question can entertain a credible myth of common descent. From this perspective, the vast majority of the sovereign states today are not nation-states, but multiethnic states. In multiethnic states, the solicitation of individual loyalty is more difficult, and sometimes impossible. In this regard, two generic types of multiethnic states need to be differentiated.

The first type is a multiethnic state created by conquest and arbitrary absorption, such as the former USSR and the vast majority of sub-Saharan African states. Ethnic minorities in a multiethnic state of this kind are reluctant to be assimilated, often actively resisting the majority group's attempts to do so. As mentioned earlier, ethnic minorities' nationalism in the USSR had been kept alive despite decades of suppression. In sub-Saharan Africa, contemporary state boundaries were created on the basis of colonial administrative units, and bear no resemblance to indigenous group identities, tribal loyalties, and traditional homelands (Asiwaju, 1985; Brass, 1984; Chabal, 1986; Mazrui, 1986; Migdal, 1988). In these situations, a contest between loyalty toward the state and loyalty toward one's own ethnic group invariably ends with the latter being more potent and long lasting.

The second type of multiethnic state is formed through voluntary immigration, such as the United States. With the exception of the importation of slaves, all other groups arrived in the United States as voluntary immigrants in search of a better life. As a consequence, they are anxious to be accepted and given full opportunity to participate in the society. They are eager to demonstrate their loyalty, especially in times of war. The strength of U.S. patriotism, despite the diversity of its population, is a testimony to the extent of the loyalty felt by its citizens toward their country.[8]

Most of the multiethnic states today are neither as successful as the United States, nor as unsuccessful as the former USSR. However, for most of them, most of the time, securing loyalty from their respective subjects is an ongoing concern. Many face some form of internal challenge in varying intensity, and must coordinate carefully the use of coercion with efforts to cultivate loyalty. Such states are not always successful, and there is no simple formula to guarantee positive results.

## The Price of Success: The Potential Instability of States

If we look at today's large-scale societies as victors in the evolutionary process of intergroup conflict and competition, the price they have paid, and are still paying, for their success is evident. Regardless of differences in levels of economic development, political ideology and institutions, size, and other factors, most states today must cope with separatist move-

---

[8]For a comparison between the USSR and the United States from the perspective of the identification mechanism, see Shaw and Wong (1989).

ments, ethnic mobilization by aggrieved minorities, and communal and regional conflicts. This is not only true for the new states in sub-Saharan Africa and other parts of the Third World, but also in parts of Europe, Asia, and North America. The phenomenon is global.[9] From an evolutionary perspective, sovereign states today, with the few exceptions of true nation-states, suffer chronic problems of instability as a result of their awesome growth in size and complexity over the last 10,000 years. The state must cope with complexities arising from cultural, ethnic, religious, linguistic, andregional differences in its population. Such differences often determine the state's elite composition, national identity, and institutions, favoring the dominant group at the expense of the minorities. Minority groups' mobilization, in turn, affects and often constrains the state's ability to balance coercion and loyalty as means to maintain the stability of the society.[10] The root cause of instability for most multiethnic states can therefore be summarized as follows: Although coercion alone is inevitably inadequate in maintaining social cohesion, the solicitation and maintenance of loyalty are extremely difficult.

## CHALLENGES AND STRATEGIC RESPONSES

Today's sovereign states are caught in a bind, victimized by their own success. Humanity must now identify and coordinate its activities with ever larger numbers of people in an increasingly impersonal context. All this is extremely alien to humanity's experience of intimate face-to-face interactions among members of extended families, which has characterized our evolutionary past. Rapid group expansion has created enormous stress on group stability.[11]

The bind is a direct consequence of two opposing forces. The first is the need to maintain cohesion and stability in large-scale societies. As argued earlier, the state must strive to be the institution where individuals' sense of belonging, identity, and social obligations are met. It must convince individuals that their well-being and survival depend on it. The

---

[9]For a discussion of ethnic mobilization in Europe, see Smith (1981). For a more global view, see van den Berghe (1981).

[10]For an informative discussion of the relationship between state and society from the perspective of ethnicity, see Brown (1989).

[11]The rise of bureaucracy has been devised as an impersonal means to administer the distribution and allocation of benefits and costs in a large-scale society. Its functions are meant to ensure that all members of the ingroup, however large, are being treated equally. As Max Weber remarked: "Bureaucracy is the means of carrying the 'community action' into rationally ordered 'societal action'" (Gerth & Mills, 1946, p. 228). But bureaucratic organizations have also created problems of rigidity, incompetence, and nepotism. For further discussions on the subject of bureaucracy and the evolution of large-scale societies see Betzig (1986) and Masters (1986).

ultimate rationale for the indispensability of the state is its claim that it can protect its citizens from predation and exploitation by other states.

The second and opposing force is the increasingly clear need for states to cooperate, giving up some of their sovereignty if necessary to respond effectively and in concert to emerging global crises (Bromley, 1992; Ostrom, 1990). But this is something that is extremely foreign to the entire evolutionary history of the sovereign state. Sovereign states have evolved primarily for competition and conflict, not cooperation. Therefore, despite clear perception of the urgent need to change their behavior, sovereign states are at a loss as to what to do.

Caught in such a bind, the behavior of sovereign states is therefore erratic and self-contradictory. In the face of clear recognition of impending environmental disasters, the vast majority of states have responded. There is no lack of international initiatives, resolutions, conferences, and protocols aimed at improving cooperation, preserving the environment, and protecting humanity's common future. The U.N. has pronounced the 1990s the "Fourth Development Decade." It completed a major international conference on the environment and development in 1992. Hardly a day goes by without some government or minister proposing, agreeing, or voting for some new resolution or joint declaration on the environment. However, these activities are mostly confined to the level of rhetoric; they are the kind of things sovereign states know how and are willing to do.

The Second Climate Conference held in Geneva in November 1990 is one such example. One hundred and thirty-seven countries participated. All agreed that a world climate treaty must be set to halt global warming, yet the conference failed to establish concrete deadlines for greenhouse gas reduction. The Americans wanted to talk about an agreement to stop deforestation before they would talk about reduction of fossil fuel use. The Brazilians, who have most of the trees, refused. The Saudi Arabians did not want to talk about carbon dioxide, which comes partly from burning their oil, but were interested in a reduction of other greenhouse gases. Thus, the conference ended and nothing was accomplished other than the usual lofty rhetoric (*The Economist*, November 1990).

The Rio Conference on the Environment and Development, despite the extensive press coverage and public attention, has basically repeated the past patterns. Many resolutions were drafted, approved, and publicized, but concrete actions are far from forthcoming. Indeed, one of the critical issues—population growth—was eliminated from the conference agenda in the early planning stages for fear of causing disharmonies among participating states.[12]

---

[12]For a discussion of the importance of the population factor in the environmental crisis, see *The Economist*, May 30, 1992, and United National Population Fund (1991).

Meantime, however, sovereign states are continuing business as usual in maintaining their monopoly of political power, enhancing their coercive capacity, and maneuvering to secure the populace's loyalty. Thus, state policies in the wealthy industrialized West continue to encourage and protect its profligate lifestyles, thereby continuing the consumption of vast amounts of natural resource and energy, and generating mountains of industrial waste and pollutants. In contrast, many of the poorest Third World countries are spending up to one half of their national incomes on equipping and expanding their armed forces, even as their economies are collapsing, their debts are rising, and their natural environments are in ruins. As political scientist Bjorn Hettne (1988) pointed out: ". . . very few governments in the Third World are concerned with development as a priority area. They are busy keeping themselves in power, fighting neighbours or suppressing rebellions" (p. 20; see also Bratton, 1989).

This situation is akin to a group of people in a lifeboat on the high seas. If they all row together in the same direction, they may have a chance to reach shore and safety. Instead, one person decides to row in one direction, another in the opposite. One starts a fire to boil and evaporate the water inside the boat, another drills holes to pump the water out. One captures the food locker and hoards it. Others pray and scold. Some decide to use the oar as weapons. As time passes and their situation becomes more precarious, they are no nearer to the shore.[13]

Although the manifestations are many and varied, the sovereign state is constrained in its behavior in two major ways. First, because of its inherent instability, the sovereign state must maintain a vigilant insistence on its monopoly of political power, with all the coercive capacity that it implies. This effectively bars individuals from interacting in international affairs as citizens of the world, rather than members of a specific sovereign state. Second, the sovereign state must diligently cultivate the loyalty of its citizens. The state must portray itself as representative of the national interests, and act in favor of groups from the most powerful and populous classes. Consequently, global priorities are ignored while national priorities are promoted and jealously guarded.[14]

Contemporary sovereign states, as powerful as they are in affecting international affairs, global events, and people's lives generally, are thus paradoxically constrained in their freedom of action. State power, however defined, has been shown time and again to be dependent on internal factors that affect how easily or difficult loyalty and social cohesion can

---

[13]This lifeboat analogy was suggested by Professor Claude Phillips of the University of Michigan at Kalamazoo.

[14]Empirical confirmation of this type of state behavior can be found in Farhi (1988) and Kaplan (1985).

be maintained, and external factors that determine degrees of international competition and conflict (Colburn, 1988; Gurr, 1988; Snider, 1987). These constraints have biased state behavior so much so that we find ourselves at the brink of global environmental disasters. Without exaggeration, sovereign states today are the most serious road blocks to realizing visions of a common humanity with a viable common future.

Are we doomed, like individual Titanics, secured in our respective steel hulk called sovereign state, rushing toward the iceberg in the darkness of the night? Does the owl of Minerva fly only at dusk? As formidable as the challenges ahead are, I do not believe there is no way out. An evolutionary analysis of social and political behavior does not imply things are somehow immutable or pre-ordained. However, it does warn against unqualified optimism and facile utopianism. The value of an evolutionary approach is precisely that it can uncover deep causes of certain human social behavior and explain why these behaviors are often extremely difficult to change. Therefore, it points to the need for strategic thinking.[15]

Although an outline of detailed, strategic alternatives requires further study, this chapter attempts to develop two principles for action—one passive and the other active. The first is the principle of avoiding tasks that, given the evolutionary perspective developed earlier, are highly unlikely to be successful. Professor Karl Deutsch's concept of an adaptive-learning state, however rational and necessary, is in all likelihood a pipe dream. All international efforts based on the premise that sovereign states would somehow learn to be genuinely altruistic and cooperative are doomed to failure. Such attempts in the past have wasted tremendous amounts of precious resources, time, and talent, producing empty rhetoric and hollow, unenforceable protocols. The principle here is to let us examine what can be done, even if at a much reduced scale, and without the pretense that sovereign states are genuinely interested in mutual assistance and cooperation. Billions of dollars are still available for international development each year. It is now time to use that money for concrete small gains, instead of gigantic failures.[16]

The second and active principle is to bypass sovereign states in environmental and development efforts. A prime example are nongovernmental organizations (NGOs). The growth of NGOs in both the developed West and Third World countries that are devoted to environmental and development issues is perhaps the most encouraging sign of our time.

---

[15]Strategic thinking here refers to the method of outmaneuvering obstacles that cannot be tackled head on. "Strategic thinking succeeds by inducing the coming together and even reversal of opposites" (Luttwak, 1987).

[16]One proposal of how this may be accomplished is outlined in a manuscript entitled, "The Silent War: Failures in International Development—Causes, Symptoms and Remedies" (Shaw & Wong, 1990).

For NGOs to be truly effective, however, they must adhere to the follow-ing criteria: retain independence from sovereign states, have as their goals global instead of parochial/regional concerns, and develop links between abstract global issues, such as the diminishing rain forestation, ozone depletion, and global warming, and humanity's deep-rooted concerns for kith and kin, such as whether one's children and grandchildren will breathe clean air and lead healthy lives free from crippling diseases and natural disasters caused by a deteriorating environment.

The need for NGOs' true independence is obvious, although it is by no means easy. Many NGOs, particularly in the developed West, are dependent on governments for funding. They are then subject to govern-ment inspection, or even subtle manipulation. They must insist on being truly independent. The same is true for NGOs in developing countries. Indeed, in most developing countries, local NGOs require prior approval of the government before they can receive funding from international sources. Such interference frequently subverts the apolitical nature of the NGOs, and undermines their effectiveness.[17] To meet the global challenge, NGOs must maintain and guard their independence vigilantly.

The case for global orientation is also obvious, although in practice many NGOs are issue or region oriented. The caveat here is that this issue/region orientation should in no way contribute to, however unwit-tingly, divisions and conflict at a global level. The role of some NGOs in famine relief in Ethiopia and Sudan, for example, has been shown to be counterproductive. Many such NGOs are evangelical in nature, and often have conflicting agency objectives (Zmolek, 1990). Only a firm commit-ment to a global orientation can provide the necessary common ground for NGOs to harmonize their efforts and objectives.

The last criterion, the need to link global problems with individuals' personal priorities, is perhaps most significant. When individuals can see clearly that their personal priorities—the welfare of their kith and kin, which is ultimately dependent on a sustainable common future—are not well served by the state as global crises loom larger and larger, there is then a chance that individuals may gradually switch their loyalty from the state to the global commons. It may well pave the way to the obso-lescence of the sovereign state.[18]

These are tall orders, and this chapter has only begun to scratch the surface in outlining these principles. NGOs are just one example consistent

---

[17]For example, Bretta (1989) observed in Kenya and Zimbabwe that the government is suspicious of and antagonistic to NGOs that are dedicated to development.

[18]Daly and Cobb (1989) worked out an intriguing economic model for environmentally sustainable development. Significantly, the primary precondition in their model is the need to return to the community, where there is strong interpersonal relations and democratic interactions and decision making.

with such principles, lest it be misunderstood that NGOs are seen as the end all and be all. There will be many more such alternatives as attention is focused in this direction. The challenge at hand is daunting, but the prospect of failing to meet the challenge is more daunting still. Herein lies my hope and optimism.

## REFERENCES

Adams, R. N. (1975). *Energy and structure: A theory of social power.* Austin: University of Texas Press.

Adelman, J. R. (1985). *Revolution, armies, and war—a political history.* Boulder, CO: Lynne Rienner.

Alexander, R. D. (1971). The search for an evolutionary philosophy of man. *Proceedings of the Royal Society of Victoria, 84,* 99–120.

Alexander, R. D. (1975). The search for a general theory of behavior. *Behavioural Science, 20,* 77–100.

Alexander, R. D. (1979). *Darwinism and human affairs.* Seattle: University of Washington Press.

Ames, E., & Rapp, R. T. (1977). The birth and death of taxes: A hypothesis. *Journal of Economic History, 37,* 161–178.

Anderson, P. (1974). *Lineages of the absolutist state.* London: New Left Book.

Asiwaju, A. I. (1985). *Partitioned Africans.* Oxford, England: Oxford University Press.

Axelrod, R. (1984). *The evolution of cooperation.* Chicago: University of Chicago Press.

Axelrod, R., & Keohane, R. O. (1985). Achieving cooperation under anarchy: Strategies and institutions. *World Politics, 38,* 226–254.

Bean, R. (1973). War and birth of nation state. *Journal of Economic History, 33,* 203–221.

Becker, E. (1986). *When the war was over.* New York: Touchstone.

Beitz, C. R. (1979). *Political theory and international relations.* Princeton, NJ: Princeton University Press.

Betzig, L. L. (1986). *Despotism and differential reproduction—a Darwinian view of history.* New York: Aldine deGruyter.

Bigelow, R. (1971). *The dawn warriors.* Boston: Little, Brown.

Brass, P. (Ed.). (1984). *Ethnic groups and the state.* London: Croom Helm.

Bratton, M. (1989). Beyond the state: Civil society and associational life in Africa. *World Politics, XLI(3),* 407–430.

Bretta, M. (1989). The politics of government–NGO relations in Africa. *World Development, 17,* 569–587.

Bromley, D. W. (Ed.). (1992). *Making the commons work—theory, practice, and policy.* San Francisco: Institute for Contemporary Studies Press.

Brown, D. (1989). Ethnic revival: Perspective on state and society. *Third World Quarterly, 11,* 1–17.

Brown, L., Flavin, C., & Postel, S. (1989). A world at risk. In *The state of the world.* Washington, DC: World Watch Institute.

Brzezinski, Z. (1989/1990). Post-communist nationalism. *Foreign Affairs, 68,* 1–25.

Carneiro, R. L. (1970). A theory of the origin of the state. *Science, 169,* 733–738.

Carneiro, R. L. (1978). Political expansion as an expression of the principle of competitive exclusion. In R. Cohen & E. R. Service (Eds.), *Origins of the state: The anthropology of political evolution* (pp. 31–48). Philadelphia: Institute for the Study of Human Issues.

Chabal, P. (Ed.). (1986). *Political domination in Africa.* London: Cambridge University Press.

Charny, I. W. (1982). *How can we commit the unthinkable? Genocide: The human cancer.* Boulder, CO: Westview.

Claessen, H. J. M., & ven de Velde, P. (Eds.). (1987). *Early state dynamics.* New York: E. J. Brill.

Cohen, Y., Brown, B. R., & Organski, A. F. K. (1981). The paradoxical nature of state making: The violent creation of order. *American Political Science Review, 75,* 901–910.

Colburn, F. D. (1988). Statism, rationality, and state centrism. *Comparative Politics, 20,* 485–492.

Connor, W. (1978). A nation is a nation, is a state, is an ethnic group, is a. . . . *Ethnic and Racial Studies, 1,* 377–399.

Cousins, N. (1987). *The pathology of power.* New York: Norton.

Daly, H. E., & Cobb, J., Jr. (1989). *For the common good: Redirecting the economy toward community, the environment and a sustainable future.* Boston: Beacon.

Deutsch, K. W. (1986). State functions and the future of the state. *International Political Science Review, 7,* 209–222.

Dumond, D. E. (1972). Population growth and political centralization. In B. Spooner (Ed.). *Population growth: Anthropological implications* (pp. 89–112). Cambridge, MA: MIT Press.

*The Economist,* November, 1990.

Farhi, F. (1988). State disintegration and urban-based revoltuonary crisis—a comparative analysis of Iran and Nicaragua. *Comparative Political Studies, 20,* 485–492.

Finkelstein, M. S., & Finkelstein, L. S. (1966). *Collective security.* New York: Harper & Row.

Geiger, G. (1988). On the evolutionary origins and function of political power. *Journal of Social and Biological Structure, 11,* 235–250.

Gilpin, R. (1981). *War and change in world politics.* London: Cambridge University Press.

Gerth, H. H., & Mills, C. W. (Eds.). (1946). *From Max Weber: Essays in sociology.* Oxford, England: Oxford University Press.

Gleick, P. H. (1993). Water and conflict. *International Security, 18,* 79–112.

*The Global and Mail,* September 16, 1988, p. A7.

Gordon, A., & Suzuki, D. (1991). *It's a matter of survival.* Cambridge, MA: Harvard University Press.

Gurr, T. R. (1986). The political origins of state violence and terror. In M. Stahle & G. A. Lopez (Eds.), *Government violence and repression: An agenda for research.* New York: Greenwood.

Gurr, T. R. (1988). War, revolution, and the growth of the coercive state. *Comparative Political Studies, 20,* 45–65.

Gurr, T. R., & Harff, B. (1988). Toward empirical theory of genocide and politicides: Identification and measurement of cases since 1945. *International Studies Quarterly, 3,* 359–371.

Hamilton, W. (1963). The evolution of altruistic behaviour. *American Naturalist, 97,* 354–364.

Hamilton, W. (1964). The genetic evolution of social behaviour: I and II. *Theoretical Biology, 7,* 1–16, 17–52.

Hampson, F. O. (1988). The climate for war. *Peace and Security, 3,* 8–9.

Harff, B. (1986). Genocide as state terrorism. In M. Stahle & G. A. Lopez, (Eds.), *Government violence and repression: A research agenda* (pp. 58–81). New York: Greenwood.

Herz, J. H. (1957). Rise and demise of the territorial state. *World Politics, 9,* 347–362.

Hettne, B. (1988). The world of crisis for the nation-state. *Development, 2/3,* 14–25.

Hinde, R. A. (1989). Patriotism: Is kin selection both necessary and sufficient? *Politics and the Life Sciences, 8,* 58–61.

Homer-Dixon, T. F. (1991). On the threshold—environmental changes as causes of acute conflict. *International Security, 16,* 76–116.

Horowitz, I. L. (1980). *Taking lives: Genocide and state power.* New Brunswick, NJ: Transaction.

Jackson, R. H., & Rosenberg, C. G. (1982). Why Africa's weak states persist: The empirical and the juridical in statehood. *World Politics, 35,* 56–78.

Johnson, G. R. (1986). Kin selection, socialization, and patriotism: An integrating theory. *Politics and the Life Sciences, 4,* 127–154.

Johnson, G. R. (1989). The role of kin recognition mechanism in patriotic socialization: Further reflections. *Politics and the Life Sciences, 8,* 62–69.

Joyce, A. (1989). The nuclear arms race: An evolutionary perspective. *Politics and the Life Sciences, 7,* 186–202.

Kaplan, M. (1985). Recent trends of the nation-state in contemporary Latin America. *International Political Science Review, 6,* 81–103.

Keohane, R. O. (1984). *After hegemony—cooperation and discord in the world economy.* Princeton, NJ: Princeton University Press.

Krasner, S. D. (1985). *Structural conflict—the Third World against global liberalism.* Berkeley: University of California Press.

Kuper, L. (1981). *Genocide: Its political use in the twentieth century.* New Haven, CT: Yale University Press.

Lewellen, T. C. (1983). *Political anthropology.* South Hadley, IL: Bergin & Garvey.

Luttwak, E. N. (1987). *Strategy.* Cambridge, MA: Harvard University Press.

*Maclean's* (1990, September 17). The environment special report, pp. 11–15.

Masters, R. D. (1986). The problem: Is bureaucracy an "unnatural" phenomenon? In E. White & J. Losco (Eds.). *Biology and bureaucracy* (pp. 28–47). Lanham, MD: University of America Press.

Masters, R. D. (1989). *The nature of politics.* New Haven, CT: Yale University Press.

Mazrui, A. A. (1986). *The Africans: A triple heritage.* London: Heinemann.

McNeill, W. H. (1982). *The pursuit of power.* Chicago: University of Chicago Press.

Migdal, J. (1988). *Strong societies and weak states.* Princeton, NJ: Princeton University Press.

Modelski, G. (1978). The long cycle of global politics and the nation state. *Comparative Studies in Society and History, 20,* 214–235.

Ophuls, W., & Boyan, A. S., Jr. (1992). *Ecology and the politics of scarcity revisited: The unraveling of the American dream.* New York: Freeman.

Ostrom, E. (1990). *Governing the commons.* Cambridge, England: Cambridge University Press.

Phillips, C. (1992). *The dynamics of political evolution.* Unpublished manuscript.

Puchala, D. J. (1971). *International politics today.* New York: Harper & Row.

Rasler, K. A., &. Thompson, W. R. (1985). War making and state making: Governmental expenditures, tax revenues, and global wars. *American Political Science Review, 79,* 491–507.

Renner, M. (1989). Enhancing security. In L. R. Brown & M. Renner (Eds.), *The state of the world.* Washington, DC: World Watch Institute.

Sahlins, M. P. (1968). *Tribesmen.* Englewood Cliffs, NJ: Prentice-Hall.

Service, E. R. (1971). *Primitive social organizations: The process of cultural evolution.* New York: Norton.

Service, E. R. (1975). *The evolution of state and civilization.* New York: Norton.

Shaw, R. P., & Wong, Y. (1989). *Genetic seeds of warfare: Evolution, nationalism and patriotism.* Boston: Unwin Hyman.

Shaw, R. P., & Wong, Y. (1990). *The silent war: Failures in international development—causes, symptoms, and remedies.* Unpublished manuscript.

Smith, A. D. (1981). *The ethnic revival.* Cambridge, England: Cambridge University Press.

Smith, A. D. (1984). Ethnic identity and the myth of ethnic descent. *Research in Social Movement, Conflict and Change, 7,* 95–130.

Smith, A. D. (1988). The myth of "modern nation" and the myth of nations. *Ethnic and Racial Studies, 11,* 1–20.

Smith, A. D. (1989). The origins of nations. *Ethnic and Racial Studies, 12,* 340–367.

Snider, L. W. (1987). Identifying elements of state power—where do we begin? *Comparative Political Studies, 20,* 314–356.

Stern, P. C., Young, O. R., & Druckman, D. (1992). *Global environmental change: Understanding the human dimension*. Commission on the Behavioral and Social Sciences and Education, National Research Council.

Strate, J. (1982). *An evolutionary view of political culture*. Unpublished doctoral dissertation, University of Michigan, Ann Arbor.

Tilly, C. (Ed.). (1979). *The formation of national states in Western Europe*. Princeton, NJ: Princeton University Press.

Tilly, C. (1979). *Sinews of war*. Presented at the annual meeting of the Council of European Studies Conference of Europeanists, Washington, DC.

United Nation Population Fund. (1991). *Population, resources and the environment—the critical challenge*. New York: Author.

van den Berghe, P. (1981). *The ethnic phenomenon*. New York: Elsevier.

Willhoite, F. H., Jr. (1986). Political evolution and legitimacy: The biocultural origins of hierarchical organizations. In E. White & J. Losco (Eds). *Biology and bureaucracy—public administration and public policy from the perspective of evolutionary, genetic, and neurobiological theory* (pp. 56–78). Lanham, MD: University Press of America.

Wirick, G. (1989). Environment and security: The case of Central America. *Peace and Security*, 4, 2–4.

Wittfogel, K. A. (1957). *Oriental despotism: A comparative study of total power*. New Haven, CT: Yale University Press.

World Commission on Environment and Development. (1987). *Our common future*. Oxford, England: Oxford University Press.

Zmolek, M. (1990, January 6). Aid agencies, NGOs, and institutionalization of famine. *Economic and Political Weekly*, pp. 37–48.

# 20

## The Evolutionary Psychology of Spatial Sex Differences

Irwin Silverman
Krista Phillips
*York University*

The creator of Fig. 20.1 was either conversant with the psychological literature on sex differences or an astute observer of behavior. Indeed, males use cardinal directions such as north and south more than females, who tend toward relative directions such as left and right (Ward, Newcombe, & Overton, 1986). This is one of a miscellany of human sex differences in the realm of spatial behavior.

Spatial sex differences are both qualitative and quantitative. *Qualitative differences* refer to disparate strategies preferred by males and females to solve specific spatial problems. The prior example was not the only difference between sexes in route learning; males also employ distance concepts more than females, who rely more on landmarks (Bever, 1992; Galea & Kimura, 1993). Thus, a male directing you to a location will more likely tell you it is, "ahead about 2 miles on the northeast corner," whereas a female is more apt to say, "just past the traffic light, across from the church."

Studies of quantitative differences tend to show a male advantage across a variety of spatial tasks. These include: mental rotation of objects, mentally constructing figures from patterns, perception of horizontality, recognition of shapes embedded in other shapes, creating designs from their parts, map reading, maze solving, and estimating the speed of a moving object. Magnitudes of sex differences vary among tests, with mental rotations showing the largest differences and three-dimensional tasks showing greater differences than two-dimensional tests (Halpern,

**SALLY FORTH**

FIG. 20.1. Sally Forth. Copyright © 1994 by The Hearst Corporation. Reprinted with special permission of King Features Syndicate.

1992; Linn & Peterson, 1985; McGee, 1979; Phillips & Silverman, 1993). In five studies from our research program, comprised of samples from the United States, Canada, and Japan, the variance accounted for by sex differences on the three-dimensional mental rotations test depicted in Fig. 20.2 ranged fairly evenly from 14% to 29%.

The study of spatial sex differences, particularly the tendency for males to excel, has traditionally been a focus of controversy in the behavioral sciences between hereditarians and environmentalists. Earlier approaches dealt mainly with socialization practices, based on the assumption that society encourages and reinforces males more than females to engage in activities that promote the development of spatial skills (Hoyenga & Hoyenga, 1979; Maccoby & Jacklin, 1974). In support of this notion, studies have demonstrated augmenting effects of training and practice on some spatial skills (e.g., Brinkmann, 1966; Connor, Shackman, & Serbin, 1978; Vandenberg, 1975). There are also data indicating that training and practice effects are greater for females, although these findings have been

FIG. 20.2. Two sample items from the Mental Rotations Test (the task is to designate which two of the four figures on the right depict the figure on the left in alternative positions.

disputed (Baenninger & Newcombe, 1989; Koslow, 1987). Recent trends, however, have shown a shift in emphasis to genetic factors based on several sources of evidence.

## EVIDENCE FOR GENETIC FACTORS

### Universality

One source of evidence is that the male advantage in spatial tasks is highly consistent across populations and situations. In addition to hundreds of studies throughout North America, spatial sex differences on a variety of tasks have been replicated in Japan (Mann, Sasanuma, Sakuma, & Masaki, 1990; England (Lynn, 1992); Scotland (Berry, 1966; Jahoda, 1980); Ghana (Jahoda, 1980); Sierra Leone (Berry, 1966); India, South Africa, and Australia (Porteous, 1965); and separately for Black and White racial groups within the United States (Samuel, 1983). The only culture where spatial sex differences have failed to appear is the Inuit of Baffin Island (Berry, 1966), where both sexes show atypically strong spatial abilities. Kagan and Kogan (1970) suggested that multiple generations of endogenous mating within this society may have resulted in a specialized gene pool.

In regard to age groups, spatial sex differences have been observed in children as young as preschoolers (McGuiness & Morley, 1991). However, the consensus is that differences do not appear reliably across tasks until early adolescence, which is generally attributed to accelerated hormonal differentiation (Burstein, Bank, & Jarvick, 1980; Johnson & Meade, 1987). One study (Willis & Schaie, 1988) has shown that, from this age, the direction and magnitude of sex differences tend to be constant throughout the life span.

The universality of spatial sex differences also extends across species. Studies with wild and laboratory rodents have shown that males consistently outperform females in maze learning tasks (Barrett & Ray, 1970; Gaulin & Fitzgerald, 1986; Joseph, Hess, & Birecree, 1978; Stewart, Skvarenina, & Pottier, 1975). Further, sex differences in route learning strategies similar to those described earlier for humans have been observed in rats. When navigating in radial-arm mazes, males tend to use distal cues such as the shape of the room, whereas females use landmarks (i.e., distinctive objects in the environment; Williams & Meck, 1991).

### Heritability

There is substantial evidence from the field of behavior genetics, most based on standard twin studies, to the effect that variation in spatial tests scores is to some degree heritable (Bouchard, Segal, & Lykken, 1990; DeFries,

Vandenberg, & McClearn, 1976; Osborne & Gregor, 1968; Plomin, Pederson, Lichtenstein, & McClearn, 1994; Tambs, Sundet, & Magnus, 1984; Vandenberg, 1969). Consistent with data on the magnitude of sex differences, the largest heritability estimates appear to be for mental rotations tasks.

O'Connor (1943) was the first to surmise that spatial abilities is a sex-linked recessive characteristic. Several studies of intrafamilial correlations have supported this contention (Ashton & Borecki, 1987; Bock & Kolakowski, 1973; Hartlage, 1970; Yen, 1975), whereas others have not (Bouchard & McGee, 1977; DeFries et al., 1976). McGee (1979) noted that the extent to which familial correlations approximate predictions based on the sex-linkage hypothesis depends on the type of spatial task used, with three-dimensional mental rotations providing the best fit.

## Hormonal Influences

Another impetus for the current emphasis on genetic factors has been the discovery of hormonal influences on spatial sex differences, operating again in parallel manner in humans and animals (see Burstein et al., 1980; Gaulin & Hoffman, 1988; Harris, 1978; Kimura & Hampson, 1993; Linn & Peterson, 1985; McGee, 1979; Reinisch, Ziemba-Davis, & Saunders, 1991; Williams & Meck, 1991)

For the most part, these studies have focused on the organizational properties of hormones; that is, hormonal influences on the ontogenetic development of spatial abilities to a stable, mature state. Organizational determinants have been experimentally manipulated in animals, and inferred in humans from such correlates as maturational level, physical characteristics, and atypical hormone production associated with medical disorders.

Recent studies, however, both human and animal, have begun to consider the activational role of hormones; shorter term effects on spatial behaviors of hormonal fluctuations due to naturally occurring cycles or other transitory occurrences (e.g., Binnie-Dawson & Cheung, 1982; Gordon, Corbin, & Lee, 1986; Hampson, 1990a, 1990b, 1990c; Kimura & Toussaint, 1991; Silverman & Phillips, 1993; Woodfield, 1984). Phillips and Silverman (1993), using menstrual cycle phase as the indicant of estrogen level, reported significantly greater activational effects for three-dimensional compared with two-dimensional spatial tests, which is congruent to the data cited earlier for both sex differences and heritability. These authors attributed the greater sex differences, heritability, and hormonal effects for three-dimensional spatial tests to their greater ecological validity. Humans and other animals develop and use their spatial behaviors in a three-dimensional world, hence this would seem to be the most salient test to study correlates of these behaviors.

Both organizational and activational studies generally show decreases in spatial abilities with increased estrogen levels, consistent with observed sex differences. Corresponding increases in spatial performance with increased testosterone levels, however, tend to occur for females, but not males. In fact, males frequently show a paradoxical, inverse effect (Gouchie & Kimura, 1991; Kimura & Toussaint, 1991; Nyborg, 1983, 1984). Nyborg (1983) attempted to explain this paradox in terms of the fact that plasma testosterone is, under some circumstances, converted to brain estrogen.

We have been measuring testosterone and estrogen levels in males by means of salivary assays and relating these, between subjects, to differences in three-dimensional mental rotations and nonspatial cognitive test scores. Thus far, we have found, for mental rotations scores only, a direct correlation with testosterone levels and an inverse correlation with estrogen levels, despite the fact that the two hormones were directly related. Compatible findings were reported by Janowsky, Oviatt, and Orwoll (1994), who found that performance on a different spatial test was enhanced with exogenous testosterone administration in males. In their study, however, increasing testosterone levels had the effect of decreasing estrogen levels. Apparently, hormonal effects and interactions are of a more complex nature than can be revealed by the current state of theory and data.

### Hemispheric Lateralization

There are a number of theories that ascribe spatial sex differences to differences in brain organization—specifically in regard to lateralization of function, whereby verbal behaviors tend to be mediated by the left hemisphere and spatial attributes by the right. One conjecture emanating from lateralization theories, first stated by Levy (1969), is that the hemispheres of males are more specialized for all lateralized functions. Supporting data come from perceptual asymmetry studies, in which visual and auditory stimuli are presented to the right or left hemispheres exclusively, and from studies of patients with unilateral hemispheric damage (see Hampson & Kimura, 1992; Kimura, 1987; McGlone, 1980).

In a variation of this concept, Waber (1976, 1977) maintained that the reason for the greater degree of functional lateralization in males was that they matured more slowly than females, allowing the hemispheres to develop a greater degree of specialization. In line with these notions, she found that late maturers of both sexes were superior in spatial ability than their early maturing counterparts.

A different perspective on lateralization effects was advanced by Annett (1985), who proposed the existence of a right-shift (rs) gene, effecting both handedness and lateralization patterns. According to Annett, individuals inheriting the gene from both parents (r++) tend to be right-handed and left-hemisphere dominant, which is disadvantageous for spatial problem solving because it biases the person toward the use of verbal strategies to solve spatial problems. She surmised further that males who are r++ are less adversely effected spatially than females because they are less prone in general toward verbal solutions. She attributed this to the slower maturation of their left hemispheres, and consequent slower development of their verbal skills, which appears antithetical to Waber's prior assumptions.

Direct tests of the right-shift theory applied to spatial sex differences have not been reported. Casey and Brabeck (1990) and Pezaris and Casey (1991), however, found data in support of their modified version of the theory, in which it is considered that r++ effects operate only in interaction with spatial problem-solving experience.

As noted by Gaulin and Hoffman (1988), one problem with lateralization theories is that they beg the question of why, if the hemispheres of males are more specialized and abilities are predicated on degree of specialization, males do not excel in verbal as well as spatial functions. The answer may reside in recent work by Kimura (1987), suggesting that sex differences in the basic elements of language reflect organizational differences in the anterior and posterior regions of the cortex, rather than in the hemispheres.

Finally, Broverman, Klaiber, Kobashi, and Vogel (1968) posed a theory of spatial sex differences based on their observation that tests that reliably differentiate the sexes, such as mental rotations and embedded figures, tend to require inhibition of attention to prominent stimulus features. They cited various sources of evidence suggesting that estrogen alters the balance among activational, sympathetic, and inhibitional parasympathetic processes in favor of the former, and they maintained that this accounts for the female disadvantage on these tests.

## EVOLUTIONARY-BASED THEORIES

### Gaulin and Fitzgerald's Theory of Mating Systems

The near universality of spatial sex differences across human cultures and their demonstrated hormonal bases, heritability, and occurrence in other species all indicate the feasibility of an evolutionary approach, but it was not recently that the first systematic attempt of this nature was reported by Gaulin and Fitzgerald (1986). These investigators proposed that spatial abilities would have been selected for more so in males than females in polygynous species only because polygynous males require navigational skills to maintain large home ranges in which to seek potential mates and/or resources to attract mates. (*Home range* refers to the area within which an animal freely travels on a regular basis.)

Gaulin and Fitzgerald tested their theory with two species of voles: one, meadow voles, which are polygynous, and the other, pine voles, which are monogamous. First, they compared sex differences in home range size between these species by tagging and following the animals daily in their natural habitats. Findings were consistent with their theory; sex differences in the direction of larger male home ranges occurred solely for meadow voles. Then they compared sex differences in spatial abilities between the species, using maze learning tasks; they found, also as predicted, a male bias for meadow voles only. In a follow-up study, Gaulin and his colleagues (Jacobs, Gaulin, Sherry, & Hoffman, 1990) compared sex differences in hippocampus size between these species (the hippocampus is assumed to have a significant role in the mediation of spatial functions). They found, again as expected, proportionally larger male hippocampi in meadow voles, but no sex differences in pine voles.

Presently, Gaulin and company are attempting to extrapolate these findings to other species showing spatial dimorphism, including humans. A 1988 article by Gaulin and Hoffman reviewed the cross-cultural literature on sex differences in home range size, showing a near universal male bias beginning at toddlerhood. It is generally held that polygynous mating systems are also characteristic of our species (Symons, 1979).

One aspect of the theory, however, may be questionable in its extrapolation to the human case—the assumption of an adaptive advantage of spatial skills for mate acquisition for males. Across human evolutionary history, females have shown greater natal dispersal (the distance traveled by an individual from natal site to first place of breeding) than their male counterparts (Koenig, 1989). If one implies from this that mobility is more directly associated with reproductive success for females than males, then, by Gaulin and Fitzgerald's reasoning, females rather than males should have been subject to stronger selection pressures for spatial abilities.

## Silverman and Eals' Theory of Division of Labor

Based in part on these considerations, Silverman and Eals (1992) posed an alternative theory, in which the critical factor in selection for human spatial sex differences was division of labor. Archeological and paleontological data demonstrate that, throughout the Pleistocene, which is considered the environment of evolutionary adaptedness (EEA) for humans, males predominantly hunted and females predominantly foraged (Tooby & DeVore, 1987).

As noted by Silverman and Eals,

The various spatial measures showing male bias (e.g., mental rotations, map reading, maze learning) correspond to attributes that would enable successful hunting. Essentially, these attributes comprise the abilities to orient oneself in relation to objects or places, in view or conceptualized across distances, and to perform the mental transformations necessary to maintain accurate orientations during movement. This would enable the pursuit of prey animals across unfamiliar territory and, also, accurate placement of projectiles to kill or stun the quarry. In fact, there have been studies based on the same evolutionary notions, demonstrating direct relationships between standardized spatial test scores and throwing accuracy (Jardine & Martin, 1983; Kolakowski & Molina, 1974). (pp. 534–535)

Silverman and Eals' contended further that if spatial attributes such as navigational skills and throwing accuracy evolved in males in conjunction with hunting, spatial specializations associated with foraging should have correspondingly evolved in females. Unlike animals, food plants are immobile, but they are embedded within complex configurations of vegetation. Successful foraging would require finding food sources within such configurations and relocating them in ensuing growing seasons (i.e., the capacity to rapidly learn and remember the contents of object arrays and the relationships in space of the objects to one another). Foraging success would also be increased by peripheral perception and incidental memory for objects and their locations, inasmuch as this would allow one to assimilate such information nonpurposively while walking about or carrying out other tasks.

Based on these conjectures, Silverman and Eals compared sexes on their abilities to learn contents and spatial configurations of object arrays, using various original test situations. In one, developed for group administration, subjects were presented with drawings of common objects in an array and asked to examine them for 1 minute. The other used an actual array. Subjects were left alone for 2 minutes in a small room (stimulus room), outfitted as a graduate student office, containing a variety of work-related and personal items. In some conditions, they were instructed to try to learn the objects in the room and their locations (directed learning); in others, they were unaware that their time in the room was related to the study (incidental learning).

Dependent variables comprised memory for items and their locations, assessed independently, using both recall and recognition as performance criteria. Females' scores consistently exceeded those of males at statistically significant levels with moderate to large effect sizes, with the largest effects occurring for incidental learning. A subsequent study by Gaulin, Silverman, Phillips, and Reiber (1995), using Silverman and Eals' group procedure, replicated these sex differences with a disparate population.

In a follow-up study, Eals and Silverman (1994) investigated whether females' advantages in recall of object arrays was based on their superior verbal skills; specifically, their greater capacity to recall object names

(Maccoby & Jacklin, 1974). It was suggested that, if this were so, it could be argued that female verbal superiority, at least in its rudimentary form, emerged also in human evolution as a product of division of labor. Similar to spatial differences, verbal sex differences are near universal and show hormonal correlates (Burstien, Bank, & Jarvick, 1980).

Eals and Silverman (1994) repeated the studies of Silverman and Eals, but with the inclusion of uncommon objects (i.e., items for which subjects would not possess verbal labels). For the group studies, all of the drawings in the array were composed of unfamiliar objects, gleaned from various catalogues and the investigators' imaginations. For the individual studies, uncommon objects, specially constructed or collected, were interspersed among familiar objects in the stimulus room, appearing as if they had some other research purpose.

The female advantage in recall of locations was wholly replicated for the group test. For the individual tests, female superiority in recall of common objects, as reported in Silverman and Eals, was also replicated, with the largest effects again occurring for incidental learning. A female bias in location recall was observed as well for uncommon objects, but only for conditions of incidental learning. Inasmuch as subjects in the group test were neither instructed nor led to attend to object locations, this also was regarded as an incidental learning condition. Thus, Eals and Silverman concluded that the strongest and most reliable sex differences in recall of object arrays, encompassing both familiar and unfamiliar objects, occurred when the learning was extraneous to the subjects' on-going activities. They also concluded that the female advantage in recall of object arrays appeared not to be mediated by verbal mechanisms.

On the basis of these stronger sex effects for incidental learning conditions, Eals and Silverman questioned whether sex differences in memory for object arrays reflect differences in attentional styles, rather than memory processes. Expanding on their original hunter–gatherer model, they reasoned that the ancestral functions of females as keepers of the habitat and caregivers of the young, as well as foragers for food, would have predisposed them to a more inclusive attentional style (i.e., they may spontaneously attend to a wider range of detail in their physical and social environments). In support of this notion, prior studies of children (Blaney, 1990) and adolescents (Windle, 1992) have suggested that males tend more than females to employ a narrowed attentional focus in various tasks. Giambra and Grodsy (1992) reported that adult women tend to have more frequent task-unrelated thought intrusions during reading than their male counterparts.

In our research program, we have begun testing the attentional style difference hypothesis with observational studies in a variety of sites where people peruse, such as museums, galleries, zoos, and so on. Thus far, consistent with expectations, we have noted a tendency for males to stop at fewer exhibits and show greater variability in time spent at those they do examine. We are also planning experimental studies directed toward the question of whether attentional style can account, at least in part, for sex differences in recall of object arrays under incidental conditions. We use a procedure adapted from Mandler, Seegmiller, and Day's (1977) method for measuring incidental learning with general attentional level controlled. Subjects are tested for location recall, but their attentions are directed to some aspect of the object array irrelevant to location (e.g., by having them estimate the prices of the items).

We are also interested in possible relationships between females' greater capacities for incidental object location recall and their propensities to use physical landmarks in spatial mapping and route learning tasks, discussed earlier. Choi (1994) found a significant positive correlation, exclusive to females, between landmark use in a map-reading task and a separate measure of object location recall. An interesting question from the standpoints of both evolutionary origins and ontogenetic development may be whether the greater use of landmarks by females in spatial mapping emanates from their greater ability for object location recall, or the reverse.

### Reconciling Evolutionary Theories

The evolutionary theories of Gaulin and Fitzgerald and Silverman and Eals may be regarded as competitive or complementary. On the one hand, there are species, such as among lions, which could provide a critical test between theories inasmuch as their mating systems are polygynous, but females do the hunting). On the other hand, the theories may be reconciled if we assume that, in a species or subspecies, any difference in selection pressures between sexes related to spatial behavior, whether it involves home range size or division of labor or some other ecological variable, may result in an evolved sexual dimorphism.

## CONTRIBUTIONS OF THE EVOLUTIONARY APPROACH

### Levels of Causation

Scientists deal with diverse levels of causation, which can be conceptualized on a continuum between proximate and ultimate. Proximate refers to more immediate causes—ultimate to those more remote. For example, if you were asked why you were reading this book, a proximate cause may be that it was recommended for a course you are taking; an ultimate explanation would be that your species is innately curious.

The theory of evolution by natural selection remains the sole scientific theory of the ultimate origins of animal and human behavior. Thus, by its virtual eschewal of this theory, traditional psychology has remained wholly proximate in its paradigms. Psychologists' attempts to understand the processes that propel and direct behavior are limited to *ontogenetic* development—events that occur during the life span of an organism. *Phylogenetic* development, comprising evolutionary origins of behavior, has an insignificant role in traditional psychological theorizing.

The issue is not whether proximate or ultimate approaches are superior. As evidenced in this chapter, evolutionary theories do not supplant proximate theories. Rather, they function to give these direction (e.g., the hippocampus size studies described earlier based on Gaulin and Fitzgerald's evolutionary model, or the studies of attentional style stemming from Silverman and Eals' theory). Evolutionary theories do not ignore questions of how proximate psychological or physiological mechanisms operate to elicit behavior. Rather, they attempt to explain how these mechanisms, as opposed to all other possible mechanisms, came to exist.

Consider one of the proximate explanations of spatial sex differences described herein; that male brains are more functionally lateralized than female brains. Without benefit of an evolutionary perspective, the reasoning seems to be that male and female brains became differentially lateralized by happenstance or some circumstance unrelated to spatial behavior, and spatial sex differences developed as an incidental effect of this divergence. Evolutionary psychology attempts to fill explanatory gaps of this nature. Basic to the theory of evolution by natural selection is the tenet that form follows function. Hands, teeth, eyes, and such were constructed by natural selection to do the things they do because the things they do conveyed adaptive advantages to their bearers, and so too were brains. If spatial sex differences were adaptive in human evolution, whether by facilitating mating strategies or division of labor, then it plausibly follows that sex differences in lateralization or any aspect of brain development that enabled these differences evolved as a result.

## Domain Specificity

Cosmides and Tooby (1992; Tooby & Cosmides, 1992) proposed a theory of the adaptive value of domain specificity in natural selection, which has potential to change the face of behavioral science in general and cognitive psychology in particular. Their model represents, "the abandonment of the axiom that evolved psychological mechanisms must be largely—or exclusively—general-purpose and free of any content or structure not put there by experience." They posited instead that,

> Both human and nonhuman minds contain—in addition to whatever general purpose machinery they may have—a large array of mechanisms that

are (to list some of the terms most frequently used) functionally specialized, content dependent, content specialized, domain specific, context specialized, special purpose, adaptively specialized, and so on. (Tooby & Cosmides, 1992, p. 93)

In a sense, Silverman and Eals' theory embodies the concept of domain specificity, in that these investigators analyzed spatial sex differences in terms of the evolution of diverse specializations, whereas most prior theories were based on the presumption of differential ability levels between sexes in the general domain of spatial ability.

Domain specificity is also fundamental to an emerging view of the present authors regarding the nature of three-dimensional mental rotations. As suggested previuosly, this ability seems to be the most salient of all measures of spatial behavior, yielding the largest and most reliable sex differences, heritability estimates, and hormonal effects, and providing the best evidence for sex-linked recessive characteristics.

Silverman and Phillips (1993) were struck by the magnitude of transient hormonal effects on three-dimensional mental rotations scores and pondered whether this faculty should continue to be included in the domain-general realm of spatial reasoning. They proposed that, "Three-dimensional mental rotations might be more accurately regarded as a 'spatial sense'; perhaps as genetically hard-wired in homo sapiens as in other animals which depend on spatial proficiencies to survive" (p. 267). Shephard and Cooper (1982) also had conceptualized three-dimensional mental rotations performance in this manner, stating that three dimensionality is one of the "most enduring and pervasive facts about our world," and hence, would be readily incorporated into "our genetically transmittable perceptual wisdom" (p. 3).

Congruent to this notion, Linn and Peterson (1986), using a meta-analysis technique based on the nature of the cognitive processes involved in solving individual spatial tests, concluded that mental rotations abilities occupy their own separate factor. Consistent also are studies of strategies for solving three-dimensional mental rotations (Cochran & Wheatley, 1989; Freedman & Rovagno, 1981; Schulz, 1991; Tapley & Bryden, 1977). The most successful strategy, employed more frequently by males, simply entails visual rotation of the test figure. Less successful strategies involve focusing on key features of test and target figures, and assessing how they compare in location, direction, angle, and so on.

Most writers regard these as alternative modes of spatial reasoning, labeling the visual rotation strategy *holistic* and the part-by-part strategies *analytical*. However, our view is that the capacity to mentally rotate a three-dimensional figure may be no more part of a general domain of spatial reasoning than the capacity of an infant to avoid crawling over precipices or a squirrel to leap between branches. We are currently engaged in studies emerging from this proposition (e.g., assessing hormonal activational effects on mental rotations strategies), and are exploring the domain specificity of other spatial behaviors.

## Nature and Nurture

Within traditional psychology, it is generally implied that when one speaks of evolutionary or innate causes, the behavior in question is fixed somehow in the gene, ready to roll out in complete and immutable form. This is usually contrasted with environmental causation, whereby behavior is assumed to occur independent of genes and can be readily altered. There are many labels for this dichotomy, such as biology versus culture, nature versus nurture, heredity versus environment, instinct versus learning, and innate versus acquired. For evolutionary psychologists, however, the division between heredity and environment is spurious. Within the evolutionary model, the complete explanation of behavior must always involve both.

It is axiomatic that there can be no function without structure, and the structures underlying psychological functions, just as those for other bodily functions, begin with genes (Dawkins, 1989). The causal sequence is that genes contain the DNA that program specific proteins, and that proteins, in turn, determine the specific nature of the cells of the body, including nerve cells. Nerve cells, of course, underlie all psychological activity. If the nerve cells mediating thoughts, feelings, or actions become impaired, then the capacities for thoughts, feelings, or actions also become impaired. If the organism dies and its nerve cells cease to function, then so too will its thoughts, feelings, and actions. Thus, genes must be regarded as integral to every aspect of behavioral development and expression.

This analysis does not rule out environment—molar psychological activity always occurs in response to environmental events—but it implies that the most feasible way to view the role of environment is in terms of its interaction with genetic constitution. All behavioral development, from the courtship song of a bird to the bond between mother and child, involves an organism programmed by its genes to react in certain ways to certain environmental events. These programs may be more or less plastic, but they will always entail genetic and environmental factors operating in concert.

Thus, evolutionary psychologists take no role in the heredity–environment debate, accepting as given that the effects of one can never be fully understood without reference to the other. Correspondingly, it is not the mission of evolutionary psychology to establish the prepotency of heredity or environment in the ontogeny of spatial sex differences. Their mission, rather, is to discover the particular nature of the interaction between heredity and environment that underlies the development of these differences.

It is also fallacious to presume that genetic causality implies immutability. Specific behaviors show considerable variation in mutability, but conventional wisdom suggests that this variation is largely irrelevant to the respective roles of heredity and environment. For example, it is probably easier to train your dog not to chase automobiles, which has direct evolutionary roots in the protection of the pack from predators, than to induce him to unlearn the trick which you may have taught him as a pup of begging for food. Many of our own species' taste preferences, such as for sweet substances or red meat, bear conspicuous evolutionary origins. These cravings, however, appear more easily controlled than cigarette smoking, although the latter undoubtedly has more of a learned component.

Hence, the establishment of an evolutionary basis for spatial sex differences has no connotation in itself regarding individual potential in any area of spatial behavior. If the evolutionary approach bears any implication for the individual, it resides solely in the premise that to act on a behavior requires foremost an accurate and complete understanding of its nature.

# REFERENCES

Annett, M. (1985). *Left, right, hand and brain: The right shift theory.* Hillsdale, NJ: Lawrence Erlbaum Associates.

Ashton, G. C., & Borecki, I. B. (1987). Further evidence for a gene influencing spatial behavior. *Behavior Genetics, 17,* 243–257.

Baenninger, M., & Newcombe, N. (1989). The role of experience in spatial test performance: A meta-analysis. *Sex Roles, 20*(5/6), 327–344.

Barrett, R. J., & Ray, O. S. (1970). Behavior in the open field, Lashley III maze, shuttle box and Sidman avoidance as a function of strain, sex, and age. *Developmental Psychology, 3,* 73–77.

Berry, J. W. (1966). Temme and Eskimo perceptual skills. *International Journal of Psychology, 1,* 207–229.

Bever, T. (1992). The logical and extrinsic sources of modularity. In M. Gunnar & M. Maratsos (Eds.), *Modularity and constraints in language and cognition* (Vol. 25, pp. 179–212). Hillsdale, NJ: Lawrence Erlbaum Associates.

Binnie-Dawson, J. L. M., & Cheung, Y. M. (1982). The effects of different types of neonatal feminization and environmental stimulation on changes in sex associated activity/spatial learning skills. *Biological Psychology, 15,* 109–140.

Blaney, N. T. (1990) Type A, effort to excel and attentional style in children: The validity of the MYTH. *Journal of Social Behavior and Personality, 5,* 159–182.

Bock, R. D., & Kolakowski, D. (1973). Further evidence of sex-linked major-gene influences on human spatial ability. *American Journal of Human Genetics, 25,* 1–14.

Bouchard, T. J., Jr., & McGee, M. G. (1977). Sex differences in human spatial ability: Not an X-linked recessive gene effect. *Social Biology, 24,* 332–335.

Bouchard, T. J., Jr., Segal, N. L., & Lykken, D. T. (1990). Genetic and environmental influences on special mental abilities in a sample of twins reared apart. *Acta Geneticae Medica Gemellologiae, 39,* 193–206.

Brinkmann, E. H. (1966). Programmed instruction as a technique for improving spatial visualization. *Journal of Applied Psychology, 50,* 179–184.

Broverman, D. M., Klaiber, E. L., Kobashi, Y., & Vogel, W. (1968). Roles of activation and inhibition in sex differences in cognitive abilities. *Psychological Review, 75,* 23–50.

Burstein, B., Bank, L., & Jarvick, L. F. (1980). Sex differences in cognitive functioning: Evidence, determinants, implications. *Human Development, 23,* 299–313.

Casey, M. B., & Brabeck, M. M. (1990). Women who excel in a spatial task: Proposed genetic and environmental factors. *Brain and Cognition, 12,* 73–84.

Choi, J. (1994). *Sex differences in spatial mapping strategies: Hormonal influences.* Unpublished master's thesis, York University, Toronto, Canada.

Cochran, K. F., & Wheatley, G. H. (1989). Ability and sex-related differences in cognitive strategies on spatial tasks. *The Journal of General Psychology, 116,* 43–55.

Connor, J. M., Shackman, M., & Serbin, L. A. (1978). Sex-related differences in response to practice on a visual-spatial test and generalization to a related test. *Child Development, 49,* 24–29.

Cosmides, L., & Tooby, J. (1992). Cognitive adaptations for social exchange. In J. H. Barkow, L. Cosmides, & J. Tooby (Eds.), *The adapted mind: Evolutionary psychology and the generation of culture* (pp. 163–228) New York: Oxford University Press.

Dawkins, R. (1989). *The selfish gene* (2nd ed.). New York: Oxford University Press.

DeFries, J., Vandenburg, S. G., & McClearn, G. E. (1976). Genetics of specific cognitive abilities. *Annual Review of Genetics, 10,* 179–207.

DeFries, J. C., Ashton, G. C., Johnson, R. C., Kuse, A. R., McClearn, G. E., Mi, M. P., Rashad, M. N., Vandenberg, S. G., & Wilson, J. R. (1976). Parent offspring resemblance for specific cognitive abilities in two ethnic groups. *Nature, 261,* 131–133.

Eals, M., & Silverman, I. (1994). The hunter-gatherer theory of spatial sex differences: Proximate factors mediating the female advantage in recall of object arrays. *Ethology and Sociobiology, 15,* 95–105.

Freedman, R. J., & Rovagno, L. (1981). Ocular dominance, cognitive strategy, and sex differences in spatial ability. *Perceptual and Motor Skills, 52,* 651–654.

Galea, L. A. M., & Kimura, D. (1993). Sex differences in route learning. *Personality and Individual Differences, 14,* 53–65.

Gaulin, S. J. C., & Fitzgerald, R. W. (1986). Sex differences in spatial ability: An evolutionary hypothesis and test. *The American Naturalist, 127,* 74–88.

Gaulin, S. J. C., & Hoffman, H. A. (1988). Evolution and development of sex differences in spatial ability. In L. Betzig, M. B. Mulder, & P. Turke (Eds.), *Human reproductive behavior: A Darwinian perspective* (pp. 129–152). Cambridge, England: Cambridge University Press.

Gaulin, S. J. C., Silverman, I., Phillips, K., & Reiber, C. (1995). *Menstrual cycle related changes in abilities and attitudes.* Unpublished manuscript.

Giambra, L. M., & Grodsky, A. (1992). The influence of age on spontaneous task-unrelated thought intrusions during reading. *Imagination, Cognition and Personality, 11,* 367–379.

Gordon, H. W., Corbin, E. D., & Lee, P. A. (1986). Changes in specialized cognitive function following changes in hormone levels. *Cortex, 22,* 399–415.

Gouchie, C., & Kimura, D. (1991). The relationship between testosterone levels and cognitive ability patterns. *Psychoneuroendocrinology, 16,* 323–324.

Halpern, D. F. (1992). *Sex differences in cognitive abilities* (2nd ed.). Hillsdale, NJ: Lawrence Erlbaum Associates.

Hampson, E. (1990a). Estrogen-related variations in human spatial and articulatory-motor skills. *Psychoneuroendocrinology, 15,* 97–111.

Hampson, E. (1990b). Variations in sex-related cognitive abilities across the menstrual cycle. *Brain and Cognition, 14,* 26–43.

Hampson, E. (1990c). Influence of gonadal hormones on cognitive function in women. *Clinical Neuropharmacology, 13,* 522–523.

Hampson, E., & Kimura, D. (1992). Sex differences and hormonal influences on cognitive function in humans. In J. B. Becker, S. M. Breedlove, & D. Crews (Eds.), *Behavioral endocrinology* (pp. 357–398). Cambridge, MA: MIT Press.

Harris, L. J. (1978). Sex differences in spatial ability: Possible environmental, genetic and neurological factors. In M. Kinsbourne (Ed.), *Asymmetric function of the brain* (pp. 465–522). Cambridge, England: Cambridge University Press.

Hartlage, L. C. (1970). Sex-linked inheritance of spatial ability. *Perceptual and Motor Skills, 31,* 610–621.

Hoyenga, K. B., & Hoyenga, K. T. (1979). *The question of sex differences: Psychological, cultural, and biological issues.* Boston: Little, Brown.

Jacobs, L. F., Gaulin, S. J. C., Sherry, D., & Hoffman, G. E. (1990). Evolution of spatial cognition: Sex-specific patterns of spatial behavior predict hippocampal size. *Proceedings of the National Academy of Science, USA, 87,* 6349–6352.

Jahoda, G. (1980). Sex and ethnic differences on a spatial-perceptual task: Some hypotheses tested. *British Journal of Psychology, 71,* 425–431.

Janowsky, J. S., Oviatt, S. K., & Orwoll, E. S. (1994). Testosterone influences spatial cognition in older men. *Behavioral Neuroscience, 108,* 325–332.

Jardine, R., & Martin, N. G. (1983). Spatial ability and throwing accuracy. *Behavior Genetics, 13,* 331–340.

Johnson, E. S., & Meade, A. C. (1987). Developmental patterns of spatial ability: An early sex difference. *Child Development, 58,* 725–740.

Joseph, R., Hess, S., & Birecree, E. (1978). Effects of hormone manipulation and exploration on sex differences in maze learning. *Behavioral Biology, 24,* 364–377.

Kagan, J., & Kogan, N. (1970). Individuality and cognitive performance. In P. Mussen & L. Carmichael (Eds.), *Manual of child psychology* (pp. 221–265). New York: Wiley.

Kimura, D. (1987). Are men's and women's brains really different? *Canadian Psychology, 28,* 133–147.

Kimura, D., & Hampson, E. (1993). Neural and hormonal mechanisms mediating sex differences in cognition. In P. A. Vernon (Ed.), *Biological approaches to the study of human intelligence* (pp. 375–397). Norwood, NJ: Ablex.

Kimura, D., & Toussaint, C. (1991, August). *Sex differences in cognitive function vary with the season.* Paper presented at the 21st annual meeting of the Society for Neuroscience, New Orleans, LA.

Koenig, W. D. (1989). Sex biased dispersal in the contemporary United States. *Ethology and Sociobiology, 10,* 263–278.

Kolakowski, D., & Molina, R. M. (1974). Spatial ability, throwing accuracy and man's hunting heritage. *Nature, 251,* 410–412.

Koslow, R. E. (1987). Sex-related differences and visual-spatial mental imagery as factors affecting symbolic motor skill acquisition. *Sex Roles, 17,* 47–60.

Levy, J. (1969). Possible basis for the evolution of lateral specialization of the human brain. *Nature, 224,* 614–615.

Linn, M. C., & Peterson, A. C. (1986). Emergence and characterization of sex differences in spatial ability: A meta-analysis. *Child Development, 56,* 1479–1498.

Lynn, R. (1992). Sex differences on the differential aptitude test in British and American adolescents. *Educational Psychology, 12,* 101–106.

Maccoby, E. E., & Jacklin, C. N. (1974). *Psychology of sex differences.* Stanford, CA: Stanford University Press.

Mandler, J. M., Seegmiller, D., & Day, J. (1977). On the coding of spatial information. *Memory & Cognition, 5*, 10–16.

Mann, V. A., Sasanuma, S., Sakuma, N., & Masaki, S. (1990). *Neuropsychologia, 28*, 1063–1077.

McGee, M. G. (1979). Human spatial abilities: Psychometric studies and environmental, genetic, hormonal and neurological influences. *Psychological Bulletin, 80*, 889–918.

McGlone, J. (1980). Sex differences in human brain asymmetry: A critical survey. *Behavioral and Brain Sciences, 3*, 215–263.

McGuiness, D., & Morley, C. (1991). Sex differences in the development of viseo-spatial abilities in pre-school children. *Journal of Mental Imagery, 15*, 143–150.

Nyborg, H. (1983). Spatial ability in men and women: Review and new theory. *Advances in Behaviour Research and Theory, 5*, 89–140.

Nyborg, H. (1984). Performances and intelligence in hormonally different groups. In G. J. DeVries, J. DeBruin, H. Uylings, & M. Cormer (Eds.), *Progress in brain research* (Vol. 61, pp. 491–508). Amsterdam, The Netherlands: Elsevier.

O'Connor, J. (1943). *Structural visualization.* Boston: Human Engineering Laboratory.

Osborne, B. T., & Gregor, A. J. (1968). Racial differences in heritability estimates for tests of spatial ability. *Perceptual and Motor Skill, 27*, 735–739.

Phillips, K., & Silverman, I. (1993, August). *Evolutionary theory and data regarding activational effects of estrogen on female spatial performance.* Presented in the symposium titled "Evolution and Human Cognition" at the meetings of the Human Behavior and Evolution Society, Binghamton, NY.

Plomin, R., Pederson, N. L., Lichtenstein, P., & McClearn, G. E. (1994). Variability and stability in cognitive abilities are largely genetic later in life. *Behavior Genetics, 24*, 207–215.

Porteous, S. D. (1965). *Porteus maze test: Fifty years application.* Palo Alto, CA: Pacific Books.

Reinisch, J., Ziemba-Davis, M., & Saunders, S. (1991). Hormonal contributions to sexually dimorphic behavioral development in humans. *Psychoneuroendocrinology, 16*, 213–278.

Samuel, W. (1983). Sex differences in spatial ability reflected in performance on I.Q. sub-tests by black or white examinees. *Personality and Individual Differences, 4*, 219–221.

Schulz, K. (1991). The contribution of solution strategy to spatial performance. *Canadian Journal of Psychology, 45*, 474–491.

Shephard, R. N., & Cooper, I. A. (1982). *Mental images and their transformation.* Cambridge, MA: MIT Press.

Silverman, I., & Eals, M. (1992). Sex differences in spatial abilities: Evolutionary theory and data. In J. H. Barkow, L. Cosmides, & J. Tooby (Eds.), *The adapted mind: Evolutionary psychology and the generation of culture* (pp. 533–549). New York: Oxford University Press.

Silverman, I., & Phillips, K. (1993). Effects of estrogen changes during the menstrual cycle on spatial performance. *Ethology and Sociobiology, 14*, 257–270.

Stewart, J., Skvarenina, A., & Pottier, J. (1975). Effects of neonatal androgens on open-field behavior and maze learning in the prepubescent and adolescent rat. *Physiological Behavior, 14*, 291–295.

Symons, D. (1979). *The evolution of human sexuality.* Oxford, England: Oxford University Press.

Tambs, K., Sundet, J. M., & Magnus, P. (1984). Heritability analysis of the WAIS subtests: A study of twins. *Intelligence, 8*, 283–293.

Tapley, S. M., & Bryden, M. P. (1977). An investigation of sex differences in spatial ability: Mental rotation of three-dimensional objects. *Canadian Journal of Psychology, 31*, 122–130.

Tooby, J., & Cosmides, L. (1992). The psychological foundations of culture. In J. H. Barkow, L. Cosmides, & J. Tooby (Eds.), *The adapted mind: Evolutionary psychology and the generation of culture* (pp. 19–136). New York: Oxford University Press.

Tooby, J., & DeVore, I. (1987). The reconstruction of hominid behavioral evolution through strategic modeling. In W. G. Kinzey (Ed.), *The evolution of human behavior: Primate models* (pp. 183–237). Albany, NY: SUNY Press.

Vandenberg, S. G. (1969, July). A twin study of spatial ability. *Multivariate Behavioral Research*, pp. 273–294.

Vandenberg, S. G. (1975). Sources of variance in performance on spatial tests. In J. Eliot & N. J. Salkind (Eds.), *Children's' spatial development* (pp. 57–66). Springfield, IL: Thomas.

Waber, D. P. (1976). Sex differences in cognition: A function of maturation rate? *Science*, *192*, 572–574.

Waber, D. P. (1977). Sex differences in mental abilities: Hemispheric lateralization and rate of physical growth in adolescence. *Developmental Psychology*, *13*, 29–38.

Ward, S. L., Newcombe, N., & Overton, W. F. (1986). Turn left at the church, or three miles north: A study of direction giving and sex differences. *Environment and Behaviour*, *18*, 192–213.

Williams, C. L., & Meck, W. H. (1991). The organizational effects of gonadal steroids on sexually dimorphic spatial ability. *Psychoneuroendocrinology*, *16*, 155–176.

Willis, S. L., & Schaie, K. W. (1988). Gender differences in spatial ability in old age: Longitudinal and intervention findings. *Sex Roles*, *18*, 189–203.

Windle, M. (1992). Revised dimensions of temperment survey (Dots-R): Simultaneous group confirmatory factor analysis for adolescent gender groups. *Psychological Assessment*, *4*, 228–234.

Woodfield, R. L. (1984). Embedded figure test performance before and after childbirth. *British Journal of Psychology*, *75*, 81–88.

# 21

## The Creation and Re-Creation of Language

Derek Bickerton
*University of Hawaii at Manoa*

Language represents a problem area for any study of the evolution of human behavior. The easiest aspects of human behavior to explain are those that we share with at least some other species. However, no other species has anything remotely like language, and no purpose can be served by pretending otherwise, although some scholars have tried to take this course, claiming an ancestry for language in animal communication systems (Hockett & Ascher, 1964) or suggesting that the performance of "linguistically" trained apes is on a continuum with human language production (Fouts, 1983).

Unique adaptations are not unknown or even particularly rare in nature (one need think only of the courting rituals of bowerbirds, the heat sensors of pit vipers, or the electromagnetic perception of certain eels). Moreover, one does not necessarily have to be able to trace a phylogenetic history for such adaptations to account for them. For instance, if no species related to bowerbirds constructed anything like a courtship bower, surely no researcher would feel obliged to claim that something else that a related species did do was somehow the same as building a bower. The whole process of bower building could have evolved among the immediate ancestors of modern bowerbirds. Moreover, there has been ample time—5 to 7 million years since the separation of human ancestors from other primates is the usual current estimate—for a specialized adaptation to develop in the hominid line, beginning from a level of basic cognitive capacity that is shared with a number of other species, by no means all of which are primates.

If an agnosticism appropriate to the phylogeny of bower building is all too often abandoned in evolutionary approaches to language, this may well be more metaphysical than scientific. Weighty edifices of theology and philosophy have been built on an assumption of absolute disconti- nuity between humans and other species. In seeking to refute this as- sumption, many researchers seem to have been driven to a kind of theoretical overkill, claiming a far more complete and literal identity between humans and other species than their case really requires.

## LANGUAGE AND PROTOLANGUAGE

The most plausible way to account for the evolution of language would go something as follows. The common ancestor of chimpanzees and humans had no greater language capacities than modern apes. However, language developed uniquely and gradually in the hominid line through a long series of those mosaic developments so familiar to students of evolution. Indeed, such an account has already been proposed. According to Pinker (1993), "There could have been on the order of 350,000 genera- tions"—7 million years, in other words—between us and the first emer- gence of language, so that "language could have had a gradual fade-in" (pp. 345–346). The scenario for original language creation proposed by Pinker and Bloom (1990) and Newmeyer (1991) envisages a wide variety of the structural components of language each evolving independently and being selected for specifically.

However, there are serious problems for any gradualist account of language evolution. Even those who do not believe that thought depends on language (e.g., Churchland, 1986; Jackendoff, 1987; Premack, 1983) agree that language must have greatly enhanced human thought. In fact, there are strong arguments supporting the claim that language was the creator of the kind of thinking that humans, as distinct from other crea- tures, do (Bickerton, 1995). Thus, if the original development of language was a gradual one, we would expect to see in the fossil records some unambiguous signs of the development of human intelligence.

In fact, after the invention of the Acheulian handaxe (which, according to Calvin, 1993, might have been a simple projectile or, according to Davidson & Noble, 1993, merely the core left when flake tools had been chipped from a stone), hominid ingenuity appeared to stand still. For over 1 million years, the design of this implement showed no changes whatsoever—a degree of conservatism quite unthinkable in any human population. It was not until 30,000 to 40,000 years ago that there emerged more sophisticated tools and objects with symbolic, rather than merely utilitarian, functions, followed swiftly by a cascade of inventions and innovations that has still not ceased. The sudden and rapid emergence of a sophisticated language faculty, after a long period of little if any linguistic development, would account for this sequence of events more plausibly than any alternative explanation.

The gradual evolution of a particular adaptation also requires that some selective pressure be maintained throughout that period. The selective pressures suggested by Pinker and Bloom (1990) and others involve competition between and within human groups. But there is no reason to believe that interactions within and between hominid groups differed significantly from the already complex interactions in other primate species (Cheney & Seyfarth, 1990; Goodall, 1978). If this was the selective pressure, why did it result in language in only one of the species concerned? Naturally, hominid interactions would have become more complex as a result of acquiring language (if you can lie, gossip, plot, and tell tales on one another, then the complexity of interactions obviously increases by orders of magnitude!). But the onus remains on proponents of gradualism to show precisely what specific increment(s) in social complexity (over and above the complexities common to all advanced primate societies) could have triggered the emergence of language among hominids only.

A more plausible proposal is that the selection pressure was competition between species: between *Homo erectus* and antecedent species for the emergence of protolanguage, between *Homo sapiens* and antecedent species for the emergence of full human language. However, such a scenario would imply a two-stage model of language evolution, rather than a single-process, gradualist, mosaic model. Indeed, both *erectus* and *sapiens* populations spread widely in a relatively short space of time—*erectus* across Africa and Eurasia in a few hundred thousand years, *sapiens* across this area plus Australia and the Americas in perhaps less than 100,000 years, and both populations effectively eliminated their predecessors, whether through warfare or mere competition for resources is immaterial here.

This rapid expansion also works against the hypothesis that competition between social groups within the same species drove linguistic evolution. It suggests that the prevailing strategy in the hominid line was not to stay and compete with one's conspecific neighbors, but to profit from the absence of serious competition from other species by colonizing new territories. Thus, competition between groups is unlikely to have been a significant factor in language evolution. To suppose the contrary can result only from an illicit back projection of conditions current in the human species only since the dawn of agriculture.

Competition within groups surely existed. But if, as suggested here, there was negligible gene flow between groups (a proposal supported, at least for our species, by the wide range of phenotypes among modern humans), no area of human development can have been significantly affected by intergroup competition. Any increment in linguistic capacity, to the extent that it involved physical changes in the human brain, would have remained within the group, and it would be bizarre to suppose that similar physical changes (the result of random recombinations and mutations) could have occurred independently in many different groups.

A further problem for a gradualist account of language evolution arises from the difficulty in hypothesizing the intermediate stages through which a gradual development of language would have had to pass. Bickerton (1990) proposed that there were only two stages in the development of language—stages equivalent to the pidgin and creole stages that occur in both spoken and signed languages when well-formed input was radically reduced or removed altogether. Intermediate varieties of language have been proposed by Premack (1985) and Pinker (1993), but there are serious problems with all of them (for a detailed critique, see Bickerton, 1986, 1995).

The type of problem that hypothetical intermediate languages encounter can be illustrated by the following example. Both Newmeyer (1991) and Pinker and Bloom (1990) suggested that earlier varieties of language may have simply lacked some of the basic principles of contemporary human language. One that both refer to is the principle of subjacency (Chomsky, 1981). Put simply, what subjacency does is prevent words being placed too far from their expected positions. For instance, in, "What did you do?" *what* is the logical object of *do* (we can, in fact, say, "You did what?"). However, you cannot move *what* out of its expected position if it occurs in one of a pair of conjoined sentences ("You played the piano and Bill sang" is fine, but not, "What did you play and Bill sang?"), in a relative-clause sentence ("The man who told me the news has left," but not, "What did the man who told me has left?"), or in various other contexts. Chomsky (1986) accounted for these phenomena by proposing that the boundaries of certain types of phrases and clauses create barriers that question words such as *what* are unable to cross.

Without subjacency, hominids would have been free to utter questions like, "Who when Ug found the hand-axes did he say that if ever they went missing again he would call the tribe together and they would all beat senseless?" The absence of subjacency would have had no other effect. Yet, if hominids had been capable of uttering such sentences, they would surely have been equally capable of interpreting them, so it is far from clear that imposing the subjacency constraint on Ug's language would have conferred any selective advantage on the group that imposed it.

An even stronger reason for rejecting the fewer principles-type of intermediate language emerges when we consider what is the most likely source of the subjacency constraint. We may reasonably assume that any such constraint must result from the way the language areas of the brain are structured or connected. Although we are still far from being able to describe such structures and connections, even in outline, it seems plausible to suppose that the constraint is due to some kind of limitation on the brain's capacity to process information—if some bits of information get too far from the place in the construction pattern that they would normally occupy, the brain simply cannot keep track of them. If this is true, then subjacency is not something that was imposed on a preexisting language, but rather a state of affairs implicit in the way language was wired up, and present from the moment that anything remotely like human language emerged from whatever pidginlike protolanguage preceded it.

The apparent evolutionary gulf between human language and animal call systems is in fact already reduced by the hypothesis that a structure-less protolanguage intervened between an original alingual state and the emergence of true language. Creatures as diverse as chimpanzees (Premack, 1972), bonobos (Greenfield & Savage-Rumbaugh, 1990), gorillas (Patterson, 1978), orangutans (Miles, 1983), sea lions (Schusterman & Krieger, 1984), dolphins (Herman, Richards, & Wolz, 1984), and African grey parrots (Pepperburg, 1987) have shown themselves able, under adequate training, to acquire symbolic systems that closely resemble human versions (pidgin, early child language) of protolanguage. All these cases exhibit phenomena of the same kind: short, meaningful utterances usually consisting of no more than three or four units strung together, without any of the hierarchical or recursive properties of true language. If a wide range of creatures are capable, under instruction, of acquiring a protolanguage, this strongly suggests convergence (among higher birds and mammals) on a stage of cognitive development that represents readiness for protolanguage, although not for true language (Bickerton, 1990). Such a finding certainly reduces the evolutionary uniqueness of language, which some writers have found so threatening.

Thus, although there are good reasons for supposing that human communicative capacity, after it transcended animal call systems, went through two phases—*protolanguage* (short bursts of words strung together in purely ad hoc ways) and *language* (words built into complex hierarchical structures)—there are no good reasons to suppose that any forms of language intermediate between these two stages ever existed. The absence of any intermediate variety of language from the contemporary limited input situations described in subsequent sections provides further evidence for this contention, as does a similar absence from the literature on the various traumatic aphasias and developmental dysphasias (Bickerton, 1995).

Nor need the prospect of a single dramatic change perturb the concerned evolutionist. Suppose that all that was needed for language to emerge from an original protolanguage was some mechanism that would connect words pairwise in a series of hierarchical steps, rather than serially and indvidually, like beads on a string (just such a change in processing is hypothesized in child development by Greenfield, 1991). Suppose that the mechanism in question was a single dedicated system of neural interconnections. All but one neural connection in that system could have been in place throughout the protolanguage era, with each component performing some nonlinguistic or merely protolinguistic function. There would have been no significant behavioral consequences for any individual whose brain contained the still incomplete system. However, the addition of a single link would have completed the system, enabling words to be uttered in hierarchical and recursive patterns, rather than merely strung together by ad hoc means. Other principles and properties of language would have then arisen simply from natural constraints on processing methods of the central nervous system—whether those constraints operated over a wide range of neural activities or were specific to the infrastructure of the linguistic system.

A two-stage model of linguistic evolution draws considerable support from two sources. From an evolutionary perspective, such a model fits far better with the fossil record (which indicates a relatively abrupt emergence of hominids, a long behavioral plateau over the lifetime of *Homo erectus*, and an even more abrupt emergence of our own species) than any gradualist account. It also avoids the problems raised by having to hypothesize viable varieties of language intermediate between protolanguage and contemporary human language. From a synchronic linguistic perspective, the two-stage model (but not a gradualist model with intermediate varieties) is fully compatible with what has been learned about situations where the normal course of language acquisition is radically interrupted. Two such situations—those that give rise to creole languages, and those that give rise to sign languages—are reviewed in the following sections. In these situations, language is clearly not learned, but re-created—and, as far as syntax is concerned, re-created practically from ground zero.

## Creole Languages

Creole languages are new languages that arose in situations where speakers of mutually unintelligible languages came into contact with one another. The following is concerned with a subset of these languages—those that were produced under conditions of plantation slavery or indentured labor. The reason for this focus is quite straightforward: In any scientific inquiry, one proceeds by limiting the number of factors involved. One factor present in most acquisition contexts is continuity of culture: The language a child acquires is normally the language of an ongoing society of which that child forms a part, and, accordingly, fluent control of such a language is a prerequisite for the child's taking part in that society. The child's linguistic energies are then wholly occupied in mastering a language that already exists (and has usually existed since time immemorial). What would happen if no preexisting language represented the "Open Sesame!" to the world the child would inhabit?

In plantation colonies, this condition was realized. Most of the inhabitants of such colonies, whether slaves or indentured laborers, had been removed from their ancestral cultures, transported for distances of often thousands of miles and mixed into new, polyglot, multicultural societies, usually under conditions of severe hardship. Adults continued to use their ancestral languages, but, in addition, it became necessary for them to acquire (or create) some means of communicating with speakers of languages other than their own. Yet social distance between the European colonizers and the rest of the population, plus the fact that the latter usually vastly outnumbered the former, made the most straightforward solution—learning the dominant language—unavailable.

According to most accounts, what happens under such circumstances is that an auxiliary language, a pidgin, develops (that this view at best oversimplifies a very complex situation has been shown by recent research; see Roberts, 1993, 1996). Such a pidgin lacks the structural complexity shared by all natural languages: It has a reduced vocabulary, one that contains few if any grammatical items (such as articles, prepositions, markers of tense or aspect, etc.), and it lacks any structure greater in complexity than a simple clause. Somehow this inadequate medium is expanded until it becomes the native language of the new society and develops the kinds of structure and vocabulary found universally among natural languages. In every case, the vocabulary of such a language comes mostly from the colonial language (English, French, Portuguese, and so on) that was dominant where and when it originated, but its grammar shows striking deviations from the grammar of that dominant language.

Given that the original inhabitants of different plantation colonies represented widely different mixes of language speakers, one might have predicted that the resultant novel languages, creoles, would have differed widely from one another in their grammatical structure. For instance, the population of Suriname, where a creole language known as Sranan is spoken, included speakers of Kwa and Western Bantu languages (Smith, 1987); the population of the Seychelles, where a creole language known as Seselwa is spoken, included speakers of Eastern Bantu, Malagasy, and some Indian languages (Corne, 1977); and the population of Hawaii, where Hawaii Creole English (HCE) is spoken, included Hawaiian, Chinese, Portuguese, and Japanese speakers (Reinecke, 1969). Because these language groupings differ typologically from one another in a variety of ways, influence from those groupings might have been expected to yield three different creoles.

Yet although the grammars of all three languages differ in certain respects, they resemble one another in many more ways than they differ, and their similarities owe little if anything to English, the dominant language in the formation of Sranan and HCE, or to features shared by English and French (the dominant language in the Seychelles). Moreover, those same similarities are found in all languages that developed in similar situations (i.e., in plantation colonies where a large majority of the population were brought in from elsewhere and where no preexisting common language was readily available; Bickerton, 1981, 1984).

The idea that a universal, species-specific grammar underlies the superficial diversity of the world's languages was first put forward by Chomsky (1965, 1968). If the similarities among creoles derived neither from their dominant languages nor from the ancestral languages of their speakers, it seemed plausible to suggest that those similarities somehow reflected that universal grammar (Bickerton, 1974). The main obstacle to a more specific spelling out of that somehow lay in the fact that the situations that gave rise to creoles had resulted from European colonial expansion—a historical process with no 20th-century equivalent. Therefore, there was nowhere one could observe the process of creolization in vivo; it had to be inferred from the contemporary state of creole languages plus the (in almost all cases) totally inadequate historical documentation of such processes in the past. However, after two decades of research, culminating in Roberts' (1993, 1996) remarkably detailed reconstruction of the creolization process in Hawaii, it is possible to state in somewhat greater detail the relationship between creole languages and the biological basis of the human language faculty.

## How Creole Was Formed in Hawaii

Imagine ways in which you might try to build a language from ground zero, assuming that there already existed meaningful symbolic units (words, manual signs, and so on) that would serve as building blocks in that language. Such units would naturally be limited to a type that, in each case, would correspond with some object, event, or quality in the real world. The simplest and most obvious way to create meaningful propositions from such units would be to simply place those units in sequence, like beads on a string, perhaps in some conventionalized order (such as agent–action–patient) that would facilitate comprehension. However, there are problems with such a schema. For instance, suppose you want to attach two propositions to make a single complex proposition:

How would you know where one proposition began and another ended? How would you know whether "John see Bill go home" should be parsed as "John see [Bill go home]" or as "John [see Bill] [go home]"—or, in other words, whether it meant, "John saw Bill who was going home" or "John saw Bill and then went home"? In principle, languages could resolve the ambiguity by repeating *John* in the second case. In fact, no human language ever limits itself to such devices.

In human language, problems of this nature are resolved by arranging units in hierarchical, rather than linear, relations (even if the end product, given the limitations of human productive and receptive faculties, inevitably takes on a superficially linear nature). That is to say, in "John see [Bill go home]," the units within the bracketed segment are not on a par with the units outside. On the contrary, the three bracketed units together form a single macrounit, and it is this macrounit that exists on the same level as *John* and *see*. In "John [see Bill] [go home]," however, the units in each of the bracketed segments join to form macrounits that are on the same level with one another (and with *John*).

In all languages, the boundaries of such macrounits are (to a greater or lesser extent) delimited and indicated by the presence of closed-class or grammatical items—things like articles, conjunctions, prepositions, relative pronouns, and the like, which do not refer directly to objects or events, but which carry information about the structure of propositions, rather than their content.

Thus, the distinction between the two meanings of our original "John see Bill go home" can be made, in language, by the contrast between "who was . . . -ing" in the first version and "and then" in the second. Not one of these latter units makes any reference to any object, quality, or event; in isolation, they have only the vaguest of meanings (e.g., "was" implies some form of past event, "then" some notion of consecutivity). But in the context of selected content words, such grammatical items serve as powerful determinants of meaning, and also allow the building of complex propositions that can be understood quite automatically and unambiguously, without any deliberate or conscious effort on the part of the hearer.

In contrast, in a simple bead-stringing process, disambiguation can only proceed by redundant specification. Thus, we can disambiguate our original utterance by saying, "John see Bill/Bill go home" or "John see Bill/John go home." But in so doing, we have simply broken down an original complex proposition into two distinct simple propositions. Without hierarchical structure, the simple proposition—with a single action or event, and one or more actors—represents the logical terminus of proposition building. Yet, hierarchical structure cannot be imposed on propositions without the grammatical items that are required to indicate where the macrounits (phrases, clauses) within such structures begin and end. It follows that if such grammatical items are absent, hierarchical structures cannot be produced.

In contacts between adults who lack a common language, communicative needs require that a small common vocabulary be built up first. Naturally, the same needs determine that such a vocabulary should consist almost entirely of content words. In such situations, grammatical items, with few exceptions, are either dropped altogether or, if used, are generally neither distinguished nor understood by hearers (Alleyne, 1971). But without grammatical items, complex hierarchical structures cannot be produced. Thus, participants in such situations are left with no recourse but to string content words together in short, monopropositional utterances, as shown previously.

Research on the situation in Hawaii by Roberts (1993, 1996), who has collected a corpus of several thousand contemporary citations drawn from court records, newspaper reports, letters, diaries, and other published and unpublished documents, has shown that (apart from a tiny handful of privileged individuals who acquired relatively fluent control of English and/or Hawaiian) all of the contacts between different ethnic groups were carried on by the structureless stringing together of words from all of the languages in contact, so that an utterance of three words might draw on the lexicons of three different languages (e.g., you [English] nani [Japanese] hanahana [Hawaiian]—literally, you what work, "What work do you do?"). Utterances of this brief and virtually structureless kind constituted the vast bulk of the non-native input to children in Hawaii during the later 19th and early 20th centuries.

It should be emphasized that, in addition to this anarchic and macaronic input, children in Hawaii also received well-formed input in one or more established languages, and many, probably most, became fluent in at least one of those languages. Common sense suggests that they would have transferred rules from these languages to supply the contact language with structure, but common sense would mislead us here, for in fact they did not (if they had, we would find varieties of creole influenced by Chinese, Japanese, Hawaiian, and so on, whereas in fact creole in Hawaii was completely homogenous from the beginning). Instead, children did two things simultaneously: They created a small but adequate stock of grammatical morphemes, and they linked propositions into complex structures that, although formally distinct from the structures of English, Hawaiian, Chinese, and so on, closely resembled the structures found in creole languages elsewhere in the world.

Grammatical items were not innovated from nothing, but rather created by changing the functions of extant vocabulary items. For instance, the numeral 1 was co-opted as an indefinite article, the past participle of *be* was co-opted as a marker of tense, the verb *stay* was used to express locative *be* (e.g., "Where the book stay?", "Where is the book?"), the preposition *for* acquired an additional function as an introducer of subordinate purpose clauses ("For I write," "So that I (can) write," and so on). (All of these precise adaptations can be found in numerous other plantation creoles, and the first and fourth are found in all of them.) In some cases (as with 1), the first recorded use is attributed to a child speaker; in others (as with *been* as a marker of tense), the item may have been used sporadically by a handful of adult speakers, but its first consistent, rule-governed uses are attributed to children.

Simultaneously, children are recorded as being the earliest producers of both complex phrases (e.g., "[One kanaka] make me [one bad thing] [inside of house]," "A Hawaiian did something bad to me inside the house") and combinations of clauses (e.g., "[You been say [[go up on roof] and [paint 'em]]] but [I no hear [you say [come down]]]—[why you no say [[when I been through] come down]]?", "You told me to go up on the roof and paint it but I didn't hear you tell me to come down—why didn't you tell me to come down when I'd finished?"). However, even after these developments had taken place (between 1895–1910), the language of adult immigrants remained as chaotic and structureless as before; indeed, many still spoke in this manner when they were interviewed in the 1970s, after everyone born in Hawaii had been speaking the creole for well over half a century (Bickerton & Odo, 1976). Thus, there can be no doubt that it was children, rather than adults, who converted the formless contact medium into a full natural language.

## Implications for Normal Acquisition

If the main driving force that underlies creolization is the inaccessibility of grammatical items, and if many characteristic phenomena of creoles result from the re-creation of such items, one would expect to find similar phenomena in normal acquisition, where, as is notorious (see Brown, 1973; Leopold, 1949, 1950), a significant stock of content words is acquired long before the first grammatical items. Moreover, for some time after the first grammatical items are acquired, the cognitive content of what a child wishes to express often transcends the child's current knowledge of the appropriate (target-language specific) means for expressing it. Under such circumstances, one might predict that creolelike phenomena would emerge, if only temporarily. Thus, children who only receive an unstructured jargon are under no pressure to revise their initial hypotheses about target language structure (and therefore go on to create stable creole languages), whereas children in normal acquisition situations continue to receive positive evidence in the shape of well-formed target-language sentences, which will at one and the same time disconfirm those initial hypotheses and supply them with the appropriate target-language forms.

Indeed, wherever children wish to express a concept, but have not yet acquired the grammatical morphology for expressing that concept, creolelike structures will emerge. For example, the English verb negator *not* is difficult for children to acquire because it so frequently merges with auxiliaries (*can't, won't, don't, didn't, isn't, aren't,* and so forth). In consequence, negation in early acquisition places the form *no* directly before the verb phrase (e.g., "He no bite you," "I no want envelope," and so on; Bellugi, 1968). Similarly, prior to the acquisition of *to* or other overt indicators of nonfinite verbs, subordinate clauses are regarded as invariably finite (as is assumed for creole languages by Mufwene & Dijkhoff, 1989), and the earliest biclausal sentences cited by Brown (1973) and Limber (1973) show "the embedded sentence appear[ing] exactly as it would if it stood alone as an independent simple sentence" (Brown, 1973, p. 21).

Indeed, the finiteness of such sentences is often confirmed by the presence of nominative morphology on the subject of the embedded sentence (compare one of Adam's earliest [age 2;11] complex sentences "D'you want he walk?," in contrast with the standard "D'you want HIM (to) walk?"). Moreover, when children wish to express negative sentences with negative indefinite subjects, they produce negative subjects with negative verbs ("Nobody don't like me"; McNeill, 1966) in defiance of the rules of English (standard and nonstandard alike) and most other languages. Creoles, however, permit or even mandate precisely this type of negative construction (e.g., Guyanese Creole "non kyat na bait non dag," "No cat bit any dog").

The features detailed in the preceding paragraphs are just a few of the similarities (too close and too numerous to be coincidental) between creoles and child language detailed in Bickerton (1981). One can go as far as to claim that, in the course of primary acquisition, there are few deviations from a mature grammar of English that would not be fully grammatical in one or more (usually more) of the 33 Anglo-Creole varieties distinguished by Hancock (1987). However, the converse situation—that of children who are currently acquiring already established creole languages making mistakes that would be grammatical in some noncreole language—seems not to exist. Although few studies of creole acquisition have yet been done, Adone (1994) found that children learning Mauritian creole (a French-based creole of the Indian Ocean) deviated from adult standards far less than children learning other kinds of languages.

Indeed, anyone who has compared the course of creolization with the course of acquisition can hardly fail to have been struck by a much wider and more general resemblance. The utterances that a child produces in the period between 18 months and 2 years (on average; the period may start earlier or later, and show a somewhat longer or shorter duration) are strikingly similar to the utterances that serve as input to the creole-creating generation: Like those, they are short, consisting generally of one, two, or three words, and the words appear to be single, discrete units, incapable of expansion (hierarchical, head-modifier constructions are vanishingly rare, and those that do occur may have been acquired as single units because the segmentation of adult utterances presents as a serious problem for young children as it does for adults in a contact situation; see Peters, 1983). In both pidgins and early child language, constituents are frequently omitted, being left to be inferred from contextual or pragmatic clues, in contrast with the systematic, rule-governed processes in adult language that serve to identify the reference of understood constituents. Although pidgins and early child language may show rough statistical regularities of ordering, these can arise as readily from a merely linear, stringing-of-beads process as from the conversion of hierarchical structures into linear sequences, the hallmark of adult language.

In short, the most parsimonious interpretation of language of those children under age 2 is that, like the precreole contact language, it lacks the hierarchical and recursive properties of adult language. If acquisitionists in general (Bowerman, 1973; Brown, 1973; Crain, 1991; Pinker 1984; see also Radford, 1991) have been reluctant to accept that interpretation, this is mainly because children quickly thereafter progress to a stage in which their language unambiguously possesses the properties of hierarchy and recursiveness. From a viewpoint that ignores the creole evidence, it might seem more parsimonious to suppose that the child's linguistic (and particularly, syntactic) capacity remains the same throughout development, but that some mysterious "production bottleneck" keeps the child's utterances at a primitive level until (usually early in the third year) this bottleneck is equally mysteriously removed.

From any other viewpoint, however, it is surprising that a bottleneck that can only be developmental general in nature (because no plausible linguistic motivation for such a bottleneck has been proposed) should be so readily accepted—doubly surprising when so many of the scholars who accept it believe that the language faculty is modular and quite disjoint from general cognition.

From a creole viewpoint, it seems more plausible to propose that a specific, biological capacity comes on line at around age 2, and that, like many biological capacities, this one has a relatively narrow developmental window—one that effectively closes prior to puberty. Before that window opens, the child can acquire language only through general-purpose learning capacities; after it closes, the adolescent (and subsequently the adult) may acquire additional languages reasonably well, provided adequate well-formed input is available, but can no longer convert structureless linguistic input into a structured language.

The phenomena surveyed in this section follow logically from such an account of the language faculty. However, no other account adequately explains the colossal difference between pidgin-speaking parents and their creole-speaking children. The evidence from creole languages and language acquisition would be striking enough if it represented the only phenomena of its kind. However, many features of that evidence also characterize sign languages and their acquisition, and accordingly the following turns to these.

## Sign Languages

What is most striking about sign languages is that they preserve, even in a different modality, all the major features that characterize spoken languages. In other words, their mere existence indicates that language is not modality specific, and therefore, unlikely to have arisen out of pre-existing sensory or motor systems (Siple & Fischer, 1991). The vast majority of native signers are profoundly deaf, therefore debarred from acquiring any form of spoken language, despite sometimes herculean (but quite misguided) efforts to instil such language (Sacks, 1989). Like spoken languages, sign languages operate with distinct classes of content items and grammatical items; like spoken languages, they evince hierarchical structure and expand utterances through recursive processes. The overall course of their normal acquisition (by deaf children from deaf parents) closely resembles the normal course of spoken-language acquisition, in that both commence with single units, progress to combinations of two units, and then, at around age 2, undergo an exponential increase in syntactic capacity.

However, there is one difference between them that has nothing to do with language per se, but a great deal to do with the distribution of deafness in the general population. In the case of spoken languages, normal acquisition (by children from parents who are speakers of an established language) is by far the most common mode. In the case of sign languages, normal acquisition of this kind is quite rare, affecting perhaps no more than 10% of speakers. The remaining 90% are born to hearing parents, and it is in the acquisition of this majority that we find the closest resemblances to the cycle of creolization discussed in the previous sections.

In fact, in some respects, the range of possibilities is richer than it is in the creole case. In the formation of creoles, children are exposed to the same inchoate linguistic mix from the earliest age, and a fairly uniform level of attainment is reached. However, the different circumstances that can attend the development of deaf children in a normal society may give rise to a wide range of outcomes. A child of hearing parents may be rigorously segregated from any opportunity to interact with signers or other deaf persons, and may (in what are wrongly supposed to be the child's best interests) be actively discouraged from signing while valiant but quite futile, efforts are made to teach some form of spoken language. In a worst-case scenario, the result is someone like Chelsea, a woman who, in her 30s, was virtually alingual in any modality, and who thereafter could acquire nothing beyond a degenerate, pidginlike form of sign (Curtiss, 1998).

More often, no such draconian policy is applied, and, although parents do not communicate with them by sign, the children are left to communicate with the hearing world as best they can. Under such circumstances, children develop what is known as *home sign*—a system of symbolic gestures that they produce without benefit of any model (Goldin-Meadow & Feldman, 1997; Mylander & Goldin-Meadow, 1991; Tervoort 1961). Although such systems show many features of natural language (e.g., such signs are seldom iconic, abstracting away from the particularities of actions and objects the way words do), they do not seem to develop into full-blown languages perhaps because the children who invent them seldom, if ever, interact with other children who, like them, are "native speakers" of sign. The factor of feedback or reinforcement from peers, which must have been a potent force in the development of creole languages, is absent here.

Still more frequently, hearing parents of deaf children try to use some form of signing—most often signed English, an artificial language that combines the syntax of spoken English with a vocabulary drawn from American Sign Language (ASL). Because signed English is not a natural language, one could argue that children forced to acquire it do not really have a native language. Other hearing parents may acquire ASL as a second language to communicate with their children. However, it is rare for a hearing adult learner to acquire the equivalent of native competence, so often what children receive is a kind of foreigner version of ASL. Normally, at some stage in their lives, children who have had signed English or non-native ASL as input come into contact with native ASL signers and attempt to acquire a full version of ASL (Gee & Mounty, 1991). However, the degree to which they are able to do this varies as a function of their age at first exposure to ASL. If this exposure is delayed until adolescence, full acquisition of ASL becomes impossible (Newport, 1990).

In particular, the syntax of ASL is quite complex, including a considerable component of what are, in fact, equivalents of grammatical morphology in spoken language—items often expressed in terms of direction of gaze or facial expressions and gestures (Reilly, McIntire, & Bellugi, 1991), which are entirely absent from signed English. It is items such as these, rather than those items (consisting mainly of handshapes and hand movements), that represent actions, objects, and qualities, which older signers find it harder to acquire. However, an interesting development occurs when deaf parents who have acquired ASL imperfectly have deaf children. Even if the latter are not exposed to any other ASL signers, they will expand and regularize their parents' ASL until they attain a level of competence comparable with that of children who have been exposed to ASL from infancy (Newport, 1990; Singleton, Morford, & Goldin-Meadow, 1993).

The similarity between such situations and those of creolization described in preceding sections did not go unnoticed in the literature. Woodward (1973) and Fischer (1978) were among the first to point out the parallels between signed English and pidgins, and between creoles and sign languages acquired from imperfect input. The analogies are not exact, of course. For instance, the zero-input situation described by Goldin-Meadow (1979) is much more severe than anything found in creolization, whereas the reduced-input situation described by Newport (1990) probably provides, in many cases, a more structured input than was received by most first-generation creole speakers. However, these differences should not be overemphasized because they are differences of degree only, on a continuum that links the alingual feral child (Malson, 1972) with the normal case of full exposure to a preexisting language.

Although it appears that children isolated from all meaningful human contact (e.g., Genie; see Curtiss, 1977) fail to develop any language at all, it would seem that at almost any other point on this continuum, language can be acquired. This strongly suggests that, in language acquisition, the contribution of the organism is greater than that of the environment, and that, given a minimum of input or even mere normal contact between individuals, language of some kind will arise. However, it may be that, where input is minimal, contact between children undergoing a similar degree of stimulus impoverishment (deaf children receiving inadequate signed input, hearing children receiving inadequate spoken input) is required if full language is to develop. Given such contact, the innate blueprint for language will do its work regardless of whatever help or hindrance it may meet from environmental factors.

The picture presented earlier finds strong support in recent events among the deaf community of Nicaragua (Kegl & Iwata, 1989). Until the overthrow of the Somoza regime in 1979, there were no schools or other institutions for the deaf in Nicaragua, therefore, deaf persons remained isolated in a hearing world, communicating as best they could in some form of home sign. Under the Sandinista regime, schools for the deaf were set up with teachers who tried to impose lip reading and speech. Ignoring this, the children (mostly older than 10) created out of their idiosyncratic home-sign systems a common language that came to be known as *Lenguaje de Signos Nicaraguense*. However, younger children who were subsequently brought into schools for the deaf and exposed to this language developed it further—making signs less iconic, adding new grammatical items, and developing more complex structures—until the difference between input and output grew so pronounced that this newest language acquired a name of its own: *Idioma de Signos Nicaraguense*. Thus, the whole cycle of language creation, from near zero to the full richness of natural language, evolved in Nicaragua in the space of a few years.

Looking at this cycle and comparing it with the creole evidence, it would seem that we can break down the continuum of acquisition into a few major stages. (Of course performance factors will blur the boundaries of these stages, and what follows should be regarded as an heuristic device, rather than a literal description.) These stages are expressed schamatically in Table 21.1.

Condition 1 corresponds to that of the feral child, Condition 2 to that observed by Goldin-Meadow and Feldman (1977), Condition 3 to that of *Lenguaje de Signos Nicaraguense*, Condition 4 to that of first-generation creole-speaking children, Condition 5 to that of *Idioma de Signos Nicaraguense* or that observed by Newport (1990), and Condition 6 is, of course, the normal case for hearing children. As Table 21.1 indicates, full language development requires input of some kind, but development of language per se requires only social contact between children and others; input is not a factor. Note that both Conditions 2 and 3 provide input for at-worst Condition 4. Hence, although the re-creation of language takes place in a single generation under Conditions 4 through 6, it would be spread over two generations where Conditions 2 or 3 are obtained. In other words, two generations represent the longest period possible for the re-creation of language, regardless of whether input is present.

TABLE 21.1
Relation of Environment to Output in Language Acquisition

| Environment | Output |
| --- | --- |
| No input, no social contact | Zero |
| No input, no social contact with peers | Rudimentary sentence structure, little morphology |
| No input, social contact with peers | More complex sentences, but morphology still incomplete |
| Radically ill-formed input, social contact with peers | Full language development (new language) |
| Mildly ill-formed input with or without peer contact | Full language development (new or preexisting language) |
| Well-formed input with or without peer contact | Full language development (preexisting language) |

It should be noted that Table 21.1 assumes that language acquisition is being carried out by children. Where adults are involved, Conditions 1–3 would yield no output at all, whereas Conditions 4 and 5 would yield a structureless output, or at least an output with no more structure than the input. Even Condition 6 does not necessarily result in full language acquisition for adults, in the absence of specific motivation to acquire a second language.

The data reviewed herein indicate that, even if linguistic input is entirely absent, no more than two stages are necessary to progress to a state of full natural language. If language can be re-created in a maximum of two stages (a single stage if a pidgin protolanguage is available), this strongly suggests that the original creation of language need have involved no more than two intervening stages between some alingual ancestor and modern humans.

## CONCLUSION

This chapter pursued two lines of argument that converge on a single solution. Although neither line might convince in isolation, this convergence strongly suggests a two-stage model for the evolution of language. Indeed, all the available facts seem to point in the same direction. Opposing them is only the belief that evolution must always and everywhere be gradual and mosaic (i.e., a religious rather than a scientific attitude).

A comparison of the ways in which creole and sign languages develop shows a number of factors common to both: marked impoverishment of input; creation of structured output even where no structured input is available; complete re-creation of language, up to the normal adult level, within one or, at the most, two generations; and absence of intermediate stages between an ad hoc stringing together of meaningful units and a fully principled system that organizes those units into hierarchical structures. The evidence gathered here is all the more striking because it is modality independent. This indicates clearly that the human language faculty is not merely some unusual development of vocal or manual skills, but represents an independent capacity that can be equally well expressed through vocal and manual channels. Moreover, the emergence and functioning of that faculty, even under the most adverse conditions, indicates that it represents no mere aptitude to learn language, but rather a specific blueprint for the re-creation of language in its entirety, regardless of the quality of input to the child. Sociality, rather than linguistic input, appears to be the crucial variable in triggering the execution of this blueprint.

In light of biological developments among other species, it makes sense to suppose that this blueprint for the re-creation of language is none other than the original design of the human brain that made language possible in the first place. There is surely nothing remarkable about this—rather, the converse would be remarkable. If we were dealing with spiders, for instance, nobody would suggest that there was an original neural design for spinning webs and a device for enabling infant spiders to learn how to spin webs; everyone would immediately assume that the two mechanisms were one and the same.

Such a simplifying assumption has at least one rather striking consequence. Countless scholars have repeated that words leave no fossils, and that the origins of language must remain forever inaccessible. Even Lenneberg (1967), in a book entitled *Biological Foundations of Language*, concluded that it was a waste of time to look at how those foundations came to be built. If the conclusions reached here are correct, the original creation of language can still be seen, repeating itself endlessly, before our very eyes. The home sign of deaf children with hearing parents, the pidgin of immigrant plantation workers, and the hesitant, structureless speech of children under age 2 represent the earliest form of language, or rather protolanguage, as it emerged in some ancestral species (probably *Homo erectus*, but see Wilkins & Dumford, 1995, on the claims of *Homo habilis*). In contrast, the signing of deaf children of deaf parents, the Creole of plantation immigrants' children, and the fluent, systematic speech of children over age 2 re-create the developments that took place when our own species first appeared.

# REFERENCES

Adone, D. (1994). *The acquisition of Mauritian Creole. Amsterdam*, The Netherlands: John Benjamins.

Alleyne, M. C. (1971). Acculturation and the cultural matrix of creolization. In D. Hymes (Ed.), *Pidginization and creolization of languages* (pp. 169–186). Cambridge, England: Cambridge University Press.

Bellugi, U. (1968). Linguistic mechanisms underlying child speech. In E. Zale (Ed.), *Language and language behavior* (pp. 36–50). New York: Appleton-Century-Crofts.

Bickerton, D. (1974). Creolization, linguistic universals, natural semantax and the brain. *University of Hawaii Working Papers in Linguistics, 6*, 125–141.

Bcikerton, D. (1981). *Roots of language*. Ann Arbor, MI: Karoma.

Bickerton, D. (1984). The language bioprogram hypothesis. *Behavioral and Brain Sciences, 7*, 173–221.

Bickerton, D. (1986). More than nature needs? A reply to Premack. *Cognition, 23*, 73–79.

Bickerton, D. (1990). *Language and species*. Chicago: University of Chicago Press.

Bickerton, D. (1995). *Language and human behavior*. Seattle: University of Washington Press.

Bickerton, D., & Odo, C. (1976). *General phonology and pidgin syntax*. Final Report on National Science Foundation Grant No. GS-39748, Vol. 1. University of Hawaii, mimeo.

Bowerman, M. (1973). *Early syntactic development*. Cambridge, England: Cambridge University Press.

Brown, R. (1973). *A first language*. Cambridge, MA: Harvard University Press.

Calvin, W. H. (1993). The unitary hypothesis: A common circuit for novel manipulations, language, plan-ahead and throwing? In K. R. Gibson & T. Ingold (Eds.), *Tools, language and cognition in human evolution* (pp. 230–250). Cambridge, England: Cambridge University Press.

Cheney, D. L., & Seyfarth, R. M. (1990). *How monkeys see the world*. Chicago: University of Chicago Press.

Chomsky, N. (1965). *Aspects of the theory of syntax*. Cambridge, MA: MIT Press.

Chomsky, N. (1968). *Language and mind*. New York: Harcourt Brace.

Chomsky, N. (1981). *Lectures on government and binding*. Dordrecht, The Netherlands: Foris.

Chomsky, N. (1986). *Barriers*. Cambridge, MA: MIT Press.

Churchland, P. S. (1986). *Neurophilosophy*. Cambridge, MA: MIT Press.

Corne, C. (1977). *Seychelles creole grammar: Elements for Indian Ocean proto-creole reconstruction*. Tubingen, Germany: Narr.

Crain, S. (1991). Language acquisition in the absence of experience. *Behavioral and Brain Sciences, 14*, 597–650.

Curtiss, S. (1977). *Genie: A psycholinguistic study of a modern day "wild child."* New York: Academic Press.

Curtiss, S. (1988). Abnormal language acquisition and the modularity of language. In F. J. Newmeyer (Ed.), *Linguistics: The Cambridge survey* (pp. 90–116). Cambridge, England: Cambridge University Press.

Davidson, I., & Noble, W. (1993). Tools and language in human evolution. In K. R. Gibson & T. Ingold (Eds.), *Tools, language and cognition in human evolution* (pp. 363–388). Cambridge, England: Cambridge University Press.

Fischer, S. D. (1978). Sign language and creoles. In P. Siple (Ed.), *Understanding language through sign language research* (pp. 309–331). New York: Academic Press.

Fouts, R. S. (1983). Chimpanzee language and elephants' tails: A theoretical synthesis. In J. de Luce & H. T. Wilder (Eds.), *Language in primates: Perspectives and implications* (pp. 63–75). New York: Springer-Verlag.

Gee, J. P., & Mounty, J. L. (1991). Nativization, variability and style-shifting in the sign language development of deaf children of hearing parents. In P. Siple & S. D. Fischer (Eds.), *Theoretical issues in sign language research* (Vol. 2, pp. 65–83). Chicago: University of Chicago Press.

Goldin-Meadow, S. (1979). Structure in a manual communication system developed without a conventional language model: Language without a helping hand. In H. Whitaker & H. A. Whitaker (Eds.), *Studies in neurolinguistics* (Vol. 4). New York: Academic Press.

Goldin-Meadow, S., & Feldman, H. (1977). The development of language-like communication without a language model. *Science, 197*, 401–403.

Goodall, J. (1978). *The chimpanzees of Gombe: Patterns of behavior*. Cambridge, MA: Harvard University Press.

Greenfield, P. M. (1991). Language, tools and the brain: The ontogeny and phylogeny of hierarchically-organized sequential behavior. *Behavioral and Brain Sciences, 14*, 531–595.

Greenfield, P. M., & Savage-Rumbaugh, E. S. (1990). Grammatical combination in Pan paniscus: Processes of learning and invention in the evolution and development of language. In S. T. Parker & K. R. Gibson (Eds.), *"Language" and intelligence in monkeys and apes: Comparative development perspectives* (pp. 540–578). Cambridge, England: Cambridge University Press.

Hancock, I. A. (1987). A preliminary classification of the Anglophone Atlantic creoles, with syntactic data from thirty-three representative dialects. In G. G. Gilbert (Ed.), *Pidgin and creole languages: Essays in memory of John E. Reinecke* (pp. 264–333). Honolulu: University of Hawaii Press.

Herman, L. M., Richards, D. G., & Wolz, J. P. (1984). Comprehension of sentences by bottle-nosed dolphins. *Cognition, 16*, 129–219.

Hockett, C. F., & Ascher, R. (1964). The human revolution. *Current Anthropology, 5,* 135–168.

Jackendoff, R. (1987). *Consciousness and the computational mind.* Cambridge, MA: MIT Press.

Kegl, J., & Iwata, G. A. (1989, April). *Lenguage de Signos Nicaraguense: A pidgin sheds light on the "creole" ASL.* Proceedings of the 4th annual meeting of the Pacific Linguistics Society, Eugene, OR.

Lenneberg, E. H. (1967). *Biological foundations of language.* New York: Wiley.

Leopold, W. (1949–1959). *Speech development of a bilingual child* (4 vols.). Evanston, IL: Northwestern University Press.

Limber, J. (1973). The genesis of complex sentences. In T. E. Moore (Ed.), *Cognitive development and the acquisition of language.* New York: Academic Press.

Malson, I. (1972). *Wolf children and the problem of human nature.* New York: Monthly Review Press.

McNeill, D. A. (1966). Developmental psycholinguistics. In F. Smith & G. A. Miller (Eds.), *The genesis of language.* Cambridge, MA: MIT Press.

Miles, H. L. (1983). Two way communication with apes and the origin of language. In E. de Grolier (Ed.), *Glossogenetics: The origin and evolution of language* (pp. 201–210). New York: Harwood.

Mufwene, S. S., & Dijkhoff, M. B. (1989). On the so-called infinitive in creoles. *Lingua, 77,* 318–352.

Mylander, C., & Goldin-Meadow, S. (1991). Home sign systems in deaf children: The development of morphology without a conventional language model. In P. Siple & S. D. Fischer (Eds.), *Theoretical issues in sign language research* (Vol. 2, pp. 41–63). Chicago: University of Chicago Press.

Newmeyer, F. J. (1991). Functional explanation in linguistics and the origin of language. *Language and Communication, 11,* 1–28.

Newport, E. L. (1990). Maturational constraints on language learning. *Cognitive Science, 14,* 11–28.

Patterson, F. G. (1978). Language capacities of a lowland gorilla. In F. C. C. Peng (Ed.), *Sign language and language acquistion in man and ape* (pp. 161–201). Boulder, CO: Westview.

Pepperburg, I. M. (1987). Acquisition of the same/different concept by an African grey parrot Psittacus erithacus. *Animal Learning and Behavior, 15,* 423–432.

Peters, A. M. (1983). *The units of language acquisition.* New York: Cambridge University Press.

Pinker, S. (1984). *Language learnability and language development.* Cambridge, MA: Harvard University Press.

Pinker, S. (1993). *The language instinct.* New York: Morrow.

Pinker, S., & Bloom, P. (1990). Natural language and natural selection. *Behavioral and Brain Sciences, 13,* 707–784.

Premack, D. (1972). Language in the chimp? *Science, 172,* 808–822.

Premack, D. (1983). The codes of men and beasts. *Behavioral and Brain Sciences, 6,* 125–167.

Premack, D. (1985). Gavagai, or the future history of the animal language controversy. *Cognition, 19,* 207–296.

Reilly, S. R., McIntire, M. L., & Bellugi, U. (1991). Baby-face: A new perspective on language universals in language acquisition. In P. Siple & S. D. Fischer (Eds.), *Theoretical issues in sign language research* (Vol. 2, pp. 9–23). Chicago: University of Chicago Press.

Reinecke, J. K. (1969). *Language and dialect in Hawaii.* Honolulu: University of Hawaii Press.

Radford, A. (1991). *The acquisition of English syntax.* New York: Cambridge University Press.

Roberts, J. (1993, June). *The transformation of Hawaiian plantation pidgin and the emergence of Hawaii Creole English.* Paper presented at the conference of the Society for Pidgin and Creole Linguistics, Amsterdam, The Netherlands.

Roberts, J. (1996). Pidgin Hawaiian: A sociohistorical study. *Journal of Pidgin and Creole Languages, 10,* 1–63.

Sacks, O. (1989). *Seeing voices: A journey into the world of the deaf.* Berkeley: University of California Press.

Schusterman, R. J., & Krieger, K. (1984). California sea-lions are capable of semantic comprehension. *The Psychological Record, 34,* 3–23.

Singleton, J. L., Morford, J. P., & Goldin-Meadow, S. (1993). Once is not enough: Standards of well-formedness in manual communication created over three different timespans. *Language, 69,* 683–715.

Siple, P., & Fischer, S. D. (Eds.). (1991). *Theoretical issues in sign language research: Vol. 2. Psychology.* Chicago: University of Chicago Press.

Smith, N. (1987). *The genesis of the creole languages of Surinam.* Unpublished doctoral dissertation, University of Amsterdam.

Tervoort, B. T. (1961). Esoteric symbolism in the communication behavior of young deaf children. *American Annals of the Deaf, 106,* 436–480.

Wilkins, W. K., & Dumford, J. (1995). Brain evolution and neurolinguistic preconditions. *Behavioral and Brain Sciences, 18,* 161–226.

Woodward, J. (1973). Some characteristics of Pidgin sign English. *Sign Language Studies, 3,* 39–46.

# Author Index

## A

Abernathey, V., 149, *153*
Abramson, P., 526
Acker, M., 533, 536, 537, *541*
Adams, R. M., 109, *125*
Adams, R. N., 579, *591*
Adelman, J. R., 584, *591*
Adone, D., 624, *631*
Agrawal, N., 214, *230*
Agyei, Y., 508, *510*, 522, *540*
Albon, H. D., 35, 36, 37, *39*
Alcock, J., 11, 30, *38*, *40*, 99, *128*, 496, *510*
Alexander, R. D., 16, *38*, 57, 63, 72, 74, 75,
        *81*, *82*, 113, 114, *121*, 133, 137, *153*,
        *154*, 167, 168, 169, 187, 192, 201,
        202, *204*, *206*, 266, *271*, 287, 297,
        299, 310, *335*, 386, *399*, 435, 448,
        *453*, 459, *480*, 501, *510*, 527, *540*,
        565, *569*, 579, *591*
Alexander, R. M., 112, *125*
Alington-MacKinnon, D., 397, *399*
Allen, J. B., 498, *510*
Allen, N. D., 479, *480*
Alley, T. R., 111, *121*, 550, 559, 564, *569*
Alleyne, M. C., 622, *631*
Ames, E., 580, *591*
Ames, M. A., 508, *511*
Anderson, J. L., 17, 20, 27, 34, 35, *38*, *39*,
        170, *205*, 225, *231*, 281, *300*, 312,
        333, *336*, 391, *400*, 486, *511*, 517,
        *541*, 550, *569*
Anderson, P., 580, *591*
Andersson, M., 91, 92, 93, 94, 95, 98, 99,
        *121*
Ankney, C. D., 110, *121*
Annett, M., 599, *608*
Appleton, J., 557, *569*
Arak, A., 97, *123*
Ardrey, R., 108, *121*

Arnheim, R., 550, *569*
Arnold, S. J., 101, 104, *125*
Aron, A., 498, *511*
Arterberry, M. E., 258, *263*
Ascher, R., 613, *633*
Ashmore, R. D., 550, 564, *569*
Ashton, G. C., 598, *608*, *609*
Asiwaju, A. I., 585, *591*
Aslin, R. N., 257, *263*
Atmar, W., 96, *121*
Axelrod, R., 67, *81*, *124*, 466, *480*, 574, *592*

## B

Badcock, C. R., 387, *400*, 457, 458, 459,
        460, 466, 467, 468, 469, 479, 480,
        *480*
Baddeley, A. D., 259, *263*
Baenninger, M., 597, *608*
Bailey, J. M., 221, *230*, 508, *510*, 522, *540*
Bailey, K., 203, *204*, 275, 276, *300*
Bailey, K. G., 202, *205*
Bailey, R. C., 143, *154*
Bajema, C. J., 553, *569*
Baker, R. R., 92, 99, 112, *121*
Bakker, T. C. M., 98, *121*
Balaban, E., 110, *127*
Ball, J. A., 165, *205*
Balmford, A., 98, *121*
Bank, L., 597, 603, *609*
Barash, D., 149, *161*, 379, 391, *400*, *403*,
        457, 459, 461, *480*
Barbaree, H. E., 529, *542*
Barbee, A. P., 423, *429*
Barker, W. B., 228, *233*
Barkow, J., 18, *38*, 118, *121*, 141, *154*, 266,
        *271*, 282, 292, *300*, 305, *335*, 539,
        *540*

# Subject Index

# R

Rape, *see* Sexual aggression
Reception efficiency (r), 49
Reciprocator recognition mechanisms, 74–76
    action component of, 74
    perception component of, 74
    production component of, 74
Reciprocity, 15–16, 50–52, 66–74, 344–348,
        *see also* Cooperation
    and altruistic behavior, 66–69
    and cheating, 16
    evolution of justice and, 344–348
    indirect, 345–346
    origins of in unrelated humans, 70–74
    and *Prisoner's dilemma paradigm*, 66–69
    selection for in humans, 346
    selective invasion versus selective mainte-
        nance, 50–52, 69–70
    Trivers' theory of reciprocal altruism,
        15–16
Recognition markers, 584, *see also* State, the
Repression, 458–460
    the repressed unconscious, 458–459
        dynamic, 459
        topographical, 458
    and self-deception 458–460
Reproduction, 136, 138–144
    current versus future, 136
    female resources and fertility, 143–144
    male resource control and fertility,
        140–143
    mating effort versus parental effort, 139
    sex differences, 138–144
Reproductive effort, 139
    mating effort, 139
    parental effort, 139
Reproductive strategies, 375, *see also* Sexual
        strategies
    and neo-Darwinian perspectives on devel-
        opment, 375
Reproductive success, 268–271
    counting babies in the past, 268–270
        and phylogenetic reconstruction, 269
    counting babies in the present, 270
    as measure of fitness, 268
    which babies to count, 270–271
Reproductive value, 374, 445
    of child, relationship to parents' fitness,
        445
Research programs, in hypothesis testing,
        306–307, 309–310, *see also* Hypothe-
        ses
Resource defense polygyny, 100
Resources, 140–145, 147–151
    allocation among offspring, 147–151

female, and fertility, 143–145
male, and fertility, 140–142
Respect for authority, 341–343, *see also* Mo-
        rality
    evolution of, 341–343
        deference, selection for, 342
        morality, implications for, 342–343
Runaway sexual selection, 90

# S

Sacrifice, 7
Sancode, 238
Selection, 546
Selective invasion versus selective mainte-
        nance, 50–52, 69–70
    of altruism, 50–52
    of reciprocity among unrelated individu-
        als, 69–70
Self-deception, 361–362, 458–460, *see also*
        Cheating
    evolution of, 361–362
    and repression, 458–460
Self-evaluation processes, 505–506
    sex differences in, 505–506
Self-interest, 434
Self-righteous bias, 362
Self-serving bias, 387
Selfish gene, 460–464
    and libido, 460–464
Senescence, 151–153, 397–398, *see also* De-
        velopmental psychology and evolution-
        ary theory
    and bequeathment, 397–398
    and life histories, 151–153
    and life span, 151–153
Sensation seeking, 29–32
Sex biases in investment, 147–149
    and life histories, 147–149
Sex differences, 101, 138–144, 410–418,
        420–425, 503–509, 519–520,
        595–608, *see also* Sexual strategies
        and Spatial sex differences
    in cognition, 503–509
        modularity and attraction, 507–509
        naturalistic cognitions about homi-
            cide, 506–507
        perceptual contrast and mate judge-
            ments, 504–505
        self-evaluation processes, 505–506
    and evolutionary psychology, 519–520
    in reproduction, 138–144
        female resources and fertility, 143–144
        male resource control and fertility,
            140–143